Culture, Resource, and Economic Activity
an introduction to economic geography

Paul F. Griffin
Professor of Geography
Oregon College of Education

Ronald L. Chatham
Professor of Geography
Oregon College of Education

Ajmer Singh
Associate Professor of Economics
Oregon College of Education

Wayne R. White
Assistant Professor of Geography
Oregon College of Education

Cartography and Artwork by
Jay S. Vanderford

Allyn and Bacon, Inc.
Boston

Cover photographs courtesy of
Standard Oil Company (N. J.), top; Japan Air Lines, left;
Embassy of Indonesia, right; Bahamas Ministry of Tourism, bottom.

contents

This book is an introduction to economic geography in particular and to social science in general, reflecting both an innovative approach and retention of well-established core materials. It is designed to provide the reader with an analytical and meaningful understanding of his environment.

Economic geography truly entails a broad scope, involving not only an interplay of the many variables compartmentalized in the various academic disciplines, but also an integration of these variables into a meaningful approach to the study of man's activities. Based on this conception, economic activities are presented through a system or model approach that depicts man as a vibrant force influencing the type and level of economic activities in the context of a space-time continuum. The system is broken into five different but interrelated frameworks—material, economic, political, social, and technological—which are analyzed and related to the dynamics of economic activity location.

The book is divided into six parts. Part I analyzes man's perceptive process of recognizing resource, the meaning of culture and society, and the relationship between culture, economy, and economic activity.

Part II presents the five frameworks, their structure, and their theoretical influence on economic activity, in addition to a chapter on *Classification of Economic Activities* and one on *Location, Theory, and Practice*. The former indicates the need for classifying activities, and describes the functional rationale underlying the various schemes of classification; the latter briefly analyzes the contributions of Von Thünen, Weber, Christaller, and others, culminating in contemporary ideas and practice.

Parts III, IV, and V illustrate the topical and regional interplay of primary, secondary, and tertiary economic activities, respectively, reflecting the influence of the five frameworks and supported where possible by relevant case studies. Since this book is written primarily for the American student, the authors have intentionally placed greater emphasis on the United States, giving less weight to other parts of the world, such as Asia and the Far East, where reliable data is limited or unavailable.

Part VI is concerned with statistical inference as a reference for spatial analysis, and urban and regional planning. Chapter 30, on statistical inference, is so written as to permit its independence from the rest of the book, yet correlated to allow its study either at the beginning or the end. It provides an introduction for those who wish to acquire basic knowledge of the quantitative and statistical aspects of the field.

More than 200 maps, graphs, drawings, and photographs have been included to clarify concepts, systematize data, and enable the student to grasp difficult material.

We are indebted to all those who have supplied materials, ideas, and criticisms, and owe special thanks to the many colleagues who have contributed to the literature of economic geography and economics, for the economic geographer must, of necessity, draw much of his data from both the natural and social sciences. We wish especially to thank the following geographers and economists who read the manuscript critically and contributed ideas that helped to improve the book: Fred Hirsch, who made several helpful suggestions regarding the basic organization of the material; James Gallagher, for his contributions on primary economic activities; Alfred Kuhn and Irving Morrisett, who offered many helpful suggestions on Part I; and Jay Vanderford, who was responsible for selecting and compiling all of the maps, graphs, drawings, and photographs. Finally, we wish to thank our students, who served as our patient critics.

Monmouth, Oregon

PAUL F. GRIFFIN
RONALD L. CHATHAM
AJMER SINGH
WAYNE R. WHITE

part I
Culture, Resource, Economic Activity

introduction

The overriding objective of all sciences, whether physically or socially oriented, is to analyze, interpret, and understand the vast system on the earth's surface composed of man and the environment. Since man developed the ability to think even before the occurrence of analytical patterns that could be properly called *science*, we[1] have directly and indirectly attempted to increase our understanding of this system. The system is indeed vast, and to the observant presents a complex assemblage containing many interrelated elements occurring with a multitude of forms and functions.

Since the phenomena of this system are too complex and numerous to permit simultaneous study of all, a division of labor has been effected among scientists, with each group directing its attention and effort to parts of the system. Within the major division (social and physical sciences) there are finer divisions, each of which is many times further subdivided, affording individuals the opportunity to specialize. Each of these general or specific divisions focuses its attention on an array of elements frequently called the *object of study*. The major criterion for differentiation among the divisions, however, is the *methods* that each employs in studying objects within the system. The significant difference between *method of study* and *object of study* is that the former represents an intellectual approach for analyzing and understanding the latter.

As one searches his mental image of the world's people and their activities, often perhaps the system appears too complex for rational understanding. However, by approaching with an analytical method the interrelated elements of this system, a sense of order, pattern, and regularity may be created. Economic geography represents one approach that offers a high degree of satisfaction toward understanding some of the characteristics of the economic phenomena of this system.

Geography

One may question the existence of an approach called *economic geography* when many of the same objects may also be examined in an approach called economics or history, etc. That is, historians, economists, political scientists, and other social scientists also examine "economic" components of man. However, as mentioned previously, the major difference among these disciplines is not *what* is examined but *how* things are examined. Therefore, prior to any specific analysis of the objects of economic geography, a statement on how and what will be considered is relevant.

Geography, of which economic geography is a subdivision, may be defined in many ways. Within all the variations, however, there are four major recurrent concepts. Generally, these are *man, environment, place,*

---

[1]The term *we* is used in the generic sense and includes all of mankind (approximately 3.8 billion people). At various places the term will be used in the same way, as well as to refer to the authors, and the authors and students; the group referred to will be evident from the context.

and *relationships*. There are several ways in which these four concepts may be organized; in most of these ways, however, the organization will not indicate the major approach of geography.

Consider for a moment the following example. If we have these concepts —John, Lion, (to) Eat—we may organize them as: "The Lion eats John"; "John eats the Lion"; "The Lion and John eat." Each of these methods of arranging the same set of concepts results in a quite different situation. Each of these may be totally irrelevant unless, of course, you are John.

Now, in the four concepts associated with geography, you are part of *man* and consequently will be a part of the organization of these concepts. Specifically, a proper manner of organizing them diagrammatically is:

Man   Relationships   Environment

Place

The concept **man** is used generically and includes all men, women, and children. It refers to *cultural man* (man within the context of culture and societal organization), and consequently includes all those characteristics of man that are components of culture and society. **Environment** is not limited to aspects of physical environment (such as soil, water, landforms, vegetation), but more importantly encompasses all phenomena that are part of the environment of any group of men. For example, if we wish to examine coffee production activities in Brazil we will need to know something of the consuming habits of people in the United States, because this latter group is part of the environment of the coffee producer. For reasons that will be developed in Chapter 1, the environment for one group (society) of men is not the same as for another group.

The concept **relationships** is placed in the central part of the diagram because it is considered to be the essential element. It includes all processes, interactions, and events that take place between man and environment; since these relationships, if they are to be understood, do not occur "any place" but "some place," they must be analyzed within the context of **place.** None of the four concepts is static. Man, environment, place, and relationships are constantly changing, as is evident from cursory examination of any one of the four. The "place" occupied by the principles of the Industrial Revolution (mass production techniques, for example) is not the same "place" today as five hundred years ago or even last year. The "relationships" of the hunting–gathering Bushman are not the same today as ten years ago, and "man" is not the same either. Not only do these concepts reflect change over time, but more important for the geographer, changes from place to place (across space) at the same time.

From this brief analysis we may attempt a conceptualization of geography: Geography is the study of the relationships between man and environment within the context of place. Thus we have added one other ingredient to this definition—the study of. As a peasant in southeast China plants rice, "geography" is not occurring! Also, mountains do not imply geography. Geography is the *study* or *analysis* of something—the relationships between man and environment within the context of place. Thus, it is only a perspective or method of analyzing some of the characteristics of man, and it can be used by a historian, political scientist, or student. However, when the historian, political scientist, or student uses this method he is "doing" geography, and hence is a geographer.

Using this concept of geography we may now develop a concept of economic geography. Just as there are different ways of conceptualizing geography (or any discipline), there are various ways of conceptualizing its subdivisions. Apparent within the concept of economic geography, perhaps, is that it must have some relationship to geography, but deals with more specific elements and in a slightly different way. One of the major items of concern to economic geographers is the set of man's activities that are generally referred to as economic.

Economic Activity

It is commonly assumed that man has social, political, economic, religious, and other types of activities and motivations. But what is an *economic* activity and how does it differ from other activities? Consider the following examples. Is casting a vote in an election a political activity, if the vote is cast for a candidate whose economic philosophy is in agreement with the voter? What if the election of the candidate results in the voter's acquiring a better job, a larger farm subsidy, or a government contract to construct a building? We may conclude that if the voting is indeed a political activity it was partly motivated by an economic consideration. Thus, how do we distinguish between the two? Also, is the individual who receives money for counting the ballots engaged in an economic or political activity?

Does the nationalization of foreign investments within a sovereign state constitute a political or economic act? If an entrepreneur decides not to invest in a particular manufacturing operation due to the political instability of the area, is this an economic or political decision? Is the priest, rabbi, or minister who receives money for his livelihood for participating in religious services engaged in an economic or religious activity? In the United States most weddings are performed by clergymen. Hence, may we conclude that weddings are religious activities even though some political entity must first issue a license?

Within the traditional Burmese village, the societal beliefs and values associated with attaining a desirable "life after death" (a religious idea?) necessitated that one give all that was possible to another member of the village.[2] Indeed, many individuals would devote a great deal of labor to such ventures as hunting, gathering, agriculture, and manufacturing, simply for the purpose of producing items to be given away during these regularly occurring events. These events, multiplied many times by many individuals, had a significant influence on the production, distribution, and consumption of materials among the villagers. Did the processes of producing these items constitute economic or religious activities? Did the actual giving away of the materials constitute an economic, social, religious, or some other activity?

[2]Margaret Mead, ed., *Cultural Patterns and Technical Change* (from the Tensions and Technology Series originally published by the United Nations Educational, Scientific, and Cultural Organization), reprinted as a Mentor Book (New York: New American Library, 1955), p. 26.

Are these people engaged in an economic activity? Are they in the process of consuming, exchanging, or producing a good or service? (Canadian Government Travel Bureau)

Perhaps as you are reading this section you are readily classifying each of these activities. However you may classify them, the major points emphasized here are:

1. All activities are interdependent with other activities.
2. Whatever classification you use for each activity is based on your prior experiences and ideas of what constitutes an economic, political, religious, etc. activity—which is not necessarily the same as what the people engaged in the activity think about it.
3. Any classification you use is arbitrary and selected because you feel most comfortable with it.

Still, we have not answered the question, "What is an economic activity and how does it differ from other human activities?" The major difficulty in arriving at a satisfactory answer is a consequence of the interdependence of all aspects of human behavior. Man's total activity (i.e., his behavioral patterns and entire way of life) is not a series of fractional parts, but is a whole or unit. Thus, when the concept economic or political is used to refer to some aspect of human behavior, it is not used in reference to something that stands alone, independent, and totally isolated from other aspects of human behavior. Rather, it is only a mentally contrived separation accomplished solely for the purpose of better understanding the wide array of interdependent and complex variables that constitute human behavior. The manifestation of human behavior is not the result of a single motivation, nor can it be characterized by a single act (such as "politically motivated economic activity"). The manifestation of the behavior and the motive are invariably results of man operating within the total characteristics of himself and his environment.

However, in attempting to examine human behavior, since it is highly complex, we must devise some system of classification for purposes of analysis and communication. Even with the overriding problems and implications discussed above, we will here define one aspect of human behavior. *Economic activity is any manifestation of human behavior associated with the production, exchange, and/or consumption of goods and services.*

The term *good* includes any material (tangible) object that man has acquired for some use. Iron ore, automobiles, buttons, houses, shoes, hoes, slingshots, buildings, potatoes, wheat, and even human excrement (usually for medical analysis or fertilizer) are examples of goods. *Service* refers to the work done by one or several people for others. A teacher, for example, does not deal in goods but services, as does a lawyer, doctor, plumber, carpenter, taxi driver, or hairdresser. However, all of these use goods—whether the good is a map, stethoscope, wrench, hammer, automobile, or comb—as they perform their services.

Production refers to the process of making or creating a good or service. However, we are not referring to the "creation" of matter, for matter is not made by man. Nevertheless, he does move, change the form of, or combine various types of matter to form goods. Man also produces (provides) services. As a barber manipulates the comb, clippers, and scissors he is engaged in producing a service, namely, that of cutting hair.

Exchange, also a process, refers to the obtaining of a good or service and includes buying, selling, and bartering, as well as the transportation of goods and services from one place to another and the transfer of ownership of goods or services. The process of *consumption* includes the employment of goods and services for the purpose of either producing or acquiring other goods and services, as well as satisfying an end want or need. For example, an automobile is considered a consumer's good if it is used in the traditional manner of a typical United States family. However, it is a producer's good when used by a taxi driver. In the first instance we are assuming that the automobile will not be used for producing any other good or service except to satisfy a desire to ride. In the latter we are assuming the owner will employ the automobile to produce a service of transporting people from place to place.

Economic Geography

Having previously discussed geography as the study of the relationships between man and environment within the context of place, and economic activity as any activity in which man engages in the production, exchange, and consumption of goods and services, we may now attempt a conceptualization of economic geography. Summarily, we are here considering economic geography as the study of economic activity. Since economic activity is a subdivision of man's behavior, *economic geography is a study of the relationships between economic activity and environment within the context of place.*

The study would be much simplified if all economic activities, all environments, all places and relationships were exactly alike. If such were the case, we could then study only one set of concepts and interpret the rest of mankind in terms of our conclusions. However, such simplicity is not the case and in order to acquire some comprehension of the economic activities of man it is necessary to analyze many different sets.

As may be apparent from this brief discussion of human behavior and economic activity, the number of variables that are of some significance is quite large. However, if we can construct a mental approach that enables us to reduce the number of variables, then the task of analyzing economic activities becomes easier.

Consider the following example. Given the set of fractions,

$$1/6 \quad 3/8 \quad 1/2 \quad 3/4 \quad 2/3$$

how can they be manipulated so as to give meaning to their relationships? With even elementary knowledge of arithmetic the task is simple—search for the common denominator, which is 24. Thus, we can rearrange the fractions in this manner:

$$4/24 \quad 9/24 \quad 12/24 \quad 18/24 \quad 16/24$$

and we have not changed their value or relationships. However, we have produced a situation in which the relationships are more apparent and perhaps more meaningful and useful. And, although we are looking (visually) at the set of fractions, the manipulations were accomplished mentally and not with a typewriter.

If there are common denominators, that is, characteristics of economic activity that are present in all economic activities, analysis of these common characteristics will enable us to better understand all economic activity as well as any one specific economic activity. Are there, for example, any characteristics common to the hunting–gathering Bushman, to you, to the individuals mining ore in northern Minnesota, and to the cattle rancher in Australia? Are there characteristics of industrial economic activities that are also present in pre-industrial economic activities? The resounding answers are yes, indeed!

The most important characteristic common to all economic activity is *man* who, in operating upon a set of elements (which may be referred to as resources), *creates economic activity*. Economic activity exists as a consequence of man's efforts to employ resources to achieve a set of objectives —a generalization that applies to all forms of economic activity. These efforts, however, are not random, but occur at specific places for specific reasons (although we may not be able to state all those reasons with specificity). The efforts and reasons for being are themselves consequences of other processes, particularly cultural processes. In commencing our investigation of economic geography, therefore, it is logical to start with the integral and functional elements that are responsible for economic activity: culture and man's concept of resource.

chapter 1

Culture and Society

The term culture refers to the learned ways of living that people have created. More specifically, *culture* is the integrated system of learned behavioral traits that are characteristics of man and are not the result of genetic inheritance. Since we are presently concerned with all of mankind, we may generalize within a global context that there is only one culture. However, as a consequence of the variations perceived within this global culture, social scientists have contrived many divisions, each of which also is referred to as *a culture*. In this context, culture refers to the integrated system of learned behavior traits that are characteristic of the members of a society and are not results of genetic inheritance.

A *trait* is a specific way of thinking, believing, or doing something, and includes customs, habits, roles, values, use of a specific language, religion, or tool. Since by definition and conceptual base, culture is not genetically or "naturally" induced, it does not occur in nature and is not an attribute of other animals.[1] It is totally a result of social invention, maintained, promoted, and transmitted exclusively through communication and learning.

The characteristics and processes of culture are quite distinct from those associated with inherited biological characteristics or other natural processes. To illustrate the distinction between a natural process and a cultural process, consider the following. One of the natural characteristics of *all* forms of life is the necessity to ingest food. This is applicable to plants, ants, and people. The processes involved in eating, whether

[1]For many centuries man very jealously clung to the "fact," based almost exclusively on teleological beliefs, that man alone possesses the ability to learn through communication. We have, however, discovered that many species of animals learn some of their behavior traits, and according to the concept of culture possess "culture." However, to distinguish between man's and other animals' learning via communication, the concept of protoculture has been developed. Thus, we are still "separate" from animals.

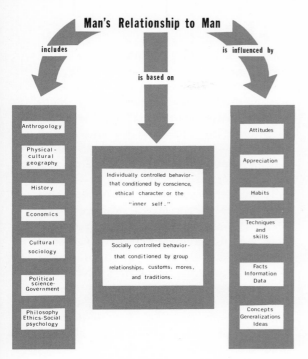

FIGURE 1.1 *The meaning of culture. (General Media Corporation)*

employing chopsticks, twigs, highly refined silver flatware, or no implements at all, are culturally induced. That is, through the medium of one's culture one makes decisions as to *how* to eat. The same principle applies to *what* is eaten. Eating eggs for breakfast (or corn flakes) is no more natural than partaking of a tasty meal of alligator tails and tubers; both are culturally induced decisions. In Chapter 2, additional references will be made to differences between cultural and natural phenomena.

SOCIETY

The concepts of society and culture are intimately interwoven and both are susceptible to a variety of interpretations. A culture is always borne by and is the reflection of a group; no one individual knows or manifests all the traits of his culture. However, society and culture

are not the same. A society is considered to be a people, whereas a culture is not people but something that people have and do (behavior which is learned). An individual belongs to a society, but not to a culture.

More specifically, *society* may be defined as a group of people interrelated by a sense or awareness of belonging together and who share social and economic interdependence—they possess a conscious awareness of belonging together. The direction and control of a society is through the medium of its culture.

Almost any set of behavioral traits may be manifest in many societies. Also, at a very general level, many different societies may have similar learned behavioral traits. However, in attempting to classify societies we invariably emphasize one set of traits at the expense of others. Democracy, industrialism, even farming, for example, are behavioral traits, but there are many democratic societies, industrial societies, and farming societies. Within the context of Western culture we may recognize such democratic societies as the United States, Canada, and Costa Rica. However, a category based on Western industrial societies would exclude Costa Rica.

Within all societies there are numerous processes that are implemented through a variety of interrelated frameworks. All societies have constructed sets of behavioral frameworks, which may be referred to as political, social, economic, and technological frameworks. As mentioned in the Introduction, however, these sets are so interdependent within the total societal milieu that we can separate them only mentally. For example, political framework does not refer to political parties or to the concept of "state." The political framework of a society is that part of the society's culture whose prime function is to direct the activities of its members in realizing societal goals. Government and state are thus only parts of the political framework. Social framework refers to the ways in which individuals of a society are organized in relation to other sets of individuals within the same society.

Each individual in a society is also a part of many different aspects of the society. For example, one may be a member of a student body, a religious organization, a book club, a fraternity or sorority, a political organization, and be employed by a grocery store. And, since the members of each of these organizations usually possess a sense of belonging and interrelatedness, each organization may be referred to as a society. Thus, every individual within any society has a wide array of interdependent relationships (either direct or indirect) with all other members of the society as well as with the culture traits that characterize it. Obviously, our main concern here is with the economic activities of society and those characteristics of society that are responsible for these activities.

SOME OVERRIDING CHARACTERISTICS OF CULTURE, SOCIETY, AND ECONOMIC ACTIVITY

Whatever diversity may be perceived among different societies, they all share several significant characteristics, which include: (1) being earth-bound, (2) having spatial distributions, and (3) spatial interactions; and they possess other sets of characteristics that may be referred to as (4) contents, (5) arrangements, (6) functions, (7) methods of preservation or maintenance, (8) objectives, and (9) change; in addition to these (10) each society has its own environment.[2] Following is a general discussion of each of these characteristics.

[2]This list is not meant to be exhaustive in terms of characteristics common to all men (and their culture, societies, and economic activities), but rather is a set of general categories that includes such characteristics as kinship systems, property, housing, child care, etc.

Earth-bound

All men, and hence all cultures, societies, and economic activities, are earth-bound. It is on the elements of the physical, as well as through the elements of the man-made environment, that man operates to provide himself with the means and commodities for living. Of all the various elements that he uses, including soil, ores, water, air, plants, animals, etc., only one—the sun—is not found at or near the surface of the earth. Consequently, the continued existence of man is dependent on his involvement in a series of processes for the acquisition of goods, especially food, from the earth. Not even the explorers of outer space are exempt from this relationship, for without sustenance produced from earth they would not only be unable to travel but also unable to sustain life.

Spatial Distribution

Culture is a result of the ability of human beings to communicate among themselves through the use of symbols. When people appear to act and think in a similar fashion, they do so because they live, talk, and work together; learn from the same individuals or organizations; talk about similar events, ideas, places, and people; and perceive similar meanings in objects of the environment. Conversely, significant differences in learning, thinking, and acting are usually consequences of the absence of common symbols of communication and the absence of shared experiences. Since continual and habitual sharing of ideas is more likely to occur among people who occupy a common area, *cultures are invariably spatially distributed.* Thus, at particular times common sets of behavior traits occupy distinct places on the earth's surface.

A group of people sharing the same cultural traits may exist in a single isolated village, in which all the members are in direct, daily, and prolonged contact with each other, or it may be distributed over a much larger area within which people, ideas, and objects circulate relatively freely and continually. The size of the space through which a set of common traits is distributed results largely from the ability and desire of a society to extend its influence.

Spatial Interaction

As a consequence of their having different locations on the earth's surface, all societies interact spatially. The movement of ideas, people, and goods from one group to another represents the spatial interaction of societies.

The degree of intensity with which interaction among different societies can or does occur is a function of *accessibility*. Accessibility, however, cannot always be measured in terms of distance, time, or cost between places. More frequently the degree of accessibility between places is a function of the characteristics of the cultures occupying those places. The interaction may be violent, as in military conflict, or peaceful, as is usually the case in most forms of international trade.

Contents

The contents of each and all cultures include both tangible and intangible items. Religion, for example, is intangible. Though one may be able to hear people singing hymns and intoning incantations, observe and feel religious edifices, sacrifices, and clerical garments, religion per se is not tangible. Likewise, other beliefs, customs, organizations, and technology are intangible. Members of societies operating within these intangible contents are what give rise to the tangible contents. This latter set of items includes all goods that are manifestations of and usually produced or acquired by a society. Houses, automobiles, chopsticks, goat-skin bags, olives, and electric generating stations are examples of tangible contents of societies.

Due to the relatively homogeneous

FIGURE 1.2   *The Apollo 11 lunar module with astronauts Neil Armstrong and Edwin Aldrin aboard. Are these men earthbound? Why? How? (NASA)*

Cominco

Mullarky Photo

Rhodesian Ministry of Home Affairs

Caterpillar Tractor Co.

Delta Air Lines

Surinam Tourist Development Board

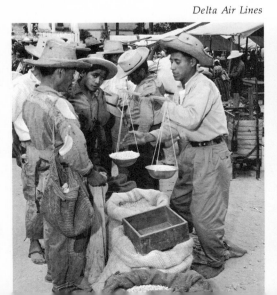

quality of the intangible contents of a society, there is usually a similarity of tangible contents in that society. Frequently, the tangible contents (material possessions) of a society are a consequence of the members' willingness and ability to direct their energies toward production and/or acquisition of goods.

Arrangement

This term refers here to the ways in which a society arranges its contents. Generally, we may perceive two major methods of arrangement: spatial and hierarchical. First, consideration will be given to the *spatial* arrangement. Previously mentioned was the characteristic of spatial distribution among different societies wherein each occupied different parts of the earth's surface. However, each society also arranges its contents spatially within the confines of the area it occupies or controls. For example, areas occupied by most societies contain agricultural landscapes, in part composed of fields, field dividers (fences), dwellings, routes of movement, and people. In the United States, these contents traditionally have been spatially arranged so that each farm family lives in a single-family dwelling, on a farm separated from other farms by field dividers, and connected with other farmers, merchants, and urban centers by the routes of movement (roads).

In most parts of the world, however, farmers live in dwellings in villages, connected to their noncontiguous parcels of farm land and to other villages by paths. Frequently, the field dividers are rows of bushes, man-created mounds of earth, or low rows of stones. Thus, although the same general set of contents is used, the spatial arrangement is quite different.

Another example is the arrangement of slums associated with cities. In most large cities in the United States, slums occur near the central city, whereas in most of the larger cities of Latin America,

slums occur near the fringes of the city. This difference in the arrangement of slums relative to the central city is primarily a manifestation of the different ways that the cities have developed. From these examples, we may generalize that although all societies have tangible contents that are spatially arranged, the same type of contents will probably have different arrangements in different societies. The other method of arrangement, *hierarchical*, or arrangement of things into hierarchies, definitely is not spatial. Hierarchical arrangement is similar to a ranking of things from high to low, from good to bad, large to small, hard to soft, etc. For example, assuming that a diamond is the hardest thing and that the inner part of a vacuum is the softest, all other items may be arranged into a hierarchy, the extremes of which will be a diamond and the inner part of a vacuum. Now, if we also assume that the diamond is the most important and that our hierarchy is to be arranged from top to bottom (vertically), with the most important at the top and the least important (softest) at the bottom, we have determined the priority of the hierarchy. Thus, each item in the arrangement will have a priority higher than anything below it, but less than anything above it.

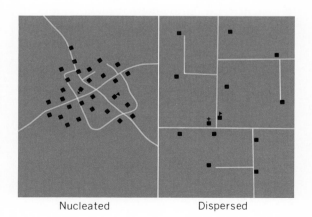

Nucleated   Dispersed

FIGURE 1.4 *A nucleated settlement and a dispersed settlement. (General Media Corporation)*

◀FIGURE 1.3 *Tools of some cultures—what roles do they play?*

FIGURE 1.5 *In what ways are the culture patterns represented here similar? What are the major functions of the personal interactions? (left—Information Service of South Africa; right—Palo Alto School System)*

All societies arrange their contents into hierarchies. Almost invariably the survival of the society is given the highest priority and other contents, whether tangible or intangible, are ranked lower. Survival is here applied not to individuals within the society but to the basic values, concepts, and other intangible contents that are deemed most important to the society as a whole. That is, the high point of the hierarchy of any society is maintenance of the basic set of values by which the society operates.

More specifically, the concept of hierarchy is expressed through the development and implementation of political organizations such as government and state. Each government, however contrived, is the result of some ordering of functions within the context of political organization. This ordering of functions and their priorities frequently results in such positions as president, vice-president, council (legislative body), constituents, etc. Religious, educational, social, and other organizations also represent hierarchies contrived by societies.

The concept *state* includes sovereign as well as nonsovereign entities. More important for our purposes, it also denotes *space* (or area), in that a state has areal extent. The United States, for example, can be thought of as a governmental organization as well as a specific portion of the earth's surface over which this organization has control. Both concepts, however, are involved in the concept "United States." Within the area of the United States we have contrived a hierarchy of areas which includes the sovereign state, the fifty states that are united, 3,049 counties, 17,105 townships, and 18,048 municipalities. Thus, there is not only a hierarchy of governmental organization but a hierarchy of areal units, each of which is integrated with its own government, is less important than any that is higher, and more important than any that is lower. One of the major characteristics of hierarchies in any society is that the number of entries in any part of the hierarchy tends to increase from top to bottom.

Within the context of U.S. society, one may well question the premise that the president is more important than any other citizen. However, the argument here is that the concept of the president, as leader of the entire society, is more important than the concept of any one other citizen—reference is not made to the value of life of individuals.

All major hierarchies in all societies are in part geared to promote the survival of those societies. It is principally through these hierarchical positions or structures, whether a village chieftain or elder, dictator, religious leader, president, premier, labor union, and so on, that societal values are implemented. Just as any individual in a society is a member of many organizations within that society, he is also a member of many hierarchies.

Function

Within any society the contents as well as their arrangement have particular functions. However, similar contents of two societies may have entirely dissimilar functions. For example, social scientists generally hold that agricultural activity for the peasant (farmer) of southern France represents a "way of life"—that the agricultural efforts are actually an end in themselves. In the United States, however, most farmers view agricultural efforts as a means of increasing their standard of living, and engage in productive agricultural enterprises to insure that they and their families can increase their consumption of goods; agriculture is not viewed as an end in itself. Just as similar contents may have dissimilar functions, similar arrangements of contents in different societies may have dissimilar functions.

Methods of Preservation

In attempting to insure unity, solidarity, and the survival of the essential traits of the culture, all societies have developed organizations or institutions whose functions include transmission of information to subsequent generations. This is to insure that culture will remain relatively intact and change will be controlled. In many societies the most important organization for such purposes is the family, extended family (clan), or tribe. Educational and religious organizations also reflect these purposes. Strictly in terms of preservation, perhaps the more obvious institutions, especially in terms of the sovereign state, are the political and military organizations.

Objectives

Each society possesses certain overriding objectives that are of some significance to all of its members. Previously mentioned were the objectives of survival and transmission of essential culture traits to subsequent generations. Another general objective of any society is to insure that its contents and functions are arranged in the manner best suited to their most beneficial use. "Most beneficial use" is not necessarily the same as "most economically productive use," but is an objective contrived from the values of each individual society.

Change

Each of the major characteristics discussed above tends to change as a result of the development of newer thought patterns.[3] Generally there are two principal processes by which change is effected in a society: by invention within the society of some idea or tool, and by diffusion of an idea or tool from one society to another.

Invention of some item by a member of a society, however, does not necessarily mean that the other members will accept and use the invention. If, within the context of societal values and past experiences, the invention is deemed undesirable (for whatever reason), then the invention probably will be rejected. Consequently, the change that might have occurred due to acceptance does not take place. Likewise, the societal evaluation of

[3]Even the characteristic of man being earth-bound, that is, requiring goods and services from earth for sustenance, is presently being re-examined. Many scientists express the possibility of man being able to live in parts of the universe other than this planet.

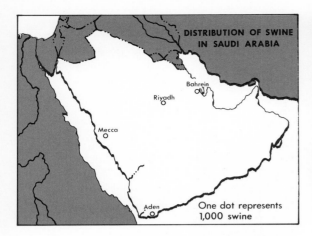

FIGURE 1.6 *Distribution of swine in a Moslem society. One dot represents 1,000 swine. (General Media Corporation)*

FIGURE 1.7 *A United States hog farm. If you change the American values associated with hogs, what changes will be made on this space? (USDA)*

an idea, whether invented within the society or introduced from another, may be totally or partly negative and hence may be wholly or partly rejected.

As an example of rejection, Moslem society generally has deemed swine to be unholy and unclean. As a consequence of this "idea," the "object" swine has been rejected, and is notably absent in any economic activity (or any other behavioral pattern) articulated by a dominantly Moslem society. Since in the United States there are no dominant societal values that exclude swine, and because we have articulated a series of activities in such a manner that this animal is deemed desirable, we have accepted it in our society. Note that the same object, swine, has been used as an example of acceptance and rejection; consequently, it is not the object that determines acceptance or rejection but the societal values toward that object. This concept will be developed more fully in Chapter 2.

In the United States we have also rejected many things—use of yaks as beasts of burden, use of camels (although they were used for a short time in the Southwest) as means of transportation, roughly hewn logs for construction of hotels, and presently we appear to be in a transitory

period of rejecting high calorie foods and accepting lower calorie ones.

The rate at which change occurs varies among societies as well as within the various social frameworks of the same society. For example, the tangible and intangible contents, arrangements, and functions within the United States are changing more rapidly than in meat hunting and gathering societies. In various frameworks of our society, also, change is more evident than in others.

Since all of these characteristics of culture, society, and economic activity have spatial arrangements, rates of change also have spatial arrangements; that is, change occurs faster or slower at different places among societies as well as at different places within the same society. Generally, over the past several decades, change has occurred more quickly in northern Italy (especially the Po Basin) than in southern Italy, more quickly in southern California than in southern Appalachia.

As ideas are invented and diffused among societies, all of these characteristics tend to change. In addition to the changes outlined, there also may be changes in the spatial arrangements of entire societies as they migrate from one place to another. So characteristic is the element of change (although the rates of change vary), that it is as gross an error to assume that any specific society or part thereof today is like it was yesterday or will be tomorrow as it is to assume that the wind does not blow.

A CONCEPT OF ENVIRONMENT

It was previously mentioned that for many reasons the environment of one society is not the same as it is for another society. However it is conceptualized, *environment* usually refers to a collection or a set of things that has some relationship to another set of things. Generally, the term is defined as the "entire set of conditions, forces, and objects that modifies or influences an organism." Thus, in this definition environment is characterized as being *conditions*, *forces*, and *objects*. Its relationship is that of modifying or influencing another thing, which here is an organism.

Note that environment is not the relationship and is not the organism, but is the set of conditions that modifies or influences the organism. Thus, the environment is outside the organism. But if the organism is a squirrel and one of the forces that modifies it is a man hunting in the forest, then the man becomes a part of the environment of the squirrel. If any activity on the part of the squirrel, such as moving to the far side of a tree, influences the man to move so as to get a better vantage point, then the squirrel is a part of the environment of the man. Each is a part of the environment of the other.

As another example, consider the process of eating and digesting. We may assume that a steak on a plate is a part of our environment. If we eat the steak it will become a part of us through digestion. When does the steak, then, cease being a part of the environment and become a part of us—when we cut it, when it enters the mouth, when it is being chewed, or digested, and on and on?

Let us return to the forest, the man, and the squirrel. Also, let us assume that we know the total conditions of the forest— conditions that have the ability to influence and modify. Is the forest the same environment for the man as it is for the squirrel? Initially, we may answer yes, obviously so; it is the *same* forest (environment) for both. If so, then the forest will influence and modify both the man and the squirrel in the same way. The man should climb a tree and perhaps eat an acorn—or the squirrel should walk along the paths and not climb a tree. When the squirrel gets tired he will leave the forest, get into a car, and drive home— or the man will climb a tree, crawl through an opening, and go to sleep.

Although the example may be absurd, if we assume that the forest is the same environment for both, our conclusions have to be valid. But we know they are not valid; consequently the assumption about the similarity of the environment also must be incorrect. Therefore, we may assume that the forest is not the same environment for both the man and the squirrel but actually represents two quite different environments. Why? There is only one forest! Perhaps there are two environments because there are two organisms—man and squirrel; each "thinks" differently concerning the forest.

Let us assume another forest, the tropical rainforest of the upper Amazon River, and two other organisms, this time two men—one from an urban society and the other from a hunting society of the rainforest. We may obviously conclude that the man from the urban society will not think about the forest in the same way as the hunter. Thus, for each of them the forest is a different environment, and each will have a different relationship with *his own* environment.

Here we may logically ask why each has a different environment, even though they are both in the same forest. The answer presently ascribed to by social scientists is that each individual has been

FIGURE 1.8   *Observe the squirrel in a forest, and men cutting trees in a forest. This is essentially the same forest—why different environments? (above—Oklahoma Department of Wildlife Conservation; below—USDA)*

raised in (influenced and modified by) different societies (environments), each of which has its own culture (which is another environment). Thus, a desert for one society is not the same as that for another; an ocean for one society is not the same as that for another; a mountain range is not the same for one society as that for another. There are as many deserts, oceans, and mountains as there are societies.

Expanding from these rather brief examples to the concepts of society, we may generalize that given the great diversity among contents, functions, arrangements, objectives, rates of change, and spatial distributions of different societies, no two societies have the same environment—even though they may occupy adjacent places and even though all occupy some place on the earth's (rather small) surface. Also, either directly or indirectly, each society is part of the environment of all other societies; hence it has relationships with these other societies.[4] In terms of the environment being those conditions and forces that influence or modify man's behavior, the most significant are his own culture and the culture of other societies.

Summary

Thus far, our analysis has focused primarily on characteristics that are common to all cultures, societies, and economic activities. However, it may be apparent that within these common traits there are reasons associated with the diversity of economic activities. Such, indeed, is the case. In Chapter 2 analysis proceeds, built on the concepts generated here, with an examination of the concept of resource within the context of culture, society, and economic activity.

[4]Automobiles, coffee, shoes, glass, clothing, aspirin, the Watusi dance, folk music, guitars, and many others are examples of ideas that have been accepted by people in the United States but which were initially used in other societies.

selected references

1. Barrows, Harland H., "Geography as Human Ecology," *Annals of the Association of American Geographers*, Vol. 13, March 1923, pp. 1–14.

2. Bredemeier, Harry C., and Stephenson, Richard M., *The Analysis of Social Systems*, New York: Holt, Rinehart, & Winston, Inc., 1962.

3. Griffin, Paul F., "Cultural Geography," Chapter 25 in *Methods of Geographic Instruction*, ed. by John W. Morris, Waltham, Mass.: Blaisdell Publishing Company, 1968, pp. 286–297.

4. Henry, Jules, *Culture Against Man*, New York: Random House, 1963.

5. Hoebel, E. Adamson, *Anthropology: The Study of Man*, 3d ed., New York: McGraw-Hill Book Company, Inc., 1966.

6. Jaeger, Gertrude, and Selznick, Philip, "A Normative Theory of Culture," *American Sociological Review*, Vol. 29, October 1964, pp. 653–669.

7. James, Preston E., *A Geography of Man*, Waltham, Mass.: Blaisdell Publishing Company, 1966.

8. Kluckhohn, Clyde, *Mirror for Man*, New York: McGraw-Hill Book Company, Inc., 1949.

9. Lebon, J. H. G., *An Introduction to Human Geography*, New York: Capricorn Books, 1966.

10. Linton, Ralph, *The Study of Man*, New York: Appleton-Century-Crofts, 1936.

11. Rodnick, David, *An Introduction to Man and His Development*, New York: Appleton-Century-Crofts, 1966.

12. Rose, Peter I., ed., *The Study of Society: An Integrated Anthology*, New York: Random House, 1967.

13. Russell, Richard J.; Kniffen, Fred B.; and Pruitt, Evelyn L., *Culture Worlds*, London: Collier-Macmillan, Ltd., 1969.

14. Thomas, William L., ed., *Man's Role in Changing the Face of the Earth*, Chicago: University of Chicago Press, 1956.

15. Wagner, Phillip, *The Human Use of the Earth*, New York: The Free Press, 1960.

chapter 2

Culture and Resource

There are many concepts associated with the term *resource*. Whatever the diversity, they all imply that resource involves the *use* of something.[1] Consequently, one may infer that resource presupposes a person. The "something" referred to is not limited to objects, but also includes processes, as well as people and ideas—all and anything that has use.

Assuming that resource involves use of something, and that use implies that the something is available, either directly or indirectly, then when similar things are available in different places, why do different societies "use" different things? Why, even when many possible resources are present, do certain groups use certain things? Since economic activities are results of people operating on resources, an answer to this question should facilitate our understanding of some other characteristics of economic activities.

THEORIES

Many theories have been postulated that attempt to explain the relationships between culture and resource.[2] Following is a brief outline of several of these theories.

Environmental Determinism

This school of thought believes that man is totally at the mercy of one or more elements of the physical environments and that these elements *determine* what man will do in a particular situation. For example, in places where temperature is relatively low, man will, because of this environmental factor, wear heavy clothing; where forests are present man

[1] One may also refer to the use by plants and animals of various foods, habitats, etc. Here, we are referring exclusively to use in terms of man.

[2] These theories may be also used to explain relationships in any situation in which man is involved, and are not limited exclusively to the relationships of culture and resource.

FIGURE 2.1   *An aerial photograph of a copra plantation in Fiji. The adjacent photo shows a nearby Fiji village. If environment determines activity, why are there two societies in the same place? (Rob Wright, Fiji Public Relations Office)*

engages in forestry; where soils are fertile man practices agriculture; where temperature and humidity are relatively high (such as in the tropics) man will be less motivated to engage in activities that industrial societies refer to as "progressive," and so forth. Generally, this theory assumes that given a certain set of physical environmental conditions, man will respond or behave in a specific predetermined pattern. From an extreme deterministic perspective, all behavioral patterns, including religious, educational, political, and economic activities, are determined by the physical environment in which man lives. Thus, within this context, resources are determined by the physical environment—not by man (or his culture). Consequently, our study, assuming we accept this premise, would focus directly and almost exclusively on the physical environment.

However, if this assumption is indeed valid, why do different societies living in similar physical environments use different resources and engage in different economic activities? More specifically, why is there not presently a hunting—gathering, limited agricultural society inhabiting the northeastern part of the

United States? This is the general type of society that was there five hundred years ago, and the physical environment (except as changed by man) is essentially the same now as then. The theory of determinism is not sufficiently flexible to allow an acceptable answer to these and similar questions.

Free-willism

Another theory associated with the relationships between culture and resource is free-willism. From this perspective man is viewed as a totally free agent— free to proceed on any course of action he desires. However, *desire* is not the same as *ability*, for the latter implies the existence of a technology capable of acquiring what is desired. The fact of desiring industrial progress does not imply the ability to acquire such progress. Hence, man is not free to effect those alternatives of progress unless he also has the ability to implement them.

Possibilism

A third concept devised in attempting to explain the relationships of culture and resource is that of possibilism. It represents a compromise between free-willism and determinism. In viewing man's activities from this perspective, it is assumed that within any given set of environmental circumstances many alternatives exist for utilizing the elements in that set. The alternatives are not static but dynamic, in that they vary with changes in the physical and/or cultural milieu. At any time in any place, a society is able to select and effect from those *possible* alternatives the ones they desire and are able to effect. Since different societies have different contents, functions, arrangements, and objectives, each will have different desires and abilities, and will not necessarily select the same alternatives from those which are possible. Also, the alternatives for one society may not be the same as for another. This particular theory (or philosophy) of analyzing and explaining man's activities has been quite useful in clarifying many questions that could not be as successfully resolved by other schools of thought.

Environmental Perception

According to our present knowledge, an individual receives information[3] through some stimulus that reaches the brain.[4] Receipt of information is generally referred to as sensing. When an individual *senses* a stimulus (from whatever source) he has received information. Perceiving involves sensing and making an interpretation of the stimulus. For example, if one hears (senses) a sound (stimulus)

but cannot attach any meaning to the stimulus, perception has not occurred. If, however, one can attach a meaning to the sound, based on past experiences with the same or a similar stimulus— that is, interpret it—then one has perceived the stimulus.

Again, referring to present knowledge associated with receiving information, all information that reaches the brain must be transmitted to it through one or several senses. Thus, perception involves both the senses and the brain, and an interpretation of stimuli (information) from any source. Environmental perception refers to the reception and interpretation of information from outside the individual—reception and interpretation of information from the environment.

For an illustration of environmental perception we will return to the example of the tropical rainforest where an individual from an urban society and one from a hunting society who is a resident of the forest are located. We have previously concluded that the forest does not represent the same environment for both individuals, but is actually two environments. If, for example, as the two are walking through the forest a sharp high-pitched sound (stimulus) is heard (sensed), the urbanite who has never heard the sound before is likely to turn abruptly toward the source of the stimulus and (depending on his interpretation) begin to "shake in his boots." However, the hunter, who also received the same stimulus, continues walking and gives no outward manifestation that he has sensed anything.

What produced the difference in their behavior patterns? Obviously, it is the same stimulus for both and they both sensed it, but behaved differently as a result. The answer is in the *interpretation* of the stimulus—that is, its perception (which involves reception and interpretation). Each perceived the same stimulus in a different way and his behavioral pattern was a consequence of the inter-

---

[3]Here *information* refers to any data gathered by an individual in any way, as by reading, seeing, hearing, touching, etc. The term information does not mean that the data gathered are either accurate or inaccurate.

[4]This is a highly generalized statement and is made in reference to information received at a conscious level. Reflex action, for example, does not involve the brain directly. However, information, societal values for example, with which we are concerned does not involve the brain.

General Media Corporation

USDA

FIGURE 2.2 *Which of these foods do you commonly eat? Are there any you do not like?*

USDA

Georgia Game and Fish Commission

pretation, not a consequence of the stimulus. Here, we may logically question why the difference in interpretation of the same stimulus. Again, referring to the present fund of knowledge associated with perception, the answer is in the experiences of the two individuals. To the hunter, the stimulus was as common as a lamp post is to the urbanite.

We have previously mentioned the different ways in which a dominantly Moslem society perceives swine, and the way in which swine are perceived in the United States. The stimuli (sight, sound, odor, etc.) from the swine are the same for both societies and both sense swine. That is, the swine has no direct effect on either of these societies. It is the perception of the stimuli that results in the behavior patterns.

Not only do objects (houses, birds, sounds, swine) from the environment provide sources of stimuli, but man-contrived intangible concepts such as price, wants, science, society, etc., also provide sources of stimuli.

Differences in perception are almost exclusively the result of differences in culture traits. The interpretation given to stimuli is based on the values, mores, customs, etc., that each individual has previously formed as a consequence of his experiences within the context of his own society. Thus, any element in the environment is perceived through the medium of culture.

Assuming the validity of environmental perception, we may here make a conclusion significant to a cultural interpretation of economic activities: *There is no "natural" influence of any element on man; all stimuli are perceived through the medium of culture*, which is not a "natural" thing. Interposed between cultural man and nature are the phenomena that have previously been identified and characterized as culture.

Generally all members of a society, since they have innumerable shared experiences, tend to perceive stimuli in much the same manner; yet even here there are differences. However, these differences within one society are relatively minor when compared to the differences among societies. Likewise, members of one society tend to be exposed to a set of stimuli that is different from the set to which another society is exposed. Thus, given different sets of stimuli and different perceptions, various societies have resulting differences in behavioral patterns.

If a society is to attain its objectives it must have adequate, accurate information about its environment. To be sure, the society does not need any more information than that which is necessary for attaining these objectives. For example, the Bushman society of the Kalahari does not need specific information related to construction of rocket engines in order to attain its objectives; consequently, one should not assume ignorance when such information is lacking. Also, being able to successfully track an antelope for many miles through a desert is not necessary to attain U.S. societal objectives (the experience may be pleasant but not necessary).

In the context of this theory, a society not only determines what elements, forces, processes, etc. (stimuli) it will perceive, but also which of the stimuli are of greater or lesser importance. That is, it constructs a hierarchy of environmental elements.

No possible source of stimuli within the environment is in itself either good or bad or hostile, nor does it possess any property which by its inherent characteristics influences a society to make decisions concerning its use. Quite the contrary, man is the dominant deciding agent and assigns values and priorities to elements of the environment based on his own interpretation of those elements. The evaluation is a function of perception. In general, societies utilize specific ele-

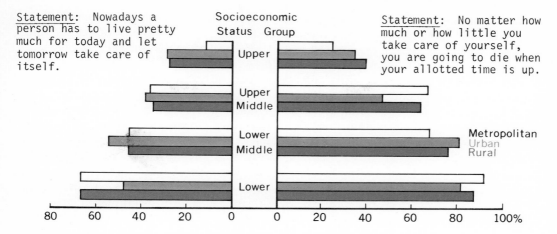

Statement: Nowadays a person has to live pretty much for today and let tomorrow take care of itself.

Socioeconomic Status Group

Statement: No matter how much or how little you take care of yourself, you are going to die when your allotted time is up.

FIGURE 2.3 *Indicators of fatalism in Appalachia; distribution of answers to a deterministic question. T. Ford, ed.,* The Southern Appalachian Region, *Lexington, Ky.: University of Kentucky Press, 1962, p. 19. (General Media Corporation)*

ments based on their own evaluation, often irrespective of the evaluation of the same element by any other society.

APPLICATION

All of these perspectives represent attempts to understand and to explain man's activities. At various times and places each of these approaches, with major or minor deviations, has played a role in the attempts to explain the activities of man.[5] Not only have these theories been employed by social scientists, viewing man's activities from a spectator position, but they are also functional, in that some societies believe these perspectives or deviations thereof are operative in their own activities. For example, some societies view their activities as being determined by forces over which they have no control; they perceive their own actions as involuntary and predetermined by their environment.

Any of the above perspectives or their variations may form the basis from which

to analyze and explain man's economic activities. Most social scientists have rejected the deterministic and free-willist perspectives as part of their methods, whatever their objects of study. Owing to the apparent success realized through the application of environmental perception, this perspective has been chosen for this text.

Still we are faced with the task of directly answering why different societies utilize different or similar elements from the environment as resources. Why do different societies develop and engage in different economic activities, even when using similar resources? In order to gain possible answers to these questions and to develop an understanding of the characteristics of economic activities, it is desirable to delve further into the concept of resource, which will be developed within the context of environmental perception.

Part of the difficulty in understanding the variations in using different elements for the same or different functions among societies results from a misunderstanding of the term resource. Use of traditional concepts, employing "natural resource" to refer to soil, rock, water, minerals, forests, and other such physical elements,

[5]The theory of environmental perception is relatively recent in its widespread application to attempts at understanding man's behavior patterns.

and "human resource" to refer to population, customs, and man-made objects, does not explain why, for example, some societies utilize the lateritic soils of the humid tropics in agriculture while others in immediately adjacent areas do not use the soils at all. Nor does this division of resources adequately explain the existence of a variety of different societies in a given place.

MAN and Nature

A thorough understanding of these questions requires a functional concept of resource. Let us assume that within the species *Homo sapiens* there are two levels of existence, which shall be referred to as man and MAN. The former represents *natural* man, literally stripped of all cultural traits—no thinking ability, no materials, religion, education, clothing, medical care, or other elements of culture. The term MAN refers to *Homo sapiens* as a *cultural* being.

Our *man* is in a state of existence similar to that preceding the development of any cultural traits. He is totally natural as a consequence of the processes of nature, and he needs and can obtain only naturally occurring elements for survival. The items he needs are:

1. *Water*—for drinking to continue the biological processes within his body
2. *Oxygen*—for maintaining life through the biological processes
3. *Land*—since his body cannot perform well or survive long in an aquatic environment
4. *Food*—containing essential minerals and vitamins
5. The presence of sufficient *heat* to maintain his bodily function, the minimum and maximum temperatures of which are relatively stable
6. *Light*—since his eyes do not function sufficiently well at night to insure survival, especially against nocturnal animals

7. A form of *internal immunity* sufficiently high to maintain bodily functions against diseases and parasites
8. A member of the *opposite sex* to insure survival of the species

Thus, the necessities of existence are indeed few. No mention is made of the quality or quantity of   of these items except that they b.   icient to maintain life. The type of food, be it snails, wasps, birds, monkeys, snakes, roots, seeds, or any other form of animal or plant life, is of no significance. Not only must these things be present at all times, but also they must be sufficiently close together so that he can acquire them through his own physical efforts. If the food is too distant from the water he will either starve or thirst to death and the species will not survive. Therefore, within the area occupied by this natural man are all the elements needed to sustain his existence in a natural context.

However, the existence of these elements within the area does not insure that the man will acquire and *use* them. The elements will remain inert and unused until operated on by man's articulating force. The most significant motivating force of man that will cause the naturally occurring elements to be used is *instinct*. Instinct is an inborn tendency to behave in a way characteristic of a species; it is a natural phenomenon contributed through *hereditary* processes and is not acquired. Without the motivation of instinct, man would be unable to obtain and subsequently use the naturally occurring elements. Thus, within the natural state, instinct that is *used* (nondeliberately) to articulate the other elements for sustenance and survival is the single major *resource* employed by our man. Within this natural state, it is principally instinct that causes the manipulation of other elements so that they then become used and hence are also resources.

All of the elements that our man uses

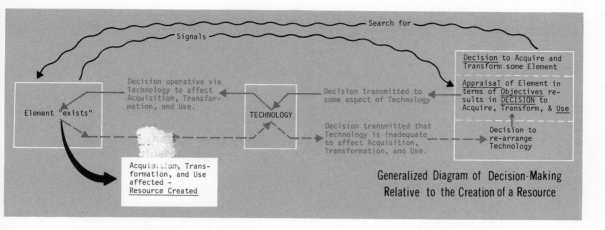

FIGURE 2.4   *The process of resource emergence. Each line represents the impact of a decision as it is operative throughout the system. Along any of the lines some relationships may demand that the decision be modified or completely changed. If the decision is "not to acquire, transform, or use," then the element will not be utilized as a resource. Thus, the major part of the process is that set of decisions made in terms of the objectives.*

Within a slightly modified context, we may substitute the political framework, social framework, etc., for technology. The "element" referred to in the diagram may be anything—the set of elements necessary to organize a mass transit system, devise a process to remove pollutants from the air, or utilize a new source of food. (General Media Corporation)

are referred to as *natural resources*—they are naturally occurring and are used in the context of and for natural processes. Within this concept of resource, each element of the environment is classified on the basis of its *use* or *function*. Elements that are not used by this man will not be called resources, since we have assumed that any resource involves use.

However, man as characterized above does not exist. All *Homo sapiens* through the processes of invention and diffusion have acquired culture traits passed from one generation to another or from one place to another during the same generation. When these acquired attitudes and behavior patterns are directed and applied to the naturally occurring elements of the environment, then those elements are used as a consequence of and for culturally generated purposes and hence are classified as *cultural resources*. With the development and use of culture traits, instinct is no longer the dominant energizing motivation.

This discussion does not imply that MAN has no "natural needs." All MEN have natural needs—the same as those of man: the natural need to eat, to eliminate wastes from the body, to drink water, to be sufficiently warm to maintain life, etc. However, in any human society, these natural needs are fulfilled through cultural media. The elements used, as well as the manner in which they are used, vary from society to society depending on the desires and technological ability of each. In some societies water is, via a series of processes, filtered, chlorinated, fluorinated, transported, and used not only for drinking, but also for cooling, heating, and washing. The existence and use of these processes and elements are not natural but culturally induced. They are not necessary to sustain life—only to maintain the essential ingredients of the societies that utilize them. Another society may acquire water by applying a hollow reed into an area of wet sand and allowing capillary action

FIGURE 2.5   *Embryo of fowl, ground grain, secretion of cow, hog meat, and ground berries—is this the way you usually think of the breakfast foods shown here?*

to raise water in the reed. Here, the process and use is also culturally induced. Likewise, steel is neither naturally occurring nor necessary to sustain man; however, it is deemed essential to modern industrial societies.

Still, some basic questions are not completely answered. Why do different societies use the same or different resources in different ways? As mentioned previously, all human activities are earthbound; their resources must come from the earth.[6] On a global scale, all MEN share the same set of *possible* resources. In addition, the quantity, quality, and type of naturally occurring elements vary significantly. However, each society has a distinct spatial distribution as well as variation in its characteristics. These variations and distributions in part account for the differences in resources.

[6]The term earth includes the geosphere, hydrosphere, and atmosphere.

In general there is a relatively common process that occurs prior to any element of the environment functioning as a resource. First, the element must *occur* or *exist*. It can be naturally occurring, man-made, or even believed to exist without actually "existing." (The *belief* by the alchemists that base metals could be transmuted to gold, and a desire for the riches associated with perfecting this process, spurred them into research that subsequently led to the development of chemistry. The belief existed, but not what was believed in; hence a "belief" may be a resource.)

Second, MAN must *recognize* (sense) and *appraise* (interpret, perceive) the element, and such appraisal must be positive. He must decide that use of the element is beneficial toward achieving his objectives. Third, he must possess the *ability to acquire* the element (technology), for if acquisition cannot be effected, the element does not function directly as a resource. Fourth, the element is actually acquired and used.

Many examples can be cited to support this concept of resource and these generalizations. Our society, for example, has selected numerous elements from our environment, modified them for specific purposes, and has used them so frequently that we have difficulty in not understanding why other societies have rejected them. Specifically, most individuals in our society have readily accepted the "wonder" drugs such as penicillin. Many pre-literate societies, however, even though they have been introduced to these drugs, have rejected them completely since they kill life (germs). Their societal values associated with the sanctity of life are considered more important than what we refer to as good health. Physicians working among peasants in Egypt discovered that trachoma and partial blindness were accepted as part of being healthy since they had always been present *and*, within the concept of the peasant, had been sent from God.[7] The Batak of Sumatra, formerly a sedentary agricultural society, have rejected their sedentary existence as a consequence of the destruction of their buffalo by tigers. The tigers, accepted by the tribe as sacred symbols, were allowed almost complete freedom among their villages.[8] Also, all societies (including our own) have rejected some potential food on the basis of their perceptions of the sources.[9]

Each of these acceptances or rejections is a reflection of perceptions based on a hierarchy of societal values. The basis of acceptance or rejection is a function of these values and not some quality

"inherent" in the thing perceived.

Two Major Sets of Resources

In the context of the theory discussed above, all things that MAN uses are resources. These include objects such as iron ore, water, buildings, jet aircraft, and tankers, as well as institutions and processes such as the family, tribe, sovereign state, government, religion, exchange arrangements, and so on.

One may argue about the inclusion of family, religion, government, technology, etc., in a list of resources. However, each of these, which are present in all societies, has specific uses or functions within the context of society. The political process and institution, for example, is frequently used as a means of directing the economic efforts of society. By offering tax incentives, special trading privileges, or access to state-owned land, political institutions can assist in economic direction. Also, the political institution represents a significant consumer of a variety of goods and services, as well as a producer of services for the general welfare of the society. Religion as well as religious organizations also have significant impact on most economic activities of a society. In many pre-industrial societies, religion is as pervasive in the economic behavior as the political institution is in an industrial society.

Summary

In order to facilitate more intensive analysis of resources, two broad sets may be created, one of which includes those resources that are used specifically to organize and direct those in the other set. The former set, entitled "frameworks," includes the social, political, technological, and economic frameworks. The latter set includes those on which the former operates: material resources, labor resources, and capital resources.

The following chapter will analyze

[7]Margaret Mead, *Cultural Patterns and Technical Change* (New York: New American Library, 1955), pp. 229–230.

[8]David Sopher, *Geography of Religions* (Englewood Cliffs, N. J., Prentice-Hall, Inc., 1967), p. 36.

[9]Some of the possible food sources we have generally rejected are dogs, cats, fertile eggs, various types of birds such as sparrows, canaries, eagles, and so on.

other general culture traits that give rise to and direct economic activity. In Part II specific attention will be devoted to the frameworks of economic activity.

selected references

1. Boulding, Kenneth E., *The Image*, Ann Arbor: University of Michigan Press, 1956.

2. Broek, Jan O. M., *Geography, Its Scope and Spirit*, Columbus, Ohio: Charles E. Merrill, Inc., 1965.

3. Chisholm, Roderick M., *Perceiving: A Philosophical Study*, Ithaca: Cornell University Press, 1957.

4. Freeman, T. W., "On the Work of Geographers," *The Geographer's Craft*, Oxford: Manchester University Press, 1967, pp. 1–18.

5. Gould, Peter R., "Man Against His Environment: A Game Theoretic Framework," *Annals of the Association of American Geographers*, Vol. 53, No. 3, September 1963, pp. 290–297.

6. Hallowell, A. Irving, *Culture and Experience*, Philadelphia: University of Pennsylvania Press, 1955.

7. Hartshorne, Richard, *Perspective on the Nature of Geography*, Chicago: Rand McNally and Company, 1959.

8. James, Preston E., and Jones, Clarence F., *American Geography: Inventory and Prospect*, Syracuse: Syracuse University Press, 1954.

9. Lewthwaite, Gordon R., "Environmentalism and Determinism: A Search for Clarification," *Annals of the Association of American Geographers*, Vol. 56, No. 1, March 1966, pp. 1–23.

10. Lowenthal, David, "Geography, Experience, and Imagination: Towards a Geographical Epistemology," *Annals of the Association of American Geographers*, Vol. 51, No. 3, September 1961, pp. 241–260.

11. Mead, Margaret, *Cultural Patterns and Technical Change*, New York: New American Library, 1955.

12. Morgan, W. B., and Moss, R. P., "Geography and Ecology: The Concept of the Community and Its Relation to Environment," *Annals of the Association of American Geographers*, Vol. 55, No. 2, June 1965, pp. 339–350.

13. Sopher, David, *Geography of Religions*, Englewood Cliffs, N. J.: Prentice-Hall, Inc., 1967.

14. Smythies, J. R., "The Problems of Perception," *British Journal for the Philosophy of Science*, Vol. 11, May 1960, pp. 224–238.

15. Wright, John K., "Terrae Incognital: The Place of the Imagination in Geography," *Annals of the Association of American Geographers*, Vol. 37, No. 1, March 1947, pp. 1–15.

Those materials that are present naturally and are directly usable by man are indeed meager. Nature, for example, does not provide housing, clothing, food, automobiles, iron ore, lead, steel, petroleum, lumber, glass, or aluminum;[1] the list can be extended almost indefinitely. If man desires any of these, as well as other resources on which his civilizations are based, he must acquire them through his own efforts complemented by his technology.

WANTS

This lack of materials directly usable by man means that *if* he is to live other than a natural existence (as characterized in Chapter 2) he must transform these naturally occurring things and hence engage in economic activity. Human wants are the mainspring of economic activity and their fulfillment is the end toward which all such activity is directed. In short, *all economic activities of all societies are contrived for a common objective —to provide the goods and services deemed desirable by all the people or a group of people in the society.*

Goods and services are acquired (through production–exchange) and consumed to give satisfaction. *Satisfaction* has many connotations and includes the innumerable motives that give rise to an activity—for example, the satisfaction derived by an individual on acquiring an automobile; the satisfaction of a Zulu after catching a scorpion for dinner; the satisfaction of a business man (in any society) after successfully concluding a transaction; the satisfaction of a Chinese peasant on acquiring nightsoil from the village latrine; or that felt by a student on graduating from college after having consumed goods (desks, chairs, maps,

chapter 3

Economy and Economic Activities

---

[1]These, as well as many other materials, do not occur either physically or chemically free in nature, but are rendered usable by mining, transporting, refining, hunting, agriculture, etc.

FIGURE 3.1 *What wants are being satisfied? (USDA)*

Characteristics of Wants

Wants, the desire to be satisfied, have two major characteristics: they are varied in time and space among all societies as well as within any society, and aggregately the desire to be satisfied is insatiable, especially over time among societies. Wants arise as a consequence of natural bodily functions mentioned in Chapter 2, and from stimuli by invention or diffusion. By far the most important wants of man result from the latter sources. Also, desire-satisfying processes frequently tend to create additional or new wants. The level of desire-satisfaction varies significantly from society to society and from time to time in all societies. Almost invariably in any society a "desirable" set of wants tends to be greater than that which presently exists.[3]

One might readily conclude that wants are traits of an individual and subsequent-

ly ask, why are economic activities of concern to society? Why does not each individual, or even family unit, produce the food, clothing, shelter, etc., that he or it will consume? An answer to these questions involves not only the characteristic of wants but the task of satisfying several wants within a short period of time.

SPECIALIZATION

Most of us are familiar with the story of Robinson Crusoe and the operation of the Crusoe economy. Mr. Crusoe, hav-

[2]This consumption is generally perceived as an investment in the student because the embodiment of education—knowledge and skills—enhances the productive capacity of the individual and also that of society.

[3]Measurements of economic level, such as per capita income, gross product, net product, etc., do not measure wants. These indices, although useful in some analyses of the performance of an activity, measure what has been accomplished, which is not necessarily the same as what was desired.

ing been shipwrecked on an uninhabited island and wanting to continue as many activities as possible, created a nearly self-sufficient economy.[4] That is, almost everything he consumed was produced through his own efforts amplified by a few basic tools. He was his own farmer, hunter, carpenter, tailor, governor, teacher, barber, and priest—in short, a jack-of-all-trades who through skillful operation of his economy provided himself with the goods and services he needed.

In addition to being nearly self-sufficient, this economy has other characteristics of importance to our discussion. The input was limited solely to the things that Mr. Crusoe could articulate through his own ideas and efforts.[5] Generally, the *input* consisted of: (1) the ideas that he had prior to being shipwrecked and those he developed on the island, which were expressed in his behavior of operating the (2) tools acquired from the ship and those he constructed, through which he manipulated the other (3) resources that he caused to emerge from his environment on the island. Also, everything that he did not previously know or possess had to be invented—since no other man was on the island diffusion of ideas could not occur. Consequently, the output, the goods and services produced and their quantity, quality, and variety, was limited by Mr. Crusoe's input.

Crusoe could perform only one operation at a time, and while thus engaged other operations were not performed. For example, time devoted to eating (consuming)[6] meant time not spent in producing food to consume; effort devoted to hunting resulted in effort not devoted to producing tools, firewood, shoes, etc. Also, utilization of other inputs, other than time and effort (use of axe to chop wood, for example), for one task meant their not being used at other tasks. Thus, Mr. Crusoe had to allocate his resources to specific operations at specific times and perform other operations later.[7]

Since the most basic and necessary of all wants are those that are perceived to insure survival, Mr. Crusoe performed the operations designed to satisfy these wants prior to performing other operations. To these he assigned the highest priority. Other wants and consequently operations to fulfill those wants were assigned lower priorities.

The limiting characteristic of Mr. Crusoe's economy was input, which determined the number of operations that could be accomplished in any unit of time. The greater the number of operations relative to the time, the greater the quantity of foods and services available at that or any subsequent time. By increasing this ratio he could then more nearly satisfy a greater range of his want hierarchy. That is, by increasing the rate at which he produced goods and services he could have access to a greater quantity and variety of services.

There were, however, significant limitations to his ability to increase the rate of production, including the limitations of knowledge, his physical strength and ability to manipulate tools, and more

---

[4]Since part of Mr. Crusoe's ability to operate his economy was a consequence of his using the tools (hoes, shovels, rifles, sailcloth, gunpowder, axes, etc.) that were taken from the ship before it sank, we may conclude that he was not *totally* self-sufficient, but was in part dependent on the work done by others in manufacturing these tools. Too, he was actually consuming these tools while employing them to produce other goods.

[5]All the ingredients that are used to produce other goods are generally referred to as *input*; the goods and services derived from the economy are referred to as *output*.

[6]Since eating was necessary, this can also be perceived as an investment that enhanced Mr. Crusoe's capacity to continue the economy.

[7]Allocation of resources must be done since all wants cannot be satisfied and are limited by "production possibilities." When Mr. Crusoe chose one alternative production over another—for example, to produce shoes instead of rope—the cost of the shoes is represented by the rope that was not produced. This is referred to as the Alternative Cost Doctrine.

FIGURE 3.2   *This is a "nearly natural" landscape. What "resources" are here? (Canadian Government Travel Bureau)*

generally his lack of specialization. This form of the Crusoe economy represents a nonspecialized economy.[8]

When Friday, a refugee from his own cannibalistic tribe, joined the Crusoe economy, there resulted a diffusion of ideas, increasing the number of operations that could be performed in any unit of time (since two people can do two things at the same time or reduce the time required for one operation), increasing the ability to articulate other resources, and hence increasing both the inputs and output of the economy. The major reason for the increased performance was the division of labor—specialization—that resulted. Generally, within certain limits, finer degrees of specialization

permit increases in inputs and in the output of an economic activity.

Specialization in its simplest form occurs as each worker in a society spends all his economic efforts in producing one good or service. One person produces cotton, another weaves cloth, and another sews the fabric into socks; or one makes arrows and another strings for bows. Each individual thus concentrates on one specific good or service, and craftsmanship can be refined to a degree of near-excellence. This type of specialization is characteristic of many pre-industrial societies. Some of the major characteristics of this degree of specialization, relative to higher degrees of specialization, are:

1. The scale of activities and the total volume of goods and services are smaller
2. The variety of any one good is smaller
3. There is a larger input of human effort and time (labor) for a smaller output of goods and services

[8]Theoretically, we may state that at any one time while performing a specific operation (shoe production), Mr. Crusoe was indeed specializing. And, he was specializing when he was producing only firewood, etc. However, in the total operation of the overall economy, which occurred during a long interval of time, the economy was nonspecialized because one specific operation was not the entire economy.

In industrial societies the degree of specialization is more intense. Whereas in the lesser degrees of specialization an individual may perform many different manipulations on a single good in the production process, in industrial societies the same manipulation is performed many times on different units of the same type of good. For example, a typical auto assembly-line worker will not produce an automobile, but devotes his entire working day to inserting thousands of the same type of bolt into slots on hundreds of different automobile frames, and the frames and bolts will be as nearly alike as standardized mass production techniques allow.

In *The Wealth of Nations* (1776), the economist Adam Smith [13] described a similar situation:

A workman not educated in this business . . . could scarcely make one pin in a day, and certainly could not make twenty. But in the way in which this business is now carried on, not only the whole work is a peculiar (specialized) trade, but it is divided into a number of (more specialized) branches . . . . One man draws out the wire, another straightens it, a third cuts it, a fourth points it, a fifth grinds it at the top for receiving the head; to make the head requires two or three distinct processes; to put it on is a peculiar business, to whiten the pins is still another; it is even a trade by itself to put them into the paper (container); and the important business of making pins is, in this matter, divided into about eighteen distinct operations, which in some manufactories, are all performed by distinct hands, though in others the same man will sometimes perform two or three of them. I have seen a small manufactory of this kind where only ten men were employed, and some of them performed two or three distinct operations. But . . . those ten persons . . . could make among them upwards of forty-eight thousand pins in a day! (pp. 4–5)

Let us analyze more closely the input and output of pins as described by Smith. In the initial situation (situation A), where one man was involved in producing pins, he "could scarcely make one pin in a day, and certainly could not make twenty." As an arbitrary output, let us assume that

this one man could make ten pins per day. Through changing the *process* of production, by introducing nine more men and then specializing the task, ten men could make 48,000 pins per day. Thus,

Situation A	Situation B
1 Man 10 Pins	10 Men 48,000 Pins
	or
	1 Man 4,800 Pins

If we consider the man-equivalency of pins (output) of B relative to that of A, in situation B one man is equivalent (in pins) to 480 men in situation A.

If our major desire is to produce a large number of pins and if the inputs are available, there is little doubt as to the process chosen—the intensive form of specialization.[9] Expanding these examples to a generalization, we may state that within certain limits an increase in the degree of specialization of any process will enable a larger number of wants to be realized.

Thus far the discussion of specialization has been in terms of a single stratum within the hierarchy of specialization. In this hierarchy there are many strata, involving for example, maintenance, personnel, workers, supervisors, researchers, administrators, etc. In modern industrial firms, hierarchical and stratum specialization have been developed to an intensity not even perceived by many pre-industrial societies (Fig. 3.3).

Specialization is characteristic not only of hierarchies but has also been imposed on space. Reflecting for a moment on the specialization resulting when Crusoe and Friday joined forces, we can illustrate a degree of spatial specialization. While Friday was preparing firewood and Crusoe engaged in sharpening an axe, each in a sense specialized, though

---

[9]It is not possible, however, to continue to increase this output with increases in input. At some level of the output/input ratio, the output increase rate will begin to decrease.

FIGURE 3.3 *Specialization of labor and space— how can this contribute to increased output (and profit)? (Cadillac Motor Car Division)*

for a short time. However, both of them occupied different spaces at the same time. Hence, in terms of the space (however small) being used by each, we may state that the space had a specialized use—that is, a space for sharpening axes and a space for cutting firewood. Specialization of labor also automatically resulted in a specialization of space used by that labor.

The same concept can be applied to the case of one or ten men involved in producing pins. In the former the labor was not specialized but the space was; in the latter each man occupied a discrete specialized space and performed a specialized part of a single process. Also, the total space occupied by the entire pin manufacturing plant represents a specialized space. The pin manufacturing plant received a part of its input from spaces outside the plant, i.e., inputs such as metal, paint, the machinery to draw the wire, sharpen it, etc. The metal, for example, was derived from another manufacturing plant and labor force specializing in metal refining, which previously

had received the metal ore from a space specializing in mining. Similarly, the machinery was derived from a variety of specialized labor forces, each occupying discrete specialized spaces devoted to the task of the labor forces.

Each of the specialized labor forces can be considered a society—a group of related individuals who share a common culture—and we can also consider the labor forces as part of a larger society, which would comprise not only the laborers and their operations, but the space they occupy. Thus, we could be describing a specialized society space devoted to the production of pins.

Previously we mentioned some of the characteristics associated with spatial distribution of cultures, societies, and economic activities. The economic activities of each society and the space that they occupy may be considered as being specialized relative to those of all other societies. Also, there are spaces of specialization within each society. Specialization for exchange is represented by the space occupied by a broker's office, a supermarket, or drugstore. Another form of exchange, transportation, has also been imposed on space in the form of railroad lines, highways, and pipelines. A coal mine, field of maize, and dairy farm represent types of economic activity which have been imposed on space. We may also conceive of a dinner table and a recreational park as specialized spaces for consumption. On a more specific basis, in the United States there are the highly specialized spaces (and associated economic activities) referred to as Corn Belt, Dairy Region, Spring Wheat Belt, and Yellowstone National Park.

In general, all parts of all economic activities and all parts of space are to some degree specialized. Specialization refers to the division of effort and space into different units, each of which has its own functions as determined by the wants and abilities of the society organizing and directing the effort and space.

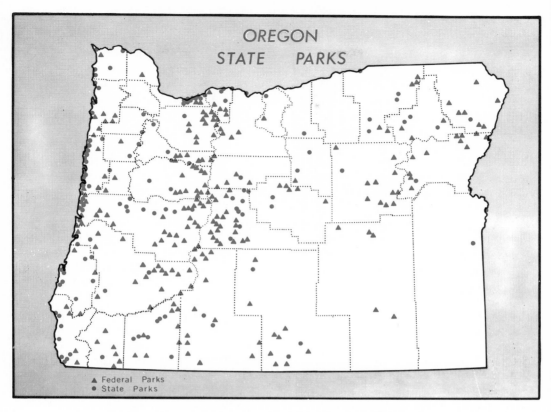

FIGURE 3.4 *Distribution of one type of specialized space (parks). (General Media Corporation)*

FIGURE 3.5 *How many types of different space functions can be recognized in this aerial view of Tananarive, Malagasy Republic? (Malagasy Director of Information)*

EXCHANGE

Specialization, even in the most simple of forms—the Crusoe–Friday economy—implies if not necessitates exchange. The spear maker cannot eat his spears, nor can the bread maker defend himself with his product. They, if they *want* other goods, must swap one good for another. This form of exchange is known as *barter*. If any regularity in the flow of goods and services is to be attained, then there must be an organization established to order not only production but also exchange, and in time of scarcity some system must exist for deciding priorities among people as well as among goods and services.

In a small isolated economy that utilizes simple specialization, the organization, although complex, may be understood and participated in by all. However, in a highly specialized industrial economy the task of getting producer and ultimate consumer together usually involves greater spaces and more people, and hence is much more complex.

Involved in this textbook, for example, are paper from lumbering; films and inks from petrochemical plants; binding material from cotton farms and textile mills; printing presses from iron ore and coal mines, iron smelters, and steel mills; rubber from rubber plantations, etc.—as well as the division of labor at the publicity office, and brokers, jobbers, wholesalers, market analysts, advertising agencies, retailers, and finally the student.

In an exchange-oriented society, there may be as many or more people engaged in services as in goods production. How does one part of the process know what the other parts want? Also, the process may break down at any point along the line, such as a strike by railroad or print shop workers, a machinery failure, or lost orders or invoices. If any part fails, failure may also occur in another part.

Barter

There are two principal means of exchanging goods and services: by barter or money. Bartering is the exchange of one good or service for another, e.g., trading eggs for potatoes, or skins for repair work on a canoe. About one-half the total population of humans does not fully participate in a barter economy. Also, this segment of man occupies more than half the entire inhabited land surface. This segment, forming many individual barter societies, is closely associated with pre-industrial activities and a simple state of specialization.

Lack of a money exchange acceptable to other societies places several restrictions on these societies with respect to their involvement in international trade. This lack, since some goods are difficult to store and "save," also results in a decreased ability to accumulate the kinds of goods necessary to develop more modern means of production and hence levels of consumption.

Money

Money is anything that serves as a medium of exchange and is acceptable to a society. The earliest forms of money were goods, such as cattle, honey, and salt. Each of these as well as many others were, at various times and spaces, of significance in establishing what we now refer to as a money economy. Our word salary, for example, is derived from the Latin for salt, which was a form of money frequently used to pay soldiers of the Roman Empire. Among the Navajo of Arizona and the Masai of East Africa, sheep and cattle respectively even now represent money as well as social status.

Money per se has little economic value; the value of money lies in what it can buy. The same applies to gold or any precious metal. The values are assigned to these goods. Also, money is not wealth—*real wealth* is the existing

physical stock and its ability to produce goods and services.

RESOURCES

Through the perspective of environmental perception we have previously defined a resource as anything that man
uses. Thus, all resources are cultural
resources, for a "natural" thing, whether
a river for power or navigation, or coal
extracted from its deposit, is used before
it assumes a cultural interpretation and
use. Without these latter events, it would
have no function for man and hence
would not be a resource.

However, resources represent a class of
objects and processes far too vast to be
discussed with any singularity. Consequently, it is advisable to divide cultural
resources into major groups. Five major
divisions appear appropriate and functional, and are generally recognized as
significant by social scientists:

1. Material resources
2. Labor resources
3. Capital resources
4. Entrepreneurship
5. Technology

Material Resources

Material resources[10] include all naturally
occurring man-transformed objects and
processes that societies use in their economic activities. These include timber,
seeds, water, fish, minerals, rivers, etc.—
all in the context of space.

Within this category the most important
is space, since space implies land as well
as minerals and many of the other material
resources. Also, control of space usually

carries with it control of the other resources *associated* therewith. However,
even in the United States this control
over space is sometimes vested at a societal level higher than the individual.
Control is *not* necessarily the same as
ownership or vice-versa. Zoning ordinances, for example, represent societal
controls over privately owned land. In
tribal societies it is frequently the village
or tribal chieftains who dictate what
shall be done with various material resources and in effect control the land—
though the "ownership," if such is recognized, is also vested in the same body.

Although the total mass of naturally
occurring objects that may function as
material resources is limited, the perceived importance of the mass and location of material resources varies considerably.

Labor Resources

Labor per se does not refer to people,
but to the expenditure of *time* and *energy*
by people in the production of goods and
services. Labor performed in a commercial
activity will generally result in one's
receiving money; whereas, in a noncommercial or barter activity the returns
may be in the form of goods. In general,
however, the labor resources of a society
also may be referred to as the working
force or economically productive group.

The quantity of labor available to any
one society, economic system, or activity is not fixed. It is principally a
function of the size of the population,
birth rate, death rate, migration, the percentage of that population in the working
force, and the hours expended by each
that the society is willing to contribute
to labor. The effectiveness of labor in
an activity is a function of its quality
and quantity. *Even in any one society* the
aptitudes, education, skills, health, co-
operativeness, ability, and willingness to
assume responsibility and adapt to change
vary widely.

[10]Using a perspective other than environmental
perception, one may classify these as natural resources. Economists frequently refer to this class
as "land," which includes everything under, in,
and on the ground not made by man; however,
only those elements that have economic use are of
practical importance.

The quality of a specific labor force is effectively measured only in terms of the activity it is to perform. For example, most of the labor force in the United States, however efficient it may be in an industrial society, would fail miserably in a pre-industrial activity such as shifting cultivation. Consequently, with respect to this latter system, the United States labor force may be said to be of low quality!

Spatial distribution of labor resources also is variable, especially as wants change, necessitating changes in the forms of production and the type of labor. As the desire for labor in one area decreases and in another increases, workers may respond by moving to the latter area. Hence, labor can be considered spatially mobile as the demand for one type of worker ceases in one area and arises in another—but with new people being trained in the latter area. Here there will be no movement of people between areas, but an areal shift in demand.

Capital Resources

Capital resources include all those resources created when labor is applied to material resources. The value of capital resources is due in part to the value assigned to material resources, but is principally a function of the value added to these by labor. Hence, capital resources are more valuable than material resources —but the latter must precede the former in any economic activity. Capital resources include such items as ploughs, hoes, shovels, railroads and locomotives, digging sticks, cranes, ships, fishing lines and hooks—in short, all items used in any form of production.

Money itself is not capital. However, in a commercial economy the possession of money is almost synonymous with the ownership of goods which the money can buy. Hence, one may consider money not as capital but as a means of gaining other goods or services held by other people.

Technology

Technology is the application of knowledge to the solution of practical problems. Thus, it is a process or technique for accomplishing an end. Technology is inexhaustible; once acquired it may be used as long as a society desires. However, as a result of the invention or diffusion of "newer" technology, "older" technology may be cast aside or altered.

A major cause of the *visible* differences among societies is the different technologies used to achieve a common end. Food production in an industrial society may be achieved through an industrial technology, and the process involves machinery, commercial fertilizer, swift

FIGURE 3.6 *The goal—food acquisition—is the same for both the man on the tractor and the men with spears hunting game. Why are their methods of pursuing the same goal different? (left—USDA; right—Australian News and Information Bureau)*

transportation systems, and the entire spectrum of other items including the retailer. A pre-industrial society landscape may consist of a few small scattered plots of land, sticks or hoes, scarecrows, and small mounds of earth in which the seeds are planted. For both societies the need is food—the means of acquiring it is different.

Entrepreneurship

Although entrepreneurship may be considered as a form of labor, here it is used in reference to a highly specialized expenditure of time and energy. Specifically, entrepreneurship is the ability of an individual or society to provide (1) high-quality management, (2) policy-making decisions, and (3) leadership to any or all aspects of the economic life of the society. An individual who possesses these qualities is referred to as an entrepreneur; a society characterized by these qualities is often called an enterprising society.

EFFECTIVENESS OF RESOURCES

Each of the above divisions of resources has distinct spatial variation in its quantity and quality. Their effectiveness in any society may be evaluated by any one or several criteria. For example, effectiveness may be evaluated on the basis of what a given society might be able to do with these resources. Almost invariably, however, members of one society tend to evaluate the characteristics of other societies on the basis of ethnocentric values.

Also, their effectiveness may be evaluated on the basis of what the *ideal economic efficiency* may be, given any specific society; or, and perhaps most important, the effectiveness of any one or all of these resources may and should be evaluated in terms of the *values* and *wants* of the society that uses the resource. A group

commonly referred to as "backward" or "primitive," for example, may not *want* the goods and services associated with an industrial society—consequently they will not organize their society to produce goods and services similar to those of an industrial society.

SOCIETAL CHOICES AND PRIORITIES

If all these resources were present everywhere at all times, and in quantities and qualities desired by all people, then the major choices of any individual or society would be associated primarily with the expenditure of time. That is, *"What do we want to do now?"* because we can do almost anything. However, these resources are limited[11] in time and space (and wants are unlimited), so decisions as to their "best" use must be made.

In making these decisions there are certain specific questions that must be answered. These questions, which all societies face and must answer within the context of their own societal values, may be effectively grouped into four general categories:

1. What goods and services shall be produced?
2. How and where shall these goods and services be produced?
3. Who will receive and consume these goods and services?
4. How will the productive capacity and capability of the society be maintained and/or increased?

What Goods and Services?

Since the resources of any society, within a given time, are limited, it is not possible to satisfy all present wants. The decision as to what shall be produced by the econ-

[11]Resources are limited because a society's wants exceed what the reserves can provide in a given time and place.

FIGURE 3.7 *Decisions! What should I buy? (Australian News and Information Bureau)*

omy is primarily a problem of deciding which wants are most important and to what degree these wants will be satisfied. Should steel, for example, which is presently available be used for production of rails, automobiles, ships, guns, or for the construction of a university? Should a portion of the steel be allocated equally toward producing all or a combination of these? Or should the steel or a portion thereof be sold and the returns used to purchase food or coal or some other good? If the decision is to use the steel for constructing one or a series of goods, then this means that other goods will not be produced from the steel. Similar questions may be asked with respect to all other resources.

If the wants of a society are to be satisfied, the society must produce those types of goods and services that are desired. Also, if societal wants as a whole are to be satisfied, then the decision-making process must be a societal one. Each society must create a system of values that reflects the want priorities of the group relative to the total range of goods and services that their economic activity can produce or acquire. The final decision of what shall be produced will be a reflection of what the society *wants* and *is able to produce.*

How Shall Goods and Services Be Produced?

Almost invariably any society has a variety of choices as to which methods to use in the production of goods and services. Societies with scientific-industrial capability have a wider variety of choices than do those with a pre-industrial technology. For example, in an industrial society iron can be produced by hand or by a variety of machine-oriented processes, including computer-assisted or operated techniques. In a pre-industrial society, iron cannot be produced by industrial machine processes, but only by hand.

Not only must the society decide which process shall be selected, but it also must decide if the process is to produce the largest quantity, the highest quality,

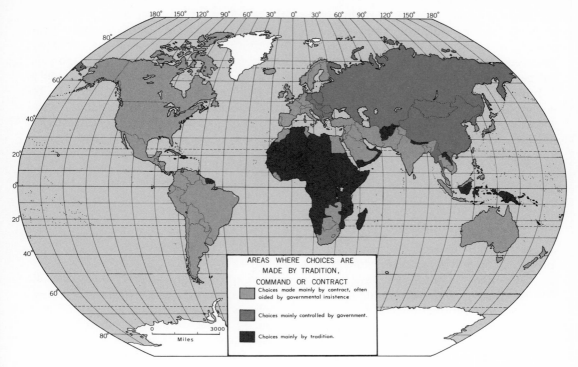

FIGURE 3.8 *World map showing where choices are made principally by (a) tradition, (b) command, and (c) contract. (General Media Corporation)*

or the greatest variety of goods and services. The process that produces the largest quantity may not be the same one that also turns out the highest quality of goods. In most societies a compromise is effected between quantity, quality, and variety of goods and services.

Who Receives the Goods and Services Produced?

Just as in resolving other questions, there are many possibilities in deciding the distribution of goods and services among the members of a society once they are produced. One possibility is to allocate to each member or family the same amount. Another is to give each member or family a set of goods and services commensurate with the needs of the member or family. A third solution is to distribute the products according to the contribution each member makes to

the process of production. Also, the goods and services may be allocated on the basis of some arbitrary dictates of a ruling individual or class of individuals. All of these methods of distribution are present in some form within any society; however, in some societies one method may be adopted more or less to the exclusion of the others.

In addition to decisions associated with methods of distribution, a society also makes decisions associated with specific products. Everyone has a place to live, but who lives in a house and who lives in an apartment; who lives near his place of work and who does not; who lives near the park and who lives near the refuse area? Also, who gets the T-bone steak and who gets the tongue and ears of the livestock? Who gets the stereo-TV console and who gets the radio? In a money-exchange society, the total amount of goods and services acquired by an individual is partially a function of the individual's income and the amount he is willing to spend for these various goods and services. Thus, the money-income is in part a means of regulating the distribution of goods and services. Also society, by its willingness or unwillingness to spend its income for various goods and services, in part determines the income of those people employed in specific activities.

How Shall Productive Capacity Be Maintained and Improved?

Every society expects to maintain its productivity and most desire to improve it. Maintenance includes keeping the productive power of the economic activities intact so that production will not fall below the present level. Improvement refers to an increase in the type, quantity, quality, and variety of products, and an increase in the techniques of production.

Material resources may be increased or changed through trial and error, scientific inquiry, and exchange with other societies. Labor resources can be increased through population increases, and development of additional or refinement of present skills through education. Capital improvement must be accomplished by diverting some resources from consumption and then using them to produce other goods. Improvements in production techniques result in a greater output of goods and services without an increase in the resources used in production.

Attempts to maintain the productivity of an activity commensurate with the society's desires may not be fruitful; hence the group may introduce changes in the activity that will result in production more compatible with their wants. Almost invariably, however, whatever changes are introduced will be made with a view to retaining as much of the traditional activity as possible. In some shifting cultivation societies, for example, newer food crops have been accepted for the realization of increased food production. However, even though productivity may be increased manyfold by other techniques being applied to the crop, the cultivators maintain the essence of their migratory economic activity. To shift to sedentary agriculture may be incompatible with their tribal organization, division of labor, religion, land tenure system, or some other societal value that is deemed as important as increasing the production of food.

MAKING THE CHOICES

These questions, of basic concern to all societies, must be resolved in some way. Each society will not only give different priority to each question, but it will also answer each question in a way different from other societies. Consequently, each will develop its own solution to providing the goods and services it deems compatible with its desires. In other words, each society develops, maintains, and promotes its own economic activities.

Within all the diversity we may perceive in the making of these choices, there are three general methods that embody most of the diversity: tradition, command or central authority, and voluntary arrangement between and among private parties.

Tradition or Custom

Most of the world's people live in societies whose economic activities are results of tradition being the major criterion in the decision-making process. What was decided and accomplished by their forebearers will be what is done now; yesterday's decisions, however realized and whatever their results (unless they pose a threat to the existence of the society), are almost exclusively the basis of what is done today and tomorrow. Within this decision-making process, over a long period of time the wants of the society remain somewhat static. Material resources, labor resources, capital, technology, and entrepreneurship all remain relatively stable; hence the economic activity, as well as the total characteristics of the society, continue almost unchanged.

Command or Central Authority

The major characteristic of this decision-making process is that a central authority (however determined, either democratically or despotically) makes the decisions and then imposes them on the society as a whole. This central authority may be benevolent toward the other members of the society; its decisions will be made in the interest of the general public. More likely the command authority may act in the interest of a special class, usually itself. A classic example of this type of decision making is the Soviet Union, in which almost all major problems are resolved in the upper portions of the party and government hierarchy.

Private Voluntary Arrangements (Contracts)

Within this process of decision making the members of a society are relatively free to act as individuals or as a group of individuals bound together voluntarily for mutual cooperation and action. The individual or groups of individuals, such as a family, corporation, etc., produce what they desire, live, work, and consume what their incomes allow. Their freedom of decision making is principally a function of the freedom that the society allows, and is limited primarily by their desire to negotiate with others for what they want. All of the negotiations or arrangements taken collectively are complex, and lest they become completely entangled and snarled must be regulated by law rather than custom.

Thus, no society or economic activity relies strictly on a single method of decision making. All societies at various levels of the hierarchy usually employ combinations of these three processes, emphasizing one and deemphasizing others.

selected references

1. Bews, John W., *Life as a Whole*, London: Longmans, Green & Co., Ltd., 1937.

2. Carol, Hans, "Stages of Technology and Their Impact Upon the Physical Environment: A Basic Problem in Cultural Geography," *Canadian Geographer*, Vol. 8, No. 1, January 1964, pp. 1-7.

3. Childs, V. G., *Man Makes Himself*, London: Watts & Co., 1936.

4. de Grazia, Sebastian, *Of Time, Work, and Leisure*, New York: The Twentieth Century Fund, 1962.

5. Ginsburg, Norton, "Natural Resources and Development," *Annals of the Association of American Geographers*, Vol. 47, No. 3, September 1957, pp. 196–212.

6. Hagen, Everett E., *On the Theory of Social Change*, Homewood, Ill.: The Dorsey Press, 1962.

7. Ken, Donald P., "The Tasks of Economic Geography," *The Canadian Geographer*, Vol. 61, No. 17, November 1960, pp. 1–9.

8. McCarty, Harold H., and Lindberg, James B., *A Preface to Economic Geography*, Englewood Cliffs, N. J.: Prentice-Hall, Inc., 1966.

9. McNee, Robert B., "The Changing Relationships of Economics and Economic Geography," *Economic Geography*, Vol. 35, No. 3, July 1959, pp. 189–198.

10. Mukeyee, Radhakamal, *Man and His Habitation: A Study in Social Ecology*, London: Longmans, Green & Co., Ltd., 1941.

11. Rostow, W. W., *The Stages of Economic Growth*, Cambridge: Cambridge University Press, 1960.

12. Samuelson, Paul A., *Economics: An Introductory Analysis*, 7th ed., New York: McGraw-Hill Book Company, Inc., 1967.

13. Smith, Adam, *The Wealth of Nations*, New York: Random House, 1937.

14. Snow, C. P., *The Two Cultures and the Scientific Revolution*, Cambridge: Cambridge University Press, 1959.

15. Thoman, Richard S.; Conkling, Edgar C.; and Yeates, Maurice H., *The Geography of Economic Activity*, 2d ed., New York: McGraw-Hill Book Company, Inc., 1968, pp. 85–101.

part II

Variables in Economic Activity

introduction

Within all societies there are numerous processes implemented through a variety of interrelated frameworks. *Framework* is used here to refer to the arrangement or structure of parts that together constitute a major portion of a society. For example, the demand, supply, markets, buyers, sellers, producers, consumers, and resources are some of the parts that constitute the economic framework of every society. The way these parts are structured and the way that the structure is operated gives direction and control to the economic activities.

In addition to the economic framework every society has a political, social, and technological framework, each of which is composed of parts interrelated with all other parts and frameworks. The frameworks of a society are those institutions the society has created in order to give overall control and direction to its activities. Here, however, we are more interested in how these frameworks are reflected in the overall economic activities of the society, as opposed to some other societal activities.

As mentioned previously, so interdependent are the parts and frameworks of a society that only in a conceptual way can we separate them for analysis. For example, in which part or framework does space belong? Obviously, it is a part of all frameworks, as are goods, services, resources, capital, and so on. Part II will analyze each of these frameworks, indicating their interrelations to each other and to the overall economic activities of society. As in previous chapters, attention will be specifically confined to the parts of frameworks that all societies have in common.[1]

---

[1] Whether or not members of a particular society recognize the importance of spatial array of material resources, market, supply, comparative advantage, political decision processes, etc. in the operation of their economy, these concepts are indeed operative.

Problems associated with the importance and relative scarcity of resources have widened from a local societal concern to include the issues of adequacy of resources, their development and conservation, and the alternative measures of meeting human needs and wants on a global scale. The significance of the relationship between economic activities and resources strongly suggests the need to understand their spatial distribution, form and quantities, and potential supplies—all of which have strong bearing on where economic activities occur and develop.

LIMITS ON THE SUPPLY OF MATERIAL RESOURCES

Land constitutes slightly less than one-third (29.3 percent) of the surface of the earth, and water more than two-thirds (70.7 percent). Man has dominion over both the vast resources perceived in the land, and the present and potentially abundant wealth of oceans. However, the land-based resources—for food, minerals, energy, water, and construction—have been and are being exploited many times more rapidly than those of the ocean. This is partly due to the relative cheapness of land-based activities under prevailing technology. But, as population pressures impinge on the limits of land-based resources, increased exploitation of ocean-based resources tends to become desirable, if not altogether feasible.[1]

chapter **4**

Materials Resource Framework

[1] Besides the ocean, man has turned to atmospheric resources for making many products. Air, once considered useless for industrial purposes, now provides raw materials for the so-called gases industry founded upon cryogenics. Revolutionary developments in the art of steel production, such as the Basic Oxygen Furnace (BOF), and other uses of products derived from air (nitrogen, argon, hydrogen), have brought into existence in the United States approximately 500 manufacturing establishments engaged in the production of air-based products. During 1966 the sales of gases and liquids was over $700 million, a volume that is expected to increase rapidly in the years ahead.

The question of feasibility is a matter of technology and the relative scarcity of the various resources. Throughout the past man has responded to challenges by adaptation or by discovering new means of meeting human demands. Although adaptations to the accomplishments of science and technology seem to be dramatically trenched against the increase of population, now running at three percent, or a doubling every twenty-four years in many developing areas, the exhaustibility of many resources is a naked fact.

LAND-BASED RESOURCES

Almost all of the earth's land surface has been explored by man, and the resources he has perceived are not only unevenly distributed but also are appropriated for diverse uses over space and time. A commonly used classification of resources is:

1. Land
2. Energy
3. Minerals
4. Water

Excluded from this list are the ice-covered wastes of Antarctica, many marshy and water-logged areas, and perhaps some parts of the deserts. These excluded items, however, are noneconomic resources only as long as present technology is insufficient to warrant their usefulness and human demand for their use is nonexistent. With this thought some scholars regard these noneconomic resources as potentially productive.

Of the 57.5 million square miles that

Table 4.1   Major Land Uses

Area		Total Area	Arable Cropland	Meadows and Pasture	Forest Land	Unused but Potentially Productive	Built upon, Wasteland, and Other
		(millions of acres)			(percentages)		
World Total		33,116.3	10.7	21.5	29.8	3.0	35.0
Continents	Percent Distribution of World Population (1967)						
Europe*	13.22	1,218.2	10.5	3.1	3.5	2.2	2.2
North America	6.43	4,870.3	15.5	9.8	18.5	21.6	14.3
Latin America	7.57	5,087.8	7.6	17.6	25.4	13.8	8.4
Near East	30.12	3,009.7	5.3	6.7	3.1	13.0	16.2
Far East*	4.59	2,760.1	19.0	3.9	10.4	2.0	6.2
Africa	9.59	6,170.1	15.1	23.7	12.4	31.9	21.7
Oceania	0.53	2,102.8	2.7	16.1	2.1	1.6	5.3
U.S.S.R.	6.90	5,535.0	16.7	12.9	22.7	2.5	14.1
Mainland China	21.05	2,362.3	7.6	6.2	1.9	11.4	11.6
Selected Nations						All Others	
Australia		1,899.4	4.8	58.4	4.6	32.2	
Canada		2,465.1	4.4	2.1	44.4	49.1	
China (Mainland)		2,362.3	11.4	18.6	8.1	61.9	
France		135.2	37.6	24.6	22.6	15.2	
India		807.5	49.7	4.5	18.7	27.1	
Japan		91.3	16.2	2.6	68.7	12.5	
United Kingdom		60.3	30.7	49.6	7.5	12.2	
United States (incl. Virgin Islands)		2,313.7	19.3	27.5	31.8	21.4	
U.S.S.R.		5,535.0	10.8	16.6	40.6	32.0	

*Populations and land-use data for the U.S.S.R. and Mainland China are not included in the totals for Europe or Asia, but are reported separately.

Source: Statistical Yearbook, 1968 (New York: United Nations, 1969), pp. 22–26, and Yearbook of Food and Agriculture, 1967 (Rome: United Nations, FAO, 1968), Vol. 21, pp. 3–8.

include continents, islands, and lakes and rivers, 55 million square miles (35.7 billion acres) are land surface. After deduction is made for the ice-covered wastes of Antarctica, more than 33 billion acres remain. As shown in Table 4.l, approximately 3.5 billion acres (10.7 percent) of this total is classified as arable land; 7.1 billion acres (21.5 percent) is classified as meadows and pastures; 9.9 billion acres (29.8 percent) is forest land; 1.0 billion acres (3.0 percent) is classified as "unused but potentially productive"; and the remaining 11.5 billion acres (35.0 percent) is built upon, wasteland, and other.

Table 4.1 shows the distribution of each resource category among the seven continents. Asia (excluding the USSR), with 55.76 percent of the world's population, has 31.9 percent of the world's arable cropland, whereas North America, with 6.4 percent of the world's population, possesses 15.5 percent of the world's arable cropland. Similar comparisons show a disproportionate distribution of people and land.

When the land controlled by any society is classified according to its various uses and is compared with land uses of other societies, the land-use distribution pattern also varies considerably. Table 4.1 shows this type of allocation for several areas. For example, India has only 4.5 percent of its area classified as meadow or pasture, while approximately half of the area in both Australia and the United Kingdom is used for this purpose.

In the United States, about one-fifth of the surface land area is arable cropland; less than one-third is in forest land, meadows, and pasture; and approximately 21 percent is built upon, wasteland, or is used for other purposes. Approximately 80 percent of the surface is used for cropland, pasture, grazing, forestry, and other, including "potentially productive."

The land-use pattern in the United States varies considerably by regions. For example, more than 50 percent of the land in the northern Great Plains and the Corn Belt is used as cropland. Pasturing and grazing dominate in the mountain, southern Plains, and northern Plains regions. Forest is the dominant land use in the Southeast, the Mississippi Delta, the Northeast, and the Appalachian, Pacific, and Lake States regions.

Data indicate that land-use patterns have changed considerably over the past several years in the United States. From the 1890s to the 1920s, agricultural acreage showed an upward trend. During this period, acreage under farm crops more than doubled; from 1920 to 1970 farm crop acreage remained much the same, but farm output has increased tremendously. This is attributed to the phenomenal increase in farm productivity, behind which lies a long list of improvements in the science of agriculture. Extensive mechanization, application of technical knowledge produced by the armies of Land Grant colleges and universities, and structural changes in agriculture are the basic factors responsible for higher U.S. farm productivity. Increases in cropland through reclamation—clearing, drainage, and irrigation—have been balanced by the abandonment and shifting of cropland to pastures and other uses. For example, between 1930 and 1950, twenty million acres of new cropland were brought into use by reclamation, but during the same period twenty-four million acres of cropland were shifted to pastures, woodland, and nonfarm uses.

Table 4.1 indicates that approximately 21 percent of the land area (486 million acres) in the United States is either built upon, wasteland, or is used for other purposes. However, within this category, authentic information is scarce pertaining to further breakdown according to land use, i.e., buildings (residential, commercial, industrial, service), highways and roads, railroad rights-of-way, mining, airports, state and national parks, wildlife areas, national defense areas, powerline lanes, and the like. According to Barlowe [1] and others,[2] the total area for these purposes during 1960 was approximately 228 million acres out of the total land area of 1,904 million acres. The breakdown of this total is given in Table 4.2.

Table 4.2   Land Use in the U.S.A., 1960

	Million Acres	Percent
Urban areas	21	9.21
Highways and roads	20	8.77
Railroad rights-of-way	3	1.32
Airports	3	1.32
Recreation	44	19.30
Reservoirs	12	5.26
Wildlife areas	15	6.58
National defense areas	22	9.65
With no specific use	88	38.59
	228	100.00

Source: Hans H. Landsberg, L. L. Fischman, and J. L. Fisher, Resources in America's Future (Baltimore: The Johns Hopkins Press, 1963), Table 18-15, p. 373, with permission of the publisher.

Generally speaking, the nonagricultural uses of land resources have been influenced heavily by technology and societal objectives. Each such use, moreover, has involved varying degrees of technology as well as a diversity of resources. For example, urban growth is a recent phenomenon resulting from much greater technological advancements. Table 4.3 shows the percent of the world's population living in cities during various years. It is obvious from this table that urbanization has gone ahead much faster and reached proportions far greater during the past century and a half than at any previous time.

Partly responsible for this rapidity of urbanization are the structural and

[2]Barlowe's data were later revised and updated by a Resources for the Future study: Hans H. Landsberg, L. L. Fischman, and J. L. Fisher, Resources in America's Future (Baltimore: The Johns Hopkins Press, 1963). The figure in Table 4.2 of 228 million acres is for the continental United States.

Table 4.3   Percentage of World's Population Living in Cities

Year	Cities of 20,000 or more, but less than 100,000	Cities of 100,000 or more
1800	2.4	1.7
1850	4.3	2.3
1900	9.2	5.5
1950	20.9	13.1
1960	25.2	17.5

technological developments in the agricultural sector. As farming becomes increasingly mechanized and rationalized, fewer people are needed to produce food and fiber. Without these technological developments, the land-use patterns of human settlement would most likely have been different. How far technology can influence land use is not known. Kingsley [14] says that

if in addition to industrialized agriculture, food and fiber come to be increasingly produced by manufacturing processes using materials that utilize the sun's energy more efficiently than do plants, there is no technological reason why nearly all of mankind could not live in conurbations of large size.

Although the rate of urbanization in developed regions is decreasing, the rate of urbanization in the world as a whole does not indicate any slowing down. This means that the urbanization gap between industrially developed and less developed regions is beginning to diminish. The percent of the world's population living in cities by regions (1960) appears in Table 4.4.

Table 4.4   Percent of World's Population Living in Cities by Regions, 1960

Region	In cities of 20,000 plus	In cities of 500,000 plus
World	25	11.7
Oceania	50	31.1
North America	57	36.2
Europe (except U.S.S.R.)	41	17.1
U.S.S.R.	36	12.5
Latin America	32	16.6
Asia (except U.S.S.R.)	17	7.9
Africa	13	3.9

These developments are merely indicative of land-use patterns for nonagricultural purposes. Unfortunately, no authentic nonagricultural land-use data are presently available, except indirect measures such as number of people, weight, or monetary worth of the commodities associated with nonagricultural land use. (Data for these measures, where available, may be used to derive the land-use estimates.) Further difficulty, however, exists in converting these measures into land-use estimates because of varying regional or national measurement standards and nomenclature. Not only are the measurement standards different for a great number of the commodities by regions, they are also different for the various commodities themselves.

ENERGY RESOURCES

The relation between economic progress and the increased use of energy is universally recognized. Considerations of where and how energy is produced, transported, or distributed are the major topics treated here.

Several sources of energy are known to mankind, and for the purpose of adding together the different energy sources, their energy value can be converted into various common denominators, such as kilowatt-hours (kwh), calories, or British thermal units (Btu).[3] Since converted data in the form of hard-coal-equivalent (h.c.e.) are readily available from United Nations sources, the same will be followed here.[4]

Energy, the force behind all work, stems from both animate and inanimate sources. The so-called animate sources consist chiefly of man and animals; also included in this category are fuel woods and agricultural wastes (such as dung, dried stems, leaves, and roots). The inanimate sources include both the fossil-orientated and nonfossil-orientated energy resources. The former include coal, crude petroleum fuel and shale oils, gas, peat, and certain metals such as those used in nuclear energy production. The nonfossil-orientated energy resources are water, wind, sun, and air. Still, one-fifth of the world's supply of energy when measured in h.c.e. is from animate sources, 65 percent of which is attributed to fuel wood and agricultural wastes.

Energy has many meanings and diverse manifestations depending upon its source and process of conversion into work.[5] Table 4.5, based on UN statistics, shows that in 1967 the world's production of energy from coal, lignite, crude petroleum, natural gas, hydro and nuclear electricity, and peat was 5,756 million metric tons h.c.e. On a per capita basis this amounts to about 1,683 kilograms h.c.e. The spatial variation in production and consumption of energy is highly significant. At one extreme, the United States, with just under 6 percent of the world's population (1967), produces over 31 percent of the world's total energy and consumes more than one-third of the world's total commercial energy supplies. Toward the other end of the range, India (not shown in the table), with almost 15 percent of the world's population, uses only

---

[3]Kwh is a unit of electrical energy or work equal to that done by one kilowatt acting for one hour. One kilowatt is equal to 1.34102 British horsepower, or the lifting of 21 short tons a foot per minute (equivalent to more than 55 Btu per minute). Btu is a unit of heat equal to 252 calories—the quantity of heat required to raise the temperature of one pound of water from 62°F to 63°F. A calorie is a unit of heat needed to raise the temperature of one gram of water one degree centigrade, called small calorie.

[4]Hard-coal-equivalent is a common denominator for various energy sources based on their calorific

value; for example, one metric ton of coal briquettes is equal to 0.67 metric ton of coal; one metric ton of crude petroleum and shale oil is equal to 1.3 metric tons of coal; 1,000 cubic meters of natural gas is equal to 1.33 metric tons of coal; and 1,000 kwh are equal to 0.125 metric ton of coal. Similarly, other sources have their conversion factors; one metric ton is 1,000 kilograms or 2,205 pounds.

[5]For detailed analysis of the nature and sources of energy, see Erich W. Zimmerman, *World Resources and Industries*, revised ed. (New York: Harper and Brothers Publishers, 1951).

Table 4.5   Production and Consumption of Energy, 1967

Region	Energy Production (millions of metric tons of h.c.e.)		Percent of World Total		Population (millions)	Percent of World Total	Per Capita Energy (kilograms h.c.e.)	
	Production	Consumption³	Production	Consumption			Production	Consumption
World total	5,755.83	5,614.35	100.00	100.00	3,420.00	100.00	1,683	1,642
North America	1,974.06	2,122.11	34.30	37.80	220.00	6.43	8,973	9,646
United States	1,817.94	1,956.95	31.58	34.86	199.00	5.82	9,135	9,834
Canada	156.09	164.76	2.71	2.93	20.00	0.59	7,804	8,238
South America	392.08	203.14	6.81	3.62	259.00	7.57	1,514	784
Western Europe	537.23	1,096.04	9.33	19.52	351.00	10.26	1,530	3,123
Middle East	663.10	51.09	11.52	0.91	157.00	4.59	4,224	325
Far East¹	208.89	502.94	3.63	8.96	1,030.00	30.12	203	488
Mainland China	266.83	266.84	4.64	4.75	720.00	21.05	371	371
Oceania	46.20	65.17	0.80	1.16	18.00	0.53	2,567	3,621
Africa	253.93	93.46	4.41	1.67	328.00	9.59	774	285
Eastern Europe²	367.23	281.42	6.38	5.01	101.00	2.96	3,636	2,786
U.S.S.R.	1,046.28	932.14	18.18	16.60	236.00	6.90	4,433	3,950

¹ Far East excludes Mainland China.
² Eastern Europe excludes U.S.S.R.
³ Bunkers supplied to foreign-going ships are excluded from Consumption.
Source: Statistical Yearbook, 1968 (New York: United Nations, 1968), pp. 349–352.

FIGURE 4.1   *Above—Nuclear reactors for production of electricity at Chinon, France. (NATO) Below—Maraetai hydro power station, New Zealand. (New Zealand National Publicity Studios)*

about 1.5 percent of the world's commercial energy. (It is recognized that this comparison is not entirely realistic, especially when energy sources such as wood, animal power, and dung are considered, which constitute a significant fraction of all the energy used in India and many other developing regions.) The Far East, with over 30 percent of the world's population, consumes only 9 percent of the world's commercial energy supplies.

Table 4.6 indicates that the relative importance of various energy sources has strikingly shifted over the past years. In 1929 solid fuels (coal and lignite) supplied almost 80 percent of the world's commercial energy. By 1967 the solid-fuel fraction had dropped to 38 percent. During the same period the share supplied by liquid fuels (crude petroleum) more than doubled, from 15 to 40 percent. The biggest gain of all was made by natural gas, which increased from 4.5 to 19 percent of the total. Although the share supplied by hydro and nuclear electric power more than doubled during the period, it still continues to be a small fraction of the total.

During these years the United States led the way in the shift from solid to liquid and gaseous fuels and strongly influenced the world totals. Oil and natural gas supplied 75 percent of all the energy consumed in the United States. In Western Europe and the U.S.S.R., coal is still important. In the U.S.S.R. there is a moderate rise in the use of liquid fuels, and in Western Europe their use has increased markedly.

The less developed and developing parts of the world depend on liquid fuels far more than do the developed regions. In 1967, liquid fuels represented more than half of the total energy consumed in the developing countries, which compares to 31 percent in 1929. Interestingly enough, historically speaking the developing countries have not followed a similar path for their energy supplies— that is, from coal to liquid fuels and from liquid fuels to hyroelectricity and natural gas. These countries are right in line with the world-wide swing to liquid fuels and natural gas from coal. There are a number of reasons for this trend:

1. Oil can be transported much more cheaply than coal over long distances.
2. The known reserves of economically mineable coal are running low.
3. To meet increasing demands for energy, alternative ways of procuring it must be sought.
4. Both natural gas and liquid fuels provide greater energy per unit of weight.

The question of adequacy of energy resources has recently attracted widespread interest. The variables that enter into this appraisal are multiplex. The demand side considers future structural changes, type and level of economic activities, and consumer tastes and preferences. The supply aspect is controlled by "know-how," and consequently the world's total energy resources are really not known. The endowment is what is actually known to exist with the prevailing technology and under the limitations of cost. Thus the measure of the resource endowment is confined to resources that are known, exploitable now, or seem likely to be in the future.

Searl [17] estimates that between 1960 and 2000 the world will have consumed approximately 435 billion metric tons of h.c.e., which means that over a forty-year period the world's energy resources will be depleted at an annual rate of 2 1/2 times that of 1960. Estimates developed by the U.S. Geological Survey indicate that a world total equivalent of 2,320 billion metric tons of recoverable coal alone are available for use, in known deposits with seams fourteen or more inches thick and lying within 3,000 feet of the surface. (This estimate does not take into consideration the allowances for discovery of new coal deposits.) Thus, if one subtracts the estimated consumption between 1960 and 2000 (435 billion metric

Table 4.6   Total and Percent Composition of Energy Use, 1929 and 1967

Energy Source	World 1929	World 1967	United States 1929	United States 1967	U.S.S.R. 1929	U.S.S.R. 1967	Western Europe 1929	Western Europe 1967	Latin America Far East Middle East Africa 1929	Latin America Far East Middle East Africa 1967
Coal and Lignite	79.8	38.3	67.9	23.0	71.5	37.0	95.2	44.8	67.3	38.5
Crude Petroleum	14.9	40.4	22.3	40.4	28.0	40.3	3.8	48.2	30.9	52.3
Natural Gas	4.5	19.0	9.3	34.5	0.4	18.6	—	3.0	1.3	5.0
Hydro and Nuclear Power	0.8	2.3	0.5	2.1	0.1	4.1	1.0	4.0	0.5	4.2
Total (in million metric tons h.c.e.)	1711	5756	777	1955	73	996	516	1096	77	580

Source: Based on *United Nations World Energy Supplies in Selected Years, 1920–1950,* Statistical Papers, Series J, No. 1 (New York: September 1952), and *Minerals Yearbook,* 1967, Vols. I–IV (Washington, D.C.: U.S. Department of the Interior, 1969).

tons h.c.e.) from 2,320, it still leaves 1885 billion metric tons h.c.e., which is sufficient to satisfy the world's total demand for energy for almost another century beyond the year 2000 at the estimated annual level of consumption in the year 2000.

The world's potential resources of oil and natural gas, as estimated by responsible authorities (U.S. Geological Survey and the Shell Development Company), are between 535 and 1,620 billion metric tons h.c.e. The former figure is based on existing standards, whereas the latter includes deposits that are considered submarginal by today's standards and whose exploitation depends on future economic and technological factors. These estimates are mere indicators and are subject to substantial upward revisions. The increase in demand and price would justify the search for new deposits and the development of new technology.

Besides, vast potential resources of oil shale and oil-bearing tar sands have been discovered. Although the present contribution of hydro, nuclear, atomic, and solar power is very small, potential progress in these areas appears promising.

Finally, it is evident that the world's need for energy could be met with fossil fuels alone for at least two or more centuries. Nevertheless, as the costs of alternative energy-producing sources decline, they will effectively compete with and substitute the fossil fuels. Thus, when the world's resources of uranium, thorium, granite, and weightless and freight-free nuclear fuels are all taken into consideration, man can be said to have within reach an almost unlimited supply of energy.

MINERALS

Minerals are the basic source for various energy fuels, chemicals, metals, and construction materials. Fuel minerals were discussed in the preceding section. Among the nonfuel nonmetallic minerals, sulphur, salt, potash, lime, borates, phosphates, gypsum, asbestos, glass, stones, and diamonds are the most common and widely explored. Similarly, among the metallic minerals, the most important are iron ore, bauxite, manganese, chromite, copper, zinc, lead, nickel, tin, titanium, vanadium, molybdenum, tungsten, and cobalt. In addition, other metals are produced:

1. Primarily as by-products of processing

other metals—antimony, arsenic tri-oxide, indium, platinum groups, cad-minium, thallium, germanium, and the like

2. Primarily as by-products of mining other metals—hafnium, titanium, be-ryllium, columbium, and tantalum

3. Wholly or largely produced and proc-essed independently—mercury, sili-con, and strontium

The nonfuel minerals in their various forms bear numerous and distinctive properties. For example, the general char-acteristics of acidity, alkalinity, solu-bility, and stability may be applied to chemicals; metals may possess the proper-ties of strength, toughness, endurance, magnetism, conductivity, and the ability to withstand the influence of weather, large loads, corrosion, and intense heat. By virtue of these properties, minerals provide the basic fabric of man's material progress. Time series data on world econ-omies indicate that the rising consump-tion of metallurgical and chemical prod-ucts is positively correlated with per capita gross national product.

The industrially developed countries, which consume the major portion of the world's minerals, depend on the less developed countries for the bulk of their supply. For instance, the United States imports all its tin, more than 90 percent of its manganese, antimony, beryllium and chromium ores, more than 85 percent of its nickel, about 75 percent of its baux-ite, and about 72 percent of its zinc and lead. On the other hand, the less devel-oped societies, recognizing the relation-ship between gross national product and the consumption of minerals in the devel-oped societies, are venturing to capture the benefits from their mineral wealth. Often, however, they face frustration in this endeavor because of the inability of their economies to effectively utilize these minerals.[6]

Behind the demand and supply esti-mates of minerals lie certain assump-tions and concepts, the understanding of which is important in the evaluation of mineral resources. The concept of resource was discussed in Chapter 2 and can be readily applied here. Other concepts relevant to minerals are grade, reserves, and substitution.

Grade. The grade or quality and the per-cent of metallic content of the ore often serve as a common criterion for the esti-mation of reserves at various locations.

Reserves. Mineral reserves have been addressed under at least three areas:

1. Known or proved reserves
2. Potential reserves
3. Ultimate or absolute reserves

Known or proved reserves are the amounts of ore (adjusted for grade) that are known to exist and are workable under the conditions of current technol-ogy. Potential reserves refer to the miner-als that will be realized in the future under improved technology. The distin-guishing factor between proved and po-tential reserves is the criterion of current feasibility and the workability of the ore. Materials that cannot be worked under present economic and technological con-straints are termed potential minerals.

Ultimate reserves are commonly de-fined as the sum of past production, current proved reserves, and reserves

[6]U.S. Joint Economic Committee, *Twenty Years After: An Appeal for the Renewal of International Economic Cooperation on a Grand Scale* (Washington, D.C.: Government Printing Office, September 1966). The United States Subcommittee on International Exchange and Payments of the Joint Economic Committee, being aware of U.S. dependence on for-eign mineral resources, the contemporary events in foreign countries endowed with these minerals, and other international trade considerations prepared this report. In the report, not only interest and dis-cussion are provoked, but also a thoughtful evalua-tion of the problem is presented to Congress and the nations who trade with the United States. The president's Materials Policy Commission, based on detailed analyses of demand and supply of minerals, expressed similar concerns during the early 1950s in *Resources for Freedom* (Washington, D.C.: U.S. Government Printing Office, 1952), Volume II.

that will be discovered in the future at the current conditions of cost and technology. All of these concepts depend upon inference based largely on indirect or geological surveys for their quantitative estimation—it is obvious that to systematically dig up even the first 100,000 feet of the earth's crust from pole to pole for precise quantitative estimation of minerals is an impossible task. The important thing is that for spatial evaluation of minerals, a *common* reserves criterion should be applied.

Substitution. Closely associated with the problem of estimating demand–supply relationships is the concept of substitution. Every ore that is mined for use occurs under a wide variety of conditions that collectively determine the demand and supply of the ore. At one pole are conditions where pure minerals are situated at the surface and located at the best possible site with respect to transportation and markets. The other represents ores of lowest possible grade, highest percentage of deleterious impurities, greatest depth, poorest location, and all other disadvantages of winning the product from the ore. Each set of conditions reflects a cost which, in the absence of improved technology, rises as the resources approach depletion or exhaustion. The cost need not be a linear function of time and depletion.

Substitution plays an important role in the effort to make materials go further. For example, when the high-quality iron ores—magnetite and hematite—in the Lake Superior region began to run out, not only were methods developed for utilizing the lower grade taconite ores found in the same area, but also steel substitutes—aluminum, magnesium, titanium, structural concrete—and a variety of strong, durable plastics resistant to heat and cold began to replace steel in many industries. Steel alloys, which have a greater tensile strength with less weight, now are being substituted for convention-

al steel. The use of aluminum is common in the construction industry. Tens of thousands of tons of aluminum are being used in barges, bridges, truck trailers, railroad cars, and automobiles. Some even project that the use of steel will be completely reversed; i.e., materials like plastics will replace steel, and steel will occupy the position held by plastics today.

The new technologies not only are making substitutions practical, but they are also giving a new meaning to the serious concerns expressed immediately after World War II toward the depletion of mineral resources. New devices and instruments—areal cameras, air-borne magnetometers, scintilometers, electromagnetic induction devices—have doubled and tripled the world's known reserves of many materials.

It is difficult to obtain reliable reserves estimates because the economic and technological factors related to local phenomena determine whether material of a given grade is or is not an ore. A material might be entered in reserve columns but may never be economically feasible to mine. Second, future substitutions and structural changes in the demand for the ore might change the whole picture, leaving the reserve estimates merely to be remembered as googol-size figures.

Perhaps the actual production of the various ores can give an accurate indication of regional endowment and productivity. The data in Table 4.7 present the total world production of twenty-four selected minerals, the leading nations, and the consumption of these minerals in the United States. It is evident from this table that:

1. Relatively few countries produce any significant share of the world's minerals. For example, only four countries account for over 50 percent of the total world output for every mineral listed.
2. The United States, a major consumer of minerals, is greatly dependent on for-

Table 4.7 Mineral Production (World, Leading Countries, and U.S.) and U.S. Consumption, 1967

Mineral	Total World Production†	Production as Percent of World Total — Four Leading Countries								U.S.	U.S. Consumption‡ as Percent of World Production	U.S. Production as Percent of U.S. Consumption
Antimony (ore content)	60.4 m.t.	Mnlnd China	20	Rep.S.Af.	20	Bolivia	19	U.S.S.R.	11	1	26.94	4.00
Asbestos (unmanufactured)	3,520.0 m.t.	Canada	40	U.S.S.R.	25	Rep.S.Af.	7	S.Rodesia	4	3	18.57	17.10
Bauxite (crude and dried)	46,350.0 m.t.	Jamaica	20	Surinam	12	Australia	11	Australia	9	5	33.25	11.40
Chromium (ore content)	2,250.0 m.t.	U.S.S.R.	29	Rep.S.Af.	23	Turkey	11	Phillippines	7	—	26.51	—
Cobalt (ore content)	18.2 m.t.	Rep. Congo	53	Morocco	11	Canada	8	Zambia	7	*	34.86	*
Copper (ore content—primary)	5,010.0 m.t.	U.S.S.R.	16	Zambia	13	Chile	13	Canada	9	17	24.28	72.28
Gold (ore and base bullion)	45,730.0 t.o.	Rep.S.Af.	67	U.S.S.R.	12	Canada	7	Canada	2	4	13.80	25.17
Iron (ore content)	339,800.0 m.t.	U.S.S.R.	27	Canada	7	France	5	Mnlnd China	5	15	20.61	66.06
Lead (ore content)	2,950.0 m.t.	U.S.S.R.	14	Australia	13	Canada	10	Mexico	6	10	20.38	20.43
Manganese (35% or more)	7,700.0 m.t.	U.S.S.R.	42	Rep.S.Af.	11	India	8	Brazil	8	*	12.78	*
Mercury	8.5 m.t.	Spain	24	Italy	15	U.S.S.R.	20	Mnlnd China	8	10	28.72	34.22
Molybdenum (ore content)	65.7 m.t.	U.S.S.R.	17	Canada	17	Chile	5	Mnlnd China	2	61	39.49	179.63
Nickel (ore content)	477.0 m.t.	Canada	47	U.S.S.R.	20	New Caled.	14	Cuba	4	3	36.11	8.80
Nitrogen (contained N)	21,576.7 m.t.	U.S.S.R.	12	France	5	W. Germany	4	Japan	4	25	28.77	108.98
Phosphate Rock (rock and apatite)	98,300.0 m.t.	U.S.S.R.	37	Morocco	10	Tunisia	3	Nauru Is.	2	37	32.08	462.23
Potash (K_2O equivalent)	15,630.0 m.t.	U.S.S.R.	18	W. Germany	16	E. Germany	14	France	12	19	24.49	79.71
Silver (ore and base bullion)	260,347.8 t.o.	Mexico	17	Peru	16	U.S.S.R.	13	Australia	9	14	80.12	14.95
Sulfur (elemental)	17,527.6 m.t.	Canada	12	Mexico	12	France	9	U.S.S.R.	9	48	34.49	75.29
Tin (ore content)	2,196.1 m.t.	Malaysia	34	Bolivia	13	U.S.S.R.	12	Thailand	11	*	18.61	*
Titanium (ilemenite concentrate)	2,685.3 m.t.	Canada	20	Australia	20	Norway	14	Malaysia	5	32	31.05	96.00
Tungsten (WO_3 content 60% basis)	36.1 m.t.	Mnlnd China	28	U.S.S.R.	22	S. Korea	8	N. Korea	7	14	22.40	66.74
Uranium (U_3O_8 content)	15.5 m.t.	Canada	22	France	19	France	5	Australia	1	53	59.76	80.75
Vanadium (V_2O_5 content)	8.9 m.t.	Rep. S.Af.	20	So.W.Af.	14	Finland	12	Mexico	7	47	48.80	96.00
Zinc (ore content)	4,916.0 m.t.	Canada	23	Canada	11	Australia	8	U.S.S.R.	10	10	30.76	34.51

*Less than 1 percent

†The weight measures in this column are metric ton (m.t.), troy ounces (t.o.), and flasks. A metric ton is equal to 1,000 kilograms, 2204.6 lb., .984 long ton, or 1.1023 short ton. The short ton is equal to 2,000 lbs.

‡The U.S. consumption was computed as the total U.S. production plus imports minus exports.

Source: Based on United Nations Statistical Yearbook 1968. (New York, 1969), and Minerals Yearbook 1967, Vol. I–II, Metals, Minerals, and Fuels (Washington, D.C.: U.S. Department of the Interior, 1968).

eign resources for many of its mineral needs. The U.S. is the leading producer of nine of the twenty-four minerals. Of these nine, only six are produced in such great quantities (over one-third of the world's supply) that the U.S. outranks all other producers. Only two are virtual monopolies of the U.S. with more than 50 percent also being mined there.

3. Although the minerals are distributed in every continent except Antarctica, the developing nations and the U.S.S.R. represent the heavier production areas of base metal (copper, lead, zinc, and tin), light metal (bauxite), and ferro-alloy metal (cobalt, manganese, nickel, and tungsten).

Although Table 4.7 represents only crude mineral (ore content) quantities, it indicates a basic pattern of mineral resource distribution. Needless to say, the columns related to consumption would change when all kinds of production, import, and export—partially or fully beneficiated material—are considered.

Various studies and evaluations relating to the adequacy of mineral resources [3, 4, 10, 16] indicate only a few supply problems and offer, in general, an optimistic outlook. With better technology resulting in new alloys, and new discoveries of mineral sites not only on land but also in the oceans, the future world mineral outlook appears promising. In addition to oil and natural gas, numerous deposits of valuable minerals have been encountered on the shelf of the epicontinental seas. These minerals include magnesium, cobalt, copper, nickel, iron, tin, coal, silver, gold, sulphur, and diamonds. Man has also speculated about the probable mineral deposits in outer space which, again, is a question of economics and technology.

WATER RESOURCES

Water is man's most abundant and most important mineral. Yet, ironically enough its spatial distribution and utilization are not properly understood. As a result, it is not uncommon to hear, on the one hand, concern over water shortage, and on the other, the assurances of practically an unlimited physical supply of water. The shortage stems from:

1. Our value system, which intractably holds water as a "free" gift from nature
2. A limited use of market price in balancing supply and demand
3. The location of water away from the established locations of people and economic activities
4. Lack of knowledge or ability to utilize the available supply of water

In this section water is evaluated and presented as a resource mineral in terms of its supply and demand patterns and the problems of utilizing the available supply.

For analytical purposes, the total hydrosphere—the sum total of water found at the surface, in the ground, and in atmospheric vapors—is divided into four categories:

1. Salt or sea water
2. Ice-locked water
3. Hydrologic cycle water
4. Depth-locked underground water

The world's water supply, that is the total water in the hydrosphere, is approximately 326,071,300 cubic miles (one cubic mile is over 1,101 billion gallons). Over 99 percent of this total is either salt water or is locked up as icecaps in Greenland and Antarctica. Salt water alone constitutes about 97.2 percent of the total. The remaining one percent is composed of that which is continually in the hydrologic cycle,[7] and that which has no direct relation to the hydrologic cycle, most of which lies at great depths not subject to replenishment except through the long-run process of geological accumulation. Thus, for all practical purposes, when we think of water supply, we are concerned with the volume of flow through the hydrologic cycle and with that of oceans.

Ocean Resources

The relative abundance of salt water was pointed out earlier. Spatial analysis of oceans involves considerations of subjectivity rights to exploitation by nations. The question of who owns the oceans includes many variables such as seaward national boundaries, consideration of land-locked countries, criteria of ownership, and management of ocean resources. Discussion of these topics is beyond the scope here; even if these topics are fully explored, developed, and implemented, it will take decades for the world to approximate the wealth hidden in the oceans. Only then will the spatial variability of ocean resources be fully realized.

Under existing arrangements, an individual nation's level of exploitation of ocean resources, which are mostly a common international property, is a combined result of the following factors:

1. The sufficiency, quality, and feasibility of land-based resources
2. Access and size of the continental shelf
3. Technology suitable for handling ocean resources
4. Conditions of light and temperature for chemical processes and the growth of plankton[8]
5. Availability of funds for oceanographic research and development

Man has extracted food, energy, minerals, and pharmacological chemicals from the oceans. Perhaps the most important resource from the oceans is food, particularly protein. (Fish meal concentrate recently approved by the United States Food and Drug Administration is an example of usability of fish at large levels.) Man presently is harvesting over 60 million short tons of fish yearly from the oceans. This is only a tiny fraction of the estimated volume actually available. Moreover, it has been demonstrated that 50 tons of algae for chicken feed can be grown annually in a single surface acre of ocean water under proper climatic conditions.

The ocean is also being used as a source of power. From the waves, tides, currents, organic matter, and from temperature differences power is being harnessed. France, for example, has in partial operation a system of turbine generators that transforms the rise and fall of the tides into electrical power. When completed the project will produce 544,000,000 kilowatt hours a year. Japan uses wave action for electric power at almost all its lighthouses, and test generators are under construction which will pipe wave energy to generating stations on land.

Since the first oil drilling rigs went to sea in the 1940s, more than $3.5 billion have been invested. Today over 16 percent of the total world oil production comes from offshore wells and is expected to increase to 25 percent by 1975. In addition to oil and supplies of natural gas, numerous minerals have been encountered in the oceans, including magnesium, cobalt, copper, nickel, iron, tin, coal, silver, gold, sulphur, and diamonds. The United States, for instance, extracts

---

[7]Hydrologic cycle is the process by which water moves from the atmosphere to the land, to the sea, and back to the atmosphere. Approximately nine percent more water evaporates over the oceans than they receive as rain and snow, and equally more rain falls on the land than that which evaporates from it; thus the volume of water carried to the sea by glaciers, rivers, and coastal springs bal-

ances out, respectively, the differential excess and loss from the land and the ocean.

[8]The favorable conditions of sunlight and temperature encourage growth of plankton, the microscopic animal and plant life found floating or drifting in the oceans or in bodies of fresh water, used as food by fish.

FIGURE 4.2 *An ancient but still used energy source is the wind, here captured by this windmill in England. (The British Travel Association)*

51,000 carats of diamonds per year from the sea, and it is estimated that there are six million tons of gold which may be removed from the ocean.

The ocean is virtually one large chemical plant providing sources of new medical discoveries. In ocean water itself, over 80 elements are present. Currently man is extracting salt, magnesium, potassium, iodine, and bromine directly from sea water. Marine pharmacologists have extracted chemicals from water and marine organisms that kill pain, inhibit the growth of certain tumors, fight viruses, and stimulate the heart. In addition, the expanding demands for recreational use of the shore, inland waters, and ocean water for swimming, sport fishing, skin diving, boating, surfing, and the like all point to the increasing value of ocean resources.

Finally, man's incessant desire for more water to satisfy his domestic and industrial needs, most of which are located on the seacoast, points to the oceans for water. Over thirty processes have been developed for desalinating ocean water. The suitability of a particular method for a given location is a function of the amount of water in demand, the source and cost of energy, the degree of salinity, and other characteristics of the ocean water, storage facilities, and the disposability and market for the by-products extractable from the brine. Distillation by the ion-exchange method using plastic membranes purifies ocean water, but has not yet been developed to the commercially feasible stage.

The specific form of distillation in the lead now is multi-stage flash (MSF) distillation—the process used in the San Diego/Guantanamo plant at a cost of about $1 per 1,000 gallons.[9] Although the MSF process produces water of slightly lesser purity than the other methods—a close runner-up is a method called long-tube vertical (LTV) distillation—it is being preferred for all three of the giant dual-purpose water and power plants under consideration: the Israeli-U.S. Mediterranean Seawater Desalination Project with an output of 32 to 40 million gallons a day (mgd) of fresh water and 175 to 200 megawatts[10] of power; Metropolitan Water District of Southern California and the U.S. Government Project to produce 150 mgd of fresh water and 1,800 megawatts of electricity from the Pacific Ocean; and the New York Project to produce 150 to 250 mgd. The above figures are indeed impressive when one compares them to current data. The 200 plants of various sizes and types desalinating water in the world today together produce only about 50 mgd of fresh water; approximately half of these plants use distillation processes. The largest is located in Aruba, an island off western Venezuela, with a capacity of 3.4 mgd and operating at three-quarters capacity.

[9] The average price for municipal water obtained from conventional sources is 30 cents per 1,000 gallons; from the same sources, irrigation water is delivered at the farmer's gate for 8 to 12 cents per 1,000 gallons.

[10] One megawatt is equal to one million kilowatt hours.

FIGURE 4.3 *A desalinization plant on the Red Sea. (Government of Israel)*

The electrodialysis process of desalination has been applied to "sweeten" brackish water. Unlike distillation, which takes water from saline water leaving brine, electrodialysis takes salt particles from saline water leaving potable water. The method of electrodialysis bears a promising hope for desalinating those waters with a low salt concentration. These include many large inland pools of brackish water.

Fresh Water Resources

Fresh water is one resource with which man has been dealing since his origin. The hydrologic cycle provides fresh water through the flow of rivers, streams, and springs, the filling of lakes and playas, and the saturation of aquifers.

The total amount of precipitation falling on the earth each year is about 380 billion acre-feet,[11] over 79 percent of which falls on the ocean and the remaining 21 percent (80 billion acre-feet) on the

[11]An acre-foot, the amount of water required to cover a level acre of land to a depth of one foot, is 325,872 gallons. Other measures commonly used for water measurement are gallons per day and cubic-feet per second (cu sec).

land. The volume of water carried to the sea by glaciers, rivers, and coastal springs is approximately 27 billion acre-feet per year with a drainage area of 25 billion acres. Another one billion acre-feet drains into inland seas, lakes, or playas, involving roughly 8 billion acres draining mostly deserts and well-watered areas. In all, more than one-half of the water that falls on the land evaporates from it each year.

Most river waters flow (run off) to the sea almost unused by man. The United States, one of the heavy water-user societies (about 1,700 gallons for all purposes per day per capita), withdraws, by diverting from streams and pumping from the ground, only slightly more than 7 percent of the total rain and snow falling annually on the United States. At the world level, about one billion acre-feet per year, less than 4 percent of the total runoff (27 billion acre-feet), is used by artificial irrigation works—the principal consumer of the world's water. This irrigates 310 million acres of land or less than one percent of the land area of the earth.

Over the conterminous United States this is an average of approximately 30

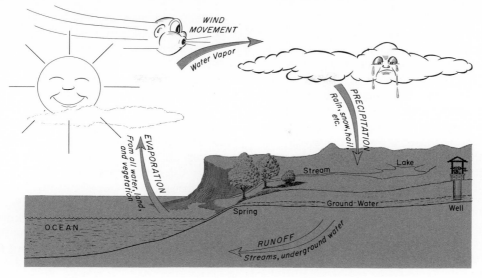

FIGURE 4.4 *Some uses by man of the hydrologic cycle. (General Media Corporation)*

inches of precipitation each year, the equivalent of over 4 billion acre-feet of water. Only about 30 percent of this total, more than one billion acre-feet per year, or about 1,100 billion gallons per day, is the gross potentially available water supply for the 48 states with which to meet various water demands. Approximately 350 billion gallons of fresh water are used daily: 171.5 billion gallons withdrawn for industrial purposes such as steam generating, electric power production, cooling, separating cellulose for paper, refining petroleum, and the like; 154.0 billion gallons for irrigating crops; and the remaining 24.5 billion gallons for domestic and public use. This, of course, does not include the huge volumes of fresh water involved with carrying off wastes, supporting inland navigation, pleasure boating and swimming, turning the generators of hydroelectric plants, and esthetic uses of water.

Supply Characteristics

In assessing a society's water supply, it is important to understand that there is no recognizable market for water at the national level because of the high cost of transporting water over long distances in comparison with its value. Thus, the mobility of water as a commodity input is localized. Another difficulty in assessing national water supply stems from the incompatibility of drainage systems and national boundaries. Here, one is concerned with the proper allocation between societies involved. Also the division of runoff water presents spatial, economic, political, and other problems which must be evaluated not only in terms of their short-run but also long-run characteristics before an estimate of the national supply of water is made.

Needless to say, not all nations may be subjected to these problems. One suggested solution is that a nation's supply of water be measured on the quantity of flow in the nation's watersheds. Indeed this approach relates the supply to the demand in a practicable fashion. But again, where the watershed is spread over two or more nations there is always the allocation problem. Thus, the watershed-basin approach undoubtedly appears to be a more logical solution.

Theoretically, the total fresh water supply of a nation is its average annual runoff including that which drains into inland seas, lakes, and playas; the effective supply is the quantity that can be made available for the various demand segments. The former is a function of the amount of precipitation, size of the drainage area, annual mean temperature, topography, and soil conditions. These factors explain the average runoff variation among regions. But at any given location there are wide variations in the average runoff. These variations are of three kinds:

1. Regular seasonal variation within a year caused by the seasonal precipitation and melting of snow
2. Irregular variations from year to year
3. Random variations caused by individual storms[12]

Table 4.8 is a consolidation of the best estimates of length, area, and discharge of the earth's thirty-eight major rivers. These rivers carry to the oceans slightly less than half of the total runoff. To answer why certain rivers are less used than others one must consider the effective supply, which is partially determined by the demand for water. The volume of water used from a river is determined by:

1. Structure and size of the demand components and the distance of demand market from the river
2. Technology, including indirect practices such as efficiency of water use, conservation and mulching methods, development of suitable crops and manufacturing processes, better lining for canals and better irrigation practices, and the attempts to modify and improve precipitation patterns by ex-

erting control over weather and climate to provide the desired amount of precipitation at the desired time and location
3. Financial ability
4. Water quality

Space does not permit a detailed analysis of each of the above factors. In general, however, in view of these factors many rivers in the economically advanced countries permit large multipurpose water developments that are economically feasible. For instance, the Ob–Yenisei project calls for a huge dam on the Ob, creating an inland sea connecting the Ob and the Yenisei, which would divert the unused flow from the Arctic to the central Soviet steppes. The Colorado and Snake project is another example of feasibility, although the political ramifications are many. Plans await leadership and agreements of all concerned for greater, more efficient utilization of such international rivers as the Rhine, Danube, Rio Grande, St. Lawrence, and the Columbia.

In most developing nations the problem of water utilization is extremely complicated. This is especially true in arid or semi-arid nations where waterlogging and salt accumulation in the soil occur in vast, nearly flat plains due to poor drainage. Another aspect pertains to willingness or reluctance to utilize the water efficiently and to solve the problem of land tenure. (An incident occurred in the desert Rajasthan state of India during the time when water from the Bakhra–Nangal dam was offered to the farmers through hundreds of miles of canals. Extension agents reported that many farmers, when told of the total process of how water was made available to them and how many kilowatts of electricity had been generated out of that water, refused to use it. The farmers reasoned that the extraction of electricity left the water "dead" and hence not usable for their crops.)

Many farmers are sharecropping tenants who have little incentive to use irri-

[12]The volume of all the runoffs when added together provides the total supply of fresh water. Runoff may be measured by the volume discharged, a theoretical measure of which is

$$D = L + A_c V_m,$$

where
D = the volume discharged,
A_c = cross sectional area of a stream or river,
V_m = mean velocity of a stream or river,
L = volume of water in the lakes and playas.

Table 4.8   Major Rivers, Their Lengths, Areas, and Discharges

Region or Continent	River	Length (in miles)	Drainage Area (square miles)	Average Discharge (cubic-feet per second)
Africa (Total)		13,053	4,215,000	
	Congo	2,900	1,425,000	2,000,000
	Niger	2,600	584,000	
	Nile	4,053	1,293,000	420,000
	Orange	1,300	400,000	
	Zambezi	2,200	513,000	
Asia, including eastern USSR (Total)		34,452	7,837,973	
	Amur	2,900	787,000	
	Brahmaputra	1,680	361,000	500,000
	Euphrates	1,700	430,000	
	Ganges	1,540	432,000	270,000
	Hwang Ho	2,700	400,000	1,116,000
	Indus	1,700	372,000	300,000
	Irrawaddy	1,250	158,000	
	Jaxartes	1,700	320,000	
	Lena	3,000	1,169,000	325,000
	MeKong	2,600	350,000	600,000
	Ob–Irtysh	3,459	1,131,273	
	Oxus	1,500	115,000	
	Salween	1,770	62,700	
	Yangtze Kiang	3,400	750,000	770,000
	Yenisei	3,553	1,000,000	
Australia (Total)		2,345	414,000	
	Murray–Darling	2,345	414,000	13,000
Europe, including western USSR (Total)		6,295	1,227,000	
	Danube	1,760	347,000	315,000
	Dnieper	1,410	202,000	
	Rhine	800	86,000	
	Volga	2,325	592,000	
North America (Total)		18,091	4,055,000	
	Churchill	1,000	140,000	
	Colorado	1,450	244,000	23,300
	Columbia	1,270	259,000	280,000
	Mackenzie–Peace	2,525	682,000	450,000
	Mississippi–Missouri	3,986	1,243,000	513,000
	Nelson–Saskatchewan	1,660	360,000	
	Rio Grande	1,800	232,000	5,180
	St. Lawrence	2,100	565,000	400,000
	Yukon	2,300	330,000	
South America (Total)		9,961	4,792,000	
	Amazon	4,000	2,772,000	7,200,000
	La Plata–Paraná	2,450	1,198,000	2,800,000
	Orinoco	1,700	570,000	
	São Francisco	1,811	252,000	

gation water and increase production. In the regions of savanna climate, which are characterized by an annual cycle of heavy rainfall during one season followed by drought the remainder of the year and by warm weather at all seasons, many millions of what are now barren acres could be brought under irrigated cultivation. The Nile project is already in progress. The basins of the Niger and the Rufiji rivers lend themselves to water utilization. Similarly, in the area extending from India east through Burma, Thailand, and Vietnam to the northern Philippines, year-round crop raising is possible. The MeKong River Plan [18] is an excellent proposal of how these countries can use their water for the development of their economies.

To capture the supply of water is not an end but merely a means. Proper use of water for those enterprises that provide higher marginal value for water is extremely important. It calls for the evaluation, analysis, and improvement of social and institutional arrangements that surround water use. The foregoing discussion has emphasized the supply of water, problems in its procurement, and man's need for it. Supplying adequate water to mankind, whose population is doubling about every 40 years, promises to be one of the major problems facing nearly all societies.

POLLUTION OF RESOURCES

For centuries man has been faced with the task of waste removal. Today, however, there is a serious lag between the upsurge in population and the means for ridding the population of its more rapidly increasing waste accumulations.

The impact of resource use upon the quality of a resource itself has become a major concern for many affluent societies engaged in mass production and consumption. The quality of resources is affected by the disposal of wastes on the land, in the water, and in the air. Air pollution in the form of smoke, dust, gases, vapors, fumes, and mists greatly affects the health and life of plants, humans, and other animals occupying the land, for polluted air contains minute

FIGURE 4.5 *Irrigation with portable lightweight sprinklers in northern Negev, Israel. (Government of Israel)*

particles of solids that finally come to rest on the land or join with water. If wastes are deposited in rivers, lakes, and bays, not only is the water supply contaminated but also adjoining land becomes less desirable for human habitation. Likewise, wastes deposited on land may pollute water through seepage and washing, and cause atmospheric contamination by producing foul odors and gases. Incinerator waste may add to air pollution and garbage grinders may turn it into a water treatment problem. Air and water treatment may leave solid or liquid wastes to be disposed of and may give off fumes into the atmosphere.

Pollution Concept

All pollution problems stem from natural laws, which usually work in a most benign fashion. Essentially, these laws decree that matter is never really consumed except, as Einstein noted, by transformation into energy. Thus, through all the operations of economic activities, matter is used, altered, and modified but it still remains as matter. Some of the residual is "thrown away" by dispersion in the environment through the actions of streams and rivers, and by the traditional methods of conversion into land enrichment or fill. The remainder escapes into the atmosphere in the form of gases, smoke, or vapors. Theoretically speaking, these residuals are simply castoff portions from the utilization of resources or what some scholars call "resources out of place."

Historically, man's thinking has been geared to a massive system of producing and distributing goods for consumption with little or no concern for what happens after the goods are used. As the earth becomes more crowded, one person's trash is being discarded in another's living space; downstream and downwind are other communities expecting fresh air and potable water. Often they must bear higher social costs for the use of resources via sewage treatment plants, air pollution control, and water purification systems.

There is a noticeable trend, however, toward recycling the "out of place" resources. In the United States more than half of the nation's steel, 56 percent of the copper, 12 percent of the rubber, and 21 percent of the paper are presently derived from scrap or reprocessed materials. The bottlenecks for recycling are sorting out, collecting, and transporting wastes for reprocessing, all of which are laborious and relatively costly. But experts look to the time when dead-heading trains, trucks, ships, and cargo planes that now move out empty after supplying the needs of our cities will carry containers filled with discarded materials. This is economically feasible by requiring householders to sort their trash, perhaps into coded baskets for collection via conveyor systems under some cities. And every new product designed for production or manufacture will be accompanied by a plan for disassembly and will be permanently labeled as to its material content.

From the ecological point of view, *pollution* is the introduction of elements able to stop, control, or redirect biological activity. These elements can set in motion a chain of adaptation that may not be revealed for many generations. Such adaptation suggests a variability in the level of tolerance of pollution elements not only over time but also over areas. The degree of environmental purity depends on the relative tolerance as a result of adaptation, and on the required standards. Air surrounding the manufacture of some electronic parts, for instance, must be considerably more pristine than that which seems quite fresh in a living room. And the water used in many industrial processes, including steam generators, in many respects must be more stringently controlled than that which comes, safe and tasty, from a kitchen tap.

No community's water supply is completely independent of the actions of the others in that watershed. Air, too, moves across political boundaries in an analogous airshed. Hence the problems of pollution, having complicated structural as well as areal interrelatedness, lend themselves to the relatively new technique of systems analysis. This technique has been applied to various pollution studies in the state of California.

From the point of view of economics, pollution is an "external effect" distorting cost curves and resulting in a misallocation of resources in an economy. The upstream plant that dumps a noxious effluent into a river has lower costs than if effluent treatment were required, and therefore finds it profitable to produce more than would otherwise be the case. The downstream plant, as a consequence, must pretreat its water, has higher costs, and does not find it profitable to produce as much. Likewise, the householder who decides to incinerate his garbage in the backyard rather than pay for collection, who chooses to skip a tune-up on his car or leaves a leaky muffler unrepaired, reduces his immediate expenses but increases cost to society. Chemicals and pesticides when used for agricultural purposes provide better yields to a group at the expense of those who face residues as part of their consumption items or inputs needing pretreatment. There are numerous other external costs associated with pollution; for example, in the United States property damage from air pollution alone is estimated at $12 billion a year.

Sources of Pollution

It is evident from the discussion above that the problem of pollution is manifold. Pollution is not one thing but a multiplicity of increasingly sophisticated substances generated by a wide variety of sources. The following classification of refuse material by kind, consumption, source, and disposal or corrective methods, suggested by the American Public Works Association [6], has been modified and expanded here to include sources for water and air pollution.

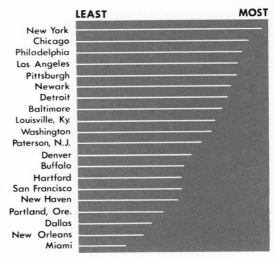

FIGURE 4.6 *Air pollution in U.S. cities, 1967, based on the relative severity of eight pollution factors. (General Media Corporation)*

1. Garbage: waste from food preparation and the handling of produce, smell from rotting
2. Rubbish: combustibles such as paper cartons, wood, branches, yard trimmings, wood furniture; noncombustibles such as metals, tin cans, glass, crockery
3. Smokes and ashes: ordinary ashes and residues from incinerating plants, smoke
4. Street refuse: sweepings, leaves, and contents of receptacles
5. Dead animals
6. Combustion engine vehicles: abandoned bodies; moving vehicles giving off exhaust, such as cars, planes, locomotives, ships
7. Industrial wastes: solid, gaseous, liquid
8. Demolition wastes: from wrecking of buildings
9. Construction waste
10. Special waste: such as hazardous solids and liquids, radioactive and pathological materials
11. Sewerage: sludge and effluent from septic tanks and sewer treatment plants
12. Agricultural pollutants: washed or

FIGURE 4.7 *A garbage dump for New York City. (New York Department of Sanitation)*

blown pesticides, herbicides, dung and urine, and the residue left in consumption items

The above twelve sources of pollution need not necessarily be the determining factors for the relative degree of pollution in a given location. Spatial variation in pollution, in general, is a function of:

1. The total population
2. The percent of population living in urban areas
3. The number, size, model, and use frequency of combustion engine vehicles
4. Type and level of economic activities
5. Type and level of human consumption
6. Human awareness, education, and sense of responsibility for pollution control
7. Topographical and meteorological factors—temperature inversion[13] and wind movements
8. Climatic factors permitting the level of BOD (biochemical oxygen demand) in the waste carrying waters

The following are a few illustrations pertaining to these factors. The effluent from the pulp and paper industry is much more than that which comes from an auto assembly plant of comparable size. The emission of contaminating substances from areas of heavy population and their attendant economic activities is larger than those areas that are sparsely populated and have relatively no industry. The nearly permanent temperature inversion in the atmosphere over the California coast is a unique phenomenon associated with the relatively stationary high pressure area over the North Pacific Ocean. Thus, as a mass of air moves down the California coast, the upper part sinks and is heated by compression. At the same time, the air next to the ocean surface is cooled from below. This process gives rise to two layers of air: above, a layer of warm, dry, descending air; and below, a layer of cold, moist, ocean-cooled air. Where these two layers meet and intermix a tem-

[13]A temperature inversion is a layer of air that shows an increase in temperature with an increase in altitude. It is called a temperature inversion since air temperature normally decreases with an increase in altitude. The effect of such a layer is to trap the air beneath it and to stop upward movement. This creates a predisposition to air pollution that is especially pronounced when there is little wind or when topographical features restrict lateral air movements.

perature inversion occurs and pollution is the result. These inversions, which man so far has been unable to alter, are now found to be quite common not only in California, but also in the major SMSAs[14] in varying degrees during peak morning and evening traffic.

Analysis of pollution has not yet advanced to a stage permitting accurate analysis of the national picture, let alone the global phenomenon. Nevertheless, the determining factors can be used to areally differentiate the pollution problem. For example, the primary sources[15] of atmospheric pollution in the United States, which account for approximately 125 million tons of pollutants each year, can be analyzed areally to provide regional pollution estimates. These studies would provide regional air quality commissions, established under the Air Quality Act of 1967, with complementary information for effective policy decisions. Policy recommendations can be further improved based on the regional distribution of the pollution content. The major contents of air pollution in the United States for one year are as follows:

Carbon monoxide	65.0 *million tons*	52.0 *percent*
Oxides of sulfur	23.0	18.4
Hydrocarbons	15.0	12.0
Particulate matter	12.0	9.6
Oxides of nitrogen	8.0	6.4
Other	2.0	1.6
	125.0	100.0

Pollution Control

With the emerging patterns of metropolitan areas and suburbia (areas in between and on the edges of metropolitan centers governed by the county), the once "no man's land" around these centers is now "somebody's" living space. This means there has to be a joint effort by parties concerned with pollution control. Three groups can build and operate pollution control facilities and can pay for them in the same or different proportion: those who require pure resources, those whose

activities "create" pollution, and the community as a whole. Each of the three takes some of the actions and pay some of the bills. A recent survey of 3,000 American corporations by the National Industrial Conference Board revealed that these corporations now have a capital investment of approximately $1 billion in facilities to reduce or control water pollution, with yearly operating expenses of $100 million. Consolidated Edison Company has recently announced its switching to less-polluting fuel for its power plants; the Tennessee Valley Authority has also announced plans to cut smoke at its electric generating plants.

The question of which units should undertake pollution control is one of technical feasibility, economic efficiency, and the maximization of welfare to the whole community watershed, region, or airshed. To propose and design alleviating measures, detailed analyses of the sources and factors of pollution content, possibilities of recycling, salvaging, or reclaiming wastes, improving the present methods and channels of disposal, and the development of new methods of disposal are important.

A major campaign to combat pollution presently is underway in the United States. A series of laws enacted during the 90th and 91st Congresses sharply expanded or initiated important programs in water, air, and solid waste management; President Nixon's declaration of "War on Pollution" in the 1970s is further testi-

[14]Standard Metropolitan Statistical Areas. The SMSA is an urban region involving one or more contiguous counties and containing a city of 50,000 or more inhabitants. The region is relatively homogeneous in terms of social and economic characteristics.

[15]In order of weight, the following are the major sources of atmospheric pollution in the United States:

Source	*Million tons (per year)*	*Percent*
Transportation	74.8	59.8
Manufacturing	23.4	18.7
Electric power	15.7	12.6
Space heating	7.8	6.2
Refuse burning	3.3	2.6
	125.0	100.0

FIGURE 4.8 *Fish killed by polluted river water. (Oregon Game Commission)*

mony to the seriousness of the problem. The attack on water pollution, which was first a subject of federal research a century ago and which received broadening support in 1948, 1956, and 1961, was significantly amplified by several measures passed in 1965 and 1966. Under the 1965 Water Resources Planning Act, a cooperative program for long-range planning for water resources in all U.S. river basins was established. The states were put on notice to set up satisfactory standards for pollution control by July 1967, lest the federal government step in. Similarly, federal air pollution control activity has also accelerated considerably since the first legislation in 1955. With the Clean Air Act of 1963, as amended in 1965, related research and regulation have been established. Regulatory vehicle emission standards have been applied to all cars built since 1968. Likewise, the Solid Waste Disposal Act of 1965, initiating federal support in this area, authorized $92 million over four years for demonstration projects and the planning of state and local programs for research and training. Stimulated by federal activity, other levels of government have stepped up their programs. Some states like New York and California have gone beyond federal requirements for water pollution control.

The battle to combat pollution is an expensive one. United States industry and government are now spending over $10 billion a year to combat pollution by factories, garbage incinerators, car fumes, sewage, etc. A whole new occupation to invent, build, test, install, and repair antipollution equipment is developing rapidly.

selected references

1. Barlowe, Raleigh, *Land Resource Economics: The Political Economy of Rural and Urban Land Resource Use,* Englewood Cliffs, N. J.: Prentice-Hall, Inc., 1958.

2. Barnett, H. J., and Morse, Chandler, *Scarcity and Growth: The Economics of Natural Resource Availability*, Baltimore: The Johns Hopkins Press, 1963.

3. Brooks, D. B., *Supply and Competition in Minor Metals*, Baltimore: The Johns Hopkins Press, 1966.

4. Brewer, Michael F., "Natural Resources Problems of the Next Decade," in *Departmental Personnel Conference Proceedings*, Washington, D.C.: U.S. Department of the Interior, 1967.

5. Clawson, M. E., *Natural Resources and International Development*, Washington, D.C.: Resources for the Future, Inc., 1964.

6. Committee on Refuse Disposal, *Municipal Refuse Disposal*, American Public Works Association, 1961.

7. Dessy, George F., and Griess, Phyllis R., "Local and Regional Differences in Long Term Bituminous Coal Production in Eastern United States," *Annals of the Association of American Geographers*, Vol. 57, No. 3, September 1967, pp. 519–533.

8. Eggleston, Wilfred, "The Nuclear Age in Canada," *Canadian Geographical Journal*, Vol. 71, No. 6, December 1965, pp. 182–191.

9. Eyre, John D., "Japan's Electric-Power Supply," *Geographical Review*, Vol. 55, No. 4, October 1965, pp. 546–562.

10. Feiss, Julian, "Minerals," *Scientific American*, Vol. 209, No. 3, September 1963, pp. 128–147.

11. Fisher, Joseph L., "Limits on the Exploitation of Natural Resources," *Technological Review*, (Alumni Association of the Massachusetts Institute of Technology), Vol. 70, No. 7, 1968.

12. Heady, Earl O., *Economics of Agricultural Production and Resource Use*, Englewood Cliffs, N. J.: Prentice-Hall, Inc., 1960.

13. Hogerton, John F., "The Arrival of Nuclear Power," *Scientific American*, Vol. 218, No. 2, February 1968, pp. 21–31.

14. Kingsley, Davis, "Rise and Growth of Cities," in *Readings in Urban Geography*, ed. by Harold M. Mayer and Clyde F. Kohin, Chicago: University of Chicago Press, 1959.

15. Kneese, Allen V., with Ayres, Robert U., *Environmental Pollution*, Joint Economic Committee, Federal Programs for the Development of Human Resources, (papers submitted to the Subcommittee on Economic Progress), 90 Cong. 2 Sess., Vol. 2, 1968.

16. Landsberg, Hans H.; Fischman, L. L.; and Fisher, J. L., *Resources in America's Future*, Baltimore: The Johns Hopkins Press, 1963.

17. Searl, F. Milton, *Production of Energy*, U.S. Atomic Energy Commission, Washington, D.C.: Government Printing Press, 1962.

18. White, Gilbert F., "The MeKong River Plan," *Scientific American*, April 1962.

The major indentifiable parts of the economic framework of any society are generally recognized under the following concepts: demand, supply, market, substitution, cost, price, and the interrelationships among these parts as a function of their spatial location. In this chapter each of these concepts or parts of the economic framework will be differentiated, analyzed, and reassembled to reflect a unified economic framework.

chapter 5

Economic Framework

DEMAND

Prices of commodities (goods or services) represent their relative desirability and availability. Prices may be determined by various means, from a perfectly competitive market to an absolute monopoly (operated by the state or private interests). Under competitive conditions, price is the result of the Law of Demand and Supply.[1] Price, representing the relative value, influences the demand and supply.

In any society, forces of demand and supply basically perform four functions:

1. Determination of the commodities and their relative quantities that are produced
2. Rationing or distribution of commodities among individuals and/or groups residing at various locations
3. Partial determination of the location and relative scale of output of the economic activities
4. Indicating sites of possible relocation of economic activities and the change in scale of output over time

Demand is the *relation* between the various amounts of the commodity that might be bought and the determinants of those amounts. The determinants reflect all hu-

[1] Alfred Marshall, *Principles of Economics*, 9th ed. New York: The Macmillan Company, 1961. Marshall's analysis assumes that the rationale behind the demand for a given commodity is its utility, which decreases as more of the commodity is acquired or consumed. Modern treatment of demand also recognizes many other factors.

man motives, desires, and aspirations for commodities. The demand can be looked at (1) as an *individual consumer's preference* for one or several commodities, and (2) as a *business firm's preference* reflecting the number of customers, where they are located, and the volume of commodities they will purchase. The former is called an *individual demand* and the latter a *market demand*. The sum of market demands of firms represents the *industry demand*. A firm, while having a market demand for its commodities, also has a business demand for its inputs, generally referred to as *derived demand*—derived from market demand and therefore immediately or ultimately dependent on it.

Overall, demand for goods and services depends on many factors. Principally these are:

1. Price of the commodity concerned
2. Prices of other commodities, especially of substitutes and complements[2]
3. Income of the buyer
4. Tastes and preferences
5. The buyer's existing stock of similar commodities
6. Future expectations of income, prices, and new commodities
7. Degree of information about the commodity wanted
8. Spatial relationship of buyers or consumers

The relative effect of any factor varies, depending upon the commodity involved, size of the area to be served, and the time period (day, month, year, etc.).

The larger the area involved, the greater the significance of the spatial distribution of customers. The trend towards growing specialization and the concentration of market demand into a few oligopolistic corporations[3] or firms illustrates the importance of the location of customers in the demand for any commodity. This is particularly so in considering the demand for spatially fixed commodities, which cannot be transported to other areas. A few examples of such commodities are outdoor recreation services and facilities (fishing, hunting, boating, park and zoo visitation, seeing fairs and festivals, watching games), education for residency degree or diploma, and hospital services.

For the sake of simplicity, the demand for a commodity has conventionally been demonstrated in terms of a *demand schedule* (Table 5.1) and *demand curve* (Fig. 5.1) A demand schedule states the relations between two variables—price and quantity. Demand curve is the transformation of demand schedule into a curve—always so called, even when it happens to be a straight line—using a two-dimensional graph.[4]

Table 5.1   A Demand Schedule

Per Unit Price	Quantity
10 cents	25
9	30
8	35
7	40
6	45
4	50
2	53

A demand schedule does not necessarily indicate price but does indicate what amounts of a commodity will be bought at different possible prices, given the market area, the time, and the commodity. Generally, the lower the price,

[2]The concept *substitution* refers to a buyer's option to do without a given good or service because he can buy a similar article that will fulfill a similar function, or because he does not need the product at all. *Complementary* refers to those products that are bought and used together. For instance, an increase in the sale of automobiles would increase the demand for gasoline; the same holds true with phonographs and records, spareribs and sauerkraut.

[3]A firm identified with oligopoly. Oligopoly as defined in Table 5.2 pertains to an industry with only a "few" firms.
[4]These are charts of a general character and hence do not represent any one commodity but can be used to represent the relations of price and quantity of any commodity. The demand schedule is in tabular form; the same data in the demand schedule is represented on the demand curve in graphic form.

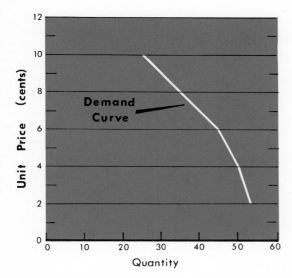

FIGURE 5.1   *A demand curve. (General Media Corporation)*

the larger the quantity that is purchased. Likewise, the higher the price, the smaller the quantity purchased. *This inverse relationship between price and quantity is often called the Law of Demand.* The law stands confirmed by many empirical investigations.

A demand schedule may be made of quantities that would be bought by customers at different possible distances. The distance, however, may not represent the actual arrangements of transport facilities, time, and conveniences. Transportation cost is often suggested as a replacement for distance. But this too, although superior to the mere distance factor, falls short of reflecting proper spatial relationships. For example, Seattle, in terms of time, might be much closer to Chicago than a town in the Shawnee Hills of southern Illinois.

For actual estimation of the demand curve, these distance complexities can be partly alleviated by introducing appropriate additional variables (factors) into the model.[5] For example, the size of population of areas would partially explain the spatial distribution of the demand, since the growth of transportation facilities

and the size of the population in general show a positive correlation.

Analysis of demand also can be helpful in explaining the location pattern of a given economic activity, its growth, and the selection of an optimum location, by:

1. Identifying the spatial distribution of the total market demand and its relation to the industry demand
2. Estimating individual market demand as related to the respective areas or clusters
3. Indicating the elasticities of these demand estimates

Elasticity, in economics, means a ratio of the relative change (generally measured as a percentage change) in two quantities or variables. The relative change is used in order to recognize the dissimilarities of the units of measurement and the scale of the two variables. The two variables may be commodity price and quantity, distance and quantity, income and quantity, price of a substitute or complementary commodity and quantity (in this case the elasticity is known as cross elasticity), transportation cost and quantity, and the like.

The data from Table 5.1 may be used to illustrate the meaning of *price elasticity.* Let E stand for elasticity, which, when expressed in numerical form is called *coefficient of elasticity:*

$$E = \frac{\text{percent change in quantity bought}}{\text{percent change in price}}.$$

Notice in the above relationship that *two observations must be known for each of the two variables;* thus, an estimate of E represents only that part or arc of the demand curve between those observation points. The E at the midpoint of the arc is considered to be the best estimate. This is called an *arc elasticity,* often simply referred to

[5] A model is a complete system of the mathematical equation(s) expressing the relationship between the given variables. The system may be as broad or as narrow as the problem being studied requires, or as the one using the model wishes.

as an elasticity. The usual formula for arc elasticity is

$$\frac{q_1 - q_2}{q_1 + q_2} \Big/ \frac{p_1 - p_2}{p_1 + p_2}$$

where q stands for quantity and p for price. Using the above formula, the E between the prices of 10 cents and 9 cents is approximately -1.73, and between 6 cents and 7 cents $-.76$. E always bears a negative sign because of the inverse relation between the two variables of the demand schedule; however, it is customary to disregard the minus sign and use only the absolute value of E. When the value of the coefficient is greater than 1, the demand is elastic; equal to 1 is unit elasticity; less than 1 but greater than 0 ($0 < E < 1$) is inelastic; and when the coefficient is zero, the demand is perfectly inelastic.

An elastic demand means that the quantity purchased is responsive to price change; that is, the percentage change in the quantity is larger than the percentage change in price. Therefore, other things being equal, it is more profitable to lower the price and sell larger quantities. An inelastic demand indicates that the percent change in quantity is smaller than the percent change in price, a situation where lowering the price is not advisable. Unit elasticity reflects an equal percent change in both the quantity and the price. The relative size of E determines how much change would occur in the volume or quantity purchased in response to certain price changes.

The illustration above shows an application of the concept of elasticity related to price and quantity. The same can be readily applied to the demand functions involving distance, transportation cost, time, income, and the like.

SUPPLY

Supply represents the total quantity of a commodity that is offered for sale within a given space and time. Assuming that the other determinants are constant, the *supply schedule* refers to pairs of possible prices and quantities offered for sale. The *supply curve*, a graphical version of the supply schedule, also can be a straight line and still be called a curve. In general, a supply curve exhibits a positive relation between prices and quantities—the higher the prices, the greater the quantities producers are willing to supply. However, this may not always be true. There can be supply schedules where larger quantities are sold at lower prices. This is evidenced in the experience of American agriculture. The farmers tend to compensate lower prices with a larger production in order to maximize their net returns. Net return is equal to the price of the commodity multiplied by the quantity, minus the total cost of production and transportation (if applicable).

The analysis of supply is similar to that of demand. The industry supply function is a horizontal summation of the individual supply functions of the firms. However, unlike the demand function, the industry supply function and the market supply function are identical for a given space.

Elasticity of supply is just as important as elasticity of demand and has the same meaning. In general, since both quantity and price (or whatever the alternative variable is) go up and down together, the elasticity of supply has a positive sign. Both time and space are more important for the elasticity of supply than they are for the elasticity of demand. The larger and longer the supply area and the period of time, respectively, the more elastic the supply is likely to be. A relatively longer period may permit the firms to readjust their costs of production, and hence their productive capacity. A larger area permits greater mobility of products for a firm in response to changes in the relevant determinant(s).

The nature and scope of the determinants of the supply function vary by commodity and location. Hence, it is difficult to offer a generalized statement about the determinants of supply. However, the following variables or determinants are considered to be the common denominators for most supply functions:

1. Price of the commodity
2. Prices of the closely related commodities and the length of time period
3. Size of supply areas
4. Technology of production
5. Future expectations and aspirations
6. Cost of production
7. Random disturbances such as those related to weather, strikes, and ephemeral incidents

These determinants, while helping to explain the supply of a given commodity, also suggest solutions as to why a given location produces a certain amount and how its level of production varies from other locations.

As an illustration, in the United States iron ore is mined from over 300 mines of various kinds and sizes. The ages of these mines range from those being opened today to those that are remarkably ancient. Some are deep and difficult to work, whereas others are shallow and convenient. Costs of operation vary from mine to mine. The result is that whatever the price of iron ore of a given grade, there will be some mines and parts of mines that can be operated profitably and some that cannot be. The industry supply curve can indicate which mines or locations are on the break-even point (where total costs are equal to total revenue), above, or below the break-even point.[6] At certain prices it will pay to operate mines capable of producing those

quantities that correspond to the price on the supply curve. As the price changes so will the areal distribution of iron mining.

For a given industry, the spatial supply functions can be utilized for effective policy. For example, United States federal farm programs and policies can assist in achieving desired objectives more effectively when modified in view of the spatial supply functions and their elasticities.

The concept of supply should not be confused with that of *production function*. The latter is the functional relationship between inputs (resources) and output (product or commodity). The conventional use of the production function is to predict the total output curve. Marginal products for individual resource inputs then can be predicted by computing the derivative of the product in respect to the particular resource. These derivatives then can be equated (1) to the resource/product price ratio, to determine the optimum quantity to use of a particular resource, and/or (2) to the resource/resource price ratio, to determine the optimum combination of resources for a particular output. Through this process the conditions of optimality and efficiency in resource use or management may be achieved. But, given other variables of production function, the existence of varying degrees of *externalities, indivisibilities*, and *factor immobilities* in resource use produce spatial variation in the production functions of the various areas, and hence the areas vary in their productive capacities as well as in actual supply of the commodity demanded.

Externalities refer to the external economies and diseconomies—changes in the long-run cost function of a firm caused by the growth of the industry—over which the firm has no control. Firms and areas enjoying external economies have lower per-unit cost of production, and those suffering from external disecono-

[6]The course of the supply curve of a firm or industry is guided largely by the marginal cost. Marginal cost at any level of output is the increase in total cost required to increase output by one unit from that level. The most profitable level of output on the supply curve is the one at which marginal cost is equal to market price.

mies have a higher cost. Educational facilities, resource pollution, ownership of resources, longevity of the firm, public facilities, and access to transportation means all influence external economies or diseconomies of the firm. The established firms have numerous advantages over their embryonic rivals in terms of easy access to capital market with favorable terms, experienced personnel, and the elimination of inappropriate policies. The ill effects of resource pollution are examples of external diseconomies. The costs of a firm downstream may be higher because of the additional cost involved in pretreating water input, which need not have been the case had a similar upstream firm not polluted the stream. Needless to say, the externalities may also appear in the consumption sector with symmetrical effects.

Indivisibility characteristic of resources or plant equipment refers to those units of inputs comprising a single complex of resources or equipment that must be employed or used as a whole, without desegmentation, in order to produce even one small range of output. An indivisible resource may be exemplified by a whole river basin, or an oil field whose development and/or exploitation is economically justified only through multipurpose project structures. Blast furnaces, refineries, and distilleries are other examples of indivisible plant equipment. In contrast, a divisible plant consists of several complexes of more or less identical equipment. This means that output can be increased by putting another machine into operation, adding another shift, or accelerating the operation. Examples are textile mills and hydroelectric plants with several units of turbines and generators. Areas vary in their adaptability and suitability for exploitation of their resources under a given technology and technical conditions. Given two areas with an identical natural resource base, different demand structures may invoke indivisi-

bility conditions on one area, limiting its comparative development. Thus, changes in capacity of a firm or area do not occur continuously, but through abrupt steps conditioned by the magnitude of indivisibilities.

Immobility of factors of production—land, labor, capital, management, and technology—may exist between occupations, firms, industries, or between geographic locations. (Under the conditions of optimality and efficiency of resource use, the marginal productivity of a particular resource must be the same in all occupations and locations.) This proposition requires that the factors of production be mobile in all respects. Consequently, the resultant distribution of economic activities exhibits a maximum degree of specialization, lending itself to the trade patterns led purely by the law of comparative advantage (discussed later in the chapter). This immobility is more pronounced between nations. The natural resource or land is immobile geographically but may not be so between various uses. The social overhead capital is relatively immobile. The other factors, too, have some degree of immobility. Impediments to free mobility materially affect the production function and hence the supply potential of an area.

An overriding determinant in both demand and supply, noted in the preceding discussion, is price, which changes as do the forces of demand and supply. Demand follows wants, and changes in wants can occur rather quickly as conditioned by the relevant determinants; but supply changes usually require production changes, or moving production and/or output, which are more time-consuming adjustments. Thus it may be concluded that *demand changes are faster and usually lead the supply to adjust accordingly.* How demand and supply balance each other and how prices are determined under spatial markets are discussed in the following section.

MARKET

The word market has diverse meanings—a *place* of business transactions, the *process* of trading a given commodity, total area occupied by consumers, and the *character* of salability. Here it is defined as a *communicative process or mechanism within which the forces of demand and supply determine the terms of transactions for a given commodity in a given area.*

Communication is an essential element of a market. The contacts may be face to face at a particular site, or by mail, telephone, or cable. The same person(s) may be in different markets for different commodities, at the same or at different times. The areal size of the market may range from that of a small settlement to the entire inhabited earth surface. Local markets can be illustrated by commodities that are too perishable and expensive (transportation cost) to be shipped very far without canning, freezing, drying, or being processed in some other way, such as fresh milk and certain fruits and vegetables. On the other hand, worldwide markets may involve wheat, sugar, tobacco, cotton, hardware, and other commodities.

What differentiates one market from another for a given product is determined by the criteria employed. Here we focus on competition as influenced by the number of firms in the industry, and the degree of product homogeneity and factor mobility to distinguish the various markets. Table 5.2 shows the conventional classification of such markets and their associated characteristics.

Table 5.2   Market Classifications and Their Characteristics

Market Type	General Characteristics
Pure Competition	Many sellers and buyers—no one "big" enough to influence the market price and the decisions of his competitors; factor mobility unrestricted; all firms in a given industry produce identical or nondifferentiable products; both sellers and buyers equally possess knowledge of the forces of demand and supply for a product; the same price faced by sellers and buyers
Imperfect Competition	
(a) Monopolistic Competition	Many sellers (same as under pure competition); each firm in a given industry produces a differentiated but substitutable product; some restrictions on factor mobility invoked by product differentiation; some control over prices
(b) Oligopoly	A few large sellers, each with a significant share of customers in the industry; factor mobility generally difficult; price controls often possible; advertising channels frequently used to increase one's share of the market; product differentiation and improvement hold effective means of market and price control
Monopoly	One seller; no close substitutes; factor mobility extremely difficult; almost total control of price; less responsive to change; sometimes practice of price discrimination*

*Price discrimination refers to different prices that exist in separate markets for the same product. The markets are separated by the relative degree of demand elasticity, which means that different prices are charged based on the earning power of the buyers, age, sex, military status, location of buyers, status, use of the product, labels and the like.

In this table markets are represented primarily from the sellers' point of view. The same characteristics apply when they are viewed from the buyers' side, except the identification changes. For example, monopsony identifies the market situation where there is one buyer. Likewise oligopsony represents a market involving few large buyers.

Any of the market types shown in Table 5.2 can exist in a given market area. How is the market area determined? The simplest criterion for market area delineation is price uniformity—commonly called Law of One Price. The law states that under competitive conditions of demand and supply the price of a given commodity tends to be equal[7] throughout the whole of the market area. (In a perfectly or purely competitive market, the price equality is very clear.) Thus, if prices of the product differ between areas by more than the cost of transporting it from one area to the other, two market areas are involved instead of one.

Improved means of transportation and related facilities continually widen market areas. As market areas expand, trade areas based on commuting patterns for shopping within the market area emerge. The establishment of trade areas reflects a situation where buyers have accepted, perhaps being unaware, the transportation cost. This often provides a partial basis for the location of economic activity. The continuous agglomeration of industry in large metropolitan areas illustrates this point.

Determination of price under the varying market types is generally a function of the forces of demand and supply. The behavior of these forces varies with the market type. Hence, different prices would be determined in different markets. A generalized mechanism of price determination, employing the schedules of demand and supply, will be offered here since analyses of individual market types are beyond the scope of this text.

The hypothetical schedule in Table 5.3 shows the amounts sellers would sell at different prices; similarly, the demand schedule in the same table shows the amounts buyers would purchase at different prices. At any given time, only that price at which the amount offered and demanded are exactly equal will affect the

Table 5.3 Hypothetical Demand and Supply Schedules in Price Determination

Number of Units Demanded	Per Unit Price	Number of Units Supplied
53	2 cents	20
50	4	30
45	6	35
40	7	30
35→	←8→	←35
30	9	40
25	10	45

transaction. This is the market price. In Table 5.3, at the per unit price of 8 cents, 35 units are demanded and the same number of units supplied; hence the market is *cleared*. There is no surplus and no shortage. Notice this *equilibrium price* of 8 cents can change as the forces of demand and supply change. Hence demand and supply can be viewed as being in constant motion, producing new equilibrium prices with every related change. Areas with more stable and steadily rising demand would attract economic activities at the expense of those with a greater degree of fluctuation in demand. With a predictable demand, it is convenient for suppliers to adjust their production.

The traditional market types of the economic framework do not consider spatial relations between buyers and buyers, sellers and sellers, and sellers and buyers, except that which is reflected by trans-

[7]The wholesale prices of a product tend to maintain equality more closely than retail prices in a given market. At wholesale level the existence of nonprice competition is practically none. And at the retail level, individual dealers may deviate from the market price by offering additional customer services and conveniences, but even then the tendency to one price is at work, setting limits beyond which deviations cannot go.

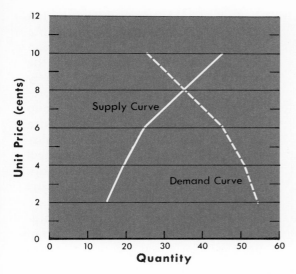

FIGURE 5.2 *Graphic representation of Table 5.3 showing hypothetical demand and supply curves. (General Media Corporation)*

portation cost and rent.[8] These spatial relations, theoretically speaking, can exist in infinite numbers. Nevertheless, these relations for any given market can be classified under four general groupings:

   I. Clustered buyers (consumers) and scattered sellers (producers)
  II. Clustered sellers and scattered buyers
 III. Both buyers and sellers scattered
 IV. Both buyers and sellers clustered

The groupings are illustrated in Fig. 5.3 with no reference to any particular market type. The spatial size and shape of the market vary, depending on the definition of the market, the commodity involved, and the communication channels. Within the general group any modification would produce a different set of spatial relations. For example, under Group III there could be even distribution of buyers and sellers in the market area, or

---

[8]Rent represents income accrued to owners of those factors of production that are limited (less than perfectly elastic in supply). This may involve land, capital, and in some cases, labor. The level of rent accrued is closely related to location and special characteristics of the factors attributed to spatial considerations.

some other modification. Any one of the market types mentioned in Table 5.2 may be assumed for each of the four spatial relations groupings. The adaptability of the various market types to the grouping or a subgroup thereof provides a predictive inference for the spatial arrangements of economic activities.

In Group I in Fig. 5.3, the conception of a spatial market where the buyers are clustered or point-located and the sellers are scattered around the buyers bears some resemblance to Von Thunen's model. Assuming an isolated area with a village type of settlement, and uniform soil fertility, climate, topography, and transportation facilities throughout the market area, he discovered that differences in land use were due to variations in transportation cost—a composite representation of the distance involved, weight, volume, perishability of the commodity, and ease of transportation. The sellers will maximize net profit by a concentrated effort to minimize (1) transportation cost for the supplies of materials, labor, and other inputs, and the delivery of the products, and (2) cost of resource inputs, especially rental cost, which is partly affected by distance from the buyers. The higher transportation cost may be offset by lower cost of materials. Since the areal location of buyers is clustered and cannot be extended, the product price would tend to be the same for all consumers irrespective of the quantity sold to any given consumer [4]. All market types are possible; however, pure competition is more likely to occur at the initial stage of development of the market with eventual blending into monopolistic competition as the rates of substitution between transportation cost and rent become equal.

The market pertaining to Group II in Fig. 5.3 reflects the situation where buyers are scattered around the production center at varying distances from the sellers. In this case sellers are maximizing profit by minimizing rental cost

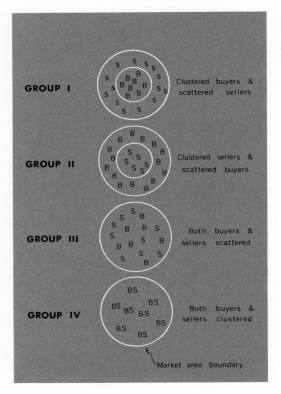

FIGURE 5.3 *A market in four general spatial relation groupings between buyers and sellers. (General Media Corporation)*

and/or by maximizing the productivity. This may involve, from the point of view of spatial strategy, agreements or cartels, extensions of the sales radius, achieving the economies of scale, and minimizing transportation cost of inputs within the production center. (The strategy of *industry-mix*, where each industry is integrated to another through using each others' intermediary products, is an example of minimizing the transportation cost of inputs by means of underground conveyors, pipes, and other methods of fast and efficient delivery.)

Transportation of products is not a variable from the seller's point of view, except in those cases where the seller absorbs part or all of the transportation cost. All firms having, in general, a similar rental cost would lean toward expanding their areal market. This can be accom-

plished through product differentiation and/or the lowering of price, assuming the buyer is paying the transportation cost of the product. If the behavior of the firms is as outlined above, then the purely competitive market does not seem to prevail under the spatial conditions of Group II. When sellers are located at a point with their customers scattered at varying distances from them, there most likely will be a strong tendency toward the development of oligopolistic and monopolistic markets.

Group III shows buyers and sellers located in some random pattern. This pattern or the particular spacing between buyers and sellers is conditioned by the spatial distribution of resources and population. Under conditions of homogeneity, the distribution of buyers and sellers would be an even one and all of the market area would be covered—the trade pattern of each buyer and seller would tend to overlap, resulting in a tendency by each firm or seller to square off his boundaries, forming a hexagonal trade area pattern within the general market area. This being a suitable structure for pure competition, as Losch [10] demonstrated, would eventually push profits to zero—a situation sellers do not relish. The most likely move for them to increase their profit would involve cutting transportation cost, resulting in some form of agglomeration and interdependence between buyers and buyers and between sellers and sellers. (This would be the result if the resources and population were heterogeneously distributed.) Since the basic spatial facts indicate the heterogeneity and sometimes indivisibility of resources, the hexagonal pattern of trade areas cannot be realistically defended. In fact, as Losch points out in his empirical work, the spatial discontinuities in economic activity would produce "hills" and "valleys" in the location of economic activities as well as of buyers and sellers. The hills represent those locations and concentrations where the re-

NATO

New York Stock Exchange

Pan American Airways

Pan American Airways

FIGURE 5.4   *What kinds of markets are represented above? Can you identify some of the spatial relations that exist between buyers and sellers?*

sources, consumers, and market type, in general, make the best combination to achieve the minimum cost of rent and transportation. These conditions point to the oligopolistic type of market, which, in fact, is the pattern of U.S. space economy.

In Fig. 5.3, Group IV is a market in which the distance factor is less important. All buyers and sellers are located adjacently. All types of the market are possible, but pure competition and monopolistic competition are more likely to prevail.

Substitution

In the section on minerals in Chapter 4, substitution was considered as a dynamic force to alleviate depletion problems. Subsequent discussion referred to substitution as a determinant of demand function. In this chapter a detailed analysis of the substitution concept is developed. The concept refers to the process by which (1) alternative locations are evaluated in terms of substitution between various transportation routes and/or means, between diverse inputs, costs and revenues, outlays in various time periods, and between a combination of these substitutions; and (2) a consumer best satisfies his wants by substitutions among various commodities and various time periods. All of these substitutions, in essence, reflect a course of rational behavior resulting in a unique combination of various inputs or outputs—a situation where no alternative move could result in a further favorable substitution, that is, in reduction in total production and delivery cost, or in the increment of utility in the case of consumers.

Production of dissimilar commodities frequently requires different ratios of inputs. Likewise, different consumers, in general, consume different proportions of various commodities, even if the total utility derived by each consumer is identical. Such differences, more pro-

nounced on the regional basis, are a result of relative prices, incomes, tastes, and beliefs.

For certain items there are no substitutes. Man must have water and salt to survive. Similarly, to raise agricultural crops a certain amount of space is a "must" input, no matter how much labor or capital have been substituted for it. Thus, within certain limits, inputs as well as outputs may be substituted for each other. The substitution may take place at various rates. A constant rate of substitution, i.e., one for one replacement or some fixed proportion, is a rare phenomenon. However, many of the substitution decisions involve a diminishing rate of substitution—sometimes referred to as *imperfect substitution*. What this imperfect substitution means and how an *ideal* substitution is achieved are illustrated by the hypothetical data in Table 5.4.

Imperfect substitutability of inputs means that as more and more of a particular input is substituted for another input in a given production process, the substituted input becomes increasingly *less* effective. In other words, the marginal rate of substitution (MRS) of any input *diminishes as the proportion of that input to other inputs increases.* [9] Marginal substitution refers to the amount of an input for which an extra unit of another input can be substituted without affecting the output. In Table 5.4, column 2, the MRS of capital (K) for labor (L) is denoted by the ratio $\Delta L/\Delta K$, where Δ refers to "change"; it is the amount of labor for which an extra unit of K can be substituted while maintaining the same output of 100 units.

Notice that any of the four combinations of K and L in Table 5.4 can yield 100 units of output. Starting with the

[9]This is a consequence of the Law of Diminishing Returns or the Principle of Variable Proportions, which says that given the state of technology and fixed quantities of all other inputs, the addition of units of a variable input will eventually lead to ever smaller increases in output. The law stands empirically proven.

Table 5.4   Combinations of Capital (K) and Labor Units (L) in Producing 100 Units of Product, Rates of Substitution, and Cost Outlays Illustrating Cost Minimization

Quantities of Inputs		Marginal Rate of K for L ($\Delta L/\Delta K$)	Substitution of L for K ($\Delta K/\Delta L$)	Unit Input Cost (C) Ratios		Total Cost (100 Units)
K	L			K = $8 C_K/C_L	L = $4 C_L/C_K	
1	10			2	0.50	$48
		4.0	0.25			
2	6			2	0.50	40
		2.0	0.50			
3	4			2	0.50	40
		1.0	1.00			
4	3			2	0.50	44

second combination, a second unit of K substitutes four units of L; the addition of a third unit of K substitutes two units of L; and finally as a fourth unit of K is added, only one unit of L can be withdrawn. This reflects that the MRS of K for L in Table 5.4 is diminishing with subsequent substitutions of K for L. Similarly the MRS of L for K (column 3), when Table 5.4 is read from the bottom up, shows a diminishing substitution.

The question of which substitution is ideal from the cost minimization point of view is answered by the relative per-unit costs of the inputs. As a general principle, the point where the MRS is inversely equal to the ratio of per-unit costs of the inputs involved represents the ideal combination. For example, Table 5.4 shows that three units of K and four units of L is the ideal combination, beyond which mutual substitution between K and L is not favorable. This is further seen from the following relationships, which use data from Table 5.4:

$$\frac{1}{\Delta L/\Delta K} = 2 = \frac{C_K}{C_L}$$ corresponds to the combination of 3K and 4L,

$$\frac{1}{\Delta K/\Delta L} = .5 = \frac{C_L}{C_K}$$ also corresponds to the same combination of 3K and 4L.

Also note that at this combination the $40 total cost is minimum.[10]

The concept of substitution as related to inputs is explained above. The same can be applied to a multitude of problems where there exists competitiveness or substitutability between existing and potential variables.

Locational Comparative Advantage

The concept of *comparative advantage* and its analysis is useful in explaining why certain areas or spaces specialize in specific types of economic activity, even though they may be suitable for other activities.

The continuous process of seeking and using those locations offering the greatest promise for the most efficient and profitable operation of an economic activity results in areal (economic) differentiation or specialization. Thus, specialization tends to become more pronounced with increasing degrees of industrialization and the broadening and deepening of knowledge of inputs. Four general types of specialization may be listed—business, task, occupational, and spatial—and all are interrelated. A specialized occupation may result in a specialized task, which in turn reflects specialization of business; specialized business gives rise to spe-

[10]The total cost is also $40 for the combination 2K and 6L. This is because the average MRS has been used in Table 5.4. If the exact rather than average MRS is used, the combination of 3K and 4L would come out as the unique one. The exact MRS can be derived by calculus, computed as a derivative with $\Delta K/\Delta L$ or $\Delta L/\Delta K$ expressed as dK/dL or dL/dK, where the change in K and L becomes infinitely small (approaches the limit zero). To accomplish this the production function must be estimated.

FIGURE 5.5 *Do you perceive that the spatial arrangement of the town and large high-way is reflected in the socioeconomic characteristics of the town? How? (New York State Department of Commerce)*

cialized location since it is established at a specific location or set of locations.

Specialization—an excellent method of using given scarce resources that provide the greatest output—in a real sense measures the economic ability of an area to compete with other areas in the production of the same or similar commodities. Thus each area bears a comparative advantage (or disadvantage) in producing the given commodity.[11] Comparative advantage is linked not only with fixed resources—favorable climate, soils, and topography—but also with favorable combinations and considerations of other inputs and societal frameworks that enter into the production process. Inadequate facilities for transporting inputs to and

commodities from their points of production often outweigh any fixed resource advantage associated with an area. Quarantine restrictions, protective tariffs, public subsidies, special tax concessions, regional price supports, and many other man-devised institutional arrangements may enhance the comparative advantage of one area at the expense of other competing areas. An abundant supply of skilled labor or management, investment and operating capital available at favorable terms, industry-mix facilities, efficient allocation and management of the factors of production, and the ingenuity and skill in marketing the outputs as well as procuring the inputs all combined may provide an area with comparative advantage.

Practically all of these considerations affecting comparative advantage are manifested in terms of costs of (1) assembling the necessary materials, processing, and marketing the output, and (2) depreciation and maintenance of capital. The costs are relative, as are the prices. Not only are costs for a particular operation affected

[11]Theoretically, each area can attain self-sufficiency for its residents with given needs and wants by employing modern technology and capital. But this would be expensive and wasteful; also, ever-increasing human wants would push towards specialization, should those wants be realized. This is particularly appropriate to situations where the productive ability of an area is definitely limited relative to the demand (e.g., deserts, mountain passes, proven mining locations, water power and reservoir areas, and other resource-oriented sites).

by the cost of other activities but also by the price of the commodity involved. It is imperative, therefore, to examine the structure of costs and prices to fully understand the concept of comparative advantage.

COSTS

For valid comparison of various locations with respect to their comparative advantage, standard cost criteria is important. The term *cost* generally refers to the outlay of funds, direct or indirect, needed for production of commodities. There are a number of concepts related to what constitutes cost. A fundamental concept is *opportunity cost* or *alternative cost*, which means that the cost of anything is the value of the alternative, or the opportunity, that is sacrificed. The alternative cost of producing fuel oil is the value of the gasoline that could have been produced from the same crude oil. The cost of lending or using capital is the interest it could earn in the next-best use of equal risk. The rent earned by land growing wheat becomes the cost of growing oats when turning the land to oats is contemplated. Similarly, the alternative cost of a given commodity represents the alternative use to which the same resources and location may be put. The foregone alternative constitutes a cost under any economic system. Thus the use of the concept of alternative cost is to compare benefits, those anticipated and those foregone. Also, this concept offers a rationale for the compensation of funds invested in the firm and the services of the entrepreneur.

A third concept is that of *money cost* or business cost. These expenses (costs) include all payments and contractual obligations by the producing unit. The full costs may be divided into *variable costs* and *fixed costs*. Variable costs vary with output. They represent the payments for materials, labor, taxes, fuel, power,

etc. Fixed costs normally do not vary with output, except when the firm's capacity is enlarged or when other administrative changes occur with respect to tenure and long-term contracts. Fixed costs or the overhead cost include certain taxes (real estate), some salaries, allowances for depreciation,[12] opportunity cost of the firm, normal profits, rent, and certain insurance payments.

The level of cost of production for a given location is influenced by:

1. Length of the time period for cost calculation and the method of prorating the cost associated with the selected time period
2. The method of allocating cost among commodities when one firm is producing more than two commodities during the same time period
3. The method of allocating cost among plants located at different points but under the same management and the output level or the size of the firm
4. The size of normal profit deemed "minimum"
5. Technical as well as economic combination of inputs
6. The types of inputs employed in the production process

Space does not permit any further evaluation of the above considerations of cost calculation. However, it must be recognized that the spatial cost variation is not only a function of input price differentials but also of the six variables listed above.

PRICES

Prices are discussed here in terms of prices of commodities, although a similar anal-

[12]Depreciation may be computed by a variety of methods. Bad debts may be estimated as a certain percentage of all sales, of charged sales alone, or of accounts receivable. Each method gives a different answer. It is important that standard criteria be applied for the comparative cost analysis.

ogy extends to input prices. Price for a given commodity at various market locations may (1) vary because of different demand–supply relationships, demand elasticity, and market type, or (2) be the same at all locations. In the former case costs are clearly relative to the commodity price. A higher price can justify a corresponding higher cost and vice versa. The latter may be a result of spatial oligopoly with scattered buyers and sellers. The conditions of this market type, in general, tend to establish a relatively stable price, limiting competition among the sellers to sales volume, occupying optimum location, and cost minimization.

Under these conditions and for the qualifying industries, two pricing systems have been operational in the United States:

1. F.O.B. (free on board) pricing
2. Basing point pricing

The former involves the sellers' price quotation consisting of the mill or factory price; freight costs are absorbed by the buyer—closer, more conveniently located buyers pay a delivered price (mill price plus freight) lower than those located at distant and remote points. In other words, production costs do not include freight charges for outbound shipments; the buyers' delivered price is composed of a constant mill price (for all sellers) plus freight charges, which are a function of distance, means of transportation, and regional freight rates. Under f.o.b. pricing arrangements, new entrants would seek a "phantom" freight advantage over established sellers by selecting a location near the periphery of buyers or one where the difference between the per-unit delivery price and the per-unit total cost is greater than, if not equal, that of his rivals.

Basing point pricing [11] refers to a system where all producers agree to quote delivery prices based upon prices assigned to some basing point (or points) plus freight. The simplest form of basing point pricing involves the single basing point system and the quoted delivered price, consisting of the agreed mill price of the sellers (irrespective of the seller's location) plus the transportation charges from the basing point. For example, if a buyer orders from a nearer seller—from where the actual freight rates are lower than from the basing point—he still pays the seller a delivered price that includes phantom freight, that is, an amount equivalent to the rate from the basing point. Similarly, if the purchase is made from a seller located where freight cost is higher than the cost from the basing point, delivery price is still based on the lower cost from the basing point.

Among the various industries associated with a single basing point pricing system, the case of the steel industry, which formerly used the so-called Pittsburgh-Plus system, perhaps has attracted the most discussion. Under this system steel prices in Birmingham, Alabama and Gary, Indiana represented the Pittsburgh price plus freight from Pittsburgh. The single basing point pricing system was ruled unlawful by the United States Supreme Court in 1948 under the provisions of anti-trust acts. Since then various modifications in the system have been suggested. Several industries including cement, gasoline, steel, and lumber have used a multiple basing point pricing system in which several regional basing points were established throughout the country instead of one single basing point. Basing points usually represent important production or distribution centers. The delivery price quoted to the buyer consists of the general mill price plus the freight cost equivalent from the nearest basing point to his location. This multiple basing point system tends to equalize or neutralize the freight advantage or disadvantage; thus it forces sellers to compete in terms of cost (devoid of outbound freight) minimization, which means greater efficiency. But the freight rate contained in the delivery price may have little relationship to the actual transportation costs charged by the hauling carriers. Furthermore, the multiple basing point system may inhibit competition by limiting the new entrants and the advantages of phantom freight.

Finally, other variations of the basing point system may be found. The "postage stamp" pricing system, for example, has a positive freight absorption—the greater the shipping distance the greater the freight absorption—on the part of sellers, and the f.o.b. mill price includes in it the freight absorbed. Note that the condition of more and more freight absorption by sellers with greater shipping distance tends to result in uniform delivery prices at all points.

TRANSPORTATION

The concept of transportation—the means of directly or indirectly connecting spatially dispersed people and their diverse activities—is indispensable in understanding social similarities, economic interdependence and development, and the levels and types of economic activities carried on in particular areas. Transportation analysis, often dwarfed in its past by current developments and future prospects, lends insight to the location and distribution of economic activities. Development of railroads, opening of various waterways, recent undertaking of freeways and turnpikes, the rapidly expanding air transportation network, and large-diameter pipelines all reflect the significant role of transportation. The economic importance of transportation is evident in the production and distribution process, the relationships that exist between transportation cost and delivery prices, the price stabilizing effect of transportation,[13] the relation between the transportation bill and gross national product, and in the general contribution of transportation toward regional economic development.

Since the distribution of economic activity partly influences freight rates or transportation costs, there exists a circular interrelationship between rates and the location of economic activity. Once this circular mechanism establishes freight rates, any deviation is resisted by those whose cost−price relations are unfavorably affected. Specifically, this involves individual firms or regions who fear a loss of their sources of incomes.

The forces which establish these rates are also the ones to initiate any change. These forces may be classified as related to

1. Carriers
2. Producers and producing areas
3. Consumers and consuming areas
4. Commodity characteristics

Transportation also helps to bring price stability for the commodity involved and encourages specialization. In general, the price rise in any market in time of local shortage is equal to the transportation cost of shipping in from the surplus areas. The surplus area, reflecting a higher degree of specialization, may even have lower production cost, and the resultant delivery price in the shortage area may remain the same, or minutely higher, than it was before the shortage.

Carrier-related forces involve competitive relations that are intramodal (between the same type of carrier firms), intermodal (between different types of carriers), or both; government control and/or subsidies; and the special privileges afforded to some carriers, routes,

---

[13]Periodic studies by the U.S. Interstate Commerce Commission show that a certain relationship exists between the transportation cost portion of the delivery price and the type of commodity transported. For example, sand and gravel transportation cost makes up over half the delivery price for those commodities; for business machines and the like, the ratio is less than one percent. Such a wide range between less than 1 percent and over 50 percent indicates the variability of the relative degree of transportation cost as a part of the delivery price, which influences the scope of the market and the distribution of a particular economic activity.

or areas. The carrier competition, besides affecting the level and structure of freight rates, may also include services such as greater speed, pick-up and delivery, more safety or less damage, and other promotional services. Public assistance granted to some carriers and routes serving certain points in the societal interest may benefit certain economic activities and areas in the form of subsidies and special privileges. These forces, individually or collectively, bring to some areas lower rates than otherwise would have been the case; the same forces also may be unfavorable to other carriers and areas, making these carriers increase their rates to offset revenue losses. Thus, the larger the ratio of freight rate and delivery price, the greater the effect of freight rate on the location of the economic activity concerned. Consequently, the relative development of the area is also affected.

Producer-related transportation forces may mean survival for some producers (or the areas where these producers are located) at the expense of lower rates for the carriers hauling their shipments. At locations[14] where competitively squeezed producers are able to convince the carriers servicing them that the closing down of production means consequent carrier's loss of traffic, the carriers are likely to accept lower freight rates in lieu of total loss of traffic, which is more painful in light of their huge overhead investment. Previously, carrier investment was often based on the competitively favorable position of the producers. Carriers affected in such circumstances may seek public assistance and subsidies.

Consumer-related transportation forces affect the location and further growth of economic activities through the relative demand elasticities of different consuming areas. For example, two competitive carriers hauling from a given point to different directions or consuming centers may encourage new entrants to that

production center, or growth of those already existing there, by lower freight rates (resulting from directional competition). Lower rates would cause lower delivery price and greater demand. (The volume of increased demand depends on demand elasticity—the more elastic the demand, the greater the increase in the volume of sales and vice versa.) To satisfy this demand the output must grow either through new entrants or by the expansion of existing producers. Consuming areas with relatively greater elastic demand are likely to be more influential in causing growth in output. The carriers linking these consuming areas not only move the production centers toward specialization, but also increase their traffic volume and revenues. This may leave the other producing areas not linked to the preferred consuming centers in a disadvantaged position; hence their locational value is downgraded for new entrants or expansion of the existing ones.

The commodities (inputs and outputs) involved in transportation also may affect locational comparative advantage. If the movement of commodities between areas is such that the carrier's service is fully utilized in both-way traffic, producers located at those points may enjoy lower freight rates and consequently be able to sell their products at lower delivered prices. These points, therefore, have cost advantage over other locations that do not have comparable return commodity flows.

Finally, assuming that inputs are mobile and can be transported to any location at a cost, the spatial cost differentials can be reduced logically to transportation cost differentials. In a sense, locations or sites are mobile; i.e., they are available anywhere but only at a different cost or rent. The rent is a function of accessibility of the site to markets, inputs, aesthetic facilities, cultural attractions including educational facilities, and the time and convenience en route. A location most accessible to the desired use involves a lower

---

[14]The point beyond which nontransportation costs cannot be lowered if they are to stay in business.

transportation cost to reach it and thus commands higher rent. Conversely, less accessible locations require higher transportation cost resulting in lower renting value. Thus, transportation costs are important in helping to explain the rationale of location of economic activity.

INTERNATIONAL TRADE

Earlier the concept of locational comparative advantage (or disadvantage) as a basis for regional trade was discussed in terms of its physical characteristics, costs, prices, and transportation forces. It was also pointed out that there are numerous other considerations that influence the comparative advantage of an area.

Although the following discussion concerns international trade in terms of its basis, significance, and effects, the same analysis lends itself to intranational trade flows. It must be recognized, however, that while the fundamental analysis of all trade is essentially the same, there are some limitations upon international trade largely because of policies of the institutions involved. Limitations may involve a certain level of output beyond which the comparative advantage becomes ineffective. Tariffs, quotas, the problems of foreign exchange, and credit restrictions in the use of certain international carriers and routes tend to discourage international specialization and trade.

It is noteworthy that the international financial institutions—International Monetary Fund (IMF), International Bank for Reconstruction and Development (IBRD), United Nations International Financial Corporation (UNIFC), Special United Nations Fund for Economic Development (SUNFED), and the United States Agency for International Development (AID)—have facilitated international trade and economic development, and assure sufficient credit in coming years to finance the free world's continued economic growth. In May 1967, the free world, by

revising the provisions of the General Agreement on Tariffs and Trade (GATT) signed in 1947, completed the greatest tariff cuts in history and laid the foundation for a vast expansion of international trade. A plan to create new "Special Drawing Rights" (SDRs) was drafted by the finance ministers of the "Group of Ten" (the United States, Great Britain, France, West Germany, Japan, Italy, Sweden, Belgium, the Netherlands, and Canada) on August 26, 1967 and submitted to the IMF in Rio de Janeiro, Brazil, September 25–30, 1967. It was approved by the IMF members early in 1970. Under the plan a specified amount of SDRs would be issued each year to member nations in accordance with each nation's demand for SDRs and the quota in the IMF. The SDRs—another name for international currency—perhaps will never be seen or used by ordinary persons. Government central banks only will use them to settle international payments along with their reserves of gold and other hard currencies.

Since different commodities require for their production different relative amounts of the various inputs, and countries (spaces) are differently endowed with these inputs, the relative supplies of the inputs are reflected in their relative prices, and the relative costs of producing different commodities reflect relative efficiency. Therefore, the variation in relative costs forms the fundamental basis of trade. (Other factors that may influence foreign trade are the satisfactions associated with the novelty of possessing or consuming "foreign makes," altruistic motives toward other countries, and the demand for foreign materials, fruits, and other food items which the country cannot procure at home.) The relation of cost to that of other commodities in the same country and to that in the other country for the same commodity determines whether a country has an equal, absolute, or comparative advantage as a basis for engaging in trade. The comparison of cost may be accomplished either through price (which normally covers the cost) or through some index representing the standard transformation of physical inputs. The former measures the social and/or market value of the commodity expressed in terms of the country's currency. The latter measures the amount of physical inputs used in producing a given amount of the commodity. Both approaches have their respective advantages and disadvantages.

The price method is convenient because of its character of being a common denominator for the various inputs, but it requires the establishment of a conversion factor—commonly called the exchange rate (the price of other currencies in terms of the local currency)—since not only do different currencies have different units of measurement, but their purchasing power also differs. The input method, however, eliminates the institutional effects (union strength, public subsidies, the degree of competitiveness in the industry concerned, and the like) from the price and represents the actual physical amount of inputs used. Differences in the quality of inputs—for example, labor—present a difficult problem.

For illustrative purposes, however, the price method will be employed. Also, for convenience let us suppose that the world contains only two countries, the United States and West Germany, and only two commodities, chemicals and steel. Let us further suppose that each country has its own monetary unit for stating prices, the dollar ($) and the mark (M.). Given the respective prices for some specified units of chemicals and steel in both the countries, and the exchange rate between the two currencies, the nature of advantage for both countries can be determined.

Equal Advantage

The hypothetical data and related equations in Table 5.5 show that the internal price ratios between steel and chemicals

in both countries are identical. If the initial exchange rate is one mark equals 25 cents, then $6.00 is the equivalent of 24M. and steel would be cheaper in Germany by 15M. (24 minus 9); similarly, chemicals would be cheaper by five marks (8 minus 3). At this exchange rate of marks for

Table 5.5 Prices of Steel and Chemicals Showing a Relation of Equal Advantage

	U.S. (prices in dollars)	West Germany (G) (prices in Marks)
Steel (S)	6	9
Chemicals (C)	2	3
	$1S_{U.S.} = 3C_{U.S.}$ $1C_{U.S.} = 1/3S_{U.S.}$	$1S_G = 3C_G$ $1C_G = 1/3S_G$

dollars (mark price of the dollars), Germany could profitably export both steel and chemicals to the United States. But one-way trade is possible only for a relatively short time. The German financial institutions dealing with foreign exchange will accumulate demand deposits in the United States banks or deplete U.S. deposits in the German banks. As the German banks continue to pile up their inventory of dollars, they will be willing to accept more dollars but only at a lower price. (At the exchange rate of 1M. = $0.25 the German banks paid four marks to get one dollar; the lower price means that to buy one dollar they will pay less than four marks.) The exchange rate of marks for dollars will continue to fall until it reaches 1.50M. = $1. At this rate steel and chemicals are equally priced in both countries, which means that there is no basis for trade, not even for one-way trade. Therefore, it may be concluded that in the absence of trade barriers, any two nations whose domestic price ratios are equal in the manner shown in Table 5.5 possess equal advantage, and hence make no net gain from engaging in mutual trade.

Comparative Advantage

Now, suppose the data in Table 5.6 represent domestic prices (which may also be referred to as costs, since prices, in general, have close association with the costs) of steel and chemicals. Note that the price

Table 5.6   Prices of Steel and Chemicals Showing a Relation of Comparative Advantage

	U.S. (prices in dollars)	West Germany (G) (prices in Marks)
Steel (S)	6	9
Chemicals (C)	2	4
	$1S_{U.S.} = 3C_{U.S.}$	$1S_G = 9/4C_G$
	$1C_{U.S.} = 1/3S_{U.S.}$	$1C_G = 4/9S_G$

or cost of S is three times the price or cost of C in the United States, while it is only nine-fourths as great as C in Germany. This means, comparatively speaking, that steel is more costly to produce in the U.S. than in Germany; similarly C is more costly to produce in Germany than in the United States. Indeed, the relative costs of the two commodities are reciprocals of each other (this can be verified from the equations at the bottom of Table 5.6). The equations show that whereas steel is relatively 4/3 times cheaper in Germany than in the United States, chemicals are relatively 4/3 times cheaper in the United States than in Germany.

Based on this information, the United States would be expected to import steel from Germany, and Germany would be expected to import chemicals from the United States in order for both countries to benefit from mutual trade. The important question, however, is on what terms the goods are to be traded. Both countries will benefit from trade if the commodities are exchanged at any ratio (terms) falling between their internal cost ratios. The United States gains no advantage when it trades three units of chemicals to obtain one unit of steel; similarly, Germany has no advantage when it trades a whole unit of steel for 9/4 units of chemicals. The United States enjoys the greatest benefit when it can receive one unit of steel by trading as few as 9/4 units of chemicals. Germany benefits most when it receives three units of chemicals in exchange for one unit of steel. There-

fore, one unit of steel must be exchanged for between $2\frac{1}{4}$ and 3 units of chemicals.

Now, let us suppose that the terms of trade are agreed upon as $1S = 2\frac{1}{2}C$. The United States gains one dollar[15] on every unit of steel imported—it costs $6 to produce one unit of steel at home and $2 to produce a unit of chemicals, but by importing one unit of steel at the expense of exporting $2\frac{1}{2}$ units of chemicals, one dollar per unit is saved $[\$6 - (\$2 \times 2\frac{1}{2})]$. In other words, the cost to the United States of an imported unit of steel is $2\frac{1}{2}$ units of chemicals, which, without trade, is 3 units of chemicals. Likewise, Germany gains one mark $[(4M. \times 2\frac{1}{2}) - 9M.]$ for every $2\frac{1}{2}$ units of chemicals imported; that is, the cost to Germany of an imported unit of chemicals is 2/5 units of steel instead of 4/9.

Examining from the view of exchange rate: if the exchange rate is $\frac{3}{2}M. = \$1$, neither country can underprice the other in steel; if the exchange rate is $2M. = \$1$, neither can underprice the other in chemicals. An effective exchange has to be within these limits (the mark price of one dollar being less than 2M. and greater than $\frac{3}{2}M.$). Suppose the rate is 1.75M. = $1.00. Stating the prices in Table 5.6 in either of the two currencies, it can easily be verified that steel is cheaper in Germany and chemicals are cheaper in the United States. At the exchange rate of 1.75M. = $1.00, the net gains of the United States and Germany are approximately $.86 and 1.29M., respectively.[16] The above exchange rate is slightly unfavorable to Germany, since 1.25M. is about $0.71. But, as American banks continue to pile up their inventory of marks, as a result of the favorable exchange rate they will be willing to accept more marks only at a lower price until an equilibrium is reached, wherein the bene-

---

[15]This gain would be affected when the relative transportation cost and other barriers to trade are taken into consideration.

[16]The net gains are computed based on the trade of 1 unit of steel with equivalent units (18/7) of chemicals.

fits of trade are identical to both nations. (The lowering of the price of the mark may be accomplished either through the exchange rate mechanism, the terms of trade, or both.)

Absolute Advantage

Absolute advantage is a special position a country may enjoy. When a space like the United States, having created a variety of efficient factors of production, is able to produce most commodities more efficiently (higher output per unit of some specified input, e.g., labor) than other countries, it enjoys the position of absolute advantage. At first thought, the general productive superiority of a country may seem to disqualify it from engaging in trade. Even though a country might have absolute advantage, however, it can best utilize its resources by specializing in producing those commodities where its comparative advantages are greatest. For example: A physician would not be expected to use his time as a nurse for rather obvious reasons, even though he may do a better nursing job, qualitatively speaking, than a trained nurse. A lawyer might be a good typist as well as a competent lawyer, giving him an absolute advantage in both fields. But the opportunity cost of his time when he is typing is much higher than what he may save (say $5,000 a year) by not hiring a professional typist. A similar analogy may be extended to a nation possessing an absolute advantage. The United States, for example, can still benefit by selling commodities to other nations where its comparative advantage is the greatest, and buying commodities from them for which their comparative disadvantage is the least.

It is evident from the above that absolute advantage is a special case of comparative advantage. The same analysis as discussed under comparative advantage also applies here. To recapitulate, the Law of Comparative Advantage states that, with no trade barriers, a nation tends to import those goods and services the relative cost of which are less abroad than at home, and exports those items the relative cost of which are greater abroad than at home. The bilateral, two-commodity trade illustration, although a simplified explanation of the process of international trade, provides the basic rationale of the process. The multiplicity of commodities in multilateral trade, coupled with the various levels and kinds of trade barriers, foreign aid, and the institutional problems of settling the balance of payments all complicate determination of the terms of trade and exchange rates. The student of geography is not concerned with the detailed process of determining exchange rates and settling problems of balance of payments. His contribution lies in analyses of resulting trade patterns and trends, and in the evaluation of the associated institutions that affect commodity flows. These flows provide an explanatory variable of why a given region has certain economic phenomena (e.g., economic activity), its volume, and degree of specialization. (Some useful devices for measuring specialization and concentration are discussed in Part VI.) The degree of specialization increases with wider markets at the expense of those activities that would have been feasible had the foreign markets not been opened. This proposition may be tested by relating the degree of specialization and/or the concentration index to the coefficient of export (exports ÷ gross product). Generally speaking, both of these measurements should reflect a positive correlation. Exceptions would be countries like the United States and the Soviet Union where domestic markets are sufficiently large to permit specialization without significant exports.

Effects

During the sixties, world trade involving an enormous variety of goods and services averaged about 10 percent of world income. This proportion doubles when data for the United States and the Soviet Union are excluded. According to the Standard International Trade Classification (SITC) adopted by the United Nations Economic and Social Council, there are 150 categories involving 570 different kinds of goods and services that make up the list of foreign trade.

During 1965 the value of exports was $165 billion currency equivalents, excluding Mainland China, the U.S.S.R. and its satellites, and United States military exports. The rate of growth in international trade has averaged about six percent since 1950, and about nine percent since 1962 [8].

These statistics, impressive as they are, have multiple repercussions on the level of real income and general economic welfare, allocation pattern of resources among various activities and locations, relative costs and prices, and the scale of production.

It goes without saying that it is invalid to conclude that if a nation's exports or imports are five percent of its national income, the latter would be affected only to this extent if foreign trade were cut off. The United States perhaps might be able to maintain its present standard of living from its vast territory and wide variety of resources, and by making numerous substitutions. Nevertheless, when one considers consumer sovereignty and preferences, types of goods and services being traded, and costs and benefit aspects of the standard of living, the effects of cutting off foreign trade become obvious. Consider the effect on the standard of living if we had to forego such items as coffee, tea, cocoa, bananas, crude rubber, tin, jute, and spices—the domestic supply of which is now totally imported. Table 4.7 in Chapter 4 shows that the United States has only two metallic minerals—magnesium and molybdenum—in sufficient quantities to meet domestic needs without importation. Substitutes could

be developed, but the costs of readjustment are great, even without taking into account benefits lost as a result of cutting off international trade.

Dynamics

In international trade, *dynamism* pertains to changes in domestic cost ratios, technology, artificial barriers, state of international relations, transportation costs, and institutional arrangements and facilities. This makes the network of world trade one of perpetual motion in terms of composition, volume, direction, and speed. Classical theory pertaining to the basis of international trade—comparative costs differences due to different production functions—stands up to empirical investigations under the short-run phenomena of trade. In the long run, production functions tend to be the same for all countries. Thus, a dynamic theory[17] of international trade, for both short- and long-run considerations, involves three variables:

1. Production function
2. Resource prices
3. Product prices

Based on the interdependent results of these variables, a country tends to export those commodities using large amounts of resources available in relatively scarce supply at home. Thus, relative resource price differentials at national levels may be attributed to relative differences in the uses of national resources. Differentials of relative demands influence relative costs for all situations where industry is either operating at an increasing or at a decreasing cost.

Although other considerations mentioned at the start of this section quite fre-

[17]The dynamic, sometimes called modern theory of international trade has come to be known as the Hackscher-Ohlin theory of trade. Bertil Ohlin, benefiting from the work by Eli Hackscher, has presented the theory in his *Interregional and International Trade* (Cambridge, Mass.: Harvard University Press, 1933).

quently influence the trade pattern, differences in relative factor endowments, relative demands, and relative production functions remain basic and dynamic forces underlying foreign trade.

SPATIAL DISPERSION AND EFFICIENCY

Spatial dispersion of economic activities is a function of the distribution of resources and consumers (both final and intermediate), the type of market, the nature of institutions, and society's goals and direction. Efficiency refers to the ratio of output and input associated with the dispersion pattern. There are numerous considerations in the measurement of efficiency. Suffice it to say that each dispersion pattern has a degree of efficiency which may or may not be the society's goal.

Given the type of market, theoretical spatial relations between the buyers and sellers were shown in Fig. 5.3. The situation of clustered buyers suggests that sellers tend to seek those locations that promise cost minimization regardless of rivals. If buyers are scattered, however, sellers seek locations that not only minimize cost but also secure a larger buyers' market. This means that sellers are faced not only with the need to determine fairly accurately the relative elasticities of demand, but also the shape of marginal cost functions, freight rates, degree and importance of amenity factors, and other institutional and custom considerations at alternative locations.

selected references

1. Balassa, B., "An Empirical Demonstration of Classical Comparative Cost Theory," *The Review of Economics and Statistics*, August 1963.

2. Brown, W. G.; Singh, Ajmer; and Castle, E. N., "Net Economic Value of the Oregon Salmon-Steelhead Sport Fishery," *The Journal of Wildlife Management*, Vol. 29, No. 2, April 1965, pp. 266–279.

3. Chisholm, Michael, *Geography and Economics*, New York: Frederick A. Praeger, 1966.

4. Greenhut, Melvin L., *Microeconomics and the Space Economy*, Glenview, Ill.: Scott, Foresman and Company, 1963.

5. Hansen, N. M., "Development of Pole Theory in a Regional Context," *Kyklos*, Vol. 32, 1965, pp. 176–190.

6. Hoover, Edgar M., *The Location of Economic Activity*, New York: McGraw-Hill Book Company, Inc., 1948.

7. Hughes, R. B., "Interregional Income Differences: Self Perpetuation," *Southern Economic Journal*, Vol. 28, 1961, pp. 41–45.

8. International Monetary Fund, *Annual Report of the Executive Directory*, for the fiscal year ending April 30, 1967, Washington, D.C.: International Monetary Fund, 1967.

9. Isard, Walter; Schooler, E. W.; and Vietosisz, T., *Industrial Complex Analysis and Regional Development*, New York: John Wiley & Sons, Inc., 1959.

10. Losch, August, *The Economics of Location*, New Haven: Yale University Press, 1954.

11. Machlup, Fritz, *The Basing Point System*, Philadelphia: The Blakiston Company, 1949.

12. Marshall, Alfred, Principles of Economics, 9th ed., New York: The Macmillan Company, 1961.

13. Nourse, Hugh O., *Regional Economics*, New York: McGraw-Hill Book Company, Inc., 1968.

14. Siehert, Horst, *Regional Economic Growth and Policy*, Scranton, Pa.: International Textbook Company, 1969.

15. Thoman, Richard S., and Conkling, E. C., *Geography of International Trade*, Englewood Cliffs, N. J.: Prentice-Hall, Inc., 1967.

16. Weber, Alfred, *Theory of the Location of Industries*, Chicago: University of Chicago Press, 1928.

The analysis of economic activity has depended traditionally on physical, economic, and occasionally on social aspects. However, the changing and spatially varying emphases and roles of various political concepts and the emergence of new states have challenged existing analyses for their ability to explain and reflect the spatial variation in economic phenomena.

The goals of governments, whether international, national, or regional and their emphases and direction are manifest in economic activity in terms of type, level, and location.[1] Countries placing high priorities on economic development tend to allocate their resources heavily toward productive capital goods; the economically advanced countries promote greater levels of research and development to find new products and processes in order to maintain a high level of consumption. Regions with declining levels of economic activity have often been observed to "catch fire" with a stimulus from government-initiated programs and activities; in a similar manner government actions may also affect the areas adversely.

The effects of political factors may be either direct and/or indirect at a given place and time. Government-owned and -operated activities are examples of direct effects. Societal values associated with property, contracts, individual opportunity and rights, modern money,[2] trade, fiscal policy (taxes, structure and level of public spending, price controls and

chapter 6

Political Framework

[1]Regions once labelled as monocultures have and are introducing diversification, partly as a result of government-directed movements for a higher degree of self-sufficiency and national security. These diversifications have been justified even at the expense of established profitable markets and benefits associated with the trade based on relative comparative advantage.

[2]Money, in the modern sense, is anything that serves as a medium of exchange, standard of value, store of value, and a standard of deferred payments; it is produced and controlled by government, which also establishes the legal mechanism for its acceptability. An ideal money is one that is durable, portable, divisible, uniform within the given denomination, recognizable, difficult to counterfeit, and relatively inexpensive to produce.

supports, production controls, subsidies, and rationing), monetary policy (discount rate, reserve requirement, and supply of money), and institutions affecting the size of economic units and the activity of labor unions are almost invariably instituted through the political framework either directly or indirectly. The structure and degree of political influences is determined by the relative political doctrines and modern concepts of the nation–state.

NATION–STATE

The concept of *nation* traditionally refers to a group of people with common language and, sometimes, religion; whereas the *state* is a territorial boundary over which a government exercises sovereignty. A nation may be stateless but a state cannot be nationless. As an illustration, Israel has existed as a nation for a long time. It was only in 1948 that she attained her statehood involving Palestine, which at one time was considered to be the Jewish State.

The classical European nation–state system, possessing the attributes of a relatively homogeneous cultural base, effectiveness of sovereignty, and loyalty and adherance to the law, is no longer realized in the same way as it was during the nineteenth century. Although some European nations still closely conform to the classical nation–state system, the two World Wars, the end of colonialism, the cold war, brush wars, and domestic instability and disharmony have produced numerous loosely structured societies, which for the sake of socioeconomic progress and survival are progressing toward reasonable facsimiles of the so-called modern nation–state.[3]

The modern nation–state is not a cohesive, homogenously structured unit. Instead, it may be referred to as a society structured through a political framework. The massive flow of government proclamations and activities are designed to stimulate and diffuse economic and social

progress and cohesiveness, and to promote unity of purpose in the political realm. Joseph L. Fisher [8], for instance, illustrates the impact of government proclamations in the U. S. as follows:

Associated with the names of most Presidents in this century have been certain watchwords. Theodore Roosevelt proclaimed his Square Deal; Wilson the New Freedom; Harding preferred Back to Normalcy; Franklin Roosevelt the New Deal; Truman the Fair Deal; Kennedy the New Frontier. Although he had no one pet phrase, Eisenhower emphasized partnership. President Johnson has proclaimed his goal for America as achieving the Great Society.
Running through these bold proclamations are several themes: a better deal for those groups suffering disadvantages; a higher level of social justice in the distribution of wealth and income among all people; the harnessing of science to economic and social development; an emphasis on freedom and range of choices in national policy; a regard for efficiency and the holding down of costs. The Great Society, it would seem, draws from all of these, but in the main, it is a restatement of American democracy in political, economic, and social terms suitable for the last third of the twentieth century. Its grandiloquent ring causes some persons to wince and others to smile; all the same, it does seem to find positive response from a much larger number of citizens who sense that to the earlier goals of individual freedom and a better deal for certain groups must now be added an all-embracing design for improvement of the whole American society. (p. 1)

The syndrome of government activity is a never-ending process in contemporary nation–states. This chapter presents the conceptualization and the effects of political factors as they influence economic activity within a spatial context. The analysis does not attempt to theorize the process of political evolution or the problem of policy making.[4]

---

[3]For further study of the concept of nation–state see Alfred Cobban, *National Self-Determinism* (Chicago: University of Chicago Press, 1944), and K. H. Silvert, *Expectant Peoples: Nationalism and Development* (New York: Random House, 1964).

[4]See Lucian W. Pye, *Aspects of Political Development* (Boston: Little, Brown and Company, 1966). An anthropological analysis of the same topic is presented by H. Morton Freid, *The Evolution of Political Society: An Essay in Political Anthropology* (New York: Random House, 1967).

POLITICAL SYSTEMS AND DIVISIONS

Where there is a state there is a government. A brief observation of governments illustrates their diversity, involving variations in how they are constituted and maintained, their relation to the governed, and the type and level of economic role they play. The spatial variation in political behavior roles is manifest in the different decision-making processes of producers and consumers, resulting in spatial variation of economic phenomena. Conceptually speaking, there are as many forms of political behavior roles as there are political entities. Yet some functional groupings can be made and analyzed. The behavior roles within these groupings may be either constitutionally defined, professionally attained, or both.

For example, it has been suggested that democratic governments act rationally within the constraints of a democratic political structure, an electorate of rational voters, and the varying degrees of uncertainty [6]. *The government* (individuals in government) rationally refers to efficiently designed strategy and actions to accomplish the selected political and economic goals of the individual(s). The constitutional and economic role of the government may be minimal, but government rationality alone is a sufficient condition to invoke spatial variability. In the totalitarian economies, the condition of rationality is stronger yet to produce the variability. However, here variability may be a result of one-directional rationality (a single party or an organization) as compared to the two-directional interplay (of the electorate and the government) found in democratic societies. At this point it is appropriate to briefly discuss the selected functional groupings or systems. In general, these politicoeconomic systems are reflected in many ways—organization, structure, development, conduct, control, and direction. Thus, we shall discuss the political system in the light of these criteria.

From the viewpoint of *organization*, three systems—capitalism, socialism, and communism—are basic. There are no universally accepted definitions of these systems; for our purposes, we shall discuss the characteristics they embody.

Capitalism

The framework of pure capitalism involves the following institutions and assumptions:

1. Private property
2. Freedom of enterprise and choice
3. Individualism
4. Competition
5. Consumer sovereignty
6. A limited role for government
7. Market-directed allocation of resources and distribution of wealth.

Under a capitalistic system, the property or means of production (material resources, buildings, plant, and equipment used in the production process) are owned by private individuals or corporate bodies. The institution of property is maintained by the legal mechanism, and the individuals or corporations holding the property may negotiate contracts and control, employ, buy, and sell the property in any market they wish. Laborers are free to sell their services wherever and to whomever they choose. There is no visible government control on the individual's choice. Nevertheless, the individual is guided by the market forces; the market conditions and coordinates individual decisions.

The consumer exercises his sovereignty by casting his votes (money) for the things he wants. The items wanted most are indicated through buying; similarly, lower prices are bid for less wanted commodities. Price is a basic organizing force through which the activities of both buyers and sellers are synchronized. The businessman, in response to consumer sovereignty, seeks to secure and organize his enterprise in such a way that it will provide profit. The allocation of the re-

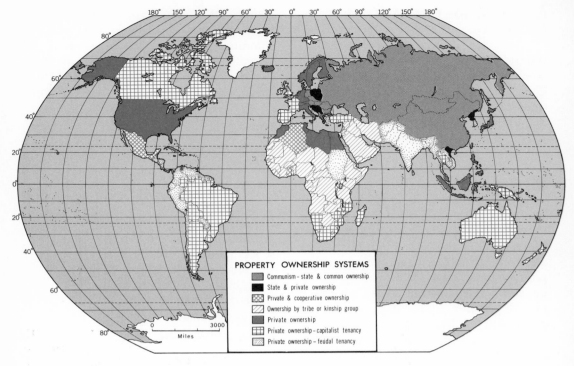

FIGURE 6.1 *World map depicting countries of different ideology. (General Media Corporation)*

sources and distribution of wealth are impersonal, primarily based on market demand and the individual's contribution. Those who pay heed to the market are rewarded and those who do not are "punished." The inequality of income distribution is justified on the basis that each person's income represents the relative value of his contribution to production.

The above outlines the major characteristics of capitalism in its pure form. However, with growing realizations of its shortcomings, many variations have occurred. These shortcomings have appeared in five areas:

1. Consumer sovereignty has been affected to the degree that the consumer has the choice to buy only those goods and services producers make available and persuade consumers to buy through advertising.
2. Decline of producer competition has

tended to increase the gap between prices and costs, thus affecting the distribution of income that would have existed under pure capitalism.
3. The tendency to monopolize in the acquiring of resources has limited resource mobility.
4. Incomes are also being earned from sources other than those directly contributing to the production process, e.g., monopoly profits, capital gains, and inheritance wealth.
5. Capitalism does not adequately provide for the production of social goods, or equitable allocation of social costs and distribution of social benefits.

Remedial actions have occurred and are occurring to alleviate these shortcomings through numerous laws and direct interventions by government. Among all of these modifications of the capitalistic system, the salient feature is that the allocation of resources and the distribution of wealth is brought about largely through the play of market forces.

Communism

The framework of communism involves:

1. Complete or nearly complete public ownership and control of the productive and distributive processes, and the property resources used therein
2. Central planning
3. Command-directed economy
4. Circumscribed freedom
5. Prescribed prices

Public ownership covers the property, means, and instruments of production and distribution—material resources, capital, transportation and communication, most retail and wholesale enterprises, banking systems, and most urban housing. The supreme authority is likened to a dictatorship interested in enhancing its own power, privilege, and prestige. Construction of the plan may or may not reflect consumer interests. The plan outlines what and how much is to be produced, where the enterprises are located, and how the output will be disposed of among the production units and consumers.

Consumer sovereignty is limited solely to the freedom to spend their income as they see fit, on those services and goods for which the central plan provides. The composition of goods and services produced as determined by the plan establishes the number and kinds of jobs available. Resource prices, set by the planning committee, vary between occupations and localities in a fashion and to a degree that provide for the needed number and types of workers in various occupations. The labor force, save occasional compulsory job assignments (and slave labor), is relatively free to choose or change jobs in response to spatial and occupational wage differentials. Product prices are used merely as a rationing tool. The planning committee or its related agency sets the consumer goods prices at levels that will clear the produced quantities leaving no shortages or surplus.

Socialism

The framework of socialism basically involves:

1. Public ownership and management[5] of all producers' goods that are strategically important to the society.
2. Large-scale production, requiring relatively large numbers of employees and great economic power
3. Equality of income distribution
4. Economic growth and elimination of business cycles
5. Reliance on market mechanism
6. Economic planning
7. "Social" democracy
8. "Meaningful" freedom

Under socialism not all property and enterprises are publicly owned and managed. Public ownership and management is limited to only those enterprises and property that hold the keys to crucial decisions regarding output, employment, resource utilization, pricing, technological development, and the location of economic activity. Control of these keys means political power, which may be exercised toward more abundant satisfaction of luxury desires and more political and social dominance. This may produce inequality of income and freedom (under the assumption that economic, social, and political liberty are inseparable —it is impossible to have one without the others), and imbalance (in favor of public goods) between social and private goods. The situation of "public opulence and private squalor" may result in continued intensification of the inequality of income

[5]The producers' goods involve a range, and each type of good on this range commands a relative degree or eligibility for socialization. Standing first in this range would be banking and public utility; second, communications; third, energy, steel, chemicals, transportation, and construction, on down the line.

distribution, and consequently, further inequality in the well-being of the society.

But in theory the public role under socialism would manifest itself in replenishing the "starved public sector," resulting in more stable economic growth, improved income distribution (since unemployed persons, who previously had no income at all, would now be earning at least something), and greater equality of opportunity and freedom to choose from various occupations, locations, and goods and services. Since the government is supposed to be elected democratically (with practically no influence from economic giants), an individuals' significance in effecting change is enhanced; thus he gains more "meaningful" freedom otherwise circumvented by the fewer rich found under pure capitalism.

Each of these political ideas—capitalism, socialism, and communism—provides a different organizational framework for viewing and resolving questions related to resource ownership and allocation, location of enterprises, and distribution of output; the spatial arrangement of economic activities tends to be different in each of these frameworks (or some modification of them). In communism, the activities tend to be resource-oriented; market-oriented under capitalism: and some mixture of resource- and market-oriented under socialism.

The *structural* aspect of a polity is closely associated with its organizational reference. For example, the capitalistic system embodying the market (and price) as the basic force of resource allocation and output distribution employs a market structure that may fall anywhere on the continuum between pure competition on one side and monopoly on the other. The spatial pattern of economic activity likely to be yielded by pure competition, monopoly, monopolistic competition, and oligopoly were discussed in Chapter 5. The structures of the communist and socialist political economies are dependent on the type and the degree of com-

mand, which may range from high centralization to complete decentralization. Each structure produces a different spatial pattern of economic activities. The control and direction of a highly centralized structure tend to develop large complexes of activities with a high degree of specialization. With decentralized control and direction of the economy, specialization may occur but is not likely to be of such a large scale as is possible under a centralized system.

A given political framework may envelop economies standing at different points in the stage and rate of economic development. Five such stages have been identified [15]:

1. Tradition
2. The preconditions for take-off
3. The take-off
4. The drive to maturity
5. High mass consumption

The traditional societies are identified as predominantly agricultural, with primitive technology, low productivity, limited entrepreneurial talent, high rate of illiteracy, high birth and death rates, limited social and economic mobility, local and provincialized political affinity, and limited trade. The second stage is transitional, reflecting a transformation of traditional ways of thinking, attitudes toward work and life, and methods of government. In this transition, political and social attitudes and economic institutions conducive to development are constructed. A spirit of nationalism emerges and moves the many nations within the state to a single nation–state.

Societies in the take-off stage reflect lowering of resistances to economic growth, increase of new and productive investments, and the use of new technology. Manufacturing is generally of increasing importance. The fourth stage reflects mass industrialization, near-literacy, increased mobility of labor, lower birth and death rates, higher productivity, and a high degree of interdependence in the economy. In the last of these stages, a society experiences income increase to a level where durable consumer goods beyond the needs for food, shelter, and clothing can be afforded. The society's resources are basically oriented toward consumer satisfaction and enjoyment. Needless to say, a given polity may have all five stages existing simultaneously within its boundaries because of spatial variations in the various components of its society.

Polities may also be differentiated by their rates of economic growth, commonly measured by the average percent increases of the real gross product from year to year. The rate of growth[6] basically depends on the proportion of the net national product invested. And, the rate of investment is a function of many factors—availability and accessibility of raw materials; availability and adoption of technology; entrepreneurship; education; social, political, and economic institutions; national solidarity and cohesion; and the general willingness of the populace to advance economically.

To recapitulate, the politicoeconomic frameworks prevailing in the contemporary world are numerous and diverse. Groupings of these polities can be accomplished wherever possible with respect to selected criteria. The list of criteria or characteristics discussed in the earlier paragraphs are by no means exhaustive. Further criteria such as freedom, justice, personal security, and social equality could also be employed, although their measurement poses many technical difficulties. Given the criteria employed and relative difficulties of measurement, functional political groupings can be delimited, the structural as well as functional understanding of which provides a background reference for the explanation of economic activity.

[6]This growth contributes towards the gain in welfare only when it exceeds the rate of population increase.

POLITICAL INSTITUTIONS

The preceding discussion demonstrates the diversity of political frameworks and some elements by which various political entities can be identified and grouped. In this section, the influence of a polity in terms of the various government institutions on its economic landscape is explored.

Basic to all political or government institutions is the individual member of the society, with his expectations, aspirations, attitudes, participation, and vigilance—qualities known to political scientists as "raw materials." With these raw materials the political individual moves to establish and direct the institutions conducive to favorable processing of his raw materials—which when organized along with the rest of the political individuals in the society may show a wide range of goals.

How are these raw materials acquired? They are related to psychological, economic, and social variables of the individual, as indicated by various studies [4, 12]. A personality that exhibits fear, suspicion, and insecurity, and shudders at uncertainty, complexity, and change, tends to seek and accept authority and leadership from others. The social experiences related to education, work, interest groups, political parties, clubs, the structure of political views of the family, religious affiliation, age, and sex influence the raw material. Katz and Lazarsfeld [11], from numerous related studies, observe a strong relationship between the character of primary groups and the political behavior of an individual. Dye [7] and Reagan [14] show that economic status and aspirations also influence the political behavior of an individual.

Given the political raw material or the micropolitics of a polity, the political system (which partially influences and molds the political raw material) influences the effect of micropolitics on macropolitics and related institutions. For instance,

FIGURE 6.2   *Which of these commercial enterprises is capitalistic? Above—Baikalsk, U.S.S.R. (Novosti Press Agency); below—Baltimore, Maryland (Hedrich-Blessing)*

capitalism coupled with democratic institutions would not only establish and maintain the supportive institutions, but also would contain the mechanism by which the micropolitics have dynamic control over the structure and direction of these institutions. Under a communist system the degree of influence of micropolitics on these institutions is perhaps minimal.

Law and the Legal System

The *law* is a sum total of rules and regulations of conduct established and enforced by authority, legislation, or custom and tradition. Thus, the concept of law involves the *legal order system* and *sociological norms*, both of which condition economic phenomena. The former is manifest in the interpretation, guarantees, protection, licensing, controls, indemnities, subsidies, prohibition, and coercion or punishment—all of which constitute "rules of the game" (the emergence and performance of economic phenomena) in which the players (entrepreneurs and managers) engage for the attainment of certain goals. The latter is an induced expression of approval or disapproval of the existence of economic activity without any outward coercive force—physical or psychological. The inducement may be a composite force of custom, religous ethics, expectation and acceptance of novelty or fashion, public opinion, and the like. The location and survival of many economic phenomena are influenced by the social-based law, discussed further in Chapter 7.[7] Just as economic activities are affected by the various political frameworks, so also are legal order systems the direct result of particular political orientations.

[7]A stimulating reading for those interested in a philosophical treatment of social-based law is Max Rheinstein, ed., *Max Weber On Law in Economy and Society,* trans. by Edward Shils and Max Rheinstein (New York: Simon and Schuster, 1967).

POLITICAL VARIABLES

The variation in national political systems provides a reference for studies related to nation–state regions. However, as in the case of the United States and other democratic countries, despite the universality of the constitutional framework, political frameworks of internal regions or states differ significantly. This differentiation is caused by the relative strength and competition of political parties, political participation, voting district apportionment, interest-group activity and strength, and factors related to the personality, role, and status of the political figures at the national level.

Our interest does not lie in political differentiation as such, but rather in its effect on the economic phenomena. For such purposes the identification of political variables is imperative. Adelman and Morris [1] have identified twelve political variables or factors that affect the level and type of economic activity of an area:

1. Degree of national integration and sense of national unity
2. Degree of centralization of political power
3. Strength of democratic institutions
4. Degree of freedom of political opposition and press
5. Degree of competitiveness of political parties
6. Predominant basis of the political party system
7. Strength of the labor movement
8. Political strength of the traditional elite
9. Degree of administrative efficiency
10. Extent of leadership commitment to economic development
11. Extent of political stability
12. Political strength and role of the military

These variables demonstrate the significant interrelationship between political patterns and economic phenomena.

The other variables having roots in the political framework include property rights (surface, subsurface, and air), tenancy and leasing, acquisition and transfer of ownership rights, bequeathing of property, protection, and guarantees, taxation, subsidies, and the employment of fiscal and monetary policies for influencing the economic performance of the region. Our interest here is to identify the relevant variables, to provide perspective for the student of economic geography and open avenues of study into discovering the precise nature and level of interrelationships between these variables and the dependent variable (economic activity). An application of these variables and others in this section will be demonstrated in Part III.

selected references

1. Adelman, Irma, and Morris, Cynthia T., *Society, Politics, and Economic Development: A Quantitative Approach*, Baltimore: The Johns Hopkins Press, 1967.

2. Alford, Robert R., *Party and Society*, Chicago: Rand McNally, 1963.

3. Cobban, Alfred, *National Self-Determination*, Chicago: University of Chicago Press, 1944.

4. Dahl, Robert, *Who Governs?* New Haven: Yale University Press, 1961.

5. Demsetz, H., "Why Regulate Utilities?" *Journal of Law and Economics*, Vol. 11, No. 1, April 1968, pp. 55–65.

6. Downs, Anthony, *An Economic Theory of Democracy* New York: Harper and Row Publishers, Inc., 1957.

7. Dye, Thomas R., *Politics, Economics, and the Public: Policy Outcomes in the American States*, Chicago: Rand McNally, 1966.

8. Fisher, J. L., *Resource Development in the Public Interest*, Annual Report, Washington, D.C.: Resources for the Future, 1965.

9. Freid, Morton H., *The Evolution of Political Society: An Essay in Political Anthropology* New York: Random House, 1967.

10. Hutton, J. P., and Hartley, K., "A Regional Payroll Tax," *Oxford Economic Pamphlet*, Vol. 20, No. 1, University of York, England, November 1968, pp. 417–426.

11. Katz, Elihu, and Lazarsfeld, Paul F., *Personal Influence*, Part I, New York: The Free Press, 1964.

12. Lipset, Seymour M., *Political Man: The Social Bases of Politics*, New York: Doubleday and Company, 1959.

13. Pye, Lucian W., *Aspects of Political Development*, Boston: Little, Brown and Company, 1966.

14. Reagan, M. D., *Politics, Economics, and the General Welfare*, Glenview, Ill.: Scott, Foresman and Company, 1965.

15. Rostow, W. W., *The Stages of Economic Growth: A Non-Communist Manifesto*, Cambridge University Press, 1960.

16. Silvert, K. H., *Expectant Peoples: Nationalism and Development*, New York: Random House, 1964.

As was pointed out in Chapter 1, cultural aspects—the sum total of all the devices and behavior produced or learned by man—are partly patterned as a consequence of communication between cultural regions. Within the limits of a society's environment, cultural factors have a direct impact on the level and type of economic activities. The impacts are relative, however, and in continuous flux due to changing technology and the level and kind of technology. Thus, culture and resources exist in a dynamic relationship.

The purpose of this chapter is to identify some of the major social factors[1] and state how they may influence the type and level of economic activities within a region. This hypothesis has been investigated by many scholars who have reached the general conclusion that social factors are highly influential in economic growth. But there are interesting philosophical and empirical differences of interpretation regarding the character and degree of these influences. Everett E. Hagen [6] has concluded that social factors (including the political factor) are *decisive* and serve as the *basic vehicle* for economic growth.[2] In any case, social factors do play a significant role in the location and growth of economic activity.

MEASUREMENT OF SOCIO-CULTURAL FACTORS

The relevance of social factors that can be identified and interpreted depends on the validity with which these factors can be measured. There have long been efforts to *enumerate* social aspects: Mary and Joseph going to Bethlehem for enumera-

chapter 7

Social Framework

---

[1]The factors of the social framework are herein considered to be: (1) population, (2) religion, (3) education, (4) perception of race, (5) family structure, and (6) personality structure.

[2]The purposes of this text do not warrant a detailed discussion on this controversy. Generally, very little empirical evidence exists on this topic; most of the work related to it has philosophical or theoretical implications.

tion, and provisions for decennial census and the State of the Union message[3] in Art. I, Sec. 2 and Art. II, Sec. 3, respectively, of the U. S. Constitution, are examples. The Hugh Moore Fund of New York (a population policy panel), the Social Science Research Council, the American Statistical Association, the Bureau of the Budget, and UNESCO (United Nations Educational, Scientific and Cultural Organization) all have made strides toward the definition and measurement of social indicators or factors. The U.S. Department of Health, Education and Welfare initiated (1961) the monthly and annual HEW Indicators, which bear promise of becoming parallel to the economic indicator series.

Progress to date along this front has involved the measurement of:

1. The spatial distribution of the population size by age, race, skill and training, marital status, and head of the household.
2. The more recent estimates of propensities to move and actual spatial mobility.
3. Estimates of present population and projections of the future, the basic variables of which are birth rates, death rates, fertility rates, and population migration.

These kinds of data, although useful for many purposes, do not reveal the overall character of a society. Many significant measures associated with value systems, beliefs, social stimuli, goals, perceptive mechanisms, dexterity, attitudes toward life, change, etc. are lacking.

The Committee on Space of the American Academy of Arts and Sciences has

prepared for the National Aeronautics and Space Administration an innovative and provocative volume, *Social Indicators* [1], in which the authors deal primarily with the social consequences or ramifications of space programs. But the substance of this volume yields valuable insight into the means by which a given society's character, as well as that of a state, can be evaluated or anticipated. Another useful by-product of this volume is that it attempts to define the type and value of social statistical series necessary for policy decisions.

To be sure, there are numerous difficulties involved in compiling social data:

1. Attempts to obtain unbiased data, especially in societies where individual freedom is highly valued and guaranteed, elicit the charge that any attempt to measure the "real" character of the society is an act of "dehumanization."
2. Presently we are unable to numericalize human values and "personal" affairs.

Aside from technical difficulties, other factors of concern include invalidity, inaccuracy, conflicting indicators, lack of data, incompatible models, and value consensus.

Invalidity refers to situations where the indicator reflects only a limited validity—the meaning of the events that generate the data does not exactly correspond to the meaning attached to the indicator, and there may be differences in the meaning of the concept at different periods. For example, a certain number of people having a particular religious affiliation does not necessarily mean that all affiliates of that particular sect represent a homogeneous affinity with its "articles of faith." Hence a social series on religious affiliations may involve invalidities. There are similar invalidities related to data on educational achievement, poverty line, and the like.

Inaccuracy is associated with sampling

[3]Historically the presidents' State of the Union messages have been dominated by the so-called "economic philistinism"—economically oriented statistics and issues—leaving the condition of the social fabric relatively minimized, if not ignored. The contemporary State of the Union messages are dominated by the Budget (required by the Budget and Accounting Act of 1921), the Economic Report (under the Employment Act of 1946), and the Manpower Report (under the Manpower Development and Training Act of 1962).

and enumeration errors and biases. *Conflicting indicators* are ones that show contradictory implications when applied or used for the same judgment or conclusion. The strengthening of the family unit in the United States holds a respectable value as a basic building block toward strengthening the democratic process; yet some contend that Social Security and welfare programs tend to weaken the family bond and thus may have an adverse effect on the national goal of a strong democracy. *Lack of data* may occur simply because of discontinuity in the series, or due to the difficulty of defining and measuring certain social aspects. *Incompatibility* of the models is related to the manner in which the indicators are statistically treated or analyzed. The difficulty of *value consensus* stems from individual differences in preferences, standards, and relative values.

Man's behavior is a composite representation of his biological structure and physiocultural environment. No attempt is made here to analyze spatial variations in the biological structure and motivational forces of man and their effects on economic phenomena. The focus is on the social factors as they develop and manifest themselves in diverse ways at different times and places; therefore, they are conceptualized as causes of spatial variation in economic phenomena.

POPULATION

The population factor has many aspects—size, density, spatial distribution, age and sex, fertility rate, birth and death rate, life expectancy, migration, and rate and trend of population growth. The implications of these aspects, manifested in varying forms and levels among the areal hierarchies of the earth, tend to produce regional differentials in the spatial distribution of economic activities and their growth patterns.

The world population now exceeds 3.5 billion, which, according to the geometric progression series of Malthus, may be looked upon as the result of two dozen individuals increasing at the rate of 0.02 percent per year over a period of approximately 100,000 years. Philip Hauser [8], using the estimates of Harrison Brown, reports that projection of the average post-World War II rate of increase of the then-existing population would give a population of fifty billion by 2160 A.D. This estimate, when extended to the middle of the twenty-eighth century, means that if all the land on earth were divided equally, each person would receive only one square foot. Can any set of economic activities support this population? Brown thinks so, assuming that technological achievements in the capturing of solar and/or nuclear energy will enable the production of energy at such a low cost that the conventional energy-producing resources will become available for other uses, including food, and the change in food habits will be such that food raised from algae farms and yeast factories will satisfy the need.

These speculations and voluminous figures may be fantasies, but they do indeed reflect one of man's crises. Table 7.1, based on United Nations statistics, shows that the rate of the world's population growth has been increasing rapidly, and future projections indicate an even faster increase.

Man can avert the population crisis or "explosion" in the same way he is creating it—through the enormous preventive as well as remedial technology that is reducing mortality and increasing life expectancy—by reducing birth rates through modification of the value systems that promote fertility and unchecked reproduction. The problems are complex, however, when viewed in terms of world societies and certain religious practices. According to the United Nations, few, if any countries are willing to commit themselves to halting of population growth (even if it is technically possible) because

Table 7.1   Size and Increases in Populations by Continental Regions

Region	Population (millions)					Average Annual Percent Increase				
	1900	1925	1950	1975*	2000*	1650–1750	1900–1925	1925–1950	1950–1975*	1975–2000*
World	1550	1907	2497	3828	6267	0.3	0.9	1.2	2.1	2.6
Africa	120	147	199	303	517	–	0.9	1.4	2.1	2.8
Asia	857	1020	1380	2210	3870	–	0.8	1.4	2.4	3.0
Europe (including USSR)	423	505	574	751	947	–	0.8	0.6	1.2	1.0
North America	81	126	168	240	312	–	2.2	1.3	1.7	1.2
South America	63	99	163	303	592	–	2.3	2.6	3.4	3.8
Oceania	6	10	13	21	29	–	2.3	1.4	2.4	1.6

*These are medium-level United Nations projections.

Source: Philip M. Hauser, "Demographic Dimensions of World Politics," in T. Morgan, G. W. Betz, and N. K. Choudry, eds., *Readings in Economic Development* (Belmont, Calif.: Wadsworth Publishing Company, Inc., 1963), p. 62, by permission of the publisher.

they fear that the "numbers game" may shortchange them in world politics. Thus, solutions to the problem are of international concern and scope. The problems are further compounded by barriers to international migration.

Table 7.1 and Fig. 7.1 demonstrate that the growth in population is occurring unevenly among the various regions, and the prospective rates of population growth

even more so. Population growth rates are a function of birth rates, death rates, and migration as shown in Table 7.2. Based on the correlations among these variables and the per capita income for a selected number of countries, it has been observed that international differentials in level of living are phenomena caused partly by these variables. For example, both death rates and birth rates are nega-

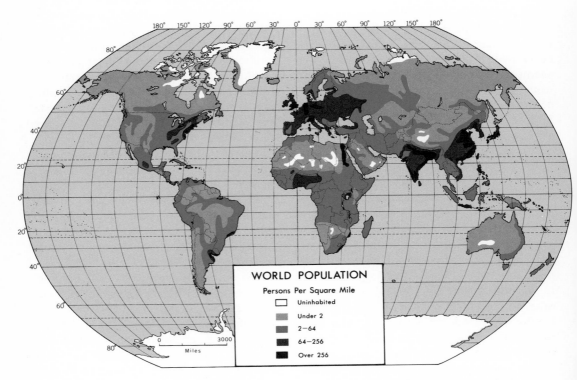

FIGURE 7.1   *World population distribution and density. (General Media Corporation)*

Table 7.2   Determinants of Population Growth

Natural Increase in a Regional Population is Affected by:

Birth Rates— *influenced by*	Death Rates— *influenced by*	Migration— *influenced by*
Fertility rate	Mortality rates	Employment opportunities
Age, sex, and income distribution	Climate	Amenity factors
Religion and cultural values	Health measures and facilities	Barriers to in-and-out migration
Technology of birth control	Education	
Working hours patterns	Environmental pollution	
Privacy	Population intensity	
Education	Caloric consumption	
Marriage rate	Type of economic activities	
Composition of food		

tively correlated to the per capita level of national income, and there are varying reasons for this relationship. In some countries, such as Ireland and Japan, the scarcity of local material resources has provided the impetus for family limitation (lower birth rates), which has been partly responsible for more efficient units of economic enterprise, resulting in higher per capita incomes. In many societies the desire for a higher standard of living has provided the impetus for family limitation.

Other aspects of the population factor, such as the structure of societies with a smaller share of the economically productive population, may mean lower total production of output. In many developing countries there is a relatively high child dependency ratio, hence a much smaller proportion of the population survives to working age. Assuming that the economically productive population of a nation is that segment between the ages of 15 and 64, poor countries average something like 55 percent of their population in this category, as compared to 65 percent for developed countries.

The size of population may or may not be a deterrent to the improvement of living standards. To a point, the increase in total population encourages exploitation of resources that would otherwise not be used or perhaps be used less efficiently. In general, the present consensus falls into the "Malthusian population trap." It reflects that at very low per capita income levels, health and nutritional

levels decline to the point where the mortality rate exceeds the birth rate. But higher incomes will bring about an increase in population under the pressure of falling mortality rate; the increase may well be faster than the rate of per capita income change until a three percent maximum limit of population increase is reached. At that point the various forces would push crash efforts to limit or decrease population and aggressive economic development in order to increase the per capita income at a faster rate. India, for example, has reached the outer end of this "trap" after having experienced reasonable rates of economic growth as a result of her various five-year plans. In summary, whether or not a society will be caught in the Malthusian trap depends basically on the levels of absolute and relative change in the rates of population and income.

Finally, the spatial variability in population density patterns directs economic activities into labor-intensive or capital-intensive categories. In general, higher population density areas tend to develop labor-intensive economic activities; low density areas are oriented toward capital-intensive activities.

RELIGION

Religion is a system of beliefs and faith in divine or supernatural powers to be revered, worshiped, and obeyed as creators, rulers, and regulators of the uni-

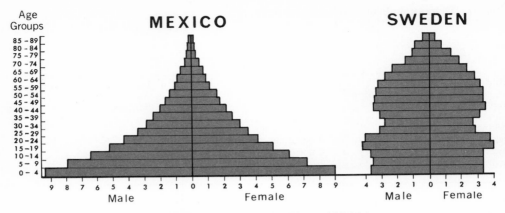

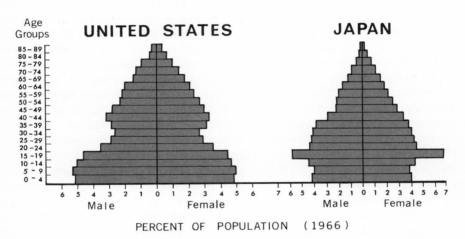

FIGURE 7.2 *Demographic pyramids of Mexico, Sweden, the United States, and Japan.*
(General Media Corporation)

verse. The expression of beliefs is manifested in manner of worship, and in associated institutions, buildings and valuables, rituals, practices, ethical codes, and expressions of conduct. No effort is made here to present a comparative analysis of the various religions and the time- and place-related changes that occur in a given religion [3, 20]. Our interest lies in the way religious aspects affect and influence resource recognition and exploitation, and resultant economic activities. Occasional inadvertency of the effects is recognized but not treated as an exogenous force.

The influences of religious factors on economic phenomena may be examined in the following ways:

1. Economic activities owned and/or operated by religion-related institutions or bodies, and the claim to income of the region
2. The regional density, structure, and coherence within and between religion(s)
3. The relation between religion and the state, and associated concessions and restrictions
4. The effect of religion on resource use and economic activities.

Property owned by religious bodies, in terms of its monetary value, location, and tax exemptions, not only restricts and conditions land use, but also helps to explain the development of commercial and population centers where religious interests were or are foci around which these centers develop. The claims on income affect economic activity through the ways this income is spent to acquire certain types of goods and services.

The extent of property ownership and claims to income that religious bodies have varies over time and place. In the United States the value of church-owned real estate was estimated at $80 billion during 1967. Estimates of the annual income flowing into religious treasuries from business profits, rentals, and dividends runs into billions. The importance of religious properties and income—exempted from the various types of taxes—is likely to increase as more and more religious bodies hold titles to various forms of economic activities. Frequently one finds churches and their agencies holding title to farms, ranches, office buildings, apartment houses, parking lots, bonds, stocks, securities, and the like. For example, a garbage dump in Chicago and the ground under Yankee Stadium in New York are owned by religious groups. With the existing tax shelters and with prudent management of properties and incomes, both resulting in lower costs, church-owned and/or -operated businesses may control greater and greater shares of the market and hence influence the types of economic activities.

Free-will offerings or voluntary contributions also provide sizable income to be expended by religious bodies. On the opposite side, the size of income left unclaimed by religious bodies may also affect the economic phenomena.

The greater the degree of density, homogeneity, and coherence within a given religion, the greater the growth and stability in the types of economic activities yielding goods and services desired by that religion—Israel is a prime example. Some regions with diversity of religious denominations or beliefs have suffered from lagging economic growth and stability because they lack a healthy social atmosphere for new business investments. The higher average rate of economic growth in West Pakistan (religiously more homogeneous than India) during the last two decades, compared to that of India, demonstrates this effect.

The relationships between religion and state and related concessions and restrictions have some bearing on the type and level of economic activity in a given region. The economies of religious states as compared to those of secular states differ significantly. Often secular states may grant concessions to religious institutions, producing results discussed earlier (e.g., the United States). Or the restrictions may penalize or discourage certain actions and manifestations of religious faith influencing the location and type of economic activities (e.g., the Soviet Union).

The effect of religion on resource use and economic activity is reflected through beliefs, taboos, and value systems—respect for authority; the status of the future; man's dominion over minerals, plants, and animals; transmigration; work and leisure; stewardship; the relation of planets to God, seasons, and holidays; worship practices; festivals, customs, and the like. Numerous illustrations can be cited to substantiate the influence of religion on economic activities. Taboos against eating particular foods and working on certain days of the week have produced vivid effects upon the economic phenomena. For over one thousand years, the Roman Catholic Church required its members to abstain from eating meat on Friday in the spirit of penance. Acting on recommendations from Catholic bishops throughout the world that renunciation of meat is not always the most effective means of practicing penance, and since meat is no longer an exceptional food,

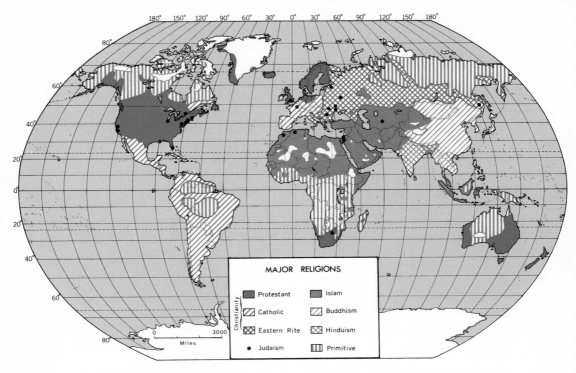

FIGURE 7.3   *World distribution of major religions. (General Media Corporation)*

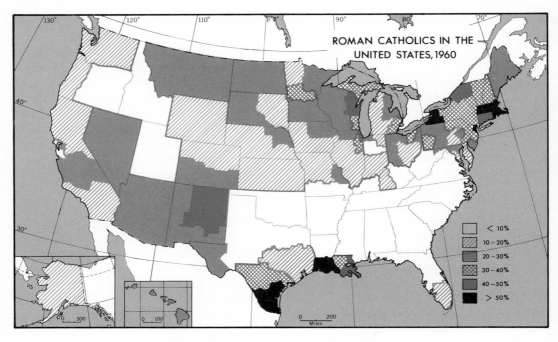

FIGURE 7.4   *(General Media Corporation)*

in February 1966, Pope Paul VI relaxed the rules on fasting and abstinence. Catholics no longer need to abstain from eating meat during Lent, except on Fridays. In addition, the Pope delegated to national conferences of local bishops the option to abolish the ban against eating meat on Fridays throughout the rest of the year. With this authority, bishops of many countries including the United States, in November 1966, terminated meatless Fridays except during Lent.

The problems of fishing industries in those countries have since been compounded by a decline in landings and thus sagging revenues, while the principal competitors of fish—meat and poultry— have been gaining. One study [2] revealed that landed prices of New England fish, on the average, were 12.5 percent lower than the normal (extrapolated from the past ten-year pattern) as a result of decreased demand for fish. This short-run decline in the demand for New England species landed (excluding lobsters, clams, oysters, and miscellaneous marine products) caused approximately $3.0 million in revenue losses to the industry over the seven-month period from December 1966 to August 1967. The economic loss is distributed among many localities (Boston, Gloucester, New Bedford, Plymouth, and Provincetown, Massachusetts, and also in Maine, Rhode Island, and Connecticut) with the greatest absolute and percentage loss of revenue to New Bedford where those species most sensitive to a lowered demand are landed. This is only one example of the economic impact of a religious factor. The Hindu belief in the transmigration of souls has resulted in keeping alive large numbers of monkeys and rats, and also cattle (which are regarded as sacred), causing both losses in crop production and the nation's agricultural carrying capacity. Without this element of belief to which approximately 66 percent of India's population adheres, the type and spatial structure of economic landscape in India would per-

haps be different. Mining explorations in Tibet were discouraged for many years by religious objections. The efforts to harness solar energy in India have partially been dwarfed by Hindu belief in the Sun god. In Moslem cultures the development of pork-raising industry does not seem to be promising becuase of religious values.

Religion itself may in some cases be weakened, but the habit, tradition, and custom patterns developed through religious culture still affect economic activity. There are many ways in which religion with all its manifestations conditions the economic landscape, a fact that numerous studies verify.

EDUCATION

Education is the sum total of knowledge (physical and social sciences, humanities, and the arts), self-awareness, recognition and appreciation of oneself and one's physical, social, economic, and political environments (ranging from home to foreign nations and outer planets) skills, and hopefulness—all of which are learned and acquired. There is marked spatial variation both in quantity and quality of education.

Studies reveal that there is a strong correlation between a region's educational development and its economic productivity and progress. Harbison [7], employing an index of educational development—enrollment in secondary schools and universities—found that for seventy-five selected countries the coefficient of correlation between educational level and per capita gross national product (GNP) is .89, which means that approximately 90 percent of the variation between those countries' per capita GNP is explained by the education factor. This conclusion, although needing further verification and qualification, indicates that the progress of a society depends significantly upon the educational level. Societies with relatively higher levels of education are

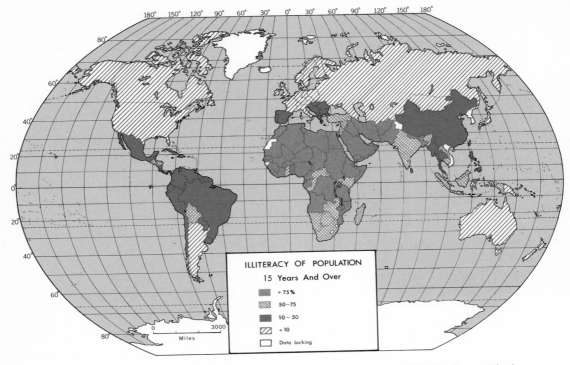

FIGURE 7.5   *Percentage of illiteracy on a world scale. (General Media Corporation)*

likely to earn a larger share of the GNP from economic activities other than primary types; also, the productivity in the primary activities would be superior.

RACIAL STRUCTURES

Racial aspects, especially the perception of the importance of race, are closely related to religion. Our interest here does not lie in the resolution of race-oriented notions —physiological differences[4] in races and their relative superiority—but rather in regional racial structure, its quantitative measurement, its perception by a society,

[4]It is noteworthy, however, that modern anthropological studies refute the centuries-old notions of physiological differences in race, and hence the racial occupational patterns related to climatic regions. The argument that blacks are better able to withstand the heat involved in cultivating cotton, sugar, and coffee is actually a cultural rather than physiological phenomenon.

and the impact of these on the economic phenomena. Kindleberger [12] states that a positive correlation exists between the percentage of white people in a nation and the per capita income. He points out that racial behavior is manifested through the cultural attitudes that condition the attitudes of a people toward occupation and the incomes earned. It is through these attitudes that a given group reflects its desire to progress. There does not, however, exist a positive relationship between the races and the types of economic activities. Why Drawidians consume more spices, and hence engage in the related economic activities, than white U.S. citizens is a cultural rather than racial reflection.

Attempts to measure racial factors for a given region may face problems of:

1. Lack of data, especially in those regions where racial enumeration and discrimination are politically illegal

2. The definition of racial stratifications
3. Difficulty of distinguishing between the race and social (class or caste) stratification
4. Construction of an index involving statistical skills

It may be argued that the variable of racial structure is not or should not be considered in economic geography because of its ethical and political implications. Yet when one looks at the results of racial tensions, the loss of energy and capacity, and economic disruptions and dislocations due to racial particularism, its impacts become evident.

FAMILY STRUCTURE

The meaning assigned to the family as a social unit or institution varies from society to society. The family involving three or more currently living generations under the same roof differs in its economic impacts from a family involving husband, wife, and children. These impacts are reflected through the social communication circle. The former, which is an "extended" family, may restrict migration, trade, flow of ideas, breaking of revered old-age roles and aspirations, and national patriotism. This type of social structure inhibits spatial communication and economic growth, and also generates ubiquitous congeries of economic units comprising basically primary types of economic activities. The latter, by virtue of the need for broader social life, breeds plasticity and mobility. These types of social changes open opportunities for increasing communication, literacy, globalism, rationality, and specificity in the relations of man to his environment. Also, the confidence and monetization of trade encouraged through the broader social circle brings specialization, which promotes easier transformation of agriculturally oriented societies into industrial and mass consumption societies.

The above generalizations, supported by many anthropologists and sociologists including Robert Redfield [17], although providing a basic framework for the role of family as a social unit, need further verification and modification, taking into account mass communication systems, cultural heritage, number of households, and the efforts to develop one national language.[5]

PERSONALITY STRUCTURE

In addition to the social indicators discussed previously, there are other factors, grouped here under the term personality structure, that affect man's economic behavior. These factors include the individual's attitudes, goals, aspirations, expectations, motivation, work, ethics, spirit of cooperation, competition, profit motive, individualism, and the values attached to security achievement, change, progress, and the like. Many of these bear the imprints of family structure, religion, education, and the perception of race within the area. But regardless of how they are classified and produced, their impact on the economic structure is frequently observed. A paramount difficulty, however, exists in quantifying these personality aspects. Complicating the analysis is the fact that the standards by which people judge or evaluate their personality aspects are relative to their experience and level of economic development. For geographic analysis involving spatial series data, data comparability is highly important. Although this concern is applicable to all spatial data, the data on personality aspects are greatly succeptible to this problem.

Based on the responses of 20,000 people from thirteen representative nations (U.S.A., West Germany, Yugoslavia, Poland, Brazil, India, Nigeria, Israel, Egypt, Cuba, the Dominican Republic, Pan-

[5]Over three-fourths of the world's states are multilingual.

ama, and the Philippines) including 600 members of the legislative bodies of some of the countries studied, Hadley Cantril [5] has presented interesting and informative data on personal concerns and expectations: personal values and character, personal economic situation, job or work situation, health, family references, political and social values, status quo, and the international situation. He concludes that the "concerns of people are patterned largely according to the phases of development they are in both culturally and ontogenetically within their society."

Professor McClelland [14] has attempted to measure human "achievement motivation" and its relation to the level of economic activity. The following is his statement of the concept:

The "achievement motive" is ordinarily measured by performing a "content analysis" on imaginative thought. The scoring criteria for the "content analysis" were derived by comparing the thought processes of people under the influence of achievement motivation with the thought processes of people not under its influence. "Thought processes" were sampled by asking subjects to write imaginative stories to pictures. It was found that they introduced more ideas of a certain kind into their stories when their motivation to achieve—to do well —was aroused than when it was not aroused. An objective coding definition has been worked out for detecting these "ideas" with high agreement among different observers. Nearly all of the "ideas" can be classified under the heading of "desiring to do well" or "competing with a standard of excellence." This then became the scoring definition for a variable which was named technically n-achievement to distinguish it from other common-sense measures of achievement motivation such as one would get from how well a person said he was trying. The n-achievement score for an individual is simply a sum of the number of instances of achievement "ideas" or images and their subtypes, and the score for a group of individuals is some measure of central tendency (the average, the mode) of the score of individuals who make up the group. In this way, it can be determined, for example, that the average n-achievement of a group of teen-age German boys is slightly but significantly lower than the average n-achievement of a

carefully matched group of American boys, or that American boys from lower class background have lower average n-achievement than boys from middle class backgrounds.

McClelland found a positive correlation between n-achievement and economic growth, and claims that by using the n-achievement measure for various regions the level of economic activity can be explained or predicted.

The analysis presented in this chapter is not of empirical rigor, but reflects conceptualization of the social framework, which plays a part in explaining the spatial variability of economic activities, both in terms of type and level.

selected references

1. Bauer, R. A. ed., *Social Indicators*, Cambridge: Massachussetts Institute of Technology, 1966.

2. Bell, Frederick W., "Economic Impact of the Abolition of Meatless Fridays," *New England Business Review*, Boston: Federal Reserve Bank of Boston, December 1967.

3. Bensen, P. H., *Religion in Contemporary Culture: A Study of Religion Through Social Science*, New York: Harper and Row Publishers, Inc., 1960.

4. Brown, Norman W., "The Sanctity of the Cow in Hinduism," *Bulletin of the Institute of Traditional Cultures*, Vol. 28, 1957, pp. 29–41.

5. Cantril, Hadley, *Patterns of Human Concerns*, New Brunswick, N. J.: Rutgers University Press, 1965.

6. Hagen, E. E., *On the Theory of Social Change: How Economic Growth Begins*, Homewood, Ill.: The Dorsey Press, Inc., 1962.

7. Harbison, Frederick, "Education for Development," *Scientific American*, Vol. 209, No. 3, September 1963, pp. 140–147.

8. Hauser, Philip M., "Demographic Dimensions of World Politics," (1959), in T. Morgan and G. W. Betz, eds., *Economic Development: Readings in Theory and Practice*, Belmont, Calif.: Wadsworth Publishing Company, Inc., 1969.

9. Isaac, Erick, "The Act and the Covenant: The Impact of Religion on the Landscape," *Landscape*, Vol. 11, Winter 1962, pp. 12–17.

10. ———, "Religion, Landscape, and Space," *Landscape*, Vol. 9, Winter 1960, p. 14.

11. ———, "The Influence of Religion on the Spread of Citrus," *Science*, Vol. 129, No. 3343, January 23, 1959, pp. 179–186.

12. Kindleberger, C. P., *Economic Development*, 2d ed., New York: McGraw-Hill Book Company, Inc., 1965.

13. Lenski, Gerhard, *The Religious Factor: Sociological Study of Religion's Impact on Politics, Economics, and Family Life*, New York: Doubleday and Company, 1961.

14. McClelland, D. C., "Community Development and the Nature of Human Motivation: Some Implications of Recent Research." (Paper presented to the Conference on Community Development and National Change, Center for International Studies, M.I.T, 1957, 20 pp. mimeo.)

15. McNeil, W. H., *The Rise of the West*, Chicago: University of Chicago Press, 1963.

16. Meinig, D. W., "The Mormon Culture Region: Strategies and Patterns in the Geography of the American West, 1847–1964," *Annals of the Association of American Geographers*, Vol. 60, 1965, pp. 191–220.

17. Redfield, R., *The Primitive World and Its Transformation*, Ithaca: Cornell University Press, 1953.

18. Schultz, T. W., "Investment in Human Capital," *American Economic Review*, March 1961; reprinted in Morgan, Betz, and Choudhry eds., *Readings in Economic Development*, Belmont, Calif.: Wadsworth Publishing Company, Inc., 1963.

19. Simmons, F. J., *Eat Not This Flesh*, Madison: University of Wisconsin Press, 1961.

20. Sopher, David E., *Geography of Religions*, Englewood Cliffs, N. J.: Prentice-Hall, Inc., 1967.

21. Tawney, R. H., *Religion and the Rise of Capitalism*, New York: Harcourt, Brace and World, 1952.

22. Weber, Max, *The Protestant Ethic and the Spirit of Capitalism*, German original 1904, New York: Charles Scribner's Sons, 1956.

chapter 8

Technological Framework

Although attention has been called to the concept of technology at several places in previous chapters, a fuller examination of its meaning and effect on economic activity is the task of this chapter.

As a generalized definition of *technology* we may use the sum total of the elements of knowledge, skills, tools, and techniques developed to satisfy human wants. Here, human wants may be divided into three parts: those related to "know-why," those related to "know-how," and the final consumer items.

KNOWLEDGE

Knowledge is developed and learned or acquired through mental processes—particularly through the ability to store, retrieve, and transmit information—and is a consequence of man's desire to attain goals. This implies that man learns through experience, and experience is a result of these processes. Human experience, especially in cumulative form, is enormous and complex. However, only when it is sorted, organized, and related to the environment does it become "something" which may be termed as useful knowledge. Thus, knowledge is that *set of human experiences which is properly sorted, organized, and related to the environment.* Knowledge in this context is only an instrument[1] applied to societal activities to achieve societal goals.

Societal goals are dynamic and culture-oriented. A society's desire for knowledge may be conceptualized as a consequence of its desire to understand, satisfy curiosity, explain, intervene, modify, control, predict, and improve its environment. It was demonstrated in Part I that culture causes both spatial as well as

---

[1]This definition of knowledge is in affinity with the "instrumentalist" school of thought, which holds that knowledge is only an instrument or means to an end—human evaluation and purposes. "Nominalism" is another related theory, which says the meaning of words (signifying knowledge) lies in the conventions that define their use.

time variations in resources, and thus in knowledge.

Learned experience or stored information is the building block for constructing knowledge. The methods of gaining knowledge are numerous, ranging from chance or "trial and error"[2] to science. The particular methodology is a function of not only the type of experience and cost restraints, but also of the already existing state of knowledge. However, the scientific method is commonly and widely used by almost all branches of learning. The scientific method is generally recognized to include the following steps:

1. A lucid statement or definition of the problem
2. A review and evaluation of related knowledge or literature
3. Selection of appropriate analytical tools
4. Construction of testable or reputable hypotheses (provisional solutions of the problem)
5. The procurement of data
6. Data synthesis and analysis
7. The testing of hypotheses
8. Derivation of conclusions
9. Recommendations
10. Distribution of results

Not all research endeavors may follow every step listed. The particular steps and sequence followed depend upon the character and scope of the research project.

SKILLS

Knowledge precedes skills. Skills refer to the *capabilities* of an individual laborer (assumed to possess no skills at the outset of his career, except intelligence to learn

skills) that can be used to perform a productive task in the economy.

There is a wide array of capabilities that constitute skill. Some skills are acquired by short periods of observation, while others require considerable training and specificity. A conventional classification of skills includes: unskilled (learned by short observation), semiskilled, skilled, administrative, organizational, clerical, and professional. The composition and relative level (quantity and quality) of skills embodied in the labor force of a society are functions of the amount of usable knowledge, processes of diffusing knowledge, social objectives, and demands for those skills. It is possible, however, that poverty of skills may occur among an affluence of knowledge. In that case, the society lacks an adequate diffusion process and perhaps lack of clarity in objectives and demands.

The United States excels not only in the development of new knowledge but also, more importantly, such knowledge is readily transformed to skills. It is no wonder that today the average American farmer produces enough food to adequately feed himself and approximately forty other people. Since World War II the productivity of American agriculture has increased at twice the rate of industry. Literally armies of scientists and extension agents based at the Land Grant colleges and universities in the United States have assisted in realizing this technological marvel. But perhaps not so readily realized are the amounts that industrial and federal government spending on research and development (R & D) activities have contributed toward the enhancement of skills. It is estimated that in 1965 the United States spent approximately $25 billion for R & D, of which the government accounted for over seventy percent.

Patent privileges tend to limit the dissemination of technology, although several government agencies and departments, as well as private organizations, are involved in diffusing technical information.

[2]Other methods include generalization from experience, logic, magic, reliance on authority, and deductive as well as inductive reasoning. Needless to say, these methods are not exclusive of each other. For example, the scientific method partially employs the mechanism of inductive and deductive paradigm, logic, and system paradigm.

For example, the National Aeronautics and Space Administration (NASA) has fashioned an elaborate system, complete with the latest computer techniques, to facilitate information transfer, which may be embodied either in the physical capital and/or in human labor. The following are a few examples of the NASA spinoff [3]:

1. NASA developed an electromagnetic hammer that removes dents from sheet metal in microseconds without structural weakening. It does not leave marks and is proving useful in activities involving metal fabrication and repair (automobile repair shops, for example).

2. Using principles developed from the Lunar-Walker, the means of locomotion of the moon's first earth visitors, a walking chair has been devised that allows paraplegics to go up and down curbs and even climb stairs.

3. Spray-on electrodes were developed to monitor the heart action of test pilots and astronauts. They are now being used for children's heart examinations and for electrocardiograms because they do not slip and provide a good electrical contact. Their potential use is impressive; for instance, coupled with a tiny transmitter they can keep a constant check on heart patients and alert a nurse if any trouble occurs.

4. NASA developed a paint that is used to the outside of space crafts. This new paint is unusually resistant to heat and scratching and has obvious commercial uses. Not too long ago, the whole thrust of government-supported research was to win a war; if peacetime uses could be found after victory, they amounted to windfall benefits. Now, however, any knowledge gained for military, space exploration, problem solving, and prestige purposes is systematically gathered, evaluated, and disseminated.

The beneficiaries of this technological spinoff include business interests, hospitals, state and local governments, and most important, those institutions offering educational and training programs for embodying skills into the labor force—in short, the entire society.

Besides the composition and relative level of skills, the degree of effectiveness and substitution of skills has great bearing on the spatial differentiation of technology and consequently on economic activity. The effectiveness of substitution depends on the suitability of skills for employment opportunities, the level of specialization, and the availability of relevant equipment and tools and their spatial mobility. Regions with incongruent skills may produce quite different sets of economic activities than otherwise might be expected.

TOOLS

Tools (technically referred to as physical capital) are labor-saving or labor-aiding objects used in human activities, which may or may not be directly operated by man; however, they are used as an extension of man's own efforts. They include hand tools, automated tools, machines and equipment, and buildings.

The determination of level, composition, and "how" of tools acquisition has long baffled social scientists, and a thorough treatment of it requires a textbook itself. Only salient features are pointed out here.

The development of tools is a function of societal objectives, knowledge, material resources, the relative size of the labor force, including entrepreneurial and organizational skills, and the arrangements of international trade and aid. Societal objectives provide the basic initiative and direction towards attaining any array of tools. Analysis of alternatives of material resources may suggest various choices. The relative quality of labor points to substitutional and complemental support for the achievement of the objec-

Eric Schwab, WHO Photos

Reynolds Metal Company

Caterpillar Tractor Co.

New Holland Division of Sperry Rand

FIGURE 8.1   *The development of agricultural implements—hand tools and machines.*

tives. For example, the United States depends on foreign nations for a major share of domestic needs for copper, lead, tin, cobalt, aluminum, columbium, tantalite, nickel, tungsten, and uranium—all of which are important ingredients in the implementation of objectives. Cobalt is used in high speed tools, jet turbines, and atomic power; columbium and tantalite are used in guided missiles, rockets, and apollos; uranium is an important fuel for generating nuclear energy.

TECHNIQUE

Technique refers to the operational or innovative aspect of technology. It is a set of instructions or steps—a computer program, convocation exercises, cookbook recipe, registration procedure, mechanical steps in operating a machine, etc.—appearing as "choices." The choices exist at various levels of economic activities. At initial stages the choices may be few, but they multiply at succeeding levels. As an illustration, energy may be generated by thermal hydro, solar, and nuclear techniques; all four represent alternative choices. But choices associated with any given technique of power generation consist of:

1. *Location*—various locations need to be evaluated in terms of spatial distribution of demand for the power, transportation cost of inputs and outputs, relative economic efficiency, and long-run considerations of the supply of raw materials to the plant.
2. *Size*—This affects the economies of scale and total transportation cost. The diseconomies of scale may be outweighed by the economies realized through lower transportation cost associated with smaller units (if possible) located in proximity to demand centers.
3. *Rate of change* of the substitution between tools and labor, which may capitalize savings during peak and slump periods.

4. *Continuity*—a plant may be run on one or multiple shifts to achieve a better substitution between labor and physical capital; when the interest rates are high resulting in higher cost of the physical capital, multiple shifts offer an economical choice in substituting labor for capital. Another aspect of continuity concerns coffee breaks, holidays and vacations, breakages and strikes. In these cases, numerous considerations and choices need to be evaluated in light of overhead costs and the loss of market during shutdowns and slowdowns.
5. *Plant life and maintenance*—this reflects on the overhead and operating costs.
6. *Input mix*—the choice between various proportions of the different inputs used with a view to increasing economic efficiency.
7. *Product mix*—here the concern is with economic efficiency.

The above list of choices can be further expanded depending on the type and detail (level) of economic activity. Each power source envelops a relatively different set of technological choices.

That technique can often be partially formulated from accumulative and diverse knowledge gives it a distinctive meaning. For example, building and use of a dolly to transport heavy objects is a technique. A person may be able to figure out how to build and use the dolly based on knowledge of the weight of the objects, physics of inclined planes, strength material (metal or wood) to be used, the distance of hauling, texture of the floor, and the like.

THE PROCESS OF TECHNOLOGICAL CHANGE

It is widely recognized that technological progress is the major factor accounting for the difference between medieval and modern standards of living, or between economically developing societies. A pertinent question may be raised as to why a certain period or place excels over another in technological progress.

Technological progress is a spectrum of changing "knowledge-accumulating" and "knowledge-utilizing" activities. Conventionally speaking, the former refers to discovery and the latter to innovation. However, these conventional terms do not adequately reflect the total process of technological progress. This process in modern meaning, contrary to popular thought that technical or scientific discovery is something that occurs in an unplanned and unpredicted fashion, encompasses integrated and interdependant involvement of three broadly identifiable activities—basic research, applied research, and "blueprinting"—commonly summed up under the label research and development.

Factors of Technology

In theory, technology is international in its occurrence, scope, and imitation. However, the sociopolitical facts, attitudes, and values remain stubbornly national, reflecting a spatial and time variability in technology. This variability is a function of many factors, particularly societal objectives, relative scarcity of resources, reward and recognition, insecurity, planning, and economic systems.

Objectives are a product of a multitude of forces, often spearheaded through political process. Certain objectives, such as improved standard of living or economic progress, are assumed to be nearly universal—they only vary in intensity and scope; while other objectives are quite distinctive, such as military power, dominance, and prestige. The seventeenth, eighteenth, and nineteenth century European drive to conquer the great centers of wealth—the "gorgeous East" and the South American El Dorado—encouraged technological progress in defense, transportation, and production. The struggle for power and empire was reflected in the invention of new methods of transportation, resources, production, and innovations in money and marketing. The goals of conquering outer space and being "first on the moon" have not only produced highly specialized technology, but have also induced a broad spectrum of research and development in numerous economic activities, and resulted in a variety of new consumer goods.

The relative scarcity of resources has strong influence on technological progress. A basic economic principle states that demand for a relatively short supply of a resource results in increased price and vice versa.[3] The increased price affects man's decisions in two ways: (1) to substitute the relatively scarce resource with something cheaper; (2) to increase the resource, which would require increasing the productive efficiency through different input proportions or through affecting the quantity or quality of the resource. In both of these choices he must resort to technology.

Automation, for example, is the result of an effort to substitute machines for higher cost labor. Also, a higher grade of labor may be realized through equipping the labor resource with additional tools and skills. These conditions are quite common in the modern Western world. It is not surprising that after reading Malthus' "An Essay on the Principle of Population as It Affects the Future Improvements of Society" (1798), Thomas Carlyle called economics "the dismal science," and William Godwin remarked that Malthus and David Ricardo had converted enthusiasm and progress appeal (churned by the stunning inventions and innovations) into gloom and despair. Both Ricardo and Malthus argued that material resources are fixed, while the population increases in a geometric progression, resulting in eventual starvation. They apparently did not consider that material

[3]The increase in price may be arranged through improved bargaining position (union) and monopoly positions. Under those circumstances, technological progress may not be as great (see Chapter 5).

resources can be increased, improved, or substituted by application of technology. Karl Marx won the praise of many intellectuals by articulately demonstrating how technological advances could increase material resources, resulting in highly unequal distribution of wealth and in class conflicts.

Rewards, in terms of related technological advances, are often conferred on a society that recognizes the value of technology. The establishment of patents,[4] copyrights, and "merit" or "incentive" systems are examples of societal recognition and reward. However, it has been argued that patent and merit policies may have adverse effects in contemporary times. The patent laws were originally conceived in affinity with nineteenth century laissez-faire philosophy to encourage the independent inventor working in his woodshed or small shop, and reward him for his personal risk and expense. Now, however, about sixty percent of all patents issued in the United States go directly into the hands of corporations. This results in diminishing the effective competition between corporations and the innovatory activities. As will be discussed later, competition tends to promote technological change and advancement.

Insecurity on the part of individuals at times tends to promote technological progress. The insecurity may be caused by either internal or external forces. Many societies, in efforts to avoid unpleasant feelings of insecurity, tend to work harder, seek greater efficiency, and to invent newer techniques and tools.

Planning is a more recent factor, which provides for technological change through systematic programming. In the Soviet Union and some other totalitarian societies, the planning factor of technology is common. Also, among the member governments of the Organization for Economic Cooperation and Development

(OECD),[5] the concept of planning for "science policy" is fast replacing an older idea that technological innovation is a purely random activity. As an illustration, to promote the systematic programming of technological progress in Italy, Spain, Turkey, and Ireland, OECD suggests the following planning process:

1. Making a complete inventory of all scientific and technical resources (including scientists and engineers)
2. Making an economic analysis to determine priorities for research
3. Formulating programs for allocating the inventoried resources among the selected priorities
4. Construction of a detailed plan for the development of all aspects and phases of pure research, applied research, and blueprinting

A meaningful coordination among all institutions is also suggested by OECD.

An economic system by virtue of its operation may affect technological progress. A competitive economic system tends to force progress and economic change. Competitors force change of each other resulting in variety and improved quality of goods and services as alternative choices to cutting prices. To produce variety and quality, technology must be favorably affected.

Research Process

The previously discussed factors are importantly reflected in the level of technology by the knowledge-accumulating and knowledge-utilizing processes—basic research, applied research, and innovation.

---

[4]In the United States, a patent is a grant of a 17-year monopoly to an inventor, giving him the right to exclude all others from duplicating his discovery for use or sale.

[5]The OECD is a 21-member international organization designed to foster permanent cooperation between member countries to harmonize national policies. Member countries include USA, UK, France, W. Germany, Canada, Japan, Greece, Norway, and others.

Basic knowledge-accumulation involves a search for the "basic" fact or relationship, which may itself serve as a resource for applied research and innovation. The process often involves highly trained scientists. Although the results of their engagement may potentially benefit all societies, political frameworks may confine the results of their activity to only certain places. The basic research partly depends on previous knowledge, tools, and technique manifest by their embodiment in capital and labor. Basic researchers also benefit from the problems associated with practical applications of and reactions to basic knowledge. Since basic research often has no immediate application, its effect on economic activity is of little significance unless the applied research and blueprinting processes are instituted. This depends on how effectively basic research findings are spun-off to potential users. The spinning-off process involves an array of activities constituting cataloging, classifying, printing, and disseminating.

Applied research infuses basic knowledge with practical considerations. Thus, the motivational force behind applied research, as contrasted to basic research appearing only in intangible forms, is the "tangible" return. Such returns may appear as physical products, tools, solutions to problems, explanations, and the like. The activity of applied research is usually larger than the basic research. If basic research is an international commodity and flows freely between societies, then poor regions tend to concentrate primarily on applied research focusing on local problems. As pointed out earlier, the results of applied research also serve as feedback to basic research.

Innovation or **blueprinting** focuses on the detailed application of basic as well as applied research outputs. This process adapts the basic and applied knowledge into techniques, plans, and consumer and investment products. The motives of direct application and diffusion are the distinguishing features of innovation. County agents, having the tools of basic and applied knowledge, quite often are engaged in innovation endeavors while adapting and diffusing knowledge to a particular situation, factory, farm, or home. Entrepreneurs, too, with the assistance of their technostructure, practice blueprinting. The practical planning profession is another instance where various bits of knowledge are brought together into an integrated whole, resulting in a technique or plan to effectively achieve the goals of the planning area.

To summarize, all three of the processes involve inputs and outputs. The processes are differentiated by the particular motivation of research and the character of the inputs and outputs. The fixity and certainty as seen in actual production processes, however, are not present in the same degree. There is always an uncertainty whether the knowledge will emerge, and if it does there is doubt as to its character and usefulness in achieving a society's goals.

Assuming technology development is measured by the dollar amount spent in R & D, the varying allocation among basic, applied, and innovative research would produce variability over space and time, even though over all of these places and during all of the time period the same dollar volume is spent. The varying allocation between these research activities will be reflected in the relative productivity and efficiency of the economic activities.

TECHNOLOGY AND ECONOMIC ACTIVITY

Technology is commonly thought to result from specific efforts or routine roles of specific segments of a society. As pointed out earlier, however, technological activities are not confined to any given segment of society, although one may do more than another. The important point

FIGURE 8.2 *The development of transport systems.*

Alcoa Steamship Company

Arabian-American Oil Company

Spanish Embassy

Reprinted from The Lamp, *Standard Oil Co. (N. J.)*

Standard Oil Co. (N. J.)

Boeing

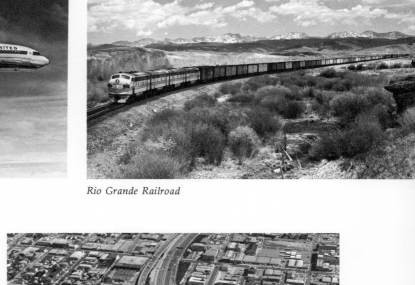

Rio Grande Railroad

Pan American Airways

is that as the knowledge-accumulation process depends, directly or indirectly, on all facets of societal activities, the resulting technology therefore affects the level and spatial dispersion of economic activities. The impact and ultimate incidence of technology upon economic institutions and activities is so significant and complex that it requires comprehensive studies of the overall relationships. Only the basic relationships are highlighted here.

Change

Change is inseparable from technology. All technology reflects change, but all change may not yield newer technology. Technological change may be an initiating force that alters not only the level and structure of economic activity, but also the socioeconomic institutions as they are modified and transformed. Technical change, as opposed to social change, is more readily acceptable by society and thus acts as a potent and practical force for causing eventual social change. Social change as a starting point is often resisted, since it directly affects the established patterns of social interaction and behavior.

For example, the technology of outer space, beside affecting the production techniques of many economic sectors and consequently affecting regional differentiation, has acted as a social diverter of various human activities. The late President John F. Kennedy's innovative idea of the Peace Corps has been labeled a "safety valve" for helping to reduce restlessness among youth—it offers an opportunity for constructive use of the energies of those students who want to "do things" for others. The substitution of iron and coal for stone and wood, respectively, were powerful change initiators for the entire spectrum of economic, social, and political activities. James Watt's steam engine of the eighteenth century produced diverse applications and caused modifications and transfor-

mation of economic as well as social aspects of the society. Thus it is logical to conclude that technology, as an entering wedge of economic change, has nourished the evolution of capitalism. Many contend that technological change is the basic resource for the economic progress of any society.

Technological change is interdependent, cumulative, and irreversible. The invention of the steam engine, for example, promoted new developments in the textile, iron, and all other types of economic activities that may possibly employ mechanical motive power. However, without the boring machine invented by John Wilkinson, the ultimate success of Watt's engine would perhaps have never become a reality.

Being cumulative in its effects, technology acts as a multiplier of economic activity producing a conglomerative complex. Nearly every technological change, irrespective of where it occurs, provides a springboard from which greater leaps may be made in other economic activities.

The irreversibility of technological change yields promise of continued economic progress. A given technological change necessitates other changes, but the process is never reversed. Thus the irreversible character of technology serves as a strong force for causing sustained economic growth of a society.

Economic Progress

Each society with its respective technology exhibits a distinctive spatial pattern of economic phenomena.[6] With technology, material resources can be increased through new techniques of procuring

[6]Lewis Mumford in his *Technics and Civilization* (New York: Harcourt, Brace and World, 1963) identified three broad overlapping and interpenetrating phases, each with a distinctive technological complex. The *eotechnic* is typified as the wood, wind, and water power complex. The *paleotechnic* is associated with the coal, steam, and iron complex. And the *neotechnic* is identified with such elements as electricity, internal combustion engines, alloys, chemicals. Each phase is thought to embody a distinct social and economic arrangement of human activities.

them, through finding feasible substitutes, or through changing proportions of resource-mix or product-mix. The reorganization or allocation of resources may result in efficiency, yielding larger output per unit of input. Labor often becomes more productive with additional education, training, and apprenticeship experiences. However, proper balance between liberal and vocational types of education must be placed to achieve the best use of technology (skills). Change in techniques of production, marketing, and distribution may result in larger demand realized through lower delivery price, which may further lower the production cost as a consequence of economies of scale.

As shown above, technological advance not only enhances the contributions of physical capital and labor, but also sparks their expansion. And through the independent, cumulative, and irreversible characteristics of technological change, economic progress tends to be self-sustained.

Since economic activities differ in their character and complexity, the relative effect of technology differs similarly. While it may propel economic progress, technology does so at varying rates among different societies.

FIGURE 8.3   *A magnesium shroud is placed on its rocket adapter as part of the Mariner spacecraft launch program to Mars. (Lockheed Missles & Space Company)*

selected references

1. Briggs, Asa, "Technology and Economic Development," *Scientific American*, Vol. 209, No. 3, September 1963, pp. 52–61.

2. Brozen, Y., "Invention, Innovation, and Imitation," *American Economic Review*, Papers and Proceedings, May 1951, pp. 239–57.

3. Chase Manhattan Bank, "Space Research Comes Down to Earth," *Business in Brief*, No. 71, December 1966.

4. Chow, G. C., "Technological Change and the Demand for Computers," *American Economic Review*, Vol. 57, No. 5, December 1967.

5. Day, R. H., "The Economics of Technological Change and the Demise of the Sharecropper," *American Economic Review*, Vol. 57, No. 3, June 1967.

6. Dewhurst, J. F., *America's Needs and Resources: A New Survey*, New York: Twentieth Century Fund, 1955.

7. Dillard, Dudley, *Economic Development of the North Atlantic Community: Historical Introduction to Modern Economics*, Englewood Cliffs, N. J.: Prentice-Hall, Inc., 1967.

8. Dunlop, John T., ed., *Automation and Technological Change*, Englewood Cliffs, N. J.: Prentice-Hall, Inc., 1962.

9. Fellner, W., "Measures of Technological Progress in the Light of Recent Growth Models," *American Economic Review*, Vol. 57, No. 5, December 1967.

10. Feuer, Lewis S., *The Scientific Intellectual*, New York: Basic Books, Inc., 1963.

11. Forbes, R. J., and Dijksterhuis, E. J., *A History of Science and Technology*, 2 Vols., Baltimore: Penguin Books, Inc., 1962.

12. Johnson, Edgar A., and Krooss, H. E., *The American Economy: Its Origins, Development, and Transformation*, Englewood Cliffs, N. J.: Prentice-Hall, Inc., 1960.

13. Kranzberg, M., and Pursell, C. W., eds., *Technology in Western Civilization*, Vol. 1, New York: Oxford University Press, 1967.

14. Metraux, Guy S., and Crouzet, Francois, eds., *The Evolution of Science*, New York: Mentor Books, 1963.

15. Nelson, Richard R.; Peck, Merton J.; and Kalcheck, Edward D., *Technology, Economic Growth, and Public Policy*, Washington, D.C.: The Brookings Institute, 1967.

In the preceding chapters, the major emphasis has been on the overriding characteristics that all societies have in common regarding economic activities. Although these chapters have been conducive to developing general theories, they have not spelled out concrete ideas about a specific economic activity. In order to make more positive statements about less general activities, it is necessary to develop categories or classes of economic activities that do not include all economic activities.

chapter 9

Classification of Economic Activities

CLASSIFICATION

The process of classification is essentially two subordinate processes: differentiation and integration. The former is a segregating of dissimilar phenomena, and the latter is the aggregating or grouping of similar phenomena. Thus, in order to contrive a classification that is the result of the *process* of classification, we must first differentiate a whole, (such as the universe) into its parts, analyze the parts, and then integrate the parts that are similar into classes and place dissimilar parts in other classes. The number of classes resulting is a function of the desire for specificity; the class to which each part is assigned is a function of the perception of differences and similarities, and the relative importance assigned to these perceptions.

The universe may be segregated into space and energy; further differentiation may result in space, time, energy, matter, and motion. Extreme differentiation will result in the smallest known parts of the universe, the *elementary particles* of which there are googols (a googol is any number with at least 100 digits). With no integration of these particles, each particle would then constitute a specific class and would have a specific name. For example, of the estimated 10^{79} protons existing in the universe, each would be in a different specific class. We may cease the process of differentiation and integration at any point between the smallest known particle and the largest whole. Man, for example, represents a class within the class organism, within the class mammal, and so on. However, without the class *man*, we could not refer to man, but indeed would have to refer to each individual by a specific name. Also, without the class tree, paramecia, etc., we would need to refer to each item by a specific name and could not even use the class oak or sycamore.

One of the major characteristics of classifications is that they are contrived by man—they are not truths that can be discovered. Consequently, there is no "true" classification, irrespective of what phenomena are included or excluded. Man literally imposes his perceptions on the phenomena being classified; he decides the level of differentiation and integration, and the attributes of the phenomena to be selected in contriving the classification. The phenomena being classified do not impose on man a particular classification, nor do they arrange themselves in classes. For example, whales and porpoises do not demand to be classified as fish rather than mammals. That both live in the water, in this classification, is totally irrelevant. They are classified with man (mammal) because of some specific biological attributes that the classifier desired to emphasize as a group.

From this example, we may also infer that, as only one phenomenon is placed in a particular class, one or several of its myriad characteristics is emphasized at the expense of others. Mammalian class emphasizes child-bearing attributes of the whale and de-emphasizes water association. Also, to differentiate man as male and female emphasizes biological functions and de-emphasizes the role of *both* as teachers, clerks, taxpayers, citizens, etc.

Whatever class a phenomenon is integrated with is a function of the criterion (or criteria) for contriving the class and the relation of the phenomenon to that criterion. For example, assume we wish to include in one class everything in the universe with a "nearly round head." The criterion for integrating or classifying is "nearly round head." Within this class we may logically include people, nails, flag poles, incandescent light bulbs, straight pins, pencil erasers, totem poles, cigars, statues of people, Halley's comet, and so on. All of these apparently totally *different* things do have something in common and consequently can be classed as being *similar*. However, a nail also can be classified under the criterion "flat head," since its head is usually flat in the dimension parallel to its shaft.[1] Also, any one of the others may be placed in numerous other classes.

Another major characteristic of any classification is that the initial criteria selected for differentiation and integration are totally arbitrary. Thus, we could select any single or several attributes of a phenomenon for the purpose of classification. However, which attributes are indeed selected should be a function of the type of information desired in the classification. Any classification should contain as much information as possible about the phenomena being classified. Consequently, even though the initial criteria are arbitrary, all subsequent decisions must be made logically on the basis of these criteria. Thus, the classification criteria must apply equally to all phenomena being classified.

The title of this text itself is indicative of phenomena that have been subjected to classification, namely economic geography (as opposed to economic history, for example). This in itself represents a class, as does each chapter and section. Here our attention is directed toward the various ways that economic activities may be classified.

---

[1]Nail could also be placed in classes with these criteria: containing metal, man-made, hard, employed in construction, elongated, etc.

The Port of New York Authority

Australian News and Information Bureau

New Zealand National Publicity

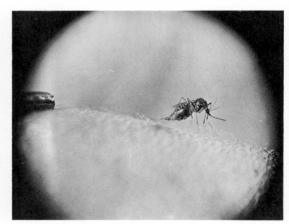

USDA

Australian News and Information Bureau

USDA

FIGURE 9.1 *How would you classify the various activities going on here? How many similar attributes can be assigned to the various spaces?*

As with any classification, we may differentiate all economic activity into its most specific parts and arrive at a name for what each man is doing in terms of his specific economic activity. From among the innumerable behavioral patterns that man exhibits, we have previously classed (defined) as economic activity all those patterns associated with the production, exchange, and consumption of goods and services. Further differentiating economic activity into its smallest parts, and contriving a specific class for each, we would arrive at a lengthy list of the specific behavior of over 3.5 billion people. This type of specificity would not, however, allow us to make any significant general propositions about either the similarities or differences among these various classes.

The section following is a discussion of some of the criteria frequently employed in the classification of economic activity. As mentioned previously, there is no inherent value or truth in any of the criteria or in the resulting classes; each one is as valid as any other.

Classification by Demand to Exchange

The societal demand to exchange[2] involves the collective demands of individuals in a society to acquire goods and services produced in another society. (Demand includes the desire, willingness, and ability to acquire.) In a theoretical sense, if there is absolutely no demand to exhange, then the activities of that society are known as *subsistent*. That is, the people involved as producers are also the only consumers of their goods and services and do not require goods and services from any other society. Thus, there is no exchange between subsistent societies, and no exchange between a subsistent and a non-subsistent society.

Again, in a theoretical sense, a society in which *all* goods and services produced are exchanged for commodities produced in another society is classed as a *commercial* society. Thus, the presence of one commercial activity necessitates the presence of at least one partly commercial society, since exchange occurs. Thus, in subsistent societies the demand to exchange is zero; in commercial societies the demand to exchange is 100 percent. However, neither of these two ideal forms exist, since all societies to a certain degree exhibit a demand to exchange. If we are to continue to use the class designations *subsistent* and *commercial*, they must be modified to reflect reality. Hence, we may state that a commercial society is one in which a large proportion of the total production is exchanged with another society. Similarly, a subsistent society is one in which a small proportion of the total production is exchanged. Whether a society is commercial or subsistent must be ascertained in relation to similar characteristics in another society.

For example, given three societies, D, E, and F, with total production of $100X$, $50X$, and $50X$, respectively, the specific products are irrelevant and may be measured in a variety of ways.[3] Which society is most commercial and which is most subsistent? Again, the categorization is a function of the specific criterion or set of criteria we wish to select. For example, a more refined statement of demand to exchange may be the total number of units exchanged away (exported). Consequently, the society that exports the most units is the most commercial, and so on.

---

[2]This criterion could also be called the "demand for no exchange." However, demand for no exchange is still a demand relative to exchange. Note that *demand* as used here does not have the same meaning as in Chapter 5, but refers to the idea of desirability.

[3]Several interesting propositions may be made concerning the theoretical data of production, exchange, and consumption. Which societies are consuming more than they produce? What are the ratios and specific inter-societal and intra-societal production, consumption, and exchange that may be relevant in the economic framework as discussed previously in Chapter 5. Is the total of all consumptions the same as the total of all productions? Is the answer to this question, as realized from the data, a reflection of "reality"?

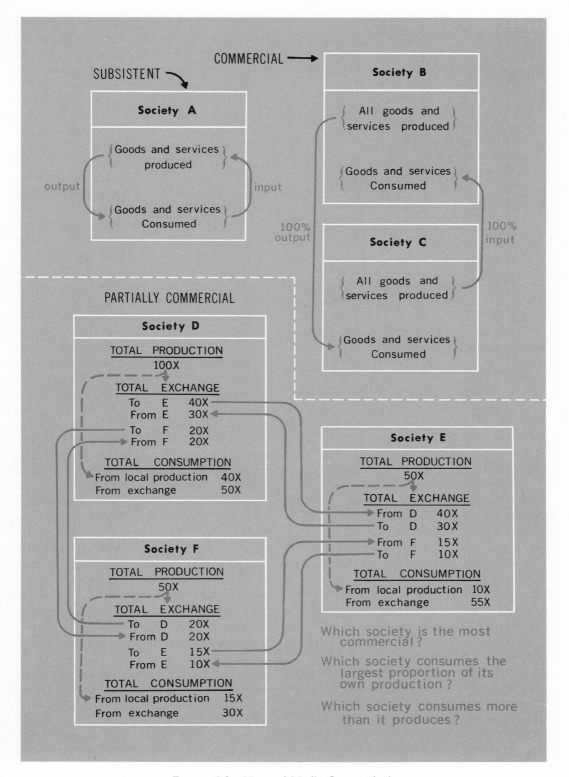

SUBSISTENT

COMMERCIAL →

Society A

{ Goods and services } produced

output

input

{ Goods and services } Consumed

Society B

{ All goods and } { services produced }

{ Goods and services } { Consumed }

100% output

100% input

Society C

{ All goods and } { services produced }

{ Goods and services } { Consumed }

PARTIALLY COMMERCIAL

Society D

TOTAL PRODUCTION
100X

TOTAL EXCHANGE
To	E	40X
From	E	30X
To	F	20X
From	F	20X

TOTAL CONSUMPTION
From local production   40X
From exchange   50X

Society E

TOTAL PRODUCTION
50X

TOTAL EXCHANGE
From	D	40X
To	D	30X
From	F	15X
To	F	10X

TOTAL CONSUMPTION
From local production 10X
From exchange   55X

Society F

TOTAL PRODUCTION
50X

TOTAL EXCHANGE
To	D	20X
From	D	20X
To	E	15X
From	E	10X

TOTAL CONSUMPTION
From local production   15X
From exchange   30X

Which society is the most commercial?

Which society consumes the largest proportion of its own production?

Which society consumes more than it produces?

FIGURE 9.2   (*General Media Corporation*)

	Society		
	D	E	F
Total Number of Units Exported	60	40	35

By this criterion, D is most commercial, then E, then F. However, if the criterion is the ratio of total units exchanged away to total production, the following relationships result:

	Society		
	D	E	F
Exchanged Away (exported) Total Production	60/100 (60%)	40/50 (80%)	35/50 (70%)

Society E is most commercial, then F, and society D is most subsistent (least commercial).

There are additional ways to contrive other ratios in order to determine the degree of subsistent or commercial demands. For example, assuming that the population of society D is 120, E is 280, and F is 100, we can arrive at a "per capita" demand to exchange, which for some purposes may be a better index of total societal demand than either of the previous indices.

In these examples we have assumed that the *total* production, exchange, and consumption of these societies is known. However, as discussed previously, in order to determine the total data (in an absolute sense) about real societies, we also must know about the depreciation, inflation, value norms, etc., in and among all exchanging societies. Although these are not known, we can isolate many variables and make some statements about demand to exchange.

As has been implied in previous statements, within any large commercial society there may be segments that are either more or less commercial than the society as a whole. For example, in the United States, which as a total society has a high demand to exchange, there are numerous segments (such as in southern Appalachia) having a demand to exchange that is lower than the demand to exchange in Manhattan. Also, in any large society there are intra-societal variations in the demand to exchange, as in India, for example. In fact, we may find in some parts of the United States a lower demand to exchange than in some parts of India.

For the remainder of this text, the concept *commercial* will be used as a substitute for the more lengthy statement that a specific society has a higher per capita demand to exchange than another or numerous other societies. The concept *subsistent* will refer to those societies that have a relatively lower per capita demand to exchange than one or numerous other societies.

Since a classification should contain information about what is being classified, what information is now contained in the class of societies known as *commercial societies* (or the behavior of those societies in an economic endeavor)? First, perhaps we know they are not (relatively) subsistent. However, this is evident from their having been assigned to a different class. Referring to the previous chapters, what types of inter- and intra-societal culture values are responsible for commercialism? From the preceding chapters, what are the implications of the various frameworks in commercial activities? in subsistent activities? By conceptually unifying the general statements in previous chapters and focusing them directly on commercial and subsistent activities, one can then acquire a great deal of information about such societies and their behavioral patterns. For example, those that are commercial have relative significant advantages (comparative, absolute) for such activity. They also have a different intra-societal framework to facilitate these advantages. Overall, their wants (one of which is demand to exchange), and consequently technology, material resources, capital, and labor, have been contrived so that the result is a higher per capita demand to exchange. A society that does not have such wants or is not able to effectuate such wants does not have a commerical economic activity.

Since societal values reflected in commercial activities are usually reflected partly as further extensions across space, one almost invariably finds that influences of commercial societies are more widespread than those of subsistent societies. With the products of a commercial society also are conveyed some of the intra-societal values of that society. In fact, as a broad generalization we may state that the more commerical a society becomes, the greater the impact it has on less commercial societies. The impact can be measured in a variety of ways, such as the relative number, value, quality, etc. of "foreign" goods, which in part reflects the values of the importer toward those goods and also toward the society from which the goods are imported.

Classification by Level of Economic Development

The answer to "Which activities are *developed?*" is as frustrating as trying to define which activities are *commercial*. This answer must also be made in a relative sense. That is, which societies are developed and which societies are consequently not developed will be a function of how "development" is defined. There is no inherently totally developed economic activity, nor is there a totally undeveloped activity.[4] Still, if we desire a classification by level of development, we are faced with the problem of contriving criteria for the concept of *developed economy*.

The following criteria (although totally adequate data for some economies are

not available) are frequently used in this classification:

1. National Product Per Capita—the total value of all final production relative to the population within the economy. A low ratio is usually deemed an indicator of low development.
2. Occupational Structure of the Labor Force—referring to the relative percentages of employees in various categories. A high percentage of employees or workers in relatively staple producing activities is deemed an index of poor development.
3. Productivity Per Employee—the ratio of total production (in some measurable unit) to total number in the labor force.
4. Consumption of Energy Supplies Per Capita.
5. Caloric Consumption Per Capita Per Day.
6. Transport and Communication Facilities Per Capita.
7. Literacy Rate—the average of years in formal education divided by the average age of the population.

Thus, if all of these criteria are discovered to be higher in one society than in another, then the former *relative* to the latter is considered more developed. If we integrate those societies that are similar in their manifestations of either individual or collective criteria into larger classes, we may speak of a class of (relatively) developed societies and a class of (relatively) undeveloped or less developed societies. Depending on the specific limits of each class, we may find that there is another set of societies that are neither as well developed as the first set nor as underdeveloped as the latter.

Now that these classes have been contrived, how much information is contained in the classification? Again, referring to previous chapters for the general propositions concerning societal values and frameworks, they may be focused

---

[4]Since in any scheme of classification there are innumerable gradations on the continuum, we may also mention the economies that are non-developed, non-developable, underdeveloped, as well as over-developed.

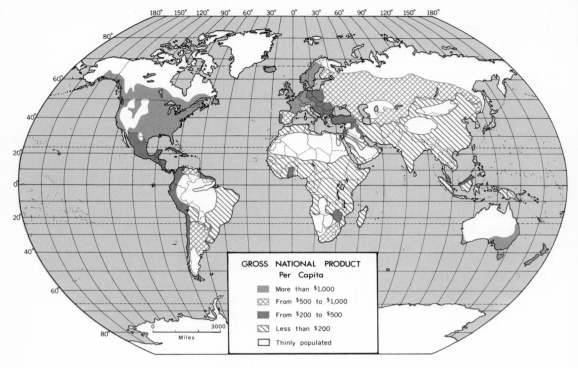

FIGURE 9.3   *World distribution of gross national product (GNP) per capita.* (*General Media Corporation*)

directly, along with the information contained in this chapter, on specific societies.

Additional Classification

In Table 9.1 is a list of other classifications that indicate the diversity with which any economic activity may be perceived. Each single criterion classification contains two classes (degrees).

Any of these criteria may be stated negatively. For example, we might have used the criterion "demand for spatial immobility," in which case the classes under "high" and "low" also would have to be reversed. Specifically, in this case the emphasis is on spatial mobility of

Table 9.1   Classification of Economic Activity by Selected Criteria and Their Degree of Occurrence

Criterion		Degree		
Societal Demand*	is	High	or	Low
Spatial Mobility of Economic Activities		Migratory		Sedentary
Diverse Goods and Services		Specialized		Diversified
Use of Machines		Mechanized		Manual
Private Control of Economic Activities		Capitalistic		Communistic

*As developed earlier, society's demand refers to its desire, willingness, and ability to articulate its resources to achieve a particular goal. If any one of these three is lacking, then a demand does not exist for that goal.

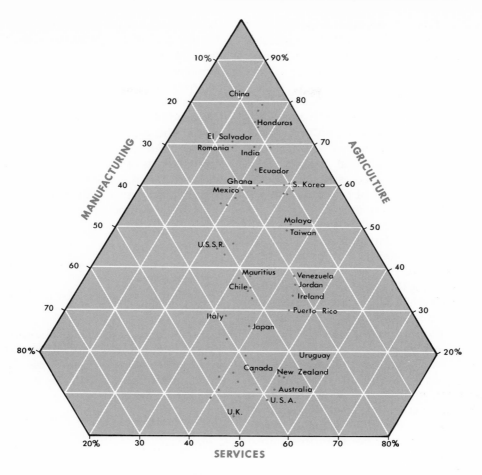

FIGURE 9.4   *Occupational structure of labor. After Broek and Webb. (General Media Corporation)*

economic activities of the society rather than on members of the society. It could well be argued that U.S. society is more migratory than the herdsmen of North Africa, and they are more sedentary. Each year, for example, the average middle class U.S. citizen will travel a greater distance than most herdsmen travel in ten years.

In applying any class (degree) to a specific economic activity, one must continually remember that these are not absolute classifications, even though they may be familiar. For each of the two classes, the single criterion classification is all-encompassing, just as were the two previous classifications. That is, all economic

activities may be classified as either specialized or generalized without reference to any other classification. Also, all economic activities may be classified as either manual or mechanized.

Each of the classifications in Table 9.1 may be further differentiated into innumerable sub-classes. For example, from the totally manual (which does not exist, for it implies no tools whatsoever) to the totally mechanized (which also does not exist, for it implies no men) there are an infinite number of blends or gradations. These may be indicated by terms such as partially-manual, quasi-manual, nearly-manual, more-nearly manual, etc. However, they may also be quantified and then subdivided, depending on the arbitrary sub-criteria that are selected for the sub-classes. Obviously, except for very specific purposes, the sub-classes quickly become redundant.

From another perspective, each of these classes may be integrated with any of the others except the one directly opposite. That is, we may decide to integrate the following to describe an activity: It is sedentary, mechanized, specialized, and capitalistic. Thus, all of these may refer to several "real" economic activities. For example, they may allude to the type of agriculture prevalent in the state of Iowa, to the General Motors Corporation, or to a stock brokers' firm on Wall Street. However, as a unit they cannot be applied to a firm in the U.S.S.R., as a consequence of the criterion "capitalistic," although we may refer to that same firm with the other three criteria.

In the remainder of the text there will be occasion to use these terms and their gradations for referring to specific types of economic activities. They will continue to be used as described here, in a *relativistic framework* rather than in an absolute sense.

As suggested previously, even elementary particles are composed of something more elementary. Also, any classification is more or less composed of classes. Thus far we have been referring to very general classes within the overall behavioral pattern of economic behavior. We will present one other general method of classification and its major sub-classes, which will represent the subsequent organization of this text.

Classification by Stage of Processing

All economic activities, however obvious their differences, also have many similarities. Significant first-order similarities have already been discussed; here lower-order similarities will be mentioned along with similar order differences. All goods

and services, as well as people, are parts of a vast process of production, exchange, and consumption. The latter represents the reenforcement of the former, which in part may be specifically made for increasing the former.

Instead of attempting to look at the vastness of the economic scene, let us use a very specific example to illustrate the interrelatedness of world economic activities —a lead pencil, which itself is recognizable as a whole or unit. A simple pencil is generally composed of four parts:

1. A hollow wooden shaft
2. Rubber eraser
3. Copper ferrule that attaches the shaft to the rubber
4. A graphite core inserted in the hollow shaft

We shall desregard the probability that the shaft is painted and impressed with an advertisement for some firm. The following questions about the pencil may logically be asked:

1. Of what is the copper composed?
2. Where did it come from?
3. How did it get attached (by whom or what) to the pencil?
4. What corporation initially invested in a copper mine, and which railroad or ocean transport company freighted the copper from mine to smelter to manufacturer?

Innumerable questions may be asked about the copper as well as the other three parts. Figure 9.5 illustrates some of the answers to these questions.

Since there is a continuous flow of information throughout the economic system, the diagram may be read from top to bottom or from bottom to top. The information flowing downward is the money (10¢) spent for the pencil. The information flowing upward is that of a pencil being manufactured and made available to a consumer. Even though several different societies may be perceived within this illustration, since this is an interrelated

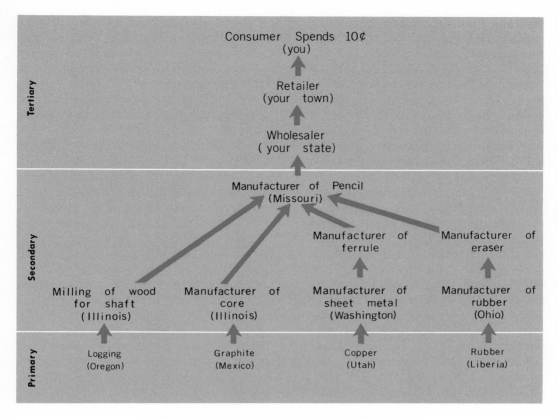

FIGURE 9.5   *A pencil—where did it come from?*

group of people, it is in itself an economically organized society. Also, the diagram of Fig. 9.5 has been greatly simplified. Not specifically indicated, for example, are the treaties between sovereign states that had to be concluded prior to exchanging goods between the United States, Mexico, and Liberia. Also not implicitly indicated are the numerous individuals working on the Liberian rubber plantation or in the mines of Utah, as well as workers in the other places who supply materials for the pencil manufacturer.

Each separate part of Fig. 9.5 literally represents scores of operations residing at a particular place. The flow lines upward represent the spatial inter-ties of transport systems—rails, highways, air routes, telegraph lines, ocean routes, postal routes, and the movements of messages and goods along these. Lest the diagram be misleading, let us remember that

this entire system was not contrived for the purpose of producing one ten cent pencil, but hundreds of millions of pencils (and thousands of miles of electrical conducting wires, thousands of homes, thousands of auto and truck tires and insulators, and so on). For, on each of these places there are numerous demands made by other members of this and other societies. Each of these firms must decide whether to allocate copper to pencils or locomotives, or wood to build houses or bridges, etc.

Given the complexity of a very simple diagram, how may we organize a workable classification of all economic activities so that each class name contains information about that class? Perhaps Fig. 9.5, which was indeed fashioned for just this purpose, lends itself to a partial answer. We have previously mentioned the ever-continuous interrelationships between production and exchange, exchange and production, production and consumption, consumption and exchange, and so on. This flow of goods and services may be referred to as a never-ending consumptive process. Thus, the loggers consume forests, the products of which are then consumed by millers, whose products are then consumed by manufacturers of pencils, whose products are then consumed by the wholesalers, then retailers, then the final (but obviously not only) consumer. Similarly, we may refer to the flow of products as a continuous exchanging process. Either of these two is as valid as any other suggestion, even the one about to be presented for further use. For what has become standard reference, the process is referred to as *production*. Thus, everyone in the flow is engaged in producing something—whether copper, ferrules, or whatever. The final consumer is engaged in *producing* demands on the process.

Three classes have also been indicated on the diagram of Fig. 9.5: primary, secondary, and tertiary. *Primary production* includes all economic activities in which the behavioral pattern of the society is that of directly extracting items from the material resources available to that society. This class includes several specific sub-classes, such as agriculture, forestry, mining, and fishing. *Secondary production* involves the transformation of material resources into another form, and is synonymous with the concept of manufacturing—whether of steel, pencils, ferrules, or bread. *Tertiary production* is the production of services. Within this class and its sub-classes, such as banking, teaching, transportation, communication, etc., societies are involved not in extracting or changing the form of matter, but in rendering or performing a service. A truck driver, for example, renders a service, as does a doctor or lawyer, or construction worker. In addition, the arrows on the

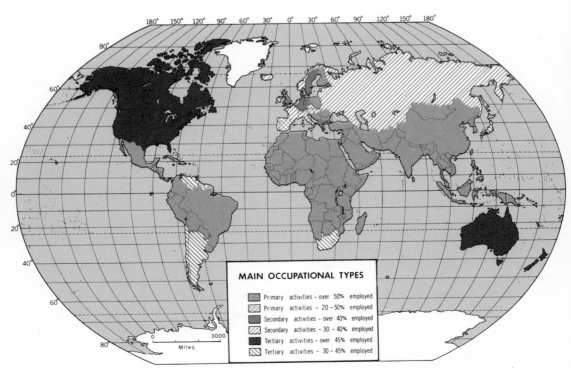

FIGURE 9.6   *Percentage of people engaged in primary, secondary, and tertiary economic activities on a world-wide basis. (General Media Corporation)*

diagram that represent flows of goods are indeed also representative of services—the transportation services.

In an attempt at unification of this classification with the preceding, the classes commercial, mechanized, specialized, etc., may readily be applied to any specific class in primary production, secondary production, or tertiary production, if it indeed has the characteristics previously assigned to both or all classes.

Figure 9.6 is a map showing the relative ratios of people involved in the major sub-classes of the production classification. In the subsequent chapters, globally important representatives of each of the classes will be examined in detail, supported where possible by specific case studies at a lower level of classification.

selected references

1. Allport, Floyd H., *Theories of Perception and the Concept of Structure*, New York: John Wiley & Sons, Inc., 1955.

2. Boulding, Kenneth E., *Beyond Economics*, Ann Arbor: University of Michigan Press, 1968.

3. Brown, Judson S., *The Motivation of Behavior*, New York: McGraw-Hill Book Company, Inc., 1961.

4. Chamberlain, Neil, *A General Theory of Economic Process*, New York: Harper & Brothers, 1955.

5. Chisholm, Michael, *Geography and Economics*, New York: Frederick A. Praeger, Inc., 1966.

6. Dember, William, *The Psychology of Perception*, New York: Holt, Rinehart & Winston, Inc., 1960.

7. Hagen, Everett E., "Analytical Models in the Study of Social Systems," *The American Journal of Sociology*, September 1961, pp. 144–151.

8. Hall, A. D., and Fagen, R. E., "Definition of System," in Walter Buckley, ed., *Modern Systems Research for the Behavioral Scientist: A Source Book*, Chicago: Aldine Publishing Company, 1968, pp. 81–92.

9. Janelle, Donald G., "Spatial Reorganization: A Model and Concept," *Annals of the Association of American Geographers*, Vol. 59, No. 2, June 1969, pp. 348–364.

10. March, James G., and Simon, Herbert A., *Organizations*, New York: John Wiley & Sons, Inc., 1958.

11. McCarty, Harold H., and Lindberg, James B., *A Preface to Economic Geography*, Englewood Cliffs, N. J.: Prentice-Hall, Inc., 1966.

12. Mundell, Robert A., *Man and Economics*, New York: McGraw-Hill Book Company, Inc., 1968.

13. Phelps, Edmund S., ed., *The Goal of Economic Growth*, New York: W. W. Norton & Company, Inc., 1962.

14. Salley, Charles M., and Murphy, Gardner, *Development of the Perceptual World*, New York: Basic Books, Inc., 1960.

15. White, Lynn, Jr., *Frontiers of Knowledge in the Study of Man*, New York: Harper & Brothers, 1956.

chapter **10**

Location, Theory, and Practice

Industry is constantly on the move, more-so in the economically developed nations than in the less developed economies. It does not locate just anywhere. Those days when the owner of a business could locate his plant primarily for personal reasons are indisputably gone. The decision of plant location has become a number-one problem for industry; as the market has become an international one, significant population shifts have occurred, transportation structure and costs have changed, and the need for new labor reserves has grown. The magnitude of the problem is indicated by the fact that some several hundred billion dollars have been spent for new plant location since the end of World War II in the United States alone, and each year the expenditures increase.

Industrial location involves complex assemblages of power, space, employees, and transportation facilities. Modern industry, moreover, is characterized not only by its diversity of specific requirements but by the quantity and quality of its organizational needs. Further, as the scale of industrial enterprises has grown, so has the *risk* of improper location become more crucial. Industrial firms committing $500 million or more to site location, as in a modern integrated steel plant, cannot gamble on improper locations. Thus, the process of industry location has become a crucial concern.

THEORIES OF ECONOMIC ACTIVITY LOCATION

The process underlying industry location is related to an integrated theory encompassing the various frameworks discussed in Part II. This process, as represented in Fig. 10.1, considers the alternative locations, given the type of production technology and scale of production, in terms of prices of inputs and outputs; the competitive structure and relations among producers, and between consumers and producers; the type, quality, and quantity

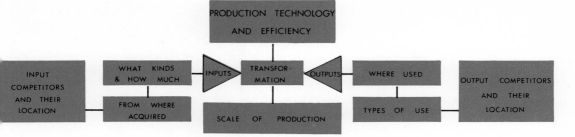

FIGURE 10.1 *The process of plant location.*

of inputs used and outputs produced; the location of inputs and market outlets; the inbound and outbound transportation costs (including means of transportation); and other factors such as labor unions, business collusions, and government regulation.

From the purely economic viewpoint, that location where economic profit is maximized[1] will be optimum for a given scale of production and time period. This means, on the one hand, the cost minimization of (1) assembling the necessary inputs, (2) the processing or tranformation, and (3) the marketing of output; on the other, revenue maximization by (1) proper product-mix, (2) proper price and delivery schedule, and (3) a better knowledge of the structure and characteristics of demand. The problem of optimum location—in terms of maximum economic profits—has attracted scholars from the various disciplines to analyze this dynamic process. As will be shown in Part III and also later in this chapter, many of the factors that influence the location of primary activity affect the secondary and tertiary activities as well; the differences are not of kind but of degree. Industry location literature has tended to follow these three major activity divisions; consequently, the following three major theory blocks have become prominent:

1. Primary activity location theory—Von Thünen
2. Secondary activity location theory—Weber
3. Tertiary activity location theory or central place theory—Christaller

Primary Activity Location Theory

The first recorded attempt to devise a systematic theory explaining the location of economic activity is generally credited to Johann Heinrich Von Thünen (1783–1850). His theory, a product of his experience in managing an agricultural estate in Germany, although directly related to land use (land-oriented materials) for primary activities, sheds light on the location patterns of other types of activities as well.

The thrust of Thünen's theory is that competition for land, reflected by the desire to maximize economic profit, tends to distribute various *types* of land use in such a way that each tract is occupied by the use that can earn the highest rent there. Different industries thus tend to settle into a pattern around the established *market centers* through the *interaction* of distance from the market and inputs (except land), product prices at the market, and the goal to maximize economic profit. Five different but related concepts are involved in Thünen's theory:

1. *Competition and economic profit.* The condition of economic profit motivates entrepreneurs to compete *rationally*

---

[1]There might be other objectives to be maximized, such as longevity, service, eventual industry control, patriotism (through meeting national needs at certain locations), and the like.

with respect to the type of activity and its location. The economic profit may be defined as

$$P = TR - TC,$$

where P is economic profit, TR is total revenue obtained by multiplying the unit price by the quantity produced, and TC is the total cost, which includes expenses for labor, equipment, supplies, taxes, inbound and outbound transportation cost, payment for the use of land, interest, and also payment to the entrepreneur for his own labor.

2. *Types of land use*. This reflects those industries and products or services desired by the market center(s) that may be produced at the locations around the center. In Thünen's conception, however, only one set of land-use types, related to the isolated market center, was considered. (He also regarded the hinterland to be homogeneous in its physical or environmental endowment.)

3. *Rent*. Economic rent is the payment or return for the use of land. It may be computed as

$$L = TR - PC,$$

where L is the economic rent, TR the total revenue, and PC the partial cost including all cost items (defined as TC) except rent.

Assuming a hypothetical situation where a producer manufactures 50 units of commodity A from a given size lot located 40 miles from the market center, receives $9 as unit price at the market center, pays $4 per unit in production cost and 10¢ per unit per mile for inbound–outbound transportation cost, then the economic rent accruing to the lot of where commodity A is produced would be

$$L = (9 \cdot 50) - (4 \cdot 50) - 40(.10 \cdot 50)$$
$$= 450 - 200 - 200$$
$$= 50.$$

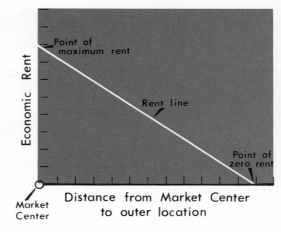

FIGURE 10.2 *The relation between rent and distance.*

Given the per unit cost of production, the activity, price, and transportation rate, the rent (Fig. 10.2) varies inversely with distance; that is, for the same activity (and thus a constant production cost and transportation rate for various locations) highest rent would accrue to locations closest to the market center. This condition, involving more than one activity, would force the lower product-price activities toward the outer spaces of the market center, and attract the higher product-price ones closer to the center.

4. *Market center*. This is the place where consumers and producers reside and determine input and output prices. (Thünen considered only an isolated market center—a city with no outside trade.)

5. *Distance*. The importance of distance, given the means of transportation, is reflected in the relative transportation cost, which is directly proportional to distance.

Based on these concepts, and the limiting assumptions of an isolated (self-sufficient) market center and homogeneity of environment of the hinterland (space around the market center), Thünen derived a pattern of land use involving six rings, as shown in Fig. 10.3. The first ring around the market center, occupied by horticulture and dairying, was found to exist because of the higher price and income yielded by these activities. The second ring was occupied by forestry. Forestry provided the basic raw material for construction and fuel; being bulky and expensive to ship by the transportation means at that time, it commanded higher price and income. The other four rings in Fig. 10.3 follow the same relative reasoning.

The symmetry of Thünen's rings would be affected by several factors:

1. Changes in or establishment of transportation routes, and varying transportation costs for different types and products from the same location
2. The heterogeneity of environment in the hinterland, and thus the comparative advantage (variable production cost for the same activity over alternative locations)
3. Changes in the economic profit maximization goal
4. The multiplicity of the market centers and their intervening force
5. The location of the labor force away from the market centers
6. Changing technology, and thus production cost
7. Changes in physical productivity, price, and cost; the occurrence of joint products
8. Public control and national security considerations

Several scholars have tested the effect of these variables on the location pattern. Losch [14], for example, tested the effect of production cost, productivity, and price, resulting in a changed pattern. Hoover [11] studied the effect of change in transportation costs, labor market structure, and national defense and security upon the location, establishing a definite relationship between these variables and location. Dunn [5], expanding on Losch's work, refined the relationship

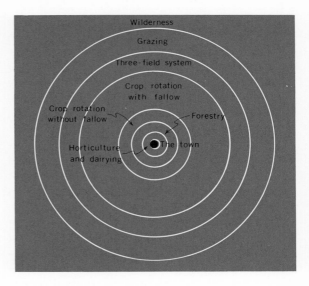

FIGURE 10.3 *Von Thünen model of land use. (General Media Corporation)*

between changes in price (through the detailed analysis of demand and supply), size of the activity, joint products, and technology. However, consideration here of Dunn's findings would distort the symmetry of Thünen's distribution pattern a great deal. Chisholm [3] has further confirmed the basic model of Thünen through extensive empirical evidence from the many developing economies. Garrison and Marble [7] demonstrated the effects of change in transport facilities and the network, multiplicity of market centers and their intervening characteristics upon the location problem.

Despite the continuing efforts of scholars to further understand location problems and patterns, Thünen's model still remains pivotal and illuminating.

Secondary Activity Location Theory

As indicated earlier, Thünen's ideas also shed some light on secondary and tertiary location. Later, Alfred Weber [19] offered his *general* theory of industrial location (manufacturing in particular) applicable to all types of economic activity and any political or economic system. Like Thünen, he developed his theory based on simplified assumptions and premises— a uniform transportation system where transportation costs vary directly with the length of haul and weight of the shipment, homogeneity of culture under a single political sovereignty, nonubiquity of labor force and wage rates (meaning nonmobility of labor and a sporadic and fixed distribution of material resources except water and sand)—and the dynamic forces of relative transport costs, labor costs, and the agglomeration factor. The agglomeration factor is a force that tends to attract industry at certain points within the region because of various economies— transportation economies, internal economies, external economies, and scale of the firm.

Weber's simplest formulation involved one input (for example, one material resource) and one market. In this model, the location is affected by the distribution of only one input, the condition of weight loss of the input in manufacturing, and the proportion of transportation charges to weight and distance. The ubiquity of the input would suggest location close to or at the market, because at that point transportation cost would be the lowest. The condition of sporadic distribution of the input and zero weight loss may result in the location being either at the source of the input or at the market. If the input is sporadic in its distribution and there is weight loss in manufacturing, then location would tend to occur at the source of the input because of the advantage in transportation cost.

However, if the analysis is extended to two inputs (material resources) and one market, the choices of location increase. Of course, the condition of ubiquitous distribution of both the inputs would suggest the location for the market. If one of the two inputs is sporadic in distribution, and there is no weight loss in either, the advantage of transportation cost would suggest locating at the market. The

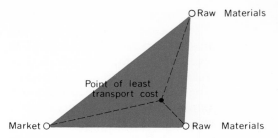

FIGURE 10.4   *Weber model of industrial location. (General Media Corporation)*

condition where both inputs are sporadically distributed and involve zero weight loss will locate the plant at the market, except when one of the inputs lies on the way of the other input being shipped to the market. In the latter case the transient point of input incidence would be equally attractive to location.

The location problem becomes more complex when both of the inputs are sporadically distributed and the weight loss condition is nonzero for both. The first step is to determine that point where manufacturing is possible with a minimum inbound and outbound transportation cost. The location from the least transport-cost input may deviate by reason of lower labor costs. If the saving in labor costs would exceed the additional transportation cost resulting from the shift, the location will move to the point offering labor-cost saving. The same holds for the saving in cost or attraction offered by the agglomeration force.

In summary, Weber offers a schematic process for choosing an overall *least-cost* location, given the distribution of materials, labor, transportation network (rates affected only by weight of the cargo and the distance of haul), the location of market, and the relative prices. Weber's analysis lacked consideration of (1) the nature and distribution of markets as demand centers, and (2) the significance of route network in terms of junctions, long-haul economies, and the group, class, commodity, and intransient rates, which all affect the transport cost—the most important variable in Weber's analysis. Palander [15] later corrected Weber's omissions and offered a more complete theory of industrial location. A restatement of Palander's work is also found in Hoover [10]. Greenhut [8] incorporates consideration of the nature and distribution of market centers into his theory of location. Finally, additional work by Isard [12], involving a multiplicity of additional factors as well as the refinement of the factors recognized earlier, has provided new stimulus and revival of this location theory.

Tertiary Activity Location Theory

Weber's theory, when expanded and refined to include the market areas and their diversity in terms of size, demand, and character, becomes directly applicable to tertiary activities. Such an attempt was perhaps first made by Walter Christaller [4], whose ideas gave initial form to what is collectively called "central place theory."[2] This theory, based on the assumptions of continuous plane, which eliminates the boundary problems and the variation in transport routes and/or facilities, even spread of "rural" population, and identical demand and purchasing power, isolates two forces:

1. *Threshold*, which represents the minimum number of people (and consequently the minimum level of demand) required to support a technically feasible establishment or firm[3]
2. *Market range*, which concerns the distance that the buyers are willing to travel to buy the good or service at a particular price

An activity will emerge and *survive* only if there is evidence of the threshold and

[2]Some of Christaller's ideas were repeated by E. Ullman, "A Theory of Location for Cities," *American Journal of Sociology*, Vol. 46 (May, 1941), pp. 853–864.

[3]The size of the establishment is determined by the dynamic forces of competitive conditions and the production function.

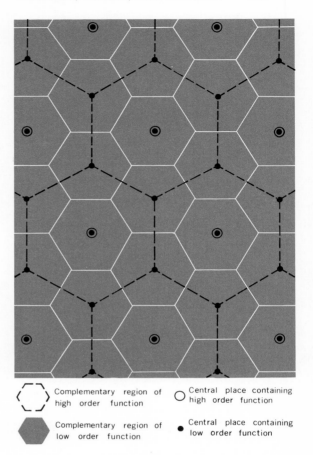

FIGURE 10.5 *Christaller model of economic activity location. (General Media Corporation)*

market range. The market range, of course, weakens with increasing distance. Since those buyers further from the activity location have to pay higher prices (price at the center plus the transfer cost), a buyer closer to the activity would be able to buy a larger number of units of the good or service than the buyer residing further away. This phenomenon reflects the weakening power of the market range as distance increases.

The emergence of the activity—made possible by the threshold and market range—would also induce other activities to locate, because since most workers associated with the initial activity tend to minimize their commuting effort they find residences closer to the activity. As they spend their incomes, further ser-

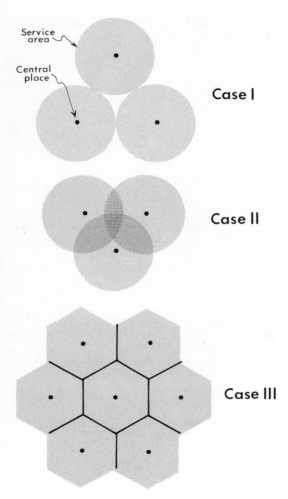

Service area

Central place

Case I

Case II

Case III

FIGURE 10.6 *Central place model with hexa-gonality of market areas. (General Media Corp-oration)*

place theory, the market range or the service area of an activity would be a circle. Figure 10.6 shows that along with the circular service areas, there will exist areas where people are residing (by assumption) but not served (case I), or areas that overlap (case II); in the same figure (case III), when assumptions of the even distribution of demand and the homogeneous transport network are slightly relaxed and adjusted, a hexagonal shape of the service area is the ideal shape, with none not served and no overlapping.

The hexagonal condition for each activity (which tends to have its own market range) may result in a hierarchical network of central place functions. However, with complete relaxation of the transport and demand assumption, the service activity locations may follow the demand and transport networks. Demand (with its varying spatial characteristics), the intervening forces, and the transport routes as "space adjusters," may give an octopus-shaped appearance to the location of central places.

Fetter [6], based on Christaller's assumptions and further assuming that the production and transport costs are identical for any two establishments or firms, each located in a different central place, demonstrated (Fig. 10.7) that the boundary between their trade areas will be a straight line perpendicularly bisecting the line connecting the two centers. If the production costs for the two firms are different, but the transport-cost structures are similar, the boundary line is curved and closer to the higher production cost area. The same reasoning applies to the situation where the production costs are similar but transport-cost structures different, resulting in a boundary closer to and curved around that location with higher transport cost.

Reilly [17] attempted to define the boundary between two centers through "retail gravitation," generally referred to as Reilly's Law of Retail Gravitation. He asserted that

vices and some permissible manufacturing activities would emerge. Thus, an agglomeration of economic activity locations and residences results, which as it serves the outlying areas becomes a central place. It should be noted that the market ranges for the various activities at the central place may not coincide. (The arrangement of economic activities and the residences at the central place is also a locational problem. Usually there is a Central Business District [CBD] conveniently linked to the residence and the supply lines).

Under the assumptions of the central

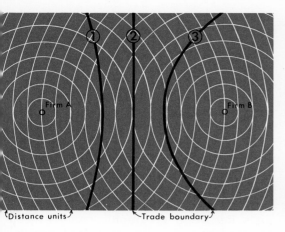

FIGURE 10.7 *Fetter model of economic activity location.*

two cities attract retail trade (*T*) from any intermediate city (*C*) or town in the vicinity of the breaking point approximately in direct proportion to the populations (*P*) of the two cities (*A* and *B*) and in inverse proportion to the squares of the distances (*D*) from these two cities to the intermediate towns.

The boundary lines may be determined by the contour lines "up to which one city excercises the dominating retail trade influences and beyond which the other city dominates." His law may be expressed as

$$\frac{T_A \leftarrow C}{T_B \leftarrow C} = \frac{P_A}{P_B}\left(\frac{D_{C-B}}{D_{C-A}}\right)^2.$$

Assuming the following hypothetical data:

P_A = population in city A = 70,000
P_B = population in city B = 50,000
D_{C-B} = distance between cities C and B
= 150 miles
D_{C-A} = distance between cities C and A
= 100 miles
$T_A \leftarrow C$ = trade to city A from city C
$T_B \leftarrow C$ = trade to city B from city C,

then, by substitution,

$$\frac{T_A \leftarrow C}{T_B \leftarrow C} = \frac{70,000}{50,000}\left(\frac{150}{100}\right)^2 = \frac{15.75}{5}.$$

This means that for every $5 of trade that goes to city *B* from city *C* there will be $15.75 worth of trade to city *A* from city *C*.

Additional work has been done by Berry and Garrison [2] to further reinforce the central place theory, extending it to explain urban agglomeration. The interaction or gravity between any two central places may be measured by Alexander's [1] formulation:

$$i = \frac{P_1 P_2}{d},$$

where *i* represents interaction, *P* is population, and *d* is the distance between cities 1 and 2. The larger the value of *i*, the greater the interaction.

In summary, the tertiary theories attempt to conceptualize the incidence of activities into a hierarchy of central place areas and the resulting interaction between them. The early theories emphasize the transportation factor, while modern theories place relatively more weight on the demand factor(s).

FACTORS OF INDUSTRY LOCATION

A paramount problem facing the executives of any large corporation is *where to locate* the plant or plants. Obtaining the best location requires consideration of a great array of interdependent factors. In general, industries often are oriented to one or a combination of three criteria—raw materials, transportation, and markets—and sometimes others. For example, industries whose raw materials lose much weight in the manufacturing process (pulp mills, packing plants, sawmills) tend to tie to their raw material source. These industries are generally classified as *resource based*. Conversely, if the product gains in bulk or weight (soft drink bottling, for example), the plant tends to orient itself near the market; such industries are often classed as *market based*. Industries whose basic material is bulky or heavy often feel compelled to locate on or near transportation facilities where lower movement costs assure them of competitive economic advantage. The industries that do not have specific orientation may be called "footloose" industries.

Power, Labor, and Capital

A number of other specific locational factors enter into the decision-making process. *Power* or *energy* is in many industries (aluminum, metallurgical) of prime importance. Both quantity and quality (skill) of labor demand observance, as in the apparel industry. *Capital* often is regarded as crucial, as witnessed by the decision of Henry Ford to install his later-to-be industrial empire in Detroit instead of Cleveland. *Industrial inertia*, or resistance to change or movement, is regarded as the classical reason that the American textile industry hesitated to separate plants.

Post-World War II industrial expansion, however, brought forth a host of new factors and modified existing ones. Perhaps this was due to the fact that, in many industries, a differential of as much as ten percent of total manufacturing and distribution costs could be affected simply by virtue of the correct spatial location—and that competition became more keen. Perhaps it was an increasing awareness of the interdependent factors that culminated in the location of a new plant, or the new role that critical self-evaluation by executives plays in site location. In any case, spatial location became as important to producers of goods as sound management and astute merchandising practices.

Climate

Among the newer factors of industrial location is that of *climate*. For some time, of course, climate has exerted control as a factor in site selection. Industries involved in flight testing, such as the aircraft industry, have often selected locations nearly devoid of the bad weather conditions that prevent flight observation and analysis. The rapid amalgamation of aircraft companies in southern California is testimony to this effect. In addition, it is recognized that lower construction and maintenance costs could be secured in locating in favorable climatic regions. The advent of technical and aerospace-oriented research added a further dimension to the role of climate. Launching of multimillion or even billion dollar capsules demanded excellent weather conditions over extended periods of time. Restricted geographic regions met such conditions, and as such influenced industrial site selection of those plants or complexes serving such functions.

In interviews with top executives as to why their companies locate in an area, "ideal climate" is invariably mentioned. Of course, ideal climate actually means nothing unless it is related to "from whose" and "for whom" points of view. Perusal of numerous advertisements of state and city chambers of commerce, public utility companies, railroads, real estate firms, "development" associations and corporations, industrial location services (both public and private), industries such as steel companies, and even banks, discloses the anomalous fact that all, regardless of what part of the world is being advertised, have an "ideal climate." To be sure, however, areas with moderate weather changes and gradual seasonal fluctuations may be indentified, and these areas have attracted industries.

Site

Actual site, too, has become a more prominent factor, particularly for industries that emit smoke, noise, or waste products. The increasing urban complexity world-over adds a further dimension to the purchase of plant sites adjacent to markets, raw materials, or transportation. Some industries, such as those involving rocket testing, are forced to acquire large tracts in isolated areas to satisfy political and conservational criticism. The site problem has undoubtedly led to the popularity of the "industrial park," a term denoting all types of privately owned industrial areas that have full-time personnel devoted to attracting industries.

Industrial parks maintain very close contacts with railroads, utilities, banks, industrial realtors, chambers of commerce, and other industrial development organizations that may be in a position to assist in locating industrial prospects. They often have very effective programs, partly because they have a great deal of leverage in dealing with industrial prospects, as compared to the purely persuasive efforts that some other agencies can employ. For example, an industrial park can make special arrangements in prices and terms, can offer "build-to-suit" and "package" deals, and can guarantee the maintenance of covenants and restrictions controlling the development of their property.

In addition to getting prospect leads from other agencies, industrial parks develop their own prospects via direct contacts, direct mail solicitation, and advertising. The national business periodicals are also used by those large-scale industrial parks that can justify such coverage. They provide detailed factual data about their sites, as well as area economic data.

Two problems of industrial parks are becoming evident that were not foreseen in their earlier years. One is the deterioration in standards that can occur when the original covenants are not strictly enforced, and when managers or tenants are succeeded by others less concerned with maintaining the intended quality of the environment. The other problem, closely related to the first, is the addition in tenants needed for expansion programs that the park management is not able to meet. There are three partial remedies for this:

1. Persuade the first tenant to take more land than he thinks he needs

2. Hold adjoining land for a tenant's future expansion

3. Have other larger sites available outside the industrial park to provide for future needs

Private land owners and developers of industrial property may operate on a local, regional, national, or international scale in the scope of their projects. In many cases, they use the services of industrial realtors for promotion and marketing of their properties; sometimes they have joint operations with railroads, universities, or municipalities; sometimes they set up complete merchandising programs of their own.

Government Spending

Defense considerations have also become factors of location practice. The U.S. Department of Defense has, since World War II, given recognized consideration to contract awarding based on regional dispersion. In several cases, plant construction of critical industries (e.g., electronics) was directly influenced by such national policy decisions. The same is true for the other types of government spending; research and development spending in a given region provides a significant stimulus or inducement for other industries to germinate in that area. Spatial separation of industries of totalitarian nations has long been an important factor in site selection—the United States merely became another of the many nations observing this consideration.

Pecuniary Incentives

Taxes are an increasingly important factor in the location of industrial plants. States and private municipalities, faced with rising costs for services and increased citizen apathy toward personal taxes, have instigated tax concessions, special deductions, and other such incentives to attract industry, which provides more jobs, more income, and consequently greater revenues. Some areas— Puerto Rico is a good example with its "Operation Bootstrap"—have created a climate of good will toward industry, which along with tax concessions and favorable loan policy has lured a number of international firms. These concessions offered by various political subdivisions usually include [20]:

1. Exemption from local or state property taxes for periods of time extending from two to ten years, frequently with the understanding that the exemption will be extended.
2. Guarantee that a new firm's property tax will not be increased for a specified number of years.
3. Exemption from state income and excise taxes. Some states accomplish this end by allowing a new firm to accelerate the depreciation of certain of its investments.
4. Exemption from property taxes on goods and materials stored for interstate shipment, a practice known as the "free-port" exemption.

In most cases, tax concessions are confined to some form of relief from property taxes, which generally means that local governments bear the entire burden of the exemption. This is one of the major disadvantages of the practice, because it leads not only to an additional burden of taxes among long-established firms, but it also limts the units of tax base of the community. Increasing the tax base and expansion by the existing industries are important objectives of a community. This presents a great dilemma for the leaders of every community. Obviously, new firms seeking locations are going to shy away from any city or location that holds a group of unhappy industrialists. The existing "happy" industrialists may accelerate more economic growth in the area by being "best advertised" than the tax incentives.

Tax concession as a financial inducement to industry has a major weakness in that it is non-selective. If offered to one industry, it must be offered to all. Furthermore, its effectiveness cannot be measured. It is believed that a large firm is more prone to place importance on tax concessions as a location factor than a small firm, merely because property taxes increase substantially as plant investment increases. Also, the appeal of tax concessions is not as great as municipal bonding to the small firm since the financing of the new plant is the immediate problem, whereas the financial advantage of tax concession is postponed.

Sub rosa tax concessions and special arrangements are often offered by local governments as inducements to industry. Some of these arrangements are legal, some are extralegal, and some may be illegal. Generally, these inducements are of two types: sub rosa tax concessions, and arrangements for free or low-cost extensions of access roads, sidewalks, utility mains, power connections, or parking lots. Some local governments provide training schools for prospective employees of a new plant. These inducements may be accompanied by assistance from community leaders in smoothing the way in zoning hearings, in waivers of code requirements, building restrictions, or fire regulations, and in modification of planning commission rulings on land–building ratios or esthetic architectural requirements. In some states, individual cities or state agencies assist industry with market research studies, special raw material or labor market studies, and other technical services, which if not obtained free would have to be purchased by the incoming firm.

Sub rosa incentives are not always accountable in dollars, but they have financial ramifications. Some communities suggest to prospective new industries that arrangements can be made to prevent the new industrial facilities from being taxed for a specified period of time after completion or that the newcomer will be underassessed. Others suggest that assessments can be stabilized at existing levels for a number of years and that the new industry need not fear future tax increases. These sub rosa arrangements, because of their confidentiality, are not assigned a dollar value, but their frequency of occurrence is believed to be rather common. Problems of such arrangements, however, are obvious:

1. Lack of accountability means that objective and accurate estimates of comparative costs cannot be determined
2. The duration of the arrangements is uncertain, since exposure and publicity may bring their cancellation
3. To the extent that arrangements are illegal or extralegal, considerable risk of exposure, litigation, and possible imposition of penalties and fines is borne by the parties that solicit, accept or assent to such arrangements.

Amenity Factors

The "good life" is rarely seen in treatises dealing with manufacturing geography but its importance is apparent, if rarely calculated. This may be considered under two phases—*casual living* and *cultural atmosphere*. Senior executives invariably stress casual living as a deciding factor in site location. While this may pose problems for those who heavily rely on detailed benefit–cost ratios for industrial site location, its persistence as a factor of geographic location is indisputable. What is meant by the term casual living? It could mean living in an area where ice and snow are minimal, if not totally absent. It could mean that the sun shines from a blue cloudless sky the day through. It could suggest homes built around a patio or garden, where many meals, particularly evening meals, are barbecued and eaten outdoors. It might suggest engineers and executives wearing cool, open throat short-sleeved sport shirts.

It might, on the contrary, suggest nearby proximity to ski slopes, scenic paths, or lakes and trout streams. But whatever it connotes—different ideas to different people—it is a factor that has definite accountability.

Cultural atmosphere is, in a sense, more definitive. Engineers, scientists, and skilled workers who comprise a significant segment of the labor force are largely an exceptionally well-educated group who desire, in fact, *insist* upon having the best of cultural advantages for themselves and their children. Among these conditions are attractive homes on large lots (even on large acreages), superior schools and libraries, efficient community government, outstanding medical and hospital facilities, active little theatre movements and, for engineers and scientists, universities and research facilities.

The interaction between industrial firms, particularly a research-based industrial complex, and educational institutions and activities are many and diverse. First, there is the demand of research and research-based manufacturing establishments for skills at various levels. Second, there is the demand of their employees, if not of the firms themselves, for better general education and for work-related specialized training. Third, there is the demand of the science complex for faculty consultants, for research performed in colleges and universities, and for other specialized services of educational institutions. Fourth, many of these science-based firms have contributed directly to vocational training by conducting their own in-house training programs; this has reduced the need for outside facilities and has added to the supply of local skills available to other firms. Finally, better opportunities and better working conditions than the traditional employments have will effect the levels of occupational and educational aspiration, occupational mobility and educational achievement.

Water

Water, always an important consideration, has taken on increasing significance in recent years as a location factor. This is partly a result of new industrial technology that has greatly intensified the demand for water. The quantity and quality of water available for industrial purposes is becoming more scarce as a result of rapid urbanization.

Traditionally, the two major sources of water are surface water from streams and lakes, and ground waters from wells and springs. Since domestic and sanitary uses normally have priorities over industrial uses, industries that require large quantities of water in their operation, such as pulp and paper, iron and steel, and food and chemical processing, may be advised to choose sites close to ample supplies of good water but away from the population centers. In most cases, these industries tend to supplement public sources by developing water systems of their own.

Of equal importance to many firms, however, is not only enough water, but water of the correct temperature, free of impurities and minerals. Hard water must usually be treated, or the corrosion and scale it would develop in pipes and circulating systems would result in excessive repair and replacement costs. Since water in a number of industries, such as steel, is necessary for cooling purposes, its temperature from the source becomes important. In certain regions (southern California is a prime example), cooling towers are required to cool the water prior to its use in the manufacturing process.

Waste Disposal

Waste disposal is also a location factor of no small import, both in terms of fluids and in regard to gases. Most states now have stringent requirements for disposal of waste material, and many cities, Los Angeles for example, go even further in efforts to reduce pollutants into the atmosphere. Dye plants and woolen mills discharge unusually heavy amounts of fluid waste material in the form of grease and suspended solids; these industries, as well as chemical industries, are usually heavily regulated by law. Consideration of the means of waste disposal, the costs of disposing, and related legal restrictions (which all vary from one place to another) are demanding a prime place in the process of industry location.

Personal Reasons

Personal reasons are probably not given the credit they deserve as an industrial location factor. The classic question, "Why did the Boeing Aircraft Company decide on Seattle for its plant location?" and the answer, "because Bill Boeing, the president, liked his home town," leads to the supposition that a key to the formation of new enterprises in particular places is the enterpreneur himself. From a location standpoint, he may appear anywhere. This is the reason that every area is presumed to have a potential for the development of "homegrown" industry. Some evidence seems to indicate that entrepreneurs are more numerous in the high-technology and high-growth industries than in others. However, he tends to start his business where he lives. He may fail if this was a poor place to start such a business, but this will probably not inhibit him. The fact that more businesses are started in urban areas is probably because more entrepreneurs live there, rather than because of any conscious relocation of such people to what is a better seedbed for new firms.

The manner in which this process takes place in the science-based industries is interesting. The scientist–entrepreneur is attracted to research and development in his graduate study period or to obtain his first job. If he is later motivated to start a business, he is already in the kind of area needed to support the activity he wants to undertake.

The importance of entrepreneurship in new business formation cannot be overestimated. The energy and enthusiasm required to get a business "off the ground" is a rare and essential ingredient that is not as well understood as it should be. An area of industrial development activity that has been neglected and that deserves study, understanding, and active support, is what might be described as the "care and feeding" of the innovator and the entrepreneur.

Community Attitudes

Often, it is true that local warmth of the populace becomes a dynamic factor of industrial location, even if tax advantages are not apparent. The rise of local industrial development corporations in small towns and the aggressive work of chambers of commerce and local bankers often swing industries, particularly the small and medium-sized firms, to locate where they are "wanted." It must be remembered that citizens of small towns and rural areas often do not want industry, or rather, do not want the accompanying changes that it brings. Firms are often highly sensitive to local feeling, and more than one community has lost a large industrial plant after town-hall meetings full of vigorous outspoken opposition. Industry must be wanted by the community; otherwise, all kinds of problems may evolve—harassment of legitimate zoning requests, resurrection of antique city ordinances that restrict operation, and measures that might make it more difficult for the firm to recruit a work force.

Firms seeking newer locations are very conscious of how they will be received in a community. They often take personal surveys of potential locations—for example, a potential industry representative walking along the main street of the various towns stopped local people to ask, "How would you like to work for company X?" In some towns he got the nearly unanimous reply, "I'd like to work for company X, especially if that fine company were located in my town." In other towns he also received an almost unanimous reply, "I'd like to work for company X, but I wish they would locate in a near-by town." There is no doubt which community the site selector chose.

Community attitude formation is the beginning of any conscientious program of industrial development. This may require organized effort to mount a campaign through all media, including personal appearances at clubs and gatherings, to spread the message about the benefits (as well as problems and effects) of industrial growth.

Summary

Basically, locating a new plant is the same as matching many shaped pegs into holes —every community is different and its unique assets must be matched up with the unique requirements of the prospective firm. The problem is that of matching the right city with the right industry. It is the question of giving expression to the law of comparative advantage inclusive of noneconomic factors.

Many cities seemingly waste time, energy, and money trying to entice industries that have no possible interest in them at all. The success in attracting industry lies first in a complete and accurate inventory of the community's resources, attitudes, comparative advantage, identification of potential sites, and then precisely knowing what the "customer" wants to buy, when he wants to buy, and what his expectations are. The industry will locate at a place matched by their requirements and the community's offering.

CHANGES IN THE MAJOR LOCATIONAL FACTORS

Using the United States as an example, various changes in the importance of the major industrial location factors of markets, labor, transportation, and material resources may be cited. Early industrialization patterns in the United States reflected a matching of the dominant locational factors of certain industries with the areas that were most favored by that factor. Thus, market-oriented industries were highly concentrated in the Northeast, on the Atlantic seaboard, and around Chicago. Raw material-oriented industries were located at the best source of those raw materials, which in many cases was the West. Many of the labor-intensive industries sought location in the South, where labor was abundant, cheap, and not affected by union activity.

Over time these factor–area relationships have been changing. Slowly at first, but accelerating since World War II, these changes are shifting the comparative advantage that certain regions have traditionally enjoyed. Nevertheless, there are still important differences in most location factors, and these are likely to persist.

Turning first to what is perhaps the dominant factor in most industries—markets—some definition is necessary. It is important to differentiate between *consumer* markets, which are generally a function of population and income patterns, and *industrial* markets, which are a function of manufacturing concentrations. There are important differences in the geographical distribution of consumer and industrial markets, although these differences are not as great as they once were. Markets, in this context, refer to *regional* markets, rather than district or local markets.

Consumer markets are still highly concentrated. As Harris [9] has pointed out, half of the retail sales in the United States are in the Northeast, from Boston to St. Louis. Some states in this area have a market density several hundred times higher than some Western states. Densities in most of the Mountain and Plains states are also very low.

That this situation is slowly changing is obvious from the higher population growth rates of Western and Southern states. However, much of this growth has, up to now, been concentrated in oasis-like areas in the West and in the South, such as southern California, Phoenix, and parts of Texas. In between, there are vast areas of very sparse consumer markets, which affect the market pull of these growth areas. While in general there is a trend toward the development of significant markets in regions other than the Northeast, the differences in regional market densities remain sizable.

Industrial markets are even more highly concentrated. About two-thirds of all manufacturing employment is still in the Northeast. These markets have traditionally been concentrated, according to industry, in certain regions or even cities. For instance, the automobile industry market has been concentrated in Detroit, the rubber industry market in Akron, and the steel industry market in Pittsburgh and the areas around Chicago.

The tendency of consumer markets to disperse has been followed by a similar but less extensive tendency for industry to broaden its locational patterns. At present rates of decentralization, however, traditional concentrations will persist for a long time.

Another factor that varies significantly among regions is wages. Wage differences as high as 25 percent between developed urban areas are not uncommon; differences between urban and rural areas are even more striking. There are forces, however, that are tending to narrow these differences. They include union organization and collective bargaining, particularly at the national level, federal minimum wage laws, and the migration of industry itself. When industry moves into an area of low wages, it increases employment. If other plants later locate close by, demand may put an upward pressure on wages and tend to reduce the differential that previously existed.

This is, of course, an imperfect mechanism. Not every industry is free to seek low wages, and many that could do so might hesitate for fear that the advantage would disappear with time. Thus, equalization does not occur as readily and completely as theory might suggest. Some authorities feel that while differences in wage levels have narrowed in recent decades, the narrowing has been quite spotty and slow.

Four additional related trends may be noted in the contemporary industry location process. Two of these are spatial in nature, reflecting shifts in the concentrations of industrial activities:

1. Regional decentralization out of the Northeast to the South and West
2. Local decentralization out of the large central cities

The other two trends are functional in nature, resulting from a variety of socioeconomic changes that have caused shifts in the relative importance of the kinds of industry locating new plants. These shifts are due to differential growth rates, which in turn reflect such changes as the rise in personal income levels, the growth of the services sector, and the increasing role of research and technology. These trends are:

3. Increasing market-orientation of industry
4. Growth of "intellect-oriented" industries

Manufacturing industry in the United States has traditionally been concentrated in the Northeast. This area, which has been referred to as the "manufacturing belt," includes the states of the New England, Middle Atlantic, and Great Lakes regions. Based on manufacturing employment, in 1870 this area accounted for 83 percent of the industrial employment of the nation.

During the past century, the growth of the Western and Southern regions of the country has generally been faster than that of the Northeast, accelerating particularly in the last two decades. In the period 1940 to 1960, while the Northeast increased its manufacturing employment 70 percent, the Southwest enjoyed an increase of 160 percent, and the Far West an increase of 200 percent.

As impressive as these growth rates are, it is important to note that they are large percentage increases on relatively small base figures. Thus, despite differences in growth, the Northeast still predominates in manufacturing. As Perloff [16] points out:

Looked at in terms of each region's share of the nation's manufacturing development, however, the enduring strength of the urban-industrial Northeast is evident. After ninety years of continuing industrial transformation, nearly two-thirds of the nation's manufacturing labor force was still located in the Northeastern industrial belt in 1960. (p. 50)

A continuation of the trend toward regional decentralization in favor of the South and West is to be expected. Inherent in this shift, which accelerates in periods of economic expansion, are opportunities for areas and communities that have heretofore lacked an industrial base.

A second trend of industrial location is that toward changes in the type of area or community selected. Traditionally, manufacturing plants were located in large cities in order to draw on a large labor force and to secure the materials and services necessary to their operation. For the past thirty years or more, however, there has been a tendency for industry to move out of the central city. In many cases, such a move was to a nearby suburban community or to some other point on the periphery of the urban concentration. In other cases, however, smaller industrialized areas or even rural towns were the favored locations.

The third trend in industrial location is that toward market orientation, based on the declining pull of other location factors, particularly the raw materials factor. Proximity to raw materials is no longer as important in the production process of the average plant as it once was. Another aspect of the increasing market orientation of industry is the relatively greater growth of market-oriented industries. As Perloff has pointed out, the resource-oriented activities of the economy have been declining in relative importance since 1870. In the past two decades, manufacturing industries, and particularly those producing consumer goods, have been proliferating and enlarging rapidly. The companies that have been building and serving these markets tend to be market-oriented by nature. As personal incomes grow and equalize across the nation, markets for the new consumer products expand. The producing companies follow these markets, giving rise to the "filling in" process described by Perloff. As fast as a regional market passes the threshold of size that permits economical operation, company after company puts branch plants into the market. Even where the economic advantages are small, when one company in an industry branches, competitiors tend to follow suit.

A plant located in the regional market it is to serve enjoys intangible marketing and public relations advantages. Regional development organizations emphasize these advantages in their promotional programs. Thus, it appears that not only have more and more industries become market-oriented in their locational decisions, but also the market-oriented industries constitute a sector that has a strong tendency toward multiplant expansion.

A final trend to be noted here concerns the growth of what might be called the "intellect-oriented" industries. This term,

admittedly vague, includes some of the so-called "footloose" industries—which are generally not footloose at all.[4] In considering this aspect of recent economic growth, the term *industry* must be broadened from its customary use as synonymous with manufacturing. While many of the companies in this field do manufacture a product, or "hardware" as it is often called, many others produce "software," which is really a service. Yet they must be considered together with manufacturing industries in defining this trend, since they are almost always "export" industries in the regional sense and thus can provide the same economic stimulation that the more traditional manufacturing activities do. Furthermore, they are among the fastest growing segments of the economy—attractive in terms of income for their employees, they have a high propensity for the generation of new business enterprises.

Essentially, this aspect includes the research and development activities of both industry and government, a thirty billion dollar business. It also includes much of the aerospace industry, parts of the electronics and precision instruments industries, and a number of other related activities. It is characterized by a high percentage of total employment in scientists, engineers, and other specialized professional categories. Its locational patterns emphasize the desires and needs of the professionals it employs, as well as the external economies that it must have to survive.

A well-recognized principle in location theory is the tendency of companies using new technologies and pioneering new fields to locate in urban environments. This principle is active here, but it pro-

---

[4]While almost all major location factors enter into most locational decisions, one factor often appears to dominate the decision in a particular industry. Thus, some studies have classified industries as market-oriented, labor-oriented, or raw material-oriented. In this classification scheme, those not fitting into one of the three groups have often been described as footloose.

vides only part of the explanation for the pattern of concentration that has emerged in the "intellect-oriented" types of industries. That concentration has been defined as consisting of five complexes centered in:

1. Southern California
2. San Francisco Bay area
3. New York–northern New Jersey
4. Boston
5. Washington, D.C.

This type of industry needs technological resources, such as those provided by universities and research organizations, and also requires many kinds of specialized services, components, and supplies. In addition, there is often a need for high-risk capital financing, and above all for a large pool of professional people from a variety of disciplines on which to draw.

With respect to the professional himself, environmental factors are also important. He wants alternative employment opportunities so that he can be assured of continuous, professionally satisfying employment. For this reason he tends to cluster with his own fellows in areas of high employment. Additionally, he wants broad recreational and cultural opportunities for himself and his family, good living conditions, and excellent educational facilities to continue his own development and to provide proper training for his children. Finally, he wants the opportunity to indulge in his hobbies and special interests. Since his is an occupation where demand is growing faster than supply, he has little difficulty in making his needs felt by those who require his services.

In light of this combination of environmental requirements for the business enterprise, as well as for the men whose capabilities are the substance of its success, the resulting pattern of urban concentration is not surprising. Rather, it is the particular urban places selected that are of interest. These places are large cities, but not all large cities are included.

Furthermore, many of the plants and most of the residences are in the more attractive suburbs. They are near centers of higher learning, but many such centers are not included. They are regionally dispersed, with most regions being represented. In each case, the reasons for the development of the complex are probably different, but the presence of entrepreneurship and the availability of risk capital are common and significant factors.

There is little reason to believe that this industry will soon disperse out of its present complexes. In fact, the R & D activity has shown a remarkable ability to resist the forces that have sought to disperse it. The industrial development significance of this industry is very great. From it come many products and technologies that will be used extensively in industries outside the identified complexes. As a technology develops and matures, its use in manufacturing need not be confined to the seedbed in which it was nurtured. In fact, it might find other, less congested areas that are far more economical places in which to carry on routine manufacturing operations. However, the urban orientation and geographical concentration of the intellect-oriented activities is expected to be a persistent trend.

case study

The U. S. Steel Corporation at Geneva, Utah

The location of an integrated iron and steel mill is an exacting experience. The expenditure is so great, upward of $500 million, that the ultimate decision must be made with extreme care. An integrated plant's location generally takes into prime consideration:

1. Convenient access to an abundant supply of iron ore, preferably of high quality
2. Convenient access to coal deposits of a quality suitable for the coking process
3. Large amounts of land near markets with heavy demand for steel products

4. Availability of large amounts of water, both in terms of quantity and quality
5. Availability of an adequate labor supply, particularly in the skilled category
6. Convenient, economical transportation facilities

Other site location factors come into consideration, including the availability of capital, but these are usually secondary.

The Geneva plant of the U. S. Steel Corporation makes an interesting analysis of plant location, since it both observed and violated the basic location factors.[5]

History

In 1941 the U.S. Government (Defense Plant Corporation) decided to construct an iron and steel plant at Geneva, Utah, near the city of Provo. For defense purposes, the site was admirable. Long-range Japanese bombers (assuming the Japanese secured a foothold on continental North America or were able to locate a carrier fleet off the Pacific coast) would have to pass through successive fighter screens from California, Oregon, Washington, Nevada, and Idaho Air Force Bases. For manufacturing purposes, the site was incredible, located 700 miles from the shipyards and defense factories that would be using its steel products. Construction faced the usual wartime problems: scarce housing, food rationing in public eating houses, overcrowded schools, difficult transportation.

However, by 1943 the $200 million plant was producing pig iron. United States Steel Corporation engineers, answering the government's call for assistance, designed and laid out the plant without regard for cost. As a result, the Geneva complex was a manufacturing dream. During the war years, U. S. Steel ran the plant for the government on a cost basis, without regard for profit to the corporation. At the close of World War II, many industry executives questioned the private operation of Geneva in the U.S. market. They pointed out that demand for steel in Utah was minimal, that the site was 900 miles from West Coast markets, necessitating rail transport, and that post-war competition of steel shipped

via the Panama Canal would be disastrous. Management at U. S. Steel disagreed, and the economic conditions bore them out. The success of the plant may be attributed to the following factors:

1. The U. S. Steel Corporation was able, under competitive bidding at the war's conclusion, to acquire this magnificently laid-out plant for $47.5 million, a sum less than 25 cents on the dollar in terms of initial cost [21].
2. Access to coal and iron ore was available at moderate cost. High quality iron ore could be obtained within 250 miles. Coal, although of marginal quality, was available from 120 miles, and fluxing limestone from 35 miles.
3. Political leaders in Utah were unwilling to let a major plant die. They worked overtime to ensure that a large corporation such as U. S. Steel could and would operate the Geneva facility and that local support for the plant's operation was sustained.
4. The Western market blossomed beyond all expectations. California was booming and steel was needed in enormous quantities —steel that Geneva could provide.

Geneva—Today

The second quarter-century of steelmaking in Utah is now underway. How has Geneva fared and what changes have occurred? First, it must be stressed that the Geneva plant has never had "smooth sailing." It began as a private enterprise, handicapped by having to ship most of its products 700–1,000 miles to market, a freight factor most of its competitors did not have to share.

Second, the situation worsened in the 1950s as competition increased and the threat of imported steel from Japan cast a new and ominous shadow over the Western market picture. Management met this challenge by improved efficiency, economies in production, higher quality products, delivery speed, and improved service to customers. The result is a plant that continues to grow with the growing market.

The Geneva Works today comprises one of the largest steelmaking facilities in the West. It operates as a fully integrated steel mill—one in which the raw materials (iron ore, coal, limestone, scrap) are processed through the

---

[5]This case study illustrates an application of the theories discussed in this chapter. However, it is not intended to be an analysis of the iron and steel industry, which is discussed in Chapter 23.

various stages into semifinished and finished products. Currently, the rated capacity is 2.5 million ingot tons annually. This requires a considerable amount of raw materials. Coal is mined in three locations—the Columbia and the Geneva mines near Dragerton, Utah, and the Somerset mine in Colorado. After mining, it is shipped by rail to Wellington, Utah, for processing through a cleaning and drying operation before shipment to the Geneva Works, thereby removing much of the waste material from the coal and controlling the moisture content. It should be noted that these coals are marginal in coking quality, making it necessary to add smaller amounts of medium and low volatile coals purchased from other sources in order to produce strong coke for use at the blast furnaces.

Although raw iron ore is still obtained from open pit mines near Cedar City, Utah, 230 miles distant, considerable blending of this ore with taconite pellets from a source near Lander, Wyoming, occurs. Limestone and dolomite from a quarry near Payson, Utah, continue to provide the Geneva Works with these necessary ingredients. Shipment is by rail for the 30-some miles necessary.

Water, a critical element in a marginal rainfall area, continues to remain adequate. The enclosure by a breakwater of a portion of Utah Lake provides a storage area of some one billion gallons. Water for this reservoir is provided by some 20 wells and from surface water sources. Economical water management causes minimal water drain over prior farm uses.

Much has been written concerning the need for highly experienced workers in the steel industry. To be sure, Geneva had its initial labor shortages and blacks, Indians, Jamaicans, and Japanese were hastily "recruited" to solve the situation. Local workers never completely satisfied the need, a problem that persists today to some degree. However, Mormon farmers and housewifes, inexperienced as they were, accredited themselves well in the long run—*desire to work* overcame inexperience.

The principal markets for Geneva products —plate, hot rolled sheets and coils, structural shapes, welded steel pipe, pig iron, coke, coal chemicals and nitrogen products for fertilizer and industrial use—continue to be the intermountain area extending east to Denver, and the West from Los Angeles to Seattle.

Approximately 80% of the Geneva products are shipped 700 miles or more to the West Coast markets.

Site Location Analysis

Was Geneva located wrongly? If so, what about its present success? These questions are, of course, matters of conjecture. It is interesting to speculate, however, on the relative success of this plant if it had been located in, say, the San Francisco Bay complex on tidewater. Skilled labor would have been more available, but probably at a higher cost; the cost of assembling raw materials at the blast furnaces would probably have been higher, but marketing costs would have been immensely lower. Who can say, too, whether California's government, with its myriad of industries, would have given the same careful attention and concern as did the Utah political organization?

What kind of conclusions are possible? Several present themselves, namely: The basic industrial location factors, while important, are not all=determinant in plant construction. Political consideration and local support often are important facets in the success of an industrial concern.

The iron and steel industry is generally regarded as a "seed industry" because it tends to spawn a host of dependent and related concerns. Hence, there are few *poor* locations in the industry—only relative good ones. Since expenditures are so huge, mistakes are irrevocable. The Geneva plant, blessed by government construction in a war era, overlooked some site location factors but still prospered. Chances are, few plants would have such fortune. The deserted or dismantled plants nationwide pay tribute to human incompetence in disregarding basic locational factors.

selected references

1. Alexander, J. W., *Economic Geography,* Englewood Cliffs, N. J.: Prentice-Hall, Inc., 1963.

2. Berry, B. J. L., and Garrison, W. L., "The Functional Bases of the Central Place Hierarchy," *Economic Geography*, Vol. 34, 1958, p. 150.

3. Chisholm, M., *Rural Settlement and Land Use: An Essay in Location, Geography Series*, London: Hutchinson University Library, 1962.

4. Christaller, Walter, *"Die Zentralen Orte in Suddeutschland*, Jena: Gustav Fischer Verlag, 1933.

5. Dunn, Edgar S., *The Location of Agricultural Production*, Gainesville: University of Florida Press, 1954.

6. Fetter, F. A., "The Economic Law of Market Areas," *Quarterly Journal of Economics*, Vol. 39, 1924, pp. 520–529.

7. Garrison, W. L., and Marble, Duane F., "The Spatial Structure of Agricultural Activities," *Annals of the Association of American Geographers*, Vol. 47, 1957, pp. 137–144.

8. Greenhut, M., *Plant Location in Theory and Practice: The Economics of Space*, Chapel Hill, N. C.: University of North Carolina Press, 1956.

9. Harris, C. D., "The Market as a Factor the Location of Industry in The United States," *Annals of the Association of American Geographers*, December 1954.

10. Hoover, Edgar M., *Location Theory and the Shoe and Leather Industries*, Cambridge: Harvard University Press, 1937.

11. ———, *The Location of Economic Activity*, New York: McGraw-Hill Book Company, Inc., 1948.

12. Isard, Walter, and Isard, P., *General Social, Political and Economic Equilibrium for a System of Regions,* Occasion Papers, Series No. 2, Philadelphia: Regional Science Research Institute, 1965.

13. Isard, Walter, *Location and Space Economy*, New York: John Wiley & Sons, Inc., 1956.

14. Losch, August, *The Economics of Location*, (first published in Germany in 1939, translated by William H. Woglam and W. F. Stopler), New Haven: Yale University Press, 1954.

15. Palander, Rord, "Beiträge zur Standortstheorie," Upsala: *Amqvist Och Wiksells Boktryckeri-a-b*, 1935.

16. Perloff, Harvey S., and Dodds, Vera W., *How a Region Grows*, New York: Committee for Economic Development, 1963.

17. Reilly, W. J., *The Law of Retail Gravitation*, New York: The Knickerbocker Press, 1931.

18. Thünen, Johann Heinrich Von, *Der Isoliterte Staat in Beziehung auf Land-wirthschaft und Nationalökonomie*, 3 vols, Hamburg and Rostock, 1826–1863.

19. Weber, Alfred, "Weber den Standort der Industrien," Part I, *Reine Theorie des Standorts*, Tubingen, 1909; translated by C. J. Friendrich as *Alfred Weber's Theory of the Location of Industries*, Chicago: University of Chicago Press, 1928.

20. Weiss, Stephen J., "Tax Structure, Tax Competition, and Tax Burden on Industry: Comparisons Across State Lines," Part I, *New England Business Review*, January 1968.

21. White, C. Langdon, "Is the West Making the Grade in the Steel Industry?" *Business Research Series No. 8*, Stanford: Stanford University School of Business, 1956.

part III
Primary Economic Activities

In Part II, Variables in Economic Activity, we enlarged on the conceptual model of man as the dynamic agent of change within the global system. Specifically, we were concerned with how the various frameworks, which are common to all societies, are contrived in order to promote the values of societies. Chapter 10 focused attention from the very general to the more specific, offering a series of classifications that are further developed in the following chapters.

Part III attempts to classify the many different types of economically productive activities. For purposes of international comparison, as discussed in Chapter 9, these may be divided into three major areas: primary, secondary, and tertiary. The primary economic activities embrace all those associated with producing or extracting from nature, and with the rearing and reproducing of animal life. Agriculture, animal husbandry, forestry, hunting and fishing, mining and quarrying are examples of *primary* economic activities. These will be discussed in Chapters 11 through 21.

introduction
to agriculture

Agriculture, the art of cultivating the ground to raise grain and other crops for man and domestic animals, is the oldest of occupations and the basis of all other arts. One can argue that the two most epochal steps in the civilization of man were the invention of the wheel and the birth of agriculture. The former initiated technology, and the latter was the start of man's reshaping of the environment to his own ends.

Origin and Dispersion

When and where did agriculture begin? For many years attention has focused on the Middle East, whose archeological remains seem to show it to be the cradle of modern man's culture. But information regarding the early domestication of plants is scarce and scattered. Recent discoveries concerning the birth of agriculture, based largely on carbon[14] datings,[1] are summarized in the map on page 172 showing spread of agriculture. The most remarkable of the discoveries indicates that agriculture appeared almost simultaneously on opposite sides of the world—in the Middle East and in Mexico. The time in both cases was roughly 7,000 B.C.

The implication is that a development such as the invention of agriculture, vital to the progress of the human species from the aboriginal to the technological stage, typically did not occur merely by chance. It was an inevitable step in the evolution of intelligent life. According to Sauer,[2] the origin of agriculture had to be linked with:

1. *A sedentary society*—for the planted land, especially among primitive cultivators, must be watched over continously against plant predators
2. The production of *surplus* and *leisure*, because famine-haunted folk lack the opportunity and incentive for the slow and continuing selection of domesticated forms; village communities in comfortable circumstances are indicated for such progressive steps
3. *Woodlands*, which permit abandonment of planting after a time to the resprouting and reseeding wild woody growth, and provide a form of rotation whereby the soil is replenished by nutrients carried up from deep-rooted trees and shrubs

A thriving agriculture appeared in the middle part of the Yellow (Hwang Ho) River valley of China during the Neolithic period. The crops in the earliest sites seem largely of local origin, with no trace of imports from the Middle East. They have survived as basic food crops in modern China: rice, millet, sorghum, and soybean. However, these finds have not been

---

[1]Carbon[14] is a radioactive form of carbon that decays slowly into nitrogen[14]. Half of a given amount of carbon[14] decays in this manner in roughly 5,600 years. The carbon[14] is produced at a constant rate by the action of cosmic rays in the high atmosphere. Since carbon likewise decays at a constant rate, there is a uniform, equilibrium level of carbon[14] in the air at all times.

[2]Carl O. Sauer, "The Agency of Man on Earth," in William L. Thomas, Jr., ed., *Man's Role in Changing the Face of the Earth* (Chicago: University of Chicago Press, 1956), p. 56.

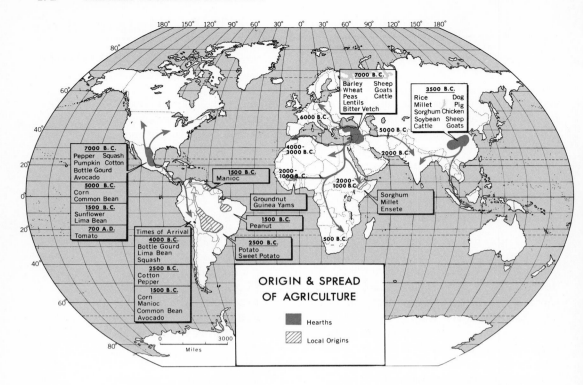

Agriculture—where it began and how it spread. (General Media Corporation)

dated by carbon[14]; hence it is impossible to relate this farming to the timetable of agricultural evolution further west.

Rice, which may have originated in the China area, appears at Indian sites 4,000 years old; these sites also show wheat, peas, beans, and lentils—all of which presumably came from the cradle of agriculture in the Middle East. This same Middle Eastern culture, centered in southeast Turkey, northeast Iraq, and the Jordan Rift valley, radiated into Europe along the southern shore of the Mediterranean, and by 3,000 B.C. had reached up the Nile as far as Khartoum.

The earliest evidence of agriculture in the Americas has been found at sites 9,000 years old in the modern Mexican states of Puebla and Tamaulipas. Crops included pumpkin, squash, annual pepper, and bottle gourd, which is also found in India and Africa. It is the only hint of a possible, dim link between the agricultural histories of those two remote regions.

The farming of Mexico seems to have spread slowly to South America. Archeological sites in the dry climate of coastal Peru show lima beans, squash, and bottle gourds from 4,000 B.C. The Peruvian region also seems to have imported root crops from the Andean highlands and eastern South America, and by 2,500 B.C. the ancient Peruvians were growing potatoes, sweet potatoes, and achira (a form of arrowroot).

The Egyptians, Babylonians, Assyrians, and Chinese are the oldest known civilizations to have systematically practiced agriculture. Many references to Egypt as a grain or corn country are found in the Old Testament, and in the earliest records of the other ancient civilizations there are many references to their agriculture.

The Greeks carried on agriculture to a limited extent, with systematic methods and good results, though their country was not well suited to this economic activity. The Romans attained greater perfection in the art and became the foremost of the ancient nations. Several of their writers produced works on agriculture, showing that they were familiar with and practiced some of the best principles and methods then in vogue. The Romans were familiar with the use of fertilizers, rotation of crops, methods of breeding domestic animals, and irrigation. Wherever they went they took their knowledge and methods of agriculture, and as a result of their conquests, this art was greatly advanced in England and a number of other countries in Europe and western Asia.

During the Middle Ages agriculture declined. Nearly all of the land in Europe was owned by the nobility, who spent their time in war and the chase, and left tilling of the soil to serfs and vassals. As a result, agriculture became almost a lost art, and it was not until the sixteenth century that it again received attention. During this century, the foundations of present methods were laid in England and other European countries. The agricultural revolution, coming on the heels of the Industrial Revolution of the eighteenth and nineteenth centuries, provided the impetus for mechanization that has been carried by Western civilization to many parts of the world.

General Characteristics

Today agriculture is practiced throughout the world—in some areas by methods not far removed from the conditions of several thousands of years ago, in others with the aid of science and mechanization, as a highly commercial endeavor. Regardless of the particular system being employed, several important generalizations about agriculture may be made:

1. Agriculture is the major sustainer of life
2. Agriculture covers a greater portion of land surface than any other economic activity
3. Every society of significance is dependent either directly or indirectly on agriculture
4. More people are engaged in agriculture than in any other economic activity
5. The total value of agricultural products exceeds the value of all other forms of economic activity (the value of animal products exceeds the value of all minerals mined)
6. Without agriculture, the type of culture with which most of the world's inhabitants are familiar could not exist
7. No other economic activity yet devised or proposed can supplant agriculture

The output (return for effort expended) of any agricultural system (and economic system) depends primarily on the following:

1. *Environmental factors* and their characteristics: All regions offer various choices, among which man is relatively free to select those he desires. Some choices are easily perceived and made; others are often subtle and appear only after intensive study, usually involving trial and error or scientific investigation.

2. The *technology* (knowledge, skills, tools, techniques) employed to transform the environmental features: This may be manifested in the woodlore of setting traps for animals, knowing what crops have better yields, or how to manufacture certain tools. It may also include the higher forms of knowledge—advanced technology such as pedology, hydrology, geology, agronomy, pathology, mineralogy, and zoology. It is perhaps obvious that those societies having the most advanced cultures will be able to increase and multiply the choices that nature does not reveal to the more primitive cultures.

Methods

The impression man makes on the physical landscape is primarily his interrelationship with the physical environment, density of population (number of people living on a given unit of land), length of residence, and tools and ideas that can be brought into play in order to change the landscape to his liking.

The ways man practices agriculture vary widely from one part of the world to another. Even though his methods are diverse, certain similarities appear that make it possible to classify agricultural efforts by the following criteria:

1. Type of tool used to till the soil, i.e., plough, hoe, stick
2. Length of residence in a locale, i.e., sedentary, migratory
3. Use made of crops or products, i.e., commercial, subsistence
4. Amount of time, labor, and land devoted to the system, i.e., extensive, intensive
5. Source of power used for tilling and harvesting, i.e., mechanized, animal, human
6. Products derived from "input," i.e., crop production, pastoralism
7. Multi-combinations of the above, i.e., intensive subsistence farming, cash-grain farming, nomadism, dairying, plantation agriculture, oases farming
8. Water availability, i.e., irrigation, dry-land, humid
9. Type of land ownership, i.e., tenancy, "suitcase," permanent, private, communal

Agricultural Systems

The foregoing discussion of methods of agriculture employed by man points out the complexity of this economic activity. The study of agriculture on a world basis further adds to the complexities. Nevertheless, it is virtually impossible to analyze the interactions between the various agricultural categories without focusing upon some sort of system that must, of necessity, be highly generalized. Whittlesey's system[3] divides agriculture in two major headings, each with several subdivisions:

[3]Derwent Whittlesey, "Major Agricultural Regions of the Earth," *Annals of the Association of American Geographers*, Vol. 26, (December 1936), pp. 199–240.

I. Pre-industrial Agriculture
   1. Nomadic hunting–gathering
   2. Nomadic herding
   3. Shifting cultivators
   4. Sedentary subsistence cultivation
   5. Intensive subsistence—rice dominant
   6. Subsistence crop and livestock

II. Industrial Agriculture
   1. Plantation
   2. Mediterranean
   3. Livestock ranching
   4. Crop farming (grain or fibers)
   5. Commercial livestock and crop farming
   6. Specialized horticulture
   7. Dairying

The above breakdown will be treated in detail in the chapters that follow.

chapter 11

Pre-industrial Agricultural Systems

Pre-industrial agriculture—an economic activity based on the use of primitive tools and weapons—may be broken down into the following agricultural systems:

1. Nomadic hunting–gathering
2. Nomadic herding
3. Shifting cultivation
4. Sedentary subsistence cultivation
5. Intensive subsistence cultivation

These five form the basis for discussion in this chapter.

NOMADIC HUNTING– GATHERING

Early man first subsisted as a hunter and gatherer. At this culture stage, which was during the Old Stone Age, hunting–gathering peoples drifted widely over the land; their tools were sufficiently specialized to suggest the conditions of procuring food in a broad regional environment. Perhaps 50,000 years ago, modern man in his present physical state appeared. Concurrently a new genre of tools became evident—the blade tools that incorporate a qualitatively higher degree of usefulness and skill in fabrication. This new man using the new tools substituted more systematic food collection and organized hunting for the simple gathering and scavenging of his predecessors. As time passed and the human population increased, men were able to adjust themselves to environments as diverse as the tropical jungle and the arctic tundra.

Today there are still people in certain areas of the world whose culture is that of the Old Stone Age, such as the Pygmies of the African rainforest, the Negritos of the Philippines, New Guinea, and Southeast Asia, the Bushmen of South Africa and Australia, and Paiutes of the western United States. These regions constitute an environment of low economic diversity; however, their great animal resources act

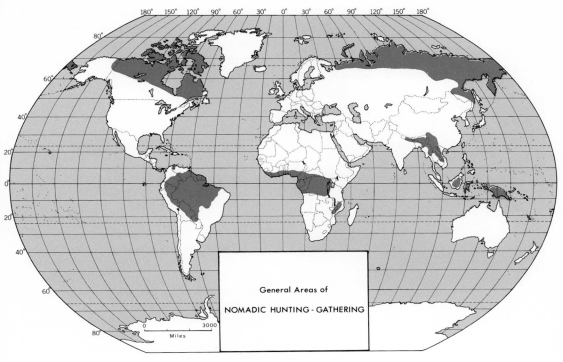

General Areas of

NOMADIC HUNTING - GATHERING

0   3000
Miles

FIGURE 11.1   *(General Media Corporation)*

as a natural staple to support the population. Much of the culture is built around this animal resource, as in the great arctic pastures of North America and Asia where caribou and reindeer are prevalent. These animals furnish most of the food, materials for clothing, shelter, tools, and weapons, and are often used as draft animals as in northern Siberia. All life and thought revolve about the principal animal resource. In just such a manner, the life and culture of the American plains Indians centered about the bison until the wave of whitemen swept across the continent, pushing both aside.

Without exception, the cultural groups that practice nomadic hunting and gathering live in the least desirable parts of the earth's surface, except for Antarctica and the highland wastes. Through bitter experience they have learned that isolation is imperative to their continued existence; only in an isolated habitat can they preserve their cultures. Generally, almost all of these hunting and gathering groups have decreased greatly within the past two hundred years, and especially in the last fifty. Invasion and introduction of diseases by whites, warfare among themselves, and the acquisition of skills that make other economies more attractive are the major reasons for this decline. Presently, approximately 300,000 are still engaged in a hunting–gathering economy. Table 11.1 shows their distribution by continents.

Table 11.1   Distribution of Hunting–Gathering Economies

North America	10,000
South America	20,000
Africa	170,000
Asia	50,000
Australia	50,000
Total	300,000

FIGURE 11.2 *A tribal chief of the Pintobe band of Australian aborigines. (Australian News and Information Bureau)*

The detailed examinations of two entirely different cultures, presented here as case studies of the hunting–gathering societies, should suffice, for their numbers are few and their impact on the world economy is slight.

case study

The Semang

The Semang, roughly 8,000 in number, inhabit the tropical rainforest of central Malaya. Daily activity begins at sunrise as the males enter the forest away from the overnight camp in search of food. Division of labor is on the basis of sex: the males hunt and the women, after cleaning up the camp site, go out in the opposite direction in search of edible plants. The tropical rainforest is well known to these people, whose social, religious, and economic customs have been handed down from generation to generation for centuries. The Semang move through the forest as easily as an urban dweller moves along a sidewalk.

The actual hunting activity takes place during the rainstorm that occurs almost daily in the forest. This helps to drown out any noise the hunters might make. Their *bows* are quite primitive; the bow strings are made of woven grass, bark, or vines. They do not know the principle of *feathering* the arrow, and thus must get quite close to the quarry to make a kill. Some Semang use the blowpipe, which was borrowed from the Senoi who live just to the south in the Malay Peninsula. The few numbers of each animal species and their relatively small size requires that the hunters range over a wide area. The major items of meat in the diet are bats, ground rodents, monkeys, snakes, birds, and lizards.

While the men are hunting animals, the women are seeking edible plants, mainly cassava, taro, plantain, flowers, seeds, and other foods high in starch. The relatively infertile lateritic soils of the tropical rainforest produce little else of food value to man. When hunting and gathering is over, usually late in the afternoon, the tribe again assembles in the area of the previous night. Here the men prepare the animals and the women the plants; both are then cooked by the women. Food consumption consists of whatever was killed or gathered during the day.

Economy

Minor details of resource use differ quite widely from area to area, and even between groups in the same area. Generally, however, most of these groups do have a similar outlook or interpretation of their environment. Their material culture is necessarily limited. Tools are rather primitive, varying from the bow and arrow and blowgun of the tropical rainforest to the boomerang of Australia or the spear of the Kalahari Bushmen. Clothing is scanty among the hunting–gathering societies of the tropics, usually consisting of loincloths made from bark, leaves, grasses, or animal skins. In the higher latitude of the tundra, the nomads dress with animal skins from caribou, seal, or reindeer carefully treated and made into parkas, mukluks, and gloves. Only in this way can they survive the subzero temperatures of these cold lands. Dwellings must be either temporary or portable, as constant movement precludes any investment in permanent structures. These also vary greatly depending upon the natural environment.

Each band of Semang, approximately twenty to thirty in number, roams in a fifteen to twenty square mile area, and its territorial claims are recognized by its neighbors. These primitive food gatherers have acquired an amazing knowledge of the rainforest flora, and have learned to make use of the leaves, flowers, seeds, nuts, berries, fruits, bark, tubers, and roots. Some have not only found ways of making poisonous vegetable substances edible but have also developed elaborate techniques of food preservation. For instance, at certain times of the year the Semang live largely on the poisonous seeds of the Piah tree, which contains hydrocyanic acid. If the seeds are needed immediately, they are boiled or roasted; otherwise they are pounded in water or rasp-packed into bark cloth or bamboo tubes, buried in wet earth for a month or more, and allowed to ferment. This treatment not only removes the poison but also preserves the food for several weeks.

Given the limited animal and plant resources of the rainforest, it is easy to see why a migratory hunting–gathering culture persists among the Semang. However primitive their existence may seem, advanced civilizations have come up with only one or possibly two other economies that might exist in the tropical rainforest and not destroy it. The Semang live very close to their environment, in a culture that cannot cope with it in any other way, and, owing to their lack of technology, they have been unable to improve it.

case study

Kalahari Bushmen

In many of the drier parts of the earth's surface, opportunity is too limited to tempt more advanced populations to settle. Therefore, the aboriginal inhabitants still maintain possession, retaining many of their age-old characteristics and clinging to most of their traditional ways of obtaining a living.

The Kalahari Bushmen are a race of primitive people who dwell in the western part of South Africa, in the immense plains bordering on the Cape of Good Hope. They are among the least-civilized peoples of the world; uniting only for defense or pillage, they have no established homes and do not cultivate the land.

The Bushmen are small people, less than five feet tall, but of excellent stature (even by Western standards), possessing strong supple arms and legs and a muscular torso. Only in the abdominal section are the Bushmen perhaps somewhat unsightly, owing to the great amount of food they must store in their bodies. Their food habits are dictated by the game supply or plant cover available to them at the moment, for the "wild" Bushmen still depend on what they can gather and the meat of the animals they kill. Feast or famine is their lot. During the short rainy season, game abounds and food is plentiful. The Bushmen then gorge themselves, grotesquely distending their stomachs. With the coming of the drought period, however, the game disappears. Since the Bushmen make no provision for the future, food scarcity and eventually famine follow. Their bodies become emaciated and they are reduced to eating even the ragged skins that clothe them.

Bushmen are hunters of consummate skill, in spite of their paleolithic equipment, which consists of throwing sticks, spears, and bows and arrows tipped with poison. Their sense of sight and hearing highly developed, they stealthily stalk game until they are close enough to kill it with their crude weapons. Even in the Kalahari there is game to hunt, quite a lot in some regions: desert animals such as gemsbok and springbok, and long-distance travelers like the giraffe, elephant, and ostrich, which often go far for water; in the less arid parts, and elsewhere during the flush that follows the rains, wildebeeste, kudu, buffalo, and pig. Parts of the Kalahari even have a fair rainfall, fifteen or twenty inches per year, but this comes during two or at most three months, and the remainder of the year is a long period of drought and thirst, great heat and winter cold.

The collection of veld foods, in which the women specialize, probably contributes more to the food supply than hunting. Even this semi-desert can provide, for those who have the knowledge and skill to seek and find them, a list of foodstuffs that is long and varied, if not particularly appetizing. It includes a considerable range of edible roots, tubers, and melons —some of which also provide water, the only available water for part of the year—wild cucumbers, berries and pulses, honey, fungi, and green-leafed vegetables, and small creatures such as lizards, desert rats, hares, tortoises,

FIGURE 11.3   *The Kalahari country—home of the Bushmen.*

termites, and snakes. But the Kalahari is, for the most part, a hostile and hungry country, where water is often a greater problem than food, and the survival of the Bushmen in such an environment must be regarded as no small achievement.

Social organization is very simple. A group consists of roughly twenty people—a man, his wives, their children and grandchildren. Polygamy is quite widespread among the Bushmen, primarily because this relationship produces more offspring than monogamy and the group is more apt to survive. Allegiance to any form of organization other than the local group is unknown. These people do not consider themselves a part of any other culture, society, association, or nationality. The existence of some idea such as a political unit, governmental control, or organization is entirely foreign, and perhaps would be catastrophic to

their culture. No other suitable economic activity has been devised that can utilize the known resources of the Kalahari so intensively as does the economic system of the Bushmen.

NOMADIC HERDING

Animal husbandry is not the same, nor can it be directly associated with, the hunting–gathering system. The Kalahari Bushmen, the Semang, and most of the Amerindians, among others, were not engaged in animal husbandry. Animal husbandry is associated only with those activities in which animals are domesticated. The Eskimo, for example, generally is not engaged in animal husbandry,

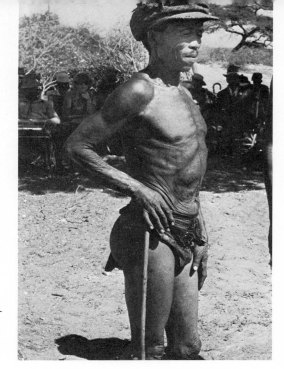

FIGURE 11.4 *A typical Kalahari Bushman. (Botswana Information Services)*

FIGURE 11.5 *An Eskimo with reindeer in Alaska—note the tundra landscape. (Alaska Travel Division)*

since he is a hunter and not a herdsman; in some cases, however, with the introduction of reindeer or domesticated caribou, the Eskimo has been induced to take up reindeer herding instead of hunting. Thus, some Eskimos have changed from hunting animals to animal husbandry.

Knowledge of the original domestication of animals is lost in the dark period of prehistory. The methods of domestication can only be surmised from such indirect evidence as the attitudes and habits of primitive peoples concerning the animals around them. Presumably the initial steps were taken largely through the widespread human practice of making pets of captured young or crippled wild animals.

People in a paleolithic (Old Stone Age) culture generally had no truly domestic animal, except perhaps the dog. Cattle and sheep were domesticated as early as 7,000 B.C. in Asia Minor. Horses first appeared as domesticated animals about 3,000 B.C., and mounted invaders from the north brought them into the Tigris–Euphrates Valley as early as 2,000 B.C. Chickens were domesticated in southeastern Asia perhaps by 2,500 B.C. Only the llama, alpaca, guinea pig, and turkey were domesticated in Latin America. American Indians north of Mexico had no domesticated animals except dogs.

Whatever and wherever the first domesticated animals were, it is quite certain that many animals in many places were domesticated for a multitude of uses. For example, in the great division of original agriculture—vegetable planting versus seed planting—animals such as cats, chickens, and ducks are considered household animals. With the seed planters go the herd animals such as camels, goats, sheep, yak, horses, and *Bos indicus*[1] and *Bos taurus*.[2]

Animals commonly associated with no-

madism were not domesticated by nomads but by sedentary agriculturalists. Nomadism originally developed *after* sedentary agriculture and *after* the domestication of sheep, cattle, goats, and camels. Therefore, the origins of nomadism are to be found not in deserts now traveled by nomads but in areas of original seed domestication and cultivation. It was primarily through the cultivation of seed (grains) able to withstand long dry periods, and animals also able to withstand long droughts, that nomadism developed from seed planting.

It is quite a tribute to early man that no major species of plants or animals have been domesticated since about 2000 B.C. All of the so-called modern plants and modern animals are not newly domesticated species, but only cross-breeds of species domesticated thousands of years ago.

Nomadism as an Economic Activity

Not only does animal husbandry cover a larger area of the world's surface than any other agricultural activity, but nomadism occupies an area larger than any other single economic activity. Nomadism is characterized by:

1. Location in semi-arid or arid regions
2. Migratory habits
3. Grazing of animals on native or wild plants
4. Almost complete dependence of man on the animal population for his transportation, food, shelter, tools, clothing, and fuel
5. A level of technology often too low to apply any principles of cross-breeding or hybridization to the animals to improve their quality
6. Near-subsistence production

In many areas, nomadism is a product of cultural associations that may be as dominant a factor in the activity as the phys-

---

[1]*Bos indicus* (zebu or humpbacked cattle) are tolerant of high temperatures and high humidity, and thrive on coarse forage. Thus, this species does well in the humid tropics.

[2]*Bos taurus* includes a wide variety of cattle breeds best adapted to the middle latitude areas where mild to cold winters alternate with cool to warm summers.

ical landscape, which greatly limits the resource base. For example, many Arabs who are Moslems prefer nomadism to a sedentary way of life because of long tradition and historic events. In other areas without the benefits of modern technology and capital investment, nomadism is the only economic system that can survive.

Perhaps one wonders why, instead of migrating from one seasonal pasture to another, the nomads do not head straight for the perennial green pastures and settle there. In many cases this has been done, as by the Israelites who settled in Canaan. Invariably, when a nomadic society attempts to inhabit an already settled area of perennial grass, warfare is the result. In many instances the warfare may not be limited only to the local area. For example, the Huns, a nomadic people from the Asiatic steppe, ravaged northwestern China for centuries. In 375 A.D. the first wave of Huns appeared in Eastern Europe, in the steppe lands north of the Caspian and Black Seas. By the end of the fifth century they swept almost to the Atlantic. The Moors, a Mohammedan Arabic-speaking race of mixed descent, overran Spain (711–713 A.D.) and pushed northward into France, until their repulse by Charles Martel at the Battle of Tours in 732, after which they practically restricted themselves to Spain south of the Ebro. In 1241 Mongol nomads invaded the West as far as Poland. Turkish nomads laid seige to the city of Vienna (1529), and during the sixteenth and seventeenth centuries the Manchus invaded China Proper.

In many instances these invasions were triggered by a series of unusually dry years in the steppe areas occupied by nomadic tribes. With no grass to eat the herds die, famine results, and the desert clans raid the oases of other clans. If the drought is prolonged, vast migrations such as those mentioned above take place. Hence, the law of survival of the fittest tends to operate to some degree in human affairs too.

Often nomads are assimilated into the existing population. The Huns, for example, never returned to eastern Asia. Instead, they were gradually absorbed into the European milieu. The Manchus, Tatars, and other such nomadic tribes of northern and eastern Asia were fused into the population of China Proper. Almost invariably, when a nomadic tribe inhabits an area of sedentary agriculture over a sustained period, the nomadic activity disappears. It blends in with the livestock–crop associations, and nomadism as a way of life ceases.

There has been a conscious effort on the part of some governments to make nomads sedentary. Egypt has attempted this with moderate success. Iran and Iraq have taken measures to permanently settle more than three million nomads. Somali, Israel, Tanzania, and the Soviet Union also have experimented with this activity. The United States did it in the past century by establishing *reservations* for the Amerindian.

The principal regions of pastoral nomadism are in the arid lands of the Old World, extending from North Africa through Saudi Arabia to inner Asia. This type of highly specialized livelihood involves frequent movement of livestock in response to the need for grazing lands and water. Settlement is generally characterized by small clusters of homesteads temporarily established near a common waterpoint and pasture. Subsistence is obtained almost entirely from domestic stock such as cattle, camels, goats, and sheep.

SHIFTING CULTIVATION

In most cases, shifting cultivators dwell in greater numbers in the tropical wet and tropical wet–dry climates. Generally, the location of these economic activities not only coincides with the above climates but also is adjacent to the hunting–gathering societies. In many instances, the reasons for the shifting cultivators being located in these relatively isolated areas are

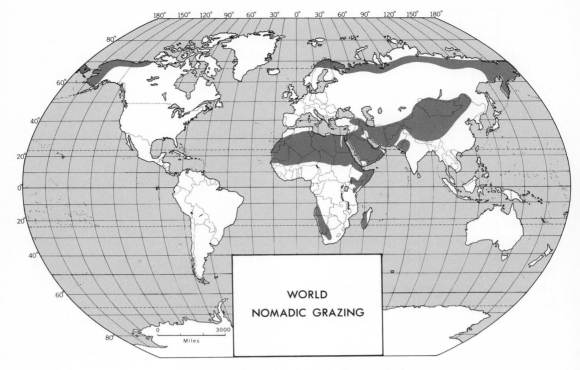

FIGURE 11.6   (General Media Corporation)

FIGURE 11.7   A grazing scene in Tunisia, North Africa. (Government of Tunisia)

the same for the hunting–gathering systems. These include:

1. A forcible exile into remote areas by advanced cultures occupying the more desirable lands
2. Self-exile to preserve cultural characteristics
3. A socioeconomic organization that can be manifested better here than elsewhere

Subtypes

Three major subtypes of shifting cultivators may be recognized. The first, or least advanced, usually consists of a hunting–gathering tribe that supplements its activities by very primitive agricultural techniques. Quite often no tools are employed, not even sticks. The ground is not plowed in any way. Wherever there is a natural clearing in the forest, seeds are placed in holes dug either by hand or stick. This subtype of shifting cultivators does not till or care for the crops. As the crops are growing they practice an economic system almost identical to the simple hunting–gathering economy. When the crops mature, however, the shifting cultivators return to harvest them. Obviously, due to insects, fungi, and other such pests, crop yields are low. In this socioeconomic system, the hunting–gathering economy is the major source of livelihood, and the very limited agriculture that is practiced is only supplementary.

The next stage or type of shifting cultivation consists of semi-permanent dwellings made of materials easily gathered from the immediate area. These dwellings usually are occupied for about three to four years and the agricultural activities occur in the adjacent area.

The third and most common subtype of migratory agriculture is that in which the tribe is relatively well settled in the same area for periods of up to twenty to thirty years. Here the forest is cleared in patches —one clearing will be used for several years, then an adjacent one. After several clearings are made and their soil resources depleted, migration must take place. The dwellings and fields are abandoned and a new area is sought.

Physical Environment

As mentioned previously, these cultures are mainly located in the wet and wet–dry tropical regions. These areas are usually unsuitable for any other type of economic activity, plantation agriculture being a possible exception. The grass sod of the wet–dry savanna is not conducive to this type of economic endeavor, for agriculture on heavy soils requires power greater than man alone. In the forests of the humid tropics the soil is heavily leached, friable, crumbles easily, and hence is possible to stir with a stick.

Level land is preferred for this type of agriculture as with most others. However, in some areas, such as the Asian tropics, competition with the more advanced rice-eaters has driven the shifting cultivators to the rough infertile uplands. The flat coastal marshes of the Guinea coast also are not sufficient; here the rather mucky, dense, and heavy soil will not yield good crops.

Agricultural Techniques

Migration cultivation, or the production of annual food or fiber crops in temporary clearings in the forest, is widespread. This practice is called *milpa* in the Amazon Valley, *fang* in the Congo Basin, and *ladang* in Southeast Asia. Trees are girdled or felled with either stone or iron axes. After they have been dried by the high temperatures, they are piled and burned. Later the ashes are spread over the ground to restore fertility. The temporarily enriched soil is stirred with a digging stick by the more primitive groups, or with a hoe among more advanced peoples, after which the crops are planted.

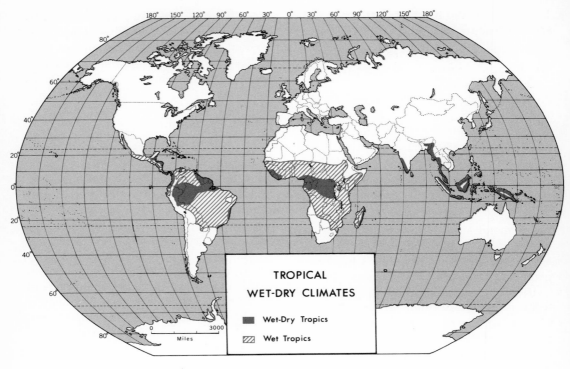

FIGURE 11.8   *(General Media Corporation)*

Crops

Usually only one or two vegetable crops are planted per family in the wet tropics—perhaps a few beans and melons, or yams, taro, and cassava—although a wide variety of tree crops (coconuts, breadfruit, oil palm, mangoes, avocados, bananas, plantains, cacao, guava) and vegetable crops (yams, sweet potatoes, pumpkins, beans, and peanuts) are cultivated throughout the area. A little rice and corn are grown in a few places where exogenous forces have introduced them. Sugar cane and millet are also grown here and there. Within a year or two, however, weeds and other pests become serious, or the fertility declines. Then the land is abandoned to forest and a new clearing is made.

Bread is made from cassava or manioc, which is a staple in the diet of the more sedentary cultivators. Bananas, yams, and sweet potatoes provide abundant starch; coconuts and oil palms supply the needed fats. But there is a dearth of protein in the diet, and these people consume too much starch, which results in protruding abdomens, even among little children.

Production and Soil Nutrients

At first glance it would appear that the tropical humid areas are rich in soil nutrients since they support a dense vegetation. In some cases this is true. However, the available nutrients, climatic conditions, and vegetative growth is such that almost all nutrients are being used or stored in the vegetation or are being leached from the soil by the constant rains.

As the plants absorb and use minerals from the soil, they are not returned to the soil until the leaves fall or until the

FIGURE 11.9 *Manioc ready for grinding into meal (flour)—a common scene throughout the tropics. (Malagasy Director of Information)*

FIGURE 11.10 *Preparing manioc to be planted in the Amazon region of Brazil. (U.S.O.M.)*

tree matures, dies, falls, and then decays. Since the growing season is year-long in the wet tropics and at least six months in the wet–dry tropics, the density of fallen decaying trees or ground vegetation is rather slight at any one time. Also, the constantly high temperatures produce a high density of organic decaying bacteria. Therefore almost all nutrients present are not available for man to use.

Thus, man must clear and burn portions of the forest to make soil nutrients available. When the vegetation is burned, the cycle of nature is broken and for a time the soil is relatively rich. Unfortunately, the bulk of these nutrients are valuable only to starchy plant foods. The period of soil enrichment is rather short. Usually the first crop yield is good; however, the second is only a fraction of the first, and the third and fourth harvests fall off appreciably. Since these people do not possess the ideas, tools, and techniques necessary to cope with this problem of soil depletion, they are forced to move on —hence their name, migratory agricul-

turists. Table 11.2 shows their general distribution and numbers.

Table 11.2 Distribution of Migratory Agriculturalists

Central America	250,000
South America	1,100,000
Africa	30,000,000
Madagascar	1,000,000
India	5,000,000
Southeast Asia	5,500,000
Philippines	200,000
New Guinea	500,000
Indonesia	10,000,000
Total	53,550,000

SEDENTARY SUBSISTENCE AGRICULTURE

Throughout the areas inhabited by hunting–gathering and shifting cultivating societies, over the centuries many groups have changed their economic systems. Quite often such changes have occurred in a more progressive direction.

In general, many of the more primitive forms have gradually evolved into sedentary subsistence agricultural systems.

People will change their entire pattern of living only when there is considerable pressure from some source to cause such a radical shift. One such example is that of population pressure—the increase of people living in a limited area—which results in:

1. A lower standard of living and a switch to other forms of resources
2. Migration to other areas
3. A change in the socioeconomic activities that will maintain the essentials of the existing patterns while transforming those of lesser necessity or tradition

Environment

The characteristics of most tropical humid soils have already been mentioned. However, there are four major soil types that are of sufficient fertility to support, with intensive agricultural techniques, a relatively dense population. These are alluvial, grassland, swamp soils, and soils of volcanic origin. *Alluvial* soils are quite fertile because of the consistent inundation of river lands by annual floodings. *Grassland* soils contain relatively large amounts of nutrients owing to inconsistent noncontinuous precipitation. *Swamp* soils are not leached of organic matter because of a high water table existing in the area. Recently developed *volcanic* soils are also quite fertile and may be replenished easily in active volcanic lands.

Variations of Sedentary Agriculture

Production of foodstuffs and other plants for local use takes many forms in terms of the products grown (rice, tubers, fruits), the techniques used (tools, irrigation, use of work animals), intensity (settled agriculture, minor gardening), organization (ownership of land, financing, work methods), and other variables. Native communities often supplement their subsistence cropping to some extent with saleable products. Growing rubber or pepper, or making copra from coconuts, for example, provides them with money to help fill their minimum needs for imported goods.

Location

Latin America. Much of the sedentary subsistence farming in Latin America is still characterized by extravagant employment of human labor, little use of machinery, forest destruction, and soil wastage and erosion. The pattern of farming usually followed consists of:

1. Felling with axes all but the largest trees, which are girdled
2. Burning of forest and ground vegetation
3. Planting with hoe or stick (such crops as corn, beans, rice, manioc, and even cotton)
4. Chopping weeds with machete
5. Harvesting a few crops, usually not more than three or four
6. Planting grasses to be grazed until scrubby trees choke them out, or simply abandoning the land for a newly-cleared plot

Africa. Traditionally, Congolese agriculture is little better than subsistence agriculture. Small family-owned farms produce cassava and plantain bananas, along with some sweet potatoes, yams, rice, and sugar cane. These are grown for home consumption.

The hoe is the most important tool in African sedentary subsistence farming. Other important agricultural implements are the axe and the bush knife, used to cut trees and shrubs when new clearings are made. The cultivated crops of the wet–dry savanna lands are mainly shrubs such as the cotton bush, small plants such as tobacco and the peanut, or domes-

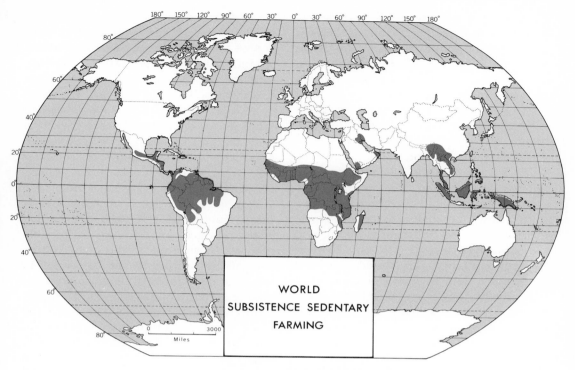

FIGURE 11.11 *(General Media Corporation)*

ticated grasses—maize and millet. Corn, wheat, barley, rice, sorghum, sweet potatoes, and various types of beans are staple items of the diet. Secondary crops commonly grown in the savanna lands are manioc, sesame, artichokes, peppers, tomatoes, pumpkins, henna, and indigo.

Asia. In south and east Asia the dominant subsistent sedentary agricultural techniques are more complex than any in the world. This is a land of real tropical farmers. Monsoon Asia's dry and cool season gives man more energy than in the wet tropics. Then, too, the task of clearing and maintaining a farm is relatively easy. The young trees and dry grass are burned near the close of the dry season. The ground is then stirred with hoes and crops are planted at the beginning of the rains. Since this is a land of grass, the crops that are planted are primarily grains, which are domesticated grasses. Rice,

many varieties of millet, guinea corn, kaffir corn, sorghums, maize (introduced by traders and missionaries), wheat, and others are sown. Cotton and sugar cane are also important. Since the rainy season is rather short, irrigation is often practiced during part of the year.

Soils, generally alluvial in nature, occur in the major drainage basins such as the Irrawaddy, Salween, Menam, Mekong, Red, Yangtze, and Si Rivers. These soils are naturally fertile, but owing to intensive tillage they require high amounts of fertilizer derived from animal and human sources. The latter is by far the most widely used in Southeast Asia, because the population is so dense that animals are relatively few.

Fields are relatively small, often averaging less than two acres per farm. Thus, in order to feed, clothe, and house a family of up to ten people, yields have to be high and methods intensive. Labor is supplied mainly by hand, although a few highly skilled groups use animal power, as in parts of South Vietnam. Due to the high labor requirements of rice cultivation (the dominant food crop), ninety percent or more of the agricultural population often is employed in the planting, cultivating, and harvesting of this important grain.

Before the monsoon rains begin, the fields are tilled (stock, hoe, or plow) and flooded with water. The rice is then planted and the fields remain flooded until a few days before harvest. Almost every member of the family, young and old, is engaged in some manner in helping to produce the rice crop. Terraces are built or mended. Soil, washed from the fields, is carried on the backs of men to the upper fields in order not to lose it. Even the water inundating the paddy field is planted with fish, which serve not only as food but also supply fertilizer for the rice.

INTENSIVE SUBSISTENCE— RICE DOMINANT

Rice is the staple food of Southeast Asia. It is so prevalent in the peasant economy that an agricultural system, based on intensive tillage, night soil, multiple cropping, and hand labor, has been developed around this dominant crop. It should be emphasized that the Southeast Asian farmer's methods of agriculture would no doubt remain the same whether the crop were rice or soybeans or manioc.

If wheat is the staff of life of the Western world, then rice is life for much of the East. More than one-third of the world's population is totally dependent upon this marsh grass for survival. Its great popularity stems from the fact that rice is relatively easy to grow and is easy to prepare. Unlike wheat or corn, it requires no milling and mixing and baking, but is simply boiled and eaten.

The very adaptability of rice has, until recent times, hampered research into the development of new varieties and improved farming techniques that would produce better yields. Today, however, with the population explosion, yield per acre must be increased as well. Although by Asian standards none of the developed countries are big rice producers, they have made the greatest advances in production. Asia, with some 208 million acres under cultivation, averages only 1,602 pounds per acre. The United States has nearly 1.8 million acres in rice, but reaps nearly 4,000 pounds per acre. That the United States produces any rice at all probably comes as a surprise to those who think only of the "amber waves" of wheat in the nation's Midwest. Even more surprising is that while the United States accounts for just over one percent of the world's total rice production, it is the second largest rice exporter, trailing only Thailand. This is because most of the world's rice goes no further than the farm where it is grown; less than five percent of the crop is traded across national frontiers.

Rice farming in developed countries such as the United States requires large-scale mechanization in order to be profitable. Seeding is done by air, fields are leveled and diked with special machines, and harvesting is accomplished by self-propelled combines that reduce a field of rice to bulk form in one brisk operation. Large amounts of chemical fertilizers are used. Obviously, the above methods account for the higher yields but are beyond the scope of pre-industrial agriculture in Southeast Asia.

Wet (Sawah) Rice

Throughout the countries bordering the South China Sea most of the cultivated land is used for the growing of lowland or wet rice. Fields must be leveled and surrounded by earth dams to impound rain water during the rainy season, or to confine the water carried to the fields through

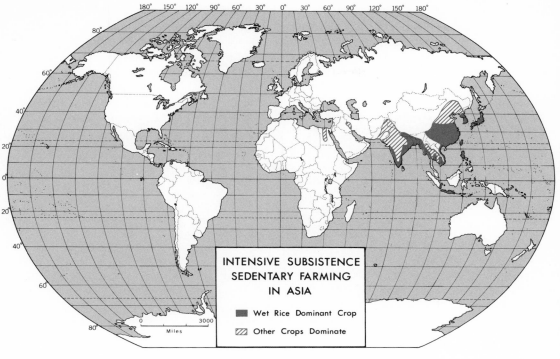

FIGURE 11.12   (General Media Corporation)

irrigation canals or lifted to the fields by mechanical means. If the field is properly leveled the surrounding dike will keep the water everywhere at the same depth. The size of the wet-rice or paddy fields and the amount of labor that is required to make them depend upon the topography of the region. In the lowlands, where no terracing is required, relatively little labor is involved in making the paddies, which are frequently large. Hilly or mountainous terrain, on the other hand, necessitates terracing, which demands greater effort and reduces the size of individual fields —the steeper the slope, the narrower the paddies.

The problems presented by the cultivation of wet or lowland rice vary from country to country, region to region, and sometimes even from village to village. Lowland rice demands a soil thoroughly soaked with water and worked into a fine

soft mud by hoeing, plowing, trampling, or harrowing. The field must remain under water until the ears of rice begin to fill and harvest time approaches. The amount of water required to grow lowland rice depends upon the particular variety of rice, length of its growing period, and the nature of the soil. There are many varieties of lowland rice. Classified on the basis of the time required from planting to harvest, these are: quick maturing (60 days), medium maturing (150–190 days), and late maturing (up to 300 days).

Regardless of where rice is grown as a subsistence crop in Southeast Asia, several generalizations about rice cultivation may be made:

1. Back-breaking labor
2. Intensive tillage
3. High moisture requirements—38 to 40

FIGURE 11.13 *Preparation of a rice seedbed in Thailand, to produce seed that will later be transplanted. The ground is stirred up by the men with heavy hoes, then puddled by the feet of the women into a smooth pasty mixture. Presoaked rice seed is then spread thickly on the puddled surface. (USDA)*

FIGURE 11.14 *Harvesting rice—the staff of life in Southeast Asia. (Embassy of Cambodia)*

inches of annual precipitation or its equivalent through irrigation
4. Relatively heavy clay soils, with relatively impervious subsoils
5. Green manuring and/or night soil
6. Use of hand tools
7. Great population density

IR-8: Key to Economic Stability?

IR-8 is a so-called miracle rice—a high yield, hybrid strain developed several years ago at the International Rice Research Institute in the Philippines. It has been cultivated in Vietnam for the past few years, initially introduced by U.S. agricultural advisers in the provinces. These officials see the rice as a key to this plundered nation's economic stability.

As recently as 1964, Vietnam was a rice-exporting nation, But, as fighting intensified, millions of peasant farmers were forced off their land and into towns and cities, cutting production while increasing market demand in the cities. South Vietnam currently is importing more than 600,000 tons of American and Thai rice per year to supplement its own production of 2.5 million tons.

Experts now believe that even when the war ends many of these peasant farmers will not return to their paddies. Thus, the farmers that remain on must have a stronger, higher-yielding rice to return the nation to self-sufficiency and, eventually, to rice exporting.

IR-8 has anywhere from two to six times the yield of local rice strains. Moreover, it is highly adaptable to seasonal changes and unlike local strains can be planted and harvested twice a year. But there are drawbacks. Aside from its lack of taste, IR-8 often requires more irrigation and considerable use of fertilizer and pesticides than local rice varieties, making it more costly to produce. Also, there is a high grain loss when it is milled, cutting down profitability. And some economists say that when the day comes that Vietnam is ready to export rice, the world may not want

IR-8. Other experts, however, insist IR-8 is the rice of the future, and they claim there already is a demand for it in several Asian, African, and South American countries.

INTENSIVE SUBSISTENCE— RICE UNIMPORTANT

Much of interior India, dry inland portions of Southeast Asia, and Mainland China north of the Yangtze, although still cultivated intensively, differ in the nature and methods of crop production. As previously discussed, where rice is dominant, water is supplied either through man-made irrigation systems or by natural rainfall and flooding. Where the natural rainfall is insufficient or undependable and man is unable to afford costly irrigation systems, grains other than rice become the staples of diet. India and China are classic examples of intensively cultivated, densely populated lands with the bulk of their labor force engaged in subsistence agriculture. As such they merit further attention.

India

Agriculture is the mainstay of India's economic life, as well as its greatest economic problem. In simple terms, India has too many people on too little land. Productivity is among the lowest in the world because of primitive techniques, poor seed, a highly seasonal distribution of rainfall, and land tenure systems that have provided little incentive to the actual cultivator. In the last decade, land reform, agricultural extension services, better seed, and a rapidly expanding use of fertilizer have put the increase in food production slightly ahead of the increase in population; however, the enormous population pressure on the land remains (there are an estimated 45 million landless agricultural laborers) and India will continue to be a food deficit nation for many years.

To a very great extent, the cultivator in India labors not for profit or a net return but for subsistence. The overcrowded population, lack of alternative means of securing a living, difficulty of finding any avenue of escape, and the early age at which man is burdened with dependents combine to force the farmer to grow food on whatever terms he can.

Illiteracy, conservatism, superstition, and fatalism—widespread among Indian farmers—play a large part in preserving India's centuries-old agricultural methods. The peasant still sows and reaps by hand; he does not make full use of the available manure from livestock and seldom uses artificial fertilizer. Approximately four-fifths of the cultivable area in India is dependent on the rainy seasons or monsoons, and crop failures in various parts of the country have been a recurrent feature of India's agriculture.

Of the major subsistence grains cultivated in the drier parts of India, sorghum, millet, and wheat occupy the greatest acreage of inefficiently worked land. Sorghum is widely distributed over the Deccan Plateau, but is most heavily concentrated on the black soils in the central part of the peninsula. Millet is the major grain in the extreme northwest and Rajasthan portions of India bordering West Pakistan. Wheat is grown mainly in the northwestern and central parts of India. Other secondary crops include gram or chickpea, which is the most widely grown pulse crop of India and extends from the Punjab plains eastward up to the delta region; peanuts, which are highly concentrated in the southern half of the peninsula; and cotton, produced mostly in the northwestern and central parts of the Deccan Plateau.

Mainland China

China, like the United States, can be divided into fairly well-defined regions. The most clear-cut separation is between north and south, and the dividing line follows generally along the Yangtze Valley. South of the Yangtze the green of South China is the green of the rice fields. Rice is the universally cultivated crop in this region, for rainfall is plentiful and the air is moist and warm almost year round.

North of the Yangtze, the green countryside dies away quite suddenly into brown, except for a momentary revival where the Yellow River forges its treacherous way to the sea. North China is a region of plains, both fertile and barren, and of bare mountains. Like the south, there is much rich soil, but the richness is less stable because of infrequent and uncertain rainfall. Prolonged droughts may come to parch the soil and burn the crops out before harvest —or, nature is fickle enough to bring sudden outbursts of rain that produce devastating floods.

Despite this climate, North China is a highly productive region. The area near the coast, the famous North China (Yellow) Plain, is one of the most densely populated and most intensively cultivated parts of the country. Better known as the winter wheat–kaoliang (a kind of sorghum) region, it comprises most of Hopei, Shantung, and Honan provinces. Because of its high percentage of cultivable land (60 percent or more under cultivation) the winter wheat–kaoliang section produces a wide variety of crops without irrigation. Fortunately, the maximum rainfall (24 inches annually) occurs during the hot summer. Winter wheat is the principal crop and occupies about 45 percent of the cultivated land. No other winter crop is planted to any extent, although barley and peas are grown in a few districts.

Kaoliang, the chief summer crop, is well adapted to the climate, producing large amounts of grain and stalks for human food and fuel. Soybeans, cotton, corn, and sweet potatoes also cover a considerable area in the summer. Delicious persimmons and hard pears are important fruits. Peanuts are cultivated in many districts, especially in Shantung and Honan, and flue-cured tobacco is grown in a few localities. No other agricultural area has so much diversification.

To the west of the winter wheat–kaoliang region are the Loess Highlands, an area of wind-blown silt deposits three hundred or more feet thick in places, with fertile soils, steep slopes, and marginal rainfall. More than one-third of the cropland is terraced, not in order to flood the fields, but to check erosion of the steep hillsides. The best agricultural districts are along the Yellow River in southern Shansi and northern Honan, extending west into Shensi. Winter wheat, the major crop, is confined to the plains and valleys; other winter crops, of only minor importance but extensively planted in some localities, are rapeseed, peas, and barley. Millet is the most widely grown summer crop, followed by corn, soybeans, sesame, and buckwheat, with cotton important in some of the better agricultural districts.

The spring wheat region forms a fringe along the Mongolian frontier, lying on either side of the Great Wall. The percentage of cultivable land is small, owing to the colder climate and a very limited rainfall. Spring wheat is the principal crop, with millet, oats, peas, flax, and buckwheat following.

SUBSISTENCE CROP AND LIVESTOCK FARMING

Subsistence crop and livestock farming occupies large tracts of semi-desert, hilly, or mountainous lands in the Anatolian and Iranian plateaus in southwest Asia, portions of Soviet Siberia bordering the Mongolian People's Republic, and small segments in Soviet Europe north of the 55th parallel. The Carpathian and Rhodope mountain areas of east-central and southeastern Europe also have small tracts of land that are still classified as subsistence crop and livestock farming. The only area of significance outside the Eurasian realm is the Mexican plateau.

People engaged in this dual activity are few. In the past, most of them followed a nomadic way of life, but inroads are constantly being made on the lands they occupy through government intervention, improvements in agricultural techniques, resettlement programs and the like. For the most part, agriculture and animal husbandry tend to become separate occupations. The mixed type of farming characteristic of many parts of the world is practiced only on a small scale, and many villages maintain one or more shepherds to look after all animals in common, while the great majority of owners devote themselves entirely to cultivation.

Herding tends to be restricted to less favorable regions. Those people who still persist in this endeavor have become semi-nomadic villagers who move their flocks in summer to hillsides or alpine mountain slopes where the animals graze until cold weather threatens. This transhumance system of vertical seasonal movement of flocks and herds is an ancient practice in Eurasia.

Because of population pressure, all lands capable of cultivation are given over to cereal growing, which produces a greater quantity of foodstuff per unit of area than land under pasture. Wherever possible, vegetables and fruits are cultivated. The Kurds of eastern Turkey and Armenia, Buryats of southeastern Siberia, and Yakuts north and west of Lake Baikal, U.S.S.R., are former nomadic herders who have become sedentary agriculturists still somewhat dependent on livestock, the latter being carried on as a semi-village function.

selected references

1. Baker, Simon, "Shifting Agriculture in Ceylon," *The Journal of Geography*, Vol. 67, No. 9, December 1968, pp. 564–568.

2. Bhatia, Shyam S., "A New Measure of Agricultural Efficiency in Uttar Pradesh, India," *Economic Geography*, Vol. 43, No. 3, July 1967, pp. 244–260.

3. Dyson-Hudson, Rada, "Subsistence Herding in Uganda," *Scientific American*, Vol. 220, No. 2, February 1969, pp. 76–89.

4. Floyd, Barry, and Adinde, Monica, "Farm Settlements in Eastern Nigeria: A Geographical Appraisal," *Economic Geography*, Vol. 43, No. 3, July 1967, pp. 231–243.

5. Harris, David R., "New Light on Plant Domestication and the Origins of Agriculture: A Review," *Geographical Review*, Vol. 57, No. 1, January 1967, pp. 90–107.

6. Henshall, Janet D., and King, Leslie J., "Some Structural Characteristics of Peasant Agriculture in Barbados," *Economic Geography*, Vol. 42, No. 1, January 1966, pp. 74–84.

7. Murdock, George Peter, "Staple Subsistence Crops of Africa," *Geographical Review*, Vol. 50, October 1960, pp. 523–540.

8. Nath, V., "The Growth of Indian Agriculture: A Regional Analysis," *Geographical Review*, Vol. 59, No. 3, July 1969, pp. 348–372.

9. Pelzer, Karl J., *Pioneer Settlement in the Asiatic Tropics*, New York: American Geographical Society, Special Publication, No. 29, 1945, especially Ch. 2, "The Shifting Cultivator," pp. 16–34, and Ch. 3, "The Sedentary Cultivator," pp. 43–78.

10. Petersen, William, *Population*, 2d. ed., New York: The Macmillan Company, 1969.

11. Pico, Rafael, "Notes on Geography and Development in the Tropics," *The Professional Geographer*, Vol. 20, No. 4, July 1968, pp. 227–229.

12. Rutherford, John, "Double Cropping of Wet Padi in Penang, Malaya," *Geographical Review*, Vol. 56, No. 2, April 1966, pp. 239–255.

13. Stenton, Jean E., "Rural Development in Malaysia," *Canadian Geographical Journal*, Vol. 77, No. 3, September 1968, pp. 84–93.

14. Vermeer, Donald E., "Geophagy Among the Tiv of Nigeria," *Annals of The Association of American Geographers*, Vol. 56, No. 2, June 1966, pp. 197–204.

15. Walters, R. F., "Some Forms of Shifting Cultivation in the South-West Pacific," *Journal of Tropical Geography*, Vol. 14, 1960, pp. 35–50.

introduction

to industrial agricultural systems

Industrial agriculture is a result of the application of industrial processes to the production of plants and animals. It presumes a productivity of commodities greater than that consumed by the producers, and therefore also assumes a marketing outlet outside the producing area. Industrial agriculture is associated almost exclusively with industrial societies, for only they possess the technology to coordinate large-scale production, storage, transportation, and marketing of agricultural goods.

The following broad systems of industrial agriculture will serve as the basis for discussion in Chapters 12 through 18:

1. Tropical commercial plantation
2. Mediterranean
3. Livestock ranching
4. Commercial grain farming
5. Commercial livestock and crop farming
6. Specialized horticulture
7. Dairying

chapter 12

Tropical Plantation Agriculture

Tropical plantation agriculture is usually a corporate enterprise that organizes the production of valuable commercial crops such as cotton, sugar cane, sugar beets, rubber, pineapple, bananas, coconut, tea, cacao, cloves, nutmeg, allspice, and citrus fruits. This is accomplished through factory-like production methods, with headquarters, a marketing organization, transport facilities, worker housing, and welfare facilities. Its *corporate organization* is the distinguishing feature from other forms of large-scale intensive agriculture.

This system is not characterized by any one special crop, but rather by the manner in which it is produced and the land managed. Neither is it strictly a phenomenon of the tropics or subtropics, for the system is employed in a wide range of extra-tropical regions. Plantations range from the production of bananas or rubber in the wet tropics to state and collective enterprises in the Soviet Union. Plantations may cultivate potatoes and sugar beets in California or grow varieties of fruits, vegetables, cotton, or tobacco in the southern United States. Monoculture no longer prevails as it once did. Even the tropical plantation system has tended toward crop diversification. For example, rubber and bananas are commonly paired, as in Haiti; citrus fruits and bananas are produced in tandem on plantations in British Honduras; cacao and oil palms in other parts of Central America; sugar cane, citrus fruit, and cattle in Florida.

Many of the crops usually identified with tropical plantations also are grown by non-plantation methods. Cacao and peanut production in Nigeria, rubber in Amazonia and Malaysia, bananas in Central America, and tea in Ceylon are produced by individual farmers, or even gathered without cultivation by individuals and sold to the plantations for export.

Diversification, although not the general rule, also is present in a plantation system. Many tropical plantation enterprises operate in several countries to minimize crop failures, destruction by hurricanes, attacks by pests or fungi, and other such destructive forces. Although the tropical plantation system of agriculture varies widely in operation, the following generalizations can be made:

1. Land in more than one geographical region, often with distinct separate tracts
2. Large land area cleared
3. Large capital investment
4. Application of scientific techniques: meteorology, soil, seed, fertilizer

5. Highly structured managerial arrangement
6. Production for commercial purposes
7. Highly integrated transportation and communication facilities

Table 12.1 shows the leading exporting and importing nations for a selected list of tropical products entering world trade.

The tropical plantation system was evolved to answer the specific need of meeting world demand for certain staple crops. It rested on acquisition by Europeans of areas of suitable land sufficient

Table 12.1   International Trade in Selected Tropical Plantation Crops (in metric tons)

Leading Exporters		Leading Importers	
Coffee			
Brazil	808,930	United States	1,280,030
Colombia	338,060	West Germany	275,940
Ivory Coast	185,650	France	217,070
Angola	159,170	Italy	120,540
Uganda	157,760	Sweden	91,910
Bananas			
Ecuador	1,200,000	United States	1,645,570
Honduras	571,560	France	830,080
Panama	335,540	West Germany	811,940
Taiwan	318,420	United Kingdom	646,910
Costa Rica	316,040	Japan	606,450
Sugar			
Cuba	5,315,600	United States	3,498,000
Brazil	760,000	U.S.S.R.	2,333,900
U.S.S.R.	656,700	United Kingdom	2,175,800
Mexico	527,700	Canada	847,200
Mainland China	362,300	France	435,400
Cacao (Cacao Beans)			
Ghana	501,920	United States	360,090
Nigeria	305,560	West Germany	166,930
Ivory Coast	126,410	Netherlands	119,340
Brazil	91,970	U.S.S.R.	88,800
Ecuador	39,280	United Kingdom	82,320
Natural Rubber			
Malaysia	1,050,620	United States	465,160
Indonesia	694,660	U.S.S.R.	271,200
Thailand	220,820	Japan	212,810
Ceylon	100,450	United Kingdom	200,340
Cambodia	68,700	West Germany	186,900

Source: United Nations, Food and Agricultural Organization, *Yearbook*, Vol. 20 (Rome, 1966), Tables 41, 58, 59, 60, and 94.

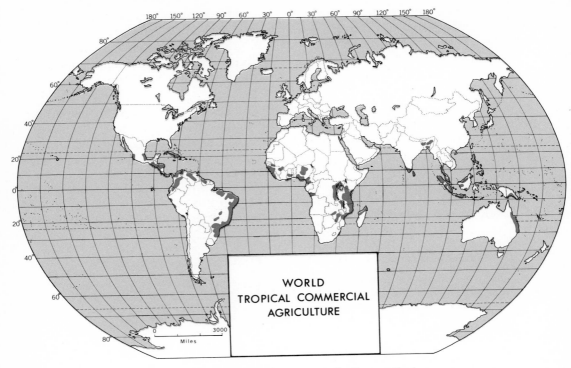

FIGURE 12.1   (*General Media Corporation*)

to make economically attractive units, where managers and assistants were established to provide commercial organization and technical direction. Manual labor had to be cheap, so that the product could be sold at a price that would ensure a large and growing volume of demand. However, the above conditions no longer are as valid as they were in the eighteenth and nineteenth centuries, when Europeans established colonial systems followed by commercial ventures in the tropical and subtropical regions of the Americas and Southeast Asia.

LOCATION

Tropical plantations occupy numerous small areas, rather than broad regions, within the low latitudes. The percentage of land occupied is rather small in relation to the total area. Plantations generally are located in the tropical lowlands—preferably near navigable rivers where the alluvial soils and water transport facilitate the growth and shipment of crops for export.

PHYSICAL ENVIRONMENT

Equatorial areas are characterized in general by heavy rainfall and high temperatures, except for the uplands and mountainous portions. Tropical lowlands near the equator receive at least 60 inches of precipitation annually, with windward slopes averaging 200 inches or more. Farther poleward (5 to 18 or 20 degrees north or south of the equator) a dry period prevails, lasting from four to six months. This Wet–Dry belt averages 30 to 60 inches annually, a hazard to commercial agriculture without irrigation. Temperatures are high year round and frost at sea level is un-

FIGURE 12.2 *Aerial view of a banana plantation on the Pacific coast plain of Guatemala. (USDA)*

known. Average daytime temperatures of 75° to 80° F. are experienced near the equator; 70° to 80° F. during the wet season in the wet–dry tropics when cloud cover and rain prevail; 80° to 90° F., or even 100° F., during the dry season. Average temperature for the coldest month in the tropical zone is 64° F. or above.

Soils

Latosols, the major soil group in the humid tropics, are highly suitable for plant growth. Under the original cover of rainforest, their fertility is maintained in a delicate equilibrium. The organic matter that falls from the trees decomposes and feeds the plant life in continuous cycle of growth and decay, with the same small capital of nutrients but rapid turnover. Once the rainforest has been cleared, the balance is upset, and soil fertility declines rapidly due to intense oxidation and leaching under high temperature and rainfall. The leached soils of the tropical zone on the whole produce low yields. This may be counterbalanced by obtain-

ing two harvests a year, but that is not possible everywhere. Furthermore, cultivation requires more labor per acre of cropland than in the middle latitudes, chiefly because of the need for frequent weeding.

Pests and Diseases

The tropical zone, with its incessantly high temperatures and humidity, offers a favorable environment for the multiplication of a wide variety of insects. Some species damage crops directly; others help to transmit infectious diseases. Many tropical plantations have been hampered or wiped out by pests and diseases. Others have been forced to move to new locations. The United Fruit Company, for example, shifted its banana plantations from the humid eastern littoral of Central America to western Central America in order to escape the dread Panama or wilt disease, which yellows and wilts the banana leaves and kills the affected shoots.

The dry season of western Central

America checks these diseases but necessitates irrigation; sigatoka, a serious leaf spot caused by a sooty mold, also has been a source of much trouble to banana plantations in Central America. The latter can be controlled by spraying with copper sulfate every three weeks, but then the harvested fruit must be dipped in sodium acid sulfate to remove the spray, followed by water to wash off the sulfate. Such attempts to eradicate disease add to production cost.

The diseases currently associated with the tropics are themselves undergoing changes in incidence and extent more rapidly than is commonly realized. The opening-up of communications by air, land, and sea, new methods of cultivation, and the extension of irrigation canals have all tended to widen the spread of some diseases hitherto localized, while the recent introduction of massive methods of control have altered the natural rhythm of others.

Winds

Heavy fruits such as the banana are easily damaged or destroyed when subjected even to light winds. A wind velocity of twenty-five miles per hour can be harmful. This is why large plantations often cultivate several separate tracts instead of one to minimize the danger of destructive winds. Since the Caribbean is the source of hurricane activity in tropical America, plantation owners are particularly vulnerable to this natural hazard.

CULTURAL ENVIRONMENT

Most tropical countries must face problems associated with the presence of an indigenous population. Not only is the native, because of his carelessness, a constant source of infection, but more important economically, he works for a smaller reward than the non-native, since his material and cultural wants are more restricted. This complication naturally has a tendency to pull down the non-native farmer's income. Theoretically, this may be overcome in various ways—for instance, by producing high-value crops that the native does not raise or by using machinery for large-scale farming. But there is always the chance that the native will imitate him and plant the same crops. As far as farming with machinery is concerned, there are various obstacles to success, especially the cultivation requirements of most tropical crops and, again, the presence of a cheap labor supply.

TRANSPORTATION

Railroads, highways, canals, and rivers are indispensable to the movement of tropical commodities to coastal ports. Ocean-going ships form the major links in the global circulation of commodities to centers of consumption. Coordination of land and sea transportation is imperative for the plantation owner, for without them he would be unable to export his surplus. Further, his shipments must be large enough to ensure a low cost per unit; otherwise his product becomes a luxury item for the average consumer.

POLITICAL FACTORS

During the eighteenth and nineteenth centuries when colonialism was at its height, thousands of Europeans were attracted to these new lands. Business soon entered the field. There were enormous profits to be made in developing virgin countries, where cheap native labor and rich natural resources might make a veritable paradise for the enterprising capitalist. Ownership of valuable properties, or long-term leasing, and the importing of expensive machinery meant that Westerners had a direct stake in these societies, one that had to be protected.

FIGURE 12.3 *Contour planting of pineapple on the island of Hawaii. (USDA)*

FIGURE 12.4 *Kona coffee grown on rockland on the island of Hawaii. Holes to plant trees are made with a jackhammer; then a handful of soil and a handful of fertilizer are placed in the hole with a seedling tree. (USDA)*

FIGURE 12.5 *A macadamia nut orchard on the island of Hawaii. (C. Brewer and Company, Ltd.)*

They looked to their home governments for such protection when it was needed. Native governments were often unaccustomed to such complex property arrangements as the Europeans brought. Political control soon led to economic domination, with plantation enterprises occupying the best sites for commercial production of tropical fruits and vegetables in great demand in the mother countries.

The dynamic agent of change was Western civilization, whose character made exertion of the driving force of power almost inevitable. The recipients were civilizations sometimes older and richer, but less dynamic. They were roughly prodded out of ancestral patterns by the forceful Europeans, and today we live in an age marked by the readjustment of these civilizations to the impact of the West, an impact they could not ignore. It has been a painful process, like all great social changes, but may give rise in the future to extraordinary things.

Nations build their economic orders on agricultural and industrial bases, and attain a particular national economy according to the interplay of resources, land, capital, and labor. World economics, like world politics, is a direct extension of domestic activity to the foreign field. Sometimes it takes the form of international enterprises, such as trusts and cartels, and organizations that regulate world prices and world markets or compete with other trusts for access to markets or raw materials. Sometimes states have tried to establish world monopolies or international control of raw materials, as Britain did with tin and rubber and Brazil with coffee.

selected references

1. Chang, Jen-hu, "The Agricultural Pattern of the Humid Tropics," *Geographical Review*, Vol. 58, No. 3, July 1968, pp. 333–361.

2. Corwin, Philip, "Top Bananas," *Barrons*, December 13, 1965, pp. 1–11.

3. Cutshall, Alden, "The Philippine Sugar Industry: Status and Problems," *The Journal of Geography*, Vol. 60, No. 1, January 1961, pp. 5–9.

4. Gregor, Howard F., "The Changing Plantation," *Annals of the Association of American Geographers*, Vol. 55, No. 2, June 1965, pp. 221–238.

5. Hessler, William H., "Coffee: Cash Crop of the Tropics," *Farm Quarterly*, Vol. 18, Summer 1963, pp. 50–61.

6. Hoy, Don R., "Trends in the Banana Export Industry of Tropical America," *The Journal of Geography*, Vol. 63, No. 3, March 1964, pp. 108–116.

7. Hutchinson, Harry W., "Village and Plantation Life in Northeastern Brazil," *American Ethnological Monograph*, Seattle: University of Washington Press, 1957.

8. Penny, D. H., and Zulkifli, M., "Estates and Small Holdings," *Journal of Farm Economics*, Vol. 45, December 1963, pp. 1017–1021.

9. Psuty, Norbert P., and Salter, Paul S., "Land Use Competition on a Geomorphic Surface: The Mango in Southern Florida," *Annals of the Association of American Geographers*, Vol. 59, No. 2, June 1969, pp. 264–279.

10. Schul, Norman W., "A Philippine Sugar Cane Plantation: Land Tenure and Sugar Cane Production," *Economic Geography*, Vol. 43, No. 2, April 1967, pp. 157–169.

11. Stevens, Rayfred L., and Brandao, Paulo Rebaucas, "Diversification of the Economy of the Cacao Coast of Bahia, Brazil," *Economic Geography*, Vol. 37, No. 3, July 1961, pp. 231–253.

12. Timoshenko, V. P., and Swerling, B. C., *The World's Sugar: Progress and Policy*, Stanford, Calif.: Food Research Institute Studies on Food, Agriculture, and World War II, No. 12, 1957.

13. Udo, R. K., "Sixty Years of Plantation Agriculture in Nigeria: 1902–1962," *Economic Geography*, Vol. 41, No. 4, October 1965, pp. 356–368.

14. Urquhart, D. H., *Cacao*, 2d. ed., London: Longmans, Green and Company, Ltd., 1959.

15. Wickizer, V. D., "The Plantation System in the Development of Tropical Economies," *Journal of Farm Economics*, Vol. 40, 1958, pp. 63–77.

The term *Mediterranean agriculture* refers to a diverse crop–livestock economic system that evolved as a major land-use pattern dating from the Roman and Greek civilizations. Four other non-Mediterranean areas—southern California, central Chile, the region about Capetown in South Africa, and southwestern Australia together with the lands about Spencer Gulf—have similar climatic patterns. This type of climate occurs on all western coasts of countries in the sub-tropics (i.e., latitudes 30° to 40°) but is usually called "Mediterranean" because it occurs most extensively about the Mediterranean Sea.

chapter 13

Mediterranean Agriculture

PHYSICAL ENVIRONMENT

Most lands within the Mediterranean sub-tropics are relatively complex in terms of their physical geography. There is a dearth of flat land; narrow coastal plains are ringed by high mountain ranges, between which are long narrow valleys. In many instances, the mountains plunge directly into the sea, forming barriers to transportation and communication. High, rugged surfaces, in many places stripped of soil and forests, steep slopes, and high relief are characteristic. Plains at various altitudes occur only in relatively small and confined sites.

Climate

The typical Mediterranean climate (near the sea) is characterized by hot, almost completely rainless summers; warm, rainy autumns; somewhat cooler and still rainy winters and springs. There are some differences between the western and central parts (Spain, Portugal, and Italy) and the eastern parts (Greece and Asia Minor): in the westernmost parts the dry summer lasts only three to four months, but lasts four to five months in the eastern parts.

The hot, dry summer is the most important climatic feature; raising summer

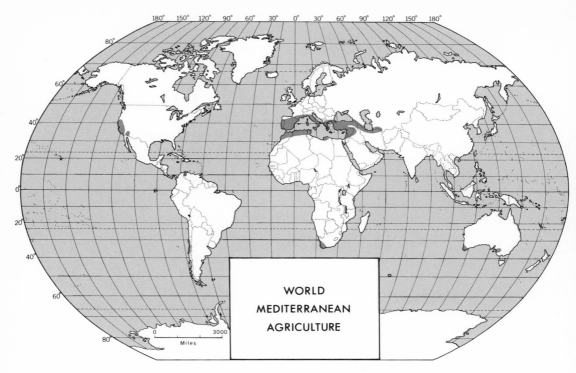

FIGURE 13.1   (General Media Corporation)

FIGURE 13.2   Aerial view of the Delta-Mendota Canal carrying water along the west side of California's San Joaquin Valley. The low rainfall of Mediterranean lands increases the need for irrigation for successful agriculture. (U.S. Bureau of Reclamation)

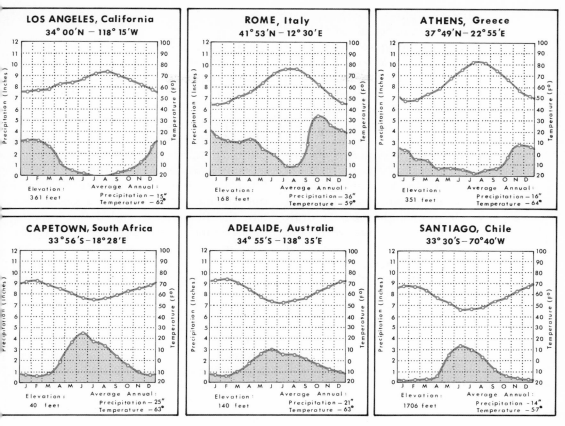

FIGURE 13.3 *Monthly temperature and precipitation graphs for selected weather stations with Mediterranean climates.*

crops is impossible without irrigation. Precipitation during the cold season also causes problems because much of the rain falls in violent storms. Torrential rains pouring down on soil that lacks the protection of vegetation or is situated on slopes in hilly country carry away fertile soil, sand, and stones, leaving only naked rocks behind; the deposit from overflowing streams and rivers is left on fields and gardens, or in the river beds where it causes further damage.

In the interior parts of the Mediterranean basin the summers are generally hotter, the winters colder, and precipitation usually less than in coastal zones. In the northern hemisphere, the first killing frosts of the season usually occur about

the beginning of December and the last through the end of March. The days are comfortably warm throughout the winter, and sunshine is abundant. During this period, radiation fogs of superficial depth are frequent in the low-lying regions. These fogs usually dissipate soon after sunrise. On the whole, however, the area might be described as having a cool climate presided over by a warm sun, so that even when temperatures range higher than usual, the relative humidity generally remains low.

Figure 13.4 shows not only the marked concentration of winter precipitation in each of the Mediterranean subtropical realms, but also the small annual totals received. Average monthly temperature and precipitation figures, however, give only a partial picture of actual conditions. They do not reveal the sharp fluctuations that can occur between consecutive years; some years are very dry, others are quite humid.

Natural Vegetation

Native plants in the Mediterranean climatic regions are adapted to the peculiar wet winters and dry summers. Trees in more moist areas and shrubs in the drier areas have deep enough roots to draw on ground water and thus withstand summer drought. Grasses make their growth in late winter and early spring, ripening in early summer before drought becomes severe. Many of the cultivated crops, however, are not suited to these conditions; for them, irrigation must be provided.

AGRICULTURAL CHARACTERISTICS

The physical environment of Mediterranean lands encourages a distinctive agriculture based on

1. Winter grains, such as wheat and barley
2. Drought-resistant perennials, such as olives, grapes, and carob (a Mediterranean evergreen whose pods are used as fodder)
3. Irrigated crops of either an annual or perennial nature, such as oranges, lemons, pomelos, deciduous fruits, corn, rice, and vegetables
4. animals

The inclusion of animals as a major feature in the agricultural economy has prompted some observers to give the name *bioculture* to Mediterranean agriculture. In no other major agricultural economy do both plants and animals occupy such an important position.

Land Use

By latitude, climate, topography, and absence of mineral resources, the Mediterranean regions are disposed more favorably to agriculture than to any other mode of life. Over half the people still depend directly on use of the soil for subsistence. The Mediterranean Basin is of special significance, because this region has been intensively settled for two thousand years. By colonization and empire building, the ancient Greeks, and to a greater extent the Romans, extended this process to the whole of southern Europe. Arable land and forest areas were exploited on a scale that in many areas led to exhaustion. The triad—grain, the olive, and the grape—became the agricultural basis of the Mediterranean civilizations.

The first major improvements in agriculture were made by the Etruscans, who advanced methods of drainage and reclamation, and in general established Roman farming on an efficient basis. During the first two centuries of the Republic, Roman society was of a patriarchal agrarian type, with the family as the primary social and economic unit. Every family had a small holding of about two acres, which it tilled with the assistance of dependents and slaves. Agricultural methods and equipment were crude, cereals and vegetables were the chief crops, and the whole system was rigorously controlled by religious concepts and rites.

The Roman conquest of Italy produced a redistribution of the land, an increase of patrician holdings, and the creation of Rome's agrarian problem. As a result, the latifundia, the great slave-work estate operated for profit by an absentee landlord, evolved. Other tenure systems such as the mesta (Spain) and the hacienda (Spanish) later developed in the Mediterranean Basin. All of these are still dominant in many areas; no real improvements have been made in agricultural methods in parts of the Mediterranean

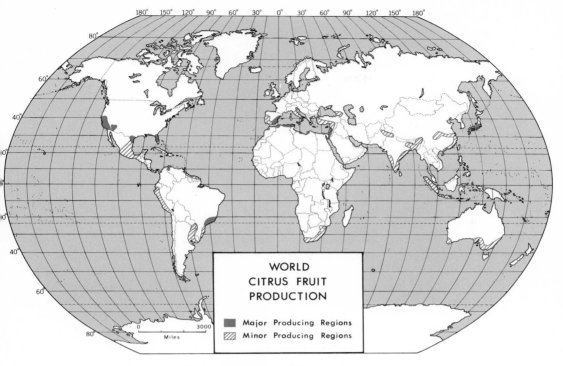

FIGURE 13.4   *(General Media Corporation)*

Basin for centuries, with the exception of commercial gardening and truck farming.

Winter Grains

Wheat, the dominant winter grain, is planted in the fall; nourished by the winter rains, it ripens in spring, and is harvested in early summer before the onset of the dry season. It is by far the most important source of starch, contributing about half of the calories in the Mediterranean diet.

But wheat yields are low compared with those obtained in other European countries; they are only about one-half the yields realized in France and one-third those of the Netherlands. Low yields in the Mediterranean Basin are due not only to natural conditions but also to the small consumption of fertilizers and the widespread use of unimproved seeds.

Mechanization so far has not been introduced to any significant extent, despite the opportunities of extending the agricultural area and improving the methods of cultivation it would provide.

Italy is the leading wheat producer in southern Europe. About one-fourth of the crop is grown on land classed as mountains, one-half on hilly land, and only one-fourth on plains. Wheat is also an important crop in Spain and other Mediterranean climates, as shown by Table 13.1.

Barley has a wider climatic range than wheat, a low warmth requirement, and can mature in a shorter period than any other grain. It is grown primarily for feed, but a considerable amount also is used for malting. Barley dominates in areas where livestock raising is important but where temperatures are too cool for corn (for feed grain). Barley and oats are competitors; the crop with the higher

Table 13.1   Wheat Acreage, Yield, and Production in Some Mediterranean-climatic Countries, 1967

Country	Acreage (1000 acres)	Yield Per Acre (bushels)	Production (million bushels)
Australia	22,711	12.2	277.3
Chile	1,730	26.8	46.4
Greece	2,315	29.3	67.9
Italy	9,913	35.6	352.6
South Africa	3,050	13.1	40.0
Spain	10,549	19.5	205.7

Source: United Nations, *Statistical Yearbook* (New York: 1968), pp. 151–152.

yield is preferred. In areas where all bread grains do poorly, barley is consumed by man as his chief cereal. In those areas where grains are grown, wheat occupies the better lands, barley the poorer. Wheat is preferred since it makes better bread and pasta—hence, it is more widely cultivated.

Winter Vegetables

The mild climate of the coastal valleys, combined with their more fertile alluvial soils, favors the growth of a number of winter vegetable crops. Some are frozen or canned, but most of them are for the fresh food market, whether it be local or at a distance. Nearly all major vegetables—carrots, turnips, tomatoes, onions, radishes, lettuce, celery, peppers, cucumbers, green beans, and squash—do well in the moist, cool Mediterranean winters. Vegetable yields per acre are high, but land is scarce and expensive, and consumption per capita is low. Hence vegetable farms are small (usually two acres or less) compared to the fields of wheat or barley.

FIGURE 13.5   *Harvesting spinach by machine in southern California. Winter vegetable production is important in the economy of Mediterranean lands. (USDA)*

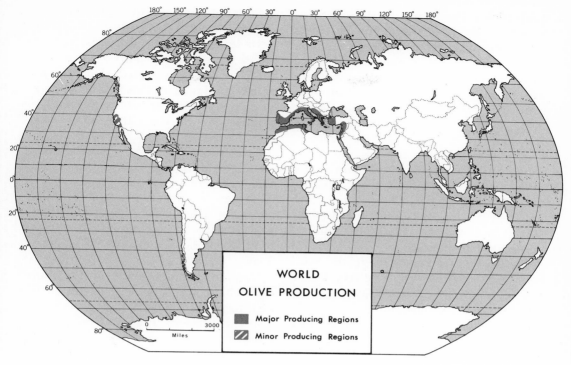

FIGURE 13.6 *(General Media Corporation)*

Summer Crops

Summer crops, planted in late spring, mature during the long, hot summer and are harvested in the dry autumn. Where irrigation is not practiced, only those crops able to withstand near-drought conditions of high temperature, little rainfall, and high evaporation rate can survive. Certain trees (olive, fig, date) and vines (grape) meet the above requirements. They are characterized by

1. Long tap roots to penetrate the water table far below the surface
2. Widespread horizontal root systems to absorb any moisture in the immediate vicinity
3. Short, thick leaves either possessing waxy or oily exteriors or minimal size to reduce transpiration and evaporation

So interwoven are these drought-resistant crops from the standpoint of cultural preferences and physical associations that they occur in all Mediterranean climates. However, the major expression of this tree and vine association in the landscape occurs in the Mediterranean Basin.

The olive tree is a characteristic evergreen of regions bordering the Mediterranean Sea where the winters are relatively mild and humid, the summers hot and dry, and the mean annual temperature is not less than 57° F. About 90 percent of the world's olive crop is harvested in the Mediterranean Basin; most of the remaining 10 percent is scattered among countries having a Mediterranean climate. Olive oil is used not only for domestic consumption but is also an important export commodity.

Spain is the largest producer and exporter of green olives and olive oil, accounting for more than one-half of the world's supply. Italy supplies between one-fourth and one-third of global production; Greece and Tunisia also are important producers of olives and olive oil in the Mediterranean Basin. California produces less than one percent of the world's total crop. Although the olive tree produces a better crop when irrigated, pressure to use the land for other crops in the Old World often forces its cultivation in the drier, stonier uplands. This, combined with low-cost labor for the care, harvesting, and pickling of the olives and extraction of the oil, plus the lack of summer pasturage (which discourages grazing and hence the production of animal fats), favors olive culture in Mediterranean lands.

The fig, a tree belonging to the mulberry family, is indigenous to Asia Minor but has been naturalized in all the countries around the Mediterranean Basin. Unlike the olive tree, the fig yields two harvests per year—one in the early summer, from the buds of the last year; the other (which is the chief harvest) in the autumn, from the buds on the spring growth. When ripe figs are dried and sugar forms on the outside, they are then packed. The best are raised in Smyrna, but good figs are produced throughout the Mediterranean Basin. *Interculture*—the cultivating of vegetable crops between rows of fig trees—is quite common in Europe.

Viticulture

The vine is cultivated in all Mediterranean lands, for wine from grapes is the ordinary drink of the people. Although Italy produces more wine than any other country except France, the quality of the wine is generally poor, and owing to imperfect preparation quickly deteriorates instead of improving with age. Vineyards not sensitive to frost in winter find a suitable climate on sheltered sunny slopes.

In the vineyard zone of Italy man's ingenuity has been tested and developed. Grapes, wheat, and mulberry trees often occupy the same ground. The trees, close-cropped to keep them producing tender, fresh leaves for the silkworms, serve as stakes for the vines. Two or three horizontal wires are fastened along the row of trees, and the vines are tied to the wires. The trees give a warmer, more even temperature for the vines than either deadwood or iron posts.

Grapes are classified as table, wine, raisin, currant, juice, and canning varieties. Specialty areas have developed over the years in various parts of the Mediterranean: wine from Algeria and Portugal, currants from Greece, table grapes from the Malaga district of southern Spain.

Despite the importance of agriculture, only about one-fifth of the land in the Mediterranean climatic regions is intensively cultivated. The remainder is too steep, too dry, too rocky, or too "something else." Thus, due to this limitation, a definite pattern of land use has evolved over the centuries. Small fruits and vegetables occupy the lowlands where temperature and soil favor such cultivation near urban markets. Wheat and barley are grown in the drier portions of the lower slopes. Tree crops and the vine dominate the upper slopes, thus reducing erosion while yielding desirable food crops. Frequently, interculture is practiced to make the most of the usable land.

ANIMAL HUSBANDRY

Livestock *grazing* is based primarily on natural vegetation. The marginal nature of so much of the land utilization in the Mediterranean, and the extent of open woodland and scrub, has stressed the importance of pastoralism. Generally, cattle tend to predominate in the wetter areas, sheep over vast areas of the arid zone, and goats in the driest, more rocky areas. Pastoralism has been divorced from agriculture, and this, together with the abrupt physical contrasts of relief

FIGURE 13.7 *Grape pickers gathering the harvest in Australia. (Australian News and Information Bureau)*

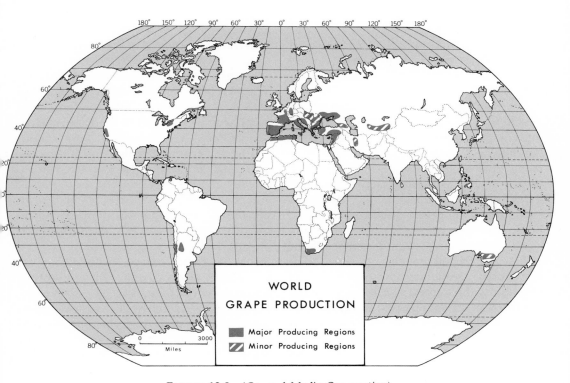

FIGURE 13.8 *(General Media Corporation)*

FIGURE 13.9   *A landscape in southern Spain—an area characterized by Mediterranean agriculture. Note the orchards mantling the hills in the background. (Spanish National Tourist Department)*

and climate, has encouraged *transhumance*. This seasonal movement from lowland to highland, traceable to remote antiquity, is a climatic response. During the winter (wet) season, the lush green lowlands with mild temperatures are ideal for grazing livestock. In summer, when the lowland pastures are dry and dormant, the cool grassy upper slopes are ideally suited to pastoral activities. Over much of the Mediterranean, sheep far outnumber all other domestic animals. The native grassland is too scanty for the large-scale grazing of cattle. In southern California, sheep ranches at one time dominated the land, and they are still numerous. In central Chile and southwest Africa, sheep ranching is very important. The breeding and raising of sheep for wool is the most important of the agricultural and pastoral activities in Australia.

Livestock *farming* is based on irrigated meadows planted in alfalfa, hay, clover, sown grasses, or other forage crops. The animals are stall fed. Meat, milk, and cheese are produced both for local consumption and export in northern Algeria, northern Italy, southern France, and southern and eastern Spain. Dairying is especially important near the larger cities. Italian cheeses (parmesan, gorgonzola, and stracchino) are highly esteemed in Western Europe and the United States. In other areas in the Mediterranean Basin, such as southern Italy, central Spain, northern Greece, Yugoslavia, Turkey, and Syria, subsistence livestock farming largely prevails.

Large-scale commercial livestock farming is important in California. Irrigated pastures and imported grain support huge dairies and meatpacking plants near Los Angeles and San Francisco.

The San Joaquin Valley acts as a large milk reservoir, serving the urban population.

CULTURAL ENVIRONMENT AND AGRICULTURE

The importance of *institutional resistance* to economic expansion is perhaps most obvious in Asia, but it is easily observed also in the Mediterranean Basin. Many institutions are active in this respect, some even decisive; the more important are mentioned here: economic privileges granted to specific groups and individuals; authoritarian relationships within an economic sector (e.g., landowner–tenant farmer); vested political power (e.g., absence of a truly representative government, an equitable taxation system, personal and economic security for the citizen and his enterprise, etc.); the glorification of frugal attitudes of mind (e.g., the impact of religious teachings leading to acquiescence to suffering and hardship).

There is some relation between religious behavior and social patterns, especially in small towns and villages where most of the agricultural population lives: big families comprising three or four generations—with many children, owing to the high birth rate—exist on the yield of small farms.

The Mediterranean type of habitation, characterized by large villages that depend exclusively on agriculture, involves long distances between the dwellings and the place of employment; several hours are wasted every day in walking to and from work. The typical village offers poor housing conditions, and is often a slum as bad as the poorer districts of towns. The present pattern of settlement nevertheless conforms to the general economic and social situation, and can hardly be changed without introducing entirely new elements in the life of the agricultural population. Such elements would involve huge investments, new services, and much higher standards of living.

Even though agricultural production has grown at a faster rate than agricultural population, the typical farmhold is normally too small to yield a reasonable income for the many individuals living on it. The number of agricultural holdings has been rising while area per unit has been decreasing. Too many people are trying to gain a living from agriculture, and because of this overpopulation the income per active person is low.

The only factor of production available in abundant quantity is manpower. The labor force is insufficiently occupied because of the existing pattern of production and the low technical standards of existing enterprises. An adjustment of mental attitudes in the widest sense is thus a necessary condition for economic growth. This implies not only better schooling and technical training, but also development of manual skills in industry and agriculture, and what is perhaps even more important, liberty in political, organizational, and economic affairs.

selected references

1. Burke, J. Henry, "Citrus Industry of Italy," *Foreign Agriculture Report*, No. 59, Washington, D.C.: United States Department of Agriculture, 1962.

2. Gregor, Howard F., "The Local Supply Agriculture of California," *Annals of the Association of American Geographers*, Vol. 47, No.3, September 1957, pp. 267–276.

3. Gregor, Howard F., "The Plantation in California," *The Professional Geographer*, Vol. 14, No. 2, March 1962, pp. 1–4.

4. ———, "The Regional Primacy of San Joaquin Valley Agricultural Production," *The Journal of Geography*, Vol. 61, No. 9, December 1962, pp. 394–399.

5. Griffin, Paul F., and Chatham, Ronald L., "Urban Impact on Agriculture in Santa Clara County, California," *Annals of the Asso-*

ciation of American Geographers, Vol. 48, No. 3, September 1958, pp. 195–208.

6. ———, "Population: A Challenge to California's Changing Citrus Industry," *Economic Geography*, Vol. 34, No. 3, July 1958, pp. 272–276.

7. Griffin, Paul F., "The Olive Industry of California," *The Journal of Geography*, Vol. 44, No. 9, December 1955, pp. 429–440.

8. Highsmith, Richard M., Jr., "Irrigated Lands of the World," *Geographical Review*, Vol. 55, No. 3, July 1965, pp. 382–389.

9. Hodgson, Robert W., "The Avocado—A Gift from the Middle Americas," *Economic Botany*, Vol. 4, No. 3, 1950, pp. 253–293.

10. Holm, Henrietta M., "The Agricultural Economy of Algeria," *Foreign Agriculture Service, FAS M-38*, Washington, D.C.: United States Department of Agriculture, 1959.

11. Isaac, Erish, "The Citron in the Mediterranean: A Study in Religious Influences," *Economic Geography*, Vol. 35, No. 1, January 1959, pp. 71–78.

12. Opitz, Karl W., "Italy's Olive Production and the Table Olive Industry," *Foreign Agricultural Service, FAS M-24*, Washington, D.C.: United States Department of Agriculture, 1957.

13. Parsons, James J., "The Acorn–Hog Economy of the Oak Woodlands of Southwestern Spain," *Geographical Review*, Vol.52, No. 1, April 1962, pp. 211–235.

14. Rubel, D. M., "The Deciduous Fruit Industry of Italy," *Foreign Agricultural Service, FAS M-55*, Washington, D.C.: United States Department of Agriculture, 1958.

15. Thompson, Kenneth, "Location and Relocation of a Tree Crop—English Walnuts in California," *Economic Geography*, Vol. 37, No. 2, April 1961, pp. 133–149.

Cattle, sheep, and goats are the major domesticated animals tended by man. This form of animal husbandry or livestock ranching is based on a much higher plane than nomadism. It is primarily the result of man's ability to add to the naturally occurring resource base by improving on its carrying capacity.

In general, livestock ranching occupies the wetter margins of steppe lands. In North America, it is an important economic activity in the drier parts of the Great Plains, stretching from Texas through the Prairie Provinces of Canada, and throughout the intermontane basins and plateaus between the Rocky Mountains and the Sierra Nevada–Cascades from Canada to central Mexico. South America has two zones. The first begins at the southern tip of the continent at Tierra del Fuego and continues for some 4,000 miles through Argentina, Uruguay, and Brazil on the east. The northern zone, much smaller in size, occupies the llanos of Colombia and Venezuela. Large cattle and sheep ranches dominate much of the interior of Africa south of Angola and Rhodesia. The greater parts of Australia and New Zealand are utilized for livestock ranching—in no other area does this economic activity occupy so much space. Except for the Kazakhistan–Turkmenia region northeast of the Caspian Sea, formerly the habitat of nomads, livestock ranching is largely absent from the Eurasian realm.

chapter 14

Livestock Ranching

CHARACTERISTICS

Livestock ranching is characterized by:

1. Relatively large land areas, as opposed to either field agriculture or livestock farming
2. Upgrading of natural vegetation
3. Erection of permanent buildings, roads, fences, etc.
4. Extensive use of the land, as opposed to intensive use, which is more com-

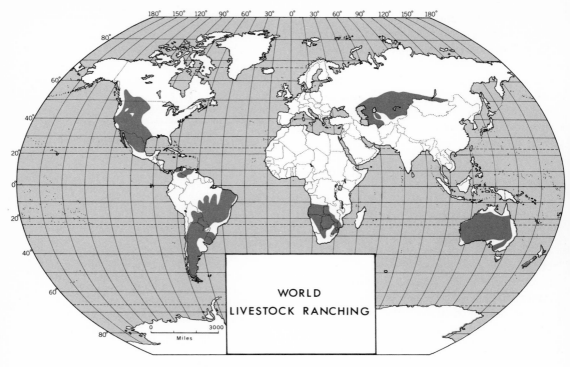

FIGURE 14.1   *(General Media Corporation)*

monly associated with livestock farming

5. Awareness of and dependence upon economic factors that in great part determine the success or failure of the venture—these factors include government policies, world market prices, financial management, application of scientific principles of animal husbandry to improve quality and quantity, production for sale, and great distances from markets (a reflection of the need for low land values)

Wool and skins are the chief revenue items. Some meat may also be sold. Most of the animals, however, are purchased by farmers who fatten them for market. This is especially true of beef cattle, which spend twelve to eighteen months on range pasture, obtaining their size and frame, before being shipped to feedlots for concentrated grain feeding prior to slaughter. *Carrying capacity*, a term used to describe the number of animals a given amount of land can support, varies considerably. In deserts, 100 acres or more are required for forage to support one steer. Steppes and mountain meadows vary from 25 to 75 acres, depending on the availability of moisture. In the subhumid part of the Great Plains, the carrying capacity improves, averaging 10 to 15 acres. Because carrying capacity is often low, large acreages are required for an economic unit. In western Texas many ranches have 20,000 acres; one ranch in southern Texas covers over 1,000 square miles. In Arizona and New Mexico many ranches have 30,000 to 40,000 acres. The world's largest ranches are found in Australia— several encompass 5,000 or more square miles; one even spreads over 12,000 square miles.

Carrying capacity may be increased by proper range management. On many ranges, grazing on all parts of the range can be systematically deferred each year,

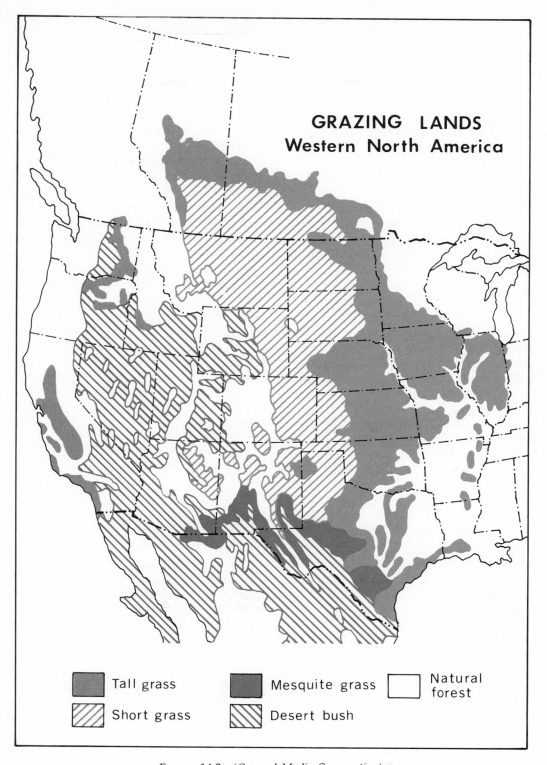

GRAZING LANDS
Western North America

Tall grass

Short grass

Mesquite grass

Desert bush

Natural forest

FIGURE 14.2   *(General Media Corporation)*

particularly during the growth season, by subdividing the range with fences. This system of controlled grazing results in additonal forage from increased plant vigor.

PHYSICAL CONDITIONS

Temperature and rainfall affect the distribution of cattle directly through their effect on the cattle themselves, and indirectly through the availability of an adequate supply of pasture and cheap forage. The taurine cattle are, in general, adapted to the middle latitudes, but different breeds are best suited to different climatic conditions. In the United States, Hereford cattle predominate in the semiarid sections of the western states, while shorthorn and Angus breeds are found in the central states where feed and pasture are plentiful. Breeding and selection in their original habitat seem to account for these differences, the Herefords having been bred so that they are adapted to sparse pasture conditions, while shorthorns must have better pasturage.

The poleward extension of beef-cattle production is limited by severe winters, which make necessary the construction of protective buildings and provision of winter forage. In regions with mild climates and year-round pasture, expenditures for these items can be almost eliminated. In the low latitudes, cattle may suffer from pests and disease, especially in the lowlands—a factor that limits cattle raising to the highlands in parts of the low latitudes.

Probably the most influential factor determining the distribution of cattle is the availability of cheap pasture and forage, found mostly in the semiarid grazing lands. Not all breeds of cattle are suited to these regions, however. Only those beef breeds such as the Hereford, which are adapted to dry conditions and land too rough for agriculture, can be grazed in these areas. This is the case in the west-

ern parts of the United States, in Australia, and in parts of Argentina.

Some of the land in Argentina that is planted in alfalfa and used for grazing is also good grain land. There is a tendency, therefore, for agriculture to encroach on these lands, leaving grazing to those lands that are unsuited to more intensive cultivation.

The annual rainfall must be at least 10 or 12 inches to maintain a sufficient cover of grass for cattle. On the arid borders of the grazing lands, where the herbage is too sparse for cattle, sheep may be grazed. In some regions, however, cattle are grazed where the rainfall is not only too light, but uncertain; in periods of drought the pastures fail, cattle suffer or die, and heavy losses and suffering result.

Climatic conditions also restrict the potential sheep-producing areas somewhat, since sheep are adapted to cool climates and the fleece tends to degenerate in regions having high temperatures. Sheep are less subject to hoof rot and parasitic diseases when raised in semiarid regions.

CULTURAL ENVIRONMENT

The dominant factor in livestock ranching is distance. Population density is sparse, varying from twenty-five people per square mile to less than two. The range or "spread" is usually measured in square miles called sections. Towns are small and far apart, and there are no big cities. In no other agricultural activity do schools, libraries, public health units, road maintenance divisions, and other social and economic agencies suffer so much from lack of an adequate population base—either these services do not exist at all or they are very costly. The settlement pattern is either dispersed, as is the case with individual ranch homes and associated buildings, or agglomerated. The latter type comprises the service centers found only in commercial

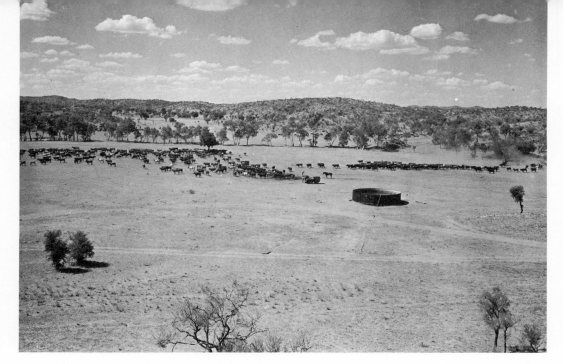

FIGURE 14.3 *A watering paddock in the Northern Territory of Australia. (Australian News and Information Bureau)*

economies. Surplus production from the surrounding ranches, such as wool, skins, etc., are collected at the service centers for shipment to major markets; here, too, ranchers secure their needed supplies.

Sociology

Livestock ranching is associated with freedom, independence, and egalitarianism. There appears, however, in actuality to be a marked class system, which differentiates into:

1. Landowners and ranch operators
2. A small middle class of merchants
3. Professional personnel
4. Public servants
5. A large body of wage workers

The elite landowners and operators generally have great influence in ranching communities. Frequently they operate or are associated with banks and other urban economic institutions, and have a strong voice in community affairs because of their prestige and economic standing.

Ranchers tend to remain in the community of their birth and pass their operations on to sons. They try to increase their holdings where they can and sell off portions only when they must.

There is usually a ranch house on each spread, but the rancher frequently spends a good part of his time in town. He is motivated to establish a residence in the community when he has children of school age. After his children grow up he may choose to remain a town dweller, still maintaining his ranch home, however, which he occupies during the summer months.

One must not overlook some of the less material aspects of ranching culture. The cowboy is a symbol of high value not only to TV-raised children but also to many adults. Significantly, the ranchers are themselves fully persuaded of the superiority of this way of life. They hold themselves to be particularly blessed and their children usually want to follow the parental occupation. This prestige is augmented by the color and romance associated with ranching, the opportunity to be outdoors, to ride horseback, to work with livestock, and to make a good profit.

Ownership

Ranchers use private land alone, or private land in combination with various forms of public land. The rancher's ability to control such land in achieving his own interests is limited by the large acreages he must police and manage, and by the control he has over the land he uses through ownership, lease, or permit.

Private fee-simple ownership normally gives the rancher a high degree of control. A rancher who operates large acreages, however, may be unable to exercise precise control in a real physical sense. In areas where big game abounds, for example, the rancher may not be able to prevent grazing by the animals. He may not be able to exclude hunters or others from access to the land. Sometimes this lack of precise control may affect greatly the product he reaps from the land.

His control over the public land he uses is subject also to the limitations imposed by the permit from the administrative agency. The reality of multiple uses then makes itself felt. Grazing on a public range allotment may be conditioned by one or more additional uses at the same time. The allotment may be open to hunters or fishermen during the grazing season, or the grazing season may be cut short to make way for a hunting season.

Ranch Management

Efficient operation of a ranch requires varied knowledge and considerable managerial skill. The successful rancher skillfully culls and improves his breeding stock; he maintains a delicate balance between the number of animals and the amount of forage on his range. He allocates his pastures in the most advanta-geous way among the different classes of livestock, as he strives to manage labor, purchase supplies, and sell ranch products profitably. Because his income varies directly with the amount and quality of surplus livestock produced, he maintains productivity of herds by the skillful use of good breeding stock and removal of relatively unprofitable animals. Earnings may be increased by grazing as many animals as the range will safely support at all times. This involves an increase in the number of livestock grazed when forage is abundant; and a reduction in size of flocks and herds when forage is scanty. Ranchmen also study the vegetation of their land to determine the proportion of cattle, sheep, and goats that make most efficient use of the range. For example, goats are more numerous on ranches having much stony, rugged, land and an abundance of shrub vegetation; they can subsist on little. Cattle graze in greatest numbers on the relatively smooth, grassy, well-watered pastures. Sheep find optimum conditions on rolling land having an abundance of both "grass" and "browse" vegetation, but do well on either the typically goat or cattle ranges.

Ranch Labor

The character of ranch labor has changed materially with the increasing intensity of the ranching industry. In pioneer days ranchers employed cowboys who could ride skillfully; rope, brand, and herd animals; and ably defend the employer's interest against thieves and rival ranchers. When the use of wire fences became widespread and law and order came to the range, the fighting ability of the cowboys lost its usefulness, and increased emphasis was given to skill in managing livestock and rangeland under modern ranching conditions. The cowboy is still a good horseman, for much of his work must be done in the saddle. His primary business is to assist in caring for the

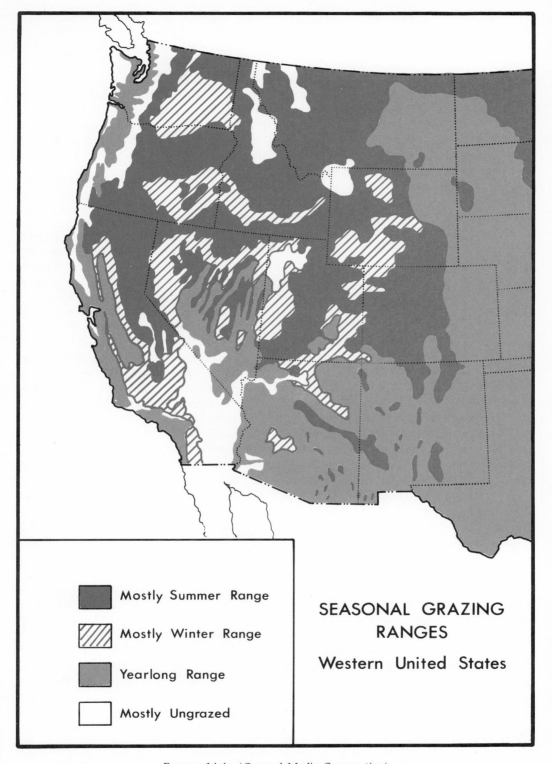

SEASONAL GRAZING
RANGES
Western United States

Mostly Summer Range

Mostly Winter Range

Yearlong Range

Mostly Ungrazed

FIGURE 14.4 (General Media Corporation)

needs of livestock and in the direction of their movements. He must possess an uncanny sense of where livestock might be feeding at any time, and be able to drive them to headquarters or another pasture as needed. He needs to be an expert with the lasso to cut out steers for market, and be able to use the branding iron quickly and efficiently, be ready to assist in the dehorning of cattle and other chores, and to be a good team member during the roundup. So professional is the character of his work, and, in his opinion, so superior to the farm hand, that he will often resign his position if asked to plow or do other agricultural labor.

MARKETS

Extensive pastoral beef production is found in Argentina, Uruguay, Australia, and the western plains of the United States. In these regions the population is relatively sparse, and the cattle graze over large tracts of land. While the number of cattle per square mile is small, the number of cattle per thousand of population is large compared to that in regions of intensive agriculture. Ranchers consume only a very small portion of their output. Since their product is far from consuming markets, producing areas located near railroads and ocean ports are vital to the industry. The two major market outlets are in the highly industrialized section of the American manufacturing belt and Western Europe.

Sheep raising is concentrated in the Southern Hemisphere, in newly developed lands having a sparse population— Australia, South Africa, New Zealand, and the South American countries of Argentina and Uruguay. The United States, the Soviet Union, and India also are important sheep-raising regions, but the sheep are so scattered in their distribution that the number per square mile is small. In the United States about two-thirds of the sheep are found in the drier regions of the Far West, chiefly in the Great Plains and Rocky Mountain states, and in portions of the Pacific Coast states. Wool, mutton, and lamb are exported from Australia, Argentina, New Zealand, and Uruguay, and wool is exported from South Africa. Both wool and mutton are shipped to European nations, especially the United Kingdom, and to the United States.

TRANSPORTATION

The development of transportation facilities and methods of preserving meat products so that they can be transported long distances has had a very important effect on the trade of these products. In some regions, the lack of transportation facilities within the country itself seriously handicaps the ranchers. For instance, in Australia, it is sometimes necessary to trail cattle overland for one thousand miles or more in order to deliver them to the seaboard markets. Poor transportation made it impossible at first for South American countries to market their animal products; the hides and tallow were exported and the carcasses left on the range. In the early nineteenth century meat-salting was introduced, and after 1820 much jerked or sun-dried beef was exported from South America. In some cases beef extract is produced; being a concentrated product, it can bear the cost of transportation to distant markets. In the latter part of the nineteenth century live cattle were exported from Argentina and the United States, this type of shipment reaching its peak about 1900. But the shipment of live animals is not only inhumane, it is also expensive because of space requirements. The cattle must be fed during transit, many of them die, and most of the animals lose weight. In addition, strict quarantine regulations must be established by the importing countries to prevent the possible introduction of diseases.

The two most significant technical

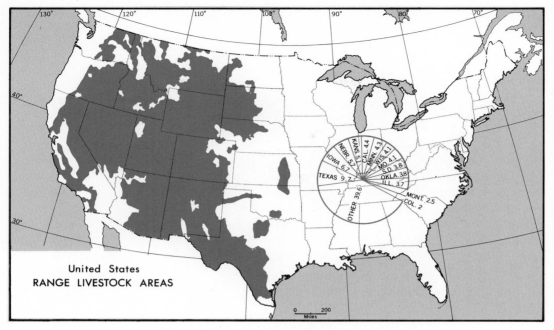

FIGURE 14.5   *(General Media Corporation)*

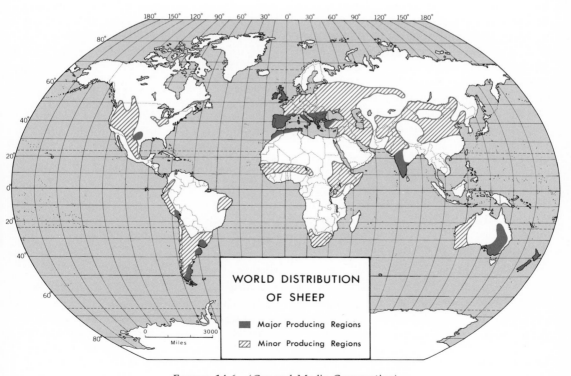

FIGURE 14.6   *(General Media Corporation)*

FIGURE 14.7   *Cattle on a trail drive in the Llanos of Venezuela.*

improvements that have affected the marketing of meat products were introduction of the hermetically sealed can, and the development of refrigeration equipment for shipping chilled or frozen meat. Chilled beef requires a temperature of 30° F.—at which temperature the meat retains its physical properties—while frozen beef is kept in a chamber at 10° to 15° F. This latter method makes the meat hard and rigid, and requires that it be thawed in a special way before being consumed. Beef exports from the United States are chilled, while those from the Southern Hemisphere are chiefly frozen, although Argentina is exporting an increasing amount of chilled beef.

case study

Livestock Ranching in the United States

Livestock ranching occupies about 30 percent of the land area in the United States, but only three percent of the nation's population dwells in the areas where this economic activity dominates. Stretching in a 500 to 1,000 mile band from Mexico to Canada, this western region has 14 percent of the cattle and 45 percent of the sheep grazed in the United States. The grazing land is too infertile, high, or dry for agricultural crops. About half of it is owned by federal and state governments, a large part of which is in national forests. Four patterns of grazing exist:

1. Year-long grazing
2. Seasonal grazing for nonmigratory use
3. Seasonal grazing for migratory use
4. Upland summer grazing

Throughout the ranch country there are mining enterprises, farming areas, and recreation centers, including dude ranches.

History

Livestock ranching historically may be divided into two periods: the *open range* and the *organized ranch*. The first dates from the mid-1700s to about 1880. This is the period that is most often portrayed in the western pulp magazines and on TV westerns. It was the era of lawlessness, cattle rustling, the six-gun, the long drive to railheads, and danger from Indians.

Cowboys' lives centered on the roundup

FIGURE 14.8

and the cattle drive. In the spring and autumn they rounded up the cattle, branded the new crop of calves, and separated the beef cattle from the rest of the herd. Then they took the steers that were to be sold and drove them over many miles of open country to the nearest railroad terminal. From there the cattle were shipped to slaughterhouses and packing plants. In the nineteenth century, railroads were few and far between. Driving the cattle was a long, hard job. The cowboys rose before sunup to start the cattle moving. They drove them all day through the heat or dust or wind, and dozed around campfires at night, still alert for trouble or for strays. The men were often on horseback fifteen hours a day.

Cowboys had to be resourceful and strong, skilled horsemen, and handy with a lariat and gun. Their distinctive clothing was designed for protection. The wide-brimmed hat was worn to shield them from the sun and dust and to shed the rain; chaps protected their legs from cactus and tumbleweed; the gun and holster provided protection against rustlers or Indian attack.

The animals on which this economy was based were brought to the New World by the Spanish, who learned ranching for the most part from the Moors. Thus, the ranching activities of the western states had their beginnings from stock bred on the nomadic grazing lands of Africa and the Iberian Peninsula.

Largely because of its natural vegetation, the Great Plains became the scene of a range-cattle industry that far exceeded in scale and results any of its predecessors in American history. The building of the Union Pacific Railroad brought hunters who supplied the construction crews with buffalo meat, and its completion in 1869 let in additional throngs who eliminated the buffalo, leaving the grasses of the plains unused.

During the years of the Civil War a vast reserve of range cattle had grown up on the Texas plains. Population growth in the East and the advance of the railroads into the Great Plains provided a market and a means for shipping these cattle. This combination of circumstances enabled the range-cattle industry to dominate the Great Plains from the late 1860s to the early 1880s. A less publicized but comparably important cattle business overflowed from the interior of the Oregon country during 1875–1885.

Starting from their breeding grounds in lower Texas, great herds of cattle were driven northward to Abilene and other shipping points in Kansas. Later herds were pushed

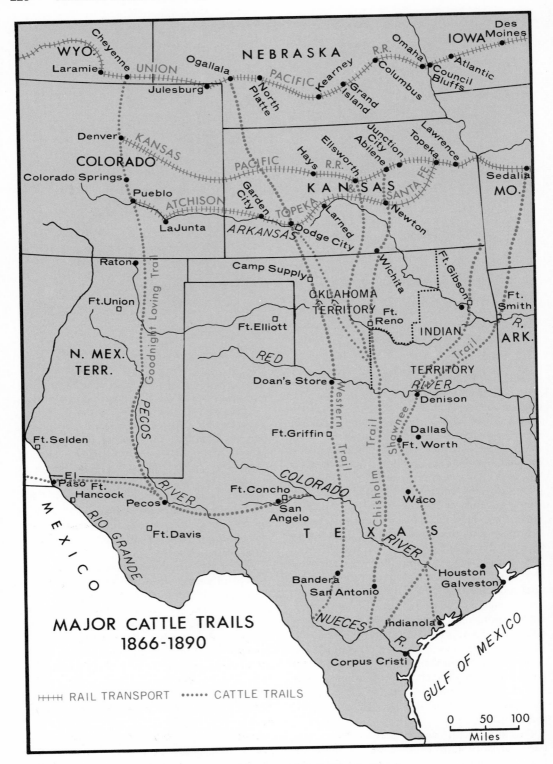

FIGURE 14.9   *(General Media Corporation)*

into Nebraska, the Dakotas, and Montana, first to provide meat for Indian reservations and military posts, and later to raise cattle for eastern markets. Incident to this business, trial-and-error experimentation developed standard procedures for trail management, the roundup, and so on, which contributed so much romance and color to American history through western novels, movies, and folklore.

Organized Ranch Period

About 1880 the boom element began to enter this cattle industry. Companies financed chiefly by outside, generally European capital entered the business. Permanent ranches soon became established with seeded and irrigated pastures. More and more railheads were built. Contacts were made with Midwest feedlots, meat-packing plants, and midwestern and eastern markets. Rotation grazing, prevention of overgrazing, dug wells and piped water for livestock, fencing of the range, and other such innovations quickly followed. Range practices were worked out, with cattle occupying the better grazing lands, sheep the less desirable areas, and goats in lands unsuited to either cattle or sheep.

A modern ranch can cover 500,000 acres of dry, desert country or 100 acres of greener country where the climate is wetter and more grass can be grown. There are big ranches and small ranches—ranches that use modern machines and are run like giant businesses, and ranches run entirely by single families, where each member of the family has a job to do and helps to decide how the ranch should be run. There are ranches in the dry, sandy deserts of Texas, on the cold plains of Montana, and in the green uplands and plateaus of Colorado.

Role of Land

Land is relatively more significant in ranching than in any other major type of farming. The forage it provides can be converted into economic uses only by grazing animals. The western livestock region covers roughly the western half of the United States. About three-fourths of all land in this region is used for grazing. The rest is in cropland, mountains, and forests that are not grazed; military and other reserved areas; and urban and industrial sites. The soils and climates, which vary markedly in this region, determine the amount and kind of forage and the season of grazing use.

Land used for grazing generally is unfit for any other agricultural use. The soil may be too poor or rocky for cultivation. The climate may be too dry and the summers too short for crops. Some areas may be too remote from market to make crop production profitable. Therefore, ranchers have little choice but to continue livestock grazing, regardless of the

FIGURE 14.10 *Sheep grazing on an irrigated pasture in western United States. The principal forage plants here are brome grass, orchard grass, and yellow sweet clover. (USDA)*

price levels for their product, the costs or operation, or the productivity of the land itself. Most of the western rangeland will continue to be used for grazing, despite competition from other livestock-producing regions, price levels, and the other hazards of ranching.

Even though most rangeland cannot be used successfully for other types of agriculture, surprisingly little land in the West is so poor that it cannot be used for grazing. There are a few nearly barren areas, like the salt flats in Utah and parts of the desert in southern California, western Arizona, and southern Nevada. A few of the rockier, more barren mountains and some of the densely forested areas of northwestern California and western Oregon and Washington have no grazing. No one knows for certain how scant vegetation has to be to preclude some kind of grazing use. Some of the near-desert land may be grazed for only a few weeks following rains. Other dry areas may be grazed only by sheep in winter, when snow provides enough water for them. Still other areas may be grazed briefly in spring or summer when water and vegetative conditions are favorable.

In general, an acre of rangeland has a relatively low productivity; many acres are needed for a reasonably efficient ranch. Even a small, family-operated ranch may have 12,000 acres. This simple fact gives ranching and the management of rangeland its unique character.

Besides the basic problems of low productivity and lack of full control, the rancher is faced also with relatively high risk and uncertainty in his use of land. The great variation in productivity of rangeland from year to year requires flexibility in number of animals and seasons of grazing, and causes a variable output. The rancher may not be able to graze his land at all times, or he might have to dispose of his livestock or obtain feed from other sources. Either may be costly.

selected references

1. Aschmann, Homer, "Indian Pastoralists of the Guajira Peninsula," *Annals of the Association of American Geographers*, Vol. 50, No. 4, December 1960, pp. 408–418.

2. Baker, Oliver E., "Agricultural Regions of North America," *Economic Geography*, Vol. 7, No. 2, April 1931, pp. 109–153; Vol. 7, No. 4, October 1931, pp. 325–364; Vol. 8, No. 4, October 1932, pp. 325–377.

3. Boonstra, C. A., "Sheep Industry of Argentina's Patagonia," *Foreign Agriculture,* Vol. 15, July 1951, pp. 143–145.

4. Carney, J. P., and Anderberg, F., "The Sheep Industry of Western Australia," *Quarterly Review of Agricultural Economics*, Australia, Vol. 11, 1958, pp. 193–200.

5. Darling, F. Fraser, "Man's Ecological Dominance through Domesticated Animals on Wild Lands," in Thomas, William L., Jr., ed., *Man's Role in Changing the Face of the Earth*, Chicago: University of Chicago Press, 1956, pp. 778–787.

6. DeGraff, Harnell, *Beef: Production and Distribution*, Norman: University of Oklahoma Press, 1960.

7. Doerr, Arthur H., and Morris, John W., "The Oklahoma Panhandle—A Cross Section of the Southern High Plains," *Economic Geography*, Vol. 36, No. 1, January 1960, pp. 70–88.

8. Fletcher, Robert H., *Free Grass to Fences: The Montana Cattle Range Story*, New York: University Publications, 1961.

9. Johnson, Charles W., "Major Changes in the Beef Industry," *The Journal of Geography*, Vol. 64, No. 2, February 1965, pp. 53–58.

10. Jordan, Terry G., "The Origin of Anglo-American Cattle Ranching in Texas: A Documentation of Diffusion from the Lower South," *Economic Geography*, Vol. 45, No. 1, January 1969, pp. 63–87.

11. King, H. W., "Transhumance Grazing in the Snow Belt of New South Wales," *The Australian Geographer*, Vol. 7, 1959, pp. 129–140.

12. Kollmorgen, Walter M., "The Woodsman's Assault on the Domain of the Cattleman," *Annals of the Association of American Geographers*, Vol. 59, No. 2, June 1969, pp. 215–239.

13. ———, and Simonett, David S., "Grazing Operations in the Flint Hills—Bluestem Pastures of Chase County, Kansas," *Annals of the Association of American Geographers*, Vol. 55, No. 2, June 1965, pp. 260–290.

14. White, C. Langdon, "Cattle Raising: A Way of Life in the Venezuelan Llanos," *Scientific Monthly*, Vol. 83, September 1956, pp. 122–129.

15. Wilson, Charles M., *Grass and People*, Gainesville: University of Florida Press, 1961.

The grain crops rank first among the food crops of the world. Especially rich in starch, they supply body fuel and energy. They are consumed directly by man in a great variety of ways, as breads, cakes and pastries, and beverages. They are also used in large quantities as feed for livestock, and so indirectly provide man with such foods as meat, dairy products, and eggs.

About 50 percent of the world's total cropland is occupied by grain crops. Wheat, rice, millet, rye, and sorghum are the major food grains for humans; oats, barley, and corn are used mainly as livestock and poultry feed. In addition to providing man's food needs, either directly or indirectly, the grains also serve as raw materials for industrial establishments.

The relative importance of any one of these grains in any particular area is dependent upon several factors, some of which are inherent in the grains, others in the people who might engage in their cultivation. Among the major factors accounting for their distribution and importance are:

1. Land capability (fertility, moisture content, temperature, precipitation)
2. Yielding capacities of the grains
3. Producer–consumer preferences (taste, tradition, uses)
4. Purchasing power of potential or real market
5. Production and marketing costs
6. Governmental policies (international trade, acreage–volume controls, parity)
7. World market prices

chapter 15

Commercial Grain Farming

LOCATION

Figure 15.1 shows that the major world regions of commercial grain farming are concentrated in the middle latitudes of the Northern and Southern Hemispheres between 30° and 55°. The percentage of land devoted to this activity—less than 5 percent of the earth's surface—is relatively small compared to that for other agricultural activities.

In North America there are several major areas of production. The largest lies in the northern Great Plains and includes the Canadian Prairie Provinces (Alberta, Saskatchewan, and Manitoba) and the Dakotas. A second area centering in Kansas continues south to include the panhandles of Texas and Oklahoma. Smaller areas occur in eastern Oregon and Washington, southern Idaho, eastern Montana, eastern Illinois, and northern Iowa.

The Pampa of Argentina is the major commercial grain area in South America. Australia has considerable acreage in the southeastern and southwestern parts of the continent. Eurasia's commercial grain area stretches from west to east for some 2,000 miles, and is 700 miles north to south. It includes all of the Ukraine except its extreme southeast corner, Crimea, much of the northern Caucasus and the irrigated regions of Central Asia and Transcaucasia, the middle and lower Volga Basin, the south Urals, western Siberia, and Kazakhstan.

WHEAT

Wheat is one of the most widely grown crops, and is being harvested in some part of the world during every month of the year. It is not grown in the hot and humid equatorial regions, in deserts (except certain oases), or in regions where the average summer temperature falls below 50° F., but it is grown throughout the mid-latitude regions and in some parts of the equatorial regions. Despite its widespread cultivation, wheat ranks among the most important commodities in international trade, both in value and volume, because in many countries production falls short of the amount needed for domestic consumption. Although Europe produces more wheat than any other continent, it nevertheless is also the largest purchaser of wheat.

The market for wheat is international in extent; the price of wheat is therefore a world price, the prices in the leading wheat exchanges (Chicago, Winnipeg, Liverpool, and Buenos Aires) moving together in response to world conditions.

Wheat has no rival as a bread grain; rye is a very poor substitute for the average taste that has been introduced to the delicacies and varieties of wheat. Due to many factors (cost, preferences, food value to animals and humans, etc.) wheat is produced and milled primarily for use in bread and pastries; only in isolated areas or in localities where production is of poor quality is wheat used significantly as a food for livestock or poultry.

Physical Environment

Temperature and precipitation, the two major elements in plant growth, are of little consequence to the wheat plant. It produces poor yields only where man attempts to cultivate it in highly marginal semiarid areas. Most varieties of wheat can mature with the following minimal requirements:

1. 90 frost-free days with average temperatures above 57° F.
2. 10 inches of reliable precipitation
3. Cool, moist germination period
4. Warm, dry period for final ripening
5. Slightly acidic, friable soils
6. Low to moderate slope

Climate

The only crops that can resist lower average temperatures than wheat are barley, rye, potatoes, and some types of grasses that are harvested before they have ripened. Wheat requires an average temperature of at least 57° F. during the three summer months, with no severe frost during the last two. This temperature requirement sets the poleward limits of wheat cultivation, and also an altitude limit wherever cultivation is carried on in highlands.

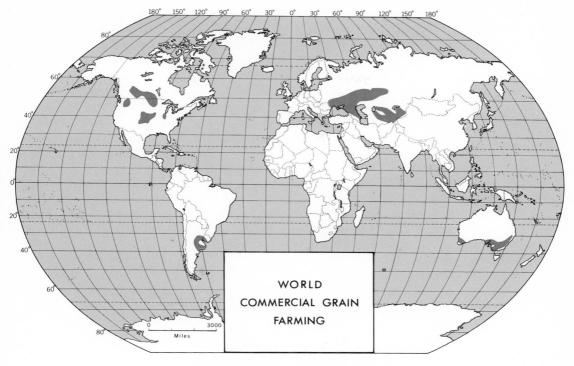

FIGURE 15.1   (*General Media Corporation*)

FIGURE 15.2   *The fields of the Gazyr State Farm, one of the largest grain-growing establishments in the southern part of the Russian Federated Soviet Socialist Republic. (Novosti Press Agency)*

Wheat can also withstand very high temperatures, if the humidity is relatively low. It is grown under such conditions in Egypt, parts of California, in northwest India, and Iraq. In a large part of the hot, low latitudes, however, high humidity and rainfall prevent wheat cultivation. Both the high and low moisture limits for possible wheat cultivation vary with temperature. In regions of low summer temperatures, wheat requires a rainfall between 10 and 40 inches annually; while in high temperature regions, the lower rainfall limit is 20 inches, and the upper, 70 inches. Thus, the temperature range is considerable, but moisture requirements restrict wheat mainly to regions with subhumid or semiarid climate.

The seasonal distribution of temperature and rainfall has important effects not only on the yield and quality of wheat, but also on the methods of cultivation. Wheat is planted in the fall or spring (the weather during the winter determining which method is followed), and in both cases is harvested during the following summer.

Spring wheat is grown in regions where the alternate freezing and thawing of the ground during the late winter and early spring would heave out of the soil, or "winter kill" wheat that had begun to grow in the fall. Spring-wheat seed must be of varieties adapted to the minimum growing season of ninety days. Thus, it must be planted after there is no danger from late spring frosts, so that it will mature before an early fall frost. Spring wheat is harvested in late summer.

Winter wheat is grown in regions where it can be planted in the fall. The plants start their growth before winter sets in, lie dormant during the winter, and continue their growth in the following spring. Winter wheat is harvested in early summer.

The ideal climatic combination for wheat growing is a cool, moist spring and a warm, sunny summer. The yield depends upon conditions during the period of early growth; the quality depends upon conditions during the ripening period. A warm, sunny summer produces a hard wheat with high nitrogen and protein content. A softer, more starchy wheat is grown in regions where the summers are cooler and moister, as in the eastern sections of the United States and in northwestern Europe. Most countries produce sufficient soft wheat to satisfy their domestic needs; it is the hard wheat, which is needed for blending purposes, that enters most largely into international trade.

Soils and Surface Features

Wheat is grown in several different types of soil, chiefly the chernozems and the gray-brownerths. The ideal soil for wheat is the chernozem, or blackerth; and the ideal crop for chernozem is wheat. It is on this soil that most of the wheat that enters international trade is grown—in the United States, Canada, the U.S.S.R., Argentina, Australia, and the Danube Basin. In Western Europe wheat is grown on the gray-brownerths.

The chernozem grassland regions are the world's prime wheat-growing lands. Since their surfaces are comparatively level and the soils friable and durable, cultivation is extensive. Large amounts of land and machinery, relatively little fertilizer, and small amounts of labor per acre are used.

Cultural Environment

Commercial wheat farming occurs in areas of low population density, usually from two to twenty-five people per square mile. Wheat has often been called a frontier crop, not only because of its distribution (Fig. 15.3), but because it is adapted to frontier conditions—scarce labor and extensive cultivation on vast tracts of land at a distance from markets. These factors explain the importance of wheat in Can-

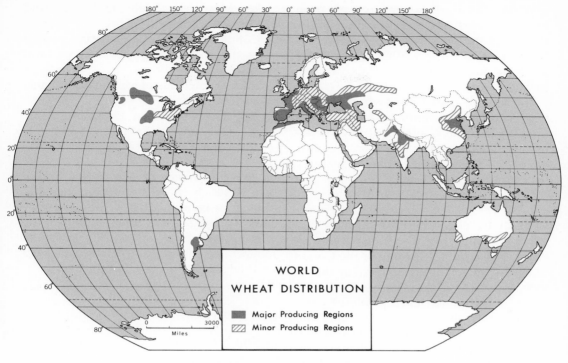

FIGURE 15.3 (*General Media Corporation*)

ada, Argentina, and Australia, where wheat is grown because there are few alternative opportunities and because the land is cheap.

Technological Factors

Technological improvements have been vital factors in determining the regions where wheat is grown, as well as the type of wheat grown and the amount produced in each region. Three technological improvements are of particular significance:

1. Well-drilling machinery made artesian water available for domestic use in the semiarid regions.
2. Railroad lines were built to make transportation facilities adequate for handling the wheat.
3. New types of agricultural machinery made it possible, in spite of a scarcity of labor, to cultivate large tracts of land in the short seasons available for seeding and harvesting.

Without these three developements it would have been impossible to bring into use the vast grasslands that have become the world's chief wheat-growing regions.

Tractor power, self-propelled combines, and other large-scale machinery enlarged the acreage that one man could handle—now about 300 acres on the eastern border of the Great Plains in the United States and 800–1,200 acres on the western edge, or even more for an especially good manager with adequate equipment. The hours of work for each acre of wheat have been reduced from 6.1 hours in 1902 to 2 hours in 1966. This includes time spent both in the field and also repairing and maintaining machinery.

Economic Factors

The acreage available for wheat production is reduced by competition for the land from other crops. Corn and cotton have much narrower limits than wheat;

thus their farm values per acre have been greater. Cotton has even narrower limits than corn, the result being that cotton has first choice of the land that is physically available for these crops, and corn has second place.

The acreage available for wheat production is, therefore, reduced by competition, and one must subtract from the potential wheat acreage that part which is better used for corn, cotton, vegetables, fruit, or other crops.

WHEAT IN THE UNITED STATES

About one crop acre in five in the United States is devoted to the production of wheat, and about one farmer in five grows wheat as a commercial crop. Wheat was a pioneer crop that accompanied land settlement as it progressed westward from the Atlantic seaboard. As each new area became a dependable source of wheat, older producing areas shifted more land to other crops, but some wheat was produced. It is still the most important crop in areas that were settled last, particularly in the Great Plains and the Pacific Northwest. In general, those are the drier areas of arable farming; wheat is grown not because the lands are especially well suited to it, but because wheat produces more grain and more income than any other crop thus far known in these areas. Except in the Palouse in Washington, yields of wheat are lower in these areas than almost anywhere else east of the Mississippi River and north of the Ohio. The Palouse country, with its cool, rainy winters and hot, dry summers, is well adapted to production of winter wheat.

There are several major areas of wheat production in the United States:

1. Spring Wheat Belt of North and South Dakota, Montana, and Minnesota, which continues into the Prairie Provinces of Canada—Alberta, Saskatchewan, and Manitoba
2. Winter Wheat Belt of Kansas, Nebras-

ka, Missouri, Oklahoma, Texas, and Colorado
3. Columbia Basin of the Pacific Northwest in Washington, Oregon, and Idaho
4. Interior lowlands of Michigan, Indiana, and Illinois
5. Appalachian area of Delaware, Georgia, Maryland, Pennsylvania, Virginia, and West Virginia

Of these five regions, the Spring Wheat Belt is much more significant than the other four combined. It is the most outstanding commercial wheat region in the world. Here as in no other area is the monoculture of grains practiced to such an intensity.

case study

Spring Wheat Belt

This region stretches for more than 1,000 miles north to south, and over 200 to 500 miles in width east to west. The northern boundary is fixed, presently because of seed requirements, by the frost-free period of ninety days and the July isotherm of 57° F. The western boundary is the foothills of the Rocky Mountains, to the east, the boundary is set by more humid climates that give rise to diseases (e.g., scab and stem rust), and competition with corn, barley, and flax; to the south by the rough topography of the Sand Hills of Nebraska used for livestock production; and to the southeast by competition with the Corn Belt and the highly valued products from beef cattle and swine.

Thus, the boundaries of the Spring Wheat Belt are set by limits both cultural (primarily economic) and physical (temperature, slope, precipitation) limits. Within most of the adjacent regions, spring wheat also could be grown profitably, however, not as profitably as other crops.

Climate

The climate is semiarid and has wide extremes. Rainfall is the greatest limitation to crop production. Moisture comes as slow rains, cloudbursts sometimes accompanied by hail, gentle

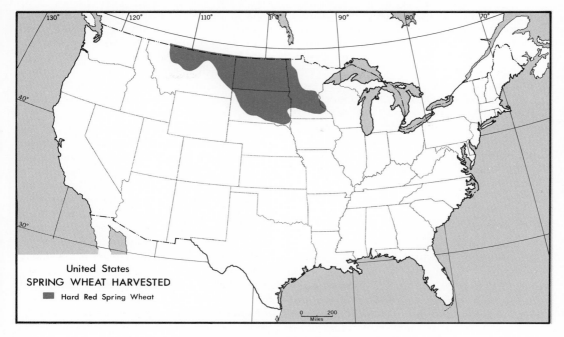

United States
SPRING WHEAT HARVESTED
■ Hard Red Spring Wheat

0   200
Miles

FIGURE 15.4 *(General Media Corporation)*

snowfalls, or intense blizzards. Annual precipitation averages slightly more than 20 inches along the eastern border, about 12 inches in north central Montana, 15 inches in southeastern Wyoming, and 15–22 inches in the Nebraska Sand Hills. About three-fourths of the annual precipitation comes during six months from April through September, nearly half in May, June, and July.

Temperatures in the Spring Wheat Belt are quite changeable. Highs of 90° to 100° F. are common during the day in summer; night temperatures of 50° F. also are to be expected during this period. Winter temperatures are considerably lower, averaging about 10–25 degrees below freezing, and on the coldest days dropping to −40° to −50° F.

In the southern portion, the frost-free period is about 120 days; the northern area 90 days. However, the shorter period in the northern part of the Spring Wheat Belt has longer hours of sunlight per day, which helps to compensate for the shorter growing period.

Soils

In the eastern part of the Spring Wheat Belt the soils are mainly loamy and sandy (cher-nozem), developed on varied glacial deposits. The western part includes the chestnut and brown soil zones, which developed on loamy and sandy glacial deposits, weathered sandstones, and loamstones and ancient river deposits.

Generally the land is a gently rolling plain, but some areas are rough and broken. Soil types and structures may vary widely. The surface features of lake beds, river valleys, plateaus, and buttes are the result of glacial action or wind erosion. Part of the area is deeply covered with glacial drift.

Production

Hard red spring wheat, the major variety here, is noted for its high protein content, which often brings a premium in the market, and for its excellent bread-making qualities. Hard red spring wheat is used extensively for blends that include weaker wheats, making a very soft and delicate flour. Red spring wheat is usually planted in early spring after the last frost. Owing to several factors, little labor is needed and one man often can handle a section of land (640 acres) with no outside labor except his machines.

Durum, a variety used chiefly for macaroni and similar pasta, is grown widely, particularly in North Dakota. The market for durum is much more limited than that for bread-type wheats.

Most farmers in the Spring Wheat Belt grow principally wheat. Often they produce other crops, usually in the fallow land as a hedge against failure of the wheat crop. Each necessary task is done with a specific piece of equipment: tractors, plows, drills, discs, harrows, weeders, combines, trucks, silo or elevator lifts, and other smaller tools.

Problems

Growing and shipping wheat are the major activities within the Belt. Nearly all residents are directly or indirectly dependent on each year's harvest. Only with the advent of the railway, the reaper, and other mechanical devices have farmers and townsmen attempted to transplant their sedentary civilization to this fickle climate.

As noted earlier, the Spring Wheat Belt is a land of climatic extremes—hot summers and cold winters—and of swift change. The region is naturally troublesome for the farmer. Though the average temperatures and rainfall are good, crops are not grown in *average* weather; they grow in the weather of the moment. Because of the dry continental climate of the spring wheat region, the crops of particular localities have often proved uncertain. One year, in large sections of South Dakota, for example, the early summer rains did not come until September. Wheat sown in April or May did not sprout until September, making not a money crop, but only a little late pasture. Dust storms, severe drought, or a hail storm in July that can level the stalks of wheat in five minutes are common hazards.

Weather Bureau records show that there are two kinds of drought: (1) those of a transitory nature, affecting a relatively small area and of comparatively short duration, frequently lasting only a year; (2) major phases of minimum precipitation covering many years and affecting large areas. When a long-run phase of mimimum precipitation prevails, there occur at short intervals what may be called "families of droughts."

If hail or drought do not ruin the wheat crop, frost may desolate it. If the season happens to be damp, rust may annihilate crops almost like fire. Grasshoppers can rise up in countless millions and devastate whole counties. And even if the crop does come through to a full, rich harvest, the grower often finds competition from a bumper crop in the Soviet Ukraine, Australia, Western Europe, or all of them.

Comparing the new settlers in the Spring Wheat Belt with the earlier settlers of Massachusetts and Pennsylvania, one finds great contrasts in economics and psychology. Instead of running a self-sufficient farm, the western settler depends on one or two money crops, selling wheat or oats or flaxseed to markets thousands of miles away, and buys everything from a store supplied largely from factories, also far away. The grower is absolutely dependent upon the railroad, which at best carries his crop only a few hundred miles, and the freight bill must be paid.

Historically, the plight of the farmer in the Spring Wheat Belt is well documented, his economic distress reflected in political dissatisfaction. In the 1870s, this region with its financial difficulties produced the "Greenback Movement." Out of it came Populism in the 1890s, in the 1920s it produced the nonpartisan League of North Dakota and the "farm bloc" in Congress; during the 1930s it supported the Townsend Plan and the New Deal.

Harvesting Wheat

Harvesting is accomplished in the greatest haste possible. A harvest crew consits of one man on a self-propelled combine, which often costs several thousand dollars, and one man in a truck behind the combine to pick up the wheat and haul it to storage. In the larger fields, there are often several dozen harvest crews of two men each. Threatening clouds necessitate working around the clock: lunch, dinner, breakfast, even drinks of water are taken on the combine and in the truck. No one can afford a single minute off from the harvest. The work is hard, the hours long, but the pay is good. Not even night stops these crews. When a crew has worked 18 to 24 hours, they are often relieved by a new crew, but the machines never stop except for refueling, refitting, or repairs. It is only on the larger, almost gigantic wheat farms that several crews

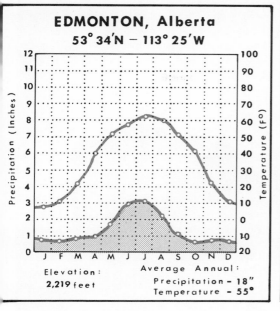
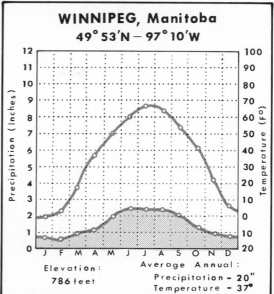

EDMONTON, Alberta
53° 34′N − 113° 25′W

Precipitation (Inches)

Temperature (F°)

J F M A M J J A S O N D

Elevation:
2,219 feet

Average Annual:
Precipitation − **18″**
Temperature − **55°**

WINNIPEG, Manitoba
49° 53′N − 97° 10′W

Precipitation (Inches)

Temperature (F°)

J F M A M J J A S O N D

Elevation:
786 feet

Average Annual:
Precipitation − **20″**
Temperature − **37°**

FIGURE 15.5   *Monthly temperature and precipitation graphs for two weather stations in the Spring Wheat Belt.*

FIGURE 15.6   *Harvesting spring wheat in Saskatchewan. (Canadian Government Travel Bureau)*

FIGURE 15.7 *Unloading Canadian grain at Chicago's port facilities. A "leg" from the elevator has been placed in the hold of the ship to unload the grain. (USDA)*

are used, for here labor is almost absent. Five crews can combine and store 600 acres of wheat in 24 hours, or less than three man hours per acre of wheat.

During the time the wheat begins to arrive at the grain elevators (storage bins), other segments of the economic structure also are busy. The elevator corporations and the rail companies are busy making bids for the storing and shipping of the grain.

Transportation

The major wheat movement from the grain elevators is by rail. Elevators have been built about ten miles apart along the major rail lines so that no major grain-producing area will be very far from an elevator or a railroad. Boxcars usually are scheduled for grain shipment six months in advance. However, unless the harvest is unusually small, there are never enough freight cars. Extra locomotives, enginemen, and other necessary personnel are brought from other sections to assist in the grain movement. When the railroads cannot handle the volume that needs to be moved, then trucks converge on the Spring Wheat Belt.

For a period of up to a month this intense activity takes place throughout the Belt. No one is idle, all machines operate day and night; the women are cooking for the combine crews. The activity is intense, for one can never be sure whether those clouds on the horizon will not destroy tens of millions of dollars worth of wheat.

CULTURAL ENVIRONMENT

Labor. Wheat farming in the major wheat areas is an "extensive" type of farming— that is, relatively few inputs are added to the land. All the plowing, planting, and harvesting of an acre of wheat in the Spring Wheat Belt, for example, can be done by only 2 hours of man labor and 1.5 hours of tractor time. In contrast, production of cotton may require as many as 100 hours of tractor work per acre. Once the wheat is seeded, particularly in the specialized producing areas, there is little more to be done until harvest. Wheat farmers sometimes spray to control weeds and insects, but ordinarily between seeding and harvest a man can do little to influence the outcome of the crop. He waits and takes what comes.

Part-time Farmers. Because wheat growing does not take their full attention for the entire year, many wheat farmers have other part-time jobs or business interests. The practice of combining other work with the farming is characteristic of the early settlement and the economic and cultural development of the Great Plains. When the Plains were first settled, the same people broke out the prairie sod and built homes, schools, churches, and stores. They now do the farming and at the same time operate the banks, machinery repair shops, and grain elevators. Many persons consider themselves farmers part of the year and during periods when crops are good. They depend on other sources of income at other times.

Settlement Pattern

This intermingling of farm and non-farm interests partly explains why many wheat farmers no longer live on the farms they operate. For many decades after settlement, most farmers lived in the open country on farms they owned or rented. More recently, particularly since World War II, many have moved to town in order to have the benefits of churches, schools, and other community services for their families.

Suitcase Farming. Because wheat farmers can now live away from their farms, land has come to have a different aspect. Farming traditionally was a business and a way of life for the farm family; each member from the time he could walk had chores or a job to do and was a working partner in the business. But business and home are separated when the family lives in town. The farm becomes so many fields of wheat, and the family's daily interests center in the town. Attitudes toward the land may change—not necessarily adversely.

Absentee operation spawned the term *suitcase farmer* for those who come to the farm from their city home and "live out of a suitcase" the few days they are seeding or harvesting.

Widespread Operations. Again, because wheat needs little attention between seeding and harvesting, the grower with the modern machinery can operate in widely separated locations. He can follow the seasons. Some individuals grow wheat in the Texas Panhandle, Nebraska, and North Dakota. The harvest begins in Texas with winter wheat and moves north into spring wheat as the summer progresses.

The ability to operate in different localities permits the farmer to work larger acreages with the same equipment, expand his scale of operations, and increase his efficiency with less equipment, overhead, and labor. Operating in separate localities also serves as a form of crop insurance against such hazards as drought and hail. The same storm is unlikely to hit both areas in the same season.

Getting a Start. The comparative ease with which young farmers can get started in farming is another characteristic of the main U.S. wheat-producing areas. Many start by using their father's machinery and renting land for a share of the crop. An industrious, dependable young man usually can rent the kind he needs. He can soon acquire his own tractor and combine if things go well. Such golden propects have attracted young farmers to the wheat sections and partly explain why the margin of cultivation has been pushed to poorer and still poorer lands. A young farmer eventually saves enough from his earnings for a downpayment on some land. As most wheat farmers do not attempt to own all the land they need to operate, he continues to rent additional land.

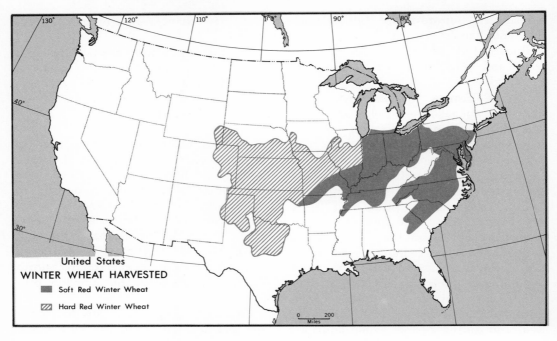

FIGURE 15.8   *(General Media Corporation)*

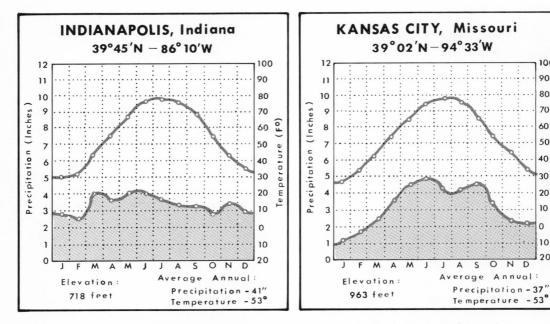

FIGURE 15.9   *Monthly temperature and precipitation graphs for two weather stations in the Winter Wheat Belt.*

Land Tenure

Part-ownership characterizes land tenure in the specialized wheat-producing regions. Part-owners—not counting paid managers and institutions—comprise more than 40 percent of the operators. Part-owner farms are larger than full-owner and full-tenant farms and have more cattle and equipment. Part-owners include the operators whose managerial capacity exceeds their possession of investment funds and those who prefer to invest more of their own funds in operating capital rather than land.

Full-owners often are small operators. They are older, and they work off the farm part of the time. Full tenants usually are the younger operators who are just getting started and who have not saved enough for a downpayment on a farm.

Land Rent

The usual rental in the specialized wheat areas is a share of the cash crops and a cash rate per acre on the forage crops and pasture. A typical *share rent* is one-third of the wheat, barley, grain, sorghum, and similar grain crops. Renting *land* is somewhat simpler, and fewer areas of conflict exist between landlord and tenant in the specialized wheat areas than in many other farm areas. That is because farming systems are simpler, production practices are more standardized, and management decisions are fewer. In a wheat-fallow area, there is no question as to the crop that will be grown. Once the crop is seeded, there are few further management decisions until harvest time.

Government Price Support

The acreage capable of growing wheat exceeds the acreage needed for domestic and foreign markets. This fact in itself would present no problem. There is also more land than is needed for producing soybeans, corn and cotton. The problem arises because wheat growing is profit-able throughout the country. In the specialized areas of the Great Plains, wheat has an unchallenged claim on the land. The competitive crops in the Eastern states have been improved by new technology. Yields have increased from use of fertilizer, weed sprays, and improved varieties. The small combine-harvester has made the Eastern wheat grower independent of the neighborhood's threshing rig. Consequently, there is excess capacity for wheat production in the United States.

This excess capacity is put to good use in times of national emergency. Wheat is a quick way to expand food supplies. It is easily transported to areas of need. At other times, however, a high production of wheat is a national problem because without price supports a great wheat surplus would lower the price of the grain to such a low level that farmers would be bankrupt. To avoid such a catastrophe, the federal government guarantees the farmer a minimum price for his grain (wheat, corn, and other grains) which is set each year by the Secretary of Agriculture. Surplus grain is purchased by the government and stored in huge cylindrical bins which are common sights in many settlements within the commercial wheat and commercial corn growing areas.

Acreage Allotments. Other acts authorize the government to subsidize exports of wheat and to pay farmers for not planting their allotted acreages of wheat. They are known as wheat programs and have an impact on wheat farmers and on the way they use their land.

COMMERCIAL GRAIN FARMING—MAJOR WORLD AREAS

Three major commercial grain regions outside Anglo-America stand out distinctly on a map.

U.S.S.R. The Soviet Union is one of the world's foremost grain-producing lands. The cereal lands form a long narrow belt, extending for nearly 3,000 miles in an east–west direction from the borders of the Eastern European states of Czechoslovakia, Hungary, and Romania across southern European Russia to the Yenisei River. This grain belt closely parallels the steppe or prairie of Russia, which is world famous for its rich blackerths, or chernozem soils. Essentially, the Soviet grain belt includes all of European Russia south of the 50th parallel to the Black Sea, and Asiatic Russia west of the Yenisei River between the 50th and 55th parallels.

The western segment, lying west of the Volga River and south of the Northwest Region, is the most productive agricultural area in the Soviet Union. It includes the Ukraine, the Moldavian Republic, the blackerth zone of the Central Industrial Region, the North Caucasian Region, and the western portion of the Volga Region. The climate is similar to the grain-growing area of Nebraska, South Dakota, and North Dakota.

Winter temperatures are mild enough to allow winter wheat to survive, and the growing season is long enough and precipitation sufficient for corn and sugar beets to mature. In terms of national acreage, it accounts for 75 percent of Soviet winter wheat, 80 percent of maturing corn, and 85 percent of sugar beets.

The eastern segment of the grain belt lying east of the Volga River is the spring wheat zone of the U.S.S.R. It includes the steppe and mixed forest areas of the eastern portion of the Volga Region, the southern Ural Region, West Siberia, and northern Kazakhstan. East of the Volga, winter temperatures gradually become more severe, precipitation becomes lighter, and the frost-free period shorter. In general, growing conditions are similar to those of the Canadian prairies.

Little winter wheat is grown, due to the extremely cold winter temperatures; also, corn and sugar beet cultivation here is extremely light. The major environmental problem for the region's specialty crop, spring wheat, is adequate moisture. In fact, droughts commonly win thousands of acres of grain. The severest type of drought is associated with the hot dry wind called *sukhovey* that originates in the deserts of Central Asia and occasionally spreads northward into the grain belt.

Argentina. The *Pampa* of Argentina, a grassy level plain, is the most productive grain region in South America. Well over half of the cultivated area is devoted to cereal grain; wheat alone occupies slightly over one-fourth of all the cropland. In total acreage it is rivaled only by alfalfa. The chief wheat area forms a giant crescent 600 miles long, stretching from Sante Fé in the north to the coastal margin east of Bahía Blanca in the south.

Although Argentina is one of the least important of the world's twelve major wheat producers, both in acreage and total output, her large wheat export is a response to a small population in relation to area and a good rail network near the ocean for shipment abroad.

Australia. Wheat is Australia's major grain crop. The wheat zone lies entirely outside the tropics and almost entirely in the areas of Mediterranean and temperate grassland climate. The chief area stretches from Adelaide inland some 1,000 miles into the Murray-Darling Basin. A second zone is located in the southwestern part of the continent. Nearly one-half the wheat is available for export; about one-fourth is shipped to the United Kingdom, much of the remainder to India, New Zealand, and Ceylon. Australian wheat has a reputation for its whiteness, and often commands the highest prices in world markets.

INTERNATIONAL TRADE

Table 15.1 shows the circulation of six major grains in world trade. Wheat is by far the most important grain commodi-

Table 15.1   1968–69 (July–June) World Trade in Cereal Grains—Leading Nations (thousand metric tons)

Exports		Imports	
Wheat Grain		World: 42,034.1	
United States	13,045.6	Japan	4,260.0
Canada	8,056.1	China (Mainland)	3,567.0
France	5,300.5	India	3,249.0
U.S.S.R.	5,166.0	United Kingdom	3,113.0
Australia	4,891.3	Brazil	1,975.0
Argentina	2,666.0	West Germany	1,913.0
		Netherlands	1,794.0
Maize		World: 27,661.2	
United States	12,977.1	Japan	4,657.0
Argentina	3,968.5	Italy	4,655.0
South Africa	2,690.0	Netherlands	3,230.0
France	2,358.7	United Kingdom	2,728.0
Thailand	1,301.5	Spain	1,740.0
*Rice (Milled)**		World: 5,032 [†]	
United States	1,748.3	Viet Nam, Rep. of	497.8
Thailand	1,047.9	India	458.2
United Arab Republic	670.9	Hong Kong	299.4
Burma	334.9[†]	Ceylon	261.5
Cambodia	172.4	Singapore	237.2
Barley		World: 6,228.8	
France	3,466.5	West Germany	960.0
U.S.S.R.	600.0	Japan	654.0
Australia	450.7	Italy	599.0
Canada	411.1	Belgium & Luxembourg	582.0
United States	249.6	Switzerland	401.0
Oats		World: 1,088.5	
Australia	333.5	Italy	160.0
Sweden	210.6	Netherlands	151.0
Argentina	200.7	West Germany	137.0
France	146.7	Belgium & Luxembourg	63.0
United States	55.7	Japan	48.0
Rye		World: 252	
Canada	105.4	Germany, Fed. Rep. of	67.6
Netherlands	34.3	Japan	47.5
United States	31.7	Norway	44.9
France	28.8	Finland	21.4
Sweden	18.3	Austria	18.8

*100 paddy units = 65 milled rice units.
[†] 1968 calendar year data.
Source: Based on the *Monthly Bulletin of Agricultural Economics and Statistics*, Vol. 19, February 1970, FAO of the United Nations, Rome; the World Agricultural Production and Trade, Statistical Report(s) August and December 1969, United States Department of Agriculture, Foreign Agricultural Service.

ty, both in terms of tonnage and value. The United States leads in wheat exports; Canada is likewise a large exporter, followed by France, the U.S.S.R., Australia, and Argentina.

selected references

1. Curtis, Byrd C., and Johnston, David R., "Hybrid Wheat," *Scientific American*, Vol. 220, No. 5, May 1969, pp. 21–29.

2. Farnsworth, Helen C., "Imbalance in the World Wheat Economy," *Journal of Political Economy*, Vol. 66, February 1958, pp. 1–23.

3. Fielding, Gordon J., "The Role of Government in New Zealand Wheat-Growing," *Annals of the Association of American Geographers*, Vol. 55, No. 1, March 1965, pp. 87–97.

4. Hewes, Leslie, "Causes of Wheat Failure in the Dry Farming Region, Central Great Plains, 1939–1957," *Economic Geography*, Vol. 41, No. 4, October 1965, pp. 313–330.

5. Hoag, Leverett P., "Location Determinants For Cash-Grain Farming in the Corn Belt," *The Professional Geographer*, Vol. 14, No. 3, May 1962, pp. 1–7.

6. Jackson, W. A. D., "Durum Wheat and the Expansion of Dry Farming in the Soviet Union," *Annals of the Association of American Geographers*, Vol. 46, No. 4, December 1956, pp. 405–410.

7. ———, "The Russian Non-Chernozem Wheat Base," *Annals of the Association of American Geographers*, Vol. 49, No. 1, June 1959, pp. 97–109.

8. Kollmorgen, Walter M., and Jenks, George F., "Sidewalk Farming in Toole County, Montana, and Trail County, North Dakota," *Annals of the Association of American Geographers*, Vol. 48, No. 3, September 1958, pp. 209–231.

9. ———, "Suitcase Farming in Sully County, South Dakota," *Annals of the Association of American Geographers*, Vol. 48, No. 4, December 1958, pp. 375–397.

10. Meinig, Donald W., "Colonization of Wheatlands: Some American and Australian Comparisons," *Australian Geographer*, Vol. 7, 1959, pp. 145–156.

11. ———, *On the Margins of the Good Earth*, Chicago: University of Chicago Press, 1962.

12. Miller, E. Joan Wilson, "Hybrid Corn and More Food for More People," *The Journal of Geography*, Vol. 63, No. 9, December 1964, pp. 413–417.

13. Rowe, Kaye, "Brandon: The Wheat City," *Canadian Geographical Journal*, Vol. 78, No. 5, May 1969, pp. 156–163.

14. Vanderhill, Burke G. "Changing Patterns in the Peace River Country," *Canadian Geographical Journal*, Vol. 77, No. 1, July 1968, pp. 2–13.

15. Willetts, H. T., "Soviet Agriculture; A Weak Link in Economic Development," *The World Today*, Vol. 16, 1960, pp. 149–160.

Commercial livestock and crop farming, often called mixed farming, is a form of extensive agriculture based on a combination of crop cultivation and animal husbandry. Half or more of the arable land is used to raise food for farm animals, which are fattened primarily for human consumption.

LOCATION

The two largest commercial livestock and crop farming regions are in the United States and Eurasia (Fig. 16.1). This activity prevails in the Midwest (Ohio, Indiana, Illinois, Iowa, Nebraska), the South (Virginia, Tennessee, Georgia), and the Southwest (Oklahoma and much of Texas). In Eurasia it encompasses much of northern Portugal and Spain, the Po Plain of Italy, a large portion of the Danube Basin countries of Hungary, Yugoslavia, and western Romania, and the Amur Valley in the U.S.S.R.

Minor regions are to be found in Argentina, southeast Brazil, south central Chile, and South Africa. Elsewhere, only occasional patches of this type of activity occur near the larger occidental cities.

CHARACTERISTICS

The commercial livestock–crop farming system concentrates on breeding and plant selection, and a well-established rotation in which legumes and hay play a part in proper soil management. Grains are produced both for sale as a cash crop and as feed for livestock. In the former case, some farmers specialize only in the growing of wheat, corn, or soybeans for sale; in the latter, corn, the major crop, is converted by animals and sold as meat for human consumption.

Farm animals utilize roughage, which may be produced in any system of mixed livestock–crop farming. On a typical Corn Belt farm with a rotation of corn,

chapter **16**

Commercial Livestock and Crop Farming

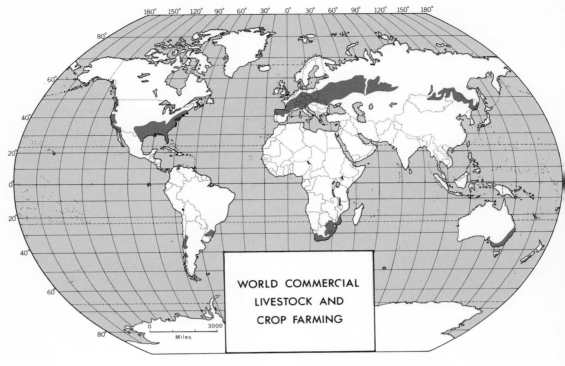

FIGURE 16.1   (*General Media Corporation*)

oats, and clover, approximately 1.75 tons of roughage are produced for every ton of grain. Animals convert these by-products of grain production, which are of little value in themselves, into products of much greater market value.

In Eurasia, root crops that are planted in rotation with the grain crops in order to maintain soil fertility are fed to farm animals. Hay is a substitute for corn in most of Eurasia; corn is an important feed crop only in the Danube Valley. Elsewhere potatoes, turnips, sugar beets, and oats are the major feed crops.

Farms in Eurasia tend to be smaller and less mechanized than their United States counterparts, with higher production per acre but lower production per worker. Average livestock–grain operations in the United States occupy approximately 150 acres (ranging from 120 to 200); in South America and South Africa they are about the same size; in Eurasia about half as large.

Livestock and crop production are complementary activities on general farms. They make possible a more even seasonal distribution of labor requirements, the heavy labor demands coming at a time when the labor is released from caring for the crops. It is for these reasons that cattle raising plays such an important role in the intensive agriculture of northwestern Europe and the Corn Belt of the United States.

case study

The United States Corn Belt

The Corn Belt or Midland Feed Region, an area of about 220 million acres, extends from central Ohio to western Nebraska and from southwestern Missouri to central Minnesota. It is bounded on the east in Ohio by the foothills of the Appalachian Mountains, and on the south by the rough topography along the Ohio River and the Ozark uplift in Illinois

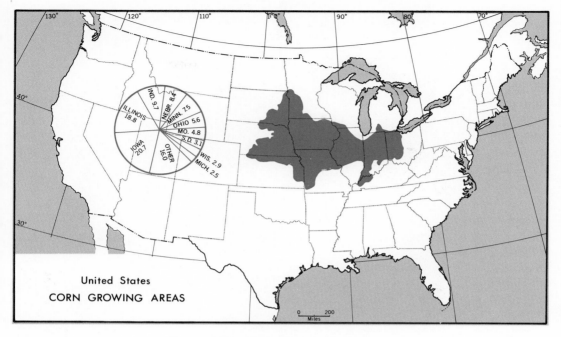

FIGURE 16.2   (*General Media Corporation*)

and Missouri. Its western and northern boundaries are established by the dry weather of
the Great Plains and the shorter growing season and cool summer nights of the Lake States
(Fig. 16.2).

Physical Environment

Most of the land in this productive region is
level to gently rolling. The deep, warm, fertile
soils are rich in organic matter and nitrogen.
They were derived chiefly from glacial and
related soil material, are relatively young and
productive, structurally good, and hold moisture well. About 60 percent of the soil was
formed under prairie vegetation.

Climate. Precipitation occurs throughout
the year, but a somewhat greater amount is
received during the summer months. The
rainfall in most of the Corn Belt is 30–40 inches
annually. The west and northwest portion
receives about 22–30 inches, but this drier
section receives about three-fourths of its
total from April to September while crops are
growing.

Summers are hot and humid. The nights
are almost as hot as the days. Daytime temper-

atures average 75° to 80° F.; night temperatures seldom drop below 60° F. Autumn days
are invigorating, with cool nights, and frosts
are frequent. Severe cold is occasionally ex-

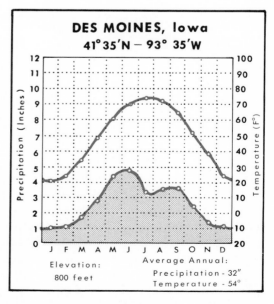

FIGURE 16.3   *Monthly temperature and precipitation for a station in the Corn Belt.*

FIGURE 16.4 *In McLain County, Illinois, a four-row planter makes a 3/4-mile row before turning around. (Standard Oil Co. of New Jersey)*

FIGURE 16.5 *Harvesting corn in the United States Corn Belt. (International Harvester Co.)*

perienced in the winter season, although on the whole the three coldest months (December, January, and February) have mean temperatures of 25° F. Much crisp, sunny weather is characteristic. Springs are unpredictable, in some years quite rainy or cold, in others, warm and sunny.

The growing season is long and warm, having about 180 frost-free days in the south and 140 frost-free days in the north. Only occasionally does corn fail to mature properly.

Work Pattern

The seasonal pattern of work on the typical Corn Belt farm is dictated to a considerable extent by seasonal variations in climate. During the winter while the ground is covered with snow and ice, emphasis is on the feeding of livestock, fence repair, and equipment overhaul. Little or no field work is possible, and traditionally winter is the time of maximum social activity among the Corn Belt farmers. With the coming of spring, attention is given to the preparation of fields and seeding of crops. During the early summer comes haying and cultivation of corn to control weeds and conserve moisture. In late summer there is a period of slack activity after the small grain harvest and prior to the corn harvest. In the fall the corn is gathered and certain crops are seeded.

Agricultural Patterns

The relatively flat topography permits an intensive corn-cropping program with modern labor-saving machinery. About three-fourths of the corn harvested for grain in the United States and about 40 percent of the world's output of corn are grown in the Corn Belt.

Corn is particularly seasonal in its use of labor and equipment. To protect or replenish the structure and productivity of his soils, and to spread the use of his labor and equipment, a Corn Belt farmer grows other crops with corn —chiefly oats, soybeans, wheat, and hay, and pasture crops—in his cropping system. He seldom grows corn on more than half of his cropland. The oat crop is seeded in the spring before work on the corn crop begins and is cut in the summer when cultivation of corn is nearly over. Soybeans, the second most prof-

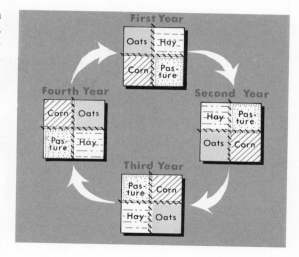

FIGURE 16.6 *A typical rotation pattern in the Corn Belt.*

itable crop in the area, are planted after corn and harvested earlier. Winter wheat is seeded in the fall when the harvest of other crops is mainly over.

Oats and *wheat* are the transitional crops in the rotation between corn or soybeans and the grass or legume soil-building crops that are essential to a program of soil maintenance and improvement. Oats and the forage crop are planted together. As the oat crop is taller and matures more quickly than grasses and legumes, the oats can be harvested without much damage to the other crop. A primary function of the oats is to serve as a companion crop to the forage crop, shading out weeds and providing some protection from wind and sun while the young forage plants become established.

The feed crops (corn, oats, and hay and pasture) and soybeans form the chief basis of the farming system in practically all parts of the region, not only in respect to the cropping program but also in selecting livestock enterprises to utilize the feed crops. The dominant crop, corn, which is primarily a meat-making feed, is used chiefly for fattening hogs and beef cattle.

Cash Grain. Cash-grain farms are the largest farms in the Corn Belt both in terms of acreage and total investment, but the smallest in hours of labor used. Corn, oats, and soybeans are grown for sale on large farms in east cen-

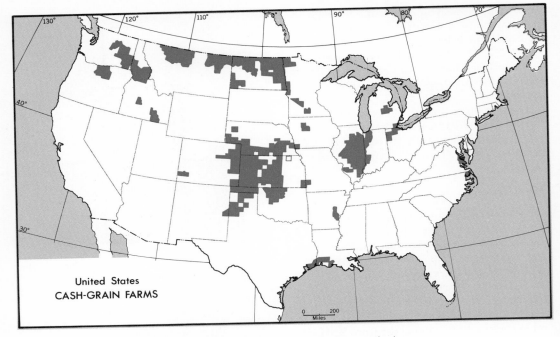

FIGURE 16.7   (*General Media Corporation*)

tral Illinois and parts of north central Iowa. Conditions that are favorable to a grain type of farming also are favorable to tenant operation of the land. Landlords usually prefer to receive a share of the crop as payment for use of the land. They also often prefer to sell their share for cash soon after harvest. Thus they frequently are not interested in providing buildings and fences, and, as their tenure is often uncertain, tenants cannot afford to put much money in the fences and equipment that are needed in livestock production. These conditions are unfavorable to development of a livestock system of farming, even though the cropping system is built mainly around feed grains.

Crop–Livestock

Hogs and beef cattle are the chief livestock enterprises dominant in three sections of the Corn Belt:

1. On the areas of loessal soils that border parts of the Missouri and Mississippi Rivers and usually are rolling
2. On the southern side of the Corn Belt—in southern Iowa, northeastern Missouri, and the adjacent counties in Illinois—where the land is rolling and there is more hay and pasture and a smaller supply of feed grains
3. On the western side of the Corn Belt, a transitional area between corn and livestock feeding, and wheat and range livestock

Hogs. Because hogs convert concentrated feeds efficiently into meat, they have first call on the corn grown. But even with an optimum-sized hog enterprise, many farms in these areas have a surplus of corn. The abundant hay and pasture are utilized better when fed to cattle in conjunction with a concentrate ration. The hog enterprise consists of about 150 hogs marketed annually, which requires farrowing about 30 litters of pigs. The ratio of spring to fall litters is about two to one. By feeding corn to hogs, farmers do a larger volume of business with only a limited addition to their investment in fixed resources. Thus, hog feeding is a method of utilizing more fully the farm operator's labor and thereby increasing his annual income.

Beef Cattle. Beef cattle usually are selected in preference to dairy cattle because they use more grain in proportion to forage than do

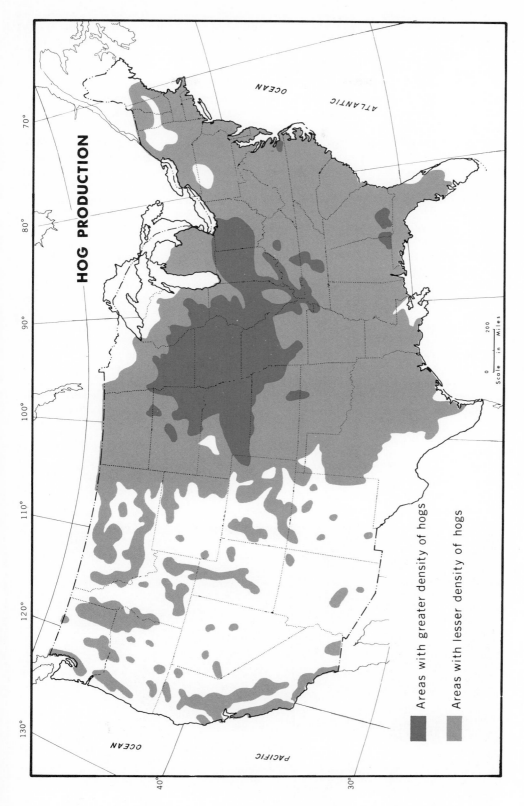

HOG PRODUCTION

Areas with greater density of hogs

Areas with lesser density of hogs

0   200
Scale in Miles

FIGURE 16.8 (General Media Corporation)

dairy cattle. Fattening cattle on grain reaches its maximum in feedlots on farms in these areas. Most of the feeder cattle are born on western ranges in the spring. Some are shipped to the Corn Belt in the fall as feeder calves weighing 350–450 pounds. Others are carried on the range over winter, grazed the following summer, and moved to the Corn Belt feedlots as 600 to 700-pound yearlings. The heaviest movement of feeders usually is in October. The yearlings are fed to various weights and grades before they are sold for slaughter. Many are marketed in late spring and early summer, the largest volume usually coming in June. Calves, which fatten more slowly than yearlings, are marketed mainly in August and September. Thus, the cattle-feeding operation has a production and investment period that may range from three to twelve months; six to eight months being the most common.

Records from a sampling of Corn Belt farms indicate that about one-half the farmers in these areas fatten cattle for market. About 10 percent of these fed lots of four carloads or more; about 50 percent fed from one to three carloads; and the rest fed less than a carload, confining their feeding operations largely to cattle of their own raising. Most of the farmers keep a small beef cattle breeding herd. Those who do not fatten large lots of cattle concentrate more on breeding herds. The typical cattle enterprise consists of about two carloads fattened for market and a small breeding herd.

Poultry and Sheep. Chickens are a minor enterprise, but farm flocks are kept on many farms. Between one-fourth and one-fifth of the poultry in the United States is in the Corn Belt. Also about half of the sheep and lambs "on feed" are fattened in the Corn Belt, and sheep are kept on a few farms.

Flexibility of Corn Belt Farms

From year to year, the fixed resources—land, buildings, and to a considerable extent machinery—of each Corn Belt farm can be utilized in many ways. Land and climate give the Corn Belt an advantage over other areas in production of several crops and several classes of livestock. The alternatives are relatively close as far as returns are concerned.

Corn and soybeans are interchangeable in the crop rotation. The typical livestock enter-

FIGURE 16.9 *Farmers using an automatic bale wagon, which can unload a bale at a time, on the go, into a feedbunk or an open pasture. Machinery such as this illustrates the increasing mechanization of the American farm. (New Holland Division of Sperry Rand)*

prises—hogs, beef cattle, fattening, and poultry—can be instituted, expanded, contracted, or liquidated in a year or two. And the emphasis of many Corn Belt herds can be shifted from "kept for beef" to "kept for milk" at any time by feeding some of the calves and marketing the milk.

Thus, the unspecialized character of the fixed resources and the relatively short period of production and investment for livestock give farmers in the Corn Belt the ability to adjust easily and quickly to changing economic conditions. A farmer may choose among his alternatives based on his expectation of future prices. A farmer who expects the price of corn to be high compared to that of livestock may curtail his livestock enterprise considerably and sell part or all of his corn. If he expects the prices of both corn and livestock to be relatively low, he may store his corn and take a price-support loan from the government. But a farmer who expects the price of hogs to be high relative to the price of corn may decide to expand his production of hogs. He may expand his cattle-feeding program if he believes that prices of fat cattle will be high compared with the current prices for feeder cattle and corn.

LIVESTOCK AND OTHER CROP FARMING AREAS

The American South

The development of commercial livestock –grain activities represents the greatest change in the South's agriculture in the period since the end of World War II. The number of dairy and beef cattle, hogs, and poultry have increased rapidly, largely because of:

1. More widespread use of recent technological developments
2. Advances in animal sciences that have led to increased production of feed crops and more extensive suitable pasturage
3. Improved financial status of a large number of Southern farmers
4. An increasing consciousness of the real possibilities of livestock enterprises among farmers, farm organizations, and land-grant college personnel

Pacific Northwest

Hay, pasture, and small grains occupy considerable acreage in the Rogue River Valley. Sheep and dairy cattle are raised to utilize the large amount of roughage. Dairy, poultry, and horticultural crops provide the three main sources of farm income in the Puget lowland. The Willamette Valley produces a large number of different crops, including grains, forage crops for hay, pasture, and silage, grass and legume seeds, vegetables, berries, tree fruits and nuts, and many specialty crops. A single farm may grow ten to fifteen different crops.

Eurasia

Considerable mixed farming is practiced in Western Europe. Livestock products (milk, pigs, eggs) form the main income, and the products of the arable land are, for the most part, fed to the livestock on the farm itself. Farms produce wheat, potatoes, sugar beets, vegetables, and fruit, and indirectly, meat, eggs, and milk.

The Danube Basin resembles the Missouri River Basin in Kansas, Nebraska, and South Dakota—a land of cold winters, hot summers, and summer rainfall maximum. It has more rough mountain land and less plain than the United States Corn Belt. Three-fifths of the entire area is devoted to field crops, pasturage, and hay; more than two-thirds of the people till the soil or raise livestock.

Millions of acres on the wide, flat plains of Hungary still serve only for pasturage, and the yields of cereal per acre is far less than in Western Europe. Corn occupies first place in Hungary and Romania, and the latter is a leading European producer. Wheat occupies first place in Bul-

FIGURE 16.10 *The Willamette Valley southwest of Salem, Oregon. Here the Willamette River bends gracefully as it flows northward to its confluence with the Columbia River near Portland. (Oregon State Highway Travel Division)*

FIGURE 16.11 *Cattle on a state farm in southeastern Yugoslavia. (Yugoslavian Information Center)*

garia and also is an important crop in Romania.

The livestock industry has suffered from the communist regimes, under which much of the grazing land has been plowed up for row crops. Fodder shortages are acute. Cattle, sheep, and hogs are present in the greatest numbers, but sheep are the most important. Hog raising is being emphasized, and more corn is now grown as feed for hogs. Cattle have declined, owing to lack of fodder, poor shelter, and their use as draft animals. The Amur Valley is one of the major grain-growing districts of the Soviet Far East. The basic crops are wheat, oats, and rye, and associated with grain farming is an intensive dairying economy.

South America

The economy of the humid subtropics of South America is basically agricultural. Livestock raising and grain farming dominate. The Pampa of Argentina produces the bulk of the nation's wheat, corn, flax, small grains, cattle, sheep, and hogs. Argentina exports nearly all the corn shipped from Latin America, principally to the United Kingdom, the Netherlands, France, Belgium, Germany, and Denmark, where it is used as feed for livestock. Wheat, too, is exported to European markets in large quantities; meat, wool, hides, and skins are other important South American trade items.

selected references

1. Coppock, J. T., "Crop, Livestock, and Enterprise Combinations in England and Wales," *Economic Geography*, Vol. 40, No. 1, January 1964, pp. 65–81.

2. Curry, Leslie, "The Climatic Resources of Intensive Grassland Farming: The Waikato, New Zealand," *Geographical Review*, Vol. 52, No. 3, July 1962, pp. 174–194.

3. Dobbins, Claud E., "Ireland's Livestock and Meat Industry," *Foreign Agricultural Service*, Washington, D.C.: United States Department of Agriculture, FAS M-130, 1962, pp. 1–13.

4. Durand, Loyal, Jr., "The Major Milksheds of the Northeastern Quarter of the United States," *Economic Geography*, Vol. 40, No. 1, January 1964, pp. 174–194.

5. Griffin, Paul F., Chatham, Ronald L., and Young, Robert N., *Anglo-America: A Systematic and Regional Geography*, 2d ed., Palo Alto, Calif.: Fearon Publishers, 1968, Ch. 12.

6. Hidore, John J., "The Relationship Between Cash–Grain Farming and Landforms," *Economic Geography*, Vol. 39, No. 1, January 1963, pp. 84–89.

7. Kernal, Willy, "The Farm of the Future," *Danish Foreign Office Journal*, No. 34, 1960, pp. 16–20.

8. Lamer, Mirko, "Economic Trends in the Soviet Dairy Industry," *FAO, Monthly Bulletin of Agricultural Economics*, Vol. 7, 1958, pp. 1–15.

9. Roepke, Howard G., "Changes in Corn Production on the Northern Margin of the Corn Belt," *Agricultural History*, Vol. 33, July 1959, pp. 126–132.

10. Rudd, Robert D., "A Beef Cattle Farm in the Corn Belt," in Richard M. Highsmith, ed., *Case Studies in World Geography: Occupance and Economy Types*, Englewood Cliffs, N. J.: Prentice-Hall, Inc., 1961, pp. 47–54.

11. Synder, David E., "An Estancia in Argentina: Commercial Livestock Raising," in Richard S. Thoman and Donald J. Patton, eds., *Focus on Geographic Activity*, New York: McGraw-Hill Book Company, Inc., 1964.

12. Stevens, A.J., "Surfaces, Soils, and Land Use in Northeast Hampshire," *Institute of British Geographers*, Publications No. 26, 1959, pp. 51–66.

13. Weaver, John C., "Crop Combinations Regions in the Middle West," *Geographical Review*, Vol. 44, No. 2, April 1954, pp. 175–200.

14. Yoke, Ralph S., "The Smallholdings of Denmark," *Foreign Agriculture*, Vol. 18, March 1959, pp. 58–59.

15. Zeuner, Frederick E., *A History of Domesticated Animals*, London: Hutchinson & Company, Ltd., 1963.

chapter **17**

Specialized Horticulture

Specialized horticulture is found in exceptionally favored spots, where fruit and vegetable growing is conducted on a large scale. Although truck farming and vineyards are widespread throughout many parts of the mid-latitudes, the areas are too small and scattered to be indicated on the map, Fig. 17.1. Because the agricultural system is much the same as in the vegetable and fruit growing of nearby oases, the irrigated areas of cotton in the lower Colorado Basin, of sugar beets in the Salt Lake oases of western United States, and sugar cane in the coastal areas of Peru and northern Argentina, these areas are classed with regions of specialized horticulture.

VEGETABLES

Vegetables play an important part in keeping a balanced diet. Some, such as beans and peas, add protein to the diet; others, such as potatoes, add starch and water. In general, they add bulk to the diet and tend to dilute the highly concentrated foods obtained in meats and cereals. Their importance has been further emphasized by the fact that they provide most of the vitamins that seem to be necessary for human health.

The increased use of vegetables, especially in the United States and Western Europe, has been due to a number of causes other than the improvement in transportation facilities. Rapid urbanization, increased purchasing power of the people, and the higher scale of living have all contributed to a greater consumption of vegetables. At the same time, technological improvements in preserving and transporting perishable products have been of great significance. The development of cold-storage methods, of refrigeration and of heated cars, improved methods of canning, preserving, quick freezing and drying, and better grading of products, have all influenced the almost revolutionary changes in diet that have

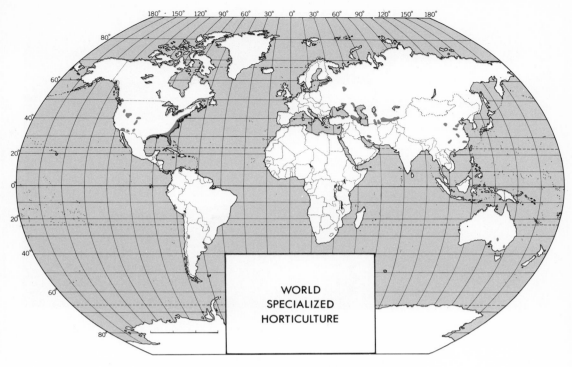

FIGURE 17.1   *(General Media Corporation)*

taken place in recent years, particularly in the industrialized sections of Europe and North America.

Climate and Soil

Most vegetables, like other crops, have definite temperature ranges. Vegetables can be grouped as cool, intermediate, and warm-season crops.[1] The vegetative season, during which the amount of heat energy is adequate to induce growth and to bring plant life to maturity, and the date of the last killing frost in the spring and the first killing frost in the fall are

important factors in limiting the region in which each type of vegetable can be successfully grown.

Among vegetable crops, only certain kinds of beans can be considered as definitely drought-resistant. All others require relatively large amounts of available water in the soil throughout the crop season. Commercial production is therefore confined chiefly to regions having either ample irrigation water or an annual rainfall of 30–40 inches or more. More important than the annual rainfall is the 20–25 inches of rainfall required during the growing season.

Almost all types of soil are used for growing vegetables, the same vegetable being grown on many different types of soil, and the same soil being used for various vegetables. Vegetables are most extensively grown on deep, well-drained, friable soils that may range in texture from fine sands to clay loams. Peat and muck are also important for certain vegetable

[1]Cool-season crops, adapted to regions with comparatively cool and short growing seasons, or to warm climates during the cooler portion of the year, are lettuce, garden peas, radishes, spinach, white potatoes, turnips, cabbage, celery, cauliflower, and kale. The warm-season crops—cucumbers, melons, squash, sweet corn, string and lima beans, sweet potatoes, tomatoes, and egg plant—require a long growing season and a high temperature. Those requiring intermediate climatic conditions are beets, carrots, onions, parsley, asparagus, and rhubarb.

FIGURE 17.2 *Vegetables growing on the sandy soils of the North Atlantic Coastal Plain. (New Jersey Department of Agriculture)*

crops. In general, a high level of readily available chemical fertility and a good supply of actively decomposing organic matter are essential.

A sandy soil yields the earliest crop, because it dries out and becomes warm earlier in the season, but it is not a fertile soil and yields are low unless heavy applications of fertilizer are used. Because a sandy soil does not hold water, irrigation is often essential. Sandy loams, clay loams, silts, mucks, and peats are progressively heavier, richer, and more retentive of moisture; yields are higher, but crops mature respectively later. Sandy soils are used when early maturity is the determining factor, but silts are used when large yields are more important.

Location

The group of plants loosely called "vegetable crops" contains many genera and species that are now being profitably grown in climatic regions very different from their native habitats. No other group of economic plants, except ornamentals,

contains so many species that are being extensively grown out of their own native environment. Despite the fact that the native range of many of these plants appears to have been exceedingly narrow and their climatic requirements rather specific and exacting, their culture may extend over 20 to 25 degrees of latitude, from sea level to 5,000 or 6,000 feet of altitude, and over a considerable range of rainfall.

Vegetables are more adaptable to extremes of latitude and altitude than most field and tree crops for several reasons, chiefly:

1. With relative ease and cheapness, seed can be produced in especially favorable locations and shipped any distance to actual growing locations.
2. Many plants produce edible crops in such a short time that they can be sown somewhere almost every month of the year.
3. In almost every locality at some season, plants encounter climatic conditions favorable for food production if not seed production.

4. The relatively low cost of bringing most short-season vegetable crops to harvest and the opportunity for speculative operations encourage production in the face of hazards that would be far too great for most long-season and perennial crops.

Thus economic forces as well as biological factors play a part in determining the geographic limits of the culture of vegetable crops.

Primarily for economic reasons, vegetables are produced on a wide-scale commericial basis only in the United States, Canada, Japan, and most of the Western European countries, and in limited areas within the vicinity of large urban centers in Argentina, Brazil, and Mexico. The bulk of the vegetables grown worldwide are not raised for sale but essentially for subsistence. This is particularly true in the tropics and subtropics.

Commercial Production

Enormous quantities of many different vegetables are grown in the countries mentioned above. Although at least a few kinds of vegetables can be grown in home and market gardens at some season in every farming region save the polar icecap, most of the extensive commercial production has developed in well-defined areas with favorable climate, soil, access to market, or some combination of these factors. Enormous developments have been made in some areas with very poor sandy soil where favorable weather permits winter culture of relatively high value crops. Certain crops, such as cauliflower, need the modifying influence of large bodies of water to prevent extreme fluctuations in temperature; others like the cantaloup need low atmospheric humidity and abundant sunshine. Other areas with poor soil have become important despite a short growing season because they are close to good markets. Thus climate is only one factor that determines the distribution of this huge

industry, but it is so far a very important one.

Generally the commercial production of vegetables is increasing throughout the developed nations of the world. This is especially true where per capita wages are relatively high, and consequently people can afford to buy vegetables nearly any time of year, winter or summer. Also, other factors such as high quality, regular supply, recognition of nutritional value, and advertisement through various media are responsible for continued consumption. In the United States, for example, the per capita consumption of vegetables is more than 400 pounds per year.

Truck farming of fruits and vegetables for wholesale marketing is a special type of commercial vegetable production generally carried on within a 24 to 36-hour trucking distance from origin to market center. The major truck farming areas of the world are:

1. Along the channel coast of France (Brittany), the Netherlands, Great Britain, and West Germany
2. The Rhone Valley, a nearly continuous area of truck farms in France and Italy
3. The oases of Algeria, Morocco, Tunisia
4. The Middle Atlantic coastal plain of the United States
5. The Gulf Coast states from Florida to Texas
6. The Imperial and Central Valleys of California
7. The Willamette Valley of Oregon

THE UNITED STATES

Commercial vegetable production is most highly developed in, but not confined to, five major regions:

1. Atlantic and Gulf region—a belt of variable width, generally nonirrigated, from Massachusetts to Texas, extending inland 100 miles or more in the Middle Atlantic and South Atlantic states
2. The Great Lakes region—a broad and

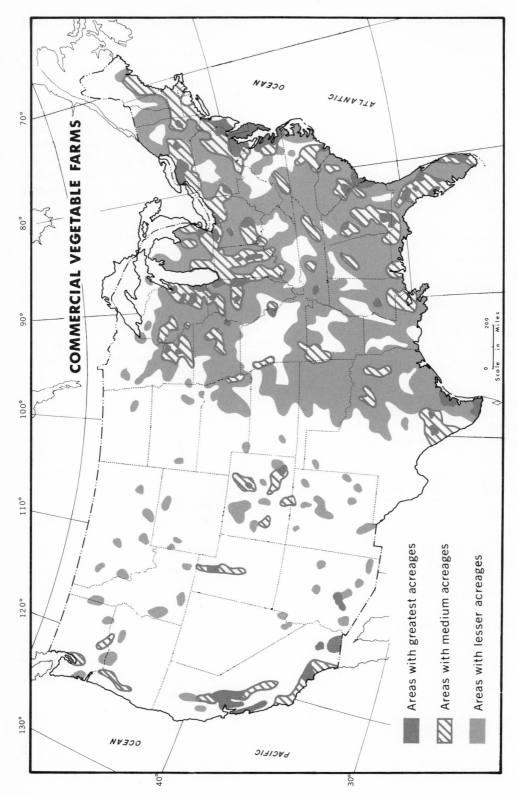

COMMERCIAL VEGETABLE FARMS

Areas with greatest acreages

Areas with medium acreages

Areas with lesser acreages

Scale in Miles
0   200

ATLANTIC OCEAN

PACIFIC OCEAN

FIGURE 17.3 (General Media Corporation)

irregular area extending from upper New York State around the Great Lakes and into Minnesota, also nonirrigated

3. Certain intermountain valleys in Colorado, Utah, and Idaho; generally irrigated except for dry-land beans and peas
4. The Rio Grande Valley of Texas, generally irrigated
5. Pacific coast and intermountain valleys of Arizona, California, and Oregon, generally irrigated

Economic Factors

Vegetable growing is a type of agriculture beset by especially heavy risks, and at times by heavy losses. The crops are easily damaged by frosts, droughts, excessive moisture, diseases and pests, with the result that replanting is often necessary. Replanting not only increases costs but delays the crop in reaching the market; in truck farming, timing the arrival of the crop at market is especially important.

The large input of hand labor in the vegetable-producing industry necessitates a rather inexpensive labor supply. In Texas, California, and Arizona, braceros or migratory Mexican laborers traditionally supplied the bulk of the field labor required. Organization of labor unions in these states, however, has resulted in demands for higher wages accompanied by union demands that braceros be stopped from working in the United States.

Mechanical Harvesting

Rising costs of labor have led to an intensive effort to mechanize the vegetable industry, with considerable progress occurring in Texas and California in the past few years. Carrots, for example, are now planted, tilled, harvested, cleaned, graded, packaged, and shipped via machines. Spinach, radishes, and potatoes are processed in a similar manner. Ma-

FIGURE 17.4 *Harvesting strawberries in the Willamette Valley of Oregon. (Oregon State Department of Agriculture)*

chines to harvest, shell, and grade beans and peas are also used. A lettuce harvester was developed by the University of California at Davis. The machine gauges the heads of lettuce and cuts those that are firm enough and large enough for harvesting. Spokes of the wheel-like device, which is a rotary elevator, grip the cut heads and lift them to the conveyor belt on the front of the machine. The belt delivers them to baskets or a packing machine.

Tomato harvesters have transformed tomato growing from total reliance on hand picking to largely mechanized harvesting since 1962. In California, where 125,000 acres are planted in tomatoes, the growers used to have to recruit 40,000 workers at the season's peak to harvest the crop by hand. With the help of an agricultural engineer and a plant biologist at the Davis campus, a tomato plant was bred that produces tomatoes of uniform size, all ripening at the same time, which can be easily detached from the vine and will not drop off prematurely. Since the

FIGURE 17.5 *The new "cube" or elongated tomato developed by the University of California. The major reason for changing from the conventional round shape is to reduce the amount of damage that occurs in machine harvesting. (Agricultural Extension Service, University of California)*

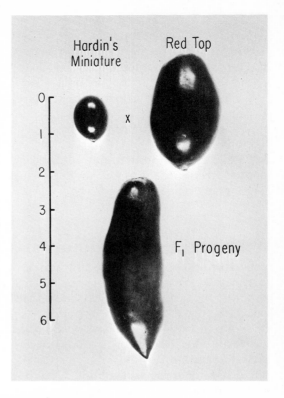

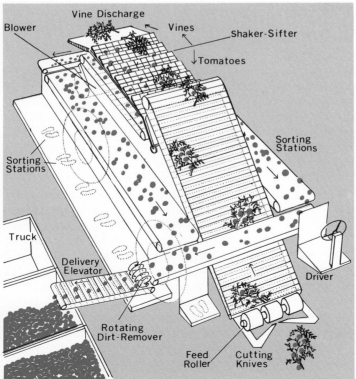

FIGURE 17.6 *A tomato harvester.*

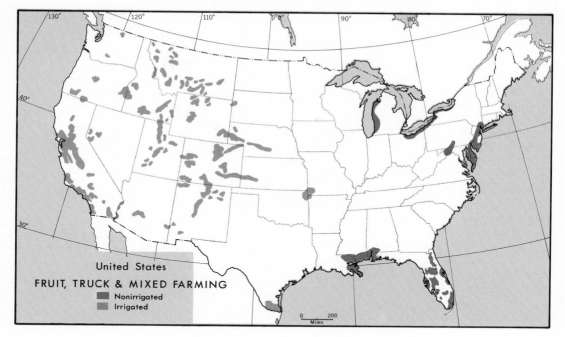

FIGURE 17.7   (*General Media Corporation*)

tomato has a skin tough enough to withstand mechanical handling, harvesters cut the whole tomato plant and convey it to the shaker-sifter, where the individual tomatoes are shaken loose. The vines are blown back onto the field; human workers stationed along the sorting belts remove tomatoes that are defective.

Market Gardening

Market gardening is an intensive type of agriculture located near densely populated metropolitan areas. It involves the growing of fresh fruits, vegetables, cut flowers, mushrooms and specialty crops that require a large expenditure in planting, cultivating, and marketing. In general, a market garden is characterized by:

1. High cost land
2. A relatively small acreage
3. Scientific principles of intensive cultivation
4. Application of high quality fertilizers
5. Successive plantings of various fruits and vegetables on the same land
6. Extremely high yields
7. A greater market demand for the products than supply

If the demand and price are sufficiently high, off-season fruits and vegetables may be grown under glass and sold as luxury items. Greenhouses are a familiar sight both on the main highways and country roads of Chester County, Pennsylvania, one of the leading areas of the nation in growing cut flowers, potted plants, foliage, and green plants produced under glass.

case study

Cleveland, Ohio: Glass House in the United States

Just to the south and southwest of Cleveland, Ohio is the major greenhouse operation in the United States, with more than 400 acres under glass. It began as an experiment by an individual urban dweller who first grew vegetables in his private garden only for himself and his family. After several years of giving the surplus to neighbors, he began to sell to grocery stores. His venture was so successful that he formed a cooperative, expanding the business to the point where today it is a large-scale enterprise, producing off-season fruits and vegetables for the Greater Cleveland and Lower Lakes market. The investment is roughly $15,000 per acre, or approximately $30,000,000 for all the acreage under glass. With such a high initial cost, it is obvious why there are few of these enterprises in the nation. Only those producers of long standing are financially able to increase their acreage and yield.

However, there are compensations for this kind of initial outlay. An acre of vegetables treated properly under glass will return about four times as much as an acre in the same vicinity not under glass. Each year, with very intensive use of the land, roughly 100 tons of vegetables can be harvested per acre— a total annual average of 40,000 tons. Of this yield, 80 percent or 32,000 tons consists of tomatoes; the retail price per pound may vary from thirty to sixty cents, depending upon locale, season, type, and demand.

Greenhouse owners must have a crop that grosses $35,000 per acre to make a fair profit, for the replacement cost of an acre of greenhouse alone is well over $100,000. The greenhouse producer must compete with such vegetable-growing areas as the Connecticut Valley, Florida, New Jersey, Texas, California, and Mexico. However, these areas must pay higher transportation costs, and their vegetables also must be picked when green in order not to spoil before reaching the market. Hence, theirs is a poorer quality for fresh market consumption than that of nearby greenhouse operations.

Canada

Canadian production, limited to summer and fall vegetables because of climate, is concentrated in the Maritime Provinces, Ontario, and British Columbia. Seasonal surpluses occur, but there is a shortage of fresh vegetables in winter and spring. Since no tariff barriers exist between the United States and Canada, growers on both sides of the border consider the two countries one market. Growers in Ontario may be shipping fresh carrots and lettuce to eastern United States markets while western Canada will be importing the same items from the Western states. Canada imports early potatoes from the States and exports seed and table potatoes during the winter.

Mexico

Major improvements in highway and rail facilities in Mexico have meant sizable increases in the production of vegetables. A large tonnage of winter and spring vegetables and melons are grown mainly for export to the United States and Canada. About half the tonnage is concentrated in the Culiacan Valley in Sinaloa. The leading crops are tomatoes, cantaloups, and watermelons; smaller quantities of onions, garlic, sweet peppers, peas, cucumbers, squash, snap beans, and eggplant are exported. Mexico limits its imports of fresh and processed vegetables, and local supplies are adequate most of the year.

Europe

Western Europe and countries of northern Africa bordering the Mediterranean form a production and marketing area, with patterns like those of North America. Production begins with winter and spring vegetables in the Mediterranean countries. Since northern Europe has the world's greatest concentration of heated and unheated glasshouses and coldframes, imports of winter vegetables are supplemented by glasshouse crops. The varieties consumed in Western Europe are similar to those of North America, but many more are eaten fresh.

Potatoes. Consumption of potatoes per capita in Europe is almost double that of the United States but has been declining. Production is high, but in some countries,

West Germany for instance, only a third is used for food. Many potatoes are used for livestock feed and for industrial products—starch, glucose, and alcohol. Yellow-fleshed potatoes are preferred in some countries for food.

Northern European countries export seed potatoes to the Mediterranean countries and import new potatoes from them in winter and spring. Trade in potatoes is extensive among these countries, but few potatoes are exported from or imported into the European area.

Onions. Onions are grown in all western countries of Europe, but climatic conditions limit production in the Scandinavian countries, the United Kingdom, and Ireland. The four principal exporting countries are the United Arab Republic, Spain, Italy, and the Netherlands. The United Arab Republic, the world's largest exporter, sends most of its crop to northern Europe in spring, and the fall crop is consumed locally. Spain exports the mild Valencia or sweet Spanish types, including some new hybrids; Italy grows many red-skinned onions. The Netherlands is a leading supplier of yellow globe onions.

Tomatoes.   Field tomatoes are produced in northern Africa, the Canary Islands, Spain, Italy, and southern France for local consumption and export in winter and spring. These supplies are supplemented with the glasshouse crops in northern Europe. Processing of tomatoes in Italy, Portugal, Spain, and France has been developing rapidly, where whole tomatoes, paste, and puree are canned.

Cabbage Family. Cabbage, broccoli, cauliflower, and Brussels sprouts are grown extensively in all countries, the largest production centered in northern Europe. Cabbage is stored in pits or in common storage, or preserved in the form of kraut.

Eastern Europe, including the Soviet Union, has encountered many problems in producing and marketing vegetable crops. Sixty-five percent of the potato and 45 percent of the vegetable produc-

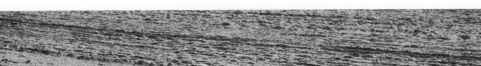

FIGURE 17.8   *Harvesting potatoes in Western Germany. (German Information Center)*

FIGURE 17.9 *A field of winter cabbages in the Coachella Valley, California. (U.S. Bureau of Reclamation)*

tion in the U.S.S.R. is grown on private plots. Cabbage follows potatoes in importance; it is marketed fresh and from storage. Carrots, beets, turnips, and rutabagas are grown extensively, especially in the northern districts. In the south—the Ukraine, Caucasus, and central Asia—cantaloups, honeydews, watermelons, and peppers are grown for local use and for shipment to northern markets. The Balkans grow tomatoes, onions, garlic, and many other crops. Poland produces a fall crop of yellow globe onions for export both east and west.

Far East

The Far East contains more than half of the world's people, with a per capita agricultural land area of half an acre. Thus, vegetables are grown on garden plots of far less than an acre, and limited transportation tends to concentrate commercial production to districts near cities.

Little or no technological research is available to growers in many of these countries; therefore, relatively small amounts of chemical fertilizers, insecticides, and fungicides are used, except in Japan and Taiwan. Growers use animal and human waste, ashes, and other materials that can be composted to improve the soils.

Sweet potatoes, cassava, and potatoes are important, particularly in the countries with a warm climate. Other vegetables are grown intensively, with five to eight crops a year on the same plot. This system requires irrigation, careful timing in planting various crops, and the use of transplants for some. Some areas will grow a crop of staked cucumbers, tomatoes, pole beans, lettuce, cabbage, Chinese cabbage, onions, peppers, or eggplant in the dry season, and a crop of paddy rice in the wet season.

In Hong Kong, a commercial vegetable farm for a family is one-third of an acre. Because Hong Kong is a free trade area, growers concentrate on vegetables that have a short growing season and for which they have a transportation advantage. Vegetables such as lettuce, Chinese cabbage, rape, mustard, tomatoes, sweet corn, and cabbage are the principal crops. Carrots, potatoes, beets, celery, and turnips are imported.

Growers deliver produce to the road, where it is picked up by a truck and hauled to one of several wholesale markets. In some other Southeast Asian countries, the produce is transported one or two baskets at a time by a person in a boat, bus, or taxi. One-third or more of the sale price is needed to pay the transportation for a distance of ten to twenty miles.

Africa

Africa is a land of contrasts and divergent societies: nomadic desert tribes, primitive jungle areas, and highly developed civilizations in the north and south. The people of the central areas depend on wild plants, cassava, yams, sweet potatoes, and watermelons. A small volume of other vegetables are grown near a few of the larger cities for local sales.

The Republic of South Africa has an extensive commercial vegetable industry, which was developed by Europeans. The supply of potatoes and other fresh and processed vegetables is good; nearly all are grown for domestic use.

South America

South American climate ranges from the northern tropical areas to the cool climates of southern Argentina and Chile. Many of the tropical areas have districts at high elevations that can grow a wide variety of vegetables. However, the better locations for vegetable culture often cannot be used because of a lack of roads and transportation.

Potatoes, cabbage, tomatoes, and corn are widely grown. Brazil is the only country that prefers yellow-fleshed potatoes,

varieties of European origin. The corn, consumed fresh, is early harvested field corn. Much of the Indian population uses vegetables for seasoning soups and stews. Onions, garlic, tomatoes, peas, and beans are popular for this purpose.

Many of the vegetable growers in Argentina are of Italian descent. They grow varieties of vegetables brought over from the homeland, such as cherry or pear-shaped tomatoes, broad beans, zucchini, leeks, artichokes, leaf lettuce, and watercress. Cabbage follows potatoes in tonnage produced.

Japanese gardeners near São Paulo, Brazil, supply vegetables for the city. Their farms are small and intensively cropped. Growers have formed a cooperative that furnishes tractors for occasional deep plowing; purchases production supplies, such as seeds, fertilizer, and spray materials; and markets the crops. Aside from tractor plowing, nearly all seeding and cultivating is done by hand. Vegetables are hauled to market by truck. Because of the elevation and moderate climate, vegetables are harvested all year in this district.

Nearly all vegetables in the South American countries are grown for domestic consumption, but Chile exports large quantities of onions and garlic to North America and Europe, and many honeydew melons to North America. Commercial processing in South America, led by Argentina, Venezuela, and Colombia, is generally limited to relatively small processors. The principal products are chili sauces, catsup, peppers, artichoke hearts, and babyfoods. A few vegetables are sun dried for home use.

Vegetable production could be expanded by making effective use of coastal plains and districts at higher elevations. Until the transportation system and marketing facilities are improved, however, low-income families will continue to use vegetables for seasoning rather than as a basic part of their diet.

FUTURE

The world's potential vegetable production is enormous. Under ideal cultural practices, yields per acre are high. As more vegetables become available, people tend to eat less cassava, sweet potatoes, and potatoes in that order. Cassava is consumed as a vegetable through necessity rather than by choice. Processing increases as the economy of a country improves.

While there is a great need in many countries of the world to expand production of vegetables, particularly the green and yellow vegetables and tomatoes, this will not happen until the economy of the country improves. Increased production requires roads, fertilizers, chemicals, farm equipment, specialized transportation equipment, and facilities for storing and marketing the crops.

selected references

1. Baker, O. E., "Agricultural Regions of North America—Part VII, The Middle Atlantic Trucking Region," *Economic Geography*, Vol. 5, No. 1, January 1929, pp. 36–39.

2. Dahlberg, Richard E., "The Concord Grape Industry of the Chautauqua–Erie Area," *Economic Geography*, Vol. 37, No. 2, April 1961, pp. 150–169.

3. "Farming on Contract," *Monthly Review,* Vol. 14, No. 6, Minneapolis, Minn.: Federal Reserve Bank, June 30, 1959, pp. 6–10.

4. Gavett, Earle E., "Truck Crop Production Practices, Imperial County, California," *Economic Research Services*, No. 128, Washington, D.C.: U.S. Department of Agriculture, September 1963.

5. Gregor, Howard F., "Farm Structure in Regional Comparison: California and New Jersey," *Economic Geography*, Vol. 45, No. 5, July 1969, pp. 209–225.

6. ———, "The Large Industrialized American Crop Farm," *Geographical Review,* Vol. 60, No. 2, April 1970, pp. 151–175.

7. Griffin, Paul F., and White, C. Langdon, "Lettuce Industry of the Salinas Valley," *Scientific Monthly*, Vol. 81, August 1955, pp. 77–84.

8. Highsmith, Richard M., ed., *Atlas of the Pacific Northwest*, 4th ed., Corvallis, Oregon: Oregon State University Press, 1968, pp. 85–90.

9. Kelly, Clarence F., "Mechanical Harvesting," *Scientific American*, Vol. 217, No. 2, August 1967, pp. 50–59.

10. King, W. C., "Gardening under Glass—A Prosperous Industry in the Netherlands," *Foreign Agriculture*, Vol. 26, November 1962, pp. 12–13.

11. Laxnal, Jon K., "The Okanagan Valley," *Canadian Geographical Journal*, Vol. 75, No. 5, November 1967, pp. 150–161.

12. Merriam, Willis B., "The Mushroom Industry at Kennett Square, Pennsylvania," *The Journal of Geography*, Vol. 61, No. 2, February 1962, pp. 68–71.

13. Olmstead, Clarence W., "American Orchard and Vineyard Regions," *Economic Geography*, Vol. 32, No. 3, July 1956, pp. 189–236.

14. Smith, Derek L., "Market Gardening at Adelaide's Urban Fringe," *Economic Geography*, Vol. 42, No. 1, January 1966, pp. 19–36.

15. Thompson, H. C., and Kelly, W. C., *Vegetable Crops*, 5th ed., New York: McGraw-Hill Book Company, Inc., 1957.

Although man's first use of milk from animals is unknown, a temple wall at Babylon thought to be 5,000 years old contains a milking scene, testimonial to its early importance. Most of the milk for human consumption comes from domestic cattle. Cows produce 90 to 95 percent of the total supply, and goats, sheep, deer, buffalo, camels, donkeys, mares, and yaks the remainder. World milk production therefore usually means cow's milk.

In some parts of the world, milking is practiced only on a limited basis because of cultural or religious taboos, economic reasons, or preference for other foods. Many tribal peoples in central Africa, for example, consider milk to be excrement from animals and hence exclude it from their diet.

chapter 18

Commercial Dairy Farming

GENERAL CHARACTERISTICS

Dairying is an intensive form of agriculture. In only a very few other agricultural activities is the amount of labor needed greater than in dairying—not in terms of total numbers of people, but in man-hours per value of product. Besides animals kept primarily for milk production, most dairy farms also stock swine, chickens, and calves. The chickens and swine are usually fed the waste products of the milking process—skim milk to poultry and whey to swine. Skim milk is a by-product of cream; whey, a by-product of cheese. Without disposing of these by raising poultry and swine, they would be useless.

Hence, many dairy farmers sell eggs and pork in addition to fluid milk. In order to keep dairy cattle functioning at their peak rate of production, they must be bred seasonally and calved. This often results in a surplus of calves on the dairy farm, which is sold as veal. Dairy cattle usually are beyond the point of high yield after twelve to fifteen years of age and are generally sold to slaughter houses

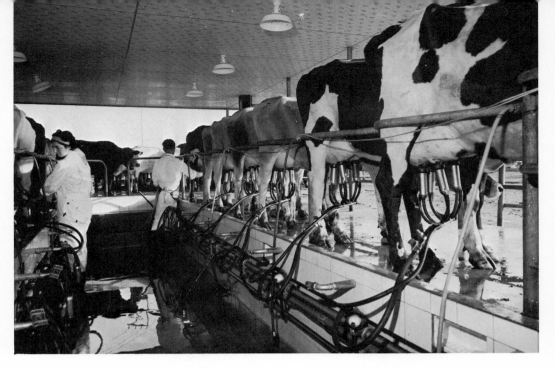

FIGURE 18.1 *A modern milking parlor. (New Zealand National Publicity Studios)*

at a very low price, owing to the low quality of the meat as compared to that of beef cattle.

Labor Requirements

Dairy cattle must be milked twice a day to produce at their maximum capacity. The milking chores alone confine the dairy farmer to his task every day of the year. In addition to the milking routine, he usually has hogs and chickens to feed. In season, other tasks include cutting and storing hay, harvesting corn and oats, preparing seedbeds for the next planting, cultivation of newly planted crops, selling animals and fluid milk, repairing equipment and machines, and many other chores.

LOCATION

The chief dairy regions of the world are in Europe, North America, and Oceania. The major producers in Europe are France, West Germany, Poland, the United Kingdom, Italy, the Netherlands, East Germany, Denmark, and the Soviet Union. In North America, the United States and Canada contribute about 95 percent of the total output. Production in Oceania is about equally divided between Australia and New Zealand.

Western Europe, North America, and Oceania—which have about 20 percent of the world's population—account for about 55 percent of total world milk production. The developing countries in Latin America, Africa, the Near East, and the Far East, with more than 60 percent of the world's population, produce about 20 percent of the world's milk.

A large part of the total world milk production (about 45 percent of annual output in the United States and Canada) is consumed in fresh and fluid form. The rest is used mainly for butter, cheese, canned milk, and dried milk. Consumption of fluid milk in North America is considerably higher than in other heavy producing areas, where distribution facilities have not been so highly developed. A rough approximation of milk utilization in sixteen of the principal dairy countries other than the United States and

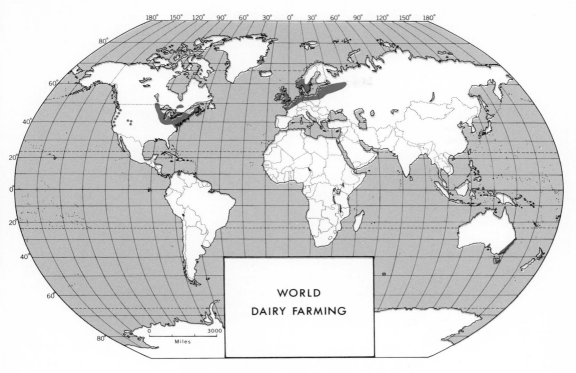

WORLD
DAIRY FARMING

0   3000
Miles

FIGURE 18.2 (*General Media Corporation*)

Canada is: about 30 percent is consumed as fluid milk, 40 percent as butter, 15 percent as cheese, and 2 percent as canned and dried whole milk. The rest goes for miscellaneous uses.

United States

In the United States there are roughly 3.1 million farms; of these, dairy farms number slightly more than 366,000, or 11.6 percent.[1] The greatest concentration is in the north and northeastern sections of the country, followed by the South Atlantic and South Central states. A third significant dairy region occurs in the Pacific Northwest. However, with a milk cow population totaling 14,662,000,[2] there are many thousands of other smaller

pockets of intensive dairy production throughout the nation. Dairying is an important economic activity near every large metropolitan area in the nation.

Europe

France, West Germany, Poland, the United Kingdom, Italy, the Netherlands, East Germany, and Denmark are the leading dairy countries in Europe, in the order named. Dairying is intensively practiced in these countries to help supply the needs of a dense industrial production. Centers of production are often located where excessive rainfall has leached the soil and left it fit for little except pasture unless intensive fertilization is utilized. In most cases, part of the food for the cattle (corn, hay, alfalfa, bean cake) is imported, and in this way the number of cattle may exceed the carrying power of the unaided local site. The manure of the cattle is an important factor in

[1]U.S. Bureau of the Census, *Statistical Abstract of the United States: 1967*, 88th ed. (Washington, D.C.: 1967), p. 651.

[2]*Ibid*, p. 651.

Table 18.1 Milk Production for Selected Countries, 1966

Area	Annual Production (1,000 Metric Tons)	Kilograms of Milk per Milking Cow
Europe		
France	28,016	2,012
Germany, West	21,357	3,649
Poland	14,221	2,365
United Kingdom	12,750	3,779
Italy	9,872	2,100
Netherlands	7,236	4,180
Germany, East	6,728	3,090
Denmark	5,306	3,913
Czechoslovakia	4,169	2,146
Belgium	3,964	3,866
Finland	3,689	3,424
Sweden	3,545	3,623
Romania	3,437	1,636
Ireland	3,232	2,308
Austria	3,216	2,915
Switzerland	3,131	3,410
Spain	2,726	1,700
Yugoslavia	2,513	1,243
Hungary	1,849	2,410
Norway	1,630	3,300
Bulgaria	1,098	1,914
U.S.S.R.	75,200	1,880
North America		
United States	54,535	3,767
Canada	8,343	2,978
Mexico	2,444	2,200
South America		
Brazil	6,903	440
Argentina	5,003	400
Colombia	2,033	273
Chile	840	1,700
Uruguay	744	410
Venezuela	694	700
Asia		
India	10,594	200
Japan	3,409	4,300
China, Mainland	2,845	—
Pakistan	2,780	—
Turkey	2,590	—
Iran	1,082	680
Israel	360	4,933
Iraq	182	—
Korea, South	106	3,400
Syria	104	—
Africa		
Republic of South Africa	2,600	—
Ethiopia	1,529	560
Sudan	1,238	560
Nigeria	617	—
United Arab Republic	408	675
Uganda	394	281
Morocco	350	370
Algeria	290	—
Oceania		
Australia	2,250	209
New Zealand	2,924	259

Source: United Nations, Food and Agricultural Organization, *Production Yearbook*, 1967, Tables 117 and 118.

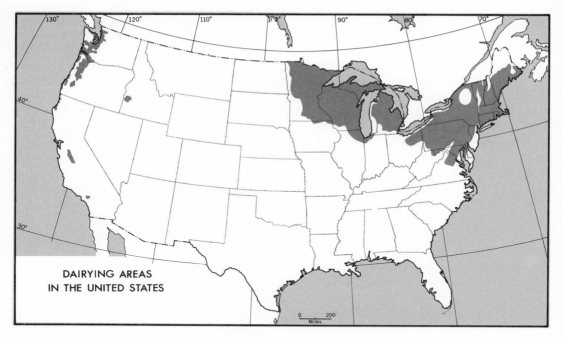

DAIRYING AREAS
IN THE UNITED STATES

FIGURE 18.3   *(General Media Corporation)*

FIGURE 18.4   *A dairy farm in Wisconsin. (USDA)*

improving the productivity of the generally poor soils.

The man–land ratio is much higher in Western Europe than in the United States. In the United Kingdom, Belgium, the Netherlands, and Germany each person has an average of about one acre of living space. Danes, Italians, and Swiss have little more. Even in relatively underpopulated France the per capita land area is only three acres. By contrast, each person in the United States has twelve acres of land. This pressure on the land results in an average farm size of 40 acres in Europe, compared to approximately 377 acres in the United States; the farm size varies greatly not only from country to country but also within individual countries. French farms, for example, vary in size anywhere from 25 to 125 acres. The average Netherlands farm is 27 acres; in Germany, 17 acres; in Denmark, 39 acres.

The British Isles and the northwestern countries from the Baltic Sea to the Alps keep a large part of their agricultural land under permanent grass. In those areas close to the sea this is due to the high gross yields permitted by the climate; inland it is due to the importance of mountain pasturage.

France is one of the largest forage-crop producers in Europe because of its satisfactory climate for hay. Additional factors include the importance of hay in French crop rotation, the growing use of cheese, butter, and milk, and the surrender under competition of poor wheat lands to forage crops, especially in Brittany, Normandy, and parts of the hilly areas of central France. Poor breeding has had its effect upon the French dairy industry. Milk yields are considerably lower than those in the Netherlands, the United Kingdom, and Germany (see Table 18.1). The fresh milk market absorbs no more than a quarter of the total production, much of which goes toward raising veal. Proximity to industrial centers has encouraged a degree of specialized milk production in certain regions—Cotentin, Bessin, Bray, Flanders, and the foothills of the Ardennes.

Outside these regions, dairying tends to be incidental to other farm activities, except in upland areas where cheese making has long been practiced. A well-known example is the Jura where Gruyère has been made since the thirteenth century. Notable cheeses are produced in the leading fresh-milk territories—Camembert and Brie—and for these France has an international reputation.

East and West Germany both have a long agricultural tradition. Dairying is an established economic activity, the milk cow utilizing much of the hay and fodder crops, and waste from the sugar beet and potato fields. Yields of milk per cow are among the highest in Europe. Agricultural self-sufficiency has always been stressed by the governments in power. Intensive dairying is especially important in the northwest and south.

Britain's milk yields are among the highest in the world, and dairy products are the country's most important single agricultural commodity. Production is widespread; marketing boards encourage dairying by guaranteed markets and a pricing policy that discounts location. In England and Wales the main dairying areas are the grasslands of Cheshire and Somerset, but production has increased in western counties and dairying has displaced livestock raising in parts of the upland margins. In Scotland, with its harsher environment and smaller population, dairying is less important, except in the southwest.

Denmark, with its small population and scientific farming, and the Netherlands and Ireland, with their areas of humid pasture, also are important dairylands. Rugged Switzerland exports dairy products to her European neighbors. Transhumance grazing is widely practiced by Swiss dairy farmers, moving their cattle to the alpine slopes in late spring and summer, and winter feeding them in the protected valleys from excess forage cut and stored for the purpose.

U.S.S.R. The Soviet Union surpasses all other nations in total milk production. However, there is no specific dairy belt. Dairying is particularly developed in the cooler, moister areas of the European portion of the Russian Soviet Federated Socialist Republic (R.S.F.S.R.), Belorussia, the Ukraine, and around the major cities.

Oceania

New Zealand's economy depends largely on agricultural production, and especially on foreign markets for livestock products. Meat, wool, and dairy products are by far the most important exports. Net returns from dairying are often higher than those obtained from sheep or cattle, especially on the smallest, most productive farms. Much of the milk produced is used in the manufacture of cheese and butter for export. About 90 percent of the dairy animals are on the North Island, where they can be grazed year round with little preserved feed and no housing. A typical farm has from 70 to 120 acres and carries 40 to 60 dairy cows. Nearly all are milked by machine. Many of the calves are sold for slaughter soon after birth; some are raised on skim milk, meat meal, and cereal meal, with limited amounts of whole milk. Approximately 85 percent of the dairy cows are Jerseys.

Australia's dairy industry will continue to play an important role in world markets. As in New Zealand, the temperate climate permits an almost continuous growth of pasture in major dairy areas and eliminates the need for housing livestock. These factors give Australia a comparative advantage in the cost of producing milk. Dairying is practiced in all states of the Commonwealth. However,

Victoria, with about 40 percent of total milk production, and New South Wales and Queensland, with about 20 percent each, are the major producing states. Dairying is largely confined to the areas of high rainfall near the east and south coasts, and to some irrigated areas; production for liquid supply is limited to areas near the main centers of population.

MANUFACTURED DAIRY PRODUCTS

Condensed or evaporated milk, butter, cheese, and other milk products can be produced at a distance from the market because they are not quickly perishable and, being concentrated, they can be more readily transported than fluid milk. Milk products are therefore largely produced where the cost of production is lowest, and in areas where fluid milk cannot be marketed profitably.

Cheese is made wherever animals are milked. A part of the supply in excess of that needed for fluid use nearly always is used for cheese. Most cheese is made from cow's milk, but smaller amounts also are made from the milk of goats, sheep, camels, reindeer, and other animals. A large percentage of the cheese produced in the United States comes from Wisconsin, the southwestern part of the state specializing in foreign cheeses, especially Swiss and limburger, while the east and north central portions produce American cheeses.

Butter is produced and consumed most extensively in temperate climates. In terms of volume and commercial significance, it is the main manufactured dairy product. Minnesota, Wisconsin, and Iowa are the leading producers of creamery butter in the United States.

Canned milk is produced in most dairying countries, but output of evaporated and condensed milk on a large scale is concentrated in a few countries, princi-

FIGURE 18.5 *Cheese being manufactured in a modern plant in Oregon. (Tillamook Cheese Association)*

FIGURE 18.6 *Half gallon cartons being filled in a modern U.S. milk plant. (USDA)*

pally the United States, the Netherlands, West Germany, and the United Kingdom.

GOVERNMENT POLICIES

Government policies affect the dairy industry in many ways, both in the production and marketing of products. For instance, in the United States all fluid milk entering the market must be pasteurized. Many markets require a regular inspection of the conditions under which individual farmers are producing milk. This inspection includes the sanitary conditions of the barns, methods of handling and cooling the milk, and other conditions that might affect the quality. Creameries and other factories producing milk products must meet certain sanitary standards. These and other requirements, although they add to the cost of the product marketed, are in the interest of the health of the consumers.

INTERNATIONAL TRADE

World trade in dairy products consists mainly of the movement of special manufactured items from a few leading suppliers to a limited number of markets. In order of economic importance, the chief dairy products in world trade are butter, cheese, dried milk (nonfat and dry whole milk), and canned whole milk. Others are ice cream mixes and infant and dietetic foods.

About three-fourths of the butter in international trade is shipped to the United Kingdom. Most of it, about a billion pounds annually, is supplied by New Zealand, Denmark, Australia, and the Netherlands. Italy and West Germany are the only other sizable importers of butter. Their imports are mainly seasonal and subject to control.

The principal markets for cheese are the United Kingdom, West Germany, the United States, Italy, and Belgium. The Netherlands generally is the largest exporter, followed by New Zealand, Denmark, France, Switzerland, and Italy. Many types of cheese enter commerce, but most of the trade is in cheddar.

International trade in canned milk is mainly between the Netherlands and the Far East, the Philippines, Hong Kong, Thailand, and Malaysia. Africa also is an important market. About two-thirds of the canned milk in world trade comes from the Netherlands; other sizable ex-

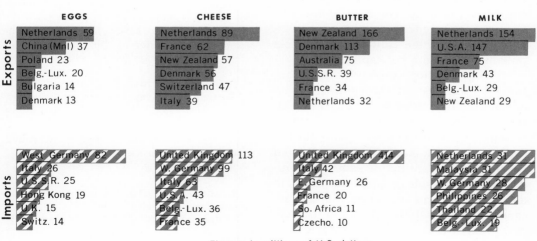

Figures in millions of U.S. dollars

FIGURE 18.7   *International trade in dairy products, 1965.*

porters are the United States, the United Kingdom, and France. Nonfat dry milk trade is carried on mainly by the United States, New Zealand, and Australia, with most of their shipments going to the United Kingdom, Mexico, the Philippines, Western European countries, Japan, and India.

Trade in such products as dry whole milk, anhydrous milk fat, dry ice cream mix, and milk-base infant and dietetic foods has been less important. More and more dry ice cream mixes have been shipped, but the importance of dry whole milk to the dairy industry as a whole has been declining.

pected to develop fast enough to absorb the total available supply. Sizable supplies of milk and milk products therefore will probably continue to move under government programs to the enormous potential markets in the developing countries.

From the standpoint of world nutritional needs, total milk production is not excessive, but from the standpoint of effective demand, there is excess production. This situation necessitates a constant review by the advanced dairy countries of national policies concerning efficiency of production and world prices for dairy products.

FUTURE

World production of milk and dairy products will probably continue to increase. While per capita consumption of certain products will go up in many countries, in all, such gains are not expected to keep pace with increases in production. A gap may continue for some time between world production and effective demand for dairy products. In the developing countries, where there are deficits of milk and dairy products to provide adequate nutrition, milk production has been growing. The rate of increase has not kept pace with population growth, however, and there continues to be less milk available on a per capita basis.

Milk production probably will continue to increase in the countries with advanced dairy industries. Yet, consumption of milk and milk products in these countries is at a high level, and further expansion of the market has only limited possibilities. Continued gains in production may result in larger surpluses of dairy products on the world market. Because of national policies both in surplus (exporting) countries and deficit (importing) countries, market expansion on a purely commercial basis is not ex-

selected references

1. Barnes, F. A., "Dairying in Anglesey, Wales," *Institute of British Geographers*, Publication No. 21, 1955, pp. 137–155.

2. Boal, F. W., and McAodha, B. S., "The Milk Industry of Northern Ireland," *Economic Geography*, Vol. 37, No. 2, April 1961, pp. 170–180.

3. Durand, Loyal, Jr., "The Dairy Industry of the Hawaiian Islands," *Economic Geography*, Vol. 35, No. 3, July 1959, pp. 228–246.

4. ——, "The Historical and Economic Geography of Dairying in the North Country of New York State," *Geographical Review*, Vol. 57, No. 1, January 1967, pp. 24–47.

5. ——, "The Major Milksheds of the Northeastern Quarter of the United States," *Economic Geography*, Vol. 40, No. 1, January 1964, pp. 9–33.

6. Fielding, Gordon J., "Dairying in Cities Designed to Keep People Out," *The Professional Geographer*, Vol. 14, No. 1, January 1962, pp. 12–17.

7. ——, "The Los Angeles Milkshed: A study of the Political Factor in Agriculture," *Geographical Review*, Vol. 44, No. 1, January 1967, pp. 1–12.

8. Gillis, F. D., "The Outlook for the Australian Dairy Industry," *Quarterly Review of Agricultural Economics*, Vol. 2, 1958, pp. 53–58.

9. Heintzelman, Oliver H., "The Evolution of an Industry: The Dairy Industry of

Tillamook County, Oregon," *The Pacific Northwest Quarterly*, Vol. 49, 1958, pp. 77–81.

10. Lambert, Audrey M., "Farm Consolidation and Improvement in the Netherlands: An Example from the Land Van Maas en Waal," *Economic Geography*, Vol. 37, No. 2, April 1961, pp. 115–123.

11. Lamer, Mirko, "Economic Trends in the Soviet Dairy Industry," FAO, *Monthly Bulletin of Agricultural Economics*, Vol. 7, 1958, pp. 1–15.

12. Lewthwaite, Gordon R., "Wisconsin Cheese and Farm Type: A Locational Hypothesis," Economic Geography, Vol. 40, No. 2, April 1964, pp. 95–112.

13. MacPhail, Donald D., "Puerto Rico Dairying: A Revolution in Tropical Agriculture," *Geographical Review*, Vol. 53, No. 2, April 1963, pp. 224–246.

14. Simpson, E. S., "Milk Production in England and Wales: A Study in the Influence of Collective Marketing," *Geographical Review*, Vol. 49, No. 1, January 1959, pp. 95–111.

15. Wilson, R. Kent, "The Distribution of Dairying in Victoria," *The Australian Geographer*, Vol. 8, March 1961, pp. 51–64.

introduction
to extractive industries

The extractive industries include those human activities that involve the removal of resources that have been stored in the environment by natural processes. Among them are fishing, logging, mining, quarrying, trapping, and hunting. Of these, the mining industries are the most noteworthy, because once minerals are consumed they are gone forever, without any possiblility of their being replenished by natural processes. At least this exhaustibility is true as far as present-day man is concerned, because it involves millions or perhaps in some cases billions of years for nature to form and concentrate sizeable mineral deposits.

Fishing and forestry industries can be maintained by propagation through restocking and or reseeding. Regulatory measures for conservation of fish and timber management must be enforced, however, if these industries are to flourish. They differ from mining endeavors in that they rely upon man's utilization of and cooperation with certain continuing processes of nature. In this sense they are reproductive industries.

Fishing, forest, and mining industries must be carried on at the point of raw material occurrence. Power, labor, capital, and transport facilities must be brought to the raw materials, and the finished product shipped from that point to the market. These industries are discussed in Chapters 19, 20, and 21.

Fishing is one of man's oldest occupations. Since he first set foot on earth, man has wrested part of his food from the water. Remains of spears, hooks, and fishnets discovered in ancient ruins indicate that Stone Age man practiced this method of food acquisition. Earliest historical paintings in caves in Europe and records from Assyria, Egypt, and China depict fishing scenes. Salt-cured fish served as field rations for Genghis Khan's hordes and the knights of the Crusades.

Although equipment has changed over the centuries, fishing methods have remained largely the same. Hooks are now made from steel rather than the bills of eagles or from bones and shells; lines and nets from synthetic fibers rather than leaves, plant stalks, and cocoon silk; fishing vessels are larger and equipped with elaborate electronic navigational equipment. The art of catching fish, however, has changed little from the days when European fishing vessels first reached the shores of North America.

Fishing industries have generally developed on a small-scale basis in each country having productive local waters. At first there was probably little incentive to go offshore to distant fishing banks; yields from local waters provided the necessary requirements of fish and shellfish. Handlining from small skiffs and sail craft enabled a daily catch; small weirs or traps in river mouths and harbors took quantities of migrating fish; shore fishermen could work the intertidal flats for oysters and shellfish. But as countries grew in population and in employment specialization, economic pressures forced fishermen to extend their activities offshore. The yield of the sea became an important commercial resource, and fisheries began to be considered so valuable a factor in national wealth that governments were careful to protect and encourage them. The right to various fisheries has often become a matter of international dispute, negotiation, and treaty.

With such a resource potential, it is

chapter 19

Fishing

FIGURE 19.1 *Haul from a trawler off the Kaikowa Coast of New Zealand. (New Zealand National Publicity Studios)*

hard to understand the relative lack of concern by many nations, including the United States, in terms of fishing research and attention to development of fisheries. While some nations, such as the U.S.S.R. and Japan, have given high priority to development of this field, most nations have been reluctant to commit national funds in appreciable amounts.

It has been noted that the last frontier of inner space lies in the world's oceans, and that man, by thrusting back this frontier, may acquire the ability to obtain almost limitless resources to feed future generations. One should not, however, forget that fishery is not analogous to agriculture. An agriculturist manipulates the environment by fertilizing the soil, weeding, eliminating pests, and selecting particular plant species for cultivation.

A fisherman generally accepts the environment as he finds it; he is, in a sense, a sea hunter. Having only rudimentary knowledge of the genetics of sea life and the occurrence of marine organisms, he cannot yet manipulate his environment.

THE FOOD WEB

The first creatures with backbones that inhabited the waters of the earth probably were "fishes." Fossilized fragments of these heavily armored, apparently cumbersome beasts have been found in deposits 450 million years old. During the next forty million-year portion of the earth's existence came the first true fishes: probably between 300 and 350 million years ago, the ancestors of the bony fishes we know today put in their first appearance.

Various fishery experts estimate there are about 40,000 kinds of fishes living in the world today. Of these, approximately 25,000 are marine varieties and the remainder inhabit fresh waters. The marine fishes are the end product of a vast food chain which has its beginning in microscopic plant and animal material called *plankton*.

As the sun's rays shine down into the upper layers of the ocean, oxygen and carbon dioxide are dissolved in it from the atmosphere. Various mineral salts, principally phosphates, nitrates, and iron compounds, along with minute amounts of essential vitamin-like substances, are meanwhile continually being poured into the sea by land erosion. These

combinations produce ideal conditions for plant growth, microscopic in size, of untold billions called phytoplankton (plant plankton). Feeding upon these minute floating plants are crustacea and other little animals ranging in size from a pin's head to somewhat larger than a grain of rice (zooplankton). All these creatures, both plant and animal, which drift more or less passively in the water, are referred to by the general term *plankton*. A great many fish—herring, pilchard, and mackerel—feed directly upon these minute plankton animals in the upper layers of the ocean. Other zooplankton, sinking to greater depths and to the sea floor, form food material for starfish, worms, sea urchins, and a host of voracious crawling animals who in turn form the food of such bottom-dwelling fish as the cod, haddock, and sole, who must

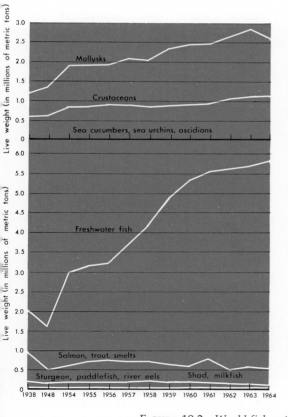
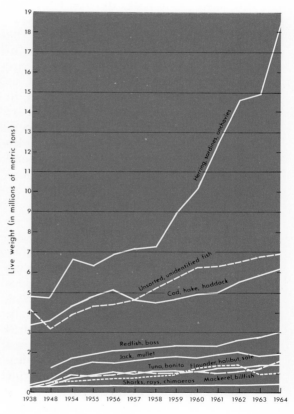

FIGURE 19.2   *World fish catch by species and varieties.*

eat ten pounds of plankton to grow one pound themselves [16]. All of these *demersal* or bottom feeding fish, as well as the *pelagic* or surface feeders, are in turn heavily preyed upon by many species of large, voracious fishes during all stages of their life.

Thus, it is easy to see the all-important role plankton play in the food web. All sea life depend on the sunlit "pastures" of floating microscopic plants for their basic food supply. In essence man, too, depends on it for his sea food. This interdependent plant and animal life chain is known as the *biotic pyramid.*

Distribution and Consumption

Although distribution of fish is worldwide, distribution of desired species is not. Differences in fertility of the sea can vary as much as that of the land, ranging from virtual deserts in mid-ocean to fantastic abundance off the Peruvian coast. In general, *shallow waters* yield the greatest quantities of fish currently in demand, but even here differences are widespread. Fish are more abundant, as far as number of species is concerned, in tropical waters; however, larger numbers of one species tend to be found concentrated in colder waters of the mid-latitudes and subpolar seas. A number of natural settings that contribute to the development of an area as an important source region for fish have been recognized.

Shallow water. Sunlight, required by all plants for photosynthesis, diminishes rapidly after 600 feet. Thus, coastal waters and the water over continental shelves or elevated areas in the seas known as *banks* are richer in plankton materials. Here, too, plant nutrients will tend to drift downward and accumulate on the sea floor where they may be affected by sunlight and regenerate nutrient material.

Some of the world's great fishing grounds are associated with coastal shallows and banks. Northwestern Europe has several hundred thousand square miles of coastal or offshore shallows, with such famous cod, herring, and flounder fishing grounds as the Dogger Banks, the waters around the Faeroe Islands and Iceland, and the coast of Norway.

Turbulence. In sea water, plant and animal remains sink toward the bottom and decomposition of this material occurs mostly in depths where photosynthesis cannot occur. Without turnover of surface and bottom water, the upper layers of the ocean would become sterile except near river mouths where nutrient salts erode from the land. In fact, however, several forces tend to provide replenishment of the upper zones, namely current mix, wind and upwellings, and winter cooling:

1. *Current Mix.* When warm and cool water currents meet, a resultant mix occurs. Generally, the warm currents glide over the cooler ones, forcing the latter downward and producing a churning effect on the lower water levels. Plant and animal plankton from both currents are intermixed and provide rich food material for fish. Most of the world's great fishing areas may be identified with a conflict of currents—for example, the Grand Banks off Newfoundland are located in an interaction point between the cold Labrador Current flowing out of Baffin Bay and the warm North Atlantic Drift (Gulf Stream) flowing from the American tropics.
2. *Wind and Upwelling.* The force of the wind itself is generally sufficient to mix waters up to several hundred feet in depth. When wind movement forces surface water away from coasts, deep water upwelling from great depths replaces it, bringing upward rich plant nutrients that support large populations of both plants and fish. The extensive fish concentrations off the

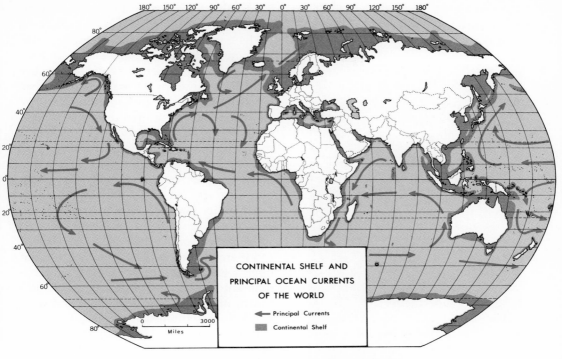

FIGURE 19.3 *(General Media Corporation)*

coast between Iquique, Chile, and Salinas, Ecuador, are a result of such wind action and resultant upwelling. Similar upwellings occur off the coasts of California, Morocco, and the west coast of South Africa.

3. *Winter Cooling.* Surface water in the higher latitudes becomes colder, and thus denser and heavier with the advent of cold weather. This surface water tends to sink and is replaced by relatively warmer water from the depths, which contains rich plant nutrients. The weather cycle thus develops a turbulence or mixing cycle that fosters renewed plant growth and the resultant food web.

Cool Water. Tropical and subtropical waters are not as productive of commercially valuable species of fish as are cool waters. Fish from warm water regions

tend to have a higher oil content, which often makes them less desirable as food. Cool water fish also tend to congregate in *schools* of one species, making it economically feasible to fish for and market *one* species, with less unit cost of production.

THE OCEAN'S PRODUCTIVITY

Although oceans cover over 70 percent of the surface of the earth, they supply little of man's food needs. In some cases, this is a function of distribution, but more often it is a case of economics, marketing practices, or transportation. Often, too, it is a function of consumer preference. The severe protein deficiencies in many low-income and highly populated nations cannot be overcome by increased fish production if demand is not present.

Five areas of the world can be identified as having high-volume fisheries.

WORLD CATCH OF FISH AND SHELLFISH BY LEADING COUNTRIES, 1955-65

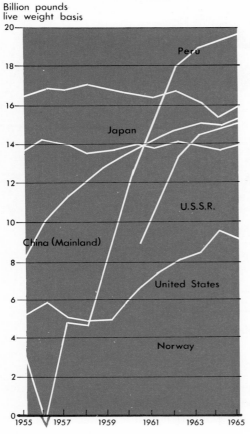

FIGURE 19.4 *The leading fishing nations of the world.*

All possess the physical characteristics previously referred to as instrumental in fishery development. Four of these are in the Northern Hemisphere and oriented to food fish; one is a recent development specializing in fish meal and fertilizer.

The Northwest Pacific

Currently, the foremost fishing area in the world is in the Northwest Pacific, encompassing seas extending from the Aleutian Islands to Indonesia. Although the principal catch is from Northern Hemisphere waters, an important segment of this fishery exists in the Southern Hemisphere between Borneo, Sumatra, and Java.

The northern part of this realm possesses a number of partially enclosed seas and a wide continental shelf, and is the meeting ground for the warm Kuroshio or Japan Current from the south and the cold Okhotsk Current from the north. Abundant fish food is present. In the north, large numbers of salmon, herring, and cod are prevalent. Salmon leads in terms of both value and weight of the catch. The five species of salmon found along the Pacific coast of North America are present here, and in addition a sixth species, the *masu*. Masu salmon occur in commercial quantities, but because of their small size are much less valuable than any of the other five species. To the south, the warmer seas around China and Japan are intensively fished, and tuna, mackerel, sardines and allied varieties, as well as great tonnage of shellfish, are annually taken. While large amounts are eaten immediately by the Japanese, who consider fish an integral part of every meal, an increasing amount is being canned for export. In the Peoples Republic of China, which like Japan annually ranks in the "Big Three" of world fishing nations and consumes most of its catch immediately, the long-range trawl ships used so extensively by Japan have as yet not been adopted. Most of China's fishing vessels are small and fish coastal waters.

An increasing utilization by the Japanese and Russians of inedible or "trash fish" for fertilizer is taking place. Their far-flung search for these items, as off the Pacific coast of North America, has created considerable vocal criticism by American fishermen.

In Southeast Asia, fish constitute a major protein source and an essential part of the daily diet. Practically all islands and coastal communities have local fishing fleets, but catches generally are small and for local immediate consumption.

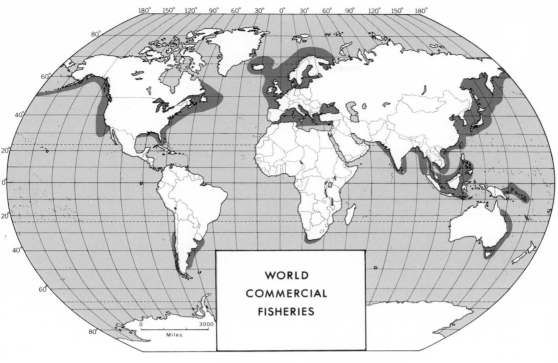

FIGURE 19.5   *(General Media Corporation)*

FIGURE 19.6   *For the Japanese, fishing has long been regarded as a primary means of procuring food. The fleet at the port of Kushiro is typical of the thousands of vessels engaged in the occupation of fishing. (Consulate of Japan)*

Seas Off Western North America

A major fishing region occurs along the Pacific coast of North America from Alaska to California. In the north, salmon dominate the catch, both in value and numbers. North Pacific waters are the true home of salmon for a very good reason. Along the shores are many cold, fresh-water streams that invite spawning and protect the abundant eggs and fry. The North Pacific Ocean into which the fingerling salmon later disappear is an ideal rearing ground because of its cooling Arctic currents and rich food supply of smaller marine organisms.

Five species of salmon inhabit the waters of the Pacific coast of North America: the pink (humpback) salmon, chinook (king) salmon, sockeye (red) salmon, coho (silver) salmon, and the chum (dog) salmon. All species of Pacific salmon are *anadromous*—the adults migrate from the ocean into fresh-water streams to spawn. This usually takes place in the summer and autumn, and in the same streams where they began life. How they manage to return to their "home stream" after their sojourn in the sea is still a mystery. The female salmon deposits her eggs in a nest, which she digs by fanning her tail in the gravel of the stream or shallow lake shore waters. Digging is alternated with egg-laying, followed by fertilization by the male salmon. In this process, the fertilized ova are covered with successive layers of gravel to a depth of several inches.

There is considerable variation in the life cycle of salmon depending upon the species and character of the fresh-water habitat. Hatching time for the eggs depends on water temperature and is usually about three months. Newly hatched fish live in the protective gravel of the nest, gradually absorbing the food in the abdominal yolk sac. At the end of this time they wriggle up through the gravel and begin the search for food.

The length of time the young stay in fresh water varies. For some species, such as pink salmon, the young begin their migration to the sea immediately. Others stay in fresh water for as long as three years. Once they reach the rich feeding grounds of the ocean, they remain there from one to four years, growing rapidly. On approaching sexual maturity, they return to fresh water to spawn and thereby complete the cycle.

California, Oregon, and Washington waters support principally a fishery for chinook, silver, and sockeye salmon. Fishing for the chinook and silver is carried on by small boats dragging skillfully fashioned hooked lures or bait that the salmon strike under the illusion of feeding. Because of their fine flavor, size, attractive appearance, and the individual care they receive in catching, chinooks command a premium price on the fresh fish market or for a salting process known as mild curing. Only a small proportion are taken by nets and canned. Chinook salmon are voracious feeders, averaging over twenty pounds in weight; specimens of fifty pounds are not uncommon, and the record size is 125 pounds.

The Alaskan fishery deals mainly in sockeye, pink, and chum salmon, in that order. Along the Alaskan coast, the halibut, a bottom fish, supports a large spring and summer fishery of unusual stability. Taken on long lines of baited hooks strung out along the bottom, halibut are marketed almost exclusively as either fresh or frozen.

A specialty fishery of some renown is the king crab operation located in the Gulf of Alaska. The crabs are taken in deep water with trawls or pots, and are very large, ranging up to eighteen pounds with a five foot spread. In the southern part of this Pacific coast region, albacore tuna, pilchards, and mackerel are taken in limited quantities.

Northwest Atlantic Region

European fishermen began exploiting the vast resources of the western Atlantic during the fifteenth century. Documentary

FIGURE 19.7 *A chinook salmon spawning in the gravel beds of an Oregon stream. (Oregon Game Commission)*

evidence recently found in England and in the Spanish archives suggests that this fishery was established even before Cabot "discovered" Canada in 1497. The Portuguese, Basque, and Bristol fishermen may all have been in this area by 1490, certainly before 1500. Nearly 500 years later, the "Spanish sailors with bearded lips" seen by Longfellow in Boston still made their appearance in this region along with the Portuguese and other Europeans. Now, Russian and Japanese fisherman swell the ranks of visiting ships.

Fishing in this region is of two types—inshore and offshore. The fisheries along Canada's Atlantic seaboard cover some 12,000 miles of bays, coves, and inlets, protruding headlands and offshore islands. The coast is dotted with fishing hamlets issuing a myriad fleet of dories, motorboats, and other vessels to reap the wealth of cod, herring, mackerel, haddock, pollack, and hake, along with shellfish such as lobster.

The offshore fishing occurs on the Grand Banks east of Newfoundland. The Grand Banks consist of a submarine plateau rising abruptly from ocean depths to general depths of less than 300 feet. The central part is quite even, but a number of isolated shoals exist between the center of the bank and the ocean deep, some as shallow as twelve feet. The Grand Banks extend as far as 230 miles eastward of Cape Lace, Newfoundland, having maximum width in an east–west direction of about 400 miles. Associated with the Grand Banks are the St. Pierre Bank and the Green Bank.

Here, on these banks, is the point where the warm, indigo Gulf Stream and the cold olive-green Labrador Current converge. A temperature range of 54° to 32° F. might take place in less than a ship's length. Along the convergence, water from the Labrador Current recurves eastward to flow parallel to the northern edge of the Gulf Stream, gradually losing its identity through mixing processes. As the cold waters of the Labrador Current chill the warm, moist southwesterly winds from the Gulf Stream, dense sea fogs are common throughout May, June, and July.

Icebergs, drifting with the Labrador Current, persist until July. The uneven ground of the shoals and banks, coupled with the strong-flowing currents, produce rough seas in bad weather or even with strong breezes.

Braving these dangers are veteran blue-water fishermen from all over the world. Even with 200,000 square miles of deep-sea grounds, the fishing pressure has been compared to the crowds in Times Square on New Year's Eve. Assembled here are otter trawlers of many varieties dragging their large cone-shaped nets, called otter trawls, across the bottom, the great ocean-going schooner fleet of Portuguese dory fishermen, and the giant factory ships of the United Kingdom and the U.S.S.R.

Great changes have taken place in the vessels and gear used to take the marine harvest. Faster vessels with powerful engines and the use of otter trawls instead of lines with hooks now provide larger catches and allow quicker trips to and from the fishing banks. The catch is no longer salted at sea, but is chilled on ice and delivered fresh to the markets. Increased efficiency in catching and handling the fish at sea and shore has resulted in expanded fishing efforts and wider markets for species previously discarded. Technological improvements have industrialized the Northwest Atlantic fisheries, resulting in a greater variety and improved quality of fish products.

Since its discovery, cod has been the principal species caught here. In recent years, haddock, halibut, hake, pollack, redfish, and assorted varieties of flatfish have also gained importance; swordfish, scallops, and seals add to the catch.

Northwestern Europe

The seas of northwestern Europe constitute probably the greatest of the world's historic fishing regions. This extensive area of fishing operations includes the Norwegian Sea, the North Sea including the famous Dogger Banks, the Barents Sea, the fiords of Norway, the Gulfs of Bothnia and Finland, the Irish and English Channels, and the waters surrounding Iceland.

Although much of these waters are in very high latitudes, sea surface temperatures are mild. The North Atlantic Drift, an extension of the Gulf Stream, is mainly responsible for the extremely favorable climate and hydrography that produce an abundance of aquatic resources. This drift results in comparatively moderate water temperatures that are suitable for the herring and bottomfishes that approach the coast on spawning or feeding migrations. As is characteristic of high-latitude waters, the number of species is not large, but the fish occur in vast schools.

The physiography of much of the adjacent coastline, particularly that of Norway, also lends itself to extensive coastal fisheries. Fiords and archipelagoes of large and small islands, islets, and rocks provide many sheltered parts and fishing grounds.

The major fish taken are herring, cod, saithe (dogfish), and allied species. Deep-water shrimp and European lobster are also secured; mackerel, flounder, halibut, and shark are taken in quantity. Some lesser operations are concerned with small whales and seals.

The fishermen of northwestern Europe are usually full-time fishermen, with the exception of Norway. The latter traditionally has had many farmer—fishermen who fish the fiords. Declining catches of coastal herring and cod have led fishermen to build larger craft and intensify distant-water fisheries. Since large craft with their high operating costs and upkeep must be kept fishing at all times, the fishing population has been steadily declining. Still, over 15,000 part-time fishermen are found in Norway alone. These individuals fish on a seasonal basis; small-scale farming and work in fish processing or other industries constitute their off-season employment.

The catch from the waters of northwestern Europe goes to a large number of countries, with the United Kingdom, West Germany, France, and Sweden the principal consumers. Fresh and frozen fish, canned fish, fish meal, and marine animal oils and fats make up the marketed items. Some of the African nations, such as Nigeria, take large quantities of dried fish. Dry-salted fish are also shipped to Portugal and some of the Latin American nations.

Western Coast of South America

In the years since World War II, attention has been focused on the rapidly developing fishery along the west coast of the South American continent. Here the emphasis has been not on fish for food but fish for fish meal. Principally in Peruvian waters, but also in Chile, the anchovy fish meal sector of the fishing industry is paramount.

Fishermen here have ready access to a rich variety of marine resources. High productivity is accounted for mainly by the movements of oceanic water masses and by associated changes due to prevailing winds. In the southeastern Pacific, there is a net eastward movement of water known as the West Wind Drift. This surface current, rich in plankton, approaches the Chilean coast at about 50° south latitude, where it divides. One branch flows southeastward around Cape Horn; the other, known as the Humboldt or Peruvian Coastal Current, flows northward along the Chilean and Peruvian coasts.

At various places along these coasts, southerly and southeasterly winds carry surface waters away from the coast and colder waters are drawn from moderate depths toward the surface, causing upwelling. These colder waters, rich in nutrient salts, further enhance the growth of the plant plankton that is the basis for the variety and abundance of aquatic resources in these waters.

The most abundant species off this coast is the anchovy, which feeds on the enormous growths of plant plankton associated with the upwelled waters of the Humboldt Current. Other pelagic surface-swimming species, such as the bonito, sardine, and jack mackerel, are found in these waters. Tuna, especially yellowfin tuna, inhabit the warmer waters to the west of the colder Humboldt Current; these generally stay offshore, except at certain times and in certain localities when the warmer waters extend inshore and cover the colder upwelled waters. Bottomfish and shellfish are negligible resources except in the northern area because of the narrowness of the Continental Shelf.

A larger variety of fish and shellfish is taken wherever the Continental Shelf broadens. The broader Continental Shelf has rich hake grounds, and other bottomfishes are also plentiful. Among the pelagic species, jack mackerel and sardine predominate. Moreover, the fishing grounds are closer to the densely populated consumer markets, and a variety of food fishes such as snake mackerel, cusk eel, and croaker are also taken in this region. Shrimp, plated lobster, clams, and sea snails are among the many shellfish available in the central region.

Whales, especially sperm whales, are abundant in waters up to 200 miles from the coast. These inhabit the rich feeding grounds of the Humboldt Current, migrating north from the Antarctic during the Southern Hemisphere's fall and winter; in spring and early summer they migrate southward from the tropics. Sperm whales yield a waxy oil for industrial use. Five species of baleen whales are also taken, the principal species being the fin and blue whales. Baleen oil is the well-known whale oil of international trade and is used mainly in the manufacture of margarine.

Export trends for fishery products have closely followed developments in the producing segments of the industry. A substantial trade in exports of fish meal and oil has been fostered with government support, with marketing in the United States, Belgium, Venezuela, West Germany, the Netherlands, and Spain, among other nations.

In a 1954 compact, Chile, Ecuador, and Peru claimed jurisdiction for conservation purposes over waters extending 200 miles from their coasts. This extensive territorial claim is in conflict with the three to twelve-mile limits recognized by most coastal countries. These three nations have adopted regulations that govern fishing and whaling in the 200-mile zone off their coast. Foreign fishing vessels planning to operate in these waters must apply to the respective governments for permits to fish and must pay duties on their catches. Special conferences sponsored by the United Nations have studied the problem of territorial waters and fishery zones, but international accord on their extent has not been reached.

OTHER MARINE RESOURCES

Several species of sea mammals make a significant contribution to either the economy of the major fishing nations or to a local economic base. Whales and seals in particular fall in this category. Whaling today is principally located in the South Pacific off Antarctica. Norway, Japan, the United Kingdom, the U.S.S.R., and the Netherlands are the major nations engaged in this operation. Modern explosive harpoons and specialized equipment, notwithstanding world conservation agreements, are rapidly depleting the fishery.

The Pribilof Islands in the Bering Sea are the chief center of the fur-seal industry. Here, strict U.S. regulation has managed to support a fairly flourishing industry.

Specialized fisheries also contribute to the world-wide fishing economy. In-

cluded here are operations for sponges, pearls, lobsters, crabs, oysters, and other crustacea. *Sponges* are obtained mainly from the waters off the West Indies, the coast of Florida, and the Red and Mediterranean Seas. While many sponges are still caught by "hooking" them with a pole in shallow water, most are now obtained by divers operating at depths less than fifty feet. The diver gathers the sponges to place in a net—when full, it is hauled to the surface. Increasing competition from synthetic and rubber articles contributes to the economic pressure facing this industry.

The major *pearl* fisheries are in the tropical waters of Australia, Southeast Asia, Ceylon, the Persian Gulf, and northern South America. The pearl, an accretion from irritation, is formed in a number of oysters or mussels. Divers gather these mussels and extract from some of them the much-valued item for decorative use. Pearl shell is, in fact, of equal or greater importance. Buttons, knife handles, and other items derive from this commodity. In certain countries, notably China and Japan, scientific pearl culture is carried on. The industry has, in recent years, faced considerable competition with artificial pearls.

Oysters, a large variety of mollusk, constitute a most valuable shellfish. The major source regions occur along the east coast of North America from Maine to Florida, in the Gulf of Mexico, along Chinese and Japanese coasts, and in Western Europe from northern Spain to the Netherlands. Chesapeake Bay, of long historic importance in the U.S. fishery, has had a lengthy period of decline due to pollution and overfishing. The bays of the Gulf Coast are heavy producers, however, and an oyster industry is developing on the coast near the state of Washington. Dredges gather most of the U.S. oyster catch.

Lobsters are found worldwide. Caught in traps or "pots" and with baited lines, at a depth of about forty feet, this seafood commands a high premium. Most of the Anglo-America catch comes from Atlantic waters from New York to Labrador. Northwest Pacific waters lead in the world catch, principally around Japan northward to Sakhalin; the Atlantic coast of Europe is also a large producer, and the waters off southwestern Africa and Chile are developing extensive lobster fisheries.

Crab and *shrimp* fishing supports a large industry, particularly in several local regions. San Francisco is a notable crab center, as is the Pacific Northwest coast including Alaska. The dungeness crab is the major species caught in the eastern Pacific; the importance of the king crab in Alaska waters has been previously noted. The shrimp, a small crustacean, is gathered extensively in the Gulf of Mexico and Mexico's Sea of Cortez, as well as worldwide for local use.

INLAND FISHING

Commercial fishing in inland waters is practiced extensively throughout the world, accounting for about six percent of the total catch. Several areas are prominent, particularly Southeast Asia. Here, lands of dense population with limited beef cattle and sheep demand a cheap protein food that is supplied by fish. "Fish farming" is widely practiced with carp and other fish, and practically all of the fresh-water fish are marketed fresh.

The U.S.S.R. also has an important fresh water fishery located in large rivers such as the Volga, Don, Dnieper, and others. Sturgeon, salmon, beam, carp, pike, and perch are representative species. The fisheries are particularly important in the delta areas of the rivers and in the inland seas.

Africa ranks high in her fresh-water fishery operation, particularly in Central Africa and Egypt. Fish constitute an important dietary item to combat the over-rich starch diet. Practically all fish are consumed fresh, due to high temperatures and lack of refrigerated storage.

Fresh-water fishing in Anglo-America is insignificant in the total world picture, but important locally. The Great Lakes and the Mississippi system constitute the major source regions of such species as perch, carp, catfish, smelt, and white bass.

The discharge of sewage, either untreated or inadequately treated, into tributary streams as well as directly into the lakes, since 1945 has destroyed great numbers of fish. The United States and Canadian governments have passed laws to stop pollution, but it will take many years to restore these waters as major fishing grounds.

A LOOK AHEAD

With the introduction during the last century of such mass fish-trapping techniques as the purse seine and the otter trawl, fishermen began harvesting the sea's bounty in increasingly larger quantities. This led to the suggestion that unrestrained netting could deplete the ocean's population. Not many believed such a thing possible. Even in 1883 the great naturalist, T. H. Huxley, observed:

I believe that the cod fishery, the herring fishery, the pilchard fishery, the mackerel fishery, and probably all the great sea fisheries are inexhaustible; that is to say nothing we do seriously affects the number of fish.

It is still not known to what extent that prophecy may have been right or wrong. Yet, marine researchers today are not at all confident that the sea's abundance is inexhaustible. Despite fishing techniques basically rooted in the past, commercial fishermen of today have become exceedingly adept at reaping the rich protein harvest of the seas. Airplanes now fly to locate schools of fish, radioing the intelligence back to commercial fisheries. Echo sounders pinpoint precise depths

FIGURE 19.8 *Seine net fishing is one of the many methods used by the Barbados fishing industry. (Barbados Tourist Board)*

at which to lay nets. And while the fishing fleets of Huxley's day consisted mostly of vessels putting out singly or in pairs, today's fleets are more like armadas. Flotillas of mother ships, spotters, and catchers work the fishing grounds for immense factory ships that process, freeze, and even can the catch.

Statistics gathered by the Food and Agricultural Organization of the United Nations give a dramatic picture of just how efficient commercial fishing has become in the years since World War II. In 1950, the world's commercial landings of all seafood totaled 46 billion pounds. By 1966, this figure had been increased by fishermen's savvy to 125 billion pounds, an increase of almost 170 percent!

According to Sir John Boyd, formerly head of the U. N. Food and Agricultural Organization, "A lifetime of malnutrition and actual hunger is the lot of at least two-thirds of mankind." Clearly, the world's demands upon its seas will increase in years to come. How will these

be met? Research and technology suggest some possibilities. A concentrate of fish protein intrigues nutritionists; at present, this powdered fish flour has only been tested as a dietary supplement in a

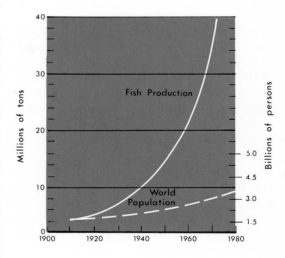

FIGURE 19.9 *Growth in world fisheries as compared with world population increases.*

few of the world's famine areas. Yet, experts contend that if produced in volume, it could supply the hungry of the world with their basic protein needs for less than half a cent a day per person. Furthermore, it would give fishermen an enormous market for fish they now ignore or throw away.

selected references

1. Craig, Alan K., "The Grouper Fishery of Cay Glory, British Honduras," *Annals of the Association of American Geographers*, Vol. 59, No. 2, June 1969, pp. 252–263.

2. de Blij, Harm Jan, "The Sea Fishing Industry of South Africa," *The Journal of Geography*, Vol. 67, No. 3, March 1958, pp. 135–142.

3. Gillespie, G. J., "The Atlantic Salmon," *Canadian Geographical Journal*, Vol. 76, No. 6, June 1968, pp. 186–199.

4. Hadgson, W. C., *The Herring and its Fishery*, London: Rutledge and Kegan Paul, 1957.

5. Helin, Ronald A., "Soviet Fishing in the Barents Sea and the North Atlantic," *Geographical Review*, Vol. 54, No. 2, July 1964, pp. 386–408.

6. Highsmith, R. M., "Food From the Sea," *Foreign Agriculture*, Vol. 24, November 1960, pp. 7–8.

7. Hull, Seabrook, *The Bountiful Sea*, Englewood Cliffs, N. J.: Prentice-Hall, Inc., 1964.

8. Koo, Teh S. Y., *Studies of Alaska Red Salmon*, Seattle: University of Washington Press, 1961.

9. Manzer, J. I., "The Sea Life of Canada's Pacific Salmon," *Canadian Geographical Journal*, Vol. 72, No. 1, January 1966, pp. 2–15.

10. Matheson, R. S., "The Japanese Salmon Fisheries: A Geographic Appraisal," *Economic Geography*, Vol. 34, No. 4, October 1958, pp. 352–361.

11. Minghi, Julian V., "The Problem of the Conservation of Salmon with Special Reference to Bristol Bay, Alaska," *Land Economics*, Vol. 36, November 1960, pp. 380–386.

12. Padgett, Herbert R., "Some Physical and Biological Relationships to the Fisheries of the Louisiana Coast," *Annals of the Association of American Geographers*, Vol. 56, No. 3, September 1966, pp. 423–439.

13. Pillsbury, Richard, "The Production of Sun-Dried Shrimp in Louisiana," *The Journal of Geography*, Vol. 63, No. 6, September 1964, pp. 251–258.

14. Sommers, Lawrence M., "Commercial Fishing in Norway," *Tydschrift Woor Economische en Sociale Geografie*, November 1962, pp. 237–242.

15. Vanstone, James W., "Commercial Whaling in the Arctic," *Pacific Northwest Quarterly*, Vol. 49, 1958, pp. 1–10.

16. Walford, Lionel A., *Living Resources of the Sea*, New York: The Ronald Press, 1958.

chapter 20

Forests and
Forest Products

Forests once covered about half the land area of the earth. They were absent or rare only in ice-capped polar regions, barren mountains, deserts, and dry grasslands. Over the centuries man has cleared forests for farming, and has overcut, overgrazed, and burned forests, so that today about one-third of the earth's land is in forest or is classified as forest land.

Of the eleven billion acres of forest land that remain in the world, one-third is unlikely to be commercially valuable, because adverse climate or soil conditions make the stands too open or too scrubby. Another third is commercially valuable and in use; the remaining third is potentially commercial but presently not used or is inaccessible.

LOCATION

The world's forests are fairly well distributed regionally. Although Europe, except the European part of the Soviet Union, has less forest than other physically larger regions, it is 30 percent forested—better than Africa (25 percent) or Asia (19 percent). The world's two most densely populated areas, Asia (without Asiatic Soviet Union) and Europe, however, have a per capita forest area of only 0.8 acre, compared with 17 acres in South America and 13.6 acres in the Soviet Union.

Accessibility

Slightly more than half of the world's forested area is deemed accessible by existing waterways, roads, railways, or other transportation. Nearly all forests in Europe are accessible and in use, but other regions have large tracts of inaccessible forest, particularly the Amazon Basin, the northern parts of the Soviet Union, and North America north of Mexico.

The accessible forests not in use are not necessarily a ready reserve from which

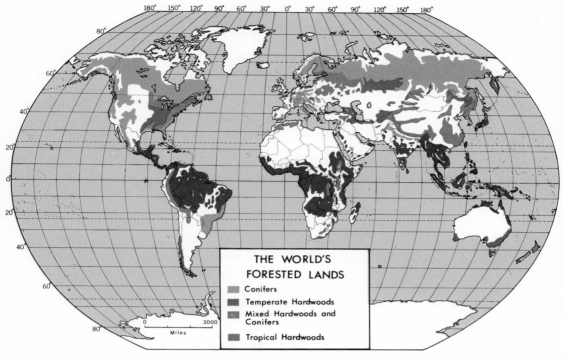

THE WORLD'S
FORESTED LANDS

- Conifers
- Temperate Hardwoods
- Mixed Hardwoods and Conifers
- Tropical Hardwoods

FIGURE 20.1   (*General Media Corporation*)

rising timber requirements will be met in the future. Generally, these forests are not in use because they grow on poorer sites, are understocked, or are stocked with species less desirable than those in use. Often they are noncommercial. Stands of scrubby alpine birch in Norway and the sparsely wooded savannas in Tanzania and the Republic of the Sudan, for example, produce little but fuelwood.

Much of the inaccessible forest in the middle and high latitudes is also noncommercial, especially where climate limits growth (as in northern Canada and the Soviet Union), in high mountains, and in dry areas. Inaccessible areas in the tropics are likely to contain good timber stands, as in the Amazon Basin, the Andes, middle Africa, and Southeast Asia.

Ownership

Most forests—especially the inaccessible and the less desirable accessible forests—

are publicly owned. More than three-fourths of the accessible forests are owned by the state or public entities. Private ownership of accessible forests is most marked in Europe (55 percent), in South America (45 percent), and in North America (43 percent). Nearly all forests are publicly owned in the communist countries, and there is a tendency toward public ownership of forest land in less-developed regions.

CLASSIFICATION OF FORESTS

Native species of trees are divided into two classes—hardwoods, which have broad leaves, and softwoods or conifers, which have scale-like leaves (as cedars) or needlelike leaves (as pines). Hardwoods, except in the warmest regions, are deciduous and shed their leaves at the end of each growing season. Native softwoods, except cypress, tamarack, and larch, are evergreen. Softwoods also are known as conifers, because all native species of softwood bear cones of one kind or another.

The terms "hardwood" and "softwood" have no direct application to the actual hardness or the softness of the wood. In fact, such hardwood trees as cottonwood and aspen have softer wood than the white pines and true firs, and certain softwoods, such as longleaf pine and Douglas fir, produce wood as hard as that of basswood and yellow poplar.

Conifers

Conifers occupy slightly more than one-third of the world's forest area, broadleaf species, slightly less than two-thirds. Conifers occur mostly north of the Tropic of Cancer. On an area basis, 98 percent of the coniferous forests, composed mainly of pine, spruce, fir, and larch, are in the Northern Hemisphere. Conifers in the Southern Hemisphere generally are mixed with broadleaf species and are not abundant. An exception is the Paraná pine, which occurs in fairly pure stands in southern Brazil and has been heavily exploited.

Plantings of the useful conifers have been made in the Southern Hemisphere. Conifers have been the mainstay of large-scale wood industries for generations because they are adaptable for many purposes, notably construction, packaging, and pulp and paper. Oddly enough, the most widely planted conifer, Monterey pine, is an import from the United States, where it occurs in a restricted area along the coast of central California and is not utilized extensively. Monterey pine has been planted in New Zealand, Australia, Chile, and South Africa.

Broadleaf

Vast tracts of tropical broadleaf forests in Latin America (including Mexico and Central America), Asia, and Africa are not in use because of inaccessibility and the bewildering number of species. Unlike temperate forests, tropical forests are generally a mixture of a great many species with low volume per acre of any one species. In the mahogany-bearing part of the Amazon rainforest, the number of marketable mahogany trees probably is less than one tree per acre.

Indonesia has at least 4,000 species of native trees that reach saw log size. Indonesian foresters estimate that about 400 of these will become commercially important because of useful wood properties or abundance. Only a few are now known in foreign markets, and not many more are used domestically, because the properties and proper use of most of these timbers are unknown or because steady supplies cannot be guaranteed.

Volume

The volume of growing stock in forests in use is estimated at 5.5 trillion cubic feet—two-thirds coniferous and one-third broadleaf; note that this proportion is just the opposite of the actual existing world supply of conifers and broadleafs. Volumes of growing stock in North America, Europe, and the Soviet Union have been estimated at 4.1 trillion cubic feet. The total volume in all forests is probably twice that of forests in use. Because a large part of the forests not in use is in the tropics, the proportion of volume in broadleaf species is large compared to coniferous stands.

Gross annual growth is estimated at 1.8 percent of the growing stock, equal to about 100 billion cubic feet. Since 1960, the drain on forests in use—removals, waste in the forest, and losses from fire, insects, disease, shifting cultivation, and transportation, especially in rafting and floating—has probably been less than the growth during the same period.

Distribution.   There appears to be no wood shortage for the world at present

FIGURE 20.2   *A Douglas fir forest in Washington state, showing patch cutting of old-growth timber. (USDA)*

consumption rates, but the uneven distribution of forests, lack of conifers locally, current quality and species requirements, high transportation costs, and waste in the woods and at processing plants produce timber shortages in certain areas.

The Soviet Union, Europe, and North America, with less than one-third of the world's population, have two-thirds of all forests, nine-tenths of the coniferous forests in use, and account for two-thirds of all removals. This roundwood volume includes more than 90 percent of the world's output of industrial wood.

PRODUCTION

Table 20.1 shows that the volume of timber removed from the world's forests in 1967 totaled about 2,100 million cubic meters (solid volume of roundwood without bark). Wood for fuel accounted for nearly three-fourths of removals in the less-developed regions—Africa, Latin America, and Asia-Pacific—but less than

one-fourth in North America, Europe, and the Soviet Union. Although a little less than half of all removals is coniferous, three-fourths of the industrial wood is coniferous and four-fifths of the fuel-wood is broadleaf.

Table 20.1   Production, Solid Volume of Roundwood Without Bark, 1967 (million cubic meters)

	Total	Coniferous	Broadleaf
World	2,100.0	1,010.0	1,090.0
Country			
U.S.S.R.	383.1	316.7	66.4
United States	324.6	231.1	93.5
Brazil	161.1*	26.8*	134.3*
China (Mainland)	136.0*	62.3*	73.7*
Canada	114.1*	103.7*	10.4*
Japan	59.6*	35.0*	24.6*
Sweden	54.0	47.1	6.9
Finland	41.1	28.2	12.9
Continent			
North America	478.0	338.5	139.5
Asia	412.4	116.5	295.9
Europe	328.9	139.2	189.7
Africa	241.8	6.9	234.9
South America	225.0	30.2	194.8

*1966 data.
Source: United Nations, *Statistical Yearbook*, 1968 (New York: United Nations, 1969), Table 49, pp. 154–155.

Coniferous Forests. These generally are utilized more completely and efficiently than broadleaf ones. Greater usable volumes per acre in coniferous forests, because of the prevalence of pure stands and the economic usability of small trees and logs, favor mechanization in logging and close utilization.

Broadleaf Forests. Rather low usable volumes per acre in broadleaf forests (particularly in the tropics), because of the mixture of species with widely varying wood properties, utility, and marketability, favor low-investment animal logging and wasteful utilization. Logging in broadleaf stands in Latin America and Asia is primitive and expensive in many places, and only choice logs of desirable species may be brought out. Other logs are left to rot in the woods. Sometimes the best logs, such as butt logs, are also left, because they are too big to handle manually.

COMMERCIAL FOREST PRODUCTS

The major processed forest products are lumber, plywood, fiberboard, and particle board (panels made from scrap wood). The order cited corresponds to the order in which those industries developed. It also corresponds to the present order of importance, measured by roundwood consumed, value of output, and direct employment afforded.

Sawmilling

Sawmilling employs two-thirds of the forest industries' labor force, uses about two-thirds of the industrial roundwood, and furnishes nearly half of the gross output value of all forest industries. The pulp and paper industry, employing one-fourth of the industrial roundwood, furnishes more than two-fifths of the gross output value.

Capital invested by the pulp and paper

industry is three to four times that of the sawmilling industry. Plants tend to be larger and more mechanized, and they yield a much higher gross value per unit of raw material used. Compared with these two giants, the wood-based panel industries—plywood, fiberboard, and particle board—are comparatively minor.

Lumber

World lumber output, estimated at 140 billion board feet, is about four-fifths coniferous. Because the wood of conifers can be readily sawed and planed and is strong in relation to its weight, it is preferred for many purposes. The Soviet Union, Europe, and North America produce most of the coniferous lumber and two-thirds of the broadleaf lumber. Temperate broadleaf species, such as oak, maple, birch, and black walnut, are used mainly in furniture, flooring, and a great variety of high-value wood products.

Tropical Woods

Tropical woods vary greatly in physical properties. Balsa, mainly from Ecuador, is lighter and softer than cork, while species of ironwood in Burma are extremely heavy and so hard that they turn nails. United States' imports of lumber or logs of tropical broadleaf species consist mainly of specialty woods. They include fine woods, whose ornamental grain and desirable physical properties make them suitable for furniture and cabinet work—among them true mahogany from Latin America, African mahogany, and some Philippine mahogany.

The United States also imports others whose unusual properties make them outstanding for different uses. *Lignum-vitae*, from Central America, is one of the hardest and heaviest of woods, and has the unique property of being self-lubricating. It is especially good for bearings under water, and is widely used for bearing or brushing blocks that line the stern tubes of propellor shafts for ships.

FIGURE 20.3 *Processing chips into finished paper products is carried on in a Toledo, Oregon plant. (Georgia-Pacific)*

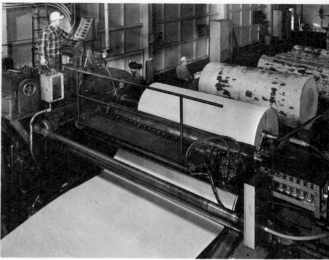

FIGURE 20.4 *Douglas fir logs are peeled into veneer for plywood on these giant lathes at Springfield, Oregon. (Georgia-Pacific)*

Lignumvitae wears better than metal and needs no lubrication in such cases. *Teak* from Southeast Asia is one of the outstanding woods of the world. Its strength, durability, and dimensional stability under varying moisture conditions make it ideal for many uses, particularly in shipbuilding.

Wood Pulp

North America and Europe account for more than four-fifths of the production. Somewhat less than one-third of the pulp is mechanical wood pulp, used mainly for newsprint and fiberboards. Nearly two-thirds is chemical and semichemical wood pulp, used chiefly in papers other than newsprint, and for paperboard and synthetic materials such as rayon, plastics, and films. About six percent of the pulp comes from nonwood sources— straw, bamboo, bagasse, and grasses such as esparto in Spain and northern Africa and sabai in India.

About 90 percent of the wood pulp is made from the long-fibered conifers, but the use of broadleaf pulp has been increasing, usually mixed with coniferous pulp.

Paper. Distribution of paper production is 19 percent newsprint; 18 percent printing and writing paper; 30 percent other paper, including tissues, wrapping paper, and wallpaper; and 33 percent paperboard, largely for corrugated containers, cardboard boxes, and food containers.

Plywood. More than half of the world's plywood is produced in North America, largely from the conifer Douglas fir. It is destined for construction and general utility purposes. Most of the plywood produced in the rest of the world is broadleaf and used for furniture, cabinetwork, or paneling. Broadleaf plywood in Europe and the United States is faced with a veneer of choice domestic species, such as black walnut and birch, or ornamental woods from tropical Latin America and Africa, such as mahogany and okoume. Japan, a major producer and exporter of broadleaf plywood, operates largely on lauan veneer logs imported from the Philippines.

The plywood category includes other products such as blockboard, battenboard, and cellular wood panels. Blockboard and battenboard consist of a thick core composed of blocks, laths, or battens glued together and surfaced with veneer. In cellular wood panels, the core consists of battens or laths spaced one from the other in either parallel or lattice form.

NONWOOD FOREST PRODUCTS

Nonwood forest products include a multitude of items collected for industrial and home use, medicine, and food. Some products are important only locally, but many enter international trade. The United States normally imports crude or slightly processed nonwood forest products valued at more than $100 million annually.

Bamboos are an essential of existence in parts of Southeast Asia. Complete houses are built solely of bamboo and without nails. Other uses include fencing, weapons, furniture, clothes, paper pulp, bridges, road surfacing, baskets, mats, domestic utensils, containers, tool handles, farm implements, binding material, fishing equipment, fuel, and food. With some exceptions, especially Ecuador, bamboos have not been extensively utilized in the Western Hemisphere. Bamboos are giant perennial grasses, some species growing more than 100 feet high and up to a foot in diameter. Like other grasses, the culms (stems), attain total height and diameter in one growing season.

Cork, the dead outer bark of the cork oak native to the Mediterranean region, was used extensively by the ancient Greeks. Cork is stripped from the trunks periodically. If the operation is carefully done with no injury to the live inner bark, the trees are not harmed and continue to produce. The product, because of its lightness and its resistance to moisture and penetration by liquids and sound, is valuable for flooring, life preservers, bottle stoppers, insulation, and compositions of various kinds.

FIGURE 20.5 A "chiclero" gashes the Zapote tree to induce the flow of sap or chicle. (Pan American Union)

Gums, Resins, and Latexes

Many gums, resins, and latexes are obtained by tapping or wounding the live inner bark or the live sapwood. *Gums*, most common in trees of drier regions, are used in adhesives, paints, candies, and medicines, and in the printing and finishing of textiles and the sizing of paper. Gum arabic, gum tragacanth, and karaya gum are the most important and better known gums.

Resins include a host of substances, such as copal, dammar, lacquer, turpentine, balsam, and elemis, that have many uses, particularly in the paint and varnish industry. The turpentine industry in the southern pine region of the United States is the world's largest producer of turpentine and resin. The flow of pine resin is often increased by spraying the chip or wound with sulfuric acid.

Guttapercha and chicle are best known among the many *latexes* tapped from wild trees. One of the important uses of guttapercha is in the construction of submarine cables, and no suitable substitute has been found. Guttapercha is a poor conductor of electricity, resistant to salt water, and pliable, yet has the right amount of rigidity. Chicle is the basis of the chewing gum industry.

Tannin extracts are prepared from the whole bark of many species, especially wattles and mangroves, and from the wood of quebracho trees in Argentina and Paraguay. Tannin also comes from the fruits of myrobalan trees in Southeast Asia, divi-divi- and tara trees in tropical America, and the acorn cups of the valonia oak of Asia Minor. It is used to tan perishable hides and skins in such a manner as to make them durable and flexible.

Quinine, valuable in the treatment of malaria, originally was extracted from the bark of cinchona trees, native to the Andes of northern South America. Most quinine now comes from large cinchona plantations in the Far East, particularly Java.

Other Nonwood Products

Curare, the arrow poison of some South American Indians, is extracted from the barks, roots, and woody stems of certain lianas. Various alkaloids found in curare are used in medicine. The demand for the fragrant *sandalwood* and sandalwood oil, an essential oil, has been so great that sandalwood has been nearly exterminated in many parts of the East.

Palms furnish fibers for brushes, cordage, hats, baskets, and mats; fatty oils are expressed from the nuts and important waxes scraped from the leaves. Carnauba wax, chiefly from northeastern Brazil, is valuable because it is hard and has a high melting point. It is used in polishes (for floors, furniture, and shoes), coatings for paper (carbon paper), phonograph records, and in pharmaceutical and cosmetic preparations.

Rattans, stems of climbing palms that may attain a length of 200 feet or more, are used for furniture, ship fenders, canes, and in plaiting or coarse weaving of many articles. Rattans occur in many tropical rainforests, but the most pliable and best quality whole and split rattan comes from Southeast Asia.

INTERNATIONAL TRADE

International trade in wood and wood products is large, mainly because forests in use are unevenly distributed in relation to population density, and forest industries are concentrated in North America and Europe. Densely populated Europe is a heavy net importer of roundwood, processed wood, and wood pulp, but a major exporter of paper and paper products. Although the Soviet Union and North America are both net exporters of wood, their different degrees of industrialization are reflected in the kind of exports—the Soviet Union exports mainly lumber and roundwood; North America, a net importer of roundwood, exports wood pulp, paper, and processed wood. The less-developed regions tend to export roundwood and import manufactured wood products, particularly paper. Because of the need for a variety of products and because the flow of raw materials in (for processing) and out (after processing), the two highly industrialized areas, North America and Europe, account for about four-fifths of international trade in wood.

Per capita consumption of wood is highest in North America. The world's industrialized areas, North America, Europe, and the Soviet Union, use much more industrial roundwood per person than fuelwood, but the reverse is true in less-developed regions, Latin America, Africa, and Asia-Pacific.

Consumption of industrial wood products varies tremendously from country to country, depending primarily on the degree of industrialization. In some less-developed countries, nearly all the wood used goes into fuelwood. For example, per capita consumption of industrial wood in the United States is more than 300 times that of Ethiopia, but fuelwood consumption in Ethiopia is six times that of the United States.

Some forest-rich countries such as Finland, the Soviet Union, Sweden, and

FIGURE 20.6 *A stand of Southern pine. (Georgia-Pacific)*

Norway use lumber as lavishly as the United States and Canada, but none come close to North America in the use of plywood and paper. North American per capita consumption of paper is three times that of Europe, twelve times that of the Soviet Union, and fifty times that of Africa.

Trends

World production trends indicate that outputs of all wood products except fuelwood will probably increase in the next decade. The output of lumber has not kept pace with the rise in general industrial output or with the increase in population. As a result, per capita consumption has been decreasing.

The pulp, paper, fiberboard, and particle board industries, unlike the sawmilling industry, are able to utilize small-size timber and frequently less valuable species. Furthermore, to an ever-increasing extent they employ wood residues from sawmills and veneer and plywood plants, and even residues from forest operations. The percentage increase in outputs of these products has been double or more that of lumber.

The particle board industry, able to operate on the cheapest raw material, has grown rapidly in the last decade, as has the plywood industry. Although large, good logs are needed for at least the face veneer, plywood has several advantages over lumber. It does not split, warps little, and can be made in large, easily used panels. Lumber is being displaced by wood-panel products as well as by masonry, metals, and plastics in construction, furniture, and other end products, and by paperboard in packaging.

Although man, in the near future, probably will clear some land suitable for agriculture, such deforestation will tend to be balanced by reforestation of denuded land near population centers, in order to avoid the expense of opening up inaccessible areas. Tropical forests contain huge supplies of wood, but increasing use of these areas will be slow because of problems of accessibility, utilization, and marketing. The increasing demand for wood products probably will quicken the current trend of better and more intensive management of forests now in use, and greater utilization of what was formerly considered unavoidable waste in the woods and at processing plants.

Man is becoming more conscious of the multiple uses of forests—wood, water, forage, recreation, wildlife, and protection from floods and soil erosion. As this understanding grows, forests, a renewable resource, will be more wisely managed for the benefit of all people.

selected references

1. Bone, Robert M., "The Soviet Forest Resource," *The Canadian Geographer*, Vol. 1, No. 2, 1966, pp. 94–116.

2. Dinsdale, Evelyn M., "Spatial Patterns of Technological Change: The Lumber Industry of Northern New York," *Economic Geography*, Vol. 41, No. 3, July 1965, pp. 252–274.

3. Fowell, H. A., *Silvics of Forest Trees of the United States*, Agriculture Handbook No. 271, Washington, D.C.: U.S. Department of Agriculture, Forest Service, 1965.

4. Gill, Tom, "Forests and Farmers," *Unasylva*, Vol. 17, No. 69, 1963, pp. 64–67.

5. Gorovili, N. S., "The Timber Industry of Northern European Russia," *Soviet Geography*, Vol. 2, No. 4, April 1961, pp. 53–59.

6. Hardwick, Walter G., "Log Towing Rates in Coastal British Columbia," *The Professional Geographer*, Vol. 13, No. 5, September 1961, pp. 1–5.

7. Harrington, Lyn, "Timber in Western Australia," *Canadian Geographical Journal*, Vol. 78, No. 1, January 1969, pp. 24–25.

8. Harrington, Robert F., "Prince George: Western White Spruce Capital of The World," *Canadian Geographical Journal*, Vol. 77, No. 3, September 1968, pp. 72–83.

9. Kromm, David E., "Sequences of Forest Utilization In Northern Michigan," *The Canadian Geographer*, Vol. 12, No. 3, 1968, pp. 144–157.

10. McDougall, Harry, "Water Bombers Protect Canadian Forests," *Canadian Geographical Journal*, Vol. 77, No. 2, August 1968, pp. 38–45.

11. Parsons, James J., "The Cork Oak Forests and the Evolution of the Cork Industry in Southern Spain and Portugal," *Economic Geography*, Vol. 38, No. 2, July 1962, pp. 195–214.

12. Prunty, Merle, Jr., "The Woodland Plantation as a Contemporary Occupance Type in the South," *Geographical Review*, Vol. 53, No. 1, January 1963, pp. 1–21.

13. Smith, David M., *The Practice of Silviculture*, 7th ed., John Wiley & Sons, Inc., 1962.

14. Wang, Chi-Wu, *The Forests of China with a Survey of Grassland and Desert Vegetation*, Cambridge, Mass.: Harvard University Press, 1961.

chapter **21**

Mining

The prosperity of modern man depends upon the natural resources at his disposal and the energy and intelligence that he applies to their utilization. The average family in the year 1800 lived, as far as material things were concerned, very much like families of hundreds of years before. The incredible changes that have come about with such rapidity in the past 170 years are due largely to the increased use of natural resources, especially minerals. Daily life for the average person has changed more during nearly any twenty-five year period within that time than it did during the entire twenty-five centuries before; mineral resources are chiefly responsible, for good or ill, for this transformation.

Minerals and rock products were used by man long before recorded history. The earliest civilizations revealed by excavation of human-settlement sites are recorded in implements made of stone. The Old Stone Age, during which tools were crudely fashioned from rocks selected for their shape and strength, was followed by the New Stone Age, when tools were more artistically shaped and were adapted to particular uses. Later, following the discovery that tin and copper could be combined to make a metal product adaptable to many uses, came the Bronze Age. Control of tin and copper deposits then became of great national consequence, as is the control of supplies of iron and petroleum today. Ancient Egypt became a world power about 4,000 B.C., in part because it controlled valuable copper deposits. Later the Roman Empire, after its conquest of Spain, built up a great civilization based in part on its control of metals valuable in the arts and to industry.

Today, industry in the Euro-American culture area is based on the exploitation of iron and coal, for this is a machine age and machines are used extensively in most occupations. In agriculture, mining, manufacturing, transportation, construction, and also in household work, steel tools and machines, smelted from iron, shaped and fashioned by energy derived largely from coal, and driven by power derived largely from coal, water, petroleum, and nuclear energy, are becoming increasingly important with every advance in technology. Therefore, to every country developing industrially the control of adequate supplies of the base minerals and rock products (coal, iron, copper, tin, zinc, lead, petroleum, bauxite, nickel, chromite, manganese, tungsten, and the like) is absolutely necessary.

Few if any countries contain within their borders all the necessary minerals and power; hence possession of minerals has been and still is one of the fundamental causes of wars, conquest, and treaties between nations. In the early days it was the precious metals, particularly gold and silver, that lured men and nations to exploration and conquest. Today greater interest is in petroleum and the essential alloy metals that are necessary in the production of certain types of steel.

OVERVIEW

From its origin either as a subsistence or a commercial activity, mining has increased in scope, area, intensity, and need until presently it is indispensable. The following are some of the more important general facts associated with mining:

1. Since 1880, world production has increased tenfold while the population has only doubled.
2. Man has mined more minerals in the past 50 years than were mined during all time previous.
3. In 1875 only a very few minerals were necessary for the machine civilization; presently, 75 minerals are considered essential.
4. No single country or major region has within its boundaries enough of these minerals, either in quantity or quality, to support the more advanced of the machine civilizations.
5. World trade in minerals has more than quadrupled during the past 25 years.

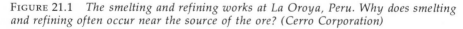

FIGURE 21.1 *The smelting and refining works at La Oroya, Peru. Why does smelting and refining often occur near the source of the ore? (Cerro Corporation)*

6. Intensive research has produced many new metal ores and new uses for others, which in time will become essential to our civilization.
7. Mining operations have changed radically from the highly selective method of mining only high-grade, easily accessible minerals to mining almost every known commercial deposit.
8. At present rates, the world's population is expected to more than double in the next 30 years; similarly, the rate of production and consumption is also expected to increase considerably, resulting in higher standards of living.

Only a few of the economically more important basic minerals—coal, iron ore, petroleum, natural gas, water, and a few selected ferroalloys—will be discussed here, for obviously it is meaningless to attempt an in-depth study of the earth's total mineral wealth.

COAL

The three main types of coal are anthracite, bituminous, and lignite. They vary in the amount of bituminous matter, the degree of hardness or softness, and the limits of fixed carbon or B.T.U. Anthracite is the hardest, burns slowly with a pale blue flame, and requires a minimum of attention. Lignite is the softest, disintegrates rapidly in air, and is liable to spontaneous combustion. Bituminous coal is the most abundant and most widely used variety, varying from medium to high rank. Medium-to-low volatile bituminous coals may be of coking quality, the property wherein the coking or caking coal softens, swells, and runs together when heated almost to its burning temperature. When further heated in a closed oven, either without oxygen or with very little, the volatile matter is driven off in the form of gas, water vapor, light oil, and tar. The gray porous residue consists largely of fixed carbon and is called coke, which is used extensively in blast furnaces for the smelting of iron ore.

Producing Areas

The bulk of the world's coal is mined in the middle latitudes of the Northern Hemisphere. Anglo-America, Europe, the U.S.S.R., and China are the largest producers, accounting for about 93 percent of the world's mined output. Only the Republic of South Africa and Australia mine coal in appreciable tonnages south of the equator (Table 21.1).

Western Europe

On the continent of Europe, a well-defined coal belt occurs about the lower Rhine of West Germany, the Sambre–Meuse field of Belgium and France, the Saar Basin of West Germany, and Silesia.

In the United Kingdom coal is produced abundantly in the Midland Valley of Scotland, the Northumberland and Durham field in northeastern England, central England on either side of the Pennine Chain (the Lancashire field on the west and the Yorkshire on the east), and in Wales, the latter producing both bituminous and anthracite.

U.S.S.R.

The Soviet Union ranks first in world production of coal, mining about one-fifth of the total output. Of the major Soviet fields, the Donets Basin has by far the best location in respect to markets and iron-producing centers. Probably because of this, it has been the largest producer since the rise of modern coal mining, even though it contains only five percent of the estimated Soviet reserves. Its actual output in 1967 was 205 million metric tons—equalling the bituminous coal production of Pennsylvania and West Virginia combined.

Table 21.1 Production of Coal—Bituminous, Anthracite, and Lignite (thousand metric tons)

Country	1960	1967	Percent Change 1960–67
World	1,962,800	1,919,800	− 2.19
Australia:			
bituminous	22,931	35,264	+ 53.78
lignite	15,207	23,759	+ 56.24
Austria: lignite	5,973	4,604	− 22.92
Belgium: bituminous and anthracite	22,469	16,435	− 26.85
Brazil: bituminous (including lignite)	1,277	1,957	+ 53.25
Bulgaria: lignite	15,416	26,739	+ 73.45
Canada:			
bituminous	8,020	8,516	+ 6.18
lignite	1,969	1,822	− 7.47
Chile: bituminous (mined)	1,297	1,357	+ 4.62
China, Mainland:			
bituminous and anthracite	420,000	227,000	− 45.95
Colombia: bituminous	2,600	3,100	+ 19.23
Czechoslovakia:			
bituminous	26,214	25,945	− 1.02
lignite	58,403	71,363	+ 22.19
Denmark: lignite	2,673	1,302	− 51.29
East Germany: lignite	214,783	242,027	+ 12.68
France:			
bituminous and anthracite	55,960	47,624	− 14.90
lignite	2,276	2,931	+ 28.78
Greece: lignite	2,550	5,162	+102.43
Hungary:			
bituminous	2,847	4,053	+ 42.36
lignite	23,676	22,976	− 2.30
India:			
bituminous	52,593	68,223	+ 29.72
lignite	47	2,929	+523.19
Indonesia: bituminous	658	207	− 69.54
Italy: lignite	794	2,201	+177.20
Japan: bituminous and anthracite	51,067	47,482	− 7.02
Mexico: bituminous	1,074	1,424	+ 32.59
Mongolia: bituminous and lignite	619	1,061	+ 71.71
Netherlands: bituminous and anthracite	12,498	8,065	− 35.07
New Zealand:			
bituminous and anthracite	813	595	− 26.81
lignite	2,247	1,813	− 19.31
North Korea:			
bituminous and anthracite	6,778	17,000	+150.81
lignite	3,842	4,400	+ 14.52
North Vietnam: anthracite	2,595	2,800	+ 7.90
Pakistan: bituminous	831	1,400	+ 68.47
Poland:			
bituminous	104,438	123,881	+ 18.62
lignite	9,327	23,922	+156.48
Rhodesia: bituminous	3,559	2,739	+ 29.94
Rumania:			
bituminous and anthracite	3,405	5,112	+ 50.13
lignite	3,363	7,852	+133.48
South Africa, Republic of:			
bituminous and anthracite	38,173	49,300	+ 29.15
South Korea: anthracite	5,350	12,436	+132.45

Table 21.1   (Continued)

Country	1960	1967	Percent Change 1960–67
Spain:			
bituminous and anthracite	13,783	12,650	− 8.22
lignite	1,762	2,650	+ 50.40
Taiwan: bituminous	3,962	5,078	+ 28.17
Thailand: lignite	108	335	+210.19
Turkey:			
bituminous	3,653	5,031	+ 37.72
lignite	1,911	3,416	+ 78.75
United Kingdom:			
bituminous and anthracite	196,711	174,898	− 11.09
U.S.S.R.:			
bituminous and anthracite	355,918	414,087	+ 16.34
lignite	134,206	141,444	+ 5.39
United States:			
bituminous and anthracite	391,526	481,164	+ 22.89
lignite	2,491	4,073	+ 63.51
West Germany:			
bituminous and anthracite	143,255	112,294	− 21.61
lignite	96,216	96,766	+ .57
Yugoslavia: lignite	21,430	25,558	+ 19.26

Source: United Nations *Statistical Yearbook*, 1968 (New York: United Nations, 1969), Tables 55 and 56, pp. 185–188.

Despite the large coal output in the Soviet Union, much of the coking coal used is high in sulfur and ash; recovery of coke per ton of coking coal is slightly more than 50 percent, as compared with 76 percent in the United States. Another problem is that much of the coal lies in thin seams, a few of which are more than a yard thick; extraction costs are therefore high, and likely to become even higher.

Anglo-America

The distribution of coal fields in the United States and Canada is extensive, with many fields still unexplored, but the largest production is concentrated in the Allegheny Plateau fields. In Canada, particularly, many coal deposits are remote from populated places where the coal can be used most efficiently, and coal is a commodity too expensive to transport long distances except in emergencies.

The United States, with about 1.8 trillion tons of coal in the ground, has one-third of the earth's known reserves. On the basis of heating value per pound, nearly 80 percent of the reserve is bituminous and subbituminous. These ranks of coal are distributed over all the United States—about one-third east of the Mississippi River, one-third in the interior, and one-third in the northern Great Plains, Rocky Mountains, and Gulf and Pacific areas. Much of this coal is of good coking quality and can be mined easily by machine methods.

Canada has 1.9 percent of the world's coal reserves, of which more than 90 percent are found in the west, chiefly in Alberta, Saskatchewan, and British Columbia. Smaller amounts also occur in the Maritime Provinces, particularly Nova Scotia and New Brunswick.

China

Coal is China's main energy-producing mineral. The country has huge coal deposits, about 95 percent of which are located in the northern areas. The major

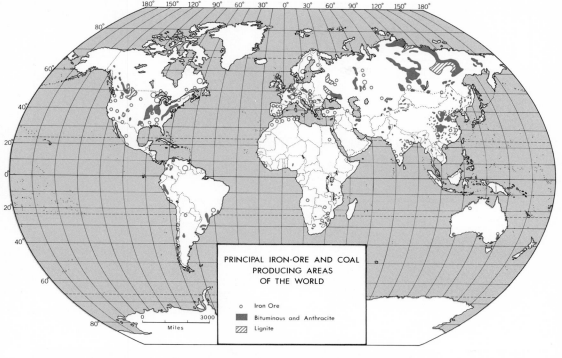

FIGURE 21.2 *(General Media Corporation)*

coal basins are:

1. Fushun in the southern part of northeast China
2. Kailan, located in Hopei Province
3. Fusin, about 93 miles from Mukden (Shenyang)
4. Tatung Basin in the province of Shansi
5. Hwainan, located south of the Hwai River in Anhwei Province

The Chinese coal industry is undergoing a period of intensive expansion, and one of the most important developments has been the large-scale introduction of hydraulic mining.

Other Coal-Producing Areas

Only a few areas outside those discussed above are conspicuous on the coal map of the world. Japan's coal reserves are moderate, and recoverable coal is estimated at about three billion tons, a very small amount compared to the United States or the Soviet Union. The major coal fields are located at opposite ends of the country, in Kyushu and Kokkaido. Japanese coal is mostly low-grade bituminous, with low heating value; the coal seams are thin, tilted, and badly broken.

India has rich deposits of coal in Bengal, Bihar, and Orissa; fortunately the deposits are close enough to large iron ore deposits to make India potentially one of the world's cheapest producers of iron and steel. In the south there are deposits of low-grade brown coal, which has not been easily used by industry in the past, but with the development of new processing and burning techniques this lignite coal will become a suitable source for thermal power.

Australia's coal discoveries in Queensland in 1960 have more than doubled the country's estimated reserves. While current published reserves are not large by

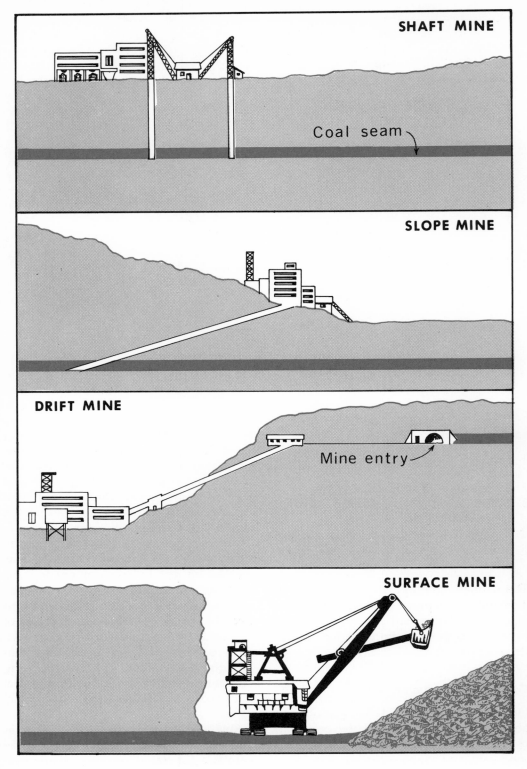

FIGURE 21.3   *Methods of mining coal.*

world standards, there is evidence that considerable veins of coal still await discovery.

Coal underlies vast areas of Transvaal and of the Orange Free State in the Republic of South Africa. With the exception of 300 million tons in Natal, however, all of this coal is non-coking and present production is relatively small.

Types of Mining

Coal mining depends upon several factors, the most important of which are

1. The area of coal available
2. Thickness and inclination of the seam and overlying strata
3. Value of surface land and other economic factors

The major coal mining methods are underground or deep mining, where coal is extracted from the seam without removal of overlying strata; strip or overcast mining, in which the strata overlying the coal seam (overburden) are removed and coal is extracted from the exposed seam; and auger mining, in which coal is recovered by means of large-diameter augers boring horizontally into the outcropping system.

Coal in World Trade

Normally, only a small proportion of the coal mined enters into world trade. Coal is heavy and bulky in proportion to its value; consequently it can bear long-distance transportation costs only under the most favorable circumstances. Most export coal moves by water, the cheapest form of transportation. If land transportation is necessary the distances covered are usually short.

The United States is both an importer and exporter of coal. Most of the imported coal comes from Canada, going from British Columbia to Washington, Montana, and Idaho, and from Nova Scotia to Maine and New Hampshire. However, compared to exports, the volume of imported coal is not great; it usually amounts to less than 200,000 tons per year. For many years Canada has been the principal customer for U.S. coal, averaging around 12 million tons per year. U.S. overseas exports, chiefly to Europe and Japan, have fluctuated widely, influenced primarily by changing rates of economic growth. Nevertheless, because of increasing energy demands and requirements for good quality coking coals in Japan, there are appreciable potentials for increased exportation of U.S. coal.

Coal production in most Western European countries has been declining in recent years, largely because of the increased use of oil for industrial purposes and the discovery of natural gas in northeastern Europe.

IRON ORE

Iron is the most useful metal of material civilization; it has made possible plants, tools, machinery, and many of the products of the Industrial Revolution. It is used principally when alloyed with other elements, notably carbon; a moderate amount produces steel, an excess produces cast iron. The availability of adequate supplies of iron ore is significant to industrial nations.

Sixty-eight countries of the world report iron ore production, and more than 150 million tons of iron ore are sold outside the country of origin each year. Seven countries, however, account for the bulk of the iron ore mined. Of these, the U.S.S.R. leads all others, followed by United States, Canada, Sweden, France, India, China, and Brazil.

Mining Methods

Open-pit and underground mining are the principal methods used in recovering iron-ore deposits. The type used depends on the position of the ore body. Deposits

Table 21.2 Production of Iron Ore (thousand metric tons)

Country	1960	1967	Percent Change 1960–67
World	256,600	339,800	+ 32.42
Algeria	1,788	1,335	− 25.34
Australia	2,859	12,273	+329.28
Austria	1,100	1,099	− 0.09
Brazil	6,355	15,163	+138.60
Canada	11,140	23,420	+110.23
Chile	3,804	6,853	+ 80.15
China, Mainland	30,250	15,400	− 49.09
Czechoslovakia	948	545	− 42.51
East Germany	408	407	− 0.24
France	21,745	15,997	− 26.42
India	10,131	15,683	+ 54.80
Japan	1,574	1,274	− 19.06
Liberia	2,192	12,575	+473.68
Luxembourg	1,926	1,715	− 10.96
Malaysia	3,209	3,044	− 5.11
Mexico	521	1,618	+210.57
Morocco	874	683	− 21.85
North Korea	1,550	3,250	+109.68
Norway	1,056	2,000	+ 89.39
Peru	3,947	4,809	+ 21.84
Philippines	638	929	+ 45.61
Poland	624	838	+ 34.29
Rumania	467	813	+ 74.09
Sierra Leone	881	1,259	+ 42.91
South Africa, Rep. of	1,965	4,910	+149.87
Spain	2,798	2,550	− 8.86
Sweden	13,014	17,596	+ 35.21
Turkey	494	881	+ 78.34
United Kingdom	4,688	3,624	− 22.70
U.S.S.R.	54,075	90,326	+ 67.04
United States	47,867	50,345	+ 5.18
Venezuela	12,474	10,959	− 12.15
West Germany	4,412	2,184	− 50.50
Yugoslavia	788	1,042	+ 32.23

Source: United Nations *Statistical Yearbook,* 1968 (New York: United Nations, 1969), Table 57, pp. 188–189.

that occur relatively near the surface are excavated by first removing the overburden with power shovels, draglines, or scrapers. Ore is then transported from the pits by rail, trucks, ships, conveyor belts, or combinations thereof; with few exceptions the choice is ruled by the grade of haul and the size of the operation.

Underground mining methods are employed where ore deposits lie deep within the earth. The large underground mines have been mechanized to the same extent as the open-pit mines, and wherever pos-

sible loaders, conveyors, and hoists have been fully automated.

Major Producing Regions

The U.S.S.R., Anglo-America, and Western Europe together account for about 70 percent of the world's iron ore production. Brazil and Venezuela are the largest producers of iron ore in South America. Asia's leaders are Mainland China and India, the sixth and seventh producing nations, respectively, in total iron ore tonnage mined. Australia's recent find in the Hamserly Range in western Australia is destined to make that area a leading world producer in the near future.

Outlook

The iron ore industry will be a vital part of the expanding industrialization brought about by rising living standards and a growing population. New mines will be opened to share in the markets created by the iron and steel industries now being planned for the recently independent, less developed nations. Others will be opened to satisfy demands foreseen for industrial areas now in existence. Those mines producing high-grade, low-silica pellets or their equivalent will tend to capture the world markets.

Technology will continue to exert strong influence on the course of the iron ore industry. Except in unusual circumstances, iron ore will be mined in open pits from the large, low-grade, easily beneficiated deposits. The trend toward larger equipment and automation of transportation and crushing plants will continue. Drilling and blasting practices in the taconite mines will improve but not at the fast rate of the last decade.

PETROLEUM AND NATURAL GAS

Petroleum, natural gas, and related bituminous minerals have been used by mankind since antiquity. In the ancient world, pitch or native asphalt was used as a binder for pavements, for waterproofing cisterns, calking ships and grain silos, and for mummification.

The first recorded production of natural gas in the United States was in western New York State in 1821, when a gas seep on the banks of Canadaway Creek was ignited accidentally, demonstrating that natural gas was an excellent fuel.

The modern petroleum industry dates from E. L. Drake's well, which was drilled near Titusville, Pennsylvania, specifically in search of oil. Oil was found at a depth of less than 70 feet on August 27, 1859. At that time, there was a demand for a better and cheaper lamp oil; whale oil was expensive, in limited supply, and unsatisfactory in other ways.

The industry has grown to the point where petroleum and natural gas and their hydrocarbon derivatives now supply three-fourths of all U.S. fuel energy needs. World consumption of petroleum continues to increase—in the United States the increase is about six percent per annum, in the rest of the free world about ten percent.

Anglo-America

Anglo-America leads the world in production of petroleum and natural gas. Not only is Anglo-America the largest producer, but also the leading consumer. The twelve major petroleum fields are Appalachia, northeast Indiana, Ohio, Michigan, Illinois, southwest Indiana, Midcontinent, Gulf Coast, Central Plains, Rocky Mountain, California, and the northern Plains Provinces in Canada. Thirty-three of the fifty states are oil or oil and gas producers, with the highest production coming from Texas, California, Louisiana, Oklahoma, Kansas, and Wyoming, in the order named. Some of the best areas, based on present knowledge, are offshore in California and Louisiana. Their development is a matter of economics, because operation costs run two to ten times those on land.

A recent oil strike on the north slope of Alaska near Prudhoe Bay, about 390 miles north of Fairbanks and 150 miles southeast of Point Barrow, may completely change the oil picture of the United States. Though the exact size of the field is undetermined, reserves are estimated at between five and ten billion barrels. If

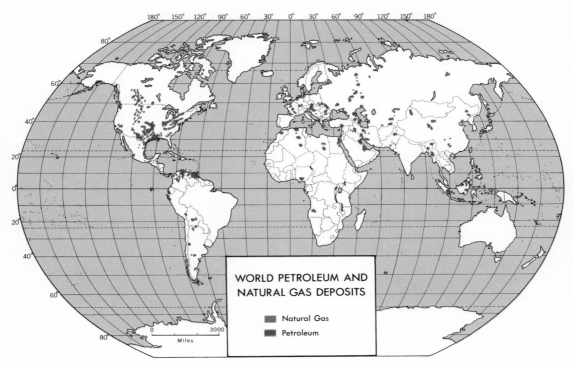

FIGURE 21.4   (General Media Corporation)

FIGURE 21.5   An offshore oil well in the Gulf of Mexico. What political ramifications are present with offshore mineral deposits?

the higher figure is correct, the field could increase United States oil reserves by 25 percent.

With about 12 percent of the proved oil reserves of the world, the United States produces roughly 40 percent of its oil. Ultimate reserves are placed at 460 billion barrels of liquid hydrocarbon (crude plus natural liquids) [16], of which perhaps some 400 billion barrels are crude alone. Allowing for past production and the possibility that even a 50 percent recovery may not be realized, a more realistic future availability of 250 billion barrels can be predicted.

Canada's petroleum reserves are estimated at nearly 3,700 million barrels, an adequate supply for the needs of that country for several decades. Although oil was discovered in 1913 in the Turner Valley field near Calgary, Alberta, the major impetus to production came in 1947 with the opening of the Leduc field near Edmonton. Spectacular exploration and development of the sedimentary basin of the Prairies followed. Commercial production in Saskatchewan, which started during World War II, passed the one million barrel mark in 1950; Manitoba, opened in 1951, passed the million barrel mark by 1954; the British Columbia fields, opened in 1955, attained an annual capacity of over one million barrels by 1961. Now, Alberta accounts for roughly 70 percent of the total Canadian output; Saskatchewan for 25 percent; Manitoba,

British Columbia, the Northwest Territories, and New Brunswick share the remaining 5 percent.

Natural Gas. Closely allied to, and often associated with petroleum are the gaseous hydrocarbons (mainly methane), or natural gas. Because of its sootless and essentially odorless qualities, low cost, ease of transmission, and high heat value (100 cubic feet equals 8 to 13 pounds of coal), natural gas is the most rapidly growing energy source in the United States. A system of pipelines totaling more than 165,000 miles distributes natural gas to all parts of the country, supplying almost 30 percent of the total fuel energy needs of the nation. Two states, Texas and Louisiana, have roughly 67 percent of the proved reserves and account for about 68 percent of the nation's natural gas production. Other large producers are Oklahoma, Kansas, New Mexico, and California. Estimated proved reserves total 260 trillion cubic feet more than adequate to meet U.S. needs for many decades.

Canada's estimated reserves of natural gas total over 33.5 trillion cubic feet—85 percent in Alberta, 11 percent in British Columbia, 3 percent in Saskatchewan, and the remaining 1 percent in Ontario, New Brunswick, and the Northwest Territories. Although natural gas is by far the cheapest source of energy in Canada, it currently supplies only about 7 percent of that nation's energy market. Nearly

Table 21.3   Production of Crude Petroleum (thousand metric tons)

Country	1960	1967	Percent Change 1960-67
World	1,053,600	1,758,700	+ 66.69
Iran	52,392	128,761	+145.76
Kuwait	81,867	115,175	+ 40.69
Libya	—	82,540	—
Saudi Arabia	62,068	129,304	+108.35
United States	347,975	434,573	+ 24.89
U.S.S.R.	147,859	288,068	+ 94.83
Venezuela	149,372	185,409	+ 24.13

Source: United Nations Statistical Yearbook, 1968 (New York: United Nations, 1969), Table 75, pp. 207–208.

one-third of the natural gas produced in Canada is marketed in the United States, being transmitted by pipeline as far as California.

The leading oil producing nations in 1967, ranked in order, were the United States, the Soviet Union, Venezuela, Saudi Arabia, Iran, and Kuwait, while the top consuming nations were the United States, the Soviet Union, Japan, West Germany, the United Kingdom, and France.

It has been estimated that by 1977 world demand for petroleum will reach 58 million barrels daily, of which the Middle East is expected to supply more than 20 million.

Although the Soviet Union is a net oil exporter, Middle East oil reserves are a main key to its political and economic goals in the Arab countries. They supply Western Europe with three-fourths of its oil and Japan with 90 percent of its needs. Soviet political domination of Arab oil-producing countries would give it an economic stranglehold on these leading industrialized parts of the free world.

The economic significance of Middle East oil to the U.S. lies in the dollar returns from American oil companies. In 1966, petroleum accounted for about 30 percent of all U.S. direct investments abroad, but produced 45 percent of the income from total U.S. direct investments. Over $1.1 billion, or more than half of all income from petroleum abroad, came from the Middle East and Libya. This amount is equivalent to more than 70 percent of the U.S. balance of payments deficit for 1966 and more than 25 percent of the 1967 balance of payments deficit. Without these earnings the deficit would have been that much higher each year, with resulting critical pressures on U.S. domestic economy.

The governments of the Arab oil-producing countries profit most from United States oil company operations. Government oil revenues average about 65 percent of the profits, in some cases going as high as 80 percent. This great new wealth has been created principally

in the last two decades and has catapulted some of the Middle East countries from feudalism into the last half of the twentieth century.

Middle East

The world's largest petroleum reserves lie in a sedimentary basin bounded by the Taurus Mountains of Turkey in the north, the mountains of Lebanon and Syria and the highlands of Saudi Arabia on the west and the mountain ranges of Iran, Muscat, and Oman on the east. The valley of the Tigris–Euphrates Rivers and the Arabian Gulf are in this basin. In terms of regional geology, the area is a structural as well as a topographic basin particularly well suited to the generation and accumulation of petroleum.

Oil was discovered in Iran before World War I, but greatest development of Middle East petroleum resources came after World War II. In 1944 the world's proved crude oil reserves were more than 50 billion barrels, of which some 30 percent occurred in the Middle East. At the beginning of 1967 the proved reserves for the world were 398 billion barrels, with 243 billion barrels, or 61 percent, in the Middle East. Most of these reserves are in countries around the Persian Gulf and in the gulf itself.

Production costs in the Middle East are the lowest in the world. Average daily production of a Middle East oil well is about 4,500 barrels, compared to an average of less than 300 barrels for Venezuelan wells and only 15 for wells in the United States. Most Middle East wells also are free flowing; oil must be pumped out of U.S. wells and a high percentage of those in other major producing areas, such as the Soviet Union and Venezuela. Additionally, much of the Middle East oil is produced from fields close to the Persian Gulf near marine shipping points. These savings more than offset the high costs of plant and equipment and other operating expenses.

The huge reserves and low production

costs inevitably have attracted more and more oil companies to seek concessions in the Persian Gulf area. Middle East governments, too, have sought a wider role in the development of their oil resources. For most of these nations, petroleum accounts for a large part of their income and foreign exchange earnings.

U.S.S.R.

Commercial petroleum production in the Soviet Union began in 1873 when the Baku oil field was discovered. This field was the major source of petroleum for decades. Great expansion in the search for new oil fields and the changeover to the use of petroleum as a major supplier of energy did not occur until the Seven Year Plan (1959–1965) got underway and particular attention was given to the development of petroleum and natural gas reserves.

Of its total crude oil production of 309 million metric tons in 1968, the Soviet Union exported 57 million tons in crude oil form and an additional 25 million tons as refined products, roughly a fourth of the total oil output.

Among the Western nations, the largest oil customers of the Soviet Union in recent years have been Italy, France, West Germany, Finland, and Sweden; Italy alone purchased more than 10 million tons of crude oil from the Soviet Union in 1967.

Large-scale Soviet oil exports began in the middle 1950s in connection with the development of rich producing fields in the Volga–Ural region between the cities of Kuibyshev and Ufa. The region now yields two-thirds of the total national output of crude oil.

The Volga–Ural region has been linked by pipeline systems with refineries both in Eastern Europe and at Omsk and Angarsk in Siberia. The present capacity of 40 million tons a year is being expanded to ultimately carry 100 million tons. The pipeline system is being used not only for oil transportation to Eastern Europe but also to supply the Soviet Union's own refineries in Europe.

Present plans call for output from the western Siberian fields of 75 million tons by 1975, out of a total planned production of 460 million tons. Surplus Siberian production will then start moving westward to European Russia by existing pipelines, reversing the present eastward flow to Siberia from the Volga–Ural fields.

A large part of the present exports by sea moves through the pipeline terminal of Ventspils in Latvia on the Baltic Sea, situated at the end of the branches of the Eastern European pipeline system.

Another new oil-producing area in the Soviet Union is the Mangyshlak Peninsula on the northeast shore of the Caspian Sea, where 37 million tons are to be produced by 1975. Transportation of Mangyshlak oil by pipeline poses problems because the oil is highly viscous and must be heated at regular intervals to keep it moving.

Discovery of new oil reserves also has been made at a great depth in the old producing area of Grozny in the Caucasus, where shallower deposits were depleted by the late 1950s. Deep drilling during the 1960s yielded new reserves whose exploitation is advantageous because of the existence of an established extraction and refining industry around Grozny. Baku, the principal producer until World War II, is still holding its own with annual production of about 20 million tons, although it has long been surpassed by the Volga–Ural fields.

The Soviet Union's petroleum needs are such that it could become a net importer in the 1970's. The problem is not entirely one of quantity but the fact that the U.S.S.R. is having to develop its new fields in areas remote from its own industrial centers as well as further and further away from its partners in Europe. Faced with mounting demand from its allies and enormous transportation problems, the Soviets have urged their Eastern-bloc partners to look beyond the U.S.S.R. for their increased needs.

Venezuela

Venezuela's proved oil reserves, estimated to contain slightly more than six percent of the total world reserves, are found in three great basins: the Maracaibo, the Orinoco, and the Barnas–Apure.

The first oil wells drilled in Venezuela were remote, shallow, and unsuccessful. The industry remained dormant for nearly half a century. Real interest dates from the completion in 1922 of the discovery well in La Rosa Field on the eastern shore of Lake Maracaibo. Today there are several thousand wells at the bottom of the lake. The oil is pumped or transported in tankers to refineries on the Paraguana Peninsula or to the Netherlands islands of Curacao and Aruba.

Of the twelve major petroleum producing companies, the largest are Creole Petroleum Company, a subsidiary of the Standard Oil Company of New Jersey, Royal Dutch Shell and the Mene Grande Oil Company, subsidiary of the Gulf Oil Corporation.

During the past forty years a farsighted partnership has been worked out between the Venezuelan government and the United States, British, and Dutch petroleum companies, which has been of mutual benefit to all. By 1960 the industry had reached such a degree of development that the public sector joined private enterprise in the industry with the creation of the Corporacion Venezolana del Petroleo (Venezuela Petroleum Corporation).

Thus the industry is now divided between the private and the public sector. The private sector includes the petroleum companies that have been holding concessions in the country, and the public sector includes the state-owned corporation, which will be in charge of continuing the process of development of the industry through more appropriate instruments such as service contracts and other similar arrangements.

The bulk of the oil produced in Venezuela is marketed mainly in the United States and Western Europe. The remainder is exported to neighboring countries in Latin America.

Other Producing Regions

As oil fields in Algeria, Libya, and Nigeria were developed, Africa became one of the major producing areas. These countries are still in an era of rapid expansion, with Libya the leading African producer. Their oil goes mainly to the nearby markets of Western Europe.

Oil was discovered in Libya in 1959 and the first commercial oil was exported in 1961. At present, cumulative Libyan oil production is well over 2 billion barrels. Seven huge oil fields have a potential ranging from 1 to 8 billion barrels.

An oil strike was made in northern Algeria in 1949, but the important discoveries at Edjeleh and Hassi Messaaud did not come until 1956, four years after the Saharan concessions were granted. By the end of 1963, proved recoverable reserves amounted to 6.5 billion barrels.

Oil was first discovered in Nigeria at Oloibiri in the Niger Delta in 1956. Since that date, nine producing oil fields have been developed and output had risen to 3.5 million tons a year prior to the Biafran revolt. Since the fall of Biafra, Nigerian production is increasing. All the oil presently produced is exported via tankers to the ocean terminal at Bonny, where tankers carry it to Great Britain and Ghana for refining.

Almost nothing is known about China, since no official figures have been released since 1959. China has only 24 oil and gas fields, with an estimated reserve of 15 billion barrels; overall output is placed at around 250,000 barrels per day. The Taching field is a large one, however, and could prove to be a world giant.

Many geologists contend that the North Slope strike in Alaska is the beginning of development of an enormous Arctic oil basin. Other undeveloped basins lie in the Latin American countries, Indonesia, Africa, and, of course, the U.S.S.R.

Table 21.4 shows the world's largest oil fields by ultimate recoverable oil, with the bulk of it in a relative handful of fields —more than half (38) of these are in the Middle East, 11 in North America, 11 in Africa, 7 in South America, 3 in Indonesia, and 1 in Australia.

Future

About fifteen years ago, the world's oil industry was dominated by American interests. The United States had the major share of known world oil reserves, produced more than half the oil consumed and most of the natural gas utilized. Refining capacity was entirely adequate for both domestic markets and export demands. The United States also supplied the bulk of the money, management, organization, and technical staff.

Recently, however, great changes have occurred in all aspects of the industry, and further changes are anticipated. Of particular significance has been the rapid shift in location of the world's major oil reserves from the United States to the Middle East, with over five-eighths of the world's proved crude oil reserves. The United States has become a net importer of oil, although its petroleum resources have continued to grow. The Persian Gulf area, because of exploration and discover-

Table 21.4   World's Largest Oil Fields by Ultimate Recoverable Oil (billions of barrels)

Rank	Field and Country	Discovered	Ultimate Recoverable Oil
Super giants—more than 10 billion barrels			
1	Greater Burgan, Kuwait	1938	62
2	Ghawar, Saudi Arabia	1948	45
3	Bolivar Coastal Field, Venezuela	1922	30
4	Safaniya-Khafji, Saudi Arabia-Neutral Zone	1951	25
5	Kirkuk, Iraq	1927	15
6	Rumaila, Iraq	1953	13.6
5 to 10 billion barrels			
7	Agha Jari, Iran	1938	9.5
8	Abqaiq, Saudi Arabia	1941	9
9	Gach Saran, Iran	1928	8
10	Sarir, Libya	1961	8
11	Raudhatain, Kuwait	1955	7.7
12	Minas, Sumatra	1944	7
13	Manifa, Saudi Arabia	1957	6
14	Marun, Iran	1964	6
15	Ahwaz, Iran	1959	6
16	East Texas, U.S.A.	1930	6
2 to 5 billion barrels			
17	Bibi Hakimch, Iran	1962	4.5
18	Sabriva, Kuwait	1958	4
19	Murban Bu Hasa, Abu Dhabi	1962	3
20	Faris, Iran	1964	3
21	Qatif, Saudi Arabia	1945	3
22	Lama, Venezuela	1957	2.7
23	Hassi Messaoud, Algeria	1956	2.7

Table 21.4   (Continued)

Rank	Field and Country	Discovered	Ultimate Recoverable Oil
24	Wilmington, California, U.S.A.	1935	2.6
25	Khursaniya, Saudi Arabia	1956	2.5
26	Wafra, Neutral Zone	1953	2.5
27	Abu Sa'fah, Saudi Arabia	1963	2.5
28	Dukhan, Qatar	1940	2.4
29	Zelten, Libya	1959	2.2
30	Poza Rica, Mexico	1930	2
31	Minagish, Kuwait	1959	2
32	Gialo, Libya	1961	2
33	Duri, Indonesia	1941	2
34	Murban Bab, Abu Dhabi	1954	2
35	Umm Shaif, Abu Dhabi	1958	2
1 to 2 billion barrels			
36	Haft Kel, Iran	1928	1.9
37	Masjid-iSulaiman, Iran	1908	1.9
38	Zubair, Iraq	1948	1.9
39	Idd el-Shargi, Qatar	1960	1.8
40	Pembina, Canada	1953	1.8
41	Amal, Libya	1959	1.7
42	Sassan, Iran	1967	1.5
43	Khurais, Saudi Arabia	1957	1.5
44	Idris A, Libya	1967	1.4
45	Elk Hills, California, U.S.A.	1920	1.4
46	Berri, Saudi Arabia	1964	1.4
47	Lamar, Venezuela	1957	1.3
48	Karanj, Iran	1963	1.3
49	Swan Hills, Canada	1957	1.3
50	Midway Sunset, California U.S.A.	1901	1.3
51	B field, Cabinda	1966	1.2
52	Yates, Texas, U.S.A.	1926	1.2
53	Idris D, Libya	1967	1.2
54	Kelly-Snyder, Texas, U.S.A.	1948	1.2
55	Huntington Beach, California, U.S.A.	1920	1.2
56	Bai Hassan, Iraq	1953	1.2
57	Oficina, Venezuela	1937	1.1
58	Maydan Mahzam, Qatar	1963	1.1
59	Ebano Panuco, Mexico	1901	1
60	Seria, Brunei	1929	1
61	Boscan, Venezuela	1946	1
62	El Morgan, Egypt	1965	1
63	La Paz, Venezuela	1925	1
64	Quiriquire, Venezuela	1928	1
65	Dammam, Saudi Arabia	1938	1
66	Kingfish, Australia	1967	1
67	Zarzaitaine, Algeria	1958	1
68	Darius, Iran	1961	1
69	Fahud, Oman	1964	1
70	Samah, Libya	1962	1
71	Rostam, Iran	1967	1

Source: Oil and Gas Journal (January 13, 1969), pp. 46–47.

ies made primarily since World War II, now has a proved oil reserve about twice that of the rest of the world. More discoveries are expected in both the Near East and North Africa because of favorable geology in these areas. Most of the operators are American oil companies, But an increasing number of European and Asian companies, some government owned, are participating. The ever-growing Middle Eastern and Venezuelan oil resources now supply one-sixth of U.S. needs and most of the liquid fuel needs of the rest of the noncommunist world. These abundant low-priced oils have altered fuel-use patterns in the United States and Europe, so that residual and distillate petroleum fuels are replacing solid fuels for both industrial and domestic uses.

Rapid growth in energy demands, due to an increasing population and expanding economy accompanied by greater per capita energy consumption, indicates that in the next few decades oil and gas will be providing a greater volume as well as a larger share of the world's fuel supply. Free world consumption during this period is predicted to double. Along with recent increases in the proved petroleum reserve there have been simultaneous increases in demand from the expanding economies of many of the previously undeveloped nations. Should present trends in world oil supply continue, petroleum and natural gas will be derived increasingly from offshore reservoirs; by liquefaction of natural gas, which is then transported as a refrigerated liquid from remote areas to energy markets; and by the production of supplemental fuels obtained from oil shale and bituminous sands when these resources, which are now economically marginal, become more competitive with oil and gas. Exactly what proportions of the oil supply will eventually be produced from these marginal resources, and the timing of such events are at present indeterminate. A substantial part of the technology needed for extraction of oil from oil shale and bituminous sands has been developed, and research and development are continuing. Success in this work will enable future economic utilization of these vast unused hydrocarbon resources that far exceed known petroleum reserves.

FERROALLOYS

Ferroalloy minerals contain elements that, when added to iron, impart some desirable quality to it. Chromium, nickel, manganese, tungsten, vanadium, molybdenum, silica, and magnesite are the ones commonly used. Depending upon the materials added and the amount of each, the steel can be made stronger, tougher, more heat resistant, or more resistant to corrosion.

Manganese is essential in purifying iron during the process of smelting. Chromium steel is used particularly in making heavy machinery parts, stainless steel, and steel that is to be subjected to high temperatures. Nickel steel is used in transportation equipment, girders, and armor plate; tungsten steel is used especially in making high-speed cutting tools. These alloy steels are often found at a distance from the steel-making centers, and therefore enter significantly into international trade.

Location

The U.S.S.R., India, Ghana, South Africa, and Brazil are the chief sources of manganese. Chromite, the ore containing chromium, is widely distributed, but three-fourths of the world's supply comes from five countries—South Africa, the U.S.S.R., Turkey, Rhodesia, and the Philippines. Canada, the U.S.S.R., New Caledonia, and Cuba together account for 90 percent of the world's nickel. China formerly supplied most of the world's tungsten; since 1949 the free world has had to rely on limited deposits in the United

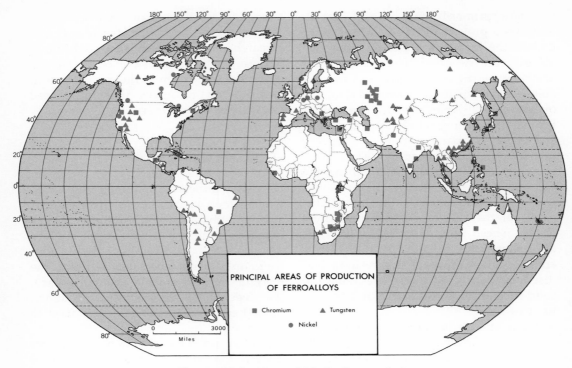

FIGURE 21.6   (*General Media Corporation*)

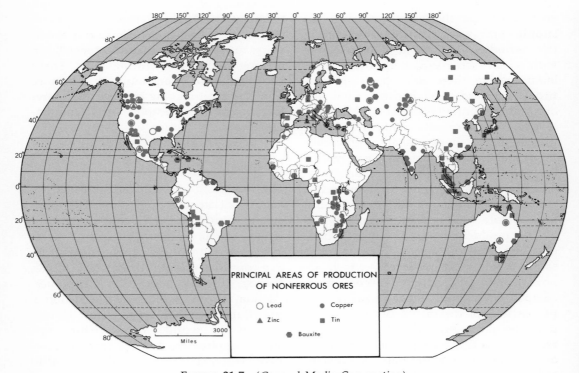

FIGURE 21.7   (*General Media Corporation*)

States, South Korea, Bolivia, Portugal, and Australia.

Growth of the ferroalloy industry roughly parallels that of steel. Individual ferroalloys fluctuate in demand due to the substitutability of many of the ferroalloys, but the majority of the output will continue to be the alloys of manganese and silicon. Overcapacity is a worldwide problem, resulting in keen competition for markets. The emergence of relatively undeveloped ore-producing countries as producers of alloys has aggravated the problem. Low profit margins result from the lower prices desired by the domestic producer to meet the competition for restricted markets from foreign imports, in addition to his domestic competition. These low-profit margins limit funds for research and engineering development for the growth of the industry.

NONFERROUS METALS

While iron and steel have supplied the largest single metallic bases for the present industrial civilization, nonferrous metals are, in the aggregate, only slightly less significant. Some of them, such as tin and zinc, find their main uses in connection with iron and steel as protective coatings. Others, such as copper and lead, owe their major consumption to the electrification of the industrial world, which has done much to increase man's productivity and comfort. Again, copper and aluminum, aside from their own uses, are alloyed with steel to give it special qualities.

Copper

The use of copper has increased rapidly in the last fifty years because, next to silver, it is the best known conductor of electricity, and also because many types of electrical equipment are made of brass, a composite of copper and zinc.

Table 21.5 Production of Copper Ore (Cu Content) by Selected Countries (metric tons)

Country	1960	1967	Percent Change 1960–67
World	4,270.0	5,010.0	+17.33
Canada	398.5	556.4	+39.62
Chile	536.4	663.9	+23.77
Peru	209.2	181.1	−13.43
United States	979.9	865.5	−11.67
U.S.S.R.	500.0	800.0	+60.00
West Germany	2.2	1.2	−45.45
Zambia	576.4	663.0	+15.02

Source: United Nations *Statistical Yearbook*, 1968 (New York: United Nations, 1969), Table 61, p. 193.

The United States leads the world in trade of copper. Crude materials, such as ores, concentrates, matte, and blister, as well as refined copper, are imported. Refined copper and fabricated copper, fabricated copper products, and manufactured goods containing copper are exported. The other leading producing countries—Chile, Canada, Zambia, Peru, and the Congo (Leopoldville)—export most of their output. The U.S.S.R. has moderate reserves of copper ore, estimated to be sufficient for several decades at present rates of production. In the past, the U.S.S.R. has regularly imported part of its copper requirements, but in 1964, with the start of production at a third major center, Almalyk, the country achieved self-sufficiency and had a net export. West Germany and the United Kingdom regularly import most of their requirements.

Bauxite

A rock consisting chiefly of aluminum hydrate or hydroxide minerals, bauxite is the principal raw material used by the world's immense aluminum industry. The aluminum industry consumes about 90 percent of the bauxite mined. The remaining 10 percent is used in making refractories, catalysts for petroleum refining, cements, abrasives, chemicals, and for other purposes.

The largest bauxite deposits are in Australia, which has 2 billion tons of reserves and about 1 billion tons of potential resources, and in Guinea, which has 1.2 billion tons of reserves and about 2.4 billion tons of potential resources. Cameroon and Mainland China each have at least 1 billion tons of potential bauxite resources that are unfavorably situated or otherwise unsuitable for mining. Jamaica, now the leading bauxite producer, has about 600 million tons of reserves and has potential resources that are nearly as large. Countries having 200 to 300 million tons of reserves include Ghana, Yugoslavia, Surinam, and the U.S.S.R.; both India and Brazil may rank with these countries when their widely distributed deposits are fully explored. Bauxite reserves in Hungary are probably about 150 million tons. Malawi, Greece, France, Guyana, Guyane, and the Dominican Republic and Haiti combined all have 50–100 million ton reserves. The United States, the largest consumer, has about 45 million tons of reserves. Most of the bauxite used in the United States is imported from Jamaica and Guyana.

Bauxite is concentrated as near as possible to the mines into commercially pure aluminum oxide, or *alumina*. In the United States, the chief concentration plants are in East St. Louis, Illinois, and Mobile, Alabama. The alumina is shipped to points that have an abundance of low cost power, and is there converted by the use of electricity into the metal, aluminum.

Lead

Because lead is not readily corroded it is widely used in the construction of electric cables, and because it is not affected by sulphuric acid it is used in storage batteries. It is also used in many other ways, but it is most significant in the electrical industry.

World trade in lead is primarily in the form of concentrates and metal. Countries producing ore in excess of smelter requirements, notably Peru, the Republic of South Africa, Canada, Australia, Mexico, Yugoslavia, and Bolivia, are suppliers

to the industrial countries having negligible or deficient output in relation to smelting capacity, such as the United Kingdom, Belgium-Luxembourg, West Germany, France, and Japan. The United States is an importer of both lead concentrates and lead metal from all of the previously mentioned countries. Communist nation trade is principally between satellite countries, although varying quantities of lead concentrates are purchased and metal is sold in trade with the free world.

Lead ranks fifth in tonnage of metals produced in the world, following steel, aluminum, copper, and zinc in that order. The United States is the world's foremost producer of lead, both as ore and as refined metal, followed by the U.S.S.R., Canada, Australia, Mexico, Yugoslavia, and Bulgaria.

Zinc

Zinc is used in many more ways than is lead. One of the most significant is in galvanizing iron and steel to resist rust. The electrical and hardwood industries use a great quantity of zinc in association with copper to make brass. Zinc compounds are also important in the manufacture of prints and wood preservatives.

Canada leads the world in zinc mined, followed by the U.S.S.R., the United States, Australia, Mexico, Japan, Peru, and Poland. The United States leads all other countries in smelter production; the U.S.S.R., Japan, Canada, Australia, Belgium, and France also rank high.

Tin

First used in bronze and later in pewter, tin-plated iron, and solders, tin shares with a few other metals the distinction of 5,000 years of use by mankind. Cassiterite, tin oxide, is the only commercial mineral of tin. Although cassiterite deposits are known throughout the world, those of economic importance are limited to a few areas, such as the placer deposits in Asia and Africa and the lode deposits in South America. There are no known tin deposits of economic grade or size in the United States.

World mine production in 1967 was 211,664 long tons, with principal contributors as follows:

Country	Long Tons
Malaysia	72,121
Bolivia	26,890
U.S.S.R.	25,000
Thailand	22,489
Mainland China	20,000
Indonesia	13,597
Nigeria	9,340

The chief uses of tin are in the production of tinplate, solder, bronze, brass, and babbitt, and in tinning; small quantities are used in metallic forms, miscellaneous alloys, and chemicals. Consumption of tin is expected to rise as the standard of living and industrialization increases throughout the world, and world mine production is expected to increase at about the same rate.

Nuclear Fuels

Uranium is the primary nuclear fuel, which, with thorium, forms the only fresh energy source developed during this century. Reserves and resources are sufficient to supply the world's long-range energy demand for many generations as gas, oil, and coal sources become depleted.

Uranium is a fairly rare element, comprising about 0.0002 percent of the earth's crust. It never occurs free in nature. More than 150 uranium-containing minerals have been identified, but the chief ones are pitchblende and coffinite. The major sources are the western United States, the Elliot Lake and Beaverlodge areas in Canada, the Republic of South Africa, France, Australia, and several areas in Communist countries.

Fertilizer Minerals

Phosphorus, potassium, nitrogen, and calcium are critical mineral elements in crop growth. In areas of intensive cultivation they tend to be depleted. Consequently, high crop yields are maintained only if these fertilizer minerals are added to the soil.

Phosphorus is largely secured from phosphate rock. It is found in several states of the United States, the largest production located in Florida and Tennessee. The United States leads the world in the production of phosphate, followed by Morocco, Tunisia, and Nauru Island in Oceania.

Potassium is one of the major elements necessary to sustain plant life. Although its chief use is as a fertilizer, there is a growing list of chemical uses for potassium compounds.

The largest deposits of potassium minerals occur in West Germany, East Germany, the U.S.S.R., and Canada; the major producing nations are the United States, West Germany, East Germany, France, and Spain. In the United States, the largest producing country, approximately 90 percent comes from New Mexico; the remainder largely from California and Utah.

Table 21.6 Uranium Oxide (U$_3$O$_8$) Production by Countries (short tons)

Country	1960	1967	Percent Change 1960–67
Australia	1,300	330	− 74.62
Canada	12,748	3,753	− 70.56
France	1,379	1,260*	− 8.63
Malagasy Republic	-	65*	-
South Africa, Republic of	6,409	3,300	− 48.51
Sweden	10	50	+400.00
United States	17,760	9,125	− 48.62

* 1966 data.

Sources: 1963 Minerals Yearbook, Metals and Minerals, Vol. 1 (Washington, D.C.: United States Government Printing Office), p. 1181; *1967 Minerals Yearbook, Metals, Minerals, and Fuels,* Vol. I–II (Washington, D.C.: United States Government Printing Office), p. 1172.

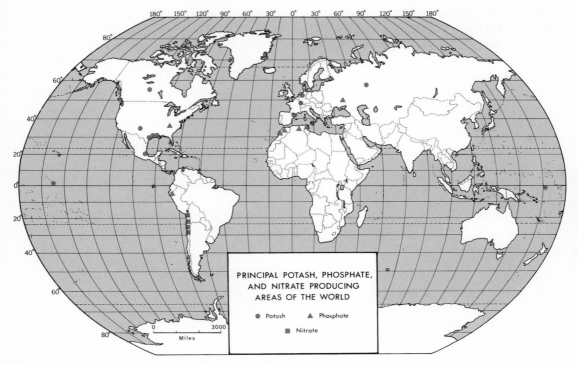

FIGURE 21.8   *(General Media Corporation)*

Nitrogen has a key role in the life cycle of plants and animals. When man devised methods to "fix" atmospheric nitrogen he achieved independence from the inadequate supply of naturally derived nitrogenous materials. The atmosphere is the main source of nitrogen supply; other sources include natural nitrates, coal, and natural organic materials such as cotton seed, tankage, bone meal, and guano.

The fertilizer industry is the largest consumer of nitrogen compounds. Ammonium sulfate, ammonium phosphate, and ammonium nitrate are components of mixed fertilizers and are produced by neutralizing the respective acids with ammonia. These compounds, as well as ammonia, both anhydrous and in solution, are sometimes applied directly to the soil or to irrigation waters to supply nitrogen to growing crops.

Calcium is obtained from limestone deposits that are widespread in farming regions. Usually the source is local; the limestone rocks are crushed and the pulverized lime is then applied to the fields. Since limestone occurs in many areas, calcium fertilizer compounds usually are locally produced; thus, no particular area achieves renown for producing it.

selected references

1. Beale, John V., "Broken Hill—A Living Legend," *Mining Engineering*, Vol. 16, October 1964, pp. 70–75.

2. Brown, L. Carson, "Ontario's Mineral Heritage," *Canadian Geographical Journal*, Vol. 76, No. 3, March 1968, pp. 80–101.

3. ———, "Elliot Lake—The World's Uranium Capital," *Canadian Geographical Journal*, Vol. 75, No. 4, October 1967, pp. 120–133.

4. Campbell, L. C., "Longwall Mining, A Breakthrough in United States Coal Production Technology," *Mining Congress Journal*, Vol. 50, August 1964, pp. 85–87.

5. Camu, Pierre, "Man and Minerals—

A Look From The Other Side," *Canadian Geographical Journal*, Vol. 75, No. 2, August 1967, pp. 38–43.

6. Earney, Fillmore C., "The Slate Industry of Western Vermont," *The Journal of Geography*, Vol. 62, No. 7, October 1963, pp. 300–310.

7. Frey, Charles W., "New Growth for Natural Gas," *The Lamp*, Vol. 48, Spring 1966, pp. 24–25.

8. Gonzalez, Richard J., "Production Depends on Economics—Not Physical Existence," *Oil and Gas Journal*, Vol. 62, March 30, 1964, pp. 59–64.

9. Hardy, Carroll F., and Laird, J. S., "Economics of Power Plant Use of Coal," *Mining Congress Journal*, Vol. 49, November 1963, pp. 38–40.

10. Knoerr, A., and Eigo, M., "Arizona's Newest Copper Producer—The Christmas Mine," *Engineering and Mining Journal*, Vol. 164, January 1963, pp. 55–67.

11. McKechnie, N. D., "The Mineral Industry in British Columbia," *Canadian Geographical Journal*, Vol. 78, No. 3, March 1969, pp. 76–89.

12. Ojala, Carl F., and Steila, Donald, "Location and Depth Zones of Major Geologic Coal Reserves in the U.S.S.R.," *The Journal of Geography*, Vol. 76, No. 9, December 1967, pp. 507–509.

13. Ross, W. Gillies, "Encroachment of the Jeffrey Mine on the Town of Asbestos, Quebec," *Geographical Review*, Vol. 57, No. 4, October 1967, pp. 522–537.

14. Stewart, Keith J., "Mineral Development In The Atlantic Provinces," *Canadian Geographical Journal*, Vol. 77, No. 6, December 1968, pp. 178–195.

15. Seindell, Kenneth, "Iron Ore Mining in West Africa: Some Recent Developments in Guinea, Sierra Leone, and Liberia," *Economic Geography*, Vol. 43, No. 4, October 1967, pp. 333–346.

16. Weeks, Lewis G., "Where Will Energy Come From in 2059?" *The Petroleum Engineer*, August 1959, pp. 29–31.

part IV
Secondary Economic Activities

introduction

The secondary economic activities involve converting material resources into intermediary or finished goods through the application of labor (including entrepreneurship and management), capital, and technology. The presence of intermediary goods characterizes the secondary activities as possessing a hierarchy whose structure and complexity are spatially differentiated. Such differentiation is involved through the composite framework discussed under Parts I and II. Although the number of secondary activities (as discussed in Chapter 9, Classification of Economic Activities) could be as large as the number of different processes and products, selection of those secondary activities for discussion here has arbitrarily been limited to a few topics.

to manufacturing

Manufacturing is the processing or combining of materials to make some desired product. It is a continuous process, carried out on a substantial scale, of transforming commodities for ultimate sale to buyers over a wide area. From the economic standpoint, manufacturing—in the sense of transformation of raw materials—historically developed universally in the form of work to provide the requirements of a house community. In this connection, it was an auxillary occupation; it first became of interest when production was carried beyond household needs.

Rise of Craft Guilds

The second mode of transforming raw materials—for other than the needs of a household—is production for sale. This originated with craft guilds, which flourished in Western Europe between 1150 and 1350 A.D.

The craft guild was an association for the promotion of its particular industry in a given town. Its economic functions were:

1. Regulation of wages
2. Fixing of prices and conditions of sale
3. Determination of the hours and condtions of labor
4. Inspection of workmanship and quality of materials

In order to accomplish these things, each craft had to obtain a local monopoly of its particular product. In general, the craft guild protected its members against competition from the product to the consumer. In addition, it served its members in time of need, provided them with opportunities for common religious and social activities, and furnished their children with schools.

Disintegration of Craft Guilds

The disintegration of the craft guilds, which took place after the close of the Middle Ages, proceeded along several lines. Certain craftsmen within the guilds rose to the position of merchant and capitalist—employer of home workers. Masters with considerable invested capital purchased the raw materials and turned over the work to their fellow guildsmen, who carried on the process of production for them and sold the finished product. The guilds were thus transformed into "livery companies," guilds of dealers in which the full members were those who produced for the market, while those who had sunk to the level of wage workers and home workers for others lost the vote in the guild and hence the share in its control.

One guild might rise at the expense of another. The fourteenth century especially is filled with struggle of the guilds for independence from other guilds. Frequently both processes ran along together; within the individual guild, certain masters rose to the position of traders, and at the same time many guilds became an organization of traders.

Development of the Domestic System

During the later Middle Ages, distinctions arose between the craft guilds. In the chief cities, both in England and on the Continent, there were a handful of industries whose guilds (or livery companies as they were later called) had come to dominate not only the other crafts but the town government as well. Thus the democracy of the guild system was attacked and weakened from another angle.

The disappearance of quality, both within and among the craft guilds, paved the way for the domestic or "putting out" system of industry inaugurated by the Commercial Revolution, when the capitalist organization of business began to develop in Western Europe during the sixteenth century.

The textile industry became the main seat of the domestic system. Its beginnings go back to the early Middle Ages. From the eleventh century on there was a struggle between linen and wool, and in the seventeenth and eighteenth centuries between wool and cotton, with the victory of the second in each case. Charlemagne wore nothing but linen, but later, with increasing demilitarization, the demand for wool increased, and at the same time with the clearing of forests the fur industry disappeared and furs became increasingly more expensive. Woolen goods were the principal commodity in the markets of the Middle Ages; they played the leading role everywhere—in France, England, and Italy. Wool was always partly worked up in the country, but became the foundation of the greatness and the economic prosperity of the medieval city; at the head of the revolutionary movements in the city of Florence marched the guilds of the wool workers. Here again one finds early traces of the putting-out system. In general, the system first appeared in Flanders, and later in England where the Flanders woolen industry called forth mass production of wool.

Typically, the stages in the growth of the domestic system were:

1. A purely factual buying monopoly of the factor (merchant and capitalist – employer) in relation to the craft worker. This was regularly established through indebtedness; the factor compelled the workers to turn their products over to him exclusively, on the ground of his knowledge as merchant. Thus the buying monopoly was connected with a selling monopoly and took possession of the market by the factor; he alone knew where the products finally were to stop.
2. Delivery of the raw material to the worker by the factor. This appeared frequently, but was not connected with the buying monopoly from the beginning. The stage was general in Europe but was seldom reached elsewhere.
3. Control of the production process. The factor had an interest in the process because he was responsible for uniformity in the quality of the product. Consequently, the delivery of the raw material to the worker was often associated with a delivery of partial products, as was the case in the nineteenth century when the Westphalian linen weavers had to work up a prescribed quantity of warp and yarn.

4. With this was also quite commonly connected the provision of the tools by the factor. In general the relation was confined to the textile industry; there were orders on a large scale for looms for the clothiers who turned them over to the weavers for a rental. Thus the worker was entirely separated from the means of production, and at the same time the entrepreneur strove to monopolize for himself the disposal of the product.

5. Sometimes the factor took the step of combining several stages in the production process; this was most likely to occur in the textile industry. He bought the raw material and put it out to the individual workman, in whose hands the product remained until it was finished. When this stage was reached the craft worker again had a master, in quite the same sense as the craftsman on an estate, except that in contrast with the latter he received a money wage and an entrepreneur producing for the market took the place of the aristocratic household.

The Factory and Its Forerunners

Shop production, which implies separation between household and industry (in contrast with home work), appears in varied forms in the course of history:

1. *Isolated* small shops are formed everywhere, especially the bazaar system, with its grouping together of a number of work shops to facilitate working together.
2. The *ergasterion* also is universal; its medieval designation was *fabrica*, an ambiguous term which may designate the cellar den leased by a group of workers and used as a shop, or a manorial institution for wage work.
3. *Unfree* shop industry on a large scale seems to have occurred particularly in later Egypt. It undoubtedly sprang from the gigantic estate of the pharaoh, out of which developed separate shops with wage labor.

In the West, the industry of the craft guilds was carried on without fixed capital, and hence required no large initial cost. But even in the Middle Ages there were branches of production that required an investment; industries were organized either through provision of capital by the guild communally, or by the town, or feudally by an overlord. Among establishments of the work shop type that existed alongside craft work organized in the guilds were included the various kinds of mills, ovens, breweries, iron foundries, and hammer mills.

THE INDUSTRIAL REVOLUTION

The roots of the Industrial Revolution run far back into the history of mankind—at least as far back as the first time man tied a stone to a club in order to make an axe to help him in his work. The most primitive man of whom we have any record used tools in his work. But tools are passive things, manipulated by human hands, dependent on a craftsman's skills, and powered by human energy. Throughout most of his history man was compelled to use his own energy to supply himself with goods and services. Later he brought into his service the domesticated work animals: the water buffalo, ox, horse, camel, and others, like the dog. But he was still dependent upon animate, living creatures for power and energy. If he or his livestock were to work, both had to be supplied with food, and part of the work was therefore lost in order to make work itself possible. Man and his beasts had to labor in order to be fed, and had to be fed in order to labor. They were caught in a cycle of food–energy–work–food, and never seemed able to push far beyond subsistence. Human slaves were no improvement because they, too, had to be fed or they could not produce.

The turning point in man's effort to be productive came about with (1) the invention of machines, and (2) the use of inanimate energy to supply power to the machines. These two things broke the cycle. A machine is a device that does much the same work as the human hand. It performs a task, more or less complicated, which prior to the invention of the machine either could not be done or could be done only with the human hand. When a machine can be powered with falling water, or with coal, gas, oil, or nuclear energy, then production can be carried on with mechanical hands and sources of energy that neither man nor his domesticated animals can consume. The falling water turning a waterwheel may be changed into a hydroelectric generator; coal, gas, oil, or nuclear energy may be utilized through steam or internal combustion engines. Whatever the method of capturing and exploiting the power, the result is always the same: men and domesticated animals are displaced by a machine driven by sources of energy other than their own. The final outcome is a great increase in productivity.

The Nature of Machinery

Though ancient and medieval people possessed machines, such as the potter's wheel and the water mill for grinding corn, their industry rested primarily on manual labor and hand tools. Furthermore, the so-called "machines" of the ancient and medieval periods did not possess all the characteristics of the true machine, which are:

1. Complexity
2. Regulation by controls that are part of it
3. Limitations and regularity in action
4. Relative independence of the operator—in its full development, the machine is automatic

The true machine as a basic element of industrial activity was a product of the Industrial Revolution. Furthermore, as the new industries expanded, machines played an even greater part in them.

Growth of the Factory System

Several basic technological inventions made possible the growth of modern industry. Among the most important were Kay's flying shuttle, Hargreave's spinning jenny, Arkwright's water frame, Crompton's spinning mule, Cartwright's power loom, Whitney's cotton gin, Howe's sewing machine, Dudley and Darby's use of coke in smelting, Smeston's air-blast, Onion and Cort's puddling process, Cort's rolling mill, Bessemer's converter, and Watt's steam engine.

The above inventions became effective in industry largely through the development of the factory system. Successor to the putting-out system, the factory system became the characteristic form of modern industrial organization. By successfully organizing the means of production, it was fully as important as machinery and the steam engine in producing the remarkable transformation of the industrial process that brought into existence a new type of society in the west.

The factory system may be regarded as the organization of labor and executives in machine-equipped plants operated by artificial power. Under it, centralization of control and the division of labor are carried to extreme limits, and the dissociation of labor from capital is almost complete. Labor is thoroughly disciplined by the pattern of the production process, and by the compulsion of the plant owners. The factory system facilitates the production of goods in large quantities for sale in world markets.

Effects of the Industrial Revolution's Diffusion

In general, the European continent began to experience the characteristic industrial changes from seventy-five to one hundred years after England. The industrial changes brought about:

1. The overthrow of the guild system where it still functioned
2. Widespread introduction of machinery and steam power
3. Rise of the factory system
4. Reduction in the relative importance of agriculture as compared with industry and commerce.

The Industrial Revolution, by introducing a new economic basis for social organization and by intensifying the rate of social change, transformed the nature of Western society. One of its primary social results was the gradual transformation of Western civilization from a rural to an urban basis—perhaps the chief social transformation in human history.

The age of the Industrial Revolution was also characterized by great population movements. Until 1865, most migrants were from Western Europe. After that date Central, Southern, and Eastern Europe began to send out millions of people. In general, the course of migration was to the United States and South America, where industry and cheap lands offered apparently unlimited possibilities to ambitious men. Curiously enough, the exodus from the old countries did not cause their population to decline, for the losses were made up by a rapid increase of the birth rate. The countries to which the migrants came benefited by the creation of a large labor supply and the transplantation of cultural forms.

These population changes in the Old World and the New were accompanied by the rapid rise of the middle class to dominance. Equally important was the appearance during the Industrial Revolution of a new social class, the industrial proletariat. By concentrating workers in the cities, the factories made it possible for the working class to achieve conscious and effective organization.

The Industrial Revolution, beginning in England about 1750 and reaching its height by 1850, was one of the major transitions in human history. Not only did it completely transform the material and social bases of Western civilization, but it also generated many strong and penetrating forces. No major development in Western civilization in the nineteenth century, nor any major movement today, is understandable without reference to the new industrial system.

Summary

More than 200 million workers in the world are engaged in manufacturing and the handicraft industries. According to population censuses, the proportion of the labor force engaged in manufacturing and handicrafts ranges from less than 10 percent in such primarily agricultural countries as Colombia, Bolivia, Iran, Egypt, Thailand, and most African countries to over 30 percent in highly industrialized countries such as the United States, Belgium, Luxembourg, West Germany, and the United Kingdom. The breadth and scope of these industries are so varied that only a few can be selected for discussion here, namely textiles, iron and steel, automotive, petrochemical, and aerospace. In each case, the United States will serve as a model, followed by a tracing of the world pattern.

The textile industries, which include the manufacture of many different kinds of cloth, are among the world's most important industrial activities. They produce articles that are a necessity for life in most regions, although in some the style factor has become equally as important as the desire for protection from the elements. Cloth is made from a wide variety of fibers, both natural and man-made, and many different articles are made from the cloth. The production of textile products is carried on in all settled parts of the world, and the methods of production differ greatly, ranging from very primitive household spinning and weaving to modern machine production.

chapter 22

Textiles

UNITED STATES

Most textile manufacturing plants are concentrated in two major regions: (1) A northeastern belt stretching from Philadelphia to lower New England, with important centers in Providence, Rhode Island, and Fall River and New Bedford, Massachusetts; (2) the Piedmont running from Virginia through North Carolina, South Carolina, Tennessee, and Georgia. In terms of employment and value added by manufacture, North Carolina, South Carolina, and Georgia are the leading textile states.

Nature of the Industry

The textile industry group is made up of over 7,000 establishments classified in 29 separate categories. Although most of the firms producing textiles are relatively small, family-owned units that manufacture a limited number of rather standardized products, the importance of this type of firm is steadily declining. Mergers, acquisitions, and internal growth have produced an increasing number of large multi-product textile firms particularly during the 1950s. However, concentration is still low, with the largest

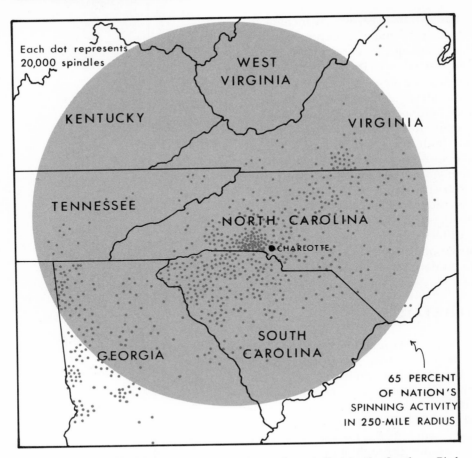

FIGURE 22.1 *Distribution of the textile industry (by spindles) in the Southern Piedmont. (General Media Corporation)*

firms accounting for less than eight percent of textile sales.

Price competition is characteristic of the textile sector, and was intensified during the 1960s by increased imports of low-cost goods. To meet this problem, textile mills are improving their efficiency by shifting to more capital-intensive manufacturing processes. In general, the industry has been relatively labor intensive. The gross value of fixed depreciable assets per worker is $7,051, considerably below the $10,188 average reported for the entire manufacturing sector.

Significant changes also have occurred in the types of fiber used. In 1958, cotton accounted for nearly 65 percent of total mill consumption of cotton, wool, and man-made fibers. By 1969, cotton had declined to 49 percent, wool fell from 5.5 to 3.5 percent, and the share of man-made fibers increased from 30 to 47 percent.

Impact on Economy

The textile industries account for roughly 3 percent of the national income originating in the manufacturing sector of U.S. economy. Textile mills employ nearly one million workers. Many plants are located in communities in which they are the only or the principal industrial employer. In addition, textile plants employ an above-average proportion of women.

The textile industries consume large amounts of fibers, thereby providing a

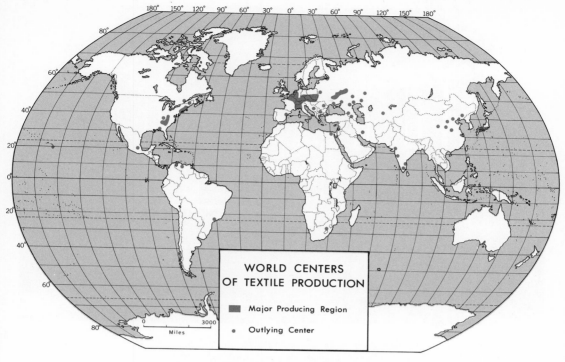

FIGURE 22.2   (*General Media Corporation*)

market for all of the raw wool, 95 percent of the man-made fibers, and 60 percent of the raw cotton produced in the United States. The textile industries also are the primary customer for domestically produced dye-stuffs and textile machinery, and supply the bulk of the fabrics used by domestic plants.

Cotton

The cotton textile industry has always migrated readily as economic conditions have changed. The industry, especially the coarser grades of yarn and cloth, seems to be particularly well-adapted to the economic conditions existing on what may be called the industrial frontier.

This industry has for more than a century and a half held a position in the vanguard of industrialization. The coarser yarns have been the first to be produced in a new region; medium and finer yarns and weaving have in some cases followed.

Older sections have been compelled to concentrate on the finer grades of yarn and cloth. This experience has been duplicated in the cases of England and New England, of New England and the Southern states, of the Occident and the Orient.

Locational Shift. The early concentration of the cotton textile industry in the New England area, and its subsequent massive shift to the South are well known. At the start of the Civil War almost 75 percent of the spindles in the United States were in the New England states. New England possessed several early advantages for cotton textile manufacture. The abundance of water power facilitated the early use of power-driven machinery. Climate played a role—humid air kept the thread from getting dry and brittle, and reduced the amount of electricity in the thread, thus eliminating snarling and tangling. These factors, combined

FIGURE 22.3 *The beginning of textile manufacturing in the "New World" was the Old Slater Mill in Pawtucket, Rhode Island. (Rhode Island Development Council)*

with the proximity of a large market and an abundance of highly skilled labor, enabled New England to become the center of the nation's cotton textile industry.

All the early advantages, however, with the possible exception of skilled labor, have been offset by the South. Simple statistics tell the tale. Between 1919 and 1939, New England lost 12.3 million cotton spindles, two-thirds of its total. Industrial misfortune on such a scale is almost unprecedented in American life. The drama of New England mill closings, of community after community racked with unemployment, fascinated editors and writers for nearly a generation.

This decline was essentially the result of two factors: (1) failure to keep the plants modern and efficient, and (2) more costly labor and shorter working hours than in the South. The losses at first were in coarse goods, but gradually the South has also encroached on finer cotton goods.

By 1962, with under 5 percent of the nation's active cotton spindles, and accounting for only 3 percent of all cotton consumed in the United States, New England could claim but small status as a cotton textile producer. Fall River, New Bedford, Lowell, and Lawrence, cities whose names were synonymous with textiles, were forced to build new economies, solidly based on diversified products.

Portions of the industry, such as finishing, however, are still centered in New England and the Middle Atlantic states. The cotton cloth market is still heavily centered in New York, with Boston ranking second. Ninety percent of the converters are located in New York, and the city remains the chief center of selling houses, mill sales departments, and the garment manufacturing industry.

Organization of the Industry. The cotton textile industry includes all mills performing one or more of the functions involved in the preparation of raw cotton for processing, spinning of cotton fibers into yarn, weaving or knitting of yarn into cloth, and finishing of the fabric. Thus the industry comprises all the stages of production and distribution, from opening the cotton bale to placing the finished cloth in the hands of its final distributor, or to manufacturing apparel and other products.

Woolens and Worsteds

The woolen and worsted industry is more localized and more stabilized as to location than the cotton industry because of the nature of the raw materials, the methods of production, and the character of the finished products.

New England is the heart of the woolen industry, employing more than half the nation's workers engaged in this enterprise. The mills are located chiefly in the Merrimack Valley, north of Boston, although concentrations are also found in Rhode Island. Boston is the great wool importing port of the nation. Nearly half the region's mills are located in Massachusetts, with the balance shared by Maine and Rhode Island.

The South. Wool manufacturing has been carried on in the South for more than a century. During most of that time, however, it lay almost dormant. The development of complete wool manufacture came about slowly. Of the 1,800 complete sets of wool machinery reported for the United States in 1845, only four were in the Southeast. In addition, scattered throughout the region were many small carding mills that processed wool brought to them by local farmers whose families then spun the yarn and wove the cloth. Most of these mills employed only one or two workers. The clothing that equipped many Confederate soldiers was made on household looms and in village workshops.

Expansion of wool manufacturing in the South did not occur on a large scale until about 1900; the greatest growth, however, has taken place since 1945. Today the South produces as much as 14 percent of all men's woolen work and dress trousers made in this country, although manufacture of men's suits and coats is still concentrated in the New York, Rochester, Boston, and Philadelphia areas, which together account for 55 percent of the nation's suit manufacture and 65 percent of its overcoat production.

Southern expansion in the manufacture of worsteds marks only the beginning of an expansion similar to the one that took place in cotton textile production.

Location Factors. Over 80 percent of the woven woolen goods are used for men's and women's clothing. Thus the demand is sensitive to style changes. This has two important results. In the first place, it is advantageous for the spinning and weaving mills to be near the market and the style centers. This is one of the reasons why the manufacture of woolens and worsteds is concentrated in the northeastern section of the United States. In the second place, the prominent role played by demands of style makes it advantageous to produce small quantities of a large number of different fabrics. In most of the woolen industry, the product is not sufficiently standardized to be produced in large quantities under conditions of large-scale production. For these reasons, the United States does not have a comparative advantage in the production of fine woolens and worsteds.

Further, the spinning and weaving of woolens and worsteds is a trade that requires highly skilled labor, which in the United States can be used more effectively in industries where it is possible to use large-scale methods of production, with a high proportion of machinery to labor. This competition for labor forces up the wage level, and the woolen industry is faced with the necessity of meeting wages that are higher than it can afford without some form of protection.

The industry in the United States is, therefore, dependent upon the tariff, and a large part of the woolen industry would disappear if the tariff were removed. The mills in the United States could probably continue to produce the staple products that are standardized and can be turned out in large quantities, but would find it difficult, without tariff protection, to compete in the finer grades of woolens and in style goods.

Man-Made Fibers

Man-made fibers are materials used by other industries, with the bulk of these fibers going into products purchased by individual consumers rather than into equipment used in industrial processing. Consequently, such factors as changes in consumer incomes and preferences have an important effect on the market for man-made fibers.

The firms that produce the bulk of the man-made fibers are located in the eastern part of the country, with the greatest concentration in Tennessee, Virginia, North Carolina, and South Carolina. They are large multi-product companies.

Rayon and acetate, made from cellulose, can be distinguished from the more recent discoveries of nylon, acrylic polyester, and other noncellulosic fibers made from petroleum, coal by-products, other minerals, or protein. Until recent years, rayon and acetate have enjoyed a meteoric growth in this county. Output rose from 400,000 pounds in 1911 to more than 1.5 billion pounds in 1960, and accounted for roughly one-fifth of total mill fiber consumption. Among man-made fibers, rayon and acetate remain the overwhelming choice of consumers, their consumption being about four times as large as that of noncellulosic fibers.

The South has shared in this growth and is now an important producing region of rayon and acetate. Since World War II, almost all the new rayon plants have been built in the South, so that to-day the area accounts for more than 50 percent of the nation's total productive capacity of rayon and acetate.

Factors Affecting Location. Because tremendous amounts of pure water are needed in the manufacture of rayon and acetate, availability of water is often the principal factor in determining a site. One viscose yarn producer, for example, uses 20 million gallons of water daily. This demand explains why rayon plants are generally found near rivers or large streams.

Their location is further influenced by the proximity to supplies of cellulose in the form of refined cotton linters and wood pulp. Most Southern plants now use cellulose made from wood pulp almost exclusively, because it is cheaper and, according to many observers, technically superior to cotton linters.

Another attraction has been the availability of chemicals. Many important producers of sulfuric acid and caustic soda are located in Alabama. These plants supply most of the chemical needs of Southern rayon producers. Cheap electricity, on the other hand, plays little or no part in attracting them because the factories generate their own electricity. Combining in-plant facilities with commercial power assures a dependable power supply, an important consideration since the nature of rayon production makes power shutdowns extremely costly.

Availability of labor also influences plant location. By locating principally outside the major cities, rayon firms have been able to draw from rural areas and nearby small communities.

Noncellulosic Organic Fibers. The noncellulosic fiber industry produces seven generic types of textile fibers—acrylic, nylon, olefin, polyestic, saran, spandex, and vinyl. Manufacturing plants are scattered from Massachusetts to Florida, with the largest concentration in Virginia, Tennessee, North Carolina, and South Carolina.

The entire noncellulosic fibers industry originated in scientific laboratories, and its future prospects depend on the success of its research and development efforts. While current research projects are carefully guarded secrets, the seven generic types of fibers now produced encompass a wide range of fiber characteristics, and it is generally expected that other fibers of the future will be modifications of existing fibers rather than completely new generic types. Recently developed fibers include a modified nylon with silk-like qualities, and bicomponent fibers made of nylon and polyester.

The research and development work of the noncellulosic fibers industry extends beyond its own products into items made from its fibers. Fiber producers develop specifications for fabrics made from their fibers, and in some cases guarantee the performance of goods made from these fabrics.

Apparel and Related Products

Since most products of the apparel industries are finished consumer goods, changes in population and in per capita income are important determinants of the total demand for the industries' products. Such changes in population composition as the rapid growth during the next decade of the 15–29 age group are expected to increase apparel sales. *Fashion* is an increasingly important element in the demand for apparel and house furnishings, as rising incomes allow more people to purchase these items for their esthetic and "status" appeal rather than for utilitarian value alone.

The apparel and related products major group of industries is made up of more than 28,000 establishments classified in 33 separate industries. The group's primary products are clothing and fabricated textile products (mostly home furnishings) made from purchased woven or knit textile fabrics and related materials such as leather, plastics, and furs. Although apparel plants are located in each of the fifty states and the District of Columbia, the northeastern and southern areas account for over 75 percent of total production, with the largest concentrations in New York and Pennsylvania.

In the past, the apparel industries have been characterized by a large number of small establishments often specializing in a single product. Average employment per establishment was less than fifty, and nearly half of all apparel establishments employed less than twenty workers. Firms were small, with single establishment, family-owned firms the most common type of operation. In recent years, however, mergers and internal growth have produced a growing number of large, multi-product firms. Although these firms account for only a relatively small proportion of the apparel sector's total output, their share is growing and the impact on the industry is much greater than their statistical share of the market.

Apparel plants employ 1.4 million workers, and the industries' combined payrolls total more than $5 billion. Nearly 80 percent of all employees are women. Although capital investment per employee is low, total value of plant and equipment, exclusive of depreciation allowances, totals over $1.2 billion. Annual investment in new plant and equipment has more than doubled since 1962 and now is in excess of $200 million.

Profits Increase But Remain Low. Price competition is characteristic of the apparel sector and has been intensified in recent years by the rapid increase in imported goods. Consequently, since 1958 earnings per dollar of sales in the apparel industries have averaged less than half those of all manufacturing corporations or of the nondurable goods sector.

Most imported goods are directly competitive with products of the domestic industry and are priced below domestic goods of comparable quality. The rising volume of low-cost imported goods is a growing threat to domestic producers, and

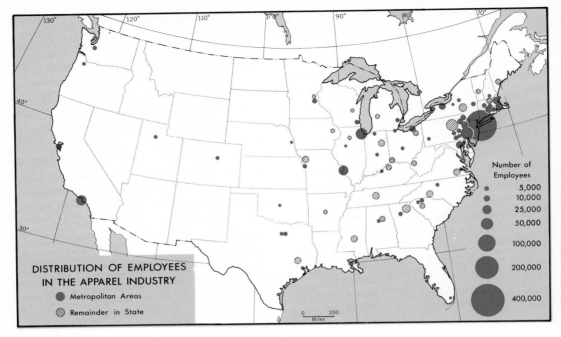

DISTRIBUTION OF EMPLOYEES
IN THE APPAREL INDUSTRY

● Metropolitan Areas

⊘ Remainder in State

Number of
Employees

5,000
10,000
25,000
50,000
100,000
200,000
400,000

FIGURE 22.4   (*General Media Corporation*)

some apparel firms are considering shifting their manufacturing facilities offshore to countries in which low wage rates would substantially reduce production costs.

Research and Development.   The apparel industries have encountered many problems in developing products with qualities desired by consumers and in improving manufacturing technology. Funds for this work have been restricted because most firms are too small to conduct independent research projects. This handicap has been partially overcome through comparative efforts centered in the Apparel Research Foundation, established jointly by the Department of Commerce and the apparel industries and continued through industry funds alone.

Advances in manufacturing technology have been slowed by the problem of designing machines capable of picking up and correctly aligning pieces of limp fabric

that are the basic material used by the industry. While prototype equipment has been developed to handle limp fabrics, a great deal of work remains to be done before it can be used economically in large-scale production. In the meantime, improvements in existing cutting and sewing equipment are steadily increasing efficiency and reducing man-hours required to produce apparel items.

COTTON TEXTILE PRODUCING COUNTRIES

Figures on the number of cotton spindles in place, on activity, and on cotton consumption give a general picture of the distribution of the spinning section of the cotton-textile industry. The number of spindles in the leading cotton-textile producing countries is shown in Table 22.1.

The United States, India, the U.S.S.R.,

Japan, and Mainland China have well over half the world's cotton spinning spindles. During the postwar years there has been a steady decline in the relative position of England and New England in the spinning industry of the world. In both there has been a decrease in the number of spindles in place, as well as in the percentage that these spindles represents of the world's total. At the same time there has been a considerable increase in the number of spindles in the southeastern states of the United States, and in India, the U.S.S.R., Japan, and Mainland China.

The United States and the U.S.S.R. also lead in the number of cotton looms, with 390,000 and 194,000, respectively. Mainland China ranks third with 160,000, followed by Japan (98,049), Italy (71,385), and West Germany (62,931).

The United States is the largest producer of cotton cloth, followed by the U.S.S.R. and India. Factory production of cloth in the U.S.S.R. and Mainland China is rising, but a larger percentage in the latter is still woven on hand looms.

U.S.S.R. The Central Industrial District is the major area of textile production in the Soviet Union. Even though under the government's planned industrial dispersion policy a number of new centers have developed in Transcaucasia and in Central Asia, Ivanovo remains the "Manchester" of the Soviet Union, the center of an important textile district. Leningrad also continues as a prominent cen-

ter of production, with about 5 percent of the country's total cotton output.

India. Under its fourth five-year plan, India hopes to increase its spindleage to 20 million and its loomage to 250,000 by 1971. Its textile industry continues to be highly labor-intensive, and the machinery used by most Indian mills is outmoded, being from 30 to 40 years old. Annual rehabilitation expenditures average $83.4 million, which is far short of requirements to build a modern industry.

Cotton milling is the largest single industry in India. There are roughly 500 mills, most of them of the composite spinning and weaving type. Over 60 percent of the spindles and looms are concentrated in Maharashtra and Gujarat, mainly in the cities of Bombay and Ahmadabad, the remainder being distributed largely in Madras, Madhya Pradesh, and Uttar Pradesh.

Export incentives schemes have been introduced, and means to overcome labor's opposition to automation are being worked out. Consumer demand for cloth in India is rising again, and better farm production is expected to increase rural purchasing power. The outlook for exports, however, is not as hopeful as for domestic offtake.

Japan's cotton textile industry has suffered badly in the past few years. Prices have been declining continuously, and both sales and profits have dropped seri-

Table 22.1 Cotton Spinning Spindles (thousands)

Country	1953	1967	Percent Change 1953–67
World	108,871	134,216	+ 23.3
China (Mainland)	4,100	12,900	+214.6
India	11,182	17,085	+ 52.8
Japan	7,502	12,614	+ 68.1
United States	22,830	20,607	− 9.7
U.S.S.R.	8,700	14,173	+ 62.9
West Germany	6,103	4,672	− 23.4

Source: United Nations *Statistical Yearbook,* 1968 (New York: United Nations, 1969), Table 96, p. 256.

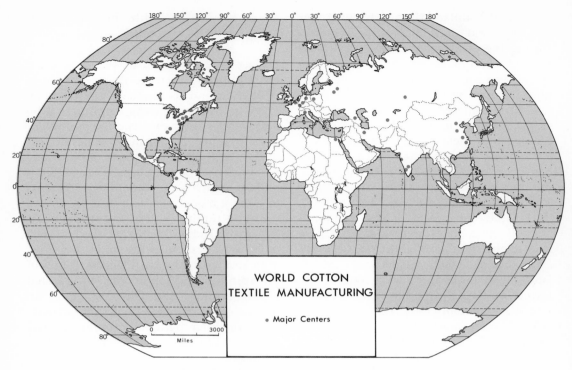

FIGURE 22.5   (General Media Corporation)

FIGURE 22.6   Aymara Indian girl spinning alpaca wool near Lake Titicaca, Bolivia. (Hal Stephens)

ously, partly due to the growing popularity of synthetic fiber production.

WORSTEDS AND WOOLENS INDUSTRY

The countries that consume the largest amounts of wool are the United States, the United Kingdom, and the U.S.S.R., followed by France, West Germany, Italy, and Japan. The relative positions of these countries fluctuate slightly from year to year, but it is evident that most of the woolen textile industry is concentrated in those countries or regions having a highly industrialized economic system; in the United States, for example, there is an extreme concentration of the woolen industries in the New England and Middle Atlantic states.

The region where woolen manufacturing is most concentrated in all the world is the West Yorkshire industrial area of England. Here, owing to local supplies of wool, near-by fuel, and proximity to market towns, local centers of manufacturing have developed and gradually expanded until now more than forty towns are included in this wood-manufacturing district of England. Because of this concentration it has been possible for certain towns to specialize in a particular type of product, and individual mills in some cases are devoted to only one stage in the manufacture of the finished product. For instance, Bradford is the central wool market and manufactures yarns that are the raw materials for factories in other towns.

The U.S.S.R. is second only to Great Britain in the number of wool spindles and looms. Pre-Soviet wool production was concentrated in the Moscow–Leningrad area for fine cloth, and in the Black Earth Center and Central Volga region, which produced coarse cloth. Since World War II, mills have been constructed nearer to the raw-material sources—Kharkov and Kremenchug in the Ukraine, Kutaisi and Tbilisi in Georgia, and Semipalatinsk in Kazakhstan.

MAN-MADE FIBERS

Japan is the second largest producer of rayon and acetate fibers, following the United States. Development of Japan's modern textile industry during the past five years has been focused on chemical fibers. Chemical textiles include regenerated fiber (rayons), semisynthetic fiber (acetate), and synthetic fiber (nylon, vinylon, and tetron). The consumption curve for chemical fibers has risen with the increased supply and demand. Through mass production, the prices have been kept low, and new preferences for Western-style home furnishings like curtains, bedding, carpeting, etc., have sent demand upward.

The price of Japanese textiles is low compared to the international average, and low at home compared to the price of other industrial products. Wholesale prices in Japan are from 50 to 60 percent cheaper than those of U.S. textiles.

selected references

1. Airov, Joseph, *The Location of the Synthetic-Fiber Industry*, New York: John Wiley & Sons, Inc., 1959.

2. Barlow, Frank D., Jr., "Cotton, Rayon, Synthetic Fibers—Competition in Western Europe," *Foreign Agricultural Report*, No. 95, Washington D.C.: United States Department of Agriculture, 1957.

3. *Changes in the American Textile Industry*, United States Department of Agriculture, Marketing Research Division, Technical Bulletin 1210, 1959.

4. Clark, Clifford D., and Olsen, Bernard M., "Technological Change in the Textile Industry," *Southern Economic Journal*, Vol. 26, October 1959, pp. 125–133.

5. Estall, R. C., *New England: A Study in Industrial Adjustment*, New York: Frederick A. Praeger Publishers, 1966.

6. "Fiber Industries," in Platt, Raze R.,

ed., *India: A Compendium*, New York: American Geographical Society, 1963, pp. 455–480.

7. Hess, Katherine P., *Textile Fibers and Their Use*, Philadelphia: J. B. Lippincott Company, 1958.

8. Hough, Richard F., "Impact of the Decline in Raw Silk on the Suwa Basin of Japan," 1968, *Economic Geography*, Vol. 44, No. 2, April 1968, pp. 95–116.

9. Hornbeck, Bernice M., "Communist China's Cotton Textile Exports—Their Growth and their Effect on World Markets," Washington, D.C.: Foreign Agricultural Service, U.S. Department of Agriculture, April 1959, FAS-M-52.

10. Karan, Pradyumna P., "Changes in Indian Industrial Location," *Annals of the Association of American Geographers*, Vol. 54, No. 3, September 1964, pp. 336–354.

11. Kenyon, James B., "The Industrial Structure of the New York Garment Industry," in Thoman, Richard S., and Patton, Donald J., eds., *Focus on Geographic Activity*, New York: McGraw-Hill Book Company, Inc., 1964, pp. 37–44.

12. Maisley, H. A., "Harris Tweed: A Growing Highland Industry," *Economic Geography*, Vol. 37, No. 4, October 1961, pp. 353–370.

13. Pryde, Phillip R., "The Areal Deconcentration of the Soviet Cotton-Textile Industry," *Geographical Review*, Vol. 58, No. 4, October 1968, pp. 575–592.

14. Rogers, H. B., "The Changing Geography of the Lancashire Cotton Industry," *Economic Geography*, Vol. 38, No. 4, October 1962, pp. 299–314.

15. ———, "The Lancashire Cotton Industry in 1840," *Institute of British Geographers, Transactions and Papers*, Vol. 28, 1960, pp. 135–153.

The iron and steel industries include both the smelting and refining of iron ore to convert it into iron and steel, and the shaping of iron and steel into products that serve as raw materials for a wide range of other industries. The companies engaged in steel production have in most cases entered related fields; they carry on mining operations and transportation, and they manufacture finished products such as ships and automobiles, as well as a variety of by-products, including coal-tar products, gas, and Portland cement.

It takes about 2.5 tons of coke, iron ore, limestone, scrap, and other materials to make a ton of ingot steel. This estimate does not include the substantial tonnage of coal and iron ore that must be washed and beneficiated to obtain the high quality materials required for efficient iron production.

chapter 23

Iron and Steel

STEELMAKING

Broadly speaking, the steelmaking processes consist in refining blast furnace iron to remove excess carbon and impurities. At the same time, the steelmaker controls the quantity of the elements other than iron that are an essential part of steel. This control usually involves removing or reducing elements already in the metal, and adding others.

Steel is stronger and more "workable" than cast iron, and can be rolled, forged, or drawn into useful shapes. Blast furnace iron, or pig iron, must be cast into shape. Steel is made by three types of processes—open hearth, bessemer, and electric.

Open Hearth

Open hearth furnaces make about 90 percent of the steel produced in the United States. The furnace is called "open hearth" because its hearth or bottom, where the metal is held, is open to the sweep of

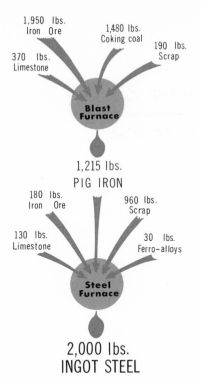

1,950 lbs. Iron Ore

1,480 lbs. Coking coal

190 lbs. Scrap

370 lbs. Limestone

Blast Furnace

1,215 lbs.
PIG IRON

180 lbs. Iron Ore

960 lbs. Scrap

130 lbs. Limestone

30 lbs. Ferro–alloys

Steel Furnace

2,000 lbs.
INGOT STEEL

FIGURE 23.1   *What it takes to make a ton of steel.*

flames that melt the steel. The hearth is shaped like a large, oval dish, and is lined with heat-resistant materials. The front side of the furnace contains doors through which the raw materials are charged. The refined steel is drawn off or "tapped" from the rear.

Gas, oil, coal, or tar may be used as fuel. To aid combustion, the fuel is mixed with hot air in burners located at each end of the furnace; these operate alternately and the flames sweep down and across the open hearth, directly above the metal bath, and out at the opposite end. The furnace is built to operate at about 3,000° Fahrenheit.

Limestone and scrap are put in the furnace. After a melting period, molten pig iron (hot metal) is poured in from a large ladle. Steel can be made in an open hearth from either scrap or pig iron, but usually is a combination of both; a frequent ratio

is 48 percent scrap and 52 percent pig iron.

The refining operation consists first of removing excess impurities from the pig iron, and then controlling the quantity of those elements other than iron that are an essential part of steel. Although the term "alloy steel" is applied only to certain steels, all steels are alloyed to some extent, for besides iron they contain carefully controlled amounts of several elements such as carbon, manganese, phosphorus, and sulphur.

The limestone melts and forms a slag that floats on top of the molten metal in the furnace. Slag is a scavenger, helping to remove the impurities that the blast furnace left in the pig iron. Most of the carbon in the metal is removed as a gas after combining with the air in the furnace. Through other chemical reactions the slag absorbs silicon and some other elements that may be present.

As much as 600 tons of steel may be made at one time in the largest open hearth furnaces. A range of 125 to 150 tons is more common, and many new furnaces have a capacity of 250 tons in one operation. Steelmen generally refer to a single furnace load of steel as a "heat" of steel.

Normally about twelve hours are required to produce a heat of open hearth steel. During the first five hours the raw materials are charged and melted; then for about six more hours the heat is allowed to "work" while the refining action takes place. During the latter part the melter, or skilled steelman operating the furnace, must exercise especially good judgment, which is gained by long experience and assisted by modern equipment.

The requirements of the countless uses of steel are so varied that steel truly must be tailor-made, and the last hour in the furnace is the climax of the melter's efforts to insure that the composition of the heat meets the particular specification. During the open hearth process, frequent

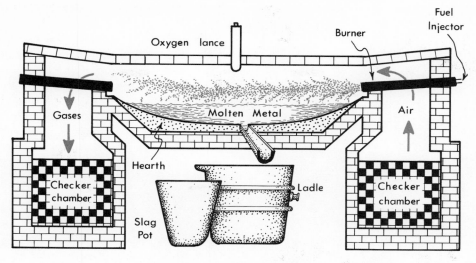

FIGURE 23.2   *An open hearth furnace.*

samples are taken for chemical analysis and other tests. The samples taken from the furnace are sent to a laboratory, and reports are quickly returned for the guidance of the melter.

When the heat is finally completed and up to specification, the furnace is "tapped" by knocking out a plug at the back of the furnace, allowing the molten metal to flow into a great ladle. The slag, which is much lighter than the steel, floats on top and overflows into a smaller ladle called a "thimble."

Because of the high temperature and the erosive effect of boiling steel and slag, special attention is essential to the design of the furnace and its extensive system of flues, called checkers. Construction of one open hearth furnace may require upwards of one million bricks of various kinds, some chosen for strength, some for heat insulation, and some because they will not disintegrate when held at a high temperature for a long time.

Bessemer

The bessemer process makes steel by blowing air through molten pig iron. Oxygen in the air combines with and burns away most of the impurities in the pig iron, thus refining it into steel.

Bessemer steel is made in a pear-shaped, tilted vessel or converter made of steel plates lined with heat resisting bricks and clay. A common size will hold 15 tons of molten pig iron. The converter has a double bottom, the lower portion of which is an air chamber. Above this is the bottom of the vessel itself, perforated with holes through which the air is blown.

In charging, the converter is tilted on its side and pig iron is poured in through the open top. It is then returned to a vertical position as the blast is turned on. Brilliant sparks burst forth, followed by dense brown flames and dark red flames which mean that the silicon and manganese are being burned out. After five minutes or so the flame becomes longer and brilliantly luminous as the carbon burns away. After ten to fifteen minutes more the flame suddenly dies down, indicating that the process has been completed, except for adding ferroalloys.

A relatively new process is oxygen steelmaking in vessels that resemble bessemer converters. A jet of high purity oxygen is directed at the surface of the molten metal

FIGURE 23.3   *Molten iron is charged into a basic oxygen furnace at this Lackawanna, New York, steel plant. The basic oxygen furnace produces high-quality steel much faster than the open-hearth furnace. (Bethlehem Steel)*

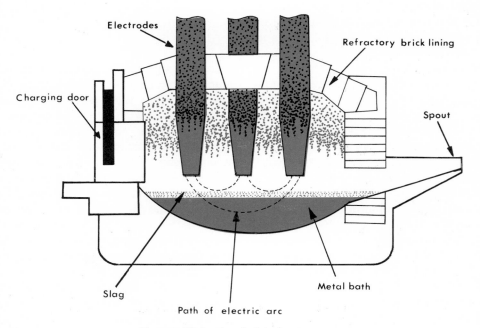

FIGURE 23.4   *An electric furnace.*

bath, helping to "burn out" the impurities.

Electric Furnace

The Electric Furnace Process of steelmaking is used for the most exacting compositions, including stainless steels, where melting and refining can be very closely controlled. The electric furnaces most widely used are steel shells, lined with heat-resisting brick. Large sticks of carbon, called electrodes, extend down through the roof of the furnace to within a few inches of the metal in the furnace. When the current is turned on, electric arcs similar to those in the arc lights used for street lighting or in home "sun lamps" are struck between the electrodes and the charge of metal, providing the heat.

Electric furnaces may use as raw material a charge consisting entirely of scrap iron and steel, although sometimes molten open hearth or bessemer steel is further refined in the electric furnace. When alloy steels are made, the alloying elements such as nickel, chromium, and tungsten are added either as pure metals or as ferroalloys. When the heat is completed, the furnace is tilted to release the steel into the ladle. About 12 percent of the steel made today is made in electric furnaces.

Steel Products

After the molten steel has been poured into ingots and allowed to cool, the subsequent processes depend upon the nature of the desired finished product. It is impossible to follow through all of these processes, and only one important section of the industry will be described.

In the production of steel sheets, the ingots are handled mechanically. They are first taken to the soaking pit, where they soak up heat until they are of a uniform temperature throughout. They are then taken to the "blooming" mill, where they are passed back and forth between rollers, which form them into thick slabs. In the rolling mill they are rolled into sheets of the desired sizes and shapes. These are the chief processes, although other steps, such as removing the "scale" also are necessary.

Many varieties of finished steel products are manufactured—sheets, plates, structural steel, pipes, rails, wire, and such specialty steel as that used for cutlery. Table 23.1 shows the percentage distribution of steel comsumption by category of use.

Table 23.1   Percentage Distribution of U.S. Steel Consumption with Projections for 1980

Category of Use	1940	1960	1980
Construction (excluding railroad)	25	31	32
Automotive	16	18	17
Rail Transportation	10	4	6
Water and Air Transportation (including military aircraft)	2	1	1
Producer Durables	9	12	18
Consumer Durables	6	6	4
Containers	8	10	7.98
Ordnance	—	—	0.2
Ferrous Castings	24	18	14
Total	100	100	100

Source: American Iron and Steel Institute, "Distribution of Steel Consumption," *Steelways*, Vol. 24, No. 2 (March–April 1968), p. 13.

Locational Factors

Three factors play a major role in determining the location of the iron and steel industry: iron ore, coal, and markets. The ratio between coal and ore and between coal and steel varies, depending on the characteristics of the original ore and the nature of the final products. It is estimated that between 1 and 1.5 tons of coal are necessary in the United States to convert one ton of ore into steel products. Low-grade ore is more weight-losing than high-grade ore. The higher the grade of ore, therefore, the greater the attractive pull of coal; on the other hand, all technological improvements in the direction of greater fuel economies reduce the attractive power of coal.

During recent years the increased use

of lower-grade ores and of ores of high phosphorus content, together with the noteworthy advances in fuel economy, have greatly reduced the "pull" of the coal fields in the steel industry. As a result there has been a decentralization of the industry. In general, however, the steel mills are still located near coal fields, although these are not necessarily fields of good coking coal (such as the Connellsville district of Pennsylvania) since coking coal forms only a portion of the coal requirements of the industry.

An additional reason why the coal fields afford the most favorable location for the steel industry will be found in a consideration of the market for steel products A large part of this market is furnished by the machine-making and machine-using industries. Since these industries need power, and since coal is an important power source, they tend to be located near the coal fields. The coal fields, therefore, exert their attractive pull on the steel industry not only directly but also indirectly through their pull on the industries that furnish the market for steel.

No general statement can be made concerning the relative importance of iron ore deposits, coal deposits, and markets as locational factors. The importance of ore and coal depend largely on the coal–ore ratio in the production of steel, which varies with the character of the ore and technological improvements.

The location of the steel plant obviously must be one with excellent transportation facilities. Bulky raw materials and finished products must be transported cheaply. The early development of Pittsburgh, Pennsylvania as a steel center was favored by its situation at the point where the Allegheny and Monongahela rivers join to form the Ohio River, which was connected by canals with Lake Erie, and then with the Hudson River through the Erie Canal. Today, Pittsburgh has excellent railroad connections with all parts of the industrial sections of the Northeast.

THE UNITED STATES STEEL INDUSTRY

The United States produces about 25 percent of the pig iron and nearly 30 percent of the steel in the world. There is enough plant capacity to produce 150 million tons, but present demand is still not sufficient to engage all this capacity.

There are now more than 275 individual companies with plants located in 300 communities in 35 states engaged in the production and finishing of iron and steel. About one-third of these companies make the raw steel required to produce their finished products. The remainder are engaged in further finishing or in semi-finished steel produced by others.

Nine-tenths of the steel made in the United States comes from the main manufacturing belt, which enjoys low-cost water transport for its raw materials: coal from Appalachia, iron ore from the Lake Superior district and Labrador, local limestone, and imported ferroalloys. The Chicago area, including Chicago, Gary (Indiana Harbor), Calumet, and East Chicago, leads all others in output. The Pittsburgh district, with many plants on the Ohio, Monongahela, and Allegheny Rivers, is second in importance. The Lake Erie district, which extends from North Tonowanda to Detroit, has nearly a dozen centers with integrated iron and steel plants, and nearly three times that many centers with rolling mills.

Other less important steel districts are:

1. The southern New England, east-central New York, and New Jersey district, which operates plants that are not fully integrated establishments, but which convert pig iron, steel scrap, and alloy metals into special steels
2. The fully integrated mills in eastern Pennsylvania (Morrisville) and Maryland (Sparrows Point), which are based on local coal and imported high grade iron ore from Venezuela and Chile

FIGURE 23.5 *Pittsburgh's famous "Golden Triangle." What two well-known rivers are pictured here? (American Air Surveys, Inc.)*

3. The Birmingham, Alabama district, which has most of the necessary raw materials for making steel within a 20 mile radius
4. The Houston and Daingerfield (northeastern Texas) integrated plants
5. The Western iron and steel districts at Pueblo, Colorado; Provo, Utah; Fontana, South San Francisco, Pittsburg, and Torrance, California; Seattle, Washington; and Portland, Oregon. Of the far western mills, only three—Provo, Fontana, and Oregon Steel Mills, Inc. of Portland—are fully integrated.

Steel's Competitive Position

Steel is facing intensified competition at home from other materials, and at the same time is confronted with increased competition from foreign steel producers in the rapidly expanding markets elsewhere in the world. Some of the traditional major steel markets, such as rail transportation, are declining in importance, while others such as containers are increasing. Domestic steels have real potential for growth because of increasing population and consumption around the world. However, full participation for U.S. companies in this growth is not assured. It depends upon continuing innovation in three important areas:

1. Research and development of new and improved products to penetrate new markets and to anticipate customer needs
2. Research to find the most effective ways of producing products in the most economical fashion
3. Development of new and improved techniques of selling

It depends also upon continued capital improvements so that American steel-making facilities will be the most modern

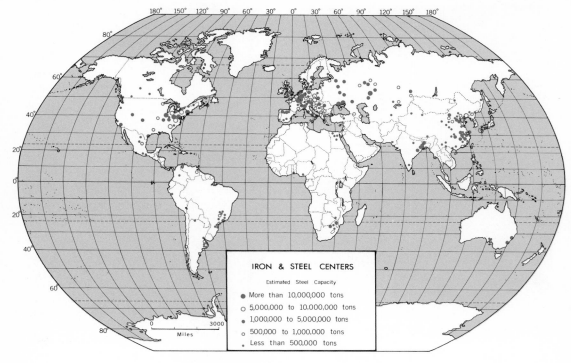

FIGURE 23.6   (*General Media Corporation*)

steelmaking facilities in the world, and this in turn requires improved profitability and improved cost performances in all phases of the business.

Trade in Steel. A rising trend in steel imports has accompanied the virtually flat pattern of United States exports of steel mill products in recent years. Despite spurts in imports, both in volume and as a proportion of steel consumption, in 1951, 1953, and 1956, the volume of steel imports showed little trend during most of the 1950s. Beginning in 1959, however, both the volume and proportion of steel consumption supplied by foreign producers rose sharply; since then the trend of imports has been inexorably upward.

In 1959, the sharp increase in imports and the market decline in exports caused the United States trade balance in steel mill products to swing from an export surplus of 1.1 million tons in 1958 to a deficit of 2.7 million tons in 1959. In 1960, the tonnage deficit narrowed to 382,000

Table 23.2   World Crude Steel Production (thousand metric tons)

Country	1953	1960	1967	Percent Change 1960–67
World	234,700	346,600	493,000	+ 42.2
ECSC	39,623	72,824	89,893	+ 23.4
Japan	7,662	22,138	62,154	+180.8
United States	101,250	90,067	115,406	+ 28.1
U.S.S.R.	38,128	65,294	102,224	+ 56.6

Source: United Nations *Statistical Yearbook,* 1968 (New York: United Nations, 1969), Table 129, p. 305.

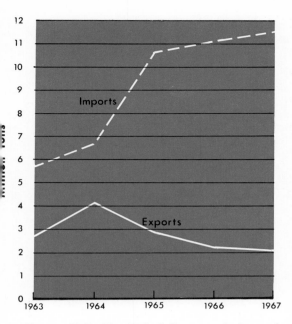

FIGURE 23.7 *The United States trade in steel, as measured by exports and imports.*

tons. Thereafter, however, the deficit began to widen considerably, and in 1965 to 1967, the tonnage deficit averaged 8.9 million tons annually.

Since 1959, the competitive position of the United States in the world steel market (as measured by percent share of the domestic as well as world steel market) has apparently deteriorated. This can be attributed largely to the sharp growth in world steel capacity and the significant price differentials between foreign and domestically produced steel.

World Trends in Steel Capacity and Consumption

Expansion in world steel capacity since 1947 has been marked by three stages of development:

1. The early post-World War II reconstruction period, when capacity especially in Europe, Japan, and the U.S.S.R., was being rebuilt
2. The period from the early 1950s to the late 1950s when capacity was ex-

panding to meet growing domestic demands for steel
3. The period since the late 1950s, when world steel capacity was growing at a rate in excess of world steel consumption

During the early postwar period, growth in world steel output and consumption kept pace with the expansion of steel capacity and there was little margin of unused capacity. In contrast, during the late 1950s world steel capacity expanded considerably faster than consumption, and utilization rates of world steel eased (but were still high).

The doubling of world steel capacity during the 1950s was accompanied by major shifts in the pattern of world steel production. The proportion of United States steel capacity to world capacity fell, and the relative proportions accounted for by Japan and the European Coal and Steel Community (ECSC)[1] countries rose. The most significant expansion in capacity occurred in the U.S.S.R., where capacity more than doubled.

Although the U.S.S.R. continued to increase her relative proportion of world steel capacity in the 1960s, the most dramatic change took place in Japan, where capacity nearly tripled and Japanese steel capacity to world capacity rose from 6.4 percent in 1960 to 12.6 percent in 1967. Sharp expansion also occurred in Canada, Latin America, and India. As a result, increased steel production in those areas, although still not adequate to meet total domestic steel needs, lessened the dependence of those countries on imports.

Declining Trend in World Prices. The dollar differential between domestic and foreign prices for selected steel products is shown in Table 23.3. The sizable differential on hot- and cold-rolled sheets and strip helps to explain the sharp

[1]European Coal and Steel Community includes Belgium, Luxembourg, West Germany, France, Italy, and the Netherlands.

Table 23.3   Differential Between U.S. Domestic Prices and Foreign Prices of Selected Steel Products

Product	Location	Price Differential Per Ton
Cold-rolled sheets	Cleveland	$18 to 21
Cold-rolled sheets	Chicago	15
Cold-rolled sheets	Philadelphia	35
Plates	Chicago	15
Hot-rolled bars	Chicago	15
Wire rods (7/32")	Cleveland	30
Hot-rolled sheets	Cleveland	30
(from service center)	West Coast	25 to 30

Source: American Iron and Steel Institute, "The Steel Import Problem," *Steelways*, Vol. 26, No. 2 (1970), p. 13.

growth in imports of that product—from nearly 1.2 million tons in 1964 to 4.3 million tons in 1967.

Price differentials between U.S. and foreign steel products are partly accounted for by differences in production costs, especially labor. For example, despite rapid growth of wages in foreign steel-producing countries, labor compensation in the United States steel industry has increased markedly in recent years. As a result, as recently as 1966 the differences in employment costs between the United States and individual major foreign steel-producing countries were as large or larger than a decade earlier. However, employment costs explain only a part of the cost differentials, as reflected by the fact that American-produced goods generally would otherwise also be priced out of many world markets—that is, in those cases where goods are produced by similarly high wage cost industries. In any product line, a number of factors in addition to employment costs also influence total costs and contribute to price differentials. In the case of steel, such factors would include differences in steel technology, as well as differences in the cost of plant and equipment, raw materials, and money capital. In recent years, although the level of output per man-hour in the U.S. is greater than in the steel industry of any major foreign country, it is apparently not sufficient for domestic

steel producers to maintain a comparative advantage in all types of steel products.

U.S. Imports. From 1958 to 1967, the volume of United States steel imports rose nearly 600 percent, while domestic consumption increased by about 60 percent. As a result of the growth in imports, by 1967 foreign producers accounted for 12 percent of the domestic steel market, compared with 2.9 percent in 1958.

During the late 1950s, Japan began a slow but steady penetration of U.S. markets, and during the import buildup in 1962 accounted for about one-fourth of United States steel imports. By 1965, Japan supplied 40 percent of U.S. imported steel products, surpassing the ECSC Countries.

Steel sheets represent the major product line in the surge of Japanese imports during the past five years. In 1967, Japan supplied 50 percent or more of wire rods, sheet and strip, plates, and pipe and tubing imported by the United States. The recent rise in Japanese exports to the United States clearly reflects the vast expansion of steel producing capacity in Japan. In 1957, steel capacity in Japan amounted to nearly 20 million tons; by 1965, capacity rose to 55 million tons. By 1972 planned expansions will increase steel capacity to an estimated 82 million ingot tons. Such capacity indicates a steel export potential of 25 to 30 million tons of steel by 1970, or practically double the annual volume exported in 1966.

OTHER MAJOR STEEL PRODUCERS

Table 23.2 shows world production of crude steel in selected years. In addition to the United States, which leads the world in steel output, other important steel manufacturing nations in order are the U.S.S.R., Japan, West Germany, the United Kingdom, and France.

The U.S.S.R. In 1928, the Soviet Union produced 4 million metric tons of steel, less than one-fifth as much as Great Britain and Germany together; in 1968, its steel output reached 107 million metric tons, approaching both that of the United States and the combined production of Great Britain and the ECSC. The largest concentrations of blast and open hearth furnaces are in the Ukraine (Zaporozhe, Donetsk, Makeyevka, Dnepropetrovsk, Dneprodzerzhinsk, Krivoi Rog, and Zhdanov), the Urals (Chelyabinsk and Magnitogorsk), and the Kuznetsk Basin (Novokuznetsk). The Ukraine and adjacent areas, with the Urals, produce more than three-fourths of Soviet iron and steel.

Recent trends point to large-scale expansion of the iron and steel industry in the Urals and northern Kazakhstan, where extensive new deposits of iron ore are being worked and large beneficiating plants have been built. The capacity of the Magnitogorsk steel facility in the Urals is being extended to 12 million tons per year and the new Karaganda facilities will have a similar capacity.

Japan. The Japanese steel industry was so badly damaged during World War II by air raids that it was virtually destroyed. In 1946, crude steel production was down to one-tenth of the prewar levels. Within seven years, however, it had regained its highest prewar level of 7,700,000 tons. The growth that followed was remarkably

FIGURE 23.8　*The Geneva works of the U.S. Steel Corporation. (U.S. Steel Corporation)*

fast: in 1956 production was 10 million tons; by 1960, 20 million; in 1963 it had risen to more than 30 million tons; and in 1966 was nearly 48 million tons.

Germany. The Lower Rhine Westphalia industrial region mines most of the bituminous and brown coal produced in West Germany. Here is by far the largest part of the nation's iron and steel facilities. The center of this heavy industrial concentration is the Ruhr, a triangle only 35 miles wide and 60 miles long, extending from Wesel to Dusseldorf to Hamm. The Ruhr industrial region is today a vast conurbation of nearly 5 million people, almost 30 percent of the Federal Republic. It is served by a labyrinth of railroads, canals, and navigable rivers, and freight moves cheaply in any direction. About one-third of the country's industrial plants are located here.

A second important steel-producing region is the Saar, which lies against the French boundary, and France has always had a deep interest in its coal mines and factories. The Saar's industries are primarily associated with the coal mines and the iron and steel works. Its peripheral location formerly tended to restrict industrial growth, but it is now central to the European community and has a brighter future.

Great Britain. Britain pioneered in the application of coal to the smelting of iron ore from the seventeenth century onward, and British inventors were responsible for the series of discoveries that led to the great expansion of steelmaking in the second half of the nineteenth century. Today, Britain is the fifth largest producer of steel.

South Wales and the northeast coast of England are the two largest steel-producing areas, together accounting for more than 40 percent of the total output. South Wales is engaged mainly in the production of flat products, and is especially noted for tinplate. In the north-

east coastal area of England, production is concentrated on heavy sections and rails, and plates for the shipbuilding and other industries. Scotland, with an annual production of over 2 million ingot tons, finds its chief internal markets in the shipbuilding and engineering industries of the Clyde Valley. Sheffield is known throughout the world for its special alloy steels. Two other areas with a substantial share of output are north Lincolnshire and Lancashire.

Britain possesses some of the most up-to-date steel plants in Europe. Notable recent developments in steelmaking include the increasing use of oxygen, not only in its application to conventional steelmaking processes, but also in the pneumatic processes. The relatively new process of continuously casting steel, which removes the necessity for the primary rolling plant, has been installed on a commercial basis by several firms.

France. French iron and steel production has also risen rapidly. Steel mills have been expanded to supply new rolling mills, such as those of Usinor at Denain and Montataire, and Sollac at Serebange and Ebange, as well as new tube-producing mills. Steel output rose from 6.2 million tons in 1938 to 19.5 million tons in 1968. The main steel-producing area is Lorraine, followed by northern France, south-central France, Normandy, and Brittany.

selected references

1. Brisby, M. D. J., Worthington, P. M., and Anderson, R. J., "Economics of Process Selection in the Iron and Steel Industry," *Iron and Steel Institute*, Vol. 202, September, 1964, pp. 721–729.

2. Case, Carl A., "Latin America's Iron and Steel Industries," *Journal of Metals*, Vol. 14, 1962, pp. 34–42.

3. Casetti, Emilio, "Optimal Location of Steel Mills Serving the Quebec and Southern

Ontario Steel Market," *The Canadian Geographer*, Vol. 10, No. 1, 1966, pp. 27–39.

4. Chilcott, Ronald H., "Spain's Iron and Steel: Renovation of an Old Industry," *Geographical Review*, Vol. 53, No. 2, April 1963, pp. 247–262.

5. Denisenko, Ivan, and Belan, Roman, "Development of the U.S.S.R. Iron and Steel Industry," *Iron and Steel Engineering*, Vol. 38, 1961, pp. 93–103.

6. Fisher, Douglas A., *The Epic of Steel*, New York: Harper & Row Publishers, 1963.

7. Fleming, Douglas K., "Coastal Steelworks in the Common Market Countries," *Geographical Review*, Vol. 57, No. 1, January 1967, pp. 48–72.

8. Hamilton, F. E. I., "Locational Factors in the Yugoslav Iron and Steel Industry," *Economic Geography*, Vol. 40, No. 1, January 1964, pp. 46–64.

9. Riley, R. C., "Changes in the Supply of Coking Coal in Belgium Since 1945," *Economic Geography*, Vol. 43, No. 3, July 1967, pp. 261–270.

10. Sharer, Cyrus J., "The Philadelphia Iron and Steel District: Its Relation to the Seaways," *Economic Geography*, Vol. 39, No. 4, October 1963, pp. 363–367.

11. Spelt, Jacob, "The Ruhr and Its Coal Industry in the Middle 60's, *Canadian Geographer*, Vol. 13, No. 1, Spring 1969, pp. 3–9.

12. Stone, Joseph K., "Oxygen in Steelmaking," *Scientific American*, Vol. 218, No. 4, April 1968, pp. 24–31.

13. "The Big Change Comes to Steel," *Business Week*, August 15, 1964, pp. 78–81.

14. Van Der Rest, P., "Europe's Steel Industry," *Steel Review*, Vol. 24, October 1961, pp. 8–20.

15. Warren, Kenneth, "The Changing Steel Industry of the European Common Market," *Economic Geography*, Vol. 43, No. 4, October 1967, pp. 314–332.

chapter 24

Metal Fabricating Industries

The process by which iron, steel, copper, aluminum, and other metals are converted into finished products is known as metal fabrication. The first step, shaping raw materials as they come from refining furnaces, is done by rolling, casting, and hammering. But these processes give only crudely shaped castings or forgings, or rolled stock such as sheets, plates, rods, and bars. For most purposes, metal parts must be accurately and precisely shaped, and this requires machine tools to do drilling, boring, planing, grinding, turning, milling, and shearing or pressing.

There are more than 200 major types of machine tools. The industry is unique in that it makes not only the machine tools used in all the metal fabricating industries, but also the machine tools that make the machines. It consists of some 500 manufacturers, heavily concentrated in Ohio, Michigan, Illinois, and southern New England. The lower Great Lakes area dominates, with about 60 percent of the national output. Many of the firms are small, and companies with less than 1,000 workers account for almost 75 percent of the total United States machine tool output.

LOCATIONAL FACTORS

Mineral products (especially iron and steel) and power are the chief resources on which the machine tool industries depend. A well-developed iron and steel industry is, therefore, a prerequisite for the establishment of large machine-producing industries. Large amounts of capital, skilled labor force, technical skill, and inventive genius are also essentials.

Some branches of the industry require tremendous capital investments—as, for instance, the electrical goods industry—and naturally tend to be located in regions where an abundant supply of capital is available at low interest rates. Both the machine tool industry and the use of machines have progressed furthest in those regions where capital is abundant and labor relatively scarce, with a resultant high wage level. Skilled labor is necessary for the production of complicated machinery, which requires great accuracy of workmanship. Even more important is the availability of men with technical education, skill, and inventiveness who can improve old machines and develop new ones, for competition demands an ability to keep in advance of competitors in technical improvements. In developing new industries, for instance, the automotive and aircraft industries, business leaders with vision toward the future of the industry are important.

MACHINE TOOLS

The foundation of the machine tool industry in the United States was laid in 1798 when Eli Whitney invented the system of interchangeable parts, the basic principle of mass production. This method of manufacturing, which permitted an unskilled man to turn out a product as good as one made by the most highly trained machinist, underlies the whole edifice of modern industry. Almost as important as his theory were the metalworking tools that Whitney designed and built to make the theory workable— among them, the jig and the fixture, limited gages, and the milling machine.

In the 1790s Samuel Slater founded for New England and the infant republic the short cut to quantity, for he was the first in the United States to set up a system of manufacture in which the successive steps of the skilled artisan were broken down into such simple components that a group of children could out-produce the finest craftsman. Whitney combined quality with quantity. Between them, these two researchers launched New England, then almost destitute of manufacturing, into a way of life that soon made

it the most highly industrialized region of the Western Hemisphere. And they also set the two basic patterns of industry that still predominate in New England —metalworking and textile manufacturing.

The research-minded Yankees who followed Slater and Whitney first transformed the face of New England, and then provided the machinery for transforming the face of America. The heart of this transformation was the machine tool— the machine for making the machines that are vital to almost every phase of manufacturing. In New England were born the jig, fixture, and limit gage, the milling machine, copying lathe, turret lathe, automatic screw machine, and cylindrical and surface grinders, to name only a few.

Utilizing these basic devices for precision metalworking, New England quickly made itself the machine shop of the new nation. In addition to turning out machine tools, New England manufacturers developed both for their own use and for sale a great variety of specialized machinery for making textiles, guns, shoes, ships, sewing machines, farm and household equipment, an ever-widening range of hardware, and many of the necessities and luxuries demanded by a rapidly expanding nation.

By 1900 the basic geographic pattern of the machine tool industry was well established. Lower New England, the Middle Atlantic, and lower Great Lakes states had essentially equal diversions of the industry; Ohio, Pennsylvania, Connecticut, and Massachusetts led in production.

The Present Pattern

The automobile industry, the largest consumer of machine tools and the prime example of mass production, has given leadership to the lower Great Lakes region, which accounts for roughly 60 percent of the total national machine tool output—Ohio alone has approximately

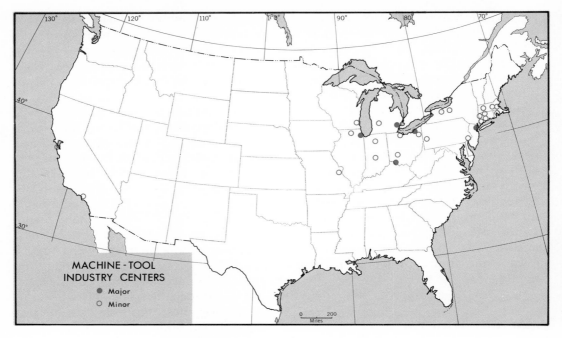

MACHINE-TOOL
INDUSTRY CENTERS
● Major
○ Minor

FIGURE 24.1   *(General Media Corporation)*

one-third of the machine tool industry. Production in the Middle Atlantic states has declined to about 10 percent of the nation's total production. New England has experienced a gradual decline, but is still an important center, especially in the electrical and textile machinery fields and in light metals manufacturing.

Output of the machine tool industry is predominantly "industrial-type" metal-cutting and metal-forming machine tools, costing over $1,000 each, and does not include any bench or portable machine tools designed for use in home work-shops, laboratories, garages, or service shops. These industrial-type machine tools are the "master tools" utilized in the manufacture of thousands of metal products important to national economy.

Metal-cutting tools produce finished parts by boring, drilling, milling, turning, and grinding to remove excess metal. Metal-forming machines shape metal by shearing, bending, stamping, or punch-ing metal into the desired shape.

Shipments of industrial machine tools are decreasing at the rate of 10 percent per year since 1966. This decrease is attributed to the cyclical economic factors inher-ent in the industry. Net new orders for machine tools reached a peak in 1966 and have since generally declined, as demand for machine tools in expansion programs apparently have passed their high-level mark. This, coupled with a softening in the demand for machines to meet defense requirements, has brought about the reduction in new orders.

Imports Significant. For lathes, milling machines, and boring machines, the num-ber of units imported averages up to 30 percent of the market, and accounts for approximately 12 to 15 percent of the value of consumption in those categories. In the United States market for light- and medium-type general purpose machine tools, foreign builders have the competi-tive advantage of lower material and labor costs. A weakening of U.S. machine tool capability in this area could affect the future mobilization base of the country. While inventories of imported machine tools remain high, the domestic producers can generally offer competitive deliveries in most kinds of machine tools, but foreign builders still have the competitive advantage of low prices.

Exports Steady. While the units of machine tools exported are low compared with the number of machine tools imported, values are high. Overseas demand for machine tools is primarily in the highly productive, technologically advanced types of machines where U.S. leadership still has a margin over foreign competition. The strength of the overseas market for U.S. machine tools lies primarily in the highly industrialized countries, whose manufacturing industries demand the cost-reducing features and quality of finished product that U.S. machines ensure.

Foreign demand for general purpose tools remains low, however, since the U.S. builder cannot compete with the lower prices of machine tools produced abroad. Expansion of United States export markets will become increasingly difficult as more models of machine tools heretofore produced exclusively in the United States are added to the product lines of foreign builders and U.S. overseas subsidiaries and licensees.

Machine Tool Technology Advances

The continued technological development of the U.S. tool industry is recognized as important to the economic and competitive well-being of the industry and the nation. To maintain her position of technological excellence and leadership in the international marketplace, the United States machine-tool industry has expended significant amounts of

FIGURE 24.2 *These giant presses which are used to form automobile hoods are representative of the varied products of the machine tool industry. (Oldsmobile Division of General Motors)*

corporate profits in continuing research of new metalworking products and processes, as well as in the further improvement of existing products. Developments attributed to the U.S. machine tool industry have been instrumental in the modernization and improvement of production processes throughout the world.

Numerically controlled machine tools are the most significant contribution to manufacturing processes made by the United States machine tool industry in the past 15 years. Other developments becoming more significant in manufacturing include complex electrical discharge machinery and electrochemical machinery. Now appearing commercially are machines using the laser beam as a cutting tool. The laser has progressed rapidly in the field of metrology, but so far its application is limited in metal re-moval techniques and is not expected to be an important factor for a long time.

Manpower Problem. Although back-logs of machine tools on order have declined steadily, there still exists a strong need for manpower with varying degrees of skill. The need for highly skilled machinists and technicians is more pressing in the machine tool industry than in many other manufacturing fields. While there have been cutbacks in production in some plants, and therefore less need for semi-skilled personnel, the need for first-class machinists and other skilled personnel remains strong. Additional skills in high demand are numerical control technicians, programmers, engineers, and service personnel. Overall trends and projections of the machine tool industry through 1968 appear in Table 24.1.

Table 24.1   Overall Trends and Projections (in millions of dollars except as noted)

Item	1960	1965	1968	Percent Change 1967−68
Machine tool industry (SIC* 3641 and 3642):				
Total shipments	1,206	2,107	2,763	2.0
Shipments of industrial-type machine tools	727	1,300	1,753	− 1.1
Exports, total	210	285	302	3.4
Imports, total	36	60	194	− 4.4
Employment:				
All employees (thousands)	81	97	107	− 0.9
Value added	816	1,343	n.a.	
Metal-cutting machine tools (SIC 3641):				
Total shipments	882	1,524	2,070	4.0
Shipments of industrial-type machine tools	520	1,021	1,392	4.2
Exports, total	128	192	194	− 3.0
Imports, total	26	50	168	− 3.5
Employment:				
All employees (thousands)	59	71	81	1.3
Value added	578	994	n.a.	
Metal-forming machine tools (SIC 3642)				
Total shipments	384	583	893	− 3.8
Shipments of industrial-type machine tools	207	369	361	−17.4
Exports, total	82	98	108	17.4
Imports, total	10	10	26	−10.4
Employment:				
All employees (thousands)	22	26	36	− 7.2
Value added	236	369	n.a.	

n.a. = not available.
*Standard Industrial Classification.
Source: U.S. Bureau of the Census, Annual Survey of Manufactures, 1968, (Washington, D.C.: U.S. Government Printing Office, 1970), Table 3, pp. 18−19.

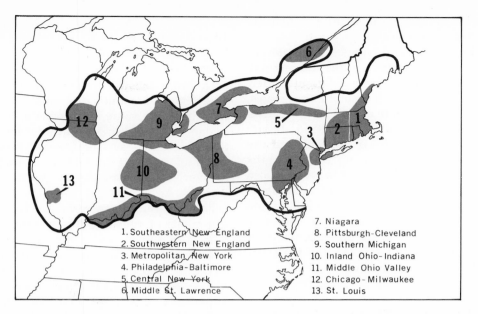

FIGURE 24.3   *The American Manufacturing Region. (General Media Corporation)*

Legend on map:
1. Southeastern New England
2. Southwestern New England
3. Metropolitan New York
4. Philadelphia-Baltimore
5. Central New York
6. Middle St. Lawrence
7. Niagara
8. Pittsburgh-Cleveland
9. Southern Michigan
10. Inland Ohio-Indiana
11. Middle Ohio Valley
12. Chicago-Milwaukee
13. St. Louis

METAL FABRICATING

The geographical distribution of steel consumption by manufacturers closely follows the distribution of steelmaking facilities. Tonnages of steel shapes consumed by metal fabricating industries are largely concentrated in a belt about 350 miles wide, running from the Mississippi River to the East Coast. The top of the belt runs just above Milwaukee and Buffalo; the bottom extends from St. Louis to Baltimore.

Located inside this 350-mile band are over two-thirds of the nation's metal fabricating plants, consuming more than three-fourths of the steel shapes used by manufacturing industries. Within the heavily industrialized belt, metal fabricating plants are even further concentrated. Over one-third of the steel mill shapes are consumed by plants in seven metropolitan areas—Detroit, Chicago, Pittsburgh, Cleveland, Philadelphia, northeastern New Jersey, and Milwaukee.

In addition to the top seven consuming areas, nearly another third of metal fabri-

cator's steel takings is consumed in thirty-two specific state economic areas inside the heavily industrialized belt. Manufacturers' use of steel mill shapes and forms in these thirty-two areas range from 200,000 to 999,999 tons. Only eight other areas in the rest of the country have steel consumption falling in this range.

Most of the nation's machinery, metalworking, automotive and other transportation equipment industries are located in this 350-mile belt. This concentration of steelmaking and steel fabricating industries, based upon the natural advantages of plentiful supplies of iron ore and coal tied together by the Great Lakes transportation system, may continue to attract a large part of the new steel-producing and steel-consuming plants to be built in years to come.

Metal-cutting Tools

Metal-cutting tools are the replaceable cutting units that are inserted into power-driven metal-cutting machine tools and that do the actual cutting or removing of metal, in the form of chips, when the machine tool is operating.

Two of the principal consumers of metal-cutting tools are the automotive and aircraft industries. Despite their increasing demand for metal-cutting tools, the domestic industry faces increased foreign competition at home and abroad, as well as a continuing trend toward use of carbide tooling, moving away from the higher priced solid-tipped to lower priced throwaway inserts. U.S. imports of metal-cutting tools amount to about $15 million per year, as West Germany, Sweden, Great Britain, and Japan become more successful in their efforts to penetrate the United States market.

Special Tools, Dies, Jigs, and Fixtures

Historically, the tool and die industry has been described as a craftsman's industry —a service industry with low-income production and high labor cost. However, the introduction of electrical discharge machines (EDM), and numerical control (N/C) machines, initiated radical changes in toolmaking processes. These technical improvements in industrial production machinery has caused a shift in the product mix of the special tool and die industry. Demand for quality tools and dies has increased while the demand for jigs and fixtures has been adversely affected. These trends, in evidence since 1963, are likely to continue.

The tool and die industry encompasses approximately 6,230 independent or contract shops employing more than 125,000 persons, predominantly tool and die makers, skilled and semi-skilled machinists. About 95 percent of the establishments in the industry have employment ranging from 1 to 49 persons; about 39 percent fall in the 1 to 4 employee range. Because the automotive industry is the tool and die industry's primary customer, most tool and die shops are concentrated in the Michigan area.

Special Industry Machinery and Equipment

Farm and construction machinery and equipment account for nearly three-fourths of the value of shipments in this category. The large volume of construction machinery and equipment exports, equal to one-third of total sales, is shipped to over 140 countries in all parts of the world.

The continuing increase in value of shipments of special industry machinery reflects to a large extent increases in size, quality, and efficiency of machines, including incorporation of advanced technology. Examples include larger and self-propelled equipment for farming, hydrostatic electric drives and hydraulically operated cranes and back-hoes for construction, textile machines with shuttle-less looms, highly sophisticated drilling equipment for oil fields, and a variety of mining and beneficiating machinery.

The value of shipments of farm machinery and equipment has almost doubled since 1960. Increased size and horsepower of tractors and more efficient allied equipment are aiding farmers to continue the upward trend in output per farm worker and per man hour. The average horsepower of tractors in use continues to increase, with total mechanical horsepower on farms still rising. The trend toward larger farms along with the shortage and rising cost of farm labor have provided impetus for the surge in demand for additional horsepower and labor-saving equipment. This trend also puts added emphasis on the production of more expensive, larger, and self-propelled equipment.

A substantial contribution to the total volume of sales continues to come from technological improvements and innovations in harvesting machinery for specialty crops, even though the sale of some types is not sufficient to justify mass production. The latter includes harvesters for many vegetable, fruit, and nut crops.

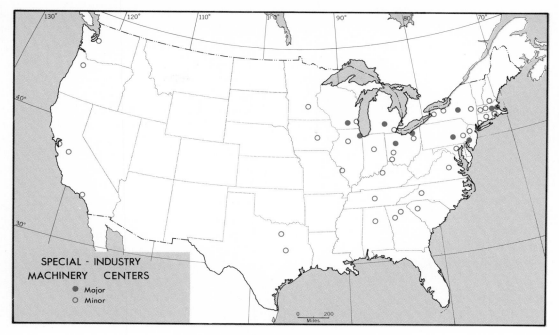

SPECIAL - INDUSTRY
MACHINERY CENTERS
● Major
○ Minor

0   200
Miles

FIGURE 24.4 (General Media Corporation)

The durability, efficiency, and sophistication of U.S. built farm machinery has given these products an unsurpassed reputation in overseas markets. However, higher production and transportation costs and other factors have contributed to the development of locally owned manufacturing facilities. In order to meet this competition, United States manufacturers have established overseas subsidiaries and licensees. This production has been concentrated in the smaller and simpler items that are economically mass produced and find a ready market in the particular country, trading block, or region of the world. U.S. facilities still supply the larger and more sophisticated types of equipment.

Production of farm machinery and equipment is concentrated in the Midwest, primarily in Ohio, Indiana, Illinois, Iowa, and Wisconsin. Eight companies out of approximately 900 producers normally account for 55 percent of the total production.

Mining Machinery and Equipment

The mining machinery industry, with annual shipments more than double those of a decade ago, has utilized progressive management, research and development, improved technology, and the efforts of an active association to bring it rapidly toward the billion dollar mark. About 190 firms own or control some 200 manufacturing establishments, which produce the machines and equipment that extract and beneficiate most of the nation's mineral output.

The primary reason for the industry's growth is the increase in mineral production in the United States, which is growing at the rate of approximately one billion dollars a year. Every ton of metallic and nonmetallic ore, and every ton of solid fuel has to be extracted from the earth and beneficiated in some way before it is ready for industrial use; a great variety of mining machinery and equipment is

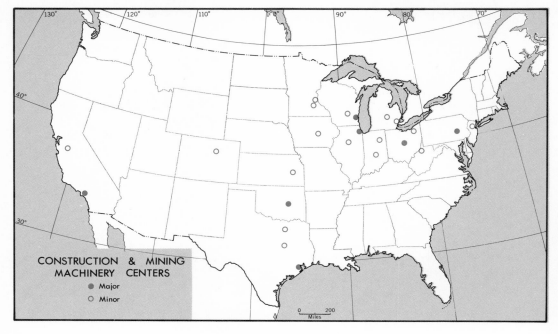

FIGURE 24.5   (*General Media Corporation*)

required. In the same way, the kind and quality of the ore, and the characteristics of the coal dictate the particular type of machinery required for proper beneficiation.

No one producer makes a complete line of products, but most manufacturers could convert their facilities to produce types they do not regularly make. The largest producing states in terms of value of shipments are Colorado, Ohio, Pennsylvania, and Wisconsin.

Oilfield Machinery and Equipment

The oilfield machinery and equipment industry consists of approximately 370 firms employing approximately 37,000 workers in 400 plants. Twenty companies account for 57 percent of the total value of shipments; 90 percent is produced by fifty of the largest companies. Products of the industry consist primarily of drilling, pumping, well-servicing, and exploratory machinery and equipment for use

in oil and gas fields or for drilling water wells. Water well equipment amounts to approximately 5 percent of the total value of shipments.

Drilling contractors account for about 95 percent of the wells completed annually in the United States; the remaining wells are drilled by the producers. Well-drilling contractors, together with well-servicing and workover contractors, account for about 90 percent of the domestic market for oilfield machinery and equipment. A change in the drilling programs of large producers inevitably affects the income of these contractors, and determines the rates of replacement of old and worn-out equipment with new and modern cost-cutting types of machinery with which to meet competition in this highly specialized field.

Productive capacity per well has been increased by the development of hydraulic fracturing and fluid injection, innovations that require new and highly specialized equipment. The increased cost of machinery has more than offset the reduction in

FIGURE 24.6 *Oilfield machinery and equipment is an important segment of the metal fabrication industry. The typical scene here is of "roughnecks" working on drill pipe on a development well. (Texas Gas Transmission Corporation)*

drilling activities, so that the value of shipments has increased.

The contract drilling industry and its techniques have undergone substantial changes during the past ten years as locations shift in the search for new oil resources. Exploration has opened less accessible land areas and offshore areas from Alaska to the Gulf of Mexico, and even in the North Sea. Work in such areas has led to the development of more highly sophisticated exploratory equipment and infinitely more complex drilling operations and equipment. A revolving drill stem is the longest direct transmission of power ever used, and only the highest quality special alloys can withstand the strain.

Oilfield machinery and equipment is exported to 115 countries, primarily to Mexico, Canada, Venezuela, Argentina, Libya, the United Kingdom, Brazil, Australia, Arabia, and Nigeria in that order. The combined exports to these countries represent 50 to 60 percent of the export market.

Food Products Machinery

Food products machinery includes a large variety of machines and equipment employed in the dairy, bakery, confectionery, meat and poultry packing, fruit and vegetable canning and packing, beverage, grain, and sugar processing industries. It also includes other commercial and industrial food products machinery, such as packing and packaging machinery.

Approximately 680 companies in the industry employ about 36,000 workers. Although 60 percent of the firms are in the small business classification, a high level of technical and production skill characterizes the entire group. Research and development expenditures of 30 to 45 percent of net income for the development of new methods and equipment is a common policy of many of the companies.

While the industry is active in foreign markets, heavy competition is encountered from food product machinery manufacturers located in the industrialized

European countries and in Japan. A significant factor holding down U.S. exports has been the establishment of foreign production facilities by various U.S. producers, from which they compete with the lower-cost foreign manufacturers on an equal basis. The nation's major export customers have been Canada, Mexico, and Europe, with steadily increasing markets in Central and South America led by Nicaragua, Panama, Venezuela, Peru, Chile, and Brazil. The South Pacific and Southeast Asian countries, led by Australia, are growing markets for machinery for the processing of food products native to those countries.

The United States also imports food product machinery from most of the industrialized European countries, led by West Germany; Japan too is making a strong entry into the U.S. markets.

METAL FABRICATING OUTSIDE THE UNITED STATES

U.S.S.R. The Soviet Union leads the world in machine tool manufacture with an annual output of 160,000 machines. This eminence has been gained recently, for as late as 1955 the U.S.S.R. was reported to have only 56 percent as many machine tools as the United States.

In pre-revolutionary Russia the share of metal fabrication and machine-building production amounted to roughly 6 percent of world production. In value, this industry was approximately four times less than textiles and six times less than that of the Soviet food industry. The technical level of machine-building factories was low, and the range of items produced very limited; mainly uncomplicated types of equipment were produced within the country.

During the pre-World War II Five Year Plans in the U.S.S.R., several large scale enterprises were constructed; the Moscow, Gorky, and Yaroslavl automobile plants; the Kramatorsk and Ural'sk heavy ma-

chine building plants; the Chelyabinsk, Kharkov, and Stalingrad (Volgograd) tractor plants; the Rostov and Tashkent agricultural machinery plants; the Ordzhonikidze machine tool plant in Moscow; the Gorky milling machine plant; the Kiev automatic machine plant; and the Moscow ball bearing plant.

Technical progress in the metal fabricating industry is manifested not only in the fundamental renewal of the range of items produced, but also in the changed technology of production itself. In foundries, the mechanization of all floor work was completed, and precision methods of casting were widely introduced— cold casting, centrifugal casting, die casting, and extraction casting.

In forge-pressing shops, free forging has been replaced by stamp forging. In machine shops, the aggregate of machine tools has been improved by the introduction of specialized machine tools, and automatic and semi-automatic machines.

West Germany. Germany long has held an important place in the world as a producer of high-quality machine tools and other fabricated metal products. German skilled labor operates at a high degree of efficiency and turns out a wide array of desired metal goods for sale on the world market for about one-third the cost of comparable quality U.S. products.

The metal fabricating industry has been accorded top priority in West Germany. Decentralization and small establishments are characteristic. The lower Rhineland associated with the Ruhr is a major production center, which includes the industrial cities of Dortmund, Cologne, Remscheid, Solingen, Düsseldorf, Duisburg, Rheydt, and München Gladbach. The Neckar Basin, a second center, contains such important industrial cities as Stuttgart, Reutlingen, Göppingen, Heilbron, and Karlsrue.

United Kingdom. Britain was the birthplace of the modern machine tool industry, and by the early 1830s had developed to an advanced stage the boring machine and screw-cutting lathe, as well as other machine tools. Today there are some 350 firms making machine tools, but the greater part of the industry's output comes from about 150 firms. The high degree of specialization makes it possible for the small firms to flourish.

The industry is centered mainly in the Midlands, Yorkshire, and Lancashire, and to a lesser extent near London and Glasgow. The Machine Tool Trades Association of Great Britain is the representative body of most of the machine tool manufacturers and importers, and is responsible for the International Machine Tool Exhibition held in Britain every four years.

Japan. Japan, the only highly industrialized nation in Asia, has not only become one of the world's leading manufacturing powers since World War II but also is the world's fifth largest exporter of material goods. Of these, the metal fabricating industry ranks high. Government tariffs allow only noncompetitive machine tools to enter the country.

Today Japan produces machine tools comparable to those made in the United States and Western Europe. Production is centered in the Tokyo–Yokohama, the Kobe–Osaka, and the Nagoya, Karatsu, and Niigata areas.

In the postwar period a large and increasing part of resources has been poured into private investment in plant and equipment. The ratio of productive investment to gross national product has risen to nearly 20 percent in recent years. Such a large investment, coupled with technological innovation, has swiftly modernized Japan's industries and raised the productivity of workers. Consequently, wage costs per unit of output in manufacturing have not increased in spite of the substantial rise in wages, and this has contributed to the improved competitiveness of Japanese commodities in world markets.

selected references

1. Adams, Walter, *The Structure of American Industry*, 3d ed., New York: The Macmillan Company, 1961.

2. Alexandersson, Gunnar, *Geography of Manufacturing,* Englewood Cliffs, N. J.: Prentice-Hall, Inc. 1967.

3. "Automation in Russia as Viewed by Soviet Engineers," *American Mechanist/Metalworking Manufacturing*, Vol. 104, March 21, 1960, pp. 125–132.

4. Chesham, Guy, "Machine Tools: A Basic British Industry," *New Commonwealth*, Vol. 36, September 1958, pp. 165–169.

5. Finney, B., "Red China Bids for a Place in the Metal Working Sun," *American Machinist,* Vol. 102, September 22, 1958, pp. 96–99.

6. "Foreign Machine Tools in U.S. Metalworking," *American Machinist*, Vol. 103, April 20, 1959, pp. 137–144.

7. Haupert, J. S., "Recent Developments in the Norwegian Metal Industries," *The Journal of Geography*, Vol. 59, No. 2, February 1960, pp. 76–80.

8. Hummell, F. E., "Market Potentials in the Machine Tool Industry—A Case Study," *Journal of Marketing*, Vol. 19, July 1954, pp. 34–41.

9. Lonsdale, R. E., and Thompson, John H., "A Map of the U.S.S.R.'s Manufacturing," *Economic Geography*, Vol. 36, No. 1, January 1960, pp. 36–52.

10. Mandell, Melvin, "The New World of Machine Tools," *Dun's Review and Modern Industry*, Vol. 78, August 1961, pp. 39–46.

11. Miller, E. Willard, *A Geography of Industrial Location*, Dubuque, Iowa: William C. Brown Company, 1970.

12. Neuweiler, N. S., "Tool Engineering in Russia; the Long-Range Plan," *Tool Engineer,* Vol. 44, February 1960, pp. 73–76.

13. Omarovskiy, A. G., "Changes in the Geography of Machine Building in the U.S.S.R.," *Soviet Geography*, Vol. 1, March 1960, pp. 42–56.

14. Smith, A. J. Gibbs, "World Machine Tool Analysis for 1957," *Times Review of Industry*, Vol. 12, November 1958, pp. 85, 87–88.

15. Sanders, Sol, "Japan—Metalworking's Sun is Rising," *American Mechanist/Metalworking Manufacturing,* Vol. 104, December 12, 1960, pp. 113–115.

chapter 25

The Automotive Industry

Automotive manufacturing in the United States originated from the driving force of three classes of inventive individuals: the bicycle makers, the buggy and wagon makers, and the blacksmith–machinists. In the mid-1890s a revolutionary vehicle made its noisy appearance on streets— the horseless carriage. The Duryea brothers of Springfield, Massachusetts, the Stanley brothers of Newton, Massachusetts, Elwood Haynes of Kokomo, Indiana, Ransom E. Olds and Henry Ford in Detroit were all racing each other to change a horseless carriage into what would later be called an automobile. The Duryea brothers are generally given credit for the first successful U.S. automobile in 1893, although Karl Benz, a German from Stuttgart, is credited with producing in 1885 what might be called the first successful gas-powered vehicle. Bicycle makers, buggy makers, and machinists rushed in to make their contributions to the long array of name emblems that were soldered onto automobile radiators.

In 1895 there were only four motor vehicles registered in the United States; in 1900, about 8,000; in 1925, 20 million; in 1954, 59 million; in 1967, 82 million. Thus, the automobile industry is largely a product of the twentieth century.

Historically, the period up to about 1910 was one of pioneering, experimentation, and early growth, during which numerous firms entered and withdrew, with no single firm able to sustain a position of prominence. The second period, 1911 through the end of World War I, was the development of a mass market, with Ford reaching prominence; still the market structure remained fluid as both new entrants and failures were high. The decade of the 1920s represented an era of standardized steel closed bodies (the open tonneau with its isinglass curtains for rainy weather became a has-been), highways were better, cars had achieved near mechanical perfection, and roadside breakdowns were no longer the hazard they once were. The era of bicycle makers,

FIGURE 25.1   *This 1912 Cadillac was the first car to use the newly invented Kettering self-starter. Hand cranking to start automobiles soon became a thing of the past. (General Motors photograph)*

FIGURE 25.2   *A modern freeway in Los Angeles County, California. (California Division of Highways)*

wagon makers, and self-made mechanics was over. In their place came college-trained mechanical engineers who knew both engines and assembly line layout methods for low-cost car manufacture, and also the super-salesmen and the capital lenders. The smaller independent car makers had shrunk in number from 88 in 1921 to 63 in the mid-twenties, and many faced the alternative of merging or going under. The next decade was to see the curtain rung on all but a few survivors. The post-World War II period has been marked by an industry concentration soaring to new heights, with General Motors attaining an increasingly dominant position.

Location

Michigan is the center of the automobile industry, and Detroit the epicenter. The industry employs 475,000 workers in Michigan—almost half of the total labor force engaged in manufacturing. Detroit alone has almost 40 percent of all auto

workers in the United States, and Flint has another 6 percent.

Although there is a tendency toward dispersal of automobile and automobile parts manufacturing, over 70 percent is concentrated in a triangular area extending from Flint and Detroit, Michigan to Cleveland, Ohio.

The triangle owes its importance in this industry largely to historical accident. Detroit, the automotive center, for example, is no better situated geographically for such production than are several other cities bordering the lower Great Lakes. Fortunately for Detroit, Henry Ford, the first successful automobile manufacturer, was born in Michigan and elected to locate his plant there.

Once the industry began, there were many favorable factors within the area to keep it there. The early models were little more than motored (horseless) carriages, and the carriage trade was a well-established local industry because of the presence of hardwood as a raw material. Marine engine building was also important, facilitating the adaptation of an engine suitable for use in automobiles. A skilled labor pool likewise was available. Also, the flat terrain made it easier for these low-powered vehicles to win public acceptance. Presence of a hilly landscape possibly would have retarded development or discouraged the pioneer builders entirely. Finally, metal fabricating was well-established and has expanded to keep pace with the growth of the automotive industry.

Other manufacturers followed in Ford's footsteps, and mass production of automobiles began on a large scale. Volume production combined with low prices put the automobile within reach of all classes. This feat was accomplished through division of labor, the use of interchangeable parts, and standardization. In 1951, the one-hundred millionth American automobile was produced. Annual output has now topped the ten million mark.

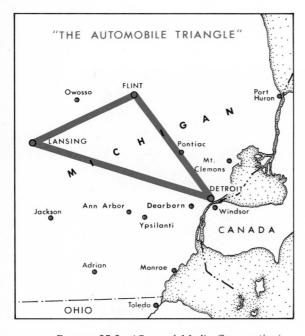

FIGURE 25.3   (*General Media Corporation*)

FIGURE 25.4 *An automotive assembly line. (Ford Motor Company of Canada, Ltd.)*

Since 1900, more than 2,700 different makes of automobiles found their way to the market place. Between 1903 and 1926, over 183 different automotive companies were started; by 1927, there were only 44 companies left; and from 1930 on, the Big Three—General Motors, Ford, and Chrysler—have produced more than 90 percent of all automobiles manufactured.

Social Changes

Few inventions have had as revolutionary an impact on society as the automobile, which has destroyed and created industries. The automobile has given rise to traffic police, motor vehicle bureaus, auto rapair and accessories businesses, road building, finance companies, insurance concerns, driver's schools, taxis, buses, trucking, and drive-in shopping centers, banks, and movies. It has caused profound economic and social changes in American life, as epitomized by the rapid development of surburban communities, as well as many problems that are results of the increased mobility, among them traffic control, traffic deaths and accidents, and problems centering on driving and drink-

ing. The automobile accounts either directly or indirectly for about one-seventh of the nation's payroll, and has ranked first as a manufactured export item since 1929. The industry is the largest consumer of gasoline, rubber, steel, lead, and nickel; it also consumes large quantities of aluminum, copper, cotton, and zinc.

Input–Output Relations

The relative importance of the auto industry in American economy is indicated by its contribution to the fluctuations of a number of major economic series. If industries closely allied to autos are also taken into account, the role of automobiles obviously would be correspondingly larger. Car sales, accessory equipment including tires, petroleum products, and the various services and fees associated with purchasing and maintaining automobiles amount to roughly 8.3 percent of Gross National Product (GNP), as compared with "auto product" as such, which accounts for about 4.2 percent of Gross National Product.

This type of measurement, however, throws little light on the interindustry relationships in which the auto industry is involved. Such relationships should be examined in order to improve understanding of both direct and indirect factors surrounding the role played by the auto industry in the economy. In recent years, development of input–output tables has facilitated the study of such industrial relationships.

Since input–output tables indicate the detailed interdependence of industries, they are, in essence, studies of production functions; in other words, input–output tables indicate how much output can result from individual industries, given certain qualities and combinations of inputs.

Auto industry purchases from and sales to various industrial groups are indicated in Table 25.1. In the table, "inputs" does not include capital equipment. All capital purchases are treated as final expenditures and are included in the "gross private fixed capital formation" category of final demand of the supplying industry

Table 25.1   Input–Output Schedule for the Auto Industry

Inputs	Percent	Outputs	Percent
Purchases from:		Sales to:	
Mining	0.1	Agriculture	0.2
Construction	0.3	Mining	*
Auto industry	29.0	Construction	*
Other manufacturing	30.1	Auto industry	29.0
Transportation, communi-cations, and public services	2.6	Other manufacturing	0.4
		Transportation, communi-cations, and public services	0.4
Wholesale and retail trade	3.1	Wholesale and retail trade	0.7
Finance, insurance and real estate	0.7	Services	4.8
Services	2.7	Govt. enterprises	0.1
Govt. enterprises	0.2		
Other industries	2.1	Total sales	35.6%
Total purchases	70.9%	Final demand:	
Value added	29.0%	Personal consumption expenditures	39.2
		Gross private fixed capital formation	15.2
		Net inventory changes	−2.3
		Gross exports	3.9
		Federal government purchases	1.3
		State and local govt. purchases	1.9
		Total final demand	59.2%
		Transfers to other industries[a]	5.0%
TOTAL INPUTS[b]	99.9%	TOTAL OUTPUTS[b]	99.8%

*Negligible

[a]Refers to the output of goods considered secondary to the industry—that is, those that would not come under the definition of goods produced by the "Motor Vehicle and Equipment" industry. Such goods are treated in this manner, rather than being redefined as the primary output of another industry, because of the difficulty of isolating the inputs necessary for the secondary goods. The assumption is made that the secondary output of an industry is a constant portion of its total output.

[b]Totals are less than 100 percent because of rounding.

Source: Office of Business Economics, U.S. Department of Commerce, "The Interindustry Structure of the United States: A Report on the 1958 Input–Output Study," Survey of Current Business (November 1964), Tables 1 and 2.

(see "output" side of the table). This is done for two reasons:

1. It is consistent with procedures used in the National Income Accounts.
2. Since capital equipment obviously will produce output for more than one year, the relationship between capital purchases and output in a particular year will not be stable.

As an illustration of how capital equipment is treated in the input–output tables, assume that General Motors buys a computer from Sperry Rand and sells a locomotive to the Northern Pacific Railroad. The purchase of the computer will be classified under the "gross private fixed capital formation" heading of final demand for the "Office, Computing, and Accounting Machines" industry. But the transaction does not affect the accounts of the automotive industry. The sale of the locomotive will be classified in the same way, but for the "Automotive" industry.

AUTOMOTIVE PRODUCTION OUTSIDE THE UNITED STATES

Canada

The Canadian automobile industry started in 1904 when the Ford Motor Company of Canada, Ltd., began to manufacture automobiles for the Canadian market and for export. In that year, 17 employees were paid $12,000 to help assemble 117 cars. All parts were ferried across the river from Detroit. Today Ford of Canada employs about 25,000 workers.

Located across the river from Detroit, Windsor, Canada shares with Oakville, Hamilton, and Oshawa the bulk of Canadian automobile manufacturing. These four cities account for 98 percent of Canada's auto and auto parts industries.

The Chrysler Corporation of Canada began production in Windsor in 1924. This company recently doubled and now employs around 9,000 people. Packard motor

FIGURE 25.5   *An aerial view of the large Ford of Canada car and truck production plant at Oakville. (Ford Motor Company of Canada, Ltd.)*

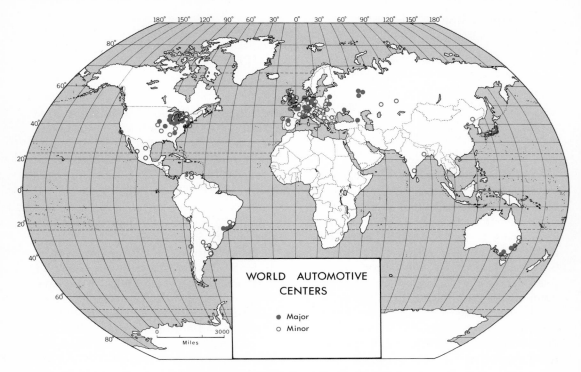

FIGURE 25.6   (*General Media Corporation*)

Table 25.2   **Motor Vehicles, Production and Assembly**

Country	Code	Production (thousands)			
		1953	*1960*	*1966*	*1967*
World	A	8,130	12,810	19,220	18,260
	B	2,360	3,690	5,440	5,650
United States	A	6,116.9	6,674.8	8,598.3	7,436.8
	B	1,206.3	1,194.5	1,731.2	1,539.5
West Germany	A	387.9	1,816.8	2,830.1	2,295.7
	B	102.4	237.8	220.5	185.2
Japan	A	8.5	165.1	877.7	1,375.8
	B	137.6	595.2	1,442.1	1,797.2
United Kingdom	A	594.8	1,352.7	1,603.7	1,552.0
	B	239.5	458.0	438.7	385.1
France	A	368.4	1,135.6	1,761.3	1,751.8
	B	129.5	233.6	262.9	257.9
Italy	A	143.7	595.9	1,282.4	1,439.2
	B	30.8	48.9	83.5	103.5
Canada	A	360.4	325.8	701.5	720.8
	B	120.6	72.0	200.6	226.5
U.S.S.R.	A	79.4	138.8	230.2	251.4
	B	300.3	501.3	654.8	697.3

A—Passenger cars
B—Commercial vehicles
Source: United Nations *Statistical Yearbook,* 1968 (New York: United Nations, 1969), Table 140, p. 317.

cars were built in Windsor from 1931 until the company joined Studebaker (1954) to become Studebaker—Packard with headquarters at Hamilton, now defunct.

Canada ranks seventh in the world in production of automobiles. In the late 1950s production began to decline drastically, and the industry started to lose its foothold in overseas markets. The small demand at home combined with foreign competition has greatly endangered the Canadian automobile economy.

West Germany, Great Britain, France, and Italy are the leading automobile producers in Europe in the order named. The industry has become an increasingly important sector of European economy—directly through its share in total output, employment, and exports, and indirectly through the growing number of dependent subsidiary industries and services.

West Germany

In a country of nearly 60 million inhabitants, motorization is gradually approaching American proportions, with cars serving both for transportation and as symbols of prestige. More than 10 million automobiles clog West German streets and *Autobahnen*—one for every six people—and pleasure is rapidly replacing business as the main buying motivation. Output and exports to all destinations are still expanding, and the flow of orders suggests that prospects for the future are good. However, a substantial shift from export sales to the domestic market has occurred, with the result that delivery times for home sales have been shortened. As incomes rise, new classes of buyers are entering the car market; for the same reason demand for large cars is growing strongly while sales of some domestically produced small and midget cars have decreased, creating difficulties for some branches of the industry.

Five companies—Volkswagen, Mercedes, Opel, Borgward, and Ford—have experienced the greatest increases. German automobiles are especially popular in the United States; since 1955 they have accounted for more than one-third of German exports to the U.S. The Volkswagen is the most popular foreign import and leads all others in total sales, challenging the U.S. compact models built to compete with it. Its place in the U.S. and world market appears to be assured. The Mercedes competes in the luxury class and is rated as one of the best in its field.

Japan

The growth of the motor industry in Japan has been spectacular. While other industries have been cutting production, motor manufacturers have maintained a 10 percent growth rate—a figure that emphasizes the dominant position they have achieved in the economy. The million mark was reached in 1963, and production has since continued to soar beyond two million. Japan now is third in world automobile production, surpassed only by the United States and West Germany.

The industry exhibits certain peculiarities when compared with those in the West. One such difference is the popularity of vehicles with small engine capacities—360 cubic centimeters or less. This type of transport was first produced in 1952; it was the result of the late arrival of motorization in Japan, coupled with the limitations imposed by the comparatively low income of the Japanese consumer. A second characteristic of the industry is the low ratio of private cars to heavier vehicles such as buses and trucks.

The heavier motor vehicles made in Japan have long been highly regarded, and now the new passenger cars rival the best that the United States and Europe can offer. Toyota and Nissan are the two leading manufacturers; others include Isuzu, Hino, Mitsubishi, Prince, Fuji, Toyo Kogyo, Daihatsu, Honda, and Suzuki. Japan leads the world in the manufacture and export of motorcycles, producing about 2,600,000 annually; Honda accounts for about 65 percent of this total. The bulk of foreign sales are made in the United States and Great Britain.

Great Britain

The British automotive industry is located mainly in the Midlands and the London area. It consists of a relatively small number of assembly firms, headed by the "Big Five" (British Motor Corporation, Ford, Rootes, Standard, and Vauxhall) and backed by a large number of specialist body and component manufacturers. The "Big Five" are responsible for about 90 percent of the output of complete vehicles of all kinds; the balance of the industry's motor production (other than tractors) consists of heavy commercial vehicles, sports, and other specialty cars.

There are roughly 20 specialty car producers. Of these, the best known are Rolls-Royce, Daimler, Armstrong Siddley, Jaguar, and Rover. They cater either to the luxury class, such as the Rolls-Royce (considered by many experts to be the finest car made), or to sports car enthusiasts, the Jaguar being one of the more popular vehicles in this field.

The largest foreign market for British-made cars is the United States, which accounts for more than one-third of total exports, followed by Canada, Australia and South Africa. The largest European market is Sweden.

Automotive research is carried out at Lindley, Warwickshire, by the Motor Research Industry Association, an autonomous body founded in 1946 and partly financed by the Department of Scientific and Industrial Research, but mainly by the industry itself. Individual firms also have their own research and development facilities.

France

Four companies produce passenger cars in France—Renault, Citroen, Simca, and Puegot; the first three have their main factories in Paris. Despite attempts since World War II to decentralize the industry, the Paris market absorbs a quarter of the cars sold in France and, like Detroit, is the center of the industry, which evolved from the coach-building and other craft enterprises involving skill in the use of metals, wood, and fabrics.

Unlike the others, Puegot makes its

FIGURE 25.7   *The Jaguar car factory in Coventry, England. (The British Travel and Holidays Association)*

cars in the provinces, with the main plant located at Sochaux (Montebeliard) on the edge of the Jura. Like other firms, Puegot also built new factories since the war at Dyon, Vesaul, and Mulhouse with subsidiaries at Lille and St. Etienne.

Automobiles have declined from 48 to 43 percent of France's total exports; although French manufacturers, in common with others, are exploring new export markets, some time will be needed for the establishment of new trade flows. The French Renault, for example, lost one-third of its sales in the U.S. market in the 1960s, and heavy stocks appear to have accumulated. However, it seems reasonable to suppose that the setback undergone by the French small car was due not so much to competition from the compact models as to the rapid advance of the Volkswagen.

The decline in sales to the United States will have to be solved, for the most part, by expanding domestic sales. In this connection, the growth of replacement demand is expected to accelerate in the near future; more than one million passenger cars (of a total of 5.6 million French cars) are over 20 years old. On the other hand, demand from first-time buyers is likely to develop only slowly, since the ratio of cars to population already is comparatively high. However, demand could be stimulated considerably by a reduction in taxation on cars and gasoline.

Italy

No country has embraced the automobile revolution with greater enthusiasm than Italy, which ranks a strong fourth in Europe. As in many other fields of engineering, production is dominated by the vast integrated concern of Fiat at Turin, where Lancia's main factory is also located. Fiat employs about 80,000 persons in the area, and makes 80 percent of the Italian motor vehicles as well as many other forms of transport. Other centers of the industry are Milan and Naples, where the

Alfa Romeo is assembled; Madena, home of the Ferrari plant; and Bolzano, where the Lancia is made. Fiat has several factories overseas, notably in South America, as well as designers and technical connections in Spain, Poland, and the U.S.S.R. Italy is second to Japan in the production and export of motorcycles, producing approximately 600,000 per year. Export trade for Italian cycles is largely with other European nations.

U.S.S.R.

Although the Soviet Union is slowly expanding car production, an automobile revolution has yet to take place in this land of 240 million people. For the foreigner a striking feature of Soviet towns is the relative absence of automobile traffic. Moscow is perhaps the only capital in the world where one can drive to the finest theater—the Bolshoi—and park his car right in front on the evening of a sold-out performance.

Although it will be some years before there is any drastic change, the government is moving to meet the rising demand for cars. Plans call for about 700,000 cars in 1970. The spurt will come largely from the new plant in Togliatti, 50 miles west of Kuibyshev and 500 miles southeast of Moscow, which the U.S.S.R. purchased from the Italian Fiat company. Other steps also are being taken: the Moscow Auto Plant, which produces small cars, is being expanded; the auto works in Izhevsk also will start producing small cars; and new models of the Volga, Moskvich, and Zaporozhets are planned.

selected references

1. Anderson, R. E., *The Story of the American Automobile*, Wahington, D.C.: Public Affairs Press, 1950.

2. "The Automobile Industry," *Italian Affairs*, Vol. 7, 1958, pp. 2045–2051.

3. Bannock, Graham, "The Motor Industry

in Western Europe: Possible Effects of a European Free Trade Area Upon the Industry," *Steel Review*, April 1958, pp. 42–47.

4. Davies, Wayne K., and Briggs, Ronald, "Automobile Establishments in Liverpool: A Steady State Distribution," *The Professional Geographer*, Vol. 19, No. 6, November 1967, pp. 323–329.

5. "French Cars Are a World Wide Hit," *France Actuelle*, Vol. 7, November 1958, pp. 1–8.

6. Goodwin, William, "Relocation of the British Motor Industry," *The Professional Geographer*, Vol. 14, No. 4, July 1962, pp. 4–8.

7. Hurley, Neil P., "The Automotive Industry: A Study in Industrial Location," *Land Economics*, Vol. 35, February 1959, pp. 1–14.

8. "The Japanese Automobile Industry," *Glimpses of Asia*, Vol. 6, May 1959, pp. 173–175.

9. Maxcy, G., and Silberston, A., *The Motor Industry*, London: George Allen and Unwin, Ltd., 1959.

10. Miller, E. Willard, *A Geography of Industrial Location*, Dubuque, Iowa: William C. Brown Company, 1970.

11. *Motor Industry of Great Britain*, Society of Motor Manufacturers and Traders, 1960.

12. Nutter, G. Warren, *The Growth of Industrial Production in the Soviet Union*, Princeton, N. J.: Princeton University Press, 1962.

13. "Red Autos, An Iron Curtain Separates Production and Demand," *American Machinist*, Vol. 103, November 1959, pp. 121–124.

14. Schwalberg, B. K., "Soviet Automobile Industry: A Current Assessment," *Automotive Industries*, Vol. 118, January 1, 1958, pp. 60–77.

15. Shabad, Theodore, "The Challenge of Soviet Industry," *Geographical Review*, Vol. 48, No. 4, October 1958, pp. 573–575.

In the world's shipbuilding competition, Japan stands alone at the head of the list, with almost 35 percent of new merchant ship construction. Sweden, Germany, and the United Kingdom follow, with about 10 percent each, then far behind, in fourteenth place, comes the United States, with less than two percent of new construction.

chapter **26**

Shipbuilding

It was not always so. During 1942–45, under the pressure of heavy wartime demand, U.S. shipyards delivered over 5,000 ships to the American and Allied merchant fleets. During that period, merchant ship construction exceeded $12 billion, and commercial shipyards employed some four million people. At their peak production rate, United States yards could have replaced the entire prewar fleet within sixteen weeks, and the entire world fleet in less than three year's time.

Today, however, the situation is different. The handful of commercial shipyards left in operation, building ships by time-honored methods for a small guaranteed market, have failed to keep up with the efficient yards built abroad since the beginning of the postwar period. The Navy's $2 to $3 billion annual spending for repair and maintenance work is spread around to keep commercial yards operating, and the fourteen shipping lines that receive federal operating subsidies are required by law to buy their new ships from American yards. But, despite a ship-replacement program that has produced 110 modern ships over the past decade, one Congressional critic claims that "72 percent of the existing merchant fleet is composed of obsolescent, inefficient, and uneconomical ships."

All in all, U.S. yards today have only 45 merchant ships under construction or on order. In terms of tonnage, American yards build less than .5 million tons annually, compared to the 4–5 million tons produced by Japanese shipyards and the 1 million tons or so constructed each year by German, British, and Swedish yards.

This feast-or-famine situation has historic parallel. During World War I, as during World War II, the nation's shipyards produced millions of tons of merchant shipping, but those ships were unable to compete two decades later with the efficient ships produced in the interim by modern yards abroad. And then as now, U.S. ships dominated the world's sea lanes in the immediate postwar period, but lost in the competition of later decades.

WHO RULES THE WAVES?

The United States in 1945 operated 60 percent of the world's merchant fleet tonnage and, even though it sold off a substantial part of that fleet over the next several years, it still accounted for 36 percent of the total in 1948. Since then, however, the U.S. active fleet has declined, from 4.5 to 4 million tons in tankers and from 8.5 to 6 million tons in dry cargo ships. Meanwhile, total world tonnage has almost quadrupled for tankers and almost doubled for dry cargo ships, so the U.S. flag share has now dropped to less than 8 percent of the total.

On the other hand, the U.S. fleet is supplemented—perhaps almost doubled—by those "flags of convenience" that are under "effective American control." Registration data are somewhat inexact for ships registered under Panamanian, Liberian, Honduran, and other convenience flags, but perhaps one half of such tonnage is owned by Greek citizens. This system permits the smaller states to gain revenue from the use of their registry, and it enables shipowners to avoid restrictions, U.S. maritime laws, and high U.S. taxes and labor costs—albeit at the sacrifice of U.S. subsidy payments as well.

Western European flags are those most commonly seen on the world's lanes today, but Japan and the U.S.S.R. hope to attain dominions in coming decades. In 1968, the British merchant fleet amounted to 20 million tons; the Liberian flag-of-convenience fleet, 23.8 million tons; the Norwegian fleet, 18.6 million tons; the U.S., 19.1 million tons; Japan, 16.1 million tons; the U.S.S.R., 8.5 million tons; and Greece, 7.1 million tons.

The U.S.S.R. today has 236 ships on order from foreign shipyards, and also has a substantial shipbuilding capability itself. According to present plans, its merchant fleet may be twice the size of the American fleet by 1972. Japanese

Table 26.1 Merchant Vessels, Tonnage Launched (thousand gross registered tons)

Country	1953	1960	1967	Percent Change 1960–67
World	5,095	8,356	15,780	+ 88.8
Denmark	142	219	488	+122.8
France	235	594	553	− 6.9
Italy	263	434	507	+ 16.8
Japan	557	1,732	7,497	+332.9
Norway	118	198	522	+163.6
Poland	—	227	400	+ 76.2
Spain	46	161	406	+152.2
Sweden	485	711	1,308	+ 84.0
United Kingdom	1,317	1,331	1,298	− 2.5
United States	528	485	242	− 50.1
West Germany	818	1,092	1,002	− 8.2
Yugoslavia	13	161	273	+ 69.6

Source: United Nations Statistical Yearbook, 1968 (New York: United Nations, 1961), Table 139, p. 316.

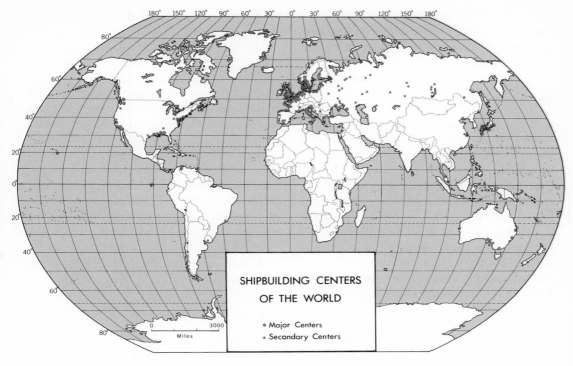

FIGURE 26.1   *(General Media Corporation)*

shipbuilders meanwhile hope to expand their fleet eight-fold by 1980, to some 120 million tons.

THE UNITED STATES

West Coast commercial shipyard employment, which plummeted from 500,000 at its wartime peak to 9000 in 1950, has since increased to about 22,000—roughly 9000 in Washington, 8000 in southern California, and 5000 in northern California yards. In the rest of the country, about 150,000 workers are now employed in ship-repair and shipbuilding (Naval shipyards, which have generally exhibited a much more stable employment pattern, now employ about 24,000 civilian workers in California and about 10,000 in Washington).

Over the past decade, East Coast yards have built 138 merchant ships, whereas Gulf Coast yards have built 40 and West Coast yards only 26 ships. The relatively poor West Coast performance reflects cost considerations that differ between the coasts. For example, a typical freighter that costs $12.0 million to build on the East Coast may cost as much as $12.6 million in West Coast yards.

According to Maritime Administration data, West Coast costs are about 5 percent higher than East Coast and about 9 percent higher than Gulf Coast costs. No trend is visible in the direction of cost equalization, since labor and materials costs have generally risen at the same rate in each region of the country.

Of the 45 merchant ship contracts awarded during the last three years, the East was low bidder 16 times, the Gulf coast 25 times, and the West Coast 4 times. But the Maritime Administration contends that geographical cost differences are "not sufficiently significant to justify any remedies to equalize costs between the coastal districts." West Coast yards formerly received a cost differential of this type, but the legislation permitting this differentiation was repealed by the 87th Congress.

Ships and Prices

Construction work in U.S. private yards centers around the Maritime Administration's 20-year, 300-ship construction program, which got underway a decade ago. About 110 of these up-to-date merchant vessels have already been delivered to U.S. shipping lines, which in return for operating subsidies are required by law to buy their new ships from high-cost American yards.

Ship prices, both here and abroad, have roughly doubled since World War II. A standard dry-cargo ship, mass-produced in World War II at $280 per ton, cost as much as $1000 per ton during the shipping crisis generated by the Suez Controversy. Prices later dropped about 25 percent below that peak, but about half of the drop has been removed since 1961.

U.S. prices have risen gradually during the last several years. Shipbuilders have been trying to regain normal profit margins, since previous assignments were relatively profitless because of competitive pressures and because of the limited amount of work available. Moreover, they have recently encountered difficulty in holding their labor force to meet current commitments as well as growing Vietnam requirements. Rising wage rates in other industries have also put pressure on shipbuilding wages and on material costs.

But foreign prices have also been rising. Japanese price levels have increased sharply under the pressure of a massive 9-million-ton backlog of orders. European prices also have reflected rising backlogs. On the other hand, European firms are strongly price competitive, since they are contract hungry because of the increased capacity made available

by recent mergers and technological improvements.

Fast Deployment

The Navy has not only turned to the Swedes for advanced techniques, but has also enlisted the aid of several technically oriented aerospace firms in developing a large fleet of high-speed transports—FDLs or Fast Deployment Logistic Ships. It has awarded three study contracts to aerospace firms to encourage the spin-off of technologically advanced techniques into the field of shipbuilding, and on the basis of these studies, it plans to award a $1-billion contract for up to thirty ships for delivery by 1972.

U.S.: Modernization

In another development, the Navy has awarded the largest blocks of ship procurement contracts since World War II, in the form of a $250-million contract for 17 landing ships and another $250-million contract for 20 destroyer escorts. The technological advances achieved through this and the FDL program should help U.S. shipyards catch up with foreign shipyards—for example, in the greater automation of steel handling (the most costly item in cargo ship construction), increased use of building docks rather than ship-ways for more concurrent outfitting, and prefabrication of increasingly large ship sections.

In yet another development, several federal agencies have recently advanced plans for the construction of three or four more nuclear merchant ships. The earlier resistance to nuclear-powered ships has declined as the technological advantages of such construction have become more apparent, and also as the cost differential in favor of non-nuclear ships has declined from 50 to roughly 20 percent. In fact, the operator of the first American nuclear merchant ship, the USS Savannah, is so

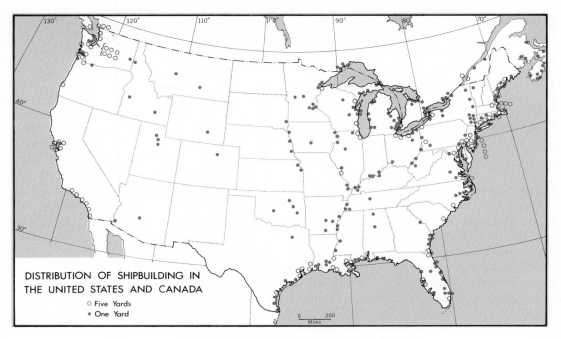

DISTRIBUTION OF SHIPBUILDING IN
THE UNITED STATES AND CANADA
○ Five Yards
● One Yard

FIGURE 26.2   (General Media Corporation)

FIGURE 26.3   A Navy ship under construction in a U.S. yard. High labor and material costs make it extremely difficult for American firms to compete with foreign ship construction yards. (Todd Shipyard Corporation)

impressed with its capabilities that he has submitted applications to the Maritime Administration for three more nuclear ships for his foreign trade routes.

OTHER SHIPBUILDING NATIONS

Japan

Japan, which accounts for more than one-third of the world's total construction, produced more than five million tons of ships in 1968. Today it has 34 yards capable of building ships of 10,000 tons or above, and it increases its yard facilities by 20 percent annually. Two-thirds of Japanese shipyard production is exported, and this $700 million in overseas sales accounts for one-tenth of the nation's total exports—a far cry from the Occupation period when Japan was completely prohibited from replacing its destroyed merchant fleet.

Mammoths. Japan's most spectacular achievement is the construction of giant ships in the 200,000-ton category. Earlier giants—the 17,000 ton tanker of two decades ago—were later outmoded by 100,000 ton giants. The latter, however, have recently been superseded in their turn through the development of new construction techniques and larger shipbuilding docks. Four Japanese yards now contain docks with 200,000-ton ship capacity, and an even larger dock is now underway.

These giant tankers are an entirely new phenomenon, resulting from the spectacular increase in world petroleum demand and the spectacular economies available in moving oil in bulk from Persian Gulf fields to Western markets. The mammoth ships are of course restricted to special-purpose runs and to specially built ports. In fact, one major firm plans to supply the European market from a million-ton tank farm on the Atlantic

Coast of Ireland, since it considers the North Sea and the English Channel to be too shallow for these Japanese super-tankers to enter.

Sweden: Technique

Sweden, like Japan, has been a pioneer in developing ship-construction techniques. As evidence of this, the U.S. recently negotiated for license rights on a number of Swedish patents after the U.S. Secretary of the Navy investigated the mechanized yards at Ardenal, Sweden.

The Ardenal yard can produce a 70,000-ton tanker with only 40 percent of the manhours required by the same firm's conventional shipyard. The new yard emphasizes prefabrication, though of course this is now a standard technique. What is unique is the use of a small work force with very advanced equipment, operating under cover along a straight production line.

The final stage of an Ardenal launching typifies the new style. The ship emerges from a covered dry dock in sections. Hydraulic jacks push the stern into the open, and hydraulic doors close around the inner end of the completed section; the next section is then assembled and joined to the first by a fast-moving welding machine, and so on. The ship is fitted-out with wiring, plumbing, and engines as it emerges into the open part of the dry dock, and the completed ship is then floated in the dry dock—not launched down-ways—and readied for sea trials within another week.

Britain has for centuries been one of the most important shipbuilding nations. Modern shipbuilding dates from the middle of the nineteenth century, when the iron-clad, steam-driven vessel replaced the earlier sailing ship. Britain led the way in the substitution of steel for iron, and in the development of the steam turbine. Between 1890 and 1913, Britain produced more than half the world's

FIGURE 26.4   *A 40,000-ton Japanese supertanker, under construction in Yokohama, Japan. (Mitsubishi Japan Heavy Industry Co., Ltd.)*

FIGURE 26.5   *Shipbuilding at Belfast, Northern Ireland. (The British Travel Association)*

new tonnage, and in 1920, launched over two million tons. In the interwar years, the problem of surplus capacity common to all shipbuilding countries caused a substantial drop in activity and periodic heavy unemployment. During World War II the industry was fully occupied in building and repairing warships and merchant ships, and a high level of activity in the building and repair of merchant ships has been maintained since 1945.

Well over three-fourths of the tonnage of ships built in Britain comes from four areas: the River Clyde in Scotland; the northeast coast of England, along the lower reaches of the Tyne, Wear, and Tees, and at West Hartlepool and Blyth; on the northwest coast of England, on the River Mersey and at Barrow-in-Furness; and Belfast, Ireland.

Over the past twenty years, traditional methods of shipbuilding have undergone radical changes, primarily due to advances in welding technique. These have led to the production of ships in large units, each 50 to 60 tons in weight, prefabricated under cover and rapidly assembled for launching.

France. The French shipbuilding industry is both concentrated and dispersed. Concentration is represented by the shipyards of the lower Loire, which possesses 60 percent of the country's shipbuilding capacity. The remaining 40 percent is distributed among many other ports. Altogether there are fourteen yards that are able to build vessels of 3,000 tons or more.

The most widely dispersed shipbuilding centers include Dunkerque, Cherbourg, Brest, Lorient, La Pallice, and Queyries. Brest and Lorient have naval bases and share some of the naval construction work with Toulon and La Seyne. France has a total capacity of some 700,000 tons, but average yearly output is only about 450,000 tons. As in Britain, the industry has had to struggle for orders in the face of foreign competiton, especially Japan.

West Germany. During the last fifty years, astonishing progress has been made in shipbuilding. Begun in order to construct warships with which to challenge Britain's mastery of the sea, the movement naturally spread to the creation of a merchant navy that would provide the experience and familiarity with the sea so necessary before a nation hitherto of landsmen could take to the ocean. Now there are large shipyards at Hamburg and its outport of Elmshorn, at Kiel, Lubeck, Bremerhaven, and Emden. The total tonnage of shipping launched has exceeded that of Great Britain since 1958.

U.S.S.R. The emergence of the Soviets as shipbuilders is new and startling. Long a major land power with little or no interest in foreign commerce, the first indication of Soviet progress in the field came in December, 1965, when a Greek businessman ordered 30 Soviet-built vessels, totaling more than 400,000 gross tons, in exchange for traditional Greek agricultural goods totaling $105 million.

Large-scale industrial shipbuilding is relatively new in the Soviet Union. Only a few years ago the bulk of new Soviet tonnage was supplied by East German and Polish yards, with many vessels ordered from Japan and Western Europe, especially West Germany, Denmark, and Finland. Since 1965 the Soviets themselves have turned out more than half of the one million tons of new tonnage that they add each year to their merchant fleet. At present the U.S.S.R. has the sixth largest and the most modern merchant fleet in the world. In 1961 it held only eleventh place. Shipyards in Nikolayev, Kherson, and Novorossisk on the Black Sea and Leningrad on the Baltic Sea are the major centers.

selected references

1. Alexandersson, Gunnar, *Geography of Manufacturing*, Englewood Cliffs, N. J.: Prentice-Hall, Inc. 1967.

2. "Britain's Shipbuilding Industry," *Labor and Industry in Britain*, Vol. 14, September 1956, pp. 110–115.

3. Duff, Peter, "Shipbuilding in Western Europe," *Steel Review*, Vol. 10, April 1958, pp. 52–62.

4. Dury, G. H., *The British Isles, A Systematic and Regional Geography*, New York: W. W. Norton & Company, Inc., 1961, pp. 254–255, 260–261, 265–266, 309–310.

5. Eskichi, Azami, "The Shipbuilding Industry: Past and Present (Japan)," *Japan Quarterly*, Vol. 5, July–September 1958, pp. 370–380.

6. Hibino, Tsuneji, *Meet Japan*, Tokyo: Charles B. Tuttle Company, 1966.

7. Jones, Leslie, *Shipbuilding in Britain*, Cardiff, Wales: University of Wales Press, 1957.

8. Kassell, B. M. "Marine Engineering Notes From the Soviet Press," *Journal of American Society of Naval Engineers*, Vol. 71, May 1959, pp. 337–346.

9. Little, C. H., "Giant Bulk Carriers," *Canadian Geographical Journal*, Vol. 77, No. 6, December 1968, pp. 196–203.

10. Lydolph, Paul E., *Geography of the U.S.S.R.*, New York: John Wiley & Sons, Inc., 1964, pp. 387–411.

11. Parkinson, J. R., *The Economics of Shipbuilding in the United Kingdom*, New York: Cambridge University Press, 1960.

12. "The Shipbuilding Industry in Western Europe," *Rotterdamsche Bank Quarterly Review*, March 1956, pp. 5–48.

13. Steed, G. P. F., "The Changing Milieu of a Firm: A Study in Manufacturing Geography," *Annals of the Association of American Geographers*, Vol. 58, No. 3, September 1968, pp. 506–525.

14. Taga, Yutaka, "Development of Shipbuilding Industry, Japan," *Contemporary Japan*, Vol. 24, 1956, pp. 68–87.

15. Theel, Gustav Adolph, *The World Shipping Scene*, Bremen: Institute for Shipping Research, 1963.

chapter 27

The Chemical Industries

The rapid expansion of the chemical industries during the last half-century represents an economic revolution the effects of which are as great as those of the mechanical revolution of the late eighteenth and early nineteenth centuries. The far-reaching nature of these effects is indicated by the fact that it is almost impossible to draw a clear-cut distinction between chemical and nonchemical industries; there are few industries of importance in which, at some stage of production, chemical changes do not take place.

Because chemical products affect almost every phase of modern life, they are essential to all industrially advanced nations. In fact, the more industrialized the nation, the more important is the role of chemical products. In the United States, for example, the chemical industries rank fourth in the economy, after petroleum refining, primary metals, and transportation equipment.

During the early part of this century, world chemical production grew at a very modest rate, reaching an estimated value of $10,000 million in the late 1930s. Production reached $50,000 million by 1955, and today it exceeds $100,000 million. Eight countries—the United States, the U.S.S.R., West Germany, the United Kingdom, France, Italy, Japan, and Canada—account for three-fourths of total world production. In 1950, the United States produced about 50 percent of the world's output, but the resurgence of the chemical industry in Europe and Japan has reduced this dominance to slightly under 40 percent today. Among the eight major producing countries, Japan is expected to undergo the greatest growth in the next decade.

NATURE OF INDUSTRY

Chemical changes involve changes in the molecular structure of matter, whereas physical changes leave the molecular structure unaltered. In the woodworking industries, for example, physical changes are brought about during the process of manufacture, but no change takes place in the molecular structure of the new material.

There are four essential characteristics of a chemical industry:

1. The industry must produce something that is different from the raw material it uses.
2. Chemical changes must be involved in a preponderance of the operations.
3. The production process must be carried out by skilled operatives who are fully aware of the chemical processes involved.
4. The industry is directed by people who have chemical training and understanding.

Raw Materials

The raw materials of the chemical industries are the elements or fundamental substances from which, by combination in various ways and in different proportions, an infinite number of compounds can be produced. Actually, however, certain compounds occur in nature; these are also considered raw materials, and new materials are formed from them by their interaction, often with the aid of electricity or heat.

Some of these raw materials, such as wood, coal, cotton, petroleum and natural gas, are of organic origin. Others are inorganic, obtained from minerals, from the gases of air, or from the dissolved salts of the sea. Among these are sulphur, pyrites supplying iron and sulphur, phosphate rock, salt, limestone, clay, neon, and nitrogen.

Factors Affecting Location

The chemical industries are characteristic of a highly developed industrial civilization, representing as they do the most intensive types of production. Large amounts of capital and a highly trained labor force are combined to bring about more complete utilization of raw materials.

Since many of the products of the chemical industries are the raw materials for other industries, those nations with a highly developed industrial system offer a powerful attraction in the form of a large market. These consuming industries are near at hand in such countries as the United States, the Soviet Union, West Germany, the United Kingdom, France, Italy, and Japan. A large market, therefore, combines with the abundant capital and trained labor force to make these nations outstanding producers of chemical products.

PETROLEUM-BASED CHEMICALS

As the chemical industries have grown over the years, the demand for basic raw materials has exceeded what can be produced readily from coal and coking operations. Accordingly, the industry has turned to petroleum as a source, and has attracted petroleum companies into what has been called the "petrochemical" industry. In general, in all industrial areas of the world, chemical raw materials based on petroleum and natural gas have exceeded the growth rate for the chemical industries as a whole.

Although the first commercial chemical based on petroleum (isopropyl alcohol) was produced in 1918, the trend did not become significant until the early 1950s. Today organic chemical products which find their origin in petroleum and natural gas constitute such a large share of the total market that the term "petrochemical" has lost most of its earlier significance. This is particularly true when referring to chemical *markets*. It is unimportant in the marketplace whether phenol, for example, originates from petro-

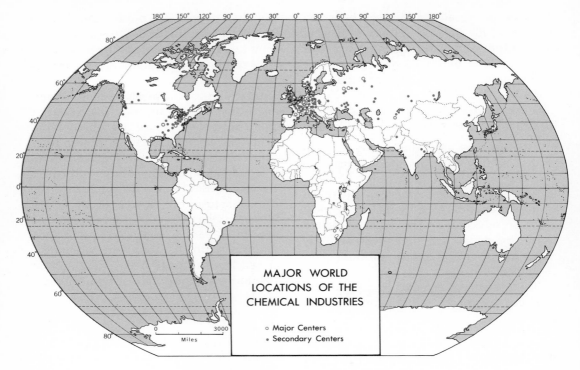

FIGURE 27.1   (*General Media Corporation*)

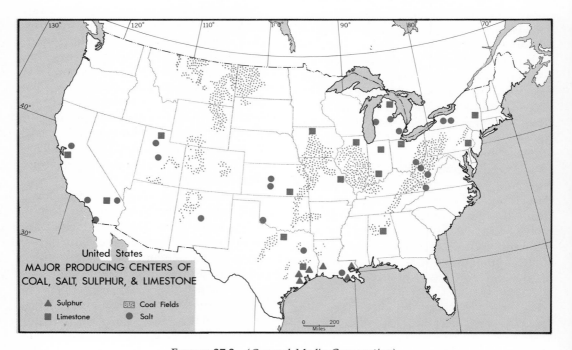

FIGURE 27.2   (*General Media Corporation*)

FIGURE 27.3 *The Baytown, Texas refining complex of Humble Oil. (Humble Oil and Refining Company)*

leum or coal. The same can be said for the vast majority of organic chemical products on the market today. The classification "petrochemicals" has thus outlived its usefulness. "Basic organic chemicals" provides a more meaningful characterization of the primary organic building blocks upon which the industry is based. The classification includes only aliphatic and aromatic hydrocarbons, excluding quantities used as fuel, and allows statistical documentation to be accurate and consistent. The importance of a raw material source—coal, oil, or vegetable—can be better appraised.

The growing importance of petroleum as a raw material source for basic organic chemicals can best be illustrated by the trend in West Germany, long a leader in chemical production from coal. Table 27.1 shows the change in the relative share of a few basic chemicals derived from petroleum from 1957 to 1968. Only benzene is still largely based on coal, in contrast with the United States where approximately 70 percent of benzene production comes from petroleum.

Production of basic organic chemicals in Western Europe reached more than 4.6

Table 27.1 Relative Share of Selected Basic Organic Chemicals Derived from Petroleum—West Germany

Chemical	Percent		
	1957	1960	1968
Methane	100	100	100
Acetylene	28	33	42
Ethylene	50	87	96
Benzene	0	1	17
Toluene	15	88	91
Xylene	0	76	77

Source: United Nations *Statistical Yearbook,* 1969, Tables 122 and 124, pp. 286, 288.

million metric tons in terms of carbon content in 1968, as shown in Table 27.2. Oil and natural gas accounted for 58 percent of this production. In the United States 93 percent, or slightly more than 12 million tons of carbon content, was derived from oil and gas.

Distribution of Petrochemical Plants

In the recent past, the petroleum-based chemical industries have shown a very high growth rate in the world economy. It is a dynamic industry, which supplies

Table 27.2   Production of Basic Organic Chemicals

	1000 Metric Tons	Percent Obtained from		
		Oil and Natural Gas	Coal	Other
Western Europe				
1967	4,045	54	43	3
1968	4,590	58	39	3
United States				
1967	11,195	93	7	0
1968	13,039	93	7	0

Source: United Nations *Statistical Yearbook*, 1969, Table 123, p. 287.

intermediate products for a number of other industries and provides substitutes for traditional materials such as steel, lumber, paper, natural fibers, soap, and other such items.

Of the approximately 1000 petroleum-base chemical plants in existence, more than 50 percent are located in the United States and Canada; over 200 are found in Western Europe, about 50 in Japan, and the rest are distributed among all other areas. Nevertheless, new plants being planned are spread more evenly among the United States, Western Europe, Japan, and developing areas. The majority of the existing plants and projects in developing countries are still concentrated in Latin America and Asia, which account for 90 percent of the total.

General characteristics of these industries include:

1. Product homogeneity and standardization
2. Process continuity and stability
3. High capital intensity

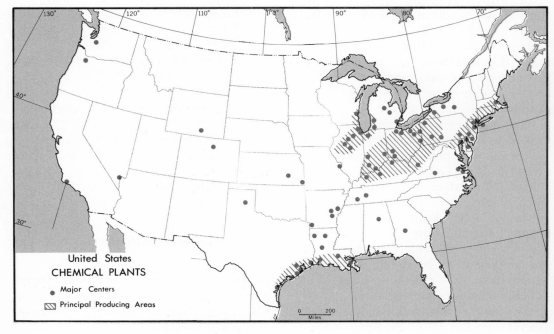

FIGURE 27.4   (*General Media Corporation*)

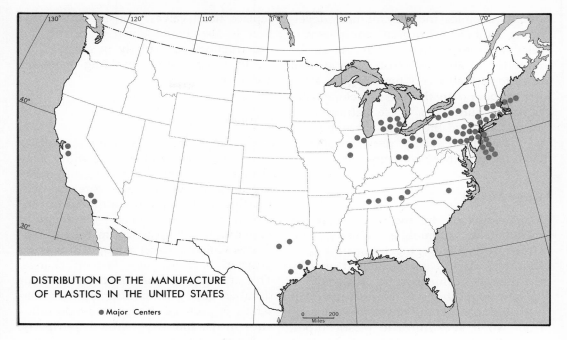

DISTRIBUTION OF THE MANUFACTURE
OF PLASTICS IN THE UNITED STATES

● Major Centers

FIGURE 27.5   (General Media Corporation)

4. High proportion of skilled labor, including technicians and scientists
5. Availability of alternative production
   processes and raw materials
6. High rate of technological change

PLASTICS

Plastics is one of the fastest growing sectors of the chemical industries, exceeding
even the growth rate of basic organic
chemicals in recent years. World production of plastics is expected to reach 20 mil-

lion tons by 1972, representing a growth
rate of about 7 percent per year. A breakdown of world production for the past
several years is presented in Table 27.3.

The United States and West Germany
account for about 47 percent of the total
world production. In fact, almost 85 percent of all plastics are produced in the
seven countries listed in Table 27.3. The
United States and Japan lead the world
as plastic users, with West Germany,
Italy, the U.S.S.R., the United Kingdom,
and France following in that order.

Plastics have provided a logical entry

Table 27.3   World Production of Plastic Materials, (1000 metric tons)

Country	1960	1961	1962	1963	1964	1965	1966	1967
World	6,770.0	7,400.0	8,965.0	10,485.0	12,480.0	14,360.0	16,640.0	17,990.0
France	347.0	375.0	448.0	508.0	611.0	695.0	800.0	890.0
Italy	345.8	467.1	572.6	660.9	812.1	930.8	997.3	1,148.4
Japan	556.1	692.6	825.9	1,069.0	1,383.8	1,608.8	2,004.2	2,688.2
United Kingdom	566.1	576.6	665.1	756.2	883.4	957.3	1,017.0	1,108.5
United States	2,849.6	2,872.3	3,602.3	4,068.0	4,582.7	5,300.1	6,162.0	5,734.8
U.S.S.R.	311.6	383.7	451.7	567.2	700.8	803.1	971.2	1,113.6
West Germany	928.2	1,080.2	1,256.7	1,434.0	1,754.3	1,998.9	2,293.0	2,630.0

Source: United Nations, Statistical Yearbook, 1968 (New York: United Nations, 1969), Table 123, p. 287.

into the chemical industry for many developing nations. Fabrication equipment is relatively inexpensive, and resins can be imported at attractive costs. The ratio of sales to capital is very high. Hence, small firms abound in the less developed nations. A number of these nations have already reached the point where demand is sufficient to justify resin production facilities, and these are being built.

Large Market

Major users of the industry's materials include the automobile industry, construction, and packaging. In the packaging industry, plastics use is limited only by the number of things to be packaged.

New applications of plastics materials are continually being developed, ranging from wood substitutes to plastic pipes. Agricultural uses include mulch film, silo covers, and irrigation pipe; medical applications are growing with the use of artificial limbs, plastic lenses, and tubing to replace heart valves. Considerable attention is also being given to plastics for construction, particularly in areas of the world where other building materials are scarce.

Outlook

The ever-improving structural qualities of plastic, along with its versatility, may change the nature of our living and working areas in future years. Already, one-fourth of all U.S. plastics are used in construction. The extremely wide range of applications of plastics materials precludes violent swings as population composition or tastes and fashion change. The strength of consumer demand for durable goods containing plastics materials is perhaps the major single influence in the industry's growth prospects, and demand is expected to remain high.

SYNTHETIC RUBBER

Synthetic rubbers are petroleum-based, and their growth has paralleled the growth of basic organic chemicals from petroleum. The 1940s saw the birth of the synthetic rubber industry due to the curtailment of natural rubber supplies as a result of the war. The industry received its greatest impetus in the United States. By 1953, synthetic rubber accounted for nearly three-fourths of total world production. Table 27.4 shows a rapidly continuing increase over natural rubber, which has remained relatively constant. This trend is expected to continue at least for several years, since natural rubber will be unable to keep up with the growing demand for rubber products.

FIGURE 27.6 *The Starr-Edwards aortic heart valve. Creation of the heart valve using plastics has prolonged the life of many people with damaged hearts. (Dr. Albert Starr)*

FERTILIZER

World fertilizer consumption has been increasing steadily and will continue its upward trend in the future. The princi-

Table 27.4   World Rubber Production (thousand metric tons)

	1953	1959	1960	1961	1962	1963	1964	1965	1966	1967
Natural	375	420	420	390	405	410	405	395	385	350
Synthetic	1015	1750	2020	2130	2400	2620	3000	3235	3235	3690

Source: United Nations, *Statistical Yearbook,* 1968 (New York: United Nations, 1969), Table 114, p. 278.

pal factor causing this trend is the increase in world population, which is expected to double by the year 2000 if the present growth rate continues. With increases projected in nutritional and other standards, the demand for food and natural fiber production in the year 2000 will be even greater than the population increase alone would indicate. Furthermore, with prospects visible for only modest increases in the land base available for agriculture, a large increase in agricultural productivity per land unit will clearly be necessary. This productivity increase will be accomplished by world-wide improvement in agricultural technology—including increased fertilization.

World population growth is shown graphically in Fig. 27.7. The shape of the curve indicates that not only is the population expanding, but it is expanding at a continually increasing rate. Between 1920 and 1930, for example, the increase was about 10 percent. The decade 1990 to 2000, however, will be a 20 percent increase.

The geographical distribution of population and regional growth rates are even more significant than the total. As shown in Table 27.5, two regions, Asia and Latin America, are growing faster than other areas. The crucial population impact will occur in Asia.

Table 27.5   Distribution of World Population

Region	Share (percent)		
	1960	1980	2000
North America	7	6	5
South America	7	8	9
Western Europe	10	8	7
Eastern Europe & U.S.S.R.	12	10	8
Africa	8	8	8
Asia	56	59	62
Oceania	1	1	1

Source: United Nations, *Studies in Petrochemicals* (New York: United Nations Publication 67, Vol. 1, 1964), p. 66.

It would be misleading to imply that population alone is the entire problem. If land resources were adequate, the population increase would represent not a problem but progress. That land resources are not adequate can be inferred from Table 27.6. Asia, with over 60 percent of the world's population in the year 2000, has today less than 30 percent of the world's agricultural land. Furthermore, prospects seem poor for major increases in good land available for agricultural use in the most densely populated Asian countries.

Production and Trade

In the last decade, world output of nitrogenous fertilizers has been increasing at the rate of about 8 percent per annum,

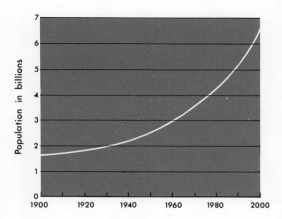

FIGURE 27.7   *World population growth.*

Table 27.6   Distribution of Agricultural Land, 1967

Region	Agricultural Land (thousand million acres)			Acres per Capita
	Cropland	Pasture	Total	
North America	0.6	0.7	1.3	6.6
South America	0.3	0.9	1.2	5.8
Western Europe	0.2	0.1	0.4	1.3
Eastern Europe & U.S.S.R.	0.7	1.0	1.6	4.8
Africa	0.6	1.5	2.0	8.5
Asia	1.1	1.1	2.1	1.3
Oceania	0.1	1.1	1.2	75.0
Total	3.5	6.4	9.8	3.4

Source: United Nations, *Production Yearbook,* 1968, Table 1, pp. 3–8.

from 4.4 million tons in 1951 to 21.2 million tons in 1967. Western Europe produces about 40 percent of the world output, and North America averages one-third.

With respect to types of fertilizers produced, ammonium nitrate and ammonium sulphate comprise about half of the total. The latter type, along with ammonium sulphate and nitrate, sodium nitrate, and calcium cyanamide have decreased their share of total output, whereas urea and complex fertilizers have been increasing

their share. Other nitrogenous fertilizers have also been increasing.

The annual rate of growth of trade has kept pace with the total production, and in the last decade exports comprised about 25–30 percent of the total output. Western Europe was the major exporter, sharing over 60 percent of the total, followed by North America. On the import side, Western Europe, North America, and Asia are the major importers. Tables 27.7, 27.8 and 27.9 show the leading producers and con-

FIGURE 27.8   *This complex at Heroya, near Porsgrunn, is Norway's largest single industrial site. It includes some of Europe's biggest and most modern fertilizer production facilities, the second largest magnesium works in the Western world, and factories producing resins as well as a variety of industrial chemicals and gases. (Norsk Hydro)*

Table 27.7   Commercial Nitrogenous Fertilizers (100 metric tons)

	Production				Consumption		
	1963	1965	1967		1963	1965	1967
United States	34,900	44,650	55,350	United States	35,644	42,080	54,871
U.S.S.R.	14,140	20,990	31,000	U.S.S.R.	10,700	17,590	26,560
Japan	11,514	13,940	18,012	France	6,828	8,605	9,900
West Germany	12,002	12,890	15,013	West Germany	7,738	7,846	8,886
France	7,459	10,819	12,235	Japan	6,893	7,240	8,500
Italy	7,254	8,363	9,501	India	3,287	5,380	8,302
United Kingdom	5,136	5,985	7,321	United Kingdom	5,411	5,960	7,604

Source: United Nations, Trade Yearbook, 1967, Tables 133–134, pp. 444–445.

Table 27.8   Commercial Phosphate Fertilizer (100 metric tons)

	Production				Consumption		
	1963	1965	1967		1963	1965	1967
United States	30,200	36,520	46,510	United States	28,804	31,745	39,280
U.S.S.R.	9,720	14,070	17,100	U.S.S.R.	8,530	12,840	16,640
France	8,230	12,175	13,330	France	10,339	12,451	13,638
Australia	6,440	8,319	9,698	Australia	5,703	8,464	9,797
West Germany	7,532	8,493	8,607	West Germany	7,100	7,901	7,918
Japan	4,763	5,970	6,552	Japan	4,519	5,090	6,300
United Kingdom	4,057	4,354	4,031	United Kingdom	4,174	4,636	4,391

Source: United Nations, Trade Yearbook, 1967, Tables 135–136, pp. 449–450, 451–454.

Table 27.9   Commercial Potash Fertilizer (100 metric tons)

	Production				Consumption		
	1963	1965	1967		1963	1965	1967
United States	23,280	25,160	28,110	United States	22,711	25,714	32,879
U.S.S.R.	13,310	18,940	26,500	U.S.S.R.	8,260	14,210	19,020
West Germany	18,965	22,290	21,197	West Germany	10,998	11,840	10,768
East Germany	17,520	18,570	20,060	France	9,097	9,696	10,243
Canada	3,587	10,672	20,000	Japan	5,378	5,790	6,400
France	16,803	18,238	18,366	United Kingdom	4,441	4,344	4,557

Source: United Nations, Trade Yearbook, 1967, Table 137–138, pp. 455–456, 457–458.

sumers of nitrogenous, phosphate, and potash fertilizers.

Fertilizers, plastics, and rubber are only a few of the sectors contributing to the growth of the world's chemical industries. Space does not permit inclusion of other sectors such as inorganics, pharmaceuticals, detergents, and the like, but their influence is nonetheless important.

selected references

1. Adams, Walter, The Structure of American Industry, 3d ed., New York: The Macmillan Company, 1961, pp. 233–310.

2. Alderfer, E. B., and Michl, H. E., Economics of American Industry, 3d ed., New York: McGraw-Hill Book Company, Inc., 1957, pp. 239–258.

3. Burck, Gilbert, "Chemicals: The Reluctant Competitors," Fortune, Vol. 68, November 1963, pp. 148–153.

4. The Chemical Industry Facts Book, Washington, D.C.: Manufacturing Chemist's Association, 1962.

5. Elford, Jean, "Sarnia, Canada's Chemical Valley," Canadian Geographical Journal, Vol. 55, November 1957, pp. 171–185.

6. Elfrod, Jean, and Phelps, Edward, "Oil, Then to Now," Canadian Geographical Journal, Vol. 77, No. 5, November 1968, pp. 164–171.

7. Hayden, H. W.; Gibson, R. C.; and Brophy, J. H., "Superplastic Metals," Scien-

tific American, Vol. 220, No. 3, March 1969, pp. 28–35.

8. Melamaid, Alexander, "Petroleum Refining and Distribution in Ethiopia," *The Professional Geographer*, Vol. 20, No. 6, November 1968, pp. 388–391.

9. Pearse, Charles R., "Athabasca Tar Sands," *Canadian Geographical Journal*, Vol. 76, No. 1, January 1968, pp. 2–9.

10. Phillips, Charles F., "The Competitive Potential of Synthetic Rubber," *Land Economics*, Vol. 36, 1960, pp. 322–332.

11. Phillips, Charles F., Jr., "Workable Competition in the Synthetic Rubber Industry," *Southern Economic Journal*, Vol. 28, October 1961, pp. 154–162.

12. *Plastics: The Story of an Industry*, New York: Society of the Plastics Industry, 1962.

13. *Rayon and Synthetic Fibers of Japan*, Tokyo: Japan Chemical Fibers Association, 1963.

14. Taylor, F. Sherwood, *A History of Industrial Chemistry*, New York: Abelard–Schuman, 1957.

15. Waller, Peter P., and Swain, Harry S., "Changing Patterns of Oil Transportation and Refining in West Germany," *Economic Geography*, Vol. 43, No. 2, April 1967, pp. 143–156.

The combined aerospace industry is one of the largest manufacturing employers in the United States. The bulk of missile and space employment is carried on as a separate operation outside aircraft plants, although many aircraft plants have shifted some of their operations to the missile and space field as they have procured government contracts. Missile component production occurs within approximately twenty different industries, but between 70 and 80 percent of total production falls in three industries—aircraft and aircraft parts, ordnance, and electrical machinery.

Scientists and engineers make up about 16 percent of total aerospace industry employment. Technicians account for 6 percent, production workers are stable at 54 percent, and the balance, 24 percent, are supervisory and other white collar workers.

Some slight shifting of aerospace workers into the Pacific Coast region is taking place. This region employs nearly 50 percent of the aerospace labor force, with Los Angeles, Seattle, and San Diego the leading centers. The Northeast accounts for about 20 percent, the South 16 percent, and the Midwest about 15 percent of the remaining workers in the industry.

SINGLE-CUSTOMER INDUSTRY

The industry is dominated by a single customer—the federal government. Although aerospace producers manufacture a number of important products for the commercial market, their major work is reserved for defense and space contracts. Moreover, the unique character of this customer–producer relationship has *significantly* affected the source and uses of funds in the rapidly changing postwar period.

The industry is principally affected by the size and shape of its dominant customer's budget—a budget that has exhibited massive structural shifts and significant ups and downs since 1945, and that exhibits a constant demand for high-quality products incorporating the latest technological breakthroughs. Many of these products of course result from advanced research and development programs, which in turn are generated by the government's demand for technological progress.

AIRCRAFT SALES PACE INDUSTRY

Sales of civilian aircraft exceeded 17,080 units in 1969 for a total value of more than $5.8 billion. In this sales total were approximately 591 commercial transports worth over $3.4 billion. Sales of aerospace vehicle components, parts, and related equipment (engines, propellers, parts, and auxiliary equipment) exceeded $12 billion.

Civil aircraft maintains leadership in production. For future re-equipment the world's airlines have on order about fifty of the huge Boeing 747s for long-range needs, but seem to be awaiting the results of the European airbus proposal before ordering either the McDonnel Douglas DC-10 or the Lockheed L-1011 U.S. airbus entries. The American airbuses are scheduled for use in late 1971. Douglas has sold twenty-five airbuses to American Airlines, which took an option on twenty-five more. If, as predicted, the Europeans do not build an airbus, there will be an opening for 500 of the U.S. advanced technology aircraft in these foreign markets.

Exports

The industry forecasts continuing foreign sales of four-engine jets (cargo, passenger, and quick change cargo-passenger); the less expensive two- and three-engine, short to medium-range jets; the smaller executive and general type aircraft; plus increased sales of the new passenger and cargo advanced technology airplanes. As Vietnam helicopter requirements ease, and as more people become informed of the advantages of rotary-winged aircraft, helicopter exports will increase rapidly.

The complexion of the world market for U.S. aircraft has not changed drastically over the years, and Europe still dominates the picture. This is not to discount the real and growing aircraft requirements of the developing countries of the Middle East, Africa, Latin America, and Asia, whose needs are not completely filled by commercial aircraft. Many of these areas have an agrarian economy and need agricultural aircraft for crop spraying, insect control, and local transport. Success in securing foothold sales in developing countries is critical to the future of U.S. aerospace exports. Financing is often the deciding factor, because of the inherent need for monetary assistance in jet transport sales.

Table 28.1   U.S. Shipments of Aerospace Vehicles, 1958, 1965, and 1969 (Value in thousands of dollars)

Item	1958		1965		1969		Percent 1965	Change 1969
	Number	Value	Number	Value	Number	Value		
Complete military aircraft	4,078	5,365,000	2,800	2,900,000	4,100	4,400,000	46.4	51.72
Complete civilian aircraft	6,882	500,129	12,543	1,577,299	17,081	5,875,801	36.2	272.52
Guided missiles & military space vehicles	n.a.	1,886,682	n.a.	4,531,000	n.a.	6,700,000	n.a.	47.87
Complete space vehicles	n.a.	n.a.	n.a.	2,449,000	n.a.	2,450,000	n.a.	0.04

Source: 1969 data estimates secured from Business and Defense Services Administration, Bureau of the Census, Current Industrial Report Series MA–175 (58–67)–2, "Shipments of Defense-oriented Industries" Washington, D.C.: Government Printing Office, 1969).

FIGURE 28.1 *From the pads of Cape Kennedy (Cape Canaveral) go missiles made for U.S. defense and for landings on the moon. (Florida News Bureau)*

Imports

Imports of aerospace vehicles and equipment continue to rise as the French Fan-Jet Falcon and other competitive executive aircraft are entering the United States market in growing numbers, while comparable American aircraft are not successfully exported. In the 10,000−33,000 pound category, imports are estimated at 99 aircraft valued at $58 million in 1969. This figure is expected to rise in 1971 by 41 percent, as imports of these airplanes reach 140.

PRODUCTION PROBLEMS

Major production delays, prevalent in early 1967, were virtually eliminated in 1968 and none occurred in 1969. Minor problems developing after delivery continue to occur, particularly with the newer, more sophisticated aircraft models. These design deficiencies, evident only after extensive use operations, are being corrected by the manufacturers who often incorporate the recommendations of the operators. Spare parts delivery dates for the older military aerospace equipment are not always met. This is the result of the long lead time for procurement of many parts. Table 28.2 shows average sales in the aerospace industry compared with all manufacturing.

World airlines require the latest equipment to remain competitive. In the past ten years of the jet era, passenger traffic tripled, freight traffic increased almost fivefold, and mail traffic increased nearly six times. Airline travel is expected to triple again in the next ten years. Currently, however, commercial airline profits are down; their rate of return on investment is decreasing as costs rise, and the yield (average revenue per ton mile) continues to drop while revenues climb.

Major carriers are taking delivery of their new equipment, adding new flights to their schedules, and laying out huge sums for stretched jet transports, as well as for the "advanced technology jetlines" or the "third generation jetliners" (airbuses). At present, new capacity is ahead of demand, but the long-range outlook continues to be good. Fewer but larger and more sophisticated units will be built at higher unit costs with little

reduction in total value of shipments and none in employment.

FOREIGN COMPETITION

Aerospace manufacturers of the large transports are meeting stiff competition from foreign manufacturers. United States transport aircraft are world renowned for economy of operation, profit-making potential, and advanced technology, but these alone are not enough to influence a sale when lower initial cost, better financing, and pooling of maintenance and parts are available from foreign manufacturers. The type of aircraft established in an area has a deciding influence on selections by adjoining countries. Sales of the large transports in the United States, and even more overseas, have been lost because of one or more of these reasons.

On the basis of its home market, the United States has hitherto supplied about 90 percent of the world's business aircraft. However, the British and French are now moving into the ranks of major

Table 28.2   Aerospace Industry Earnings, 1959–1969

Year	Profits After Taxes As Percent of Sales		Profits After Taxes As Percent of Stockholders' Equity	
	Aircraft and Parts Industry*	All Manufacturing	Aircraft and Parts Industry*	All Manufacturing
1959	1.6	4.8	8.0	10.2
1960	1.4	4.4	7.2	9.1
1961	1.8	4.3	9.2	8.7
1962	2.4	4.5	12.2	9.6
1963	2.3	4.7	11.1	10.1
1964	2.6	5.2	11.9	11.4
1965	3.2	5.6	15.1	13.0
1966	3.0	5.6	14.4	13.5
1967	2.7	5.0	12.8	11.7
1968	3.2	5.0	14.2	12.1
1969	3.0	4.8	10.6	11.5

*Includes data only for companies classified as aircraft, parts, and accessories.
Source: Compiled from Tables 2–6 of the individual Quarterly Financial Reports (4th quarter 1959– 4th quarter 1969), Security and Exchange Commission, Federal Trade Commission (Washington, D.C.: Government Printing Office).

FIGURE 28.2 *The Boeing 747 Superjet in flight over the Puget Sound area of western Washington state. This is currently the largest commercial jetliner in the world. (The Boeing Company)*

suppliers of executive turbine aircraft. The improved outlook for sales of corporate jets has influenced at least three United States manufacturers to incorporate advanced technologies in turbine power aircraft designs for market entry in the early 1970s.

case study

SST: At the Sound Barrier

The supersonic transport program may well be, as its supporters claim, one of the most remarkable transport advances of our time. On the other hand, some critics contend it will be an ear-shattering, budget-shattering disaster that fails to provide any of the efficiencies normally associated with advances in the aircraft art.

Success of the SST program undoubtedly would reinforce a national asset of immense value—the U.S. supremacy in aerospace capability. This plane with its capability for

carrying 350 passengers over 4,000 miles at a speed of 1,800 miles per hour, would be one of the most productive long-range vehicles in history. It would reshape geography, making Asia as close as Europe is today, and making Europe much closer than the two coasts of this country are now.

Even so, the SST is an exception to the historic rule that a new model plane is always superior to its predecessors in terms of benefits and costs. It meets these tests vis-á-vis the jet transports operating today, but its 2.5 cent seat per mile operating cost would be substantially above the cost of the large and efficient 747 transport which made its debut in late 1969.

Anglo-French Concorde

Major interest in the development of a supersonic transport first developed abroad, and has now culminated in the production of the Anglo-French Concorde, which is scheduled to go into service in the early 1970s. The British and French governments became interested in this type of plane when they found that the market for long-range subsonic jets had been preempted by the American 707 and DC-8, and were reinforced in their decision when their entries in the short-haul market (the Britannia and the Caravelle) were outdistanced by the American 727 and DC-9.

Almost against their will, European designers found themselves being forced across the sound barrier. The result was the Anglo-French agreement in late 1962 to share the design and construction costs of the Concorde. Seventy-two firm orders are now in hand for this $16 million plane, which is built to carry 136 passengers at a speed of 1,450 miles per hour. However, if and when the American SST becomes a commercial reality, the smaller, slower, and less technically advanced Concorde may find itself at a distinct disadvantage.

United States Government Role

The Federal Aviation Agency initiated an $11 million exploratory SST study in 1961. In 1963, the day after a U.S. airline ordered six Concordes, President Kennedy pushed the program forward, declaring that the SST was "essential to a strong and forward-looking nation." In mid-1965, President Johnson accelerated the design competition, and this phase came to an end at the beginning of 1967 with the choice of a winning aircraft design awarded to the Boeing Company in Seattle, Washing-

FIGURE 28.3 *The Boeing supersonic transport's variable-sweep wing is demonstrated in this multiple-exposure photo of the full-scale mockup. (The Boeing Company)*

ton. Thus, the United States government is paying for most of the SST development costs.

Air: The New Medium

The SST concept involves an interesting engineering challenge, since the difference between supersonic and subsonic vehicles is comparable to the difference between surface ships and submarines. The air at this speed behaves like a new medium and it requires the development of radical designs and materials to cope with these new physical forces.

As the plane approaches the speed of sound —about 660 miles per hour at high altitude— the force required to push it through the air rises abruptly. The sound waves cannot outspeed the supersonic plane, so the air in front of the plane is undisturbed until the plane pushes it aside. This fact accounts not only for an intense sonic boom but also for heat and pressure problems that give the aircraft peculiar handling problems.

At the speed designed for the SST, it will be operating in a so-called "thermal thicket" in a region where the aircraft cannot dissipate the heat generated by air friction. As a solution, aircraft fuel can be used as a heat sink, with the engine fuel made to flow between vital areas to keep aircraft parts from melting, but intense heat problems still develop when the fuel to the engines is cut for descent.

Problems of stress would also develop at the plane's cruising altitude, especially around the cabin-pressure seals at door joints and windows. A technical solution is feasible— no windows—but this in turn might create psychological problems for passengers. Stresses could also build up at the pivot of the plane's folding wing, which ranges from a 20-degree sweep at takeoff to a 72-degree sweep at maximum speed.

Sound: A New Problem

The major technical (and cost) problem is that of sonic boom—the explosive sound created when an object moves through the atmosphere at supersonic speed because of the inability of air molecules to move faster than the speed of sound. The intensity of the boom is influenced by temperature and wind variation, but mostly by the plane's altitude, weight, and shape—the greater the weight, the greater the boom.

Sonic-boom intensity is measured by pounds per square foot "over-pressure"—the excess over the normal weight of the atmosphere. The SST would probably exert 2 PSF over-pressure in accelerating to its cruising speed. In order to reduce this somewhat painful noise to the more bearable range of 1 PSF over-pressure, either a smaller plane would have to be designed or the plane would have to fly at subsonic speed over population centers, or not fly over such centers at all.

However, seat-mile operating costs would soar with the use of small planes or with substantial restrictions on supersonic flight, so that airlines might avoid purchasing such planes on economic grounds alone.

MISSILE PROGRAMS

Missile shipments continue to rise with the procurement of tactical missiles for Vietnam. United States aerospace manufacturers are increasing their share of world markets through greater use of agreements with foreign manufacturers and governments. Existing agreements include provisions for assembly of finished products outside the United States, licenses to manufacture, and "trade-off" or "off-set" as conditions for sale. Consortium for joint efforts, extending from research and development through production, are becoming more popular with manufacturers.

European countries are finding production and associated costs of new generation aerospace products so enormous that they, too, are joining together to compete with the United States. These joint ventures provide ready markets for their products. The Italian-made fuselage panels and the Canadian-manufactured wings, empennages, ailerons, flaps, tail cones, and floor panels for the McDonnell Douglas C-9 are current examples of foreign-made content in U.S. aircraft.

FIGURE 28.4 *Astronaut Edwin Aldrin, lunar module pilot, is photographed during the Apollo 11 extravehicular activity on the Moon. He has just deployed the Early Apollo Scientific Experiments Package; in the far right background is the Lunar Module. (NASA)*

OUTLOOK

A huge backlog, coupled with a stable labor environment, is providing the incentive for continued capital investment and aerospace industry growth. Little change is expected in the post-Vietnam period, as resources borrowed to support that effort are returned to peacetime civilian and defense production. Trends away from dependence on defense production will continue, and further application of aerospace technology to civilian areas will take place.

Moon Landing Highlights Aerospace Program

Columbus and Magellan are names familiar to most school children; spaceflight has added a new frontier and new names for tomorrow's history books—Gagarin, Shepard, Glenn, and now Armstrong, Aldrin, and Collins.

Neil A. Armstrong is the first man to set foot on the moon. The historic Apollo 11 flight enabled the lunar module Eagle to land on the moon's Tranquility Base on July 20, 1969 at 4:17 p.m. (EDT). This modern explorer, civilian, ex-pilot of the X-15 rocket research plane, and commander of Gemini 8 (which he dramatically brought back to earth after it started tumbling in space) commanded Apollo 11. Beginning in 1961 with Alan Shepard's first probe into outer space, man entered an interplanetary space age when he landed successfully on the moon and then returned safely to earth. The total cost of the space program from Shepard through Armstrong was $25 billion. Only time will tell whether or not such an expenditure was worthwhile, but the fallout from the technology of the space program alone should greatly exceed the total cost. The horizons of the space age appear limitless, now that man is no longer earth bound.

selected references

1. Adams, Walter, *The Structure of American Industry*, New York: The Macmillan Company, 1961, pp. 468–508.

2. Adams, W., and Gray, H. M., *Monopoly in America—The Government As Promoter*, New York: The Macmillan Company, 1955.

3. Alderfer, E. B., and Micl, H. E., *Economics of American Industry*, New York: McGraw-Hill Book Company, Inc., 1957, pp. 167–180.

4. Caves, R. E., *Air Transport and Its Regulators*, Cambridge: Harvard University Press, 1962.

5. Kibal' Chich, O. A., "The Distribution of Population and Related Indicators in Long-term Planning of Passenger Traffic," *Soviet Geography*, Vol. 4, September 1963, pp. 26–36.

6. Kish, George, "Soviet Air Transport," *Geographical Review*, Vol. 48, No. 3, July 1958, pp. 309–320.

7. McDougall, Harry, and McDougall, Charlotte, "Canada's Principal Airlines," *Canadian Geographical Journal*, Vol. 78, No. 6, June 1969, pp. 188–203.

8. Sealy, Kenneth R., *The Geography of Air Transport*, Chicago: Aldine Publishing Company, 1968.

9. Taaffee, Edward J., "United States Air Transportation and Urban Distribution," *Geographical Review*, Vol. 46, No. 2, April 1956, pp. 219–238.

10. ———, "Trends in Airline Passenger Traffic," *Annals of the Association of American Geographers*, Vol. 49, No. 4, December 1959, pp. 395–408.

11. ———, "The Urban Hierarchy: An Air Passenger Definition," *Economic Geography*, Vol. 38, No. 1, January 1962, pp. 1–14.

12. Van Dongen, I. S., *The British East Africa Transport Complex*, Chicago: University of Chicago Research Paper No. 38, 1954.

13. Westmeyer, R. E., *Economics of Transportation*, New York: Prentice-Hall Inc., 1952.

14. Wilson, G. L., and Bryan, L. A., *Air Transportation*, New York: Prentice-Hall, Inc., 1949.

15. Wheatcroft, S., *The Economics of European Air Transport*, Manchester: Manchester University Press, 1956.

part V

Tertiary Economic Activity

introduction

The goods yielded by primary and secondary types of economic activities are *things* that can be seen and measured in conventional weights and measures and employment. Services are "immaterials" or intangibles that are felt or sensed in the process of their consumption; they may be measured through the satisfaction derived from their consumption, which in turn may be translated into monetary units and/or employment figures. Services, therefore, include government, circulation, utilities, banking, finance, insurance, real estate, recreation, retail and wholesale, hair salons, medical and hospital care, repairs, motel and hotel services, specialized technical services, and the like. The service activities may involve in their operation goods produced by the primary and secondary types of activities.

The fact that services are measured in terms of the direct satisfaction derived in the process of their consumption suggests a closer spatial proximity between the consumers and suppliers of services; that buying and consumption take place simultaneously suggests "perishability"—that is, they do not easily lend themselves to circulation.

The spatial distribution of services tends to follow that of demand. Besides being related to the number of consumers, demand for services is a function of purchasing power, culture, and productivity levels in the primary and secondary activities, and intensity and frequency of human circulation.

Services are economic in function, since they satisfy human wants. They possess the characteristics of ubiquity, "perishability" (in the sense that most services need to be performed close to their buyers), market orientation, interlocking force between production and consumption, centrality, a hierarchical pattern (convenience shops, neighborhood centers, community centers, villages, towns, cities, metropolis, megalopolis), and they can be functionally classified. In this chapter a selected set of services is discussed in terms of location, characteristics, and interrelationships.

chapter 29

Service Activities

CIRCULATION

Distance is a key factor in the spatial distribution of economic phenomena, and circulation is a means of overcoming the limitations and constraints that distance imposes.[1] Circulation involves the transport of goods, people, and messages.[2] The significance of one element, transportation, as a factor affecting the location of economic activities was discussed in Chapter 5.

Circulation includes services related with railways, waterways, highways, airways, telephone, telegraph, satellites, newspapers, radio and television, postal networks, and the primitive types of manual network information dissemination. Indeed, these services are means of "circulating" the various types of items being traded. Thus, an analysis of circulation service activities must deal not only with the *means of circulation* but also the *associated trade patterns*. This interdependence between the means and the related trade patterns, although recognized, has not been widely used in geographic anal-

[1]The term circulation is used to describe all *transportation* and *communication* systems which play such a vital role in the world's economy.

[2]Language as an art of communication is not included here, although the activities associated with the development of and training for the art are service activities.

ysis. Such inspection yields helpful information in understanding the location patterns of various types of activities.

The underlying motivation for the prevalence of any form of circulation is the need to meet the wants of spatially dispersed producers, consumers, buyers, and sellers through the acts of collecting, rearranging, moving, storing, and selling. On the one hand, circulation flow patterns often serve as a permissive factor in the location or occurrence of an activity at a particular location. On the other, a particular activity located at a certain place may give rise to a flow pattern of circulation involving a specific form of transport or communication media, and may influence its level of activity.

Various investigations reveal that the availability of suitable means of circulation are instrumental in the location of economic activities: the location, type, capacity, and development of a particular circulation system or route depends upon existing or potential long-range traffic or use flows, relative benefits and costs, alternatives available to potential users, and political and social considerations. It is difficult to say which is the cause and which is an effect. The question of whether the circulation system is based on the expected traffic flow or vice versa is so complex that studies have attempted to discover the relationship by holding one of the two constant—resulting in a finding that both are highly interdependent. However, current research[3] has leaned heavily towards explaining the existing circulation patterns and their impact on the location of economic activity.

Waterways

The usefulness and convenience of water as a transport medium evidently occurred to man early in his history. Although the extent of use varies widely among nations, worldwide importance for domestic and international trade remains high. As Fig. 29.1 shows, there are basically two types of waterways: ocean and inland.

Oceanways are determined by a multiplicity of factors:

1. *Direction.* In general, the major ocean routes follow east-west directions linking the chief industrial nations and their markets. The north-south routes tend to hug the shoreline, taking advantage of prevailing currents.
2. *Distance.* Quite naturally the routes follow the shortest possible distance between any two points.
3. *Navigation hazards.* Ocean routes follow deep waters, avoiding shoals, rocks, icebergs, and where possible fogs and storms.
4. *Harbor facilities.* Natural as well as man-made harbor facilities, including fueling and cargo-handling factors, play a decisive role in the location of ocean routes.
5. *Volume, perishability, and location of goods destined for international trade.* Recent United Nations statistics indicate that Anglo-America and Western Europe account for approximately two-thirds of the world's trade, most of it via ocean carriers. European nations, including the U.S.S.R., account for about one-half of the world total.
6. *Technology.* With the advanced technology of ocean trade, many of the difficulties imposed by physical factors have been eliminated. For example, the invention and application of the mariner's compass, radar, and loran; larger capacity, length, and draft[4] of

[3]Various studies dealing with the analysis of communication systems frequently employ the tools of network geometry and graph theory. Through these tools, the circulation system as an integrated whole, comprising the various means, is depicted in terms of series of links or edges (routes), and nodes or vertices (cities or towns), where changes in one part of the system affect all other parts of the total network. The links and edges provide information about the efficiency and degree of connectivity of the system.

[4]Larger draft vessels are producing "side effects" in that they cannot visit shallower harbors. The modern super-sized tankers have approximately 50-foot drafts, and there are few harbors deep enough to accommodate them. This necessitates either rerouting the ocean ways or deepening the existing harbors.

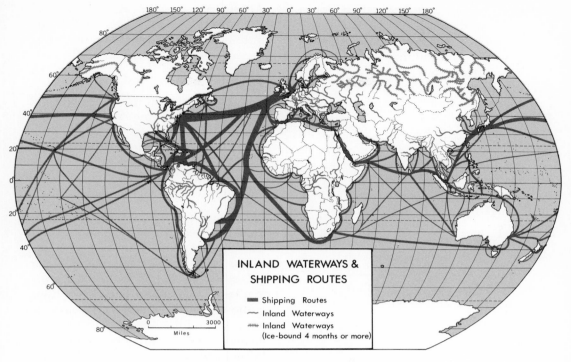

INLAND WATERWAYS &
SHIPPING ROUTES

▬▬ Shipping Routes
〜 Inland Waterways
〰 Inland Waterways
(Ice-bound 4 months or more)

FIGURE 29.1   (*General Media Corporation*)

vessels; refrigeration facilities; internal combustion engines; mechanical loading and unloading facilities—all are technological factors that influence ocean routes and the kinds of carriers used.

There are three kinds of ocean carriers—the liner, the tramp, and the tanker. Liners are ships in a fleet or line which ply regularly between scheduled ports regardless of the load available. The tramp is the slow dredge of the sea, carrying cumbersome cargoes of great weight or bulk in proportion to value, having no definite sailing schedules, and operating as a single unit of transport. Tankers are carriers of "uncartoned" or "unboxed" quantities—oil, ore, grain, etc.

Figure 29.1 shows the world's major ocean shipping routes, the most prominent being:

1. North Atlantic
2. Mediterranean−Asiatic
3. European−eastern South America
4. Panama Canal
5. Cape of Good Hope
6. North Pacific

The North Atlantic route links Western Europe and eastern North America. Since 1838, when the first transatlantic steamship line commenced operations in the North Atlantic Ocean, a well-defined trade pattern has evolved. Until today this route is the busiest of all shipping lanes, with two major lanes (east to west and west to east) sixty miles apart, mandatorily followed by all the carriers under the North Atlantic Track Agreement.

The Mediterranean−Asiatic route, the world's longest single trade route, links Asia and Europe through the Suez Canal.[5] The route is characterized by an unusually large number of integrating branch lines; i.e., the Mediterranean and Black Sea; northwestern Europe and the Medi-

[5]Temporarily closed because of obstructions due to the Arab−Israeli conflict.

terranean; Europe and the Far East, South East, and Middle East.

The European–eastern South America route, which links Europe with eastern South American ports, is gaining prominence with the expanding trade between Latin American countries and Europe. The Panama Canal route connects the eastern United States with the west coasts of both South America and the United States, as well as Australia with Europe, and the eastern United States with the Far East. As the name of the route reflects, the Panama Canal, opened in 1914, is the key to the route.

The Cape of Good Hope route links eastern United States and Western Europe with the western, southern, and eastern coasts of Africa, and connects Europe with Southeast Asia and Australia. The congestion on this route is affected by the conditions surrounding the traffic flow through the Suez Canal. During the times when the Suez Canal is closed, the traffic that normally goes through it is directed toward the Cape of Good Hope route. The North Pacific route links the west coast of North America with Eastern Asia. The increasing importance of Eastern economies to the United States has recently intensified traffic on this route.

Inland Waterways, in contrast to oceanways, require frequent dredging, widening, and embankment; also, their role is keenly competitive with other means of transportation—railways, airways, highways, and pipelines. The incidence of inland waterways is determined by:

1. Depth, length, and width of the channel.
2. Perpetuality of stream flow.
3. Frequency and height of falls and locks.
4. Speed of water flow—higher currents not only fill the stream faster, but also cut the banks and alter the stream beds making navigation difficult.
5. Vegetation—rivers with heavy vegetation make it virtually impossible for boats to get through.

6. Alternative uses of the streams and rivers—if alternative uses of the flow outbid the navigational use, the waterways may not be economically justifiable.
7. Technology.
8. Religious and cultural values attached to water flows. Some cultures may not permit the use and development of rivers for navigation. The Ganges River, for example, is a sacred river to most Hindus who would regard its use for navigation as sacriligeous.

Waterways are preferred to other means of transport because the cost per ton-mile is considerably less. This is particularly true for oceanways. The inland waterways, however, due to the keen competition offered by alternative means of transportation, specialize in carrying heavy and bulky commodities—petroleum products, coal and coke, sand, gravel and stone, iron ore, iron and steel, logs and lumber, seashells, chemicals, and grains.

Railways

Railways as means of circulation not only play an important role in the initial stages of economic development, but also help to sustain the achieved development. Their location is determined by:

1. *Collective* initiative and action taken either by private enterprise or by government. Collective action is needed because of the relatively large investment involved, which may be provided through private enterprise, if it is large enough, or subsidized by the government.
2. Suitability and cost of alternative or competing forms of transportation.
3. Terrain and other natural obstacles—areas with high mountains, lakes and streams, and infested areas often discourage the location of railways.
4. Length of haul.
5. Weight of consignment.
6. Locomotive and related technology.

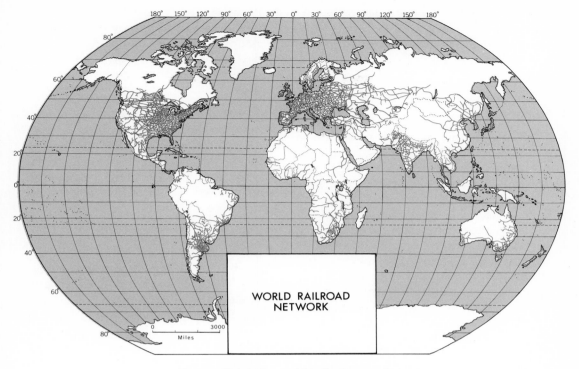

FIGURE 29.2   (*General Media Corporation*)

7. Traffic density—regions with a relatively higher degree of traffic density (water, air, and land) tend to intensify rail transportation.
8. Speed and safety.
9. The availability of steel.

As might be expected, railways are most heavily concentrated in the industrialized areas of the world—Western Europe and the eastern United States; Argentina, India, and eastern Australia also have extensive rail networks.

The gauge or width of the tracks is not universally uniform; in fact, it varies, ranging from three feet in some countries to six feet in others. In 1871 there were twenty-eight different gauges. The "standard gauge" now used in North America and most of Western Europe is 4 feet, 8½ inches. In Spain and Portugal the gauge is 5 feet, 6½ inches; 5 feet in the Soviet Union; in most of South America 3 feet, 3⅛ inches; in India it is partly 5 feet, 6 inches and partly 3 feet, 3⅛ inches, as well as other narrow gauges. The diversity in gauge sizes is a function of relative topography, source(s) of power, the length of the railway routes, technology, the type of traffic, speed, provincialism, and trade. This diversity makes it very difficult for a network to emerge and operate. Where tracks of different gauges meet, entire trainloads of goods need to be transferred through loading operations or through some adjusting track mechanism.

In comparing the relative cost figures between the regional railways, it is particularly important to consider freight rate territories (different rates for different territories), and the group, class, commodity, and in-transit rates. A single group rate applies to all points in a given territory, class rate to small quantity consignments, commodity rate to large consignments; the in-transit rate is a special privilege granted by some authority: the same long route rate schedule is applied as if there were no intervening stoppages, although the intervening stoppages may mean adding to the value (through further processing and altering) of the consignment.

Highways

Highways are means of transportation to produce networks for moving light loads over short distances involving the least amount of time, although the interstate highway system of the United States and Europe also make long hauls feasible.

The location of highways is determined by such factors as topography, availability of gravel and cement, technology, and competitive position of alternative means of transportation, the intensity of traffic (higher intensities of traffic would tend to make railways more feasible), collective initiative and action, environmental pollution, and alternative uses of land. Like railways, highways vary in width, though to a greater degree. Not only are highways differentiated by the number of lanes, type of pavement, bridges, curves, signs, overpasses, and the like, but also by the relative scenery.

Airways

Airways are the most versatile and unrivaled means of moving light and highly valued objects (including perishables like flowers, fresh vegetables and fruits, and seafoods), utilizing advanced technology of containerization, refrigeration, and other devices for speedy handling.

The air route or lane location (both vertically and horizontally) is influenced by:

1. Location of population and industrial centers[6]
2. Location of airports

3. Weather and climate, including the incidence and frequency of fog, heavy clouds, wind, hail, and storms; terrain; navigational technology; size of aircrafts; air pollution; government controls

Figure 29.4 shows the location of major air routes. The intensity of air routes is heaviest in the United States and Western Europe. However, in regions where alternative forms of transportation are few and nebulous, air transportation is of great significance.

The air routes and the carriers, at present, are basically engaged in the moving of people with only a nominal movement of goods. During most of the decade of the sixties, less than one percent of the freight-ton-mileage was handled by the air carriers. However, with the increasing size of aircraft, regional specialization, and the demand for fresh produce, the trend is toward greater utilization of airways for moving goods.

Pipelines

Pipelines, often unseen, are important means of transporting crude oil, natural gas, refined petroleum products, water, and solids in suspension (such as pulverized coal mixed with water).

The location of pipelines is determined by the location of resources and markets; terrain, the dependability and cost of alternative means of transportation, transit "shrinkage," related technology, and the frequency of earthquakes.

As Fig. 29.5 shows, most of the world's pipelines are a phenomenon of the United States, Europe, Canada, and the Middle East. The importance of pipelines in the United States is evidenced by the fact that in 1968 approximately 20 percent of freight-ton-mileage was by pipeline.

[6]Students interested in detailed analysis of air routes use may wish to calculate the ratio between the number of airline passenger departures (or the tonnage shipped) and population of airport cities. The larger the ratio the greater the intensity of air route use and vice versa. The analysis may further be expanded by calculating ratios for various destinations.

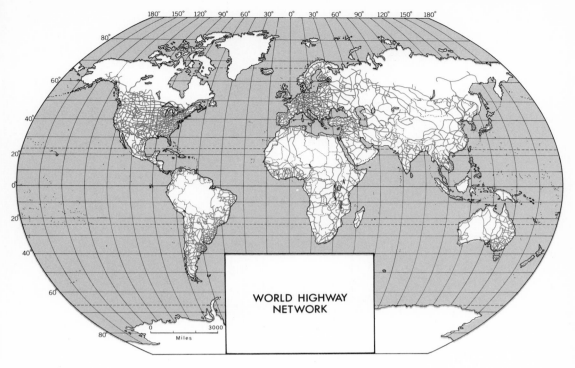

FIGURE 29.3   (*General Media Corporation*)

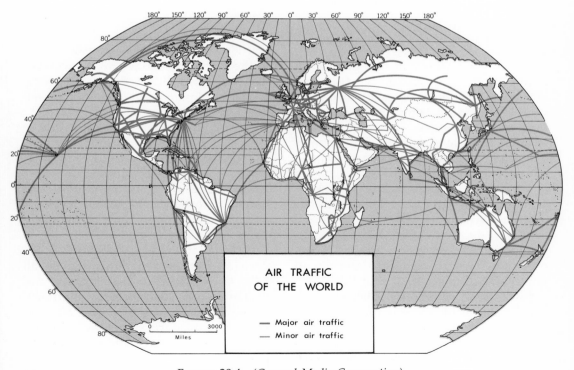

FIGURE 29.4   (*General Media Corporation*)

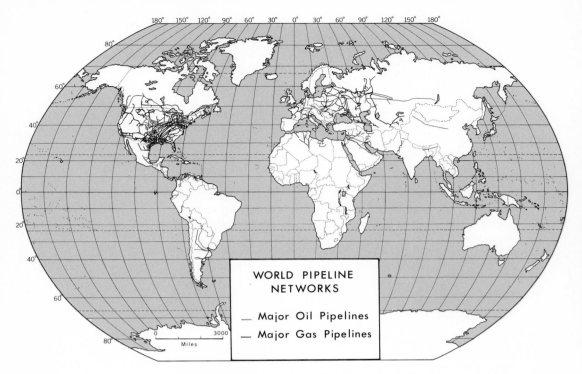

FIGURE 29.5   (*General Media Corporation*)

Telephone, Telegraph and Postal Mail

Telephone and telegraph communication differs from the previously discussed means in that their flows involve electrical impulses carrying messages rather than goods or people. The incidence and location of these services is a function of a multiplicity of factors: distance, income, education, age, degree of specialization and level of trade, structure of the family, spatial mobility and dispersion of friends and family, homogeneity of culture and language, degree of advertising and political activity, alternative means of transportation, terrain, and the intensity of winds and storms.

Postal mail is directly related to the various means of transportation. The distribution and location of post offices is affected by mail traffic, and this, in turn, is affected by the factors listed above.

The pattern of distribution of telephone and telegraph lines is extremely intense, which precludes a meaningful visual display. However, quantitative data reflecting the frequency and length of messages relayed can be used to obtain indications of regional dominance, and social as well as spatial interactions.

Radio and Television

Because of the nature of radio and television messages or communication, the "routes" are nonidentifiable, although radio or television waves intricately thread the atmosphere.

The incidence and location of radio and television stations are influenced by all of the factors listed under telephone and telegraph with the following additional factors: availability of entertainment talent, the nature and size of the audience, the location of airports, and satellite relay systems.

Radio and television facilities are found

primarily in relatively wealthy nations. As the selected 1967 data below show, the United States leads all other countries in the use of radio and television receivers.

Table 29.1 Distribution of Receiver Sets (thousands)

Country	Television	Radio
Australia	2,234	2,538
Canada	5,700*	12,050
India	6	7,579
Japan	19,002*	24,787*
United Kingdom	14,463	17,493
United States	78,000	285,000
U.S.S.R.	22,700	80,700
West Germany	13,806	27,800

*1966 data.

Source: United Nations *Statistical Yearbook*, 1968 (New York, United Nations, 1969), pp. 782–85.

FINANCE, INSURANCE, AND REAL ESTATE

The importance of finance, insurance, and real estate as service industries is well established, in that they facilitate trade, provide security (and thus business confidence), and contribute toward the overall efficiency of the economy. The category varies in terms of percent of national income and/or employment attributed to it; in the United States, for example, about 5 percent of the total employment is attributed to this category.

Banking

Banking as a service industry is characterized by the assets, mostly consisting of bonds and promissory notes, and by its task of accumulating idle funds to be channeled to those who demand them at specific times and places. The task of extending "credit" is preceded by the linking of savers and investors, where these two groups are generally unknown to each other. Banks, the place where people deposit funds and seek loans, have

learned over the past that their function to channel idle funds to those who demand them at certain times and places is enhanced through some sort of coordination of the banking system. Almost all economies have a controlled and coordinated banking system, even those economies where the financial enterprises are privately owned.

The location pattern for banks follows that of population, and is influenced by the availability of police protection, public confidence, communications, and the continuing prospects of economic growth. The banking system may be divided into two major categories: the central bank and the financial intermediaries.

The Central Bank. This controls the money supply and credit through the tools of *discount rates* (the interest rate charged to the banks borrowing from the central bank), the *reserve ratio* (the proportion of the bank deposits required to be kept with the central bank as a legal reserve), and the issuance of money. The structural and operational features of the central bank vary from one country to another—the Federal Reserve System (FRS) of the United States is taken as an example here.

The central structure of the FRS is the Federal Reserve Board of Governors, consisting of seven governors appointed by the President of the United States for fourteen-year terms staggered so that one governor's term expires every other year. The Board—with the advice of FRS auxiliaries (the Federal Open Market Committee and the Federal Advisory Council)—coordinates and directs the activities of the system. Figure 29.7 shows the country divided into twelve Federal Reserve Districts, each with a Federal Reserve Bank. There are also twenty-four Federal Reserve Bank Branches serving particular areas within the districts. Cities with Federal Reserve head offices in the official numerical order are: Boston, New York, Philadelphia, Cleveland, Richmond,

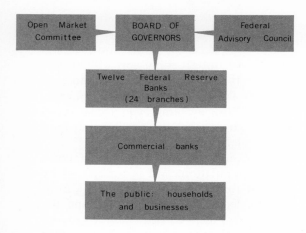

FIGURE 29.6   *The U.S. Federal Reserve system.*

Atlanta, Chicago, St. Louis, Minneapolis, Kansas City, Dallas, and San Francisco. These thirty-six Reserve Banks, including the branches, comprise the second level of the pyramid. So that the Board may be generally representative of the country as a whole, the law requires that not more than one governor may come from any

one Federal Reserve district, and also that due representation be given to various industrial, financial, commercial, and agricultural interests.

The Federal Open Market Committee is composed of twelve members, consisting of the Board of Governors and five representatives chosen by the twelve district banks in the manner that New York has one member; Boston, Philadelphia, and Richmond one; Cleveland and Chicago one; Atlanta, Dallas, and St. Louis one; and the district of Minneapolis, Kansas City, and San Francisco one. The Committee buys and sells securities through the Federal Reserve Bank of New York as a means of controlling the money in circulation.

The Federal Advisory Council, composed of a representative from each district bank, meets at least four times a year with the Board to keep the Board appraised of the situation and problems of the various districts.

There are thousands of member banks (by application). They buy stock in the

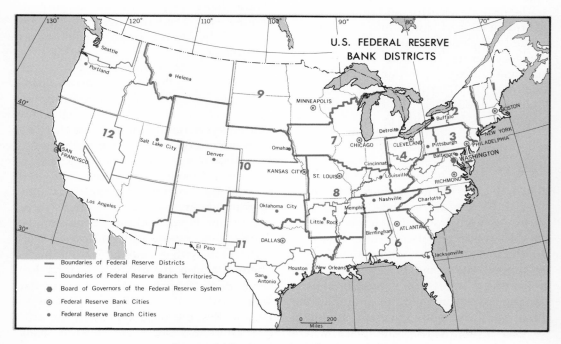

FIGURE 29.7   *(General Media Corporation)*

Federal Reserve Banks, and agree to abide by the rules of Federal Reserve authorities and accept examinations by Federal Reserve officials.

The FRS performs numerous monetary, service, and policy functions for the sake of maintaining a healthy and stable economy. These functions include: currency distribution and control, maintenance of legal reserve accounts (required by legal reserve requirements) for the member banks to control the money supply, provision of a fiscal agent for the U.S. Treasury, which spends hundreds of billions of dollars a year, the inspection of member banks to maintain their solvency and standing with the FRS, a banker's bank to clear checks and to issue loans at a lower interest rate (usually called discount rate) than what prevails in the market, and the control of money in circulation through the buying and selling of securities by the Committee. All of these functions of the FRS, as mentioned earlier, are geared toward encouraging the stability of the economy and to promote economic growth.

The Financial Intermediaries. These are the operational ends of the total banking system (not all intermediaries are members of FRS). They are called intermediaries because of their role as institutions serving the consumers, savers, and investors under the direct or indirect control of the central bank. The major types of the intermediaries are: commercial banks, savings and loan associations, mutual savings banks, insurance companies, finance companies, investment banks, trust companies, stock exchanges, and holding companies. Each intermediary specializes in certain functions, thus contributing to the overall efficiency of the banking system.

Insurance

Insurance is a means of protection against risks and insecurity inherent in certain economic systems of which the United States is an example. The risks and insecurity might be voluntary or involuntary; private insurance services are offered mostly against involuntary risks and insecurity. The insurance services are characterized by:

1. A large number of customers to permit a smaller ratio of claims paid and premium collected
2. Chances of possible risks and insecurities for all customers largely independent of each other
3. Risks and insecurities uncertain or unplanned beyond the control of the insured
4. The insurance claims tending to pay only up to the present market value of the insured objects

Factors affecting the location of insurance services are the same as for banking, with the following additions:

1. The type of economic system (e.g., capitalistic economies would require higher insurance services)
2. The tax advantages
3. The family bond and mutual responsibility
4. Church responsibility and the stand towards helping the destitute
5. The degree of government involvement in welfare assistance
6. The incidence of casualities

The locational patterns of insurance services may follow those that are insured, the offices of the agents, and the central headquarters. The latter follows a hierarchical pattern starting from the central offices located in large population centers and down to insurance agents. In fact, there appears to exist an agglomeration pattern of the various insurance agencies.

Real Estate

Real estate brokers serve as a "clearing house" between the buyers and sellers of real estate property. In the clearing house function, the listing of property for sale, appraisal, and other functions associated with the transfer of real estate is involved.

The location of real estate services is strictly "demand" oriented, and they tend to locate independently of each other. However, it seems that the intensity of real estate services would vary with the levels of education or training of the society (more educated or trained people tend to move frequently, because they are acquainted more fully with the job market), population mobility, the shifts in economic activity (temporary but expanding economic activities would attract a higher level of real estate services), and zoning regulations (zoned out regions would perhaps have lesser levels of real estate services).

RECREATION

Recreation services provide opportunities for satisfying human wants,[7] relaxation, appreciation, mental refreshment, and the like, which emerge from leisure or time not spent earning a living and performing daily chores and functions. Conceptually speaking, there are two types of recreational services—direct and indirect. Direct services include situations where the recreationist is directly involved in the experience of recreation. Indirect services include the production or manufacturing processes that cater to the recreation services but with practically no meaningful or direct involvement of the recreationists. Our discussion is concerned with the former.

The direct recreation services may be divided into:

1. Indoor—outdoor household activities occurring in or around the residential quarters
2. Indoor–outdoor entertainment, such as theaters, symphonies, sidewalk shows or performances, etc.
3. Indoor–outdoor participation activities, such as local game leagues, fishing, hiking, golf, swimming, surfing, camping, horseback riding, etc.

A person's engagement in a particular type of recreation activity at a particular place is a function of the availability and length of his leisure time, tastes and preferences, income, occupation, education, sex, age—as well as the availability of alternative recreation facilities translated in terms of time, distance, and cost, population of the recreationist's locale, and incidence and frequency of intervening recreation facilities. This list of factors suggests that the location of recreation is demand oriented; further evidence from findings of the U.S. Outdoor Recreation Resources Review Commission (ORRRC)[8] support the thesis that the availability of recreation resources (particularly outdoors) play a dominant role in the locational patterns of recreation activities. The ORRRC [14] further asserts:

Natural endowment is relevant and may be important, but it needs to be considered in relation to other relevant aspects of the location problem to be given its proper weight in analysis bearing on outdoor recreation development.

The implications of natural endowment for location are brought into sharper focus by recognizing again one important distinction between outdoor recreation services produced at a site and the more usual type of good or service produced in an economy. This is, that the final outdoor recreation product is not

---

[7]Human wants oriented toward recreation are very subjective and personal, varying from one individual to another; thus they are devoid of any specific definition.

[8]The U.S. Outdoor Recreation Resources Review Commission, created in 1958, has attempted to study the recreation wants and needs of Americans now, with future projections for 1976 and 2000; the avail-

able resources to fill those needs; and policies and programs needed to insure that the recreation needs of the present and future are adequately and efficiently met. The commission's findings, conclusions, and recommendations, contained in a series of reports submitted to the President and Congress, highlight the ever-increasing participation in recreation, the shortage of needed resources, and the steps needed to alleviate this imbalance.

transportable. Final consumers of outdoor recreation services must consume these services at the site of production. The large bulk of ordinary goods produced has incorporated in its production a certain amount of transportation, and cost of transportation becomes an essential component of cost of production. Ordinary goods are, on the whole, transported to consumers. In outdoor recreation, on the other hand, consumers transport themselves to the product. This distinction takes on some importance with reference to measurement of demand for recreation. (p. 24)

Various studies [6, 10, 14] to measure the demand (in terms of participation or visitor days) for outdoor recreation confirm the relevance of the above-listed factors influencing location of outdoor recreation activities. The demand for entertainment activities is heavily influenced by population thresholds. Thus the location of recreational activities is basically demand determined—that is, recreation activity is realized only if participated in by individuals. A natural recreation site, although tending to attract recreationists, may not be visited at all, resulting in a zero recreation activity.

Difficulties in the specification and measurement of demand for recreation basically stem from the contention that values of recreation cannot be adequately measured in monetary terms—who can estimate the value of a walk through majestic and serene woods, the sight of sunset on the ocean, or the thrill of catching a fifteen pounder? However, assuming that recreationists obtain enjoyment worth the money spent for experiencing recreation, plus the amount they would have earned had they not chosen to recreate, many state agencies and the U.S. Bureau of Outdoor Recreation have developed expenditures data. These data along with employment and participation rates may be used for detailed analyses of outdoor recreation.

PUBLIC UTILITIES

Utilities services—electricity, steam, gas, water, and waste disposal—are provided either by publicly owned or franchised agencies. Their monopolistic nature is justified by the economies of scale and the indivisibility of the flow system of the services involved.

The spatial incidence and level of utilities services are determined by:

1. The size and density of population
2. Proximity to service production facilities
3. Political strength and pressure
4. Public initiative and action
5. Culture—certain cultures shun the use of indoor toilets for the sake of maintaining soil fertility, or may be reluctant to use utilities-oriented resources because of religious values
6. Availability of revenues for construction and maintenance of the facilities

Although public utilities are common in larger, well-to-do communities, a determined and willing group of people, through collective action, may provide these services even in smaller communities. Indeed, the smaller communities bear a higher cost because of the diseconomies of scale. However, this cost coupled with the relative poverty of a community still may not deter a collective effort. These patterns are emerging in developing economies where the will of people to enjoy these services is created through various self-help programs.

GOVERNMENT INSTITUTIONS

Government is a composite act, performed by men, of providing protection against internal and external threats, controlling and directing the ascribed and defined affairs, and assisting its citizens to achieve fulfillment of life's goals and values. From the point of view of its overall nature and structure, government may be any one of the three forms—autocracy (one individual responsible for making all basic decisions), oligarchy (a group of men making basic decisions), and democracy (all people of age making basic decisions through their elected representatives—or some modification or combination of the three.

The level and structure of government is determined not only by its political form but also by the type of economic system present—capitalism, communism, socialism, and fascism. (A given political system may have any one or a combination of these economic systems.) Under a system of pure capitalism, government activity is limited to defense, justice, protection, and minimum possible intervention into the "business" sector. Under communism every activity, by definition, is government.

The magnitude and spatial distribution of government activity at various levels (national, multi-state, state, county, city, or the Standard Metropolitan Statistical Area) are determined by:

1. Density and mobility of population
2. Cost—given the level of government, government activities tend to locate where the initial and operating costs are minimum
3. Political pressures and strength (this factor often plays a dominant role in the location process)
4. Social structures—certain social conditions (disorders, disease, age composition, religious beliefs, racial structures) may influence the level and location of government activity
5. The economic system
6. National defense objectives
7. Control and communication—a system of location that maximizes communication, and in some cases maximizes control, would enter into consideration of government activity location

The above list of general factors may vary depending upon the particular government activity in question. For example, government activity in the fields of education[9] and health may be heavily affected by the local (districts, counties, and states) revenue and political aspects.

Interesting patterns may be developed by computing a ratio between the income paid to government employees and the total income of the areas to demonstrate the effects of the above-listed factors.

RESEARCH AND DEVELOPMENT

Research and Development (R & D), an activity rendered by highly skilled personnel, is increasing rapidly in the developed economies as a consequence of the greater realization that R & D is perhaps the only answer for achieving higher economic growth rates and consequently improving the standard of living. The activity involves research and exploration of new ideas, products, processes, and areas (including outer space).

The concept of R & D is an extension of the concept of technology—which supposedly does not include the actual testing, application, and the relevancy of the discovery—encompassing broader scopes, virtually applying to every human activity. The term R & D, as defined by the Organization for Economic Cooperation and Development,

. . . covers all work undertaken for the advancement of scientific knowledge, undertaken with or without a specific practical aim in view (applied and basic research), and the use of the results of basic and applied research directed to the introduction of new products and processes or the improvement of existing ones.

A measure of the activity may be the employment figures as used for most of the other economic activities. However, for various structural reasons, and simply for lack of the adequacy of such data, expenditures figures have frequently been used to reflect its extent and location.

Presently the United States is spending approximately 4 percent of its Gross Na-

[9]Parochial educational institutions tend usually to locate in proximity to the concentrations of their supporters.

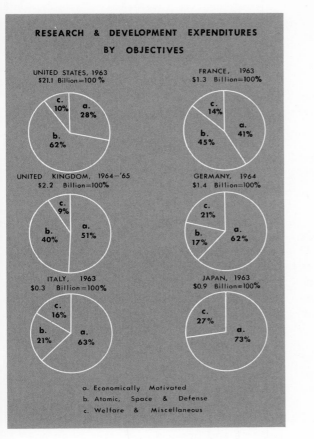

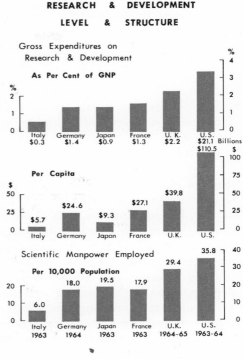

FIGURE 29.8 *R & D expenditures by selected countries.*

tional Product (GNP) on research and development, contrasted to over 2 percent in the United Kingdom, and less than 2 percent in Japan, Germany, and France. During 1968, the United States spent over $32 billion on R & D—about two-thirds in atomic, space, and defense, about one-fourth in economically motivated objectives, and the remainder for welfare and miscellaneous objectives. Germany, Japan, the United Kingdom, France, and Italy spent from one-half to three-fourths of their total R & D funds for economically motivated objectives. These governments have contributed over 60 percent of the total R & D spending.

The chief industrial recipient of government funds for the support of R & D activities in the United States, United Kingdom, and France is the aircraft industry, which receives respectively 60.6 percent, 70.3 percent, and 59.1 percent of R & D funds provided by the government to industry [13].

Factors affecting the location of R & D activity are:

1. The location of industries using R & D (regions with aircraft and missiles, electrical and communication equipment, chemicals, machinery, transportation equipment, and other major manufacturing industries have attracted higher levels of R & D)
2. Per capita income
3. Political commitments

4. Locale of "raw materials"—the universities, technical and professional personnel
5. The commitment towards higher economic growth
6. Culture (a culture committed and receptive to change would attract a higher level of R & D)
7. Level of defense budget
8. Size of business organizations (larger business sizes permit a higher level of R & D)
9. Amenity factors

Regional characters change significantly over time with the presence of R & D activity. Expenditures on R & D tend to have both short-run and long-run effects. Short-run effects of R & D expenditures in a region are realized in terms of newer jobs and incomes, and consequently further expansion in the induced activities.

Although data on long-run effects of R & D expenditures on regional economies are limited, available studies generally indicate that

regions that are relatively rich in scientific talent will derive subsequent economic benefit, and those that are relatively poor in scientific talent will suffer subsequent economic loss. In the technological era in which we live it would, therefore, appear that the distribution of scientific talent does indeed raise economic issues that should not be ignored. [11, p. 231]

There is evidence to suggest that as available scientific talent in a region increases, a more than proportional increase in R & D funds tends to follow. In addition, regions with large R & D efforts appear to have more consistent economic growth than do other regions—resulting from new industries and firms "spinning-off" from the R & D expenditures in the same area.

In 1963 and 1965, ten states received more than 70 percent of all federal R & D grants, which represents about two-thirds of the funds for domestic research and development. This reflects a relatively high degree of concentration in the regional distribution of R & D funds.

It may be concluded that R & D activity, since it tends to follow regions with particular industries, helps to maintain and perhaps accentuate existing regional economic differences. The discovery of these patterns and impacts may serve as an enlightening source for policy decisions to help depressed areas.

Table 29.2 Distribution of Federal Research and Development Obligations, Ten Leading States

States	Total Obligations (millions of dollars) 1963	1965	Percent Distribution 1963	1965
Total	$12,250	$14,357	100.0%	100.0%
California	4,283	4,553	35.0	31.7
New York	944	1,289	7.7	9.0
Maryland	676	877	5.5	6.1
Massachusetts	515	734	4.2	5.1
Texas	398	731	3.2	5.1
Pennsylvania	435	529	3.6	3.7
Florida	341	460	2.8	3.2
New Mexico	346	425	2.8	3.0
New Jersey	410	411	3.3	2.9
Ohio	304	379	2.5	2.6

Source: National Science Foundation, *Geographic Distribution of Federal Funds for Research and Development,* Fiscal Year 1965 (Washington, D.C.: U.S. Government Printing Office, 1967).

MARKETING ACTIVITIES

Marketing activities involve the process of transferring a good or service from one possessor to another. In this process, services are performed to create five different kinds of utility values:

1. Form—grading, variety, cleaning, minor processing, etc.
2. Place—procurement and delivery of goods and services
3. Time—storing the goods and services to be made available when demanded
4. Convenience—closeness to residences to reduce transfer cost[10]
5. Possession—provide quick possession at one place (for example, the checkout line) of various kinds of goods and services

Numerous categories of people are involved in creating these utilities—wholesalers, retailers, auctioneers, salesmen, brokers, creditors, jobbers, lawyers, employment agencies, advertisers, and so on. All these people—"middlemen"—are performing a service in assisting the transferring of goods and services from one possessor to another. It is a service because it adds one or more of the above-listed utility values.

The location patterns of marketing activities are influenced by the following generic factors; each subactivity under the marketing title would indeed have more specific or different factors.

Accessibility. Marketing centers or activities tend to locate at places most accessible to consumers or buyers of the services in terms of time, proximity, convenience, means of communication, and transfer cost. Population and the factors governing their demand are influential in location patterns.

Agglomeration. Marketing activities tend to concentrate at a single location (e.g., service centers) to permit one-stop shopping, to minimize transfer cost, meet buyers' desires to compare prices and quality as well as to let the sellers effectively compete, reduce overhead cost of buildings, utilities, night watching, and parking, to minimize the risks of robbery, vandalism, and to reduce some advertising costs by sharing commonly sponsored advertising attractions such as circuses, children's amusements, special shows, etc.

Space requirements. Space needed for the performance of service often influences the location of marketing services. For example, furniture stores and automobile dealers would choose locations of relatively lower cost.

Homogeneity or heterogeneity of the products or services sold. The services dealing with fairly homogeneous products (groceries, gasoline, laundry and dry cleaning, etc.) tend to follow the residential patterns; services dealing with heterogeneous objects tend to follow the shopping center pattern to permit convenient and quick comparisons of merchandise.

Spatial interdependence. The level and structure of marketing activities at one location are directly dependent upon the facilities and attractions at alternative or surrounding locations. The considerations of spatial interdependence partly explains the hierarchical arrangements of wholesaling, retailing, shopping centers, advertising, etc. Within this hierarchical system, a metropolis (as a service center) encompasses the city, and the city encompasses the town, and so on down to neighborhood centers.

Zoning ordinances. The zoning ordi-

---

[10]The concept of *transfer cost* applies to the cost associated with the effort, time, and pecuniary aspects of acquiring a good or service. Transfer cost is over and above the store, sticker, or stamped price. Often buyers are not explicitly aware of this aspect of the total price; they tend only to compare store prices.

nances are political influences that shape the pattern activity locations.

Transportation. Transportation, in particular the network of superhighways, is influencing the emergence of huge shopping centers in the "middle of nowhere." These communication-oriented service locations are also motivated by accessibility and agglomeration factors.

To conclude, marketing activities seek locations of proximity to customers, taking into consideration the nature and size of demand, in harmony with the sellers' objectives—minimum internal cost, maximum external profit, and perhaps other long-range economic, social and political objectives.

Conclusion

The above presentation yields the following generalizations:

1. A strong affinity exists between the distributions of demand and services.
2. The distribution of services within a particular population center is complex and intricately influenced by numerous factors.
3. The location pattern for each type of service varies not only in spatial but also in hierarchical structure.
4. Agglomerate service centers are becoming more predominantly characteristic of marketing activities.

This discussion by no means exhausts the list of service activities. In fact, with increasing specialization, leisure time, and income, the list is expanding every day. Never before have we used so broad a variety of services in our daily lives. The rise in the demand for services has outpaced and is likely to continue to outpace the demand for goods.

Services not only provide a bulk of the employment in the developed countries, but they are also sensitive reflectors of price changes. For example, in the three year period, 1965 to 1968, the overall U.S. consumer price index rose 11.4 percent, but within that index service costs rose much higher, and hospital costs rose 52 percent.

selected references

1. Belshaw, C. S., *Traditional Exchange and Modern Markets*, Englewood Cliffs, N. J.: Prentice-Hall, Inc., 1965.

2. Berry, J. L. B., *Geography of Market Centers and Retail Distribution*, Englewood Cliffs, N. J.: Prentice-Hall, Inc., 1967.

3. ———, "Retail Location and Consumer Behavior", *Papers and Proceedings of the Regional Science Association*, Vol. 9, 1962, pp. 65–106.

4. Bollens, J. C. and Schmandt, H. J., *The Metropolis: Its People, Politics, and Economic Life*, New York: Harper and Row Publishers, 1965.

5. Burton, Ian, "A Restatement of the Dispersed City Hypothesis," *Annals of the Association of American Geographers*, Vol. 56, September 1963, pp. 285–89.

6. Clawson, M., *Methods of Measuring Demand for the Value of Outdoor Recreation*, Washington, D.C.: The Resources for the Future, 1962.

7. Dacey, M. F., "The Geometry of Central Place Theory," *Geografisha Annaler*, Vol. 47B, 1965, pp. 111–124.

8. Duncan, O. D., "Service Industries and the Urban Hierarchy," *Papers and Proceedings of the Regional Science Association*, Vol. 5, 1959, pp. 105–120.

9. Gibbs, Jack P., "The Evolution of Population Concentration," *Economic Geography*, Vol. 39, No. 2, April 1963, pp. 119–129.

10. Gillespie, G. A. and Brewer, D., "Effects of Nonprice Variables Upon Participation in Water-oriented Outdoor Recreation," *American Journal of Agricultural Economics*, Vol. 50, No. 1, February 1968, pp. 82–95.

11. Horowitz, Ina, "Some Aspects of the Effects of the Regional Distribution of Scientific Talent on Regional Economic Activity," *Management Science*, Vol. 13, 1966.

12. Huff, D. L., "A Probability Analysis of Shopping Center Trading Areas," *Land Economics*, Vol. 53, February 1963, pp. 81–90.

13. National Industrial Conference Board, "R & D: Level and Structure in Selected Countries," *Road Maps*, No. 1585, January 1, 1968.

14. Outdoor Recreation Resources Review Commission, *Economic Studies of Outdoor Recreation,* Study Report 24, Washington, D.C., 1962.

15. Patmore, J. Allan, "The British Railway Network in the Beeching Era," *Economic Geography,* Vol. 41, No. 1, January 1965, pp. 71–81.

16. Wallace, William H., "The Bridge Line: A Distinctive Type of Anglo-American Railroad," *Economic Geography,* Vol. 41, No. 1, January 1965, pp. 1–38.

part VI
Reference, Policy, and Planning

introduction

In Parts I and II, we dealt with culture, resource, and economic activity, and variables in economic activity, in order to set the stage for Parts III through V, which implement by example the principles established previously.

Now we turn our attention to another array of ideas that are also pertinent to all economic activities, that is, measurement and measurement process, measures of dispersion, variance, and standard deviation, systems analysis, and linear programming in Chapter 30.

In Chapter 31 we will be concerned with the field of urban and regional planning, and will attempt to formulate statements that directly relate to better ways for man to utilize the space he occupies.

History supports the view that the economic significance or usefulness of an academic field advances in conjunction with the increasing degree of positivity[1] and "quantitative" sophistication employed by the field. Although a statistical orientation increases the level of abstraction, thoughtful comments by some leading geographers [1, 2, 4, 8, 10, 12, 14, 15] document the strong need for it. It should be noted that statistical orientation is not the same thing as quantitative orientation, although a definite relationship exists between the two, since the latter connotes quantification of various geographic variables. Statistical orientation is helpful in constructing conceptual frameworks of economic phenomena and in generalizing from particular events. Thus, theoretical behavior patterns of spatial phenomena can be built against the observed distributions and patterns, and space relations can be tested. Knowledge of the *what, where, how, when,* and *why* of economic phenomena can be quantitatively expressed and communicated. This is possible because, for the most part, areal content is observable and subject to some form of classification; each classification reflects the attributes of pattern, density, scatter, level or extent, distribution, shape, and changes over time. The classifications or variables may also show interaction and/or correlation. Thus, both quantitative as well as statistical orientation are necessary for spatial analyses. Our concern here is to introduce the basic concepts and illustrate their usefulness.

MEASUREMENT

Measurement of economic activity involves the consideration of:

1. The process of measurement
2. The choice of unit of measurement

---

[1]*Positivity* refers to approaches dealing with "what is" instead of "what ought to be." The latter is the concern of normative approaches.

chapter **30**

Statistical Concepts for Spatial Analysis

3. The scale of measurement
4. The type of measurement

Measurement Process

The process of measurement is the scheme of assigning value to the level or state of some attribute of a phenomenon. There are three recognized systems of measurement: metric, ordinal, and nominal.

The *metric* system employs a unit of measure such as grams, meters, and liters. However, metric measure may be expressed either as an interval or a ratio system. The former involves a measuring scale whose zero point is arbitrary. For example, the zero point on the Fahrenheit scale does not mean absence of heat. The latter employs a scale whose zero point means an absence of the attribute that is being measured. The choice between the interval and the ratio metric systems is a function of the objectives. The interval system, for instance, often is used only when interest is in a part of the total range of the variable. Spatial analysis of family incomes between $6,000 and $12,000 may employ a scale whose zero point represents $6,000. Indeed the interval system is expedient, given the objectives.

The *ordinal* measuring system employs comparative ranking as values of the attribute being measured. An example would be a ranking of regions (first, second, third, etc.) in terms of their employment, production, amenity, and the like. The ranking may be based on the metric measures of the phenomena or on a qualitative assessment. Geographers have extensively used the ordinal system to simplify and to reduce mountains of data into easily digestible presentations.

The *nominal* measuring system involves categorizing phenomena into predetermined characters. Although multinominal systems are possible, the most commonly used is the binominal system, which employs two-sided characters: human, male or female; insects, dead or alive; places, ru-

ral or urban; an answer to a question, yes or no; fruit, ripe or unripe; water, hot or cold; coin, head or tail, and the like. An observation assumes one or the other character—after, of course, the process of identifying, discerning, and designating has taken place. The nominal measuring system is employed when the phenomenon being observed is qualitative; very little use of this system has been made in geography because most geographic phenomena lend themselves to the metric and ordinal measuring systems.

All three kinds of measuring systems can be subjected to statistical analyses. The quality of results provided by these analyses depends upon the validity and reliability of the measurement. *Validity* deals with the appropriateness of the measurement employed, given the objectives, while *reliability* concerns the precision, objectivity, and trustworthiness with which a particular measure is obtained. Students may wish to refer to Chapter 8 to review the section on scientific objectivity.

Unit Choice

The metric system involves a unit of measurement. But the question of choice is crucial. Not only do the units tend to vary from one area to another—influenced by cultural values and standards and national policies—but also the meaning assigned to a given unit may vary. For example, liquid is measured in gallons, cups, buckets, jugs, or cubic feet. The capacity of the gallon also varies—the imperial gallon (5 quarts), the U.S. gallon (4 quarts). A bushel of apples has all kinds of varying weights.

The economic geographer, by the nature of his task (dealing with spatial data), is often faced with the problem of choosing (or standardizing) the proper units that provide valid and reliable measures. Standardized measures for weights, volumes, and distances (quantitative measurement) can be developed by the use of conversion factors: 1 hectare = 2.471 acres; 1 imperial gallon ≅ 5/4 U.S. gallons; one U.S. dollar ≅ .9001 Australian dollar; one mile ≅ 1.61 kilometers; one metric ton = .984 long ton = 1.1023 short tons (used in the U.S.) = 1000 kilograms; one British thermal unit (BTU) = 252 calories; and the like.[2] But the task of standardizing the *quality* differences of commodities often presents problems. How many Italian cars are equivalent to one Rolls Royce or to one Cadillac? How many Japanese crescent wrenches are equal to a given size U.S.-made crescent wrench? How many Indian Bata shoes are equal to a pair of Nunnbush or Florsheim? These problems, although they do not lend themselves to satisfactory solutions, may be tackled through the use of quality weights—horsepower, durability, content, international value approximated through exchange rates, and other such measures of quality.

Measurement Scale

As indicated earlier, any statistical concept or method can be applied to all kinds of measurements. Scale is not a measurement; it is a concept that expresses a relationship between the actual data and their visual presentation. The quantitative size of spatial data is large and cumbersome. Thus, it is expedient to scale it to meaningful and practical expressions: so many miles per inch on a map; so many units per graph paper block; so many inhabitants per circle (or some other shape), or per circle size.

Scale works both ways: On the one hand it may be used to reduce the size of the variables; on the other it may be used to explode the variables. The particular scale (type and/or level) used depends upon the objectives. It is important to recognize that the particular shape and nature of tabular, graphic, or pictorial display is a result of the specific scale

used; consequently the conclusions differ with the scale employed.

Type of Measurement

There are basically two types of measurements: descriptive and analytical. The former provides answers for the questions related to the level, location, or the characteristics of geographic phenomena; the latter is based on the former, and it concerns the nature and extent of relationship between them.

Geographic measurement is no different than that made in other social sciences, except that its measurements are related to areas, or points on the earth's surface, or the environment of activities carried out on or about the earth's surface.

The descriptive and analytical titles as the types of measurement are general and interactive. It is expedient to look at the measurement types from a functional point of view. Thus the measurement types may be functionally classified as:

1. Data and their representations
2. Measures of central tendency
3. Measures of dispersion
4. Measures of interrelationships

DATA AND THEIR REPRESENTATIONS

Data are the numerical values (metric, ordinal, or cardinal) for any defined activity and area and time over which the activity is distributed. A complete set of data is described as population. Based on these data or on sample data taken from the population, numerous representations can be developed—namely, tables, frequency distributions, histograms, line graphs, pictographs, scattergraphs, bar charts, pie charts, maps, and the like.

Data may involve any activity or any aspect of it: population, income, employment, production, trade, prices, retailing,

---

[2] ≅ means approximately equal to.

Table 30.1   Per Capita Income Received From All Sources, 1965
(Selected States)

State Number	State	Per Capita Income	Rank	Percent of U.S. Per Capita Income
	United States	$2,746		100
1	Alaska	3,187	6	116
2	California	3,258	5	119
3	Connecticut	3,401	1	124
4	Delaware	3,392	2	124
5	Hawaii	2,879	7	105
6	Indiana	2,846	8	104
7	Mississippi	1,608	13	59
8	Nevada	3,311	3	121
9	New Hampshire	2,547	10	93
10	New York	3,278	4	119
11	North Carolina	2,041	11	74
12	West Virginia	2,027	12	74
13	Wyoming	2,558	9	93

Source: U.S. Department of Commerce, Office of Business Economics, *Pocket Data Book: USA 1967* (Washington, D.C.: Government Printing Office, December 1966), p. 189.

settlements, taxation, and so on. Let us look at the selected state personal (per capita) incomes for the United States to demonstrate these representations. The first thing that could be done is to arrange this data into a table. A table should communicate clearly the information it contains so that no additional instructions will be required to understand it. The 1965 state personal incomes are tabulated in Table 30.1.

The data in Table 30.1 might then be scaled to $1000 = $1.00 and arranged into a frequency distribution as shown in Table 30.2. The frequency distribution may be used to construct a histogram (Fig. 30.1). The income differentiation may also be shown on a map. The column of relative frequency may be used to construct a pie chart or a pictograph.

A scattergraph, using the data of Table 30.1, is shown in Fig. 30.2. The scatter-

Table 30.2   Frequency Distribution of Scaled Personal Income

Scaled Income (rounded)	Absolute Frequency	Relative Frequency
1.6	1	.0769
2.0	2	0.1538
2.5	1	0.0769
2.6	1	0.0769
2.8	1	0.0769
2.9	1	0.0769
3.2	1	0.0769
3.3	3	0.2308
3.4	2	0.1538
Total	13	1.0000

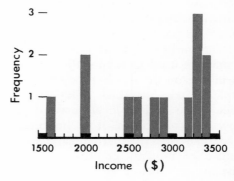

FIGURE 30.1   *Histogram of scaled personal income.*

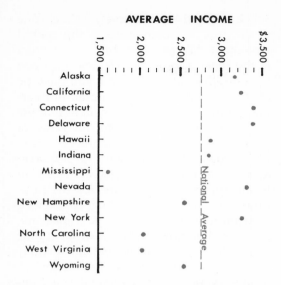

FIGURE 30.2   *Scattergraph of scaled personal income.*

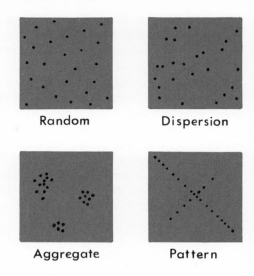

FIGURE 30.3   *Density—random, dispersion, aggregate, and pattern.*

graph, in general, presents the spatial distribution of data reflecting the visual conception of the phenomena. In geographic terminology, these conceptions are termed density and dispersion. *Density* is the degree of overall frequency of occurrence of a spatial variate relative to the size of the region or area. The personal dollar income density may be approximated as:

$$\text{density} = \frac{\text{personal income} \times \text{population}}{\text{area}}.$$

Dispersion is the degree of spread of a spatial variate relative to the size of the region. The dispersion may reflect random, aggregate, or a specific pattern type of distribution (Fig. 30.3).

MEASURES OF CENTRAL TENDENCY

Several measures of central tendency, each suited for a particular problem and computed differently, are used in geographic research. These are mode, median, and mean.

The *mode* is defined as the most frequently occurring value. This value is easily recognized from a frequency distribution of noncategorized data, such as in Table 30.2 where the mode is 3.3. For categorized data, additional computations (interpolation) are needed to obtain a single value for the mode. In some cases, more than one mode may be present.

The *median* is the middle value in a set of ranked data. In an odd number of data observations the median is identified as the $(n + 1)/2$th element, where n is the number of observations. In Table 30.2, $n = 13$, and the median value is $(13 + 1)/2$, or the 7th ranked observation, which is 2.9 (scaled and rounded). In the case of an even number of data observations, there are two median values corresponding to the $n/2$th and $(n + 2)/2$th observations. Supposing Table 30.2 had fourteen observations instead of thirteen, then the median values would be 2.9 (14/2th observation) and 3.2 [(14 + 2)/2th observation].

As is evident from Table 30.2, the median is affected solely by the values of observations in the median range; the values outside this range have no effect *whatsoever* on the median. Median is considered an appropriate measure of central tendency for populations that are skewed in distribution. The distribution represented by the histogram (Fig. 30.1) represents a skewed distribution. Why does a median provide a better measure for the skewed distributions? An answer to this question is delayed until after the discussion of mean.

Mean may be simple mean, harmonic mean, or a geometric mean. All three are arithmetically derived. *Simple mean* is the average of all observations taken, each observation given the same weight. The simple mean is symbolically expressed as

$$\bar{x} = \sum_{i=1}^{n} x_i/n, \qquad (1)$$

where n = number of observations,
   x = the value of observations,
   $i = 1, 2, 3, \ldots, n,$
   Σ = "the sum of."

This expression means that all of the observations 1, 2, 3, . . . and including the nth are to be summed and then divided by the number of observations. Formula 1 is used to derive simple mean for data not arranged in a frequency table.

For the data arranged in a frequency table the following formula would be suitable.

$$\bar{x} = \sum_{j=1}^{k} f_j x_j / \Sigma j, \qquad (2)$$

where f = frequency (the number of times) by which an observation is repeated in the data,
   k = the number of individual f,
   $j = 1, 2, 3, \ldots, k,$
   $\Sigma j = n.$

The data of Table 30.1, when substituted into formula 1, yield the simple mean of $36,333/13 = 2,795$, which when scaled and rounded is 2.8. The same result, except for rounding errors, is obtained using formula 2. (Formula 2 presupposes that the data are arranged in the form of a frequency table as in Table 30.2.)

To recapitulate, the computed values of mode, median, and simple mean are 3.3, 2.9, and 2.8 respectively. Which one is the true representative of the central tendency? All three are, but one of them is the most appropriate depending upon the objectives of the research and the type of data distribution. As pointed out earlier, mode is a crude approximation of the central tendency; it shows the value of the observation most frequently occurring in the data. Mode is never a sufficient measure of central tendency alone. Mean is an appropriate measure for distributions not skewed. For highly skewed distributions the mean is a poor measure, because although only a few observations can influence the mean, yet it still may not be representative of the "majority" of observations. As a general rule, statistics pertaining to income, precipitation, and wealth are skewed; they are better represented in terms of median.

The *geometric mean* is defined as

$$\log \bar{x} = \sum_{i=1}^{n} \log x_i/n, \qquad (3)$$

which means that n observations expressed in logarithms[3] are added, and then divided by the number of observations to produce a mean in logarithmic number. An antilog of this logarithmic mean is the geometric mean. Table 30.3

[3]If b is any positive number and $b^l = a$, l may be called the logarithm of a to the base of b. This reflects that any positive number can serve as a base. From the practical point of view, however, two bases are commonly used. One is 10, which serves as a base for conventionally named *common* logarithms; it is used for ordinary computational purposes. The other is an irrational number, 2.718+ (commonly expressed as e), which serves as a base for natural logarithms; it is used for analytical purposes.

The common logarithm of a number is the exponent of the power to which 10 must be raised to yield that number. For example, $\log_{10} 1000 = 3$ means that the base 10 must be raised to the power of 3 to yield 1000. The antilog of the logarithmic number 3 is 1000. Logarithm tables are commonly available for use; students may wish to refer to these tables and the mechanical steps to locate the logarithms and antilogarithms.

The logarithmic method of dealing with numbers not only makes the computation easier and less cumbersome, but it also provides a means of transforming positively skewed distributions into approximate symmetrical distributions.

Table 30.3   Computation of Geometric Mean

Scaled Income (rounded)	log₁₀ of Scaled Income (x)
1.6	0.2041
2.0	0.3010
2.0	0.3010
2.5	0.3979
2.6	0.4150
2.8	0.4472
2.9	0.4624
3.2	0.5051
3.3	0.5185
3.3	0.5185
3.3	0.5185
3.4	0.5315
3.4	0.5315
	$\Sigma = 5.6522$

illustrates the logarithms to the base 10 of the observations of Table 30.2. Formula 3 may be written as

$$\log_{10} \bar{x} = \frac{5.5622}{13} \cong .4348.$$

The antilog of .4348 $\cong$ 2.724, which is the geometric mean.

The geometric mean is a useful measure of central tendency for certain *positively* skewed distributions such as income and wealth. Also, all observations need to be positive and nonzero before they can be subjected to geometric mean. This kind of mean is less sensitive to extremely large values (which no doubt affect the simple mean toward a higher estimate), and consequently produces an appropriate although conservative estimate of the central tendency. Logarithms, by virtue of their method of special scaling, serve only as a technique to adjust the weight of positive extreme values in the data. They do not affect the arithmetic mechanics of deriving the mean, however.

The *harmonic mean* (hm) is defined as the reciprocal of the arithmetic average of the reciprocals. Symbolically it is written as

$$\bar{x}_{hm} = \frac{n}{\sum\limits_{i=1}^{n} \dfrac{1}{x_i}} = \frac{1}{\dfrac{1}{n}\left(\sum\limits_{i=1}^{n} \dfrac{1}{x_i}\right)}. \qquad (4)$$

To compute harmonic mean, the reciprocal of each observation is taken, then the mean of these reciprocals is computed, and finally the reciprocal of this mean is taken; the resulting mean is the harmonic mean. The scaled and rounded observations of Table 30.2 are used in Table 30.4 to illustrate the mechanics of computation.

Table 30.4   Computation of Harmonic Mean

x	1/x
1.6	0.6250
2.0	0.5000
2.0	0.5000
2.5	0.4000
2.6	0.3846
2.8	0.3571
2.9	0.3448
3.2	0.3125
3.3	0.3030
3.3	0.3030
3.3	0.3030
3.4	0.2941
3.4	0.2941
	$\Sigma = 4.9212$

$$\bar{x}_{hm} = \frac{13}{4.9212} \cong 2.642$$

Harmonic mean is used in special cases where the data are expressed in two different units of measure: feet per second, units of output per minute, and so on. One of the two is constant and the other varies. For example, if the income data of Table 30.2 were expressed as income produced per hour—income and time being the two characteristics—the data are read as shown in Table 30.5.

It is evident that the number of hours is constant—Alaska produces $3.20 on the *average* per hour, California $3.30, Connecticut $3.40, and so on. The simple mean would, if taken, implicitly give equal weight to each state's earning rate. In actuality, however, the productivity is different for different states (and workers) for a specified time period (one hour in this case). The harmonic mean alleviates this problem by converting the data into time spent per dollar earned through the taking of reciprocals. The second recipro-

Table 30.5   Per hour Personal Income

States	Dollars of Income Produced Per Hour (scaled and rounded)
Alaska	3.20
California	3.30
Connecticut	3.40
Delaware	3.40
Hawaii	2.90
Indiana	2.80
Mississippi	1.60
Nevada	3.30
New Hampshire	2.50
New York	3.30
North Carolina	2.00
West Virginia	2.00
Wyoming	2.60

cal brings the result back to dollars per hour.

It is important to note that the harmonic mean can be applied only when (1) the observations are expressed as rates of change involving two different characteristics, and (2) when no observation in the data is equal to zero, since division by zero is undefined.

The simple, geometric, and harmonic means may be derived by using appropriate weights when data appear as averages for various groups of observations. The mean so derived is called *weighted mean.* Assuming the data in Table 30.1 reflect average per capita income by states, the weights in this case would be the respective state populations. The weighting process is shown in Table 30.6.

Each state's average per capita income is weighted by multiplying it by the number of residents of that state, the resulting product is added and then divided by the sum of the populations (weights) of the thirteen states. Symbolically the weighted mean is expressed as

$$\bar{x}_w = \sum_{i=1}^{n} w_i x_i / \Sigma w_i, \qquad (5)$$

where w is the weight. Substituting the computed values, we obtain

$$\bar{x}_w = \frac{172.299}{57.06} = 3.020$$

as the weighted simple mean. The weighted geometric and harmonic means can be similarly obtained by performing the needed operations.

As a summary, the various computed estimates of central tendency utilizing the data of Table 30.1 may be listed as follows:

Mode: 3.30   or $3,300

Table 30.6   Weighted Personal Income

State	1965 Average Per Capita Income (scaled and rounded)	1966 State Population (millions)	Population × Per Capita Income
Alaska	3.2	0.27	0.864
California	3.3	18.92	62.436
Connecticut	3.4	2.88	9.792
Delaware	3.4	0.51	1.734
Hawaii	2.9	0.72	2.088
Indiana	2.8	4.92	13.776
Mississippi	1.6	2.33	3.728
Nevada	3.3	0.45	1.485
New Hampshire	2.5	0.68	1.700
New York	3.3	18.26	60.258
North Carolina	2.0	5.00	10.000
West Virginia	2.0	1.79	3.580
Wyoming	2.6	0.33	0.858
Σ		57.06	172.299

Median:	2.90	or	$2,900
Mean:			
simple	2.795	or	$2,795
geometric	2.724	or	$2,724
harmonic	2.642	or	$2,642
weighted (simple)	3.020	or	$3,020

It was pointed out that, given the nature of the data in Table 30.1 and their distribution, median is the best overall measure of the central tendency. The applicability of the other measures of central tendency was pointed out earlier.

MEASURES OF DISPERSION

The various measures of central tendency are descriptive, but they by no means completely describe the phenomena or data. They provide no idea of the *spread* in the data. For example, three samples— 0,1,11; 4,4,4; and 6,2,4—have identical simple means;[4] the mean for each of the three samples is 4. Undoubtedly a glance at the data suggests that the mean alone is not sufficient for description and comparison of the three samples. The measures of variability or dispersion provide information for the relative spreads. There are basically three measures of dispersion:

1. Range
2. Variance and/or standard deviation
3. Coefficient of variation

Range

Range is the simplest and most convenient way to measure dispersion. It is defined as the difference between the absolute values of the largest and the smallest observations. Symbolically it may be expressed as

$$[|x_l| - |x_s|], \qquad (6)$$

where l represents the largest observation, s the smallest observation, and the two vertical bars indicate use of absolute value (without any plus or minus signs). Using the data of Table 30.2, the range is

$3.4 - 1.6 = 1.8$. Although it is much easier to calculate, range lacks in providing information about the intensity of the spread, since only the extreme observations enter into the calculation. It does not estimate the extent to which the observations cluster about the mean.

Variance and Standard Deviation

Deviation—the difference between the observation and mean—is a better measure than range, since it answers the question, "How far is the observation from the mean?" There will be as many deviations as there are observations. Since mean has half of the weight of observations on one side and half on the other side, it may seem reasonable to take the average of the deviations to estimate dispersion. This may be written as

$$\bar{d} = \sum_{i=1}^{n} (x_i - \bar{x})/n, \qquad (7)$$

where $\bar{d}$ is the average deviation. Using the data of Table 30.2, Table 30.7 shows computation of the average deviations.

The zero average deviation in Table 30.7 is not a surprising result, since the observations greater than mean have positive deviations which when added to the negative deviations (due to the observations below the mean) cancel each other out, resulting in a zero sum.[5] This does not reflect that there is no dispersion in the data, but rather that the "average deviation" as a measure is incapable of estimating dispersion. Nevertheless, the deviations (1) could be added together, assuming there was not any minus sign, and average or mean deviation be obtained, or (2) the deviations could be squared, which would eliminate the minus sign (minus figures when squared

---

[4]For the remainder of this chapter, the statistical term *mean* refers to simple (arithmetic) mean.

[5]The actual sum of the deviations here is equal to −0.01; the 1 percent discrepancy is due to rounding. The sum of deviations is always equal to zero.

Table 30.7   Computation of Average Deviation

x	$(x - \bar{x})$
1.6	$1.6 - 2.8 = -1.2$
2.0	$2.0 - 2.8 = -0.8$
2.0	$2.0 - 2.8 = -0.8$
2.5	$2.5 - 2.8 = -0.3$
2.6	$2.6 - 2.8 = -0.2$
2.8	$2.8 - 2.8 =\ \ \ 0.0$
2.9	$2.9 - 2.8 =\ \ \ 0.1$
3.2	$3.2 - 2.8 =\ \ \ 0.4$
3.3	$3.3 - 2.8 =\ \ \ 0.5$
3.3	$3.3 - 2.8 =\ \ \ 0.5$
3.3	$3.3 - 2.8 =\ \ \ 0.5$
3.4	$3.4 - 2.8 =\ \ \ 0.6$
3.4	$3.4 - 2.8 =\ \ \ 0.6$
	$\Sigma \cong -0.01$
	$\bar{d} \cong -0.01/13 \cong 0.0$

yield a positive result, and then added up and divided by n[7]. The first method using the data from Table 30.7 would yield

$$\bar{d} = \frac{6.5}{13} = .50.$$

The second method, however, has greater appeal from the statistical point of view. It may be written as

$$v^2 = \sum_{i=1}^{n} (x_i - \bar{x})^2/(n - 1), \qquad (8)$$

where v^2 stands for variance.[6] This expression is the measure of *variance*,[7] which shows that the deviations are squared, added, and then divided by the $(n - 1)$th number of observations. Using the data of Table 30.7:

$$v^2 = \frac{4.49}{12} = .3742.$$

Since the deviations were squared, the variance no longer has the same type of units as the original data. To bring it back to the units of original data, square root of v^2 would be required; thus

$$v = \sqrt{v^2} = \sqrt{\text{equation (8)}} = \sqrt{.3742} = .611719,$$

which is called *standard deviation*. This figure says that the income between states varies, on the average, by .572276 (which is $572.28 when descaled).

The reliability of the mean is revealed

by the standard deviation—the greater the dispersion, the less representative the mean becomes. With larger dispersion, a single interpretation or description of the phenomena represented by the data is difficult, and thus a multiplicity of policy and programs is needed.

Coefficient of Variation

The range, mean deviation, variance, and standard deviation are all expressed in the same units as the original data. However, in situations where different scales are used and the task is to compare the measures of dispersion for the various distributions involving separate data, use of the coefficient of variation c_v is imperative. The coefficient of variation is defined as a ratio between the standard deviation and the corresponding mean, that is, $v/\bar{x}$, which gives an expression of relative variability. Often it is expressed as a percentage; it has no unit of measurement. For example, if c_v is .50 for a given set of data, the standard deviation is one-half as large as the mean.

MEASURES OF INTERRELATIONSHIPS

Geographic statistics necessarily are reflections of events that have already occurred. Since these events have occurred, man no longer has any control over them. However, if these statistics are found to

[6]From the statistical point of view, when dealing with the sample data, $n - 1$ as a divisor is a better figure. This condition is caused by the fact that $\Sigma_{i=1}^{n}(x_i - \bar{x})$ is always zero and the last deviation can be known with complete accuracy without reference to the data. This $n - 1$ as divisor produces a relatively larger estimate of the variance, compensating for the bias associated with deviations.

[7]For the purposes of desk calculations of variance, an easier formula is available:

$$\frac{\Sigma x^2 - [(\Sigma x)^2/n]}{n - 1},$$

which is precisely equal to formula 8. Those interested in the proof may consult any standard statistics text. This formula also eliminates many rounding errors.

show some relationships, patterns, or co-variances, etc., they may act as important tools for predicting future events over which man can exercise control.

It is perhaps a commonly known fact that all phenomena, including spatial, are interrelated, but the knowledge about these interrelationships is not common. In fact, the real task lies in discovering the nature and extent of these interrelationships, which involves certain tools or techniques. In the physical sciences, these tools are generally mathematical in nature, but in behavioral sciences, statistical formulations or models (involving the theory of probability) are appropriate. The following techniques shall be discussed:

1. Regression analysis
2. Correlation—rank and order
3. Location or distribution quotient
4. Input–output matrix
5. Linear programming
6. Systems analysis
7. Factor analysis
8. Ratio maps
9. Concentration index

Regression Analysis

Regression analysis estimates the functional relationship between variables. Simple regression involves the estimation of the linear or straight-line relationship between two variables. As the number of variables is increased and/or a curvilinear estimation is sought, the analysis becomes complex, although the basic principle involved is the same. Our discussion here is limited only to simple regression analysis.

Table 30.8 presents hypothetical data on the annual amount spent in a city per 1,000 population (y) residing at various distances or zones (x) from the city. We are interested in understanding the relationship between x and y.

The first thing we could do is to plot these variables in a scatter diagram as in Fig. 30.2, where the vertical coordinate measures y and horizontal coordinate measures x. (Notice the operation of scale in

Table 30.8 Hypothetical Amount Spent Annually in a City Per 1,000 Population Residing at Various Distances or Zones from the City

Zone	$ Spent Annually Per 1000 Population (in millions)	Distance (miles)
i	y	x
1	3.00	2
2	2.00	5
3	1.20	7
4	0.90	10
5	0.80	12
6	0.60	15
7	0.40	18
8	0.20	20
9	0.15	22
10	0.10	25

this figure.) It appears from this figure that as the values of x increase the values of y decrease, reflecting an inverse relationship. This visual display of the relationship, although providing a rough idea about the relationship, suffers fron inefficiency of time consumed in constructing the scatter diagram, particularly when the sample size is large, and from lack of precision of interpretation.[8]

The linear regression line (a computing method discussed later) is the locus of the means of the arrays of y observations. This regression line may be estimated by the equation

$$\hat{y} = a + bx, \tag{9}$$

where $\hat{y}$ (predicted) is the dependent variable, x is the independent variable,[9] a and b are parameters or regression coefficients.

[8]There are several other visual means of understanding relationships, namely overlay and isopleth maps. An overlay map shows proportionate symbols for the various variables superimposed on the same map or drawn on different maps. An isopleth map shows the location of lines (isopleths). An isopleth line passes through the points of equal values of the variables. Both of these approaches have not been successful in yielding trustworthy and convenient interpretations.

[9]The distinction between the dependent and independent variables is determined by the particular research problem, theory, and objectives. The variables that logically are causal in nature would be independent, and those that appear as effects would be dependent.

Table 30.9   Estimation of Parameters

	(1)	(2)	(3)	(4)	(5)	(6)
						Residuals
	x	y	x^2	xy	y	$(y - y)$
	2	3.00	4	6.00	2.21	0.79
	5	2.00	25	10.00	1.88	0.12
	7	1.20	49	8.40	1.66	−0.46
	10	0.90	100	9.00	1.33	−0.43
	12	0.80	144	9.60	1.11	−0.31
	15	0.60	225	9.00	0.78	−0.18
	18	0.40	324	7.20	0.45	−0.05
	20	0.20	400	4.00	0.23	−0.03
	22	0.15	484	3.30	0.01	0.14
	25	0.10	625	2.50	−0.31	0.41
Σ	136	9.35	2380	69.00	9.35	0.0

The parameter a is a measure of the level of y when x is zero, and b reflects the rate of change in y as a result of the change in x.

The estimation of parameters may be obtained by the process shown in Table 30.9, using the following equations:

$$b = \frac{\Sigma xy - [(\Sigma x)(\Sigma y)/n]}{\Sigma x^2 - [(\Sigma x)^2/n]}, \qquad (10)$$

$$a = \bar{y} - b\bar{x}. \qquad (11)$$

Based on the data in Table 30.9, the following computational steps produce the parameters (equation 12) for formula 11:

$$\bar{x} = \frac{136}{10} = 13.6; \ (\Sigma x)^2 = 18496$$

$$\bar{y} = \frac{9.35}{10} = .935; \ (\Sigma x)(\Sigma y) = 1271.60$$

$$b = \frac{69 - (1271.60/10)}{2380 - (18496/10)} = \frac{69 - 127.16}{2380 - 1849.60}$$

$$= \frac{-58.16}{530.40}$$

$$= -.10965,$$

$$a = .935 - [(-.10965)(13.6)] = 2.42628,$$

$$\hat{y} = 2.42628 - .10965x. \qquad (12)$$

Notice that the equations above do not carry subscripts for the sake of clarity. Also, the formulations are those that suit the desk calculations. Column 5 shows the predicted values of y, which are yielded by the computed equation 12. Columns 1

and 5 when plotted show the regression line, depicting the average relationship between x and y.

The results may be interpreted as: the 1,000 residents as a unit at zero distance from the city spend $2,426,280 on the average in that city, and this level of spending is reduced by $109,650 for each mile of residence away from the city. These results are specific as compared to the multiplicity of conclusions yielded by the scatter diagram.

We now might ask, "Is distance the only factor affecting the sales of the city?" No, there may be other factors such as income, transportation facilities, alternative opportunities, the type and level of media of communication between the city and the surrounding habitations, commuting patterns, and the like.[10] When an attempt is made to measure the influence of these additional factors on the sales of the city, we are dealing with multivariate regression analysis, which requires knowledge of matrix algebra and lengthy calculations though the various parameters are similarly interpreted.

[10]A further analysis of the residuals $(y - \hat{y})$ is helpful in identifying the additional variables. In regard to this topic students may wish to refer to E. N. Thomas, "Maps of Residuals and Regressions: Their Characteristics and Uses in Geographic Research," Monograph No. 2, Department of Geography, University of Iowa, 1960; and E. J. Taaffe, R. L. Morrill, and P. R. Gould, "Transport Expansion in Underdeveloped Countries; A Comparative Analysis," Geographical Review, Vol. 53, 1963.

Correlation

Correlation analysis has many meanings and interpretations depending on the context in which it is used. However, none of the correlation analyses involve dependence and independence of variables; they concern the covariance of the variables. We shall discuss two types: a Pearson product moment coefficient of correlation, and Spearman's rank correlation coefficient. The correlation coefficient, r_{xy}, is defined as

$$r_{xy} = \frac{[\Sigma xy - (\Sigma x)(\Sigma y)/n]}{\sqrt{[\Sigma x^2 - (\Sigma x)^2/n][\Sigma y^2 - (\Sigma y)^2/n]}} .$$

(13)

Substituting the calculations based on the data on Table 30.9, equation 13 may be written as

$$r_{xy} = \frac{69.00 - (1271.60/10)}{\sqrt{\left(2340 - \dfrac{18496}{10}\right)\left(16.4825 - \dfrac{87.4225}{10}\right)}}$$

$$= \frac{(-58.16)}{\sqrt{(530.40)\,(7.7402)}}$$

$$= \frac{-58.16}{64.0734116}$$

$$= -0.90771.$$

The resulting number has a minus sign, which indicates that y decreases as x increases. A positive r indicates that y increases as x increases. The statistic r, similar to the coefficient of variation, is an abstract number not related to any specific unit of measurement. It must be emphasized that r is a measure of the *strength* of linear association, not an indicator of causality between x and y. The strength of association, since it concerns the relationship between x and y, can be estimated by squaring the r, yielding r^2, which is called the coefficient of determination. The level of r^2 indicates the level of variation in the dependent variable accounted for by the covariation of the independent variable. Thus $r_{xy}^2 = .8239$ is interpreted as 82.39 percent of the variation in y is explained by the covariation of x. The values of r^2 range between -1 and $+1$. Negative 1 indicates that there is perfect negative correlation, positive 1 reflects perfect positive correlation, and zero shows no correlation; the other values between -1, 0, and $+1$ represent the respective levels of correlation.

In situations when the data are qualitative, the estimate of correlation may be obtained through Spearman's rank correlation coefficient (r_r):

$$r_r = 1 - \frac{6\sum_{i=1}^{n} d_i^2}{n^3 - n} .$$

(14)

Suppose we are interested in estimating the association (r_r) between the cultural qualities and the respective populations of various cities of a region. The variable of cultural quality is a reflection of "judgment" showing the data as ranked 1, 2, 3, and so on, with the highest quality represented by 1. Similarly the populations of the cities are ranked 1, 2, 3, . . ., the most populated city represented by 1. Thus the data may appear as shown in Table 30.10.

Table 30.10   Computation of Spearman's Rank Correlation Coefficient

(1)	(2)	(3)	(4)	(5)
	x_i	y_i	d_i	d_i^2
	Cultural Quality	*Population*		
City	*Rank*	*Size Rank*	$(x_i - y_i)$	
A	1	4	−3	9
B	2	2	0	0
C	3	1	+2	4
D	4	5	−1	1
E	5	6	−1	1
F	6	3	+3	9
Σ	21	21	0	24

Substituting the needed computations into equation 14, the estimate is

$$r_r = 1 - \frac{6(24)}{216 - 6} = 1 - \frac{44}{210} \cong .3143,$$

$$r_r^2 = (.3143)^2 = .09878.$$

Interested students may wish to verify that equations 13 and 14 are identical. That is, columns 2 and 3 in Table 30.10 as x and y when used through the process of formula 13 will give identical results. Recognizing that in rank correlation $\Sigma x_i = \Sigma y_i$ and $\Sigma x_i^2 = \Sigma y_i^2$, formula 14 is a shortcut method of computing r_r.

Location Quotient

Location quotient (L_q), sometimes called coefficient of localization or specialization, is a ratio that approximates the relative position of an activity (m) in an area (z) as compared to the same activity occurring in a broader region. It may be written as

$$L_q = \frac{\dfrac{\text{activity } m \text{ in area } z}{\text{total activity in area } z}}{\dfrac{\text{activity } m \text{ in the whole region}}{\text{total activity in the whole region}}}. \quad (15)$$

Assuming that the broader regional boundaries correspond to the nation and the components are the respective states, we can estimate, for example, the relative extent of electronic industry in each state by using employment figures (or some other measure). The hypothetical figures, when substituted into equation 15, will produce:

$$L_q = \frac{\dfrac{\text{state's employment in electronic industry}}{\text{state's total employment in all industries}}}{\dfrac{\text{U.S. employment in electronic industry}}{\text{U.S. total employment in all industries}}},$$

$$L_q = \frac{\dfrac{500}{1,200,200}}{\dfrac{500,000}{70,000,000}} = \frac{.000416597}{.007142857} = .058.$$

The .058 location quotient is only for one state. There would be as many location quotients as there are states. If the L_q exceeds 1.00, it shows that that state has higher specialization of localization in the electronic industry than the nation; similarly, if the L_q is less than 1.00 (as .058 in the above example), the degree of

specialization in that area is smaller than that of the nation. Thus the relative degree of specialization depends on the size of L_q—the larger the L_q, the greater the specialization and vice versa.[11]

Concentration Index

Like the location quotient, concentration index is another measure concerned with the relative distribution of economic activity. It reflects the degree to which a given activity is spatially concentrated with respect to population. If a certain percent (most commonly used is 50%) of the total national activity is located in certain areas involving only a relatively small share of the national population, it would indicate a greater concentration index.

To illustrate the computation of the index the following hypothetical data may be used:

Total population
of a hypothetical nation = 100,000,000
Total employment
in agricultural machinery
in that nation =   400,000
Total number
of regions or states =   10

Further assume that we are interested in starting with 50% of the activity as a basis of our index. Column 4 in Table 30.11 shows the ratio of agricultural machinery employment to population. The higher the ratio, the higher the employment activity in agricultural machinery in relation to the population. As we add the state agricultural machinery employment of states 1, 9, 4, 7—the highest

[11]It needs to be reemphasized that the location quotient as presented is only a rough measure. It suffers from many drawbacks, which originate from the various implicit assumptions behind the location quotient—the uniformity of demand and productivity throughout the nation, and the use of Standard Industrial Classification (the structure of this classification varies from state to state).

Table 30.11   Computation of Concentration Index

(1) States	(2) Population	(3) Employment in Agricultural Machinery	(4) Col. (3)/Col. (2)
1	12,000,000	80,000	0.0067
2	11,000,000	20,000	0.0018
3	7,000,000	10,000	0.0014
4	8,000,000	50,000	0.0063
5	12,000,000	70,000	0.0058
6	15,000,000	10,000	0.0007
7	5,000,000	30,000	0.0060
8	14,000,000	50,000	0.0036
9	6,000,000	40,000	0.0067
10	10,000,000	40,000	0.0040
	100,000,000	400,000	

states in terms of the ratio of employment and population—in that order, we obtain 200,000, which is one-half of the national employment in that industry. (Had we not reached 200,000 by adding the employment in state 7, we then would have gone to the state with the next highest ratio. (In the case where the cumulative sum does not exactly come to one-half of the national employment in the industry, the state employment of the last state must be prorated.)

Now, adding the corresponding populations of states 1, 9, 4, and 7, it comes to 31 million or 31% of the national population. Relating this to the employment figures, it may be concluded that half (200,000) of the agricultural machinery workers in the nation are concentrated in areas that have only 31% of the nation's population. The index of concentration is 69 (100 minus 31).

The closer the index is to 50, the closer the industry is to being a ubiquitous industry. The index may range between 50 and less than 100. It cannot conceptually be 100, because 100 means that all of the employment in a given industry exists in an area with no people. (Of course, if the 50% base is altered, the results would be different and thus need to be interpreted differently.)

Ratio Mapping

Ratio mapping is a technique of roughly discovering the relationship between two variables.[12] Ratios of the various values of the two variables are computed, ranked, and categorized. The number of categories is dependent on the objectives; however, four to six categories are used quite commonly—the larger the number of categories, the more complicated and cumbersome the map becomes. Based on the hypothetical data of Table 30.12, the ratio map (Fig. 30.4) may be constructed. Although in the data of Table 30.12 there are only one or two counties in a category, there would be many more sub-area values grouped into individual categories for large samples.

From Table 30.12 it can be seen that one-half of the counties have higher ratios (x/y) than the state ratio; the other half have ratios below it. The same pattern is visible from the ratio map. Indeed, the purpose of the ratio mapping is to show concisely the relationship of variables in a manner easily digestible and understood.

[12]In instances of more than two variables, multiple ratios may be used.

Table 30.12   Computation of Ratio Map

State Counties	Variable x	Variable y	x/y(100)	
	200	600	33.00	
1	20	20	100.00	category 1
2	30	40	75.00 ⎤	category 2
3	35	50	70.00 ⎦	
4	40	90	44.44 ⎤	category 3
5	25	60	41.67 ⎦	
6	15	60	25.00 ⎤	category 4
7	20	100	20.00 ⎦	
8	10	80	12.50 ⎤	category 5
9	5	70	7.14 ⎦	
10	0	30	0.0	category 6

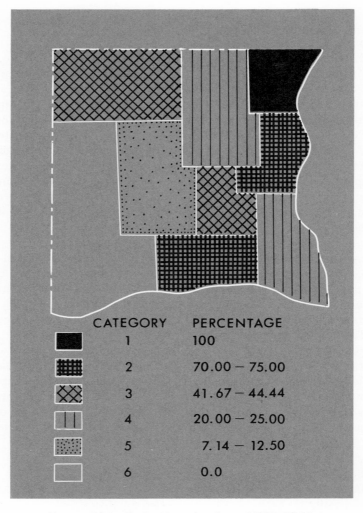

CATEGORY	PERCENTAGE
1	100
2	70.00 − 75.00
3	41.67 − 44.44
4	20.00 − 25.00
5	7.14 − 12.50
6	0.0

FIGURE 30.4   *Ratio map using data of Table 30.12.*

Other Methods

There are several other techniques that have been applied to research in economic geography. Because of their detail and complexity and the limited objective of this chapter, only selected techniques are briefly mentioned below.

Trend Surface Analysis. This analysis is a special case of regression analysis involving two independent variables, both appearing as linear and quadratic terms.[13] The dependent variable measured at discrete location points when regressed against the independent variables provides the respective regression coefficients (parameters). The equation and the parameters so estimated can be used to map a trend for the space and time under observation, and may also be used to predict spatial patterns.

Systems Analysis.   This is a technique of studying the complex interrelated *whole space-economy*, as opposed to the study of the individual parts separately. The space-economy is further decomposed into major and functional subsystems—resources, agriculture, manufacturing, distribution, consumption, etc.—to analyze their components and interrelationships. (The particular type and number of subsystems may vary depending on the objectives and data availabilites.) The components involve the explicit consideration of the quantitative and qualitative influences of various physical, political, social, and economic factors and inter-intra regional flows. Indeed, the technique of systems analysis is complex and detailed, and requires the participation of scholars from various fields.[14]

[13]These variables in some cases may even go to higher and interactive terms.

[14]For further discussion, students are referred to: Commission on College Geography, "A Systems Analytic Approach to Economic Geography," Publication No. 8 (American Association of Geographers, Washington, D.C., 1968).

Factor Analysis.   Factor analysis and a related method, principal components analysis, are specialized methods in dealing with

1. A large number of variables
2. Situations where assumptions of independence among the independent variables is not satisfied
3. Instances where the distinction between dependent and independent variables is not clear

Although the two techniques are different in their conceptual and statistical formulations, they seek to reduce a large set of intercorrelated variables into a smaller number of linear dimensions in terms of hypothetical factors, and describe the factors in terms of observed variables.

Input–Output Analysis.   This analysis shows how the output of each activity, however defined, is distributed (as input) among other activities of the space economy. Through the use of matrix algebra, the system demonstrates the patterns of dependence, interdependence, hierarchy, and circularity. With quantitative knowledge of these aspects of the system of economic activities, it is possible to predict and project appropriate courses of action to achieve the goals of society.

Linear Programming.   This technique deals with the problems of optimization (maximization or minimization) faced by regional planners and decision makers who are often confronted with certain resource, institutional, or cultural quantifiable restraints. Given these restraints and the goals—profit maximization, cost minimization, least-cost spatial arrangements of marketing routes, or a desirable redistribution and location of economic activities—linear programming techniques provide the best solutions for the problems. The process is strictly mathematical in character and operation.

selected references

1. Ackerman, E. A., *Geography as a Fundamental Research Discipline*, Research Paper No. 53, Chicago: Department of Geography, University of Chicago, 1958.

2. Berry, J. L. B., and Marble, D. F., *Spatial Analysis: A Reader in Statistical Geography*, Englewood Cliffs, N. J.: Prentice-Hall, Inc., 1968.

3. Commission on College Geography, "A Systems Analytic Approach to Economic Geography," Publication No. 8, Washington, D.C.: Association of American Geographers, 1968.

4. Duncan, O. D. C.; Cuzzort, R. P.; and Duncan, B., *Statistical Geography*, New York: The Free Press, 1961.

5. Garrison, William L., "Spatial Structure of the Economy: I," *Annals of the Association of American Geographers*, Vol. 49, No. 2, June 1959, pp. 232–239.

6. ———, "Spatial Structure of the Economy: II," *Annals of the Association of American Geographers*, Vol. 49, No. 4, December 1959, pp. 471–482.

7. ———, "Spatial Structure of the Economy: III," *Annals of the Association of American Geographers*, Vol. 50, No. 3, September 1960, pp. 357–373.

8. Gregory, S., *Statistical Methods and the Geographer*, London: Longmans, Green & Co., 1963.

9. Hare, VanCourt, *Systems Analysis: A Diagnostic Approach*, New York: Harcourt, Brace and World, Inc. 1967.

10. King, J. L., *Statistical Analysis in Geography*, Englewood Cliffs, N. J.: Prentice-Hall, Inc., 1969.

11. Miernyk, W. H., *The Elements of Input–Output Analysis*, New York: Random House, 1965.

12. Neft, David S., *Statistical Analysis for Areal Distributions*, Monograph Series No. 2, Philadelphia: Regional Science Research Institute, 1966.

13. Spivey, W. A., *Linear Programming: An Introduction*, London: The Macmillan Company, 1969.

14. Warntz, W., and Neft, D. S., "Contributions to a Statistical Methodology for Areal Distributions," *Journal of Regional Science*, Vol. 2, 1960.

15. L. Zobler, "Statistical Testing of Regional Boundaries," *Annals of the Association of American Geographers*, Vol. 47, No. 1, March 1957, pp. 83–96.

Long before the United States was formed, the tiny Atlantic Coast colonial settlements were adopting measures to restrain the people from using their land in ways that would cause injury to others or to the community. The earliest measures grew out of unhappy experiences with explosions and fires, and were simple regulations to keep gunpowder mills and storehouses outside the settlement. Market towns, like Boston, were authorized to assign locations for slaughterhouses, stillhouses, and buildings in which tallow was tried and leather was tanned.

The early laws were passed in the interest of people's health, comfort, and safety. No more restraint was placed on the use of private property than was deemed necessary to protect the rights of others. As the country grew, both cities and problems arose. The way that people use their land sometimes harms others. Areas with mixtures of homes, stores, and factories sometimes end as slums, which are hazards to health, safety, morals, and the general welfare.

As was the case many years ago, vexing land-use problems resulted in the shaping of corrective measures. Separate zoning districts were created for homes, for business, and for industry. Conflicting land uses were thus set apart. Other zoning regulations were shaped to prevent overcrowding. This was done by limiting the height and size of buildings. The same object was attained by regulating the size of building tracts and yards. Larger lots with ample yards allow for few houses and fewer persons per acre.

A bursting of city boundaries in the booming 1920s brought unguided growth to the fringes of cities, but was gentle compared to what was to come later. Urban expansion became an explosion after World War II. All over the country new forces reformed rural communities. Good roads and automobiles permitted city dwellers to spread over the countryside. Rural people in great numbers found employment and new homes in and

chapter 31

Urban and Regional Planning

around urban centers. Trade areas and daily commuting distances came to be measured in terms of travel time rather than in miles. Millions of people began to make hour-long morning and evening trips between home and work. Expressways and higher permissible speeds brought outlying areas within commuting zones. New suburbs burgeoned beyond suburbs, and scattered subdivisions soon were extended farther from the central city.

New communities took shape in forms that could not be foreseen. Urban expansion meant the building of many well-planned business and industrial districts and attractive residential suburbs, but it also brought ugly areas of haphazard growth and mixed-use ribbon districts of roadside blight, dreary miles of honky-tonks, billboards, gas stations, junkyards, shops, and homes. Yesterday's good residential areas began to look like untended orphan tracts. In places there was a helter-skelter peppering of nonfarm dwellings on small rural tracts, premature subdivisions that were not sold, and scattered housing strung out along country roads.

Mushrooming communities developed fiscal ailments. Many improvements—roads, streets, schools, libraries, water and sewage facilities, and so on—were all needed at once. Many citizens encountered unexpected increases in assessments and taxes to pay for the necessary public services. Crowded highways and road hazards presented dangers.

Some farmers faced new problems as subdivisions engulfed their lands. A few moved away with windfall profits from the sale of their farms at high prices; those who remained had higher taxes for public improvements and services that they did not need or want. Their farm plants were damaged, and their operating costs increased.

As in colonial days, the problems stem from unwise relationships in the uses of neighboring tracts of land. In colonial days, however, the problems were obvious, and the corrective restraints were simple. Today's problems are a complex mixture of fiscal matters, public services, the use and changing values of land, health, pollution, safety, and attitudes. And here *planning* is needed.

PLANNING CONCEPT

One of the first principles of law is that a piece of land is a unique sort of property. Unlike money, or most other physical objects, no two pieces of real estate are ever exactly the same. Each piece of land has its own relative advantages and disadvantages, which are never quite identical to any other. In areas of human habitation, parcels of land take on unique characteristics and advantages, depending on their relative relationship to other buildings and facilities in the community.

In light of these facts, it seems only rational that land uses be coordinated to secure the greatest possible well-being of the community to the highest advantage, for once land is committed to use, it is not only difficult to change but it may also be contrary to collective goals. The concept of planning concerns:

1. Assessment of regional resources and goals
2. Evaluation of comparative effectiveness of alternative land-use patterns
3. Coordination or synchronization of resources and goals for now and the future

Four key words are found in the above definition—*goals, resources, region,* and *coordination.* The meaning of resources was discussed in Chapter 2.

What is a Region?

Definitions of the word region vary depending upon the objectives and criteria chosen for delineation. Nevertheless,

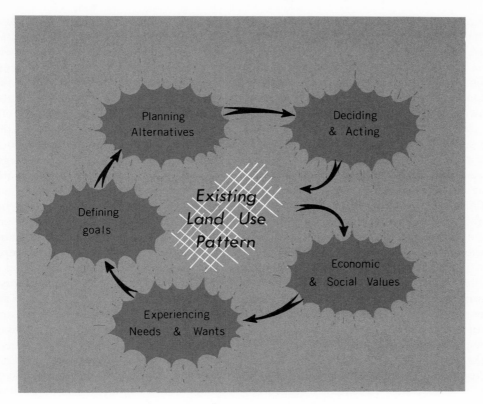

FIGURE 31.1   *The meaning of planning.*

any region basically involves four characteristics:

1. Territorial extensions or grouping of contiguous space.[1]
2. Complementation and reciprocity of some activities between the component areas of the region.
3. Some degree of uniformity and homogeneity is invoked by the chosen criteria.
4. Time dimension—that is, regions are functional and meaningful for a certain period of time; interrelationships continuously change and suggest adjustments in the boundary lines.

[1]The condition of contiguity may not apply in some cases; for example, regions delineated on the basis of international political ideologies may be noncontiguous.

The relative degree and importance of these characteristics differ for varying purposes and the type of region. For example, physiographic regional boundaries are more durable than economic boundaries; regional boundaries involving multinational sovereignty exhibit a restricted form of complementation and reciprocity, as in the case of the European Economic Community (ECC) region; multipurpose regions are larger than single-purpose regions; homogeneous regions representing direct recognition of the spatial distribution of economic activity have been best used for economic analysis, while the nodal concept of regionalism, embodying a metropolitan system, has often been used by demographers, sociologists, planners, and others.

Region may be generally defined as: A spatial study area containing an observable[2] series of resources and commodity flows of specified internal consistency. A region exhibits a marked internal interdependence and linkage of the specified elements through flow phenomena. Often, the data necessary to measure flow phenomena are not available. Even though data availability places constraints on the precise definition of study areas, there is some latitude of choice. Efforts have been made to delineate regions using standard sources of data. Such efforts are discussed in the following section.

Another aspect of the definition of a region is the accompanying set of criteria on the basis of which boundaries are determined. In other words, the criteria determine the type and scope of the given set of regions. Various types of systems of regions—physiographic regions, labor market areas, nodal regions, Standard Metropolitan Statistical Areas (SMSA)[3] and State Economic Areas (SEA), resource regions, trade regions, climatic regions, agricultural regions, manufacturing regions, political and administrative regions (state, district, and country), planning regions, soil regions, drainage areas, and regions based on standard of living, race, international political ideologies and trade, demographic factors, etc.— reflecting different reasons and purposes for area divisions and assemblages, are being used for research, control, communication and administration purposes.

Each set of criteria, for a given time period, may or may not satisfy more than one purpose, depending upon the individual situation, the quality of results desired, and the added pecuniary cost involved in defining the regions. Building on earlier works of McKenzie [11] and the National Resources Committee [12], Donald J. Bogue [1, 2] attempted to present a multipurpose standardized system of regions, resulting in the division of the United States into 506 "State Economic Areas." These consist of one or more counties with similar (homogeneous) economic and social characteristics, including a special class of "Metropolitan State Economic Areas," which with some exceptions are equivalent to the SMSA as defined by the U.S. Bureau of Census.

The need to improvise regional delineation stems from several considerations. First, the traditional divisions and boundaries are either too small or too large to manifest meaningful analytical relationships. It is especially true of smaller units. For example, the counties, which themselves are arbitrary units and are generally too small to be of economic or geographic significance, seldom reflect lucid impacts of the broader forces affecting social and economic change in the area. Only in larger aggregations are relationships manifest. However, too large an area may offer a great many impracticalities. To construct an econometric model of the world economy is a gigantic project, and even if the system of equations is saturated with statistics and data its validity is ever questionable. Resources are less diversified for smaller areas within a nation; hence the economies of these areas taken as units tend to be more specialized. In other words, some forms of economic activity represent specialized production located at certain sporadically distributed points,[4] which tend to become pivots for social masses (concentration of industry, people, and institutions superstructured on smaller space) conforming to a regional character. For most metropolitan areas, the varying degrees of specialization, economic interdependence, and the

---

[2]Subject to observation and measurement.

[3]The metropolitan system of regions does not exhaust the whole geographic area, but rather delineates selective units. This is based on a central city or cities, with the boundaries seeking to encompass the economic integration of working and living in the center and its environs.

[4]Sporadic locations of economic phenomena contrast with the ubiquitous industries that are present in all localities. For example, in a given locality, a grocery store may be called a ubiquitous type of economic activity, while the building of ships would be considered a sporadic industry.

proportion of local output exported all tend to regionalize the location of economic phenomena. Finally, the sheer prevalence of "mountains," "hills," and "valleys" of standards of living or economic prosperity suggest regionalization for effective analysis and policy.

The task of area delineation, while heavily influenced by study objectives, requires judgment in the selection of criteria and method in outlining a region. Four major classifications have been used in various studies:

1. Homogeneous regions
2. Nodal regions
3. Trade regions
4. Political or administrative regions

Regions based on *homogeneity* criteria cover areas with the same key characteristics and with approximately the same degree of intensity—for example, the central city being a focus (or foci) and the surrounding area with its environs tied to the focus by various interdependencies. The *nodal* region rests on the gravitational processes concerning the spatial movement of people, resources, and goods. The *trade* region is a special case of nodal arrangements of habitat and activities, since trade is a process of interdependence between the city and its hinterland. The *political* region reflects the administrative, legislative, social, and policy considerations. Ordinarily, there is spatial hierarchy of at least three or four levels of these divisions—state, county, city, township, section, district, and neighborhood. Thus the definition of a region is objective(s) oriented. The word "local" generally refers to areas such as city, county, and Standard Metropolitan Statistical Area (SMSA).

Goals

The establishment of a goal or goals—time and activity-related targets—is a necessary step in planning. How they are arrived at or who determines them varies from one place to another.

The process of establishing goals generally starts with the derivation of commonly agreeable general or broad titles—full employment of the labor force, social cohesion, clean environment, economic progress, and so on—through public concensus or government officials. Generally a government body, commonly called a planning commission, initiates this process. Once the general goals are identified, then the subgoals may be expressed in terms of activity levels and targets, the number of residential units at such and such a place and time, the jobs needed to absorb the labor force at various time periods, and the level of increase in the productivity and economic progress of the region.

The goals, subgoals, and objectives are directional guideposts needed for the identification of the level, structure, and performance of economic activities.

Resource Inventory

Once goals are identified and broken into subgoals, and the subgoals into specific objectives, the task of resource inventory is a routine but complex, expensive, and time-consuming chore. This actually involves collection of relevant data about almost every aspect of the environment. The detail of the data, of course, depends on the objectives. Data concerning demography, housing, utilities, transportation, economic structure, political structure and process, health, spatial patterns, trade, and education often form the basic set of required information. These data may be available in published form, and every effort should be made to secure already collected or published material. The original data collection is an expensive item.

Coordination

At this stage, goals and resources are brought together and translated into a functional plan. Various tools, such as

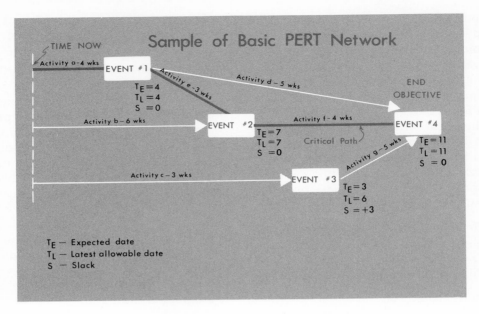

FIGURE 31.2   *PERT, a tool in planning.*

systems and input–output analyses, are used to find the interrelations between the various activities. Planners also use a technique, Program Evaluation Review Technique (PERT), to plan effectively. PERT is a diagrammatical representation of the flow, sequence, and interdependency of operations needed to produce a plan, product, or event, showing estimated completion time and cost figures for the activities in the flow. The usefulness of PERT is not limited only to planning; it also is being used extensively by the National Aeronautics and Space Administration (NASA) and by industry to enhance achievement of goals.

Numerous other operations, such as projections, trend analysis, overlays, and statistical correlations, can also be utilized. The process of coordination is highly technical and requires knowledge of advanced statistics, operations research, and other tools mentioned above.

Planning in totalitarian societies involves government participation, not only in the development of a plan but also in its execution. However, in a society like the United States, the underlying motiva-

tion behind planning is the *coordination* of privately-run activities towards the achievement of collectively agreed upon goals. This involves the determination of specific recommendations, which are translated into policy through law. Planning is sterile without policy. Therefore, any plan must lend itself to policy consideration and application.

The process of planning is dynamic. As times change, so do the resources and goals. Consequently the plan or plans must be ever-evolving concepts.

LOCAL PLANNING

The function of local planning is to promote the orderly renovation and development of the community by anticipating the physical environment that will best serve the needs of the people living and working there. A planning commission commonly serves in an advisory capacity to the local governing body. In order to adequately fulfill this function of guidance, the commission is charged with developing a planning program that will define development problems, clarify the best possible solutions, and establish patterns for orderly development from the standpoint of the common good of the entire community. Since planning involves the future, a good deal must depend on intelligent forethought. Consider, for example, the effect of 100 new families on a community:[5]

450 new people
50 new children in elementary school
25 new children in junior high school
25 new children in senior high school
2.2 new grade school rooms needed
1.65 new high school rooms needed
4 new school teachers needed
$40,000 a year added to the school operating budget
$200,000 added for school construction
Four additional acres of land to be purchased by the community: one acre for the grammar school, one acre for the high school, one acre for parks, and one acre for playgrounds
One additional policeman
Nearly one additional fireman
Four additional city employees other than fire and police
10,000 additional gallons of city water needed daily
500 new library volumes for the city library and on and on . . .

All residents of the community have common interests, e.g., that the streets are safe to walk at night, that water is available for drinking, washing, and cooking purposes. Each one, too, has special interests:

As a home owner	Will a supermarket be located on your block?
As a small retailer	Will a new shopping plaza be constructed across the street?
As a factory owner	Will you be unable to expand the size or number of your buildings because all available land around
As a motorist?	you has been subdivided into residential development? Will you have more dented fenders reminding you of bumper-to-bumper rush hour traffic?
As a citizen	Will you have that Sunday picnic in the park cancelled because there's no more room?

The local planning program is based on a general statement of goals and objectives. Basically, to satisfactorily pursue a course that will accomplish an orderly pattern of development through comprehensive planning, the local planning process includes:

1. Preparation, as a guide for long-range development, of general physical plans with respect to the pattern and intensity of land use, including provision for public facilities, together with long-range fiscal plans for such development.
2. Programming of capital improvements, based on a determination of relative urgency, together with definite financing plans for the improvements to be constructed in the earlier years of the program.
3. Coordination of all related plans of the departments or subdivisions of the government concerned.
4. Intergovernmental coordination of all related planned activities among the state and local government agencies concerned.
5. Preparation of regulatory and administrative measures in support of the foregoing.

Comprehensive Planning

Generally, a comprehensive master planning program is composed of three stages: (1) basic inventory, (2) planning proposals, and (3) regulatory measures. The

[5]Adopted from "Community Planning," *Official Newsletter* (Washington, D.C.: American Institute of Planners, April 1955).

details of the program *will be varied by the individual complexities of the area involved.* Also, quite often a community starting its initial planning effort will proceed by stages rather than attempting to produce a complete plan in its initial effort.

1. *Basic Inventory.* The collection, review and compilation of all data basic to the preparation and effectuation of a plan.

   a. *Preparation of Base Maps.* A set of detailed maps at a scale of 200 to possibly 300 feet/inch depending on the area involved; a topographic map of the area; a one sheet map of the area; aerial photographs of the entire area. These maps will serve as the base for presentation of information and plans.

   b. *Economic Base Study.* An investigation of the labor force, employment, buying power, marketing habits, manufacturing, retail and wholesale trade, and other causes and potentials of the local economy.

   c. *Population Studies.* Examine all available population information including age; sex; cultural, ethnic, racial, and religious groupings; family size; birth and mortality rates; and density patterns. Analyze the population trends, estimating future population and determining where it is most likely to occur based on past trends and economic potentials.

   d. *Existing Land-use Study.* Mapping the existing use of all property and analyzing this information to form a clear picture of the extent and character of development.

   e. *Physical Studies.* Investigate topographic and geographic conditions, soil and natural resources; review other elements of the proposed master plan in relation to these physical features.

   f. *Circulation and Transportation.* Study all transportation facilities—automobile, rail, ship, and air—including location, traffic volumes, service, capacity, and problems.

   g. *Community Services and Facilities.* Study all existing services and facilities such as schools, libraries, fire stations, parks, hospitals, water systems, utilities, sewerage, etc. This study will show among other things, location, size, areas of service, and adequacy of facilities.

   h. *Financial Studies.* Investigate the fiscal structure of the area including land values, assessment ratios, tax rates, bonding and debt limitations, costs of services, etc. Analysis will include existing problems and conditions, trends and future fiscal potentials, as they relate to a capital improvement program.

   i. *Housing Conditions and Neighborhood Analysis.* Analyze neighborhood groupings, predominant characteristics, housing conditions, need for additional housing, and development pressures—all with the purpose of identifying blighted areas, indicating future development potentials, and projecting requirements for governmental facilities and services.

2. *Planning Proposals.*

   a. *Comprehensive Master or Development Plan.* A composite of the mapped and written proposals recommending the pattern of physical development. Generally, the following three basic components comprise the master plan:

      Land Use Plan. Showing the proposed location, extent, and intensity of development of land to be used in the future for residential, commercial, industrial, public, and other purposes.

      Circulation Plan. Showing proposed location of streets, highways, railroads, transit facilities, docks, airports, and other transportation facilities.

      Community Facilities Plan. Showing the location and extent of facilities such as schools, parks, hospitals, fire and police stations, sewerage, water supply, municipal buildings, etc.

   b. *Capital Improvements Program.* Identifies needed improvements and recommends priorities to meet the objectives established in the other planning proposals. A detailed program of improvements and financing is generally established for the first six years of the program.

   c. *Urban Renewal Recommendations* (pending the granting of urban renewal powers to communities). For renewal programs to eliminate or prevent the spread of blight, for neighborhood conservation measures, for specific renewal projects if needed, for a workable program including the preparation of the elements concerned with the master plan and the neighborhood analysis.

3. *Regulatory Measures.*
   a. *Zoning Ordinance and Map.* Preparation of an ordinance to be adopted by the governing body that will establish land-use controls for promoting orderly development guided by the master plan.
   b. *Subdivision Ordinance.* Preparation of regulations to be adopted by the governing body that will establish standards for guiding all future subdivision of land.

Plan or No Plan

A community may choose the pattern of its growth, can sit idly by and allow the development of a haphazard mixture of conflicting resource uses, or it can guide growth in such a way as to prevent uses that will be harmful to other landowners and to the community.

Proper planning will forestall a mixture of factories, stores, junkyards, and homes, and lead to the development of desirable residential districts, protecting them with zoning regulations. A minimum lot size is essential to prevent overcrowding. Productive agricultural areas can be enclosed on the urban fringe in districts from which unwanted business and industry are excluded. All of the above may be accomplished for the local community through proper planning and and zoning.

Everyone plans. One hears daily, "I plan to build a new house." "We plan to save our money for a vacation." "We plan to build a new school." Each time, the speaker has examined what he possesses and has considered ways for obtaining what he or the group wants. Each plan embraces problems, needs, and goals.

A community plan is only a large-

FIGURE 31.3 *Ingredients to consider in a good plan.*

scale version of a family or group plan. The basic steps in preparing it are the same. First, the community makes a careful study of what it has now. Second, it gives thought to its current and future problems and needs, and to its potential. It decides what it wants in the future. This step involves the preparation of a master plan. The final step is for the community to develop practical ways to put the master plan into effect.

The New Town Concept

Urban sprawl and the increasing problems of congestion both in the United States and abroad have led to the development of the "New Town" concept—i.e., the construction of an entire city according to a predetermined plan. Actually, the idea is not new; the self-contained "garden city" of Letchworth, England, was built some sixty years ago on a site north of London, and scores of modified New Towns have since been constructed in

England, Scandinavia, the U.S.S.R., and other European nations.

In the United States, however, the idea has been slower to develop, largely because of lack of assistance by government agencies. In Europe, government financial backing and land condemnation has smoothed the way to an extent unknown in America. Two private developments recently under construction near Washington, D.C., however, hold some promise.

The New Town of Columbia, between Washington, D.C. and Baltimore, is located on a 25-square mile tract of countryside, with plans for 125,000 people by 1980, along with sufficient offices, industries, and stores to employ almost all of the resident working force. The other U.S. New Town, at a more advanced construction stage, is Reston, Virginia, located on an 11-square mile site 17 miles northwest of Washington. This planned city is designed to hold 75,000 people in townhouses, detached single-family homes, and high-rise apartments. Residents will overlook a 33-acre artificial lake, and enjoy pleasant paths crisscrossing the community.

The difficulties of these New Towns, both European and American, is that they are experiencing problems in becoming a truly self-contained community. For example, only 25 percent of the people presently working in Reston live in the town; thus it is not fulfilling one of its primary goals—the creation of a community where most people live close to their work.

STATE PLANNING

State planning, besides providing state-level coordination, may be of help in a number of ways to assist local communities in coordinating their efforts and avoiding conflicts. It can also provide planning services to rural areas that lack trained personnel. Unfortunately, in most states the planning agencies have not been given sufficient funds or power to do an effective job. There is currently a revival and strengthening of their position. Hawaii, California, Tennessee, and Oregon are good cases in point.

It is important to note that the state planning agency is not a substitute for local government in taking the responsibility for local development plans. State planning helps in the creation of local and regional agencies, coordination of local plans, and establishment of liaison between local planning agencies in the development of state plans. The process of state planning follows practically the same methods as outlined earlier.

The same need to look at the problem, rather than at the political boundary, will produce cooperative planning arrangements among the states to deal with regions that straddle state lines. Such arrangements have been put to effective use in adopting joint operations for a variety of interstate services. Interstate compacts, agreements, and parallel legislation adopted in adjacent states have brought an accumulation of experience with cooperative work on transportation, recreation, water resources, and other specific functions.

Some cooperative interstate planning has also been accomplished, but it has been limited to planning for one or another of these specialized activities. These interstate arrangements are available, although now largely unused, for joint comprehensive planning by the states or by local governments. Local governments can undertake joint efforts with neighbors across a state line on their own initiative, provided there are statutes that permit it.

Another responsibility of state planning programs may be realized in the balanced development of urban and rural areas. Urban areas are increasing in dependence upon rural activities, and urban people will want the conservation of farmland or open space, of forests or well-tended but lightly developed countryside. Rural areas are increasing in dependence upon urban areas, and rural people will want to see their urban centers prosper as creators of jobs and markets. Both are concerned with the form of cities and the edges of urban development, where rural and urban land-use problems become, most vividly, one problem. A narrowly urban view of land-use problems can be tempered by the comprehensive view of a state planning agency.

REGIONAL PLANNING

Axiomatic to the concept of a need for local planning is a realization that local communities do not live or exist in a vacuum. They are constantly operating and relating with a host of spatially identifiable other communities, districts, and organizational entities. They are constantly drawing on and in turn supplying a multitude of resources within an areal expanse. Thus, awareness of the interrelationship among all resources—animal, vegetable, and mineral—within an identifiable region leads to the realization that utilizing the regional planning approach will improve the process of intergovernmental action and better integrate urban and resources planning. Regional planning will coordinate local or statewide planning, and will in turn be coordinated by national planning endeavors. Therefore, the multi-area levels are complimentary to one another.

The term *regional planning*, particularly as it is used in the United States, has a variety of connotations. This results not only from the various meanings ascribed to it by different people, but also from the fact that there have been several separate streams of professional thought on the subject over the last thirty years.

One of these had its beginning during the Depression and was oriented initially to the development problems of the South. It perceived a region as being relatively geographically united (multistate), and distinctive in that it possessed "the largest possible degree of homogeneity measured by the largest possible number of economic, cultural, administrative, and functional indices for the largest possible number of objectives." [14] The focus was thus on rural, relatively underdeveloped areas. This concept of regional planning was basic to the work of the National Resources Planning Board and to most of the river basin development agencies, such as TVA. It was fundamentally economic in nature and heavily oriented to resource development. A current and somewhat modified expression of this concept is found in the Appalachian Regional Commission.

A second stream of thought in regional planning is based on the land control activities of city planners, and resulted from the increasing urbanization of the U.S. population. Interest in this type of regional planning grew very rapidly in the post-World War II period, when the urban areas of the United States grew at an unprecedented rate. Its primary concern has been the physical use of space, and its action programs have involved spatial planning on the one hand, and use controls such as zoning, on the other. In recent years, the focus of this thinking has tended to be placed on metropolitan regions rather than on cities, as city limits have, for many purposes, lost their meaning. While it has been suggested by Freidmann that the emphasis of planning in the future may shift increasingly to the relations among metropolitan regions, planning for the total economic development of rural and remote areas will continue to demand the attention of geographers and other land resource specialists. Friedmann [6] states:

Although as much as 90 percent of the total population of the country may eventually reside within city regions, there will be large areas of sparsely settled land that fall outside the immediate influence of central cities. Such areas as the Cumberland Plateau, the Blue Ridge Mountains, the Ozarks, the Great Lakes cut-over regions, parts of northern New England, and large sections of the Southwest and West fall in this category. They pose special planning problems due to the poverty of their population and their limited resources. An extensive type of development through recreation, forestry, or grazing will often form the basic approach to these areas. They are regions characterized by special physical disadvantage for more intensive development. They may be called "functional regions" when public policy addresses itself specifically to problems related to the development of their resources.

Considered on a world-wide scale, however, it seems only logical to be concerned with regional planning in the sense of the first definition given. As differentiated from that of metropolitan regional planning, it is resource-oriented and economic in nature.

The parts of a planning region are linked by common problems or common opportunities. The people of the region are interdependent, economically and socially; they do business with each other, often read the same newspaper, perhaps use the same hospital; they decline or prosper together. With widely diverse careers as individuals, people nevertheless share, in some measure, a single regional destiny.

To achieve a destiny that will be of our choosing, we have come to accept the need to plan our environment. We are accepting planning despite an ingrained urge to decide individually how each plot of ground is to be used. We find it less possible to make individual decisions stick. Many changes among people and in jobs and technology have been taking this power of decision away from individuals. Through regional planning we are trying to regain control over the way our land resources will work for us.

The uses to which we put land have become more demanding by standards of quality, location, and extent. Consider, for example, a recent projection by Robert M. Reeser of Ohio State University, applying present development standards to the future development of Ohio. He found that 22 million people in Ohio by the year 2000 (the 1960 population was near 10 million) would require more than 33.5 million acres to supply space for agriculture, industry, houses, roads, recreation, shops and other land uses. *This is 7.25 million more acres than there are in Ohio!*

Will we reduce our future population? lower standards? invent new ways to get along with less land? squeeze out some uses of land? change our forecasts? Events will give us an answer if we let the future just happen. If we prefer to exercise choice among the possible answers and work for a combination of alternatives that suit us, we will undertake to design and execute regional plans.

Prospects of Planning

History shows that planning endeavors have not been wholly effective. A myriad of reasons can be offered. A rational explanation is the simple fact that often there is no strong political structure comparable in scope to the "region," and experience has shown that the scope of planning is typically only as broad as the scope of the government it serves. Another more subtle but related deterrent to a regional approach to regional problems may be the psychological barrier of fear born of ignorance—without the benefit of government in the regional decision-making process, professional as well as the political personnel tend to seek safety in opposition.

Considering the multiplicity of national, state, and local agencies that are actively engaged in varying degrees with "regional planning" or in some way making decisions with regional impact, a primary function of an effective regional planning process must also include program coordination and integration. The result of elevating *systematic coordination* to a position of sufficient importance in the conduct of government operations is in itself reason enough to strive for a regional decision-

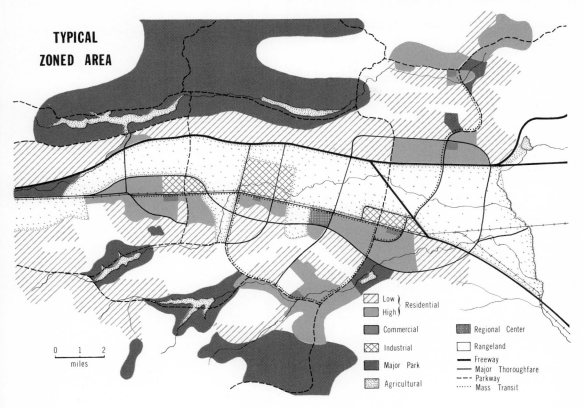

TYPICAL ZONED AREA

Low }
High } Residential

Commercial

Industrial

Major Park

Agricultural

Regional Center

Rangeland

Freeway
Major Thoroughfare
Parkway
Mass Transit

0 1 2
miles

FIGURE 31.4 *A zoned area as a result of planning.*

making process. This process will be a mere toy, however, unless the mechanism includes an intergovernmental structure capable of policy formulation and implementation at the regional level.

selected references

1. Boal, Frederick W., "Technology and Urban Form," *The Journal of Geography,* Vol. 67, No. 4, April 1968, pp. 229–236.

2. Bogue, B. J., *The Structure of the Metropolitan Community: A Study of Dominance and Subdominance* (Ann Arbor: University of Michigan, Horace H. Rackham School of Graduate Studies, 1949).

3. ——, and Beale, Calvin L., *Economic Subregions of the United States Farm Population,* Series Census-BAE No. 19, Washington, D.C.: Government Printing Office, June 1953.

4. Borchert, John R., "American Metro-politan Evolution," *Geographical Review,* Vol. 57, No. 3, July 1967, pp. 301–332.

5. Cooper, Sherwin H., "Theoretical Geography, Applied Geography, and Planning," *The Professional Geographer,* Vol. 18, No. 1, January 1966, pp. 1–2.

6. Friedman, John, "The Concept of a Planning Region—The Evolution of an Idea in the United States," *Land Economics,* Vol. 32, February 1956, pp. 1–13.

7. Hurter, A. P. and Moses, M. A., "Price and Productive Uncertainties in Dynamic Planning," *Journal of Regional Science,* Vol. 7, No. 1, Summer 1967, pp. 33–48.

8. Jackson, John N., "Geography and Planning," *The Canadian Geographer,* Vol. 11, No. 4, 1967, pp. 357–365.

9. Lampe, Fred A., and Schaefer, Orval C., Jr., "Land Use Patterns in the City," *The Journal of Geography,* Vol. 68, No. 5, May 1969, pp. 301–306.

10. Mayer, Harold M., "Cities and Urban Geography," *The Journal of Geography,* Vol. 68, No. 1, January 1969, pp. 6–18.

11. McKenzie, R. D., *The Metropolitan Com-

munity, New York: McGraw-Hill Book Company, Inc., 1933.

12. National Resources Committee, *Regional Factors in Planning,* Washington, D.C.: Government Printing Office, December 1935.

13. Nelson, Howard J., "The Form and Structure of Cities: Urban Growth Patterns," *The Journal of Geography,* Vol. 68, No. 4, April 1969, pp. 198–207.

14. Odum, Howard W., and Moore, Harry E., *American Regionalism,* New York: Henry Holt and Company, 1938.

15. Penny, P., "Town Planning, Urban Renewal and Economics," *South African Journal of Economics,* Vol. 36, No. 2, June 1968, pp. 156–170.

16. Perloff, Harvey S., "Key Features of Regional Planning," *Journal of the American Institute of Planners,* Vol. 34, May 1968.

17. Preston, Richard E., "The Zone in Transition: A Study of Urban Land Use Patterns," *Economic Geography,* Vol. 42, No. 3, July 1966, pp. 236–260.

18. Thompson, W. R., *A Preface to Urban Economics,* Baltimore: The John Hopkins Press, 1967.

Throughout this book man has been depicted as a vibrant force that influences and determines the type, level, and location of economic activities through the vehicle of his culture. The concept of culture is that of multi-personality. Selected aspects of the culture-personality were analyzed in terms of the various frameworks—material, economic, social, political, technological—using a system or model approach. The influence of these frameworks was demonstrated through the selected topical (primary, secondary, and tertiary activities) and regional interplay.

Since analysis lends itself to quantitative and statistical treatment, a separate chapter was devoted to statistical inference for spatial analysis. Concern over the increasing quantitative and statistical orientation of economic geography, that this trend might be leading to abstraction, has been expressed by some. Yet it is through abstraction that depth and clarity are recognized. Until recently, economic geography has lacked adequate inclusion of supportive quantitative and statistical tools, which not only increase the precision of measuring geographic signals, but also enhance the description and interpretation of the phenomena. Increasing quantification of economic geography as an academic field is a trend that is likely to continue.

Distance—a function of time and space—has been viewed as a basic fabric over which the spatial variation of economic phenomena was recognized and analyzed. Some, seeing distance shrinking as a result of ever-improving means of circulation, express fear that the fabric might be deteriorating, and consequently that it might be reduced in scope. In fact, improved circulation actually builds a stronger fabric for economic geography.

A greater level of circulation carries with it higher levels of trade and specialization. These, in turn, not only tend to produce a greater degree of spatial variability in economic phenomena, but also mean higher productivity, income, and leisure. Increasing income and leisure are likely to result in more service activities. However, the type and level of service activity will depend on the technological advances in providing "do-it-yourself" conveniences as substitutes for the many commercial service activities.

The location of service activities has tended to follow the population. Today, however, newer patterns are emerging, e.g., crossroad complexes away from residential areas, recreation facilities, shopping centers, and the like. One of the most logical and practical applications of economic geography has been found in the fields of industry location and planning. These topics were included to orient the student toward the practice and policy aspects of the field.

The question of spatial location of man's activities—both economic and noneconomic—has become a more crucial concern to him than ever before for several reasons: Man's landing on the moon has added a vertical dimension to the concept of space, which previously has been perceived horizontally as far as economic phenomena are concerned. Increasing population pressures, the drastic variation in land–man ratios, and vulnerability to complete devastation by nuclear attack place higher demands not only on our understanding of location patterns, but also on the arrangement of economic activities, so that they meet human needs and goals with the greatest level of efficiency.

The above challenge presents a dilemma—on the one hand, it requires a concentrated and specialized effort on the part of geographers to gain adequate insight into the problem; on the other, by virtue of its complexity the problem requires a broader treatment involving many other disciplines. One resolution has been suggested in what is called an "orchestration" approach. This approach recognizes each disciplines' contribution and requires that they interrelate harmoniously with the others to achieve a common goal of effectively satisfying human wants, whatever their structure. Of course, the question remains, "Who should play the conductor's role?" Perhaps the conductor should be the goal—a *better* society.